The author, Russ Goodenough, at the controls of his F-4C Phantom II.

Endorsements

"'Why Johnny Came Marching Home' relates a patriot's personal journey into a war on behalf of his country and the painful disillusionment he experienced as a result. I greatly admire Russ Goodenough's willingness to put himself at risk in combat the way he did. The courage he demonstrated in so many ways in and around the war is only matched by the courage he showed in examining, dissecting and exposing the hidden depths of ineptitude, the lies, the ignorance and the arrogance that caused so much human carnage in that misbegotten American exercise in futility." — Mike Farrell

Mike Farrell is a writer, director, producer and actor best known as "B.J. Hunnicutt" of TV's M*A*S*H. An ex-Marine and an anti-war activist involved in many issues pertaining to human rights and social justice, he is the author of "Just Call Me Mike: A Journey to Actor and Activist," and "Of Mule and Man."

"I am of the strong opinion that this well-researched and scholarly written book will ultimately become a necessary research source for those in the future who wish to learn about the "real facts" of a war that was poorly understood; a war the United States government had no desire to properly conduct; a war that never had a real mission statement; and a war that in other times would have charged our then-Secretary of State with treason, obviously with the full knowledge and consent of the President of the United States. Those treasonous actions directly led to numerous needless deaths and imprisonment of many U.S. Air Force and U.S. Navy tactical aircrews." — USAF Lt. Colonel (ret.) Alexander H.C. Harwick, MPA

Combat Fighter Pilot (F-4C, D & E, RF-4C) in SEA Air Wars; Author of several books.
Colonel Harwick for many years had more flying hours in the F-4 Phantom II than any pilot in the world. In Southeast Asia, he flew a total of 259 combat missions, including 125 Fast FAC (Forward Air Controller) missions, 119 operational missions (bombing, rocketry and cannon), and 15 sorties in the reconnaissance version, the RF-4. Among other decorations, he earned five DFCs and 27 Air Medals while leading the "Laredo" Fast FACs flying the F-4D out of Udorn, Thailand against Laos and The North.

"Using his personal combat logs and correspondence, Russ Goodenough creates an unparalleled account of the air wars in Vietnam and Laos during the mid-1960s, which beyond providing pinpoint details of combat operations, convincingly conveys the terror, exhaustion, and frustration experienced by American fighter pilots. His work goes far beyond the war story and stands as a damning condemnation of the political decisions that exposed aircrews to totally unnecessary levels of risk and the appalling loss of airplanes and lives.

"Although the knowledge I gained during a 1965 Pentagon assignment directed toward assessing the potential for escalation left me with serious doubts about the conduct of the war, I never understood the magnitude of the consequences until I read Russ' book. This is a landmark piece of literature that should be read by anyone concerned with the politics of war." — Robert F. Davey, MBA, PhD

USAF Instructor Pilot (F-5) during time of SEA Air Wars; Author of "Moon War"; Professor Emeritus, Aerospace Engineering, California State Polytechnic University

"This is a serious document about war, its history, its conduct, its folly, with lessons learned for soldiers, sailors, airmen and politicians. Russ Goodenough writes with passion. He knows of which he speaks. He has been there, done that. Feel the G's, smell the cordite. Strap in with Russ for a wild and dangerous ride through aerial combat in the Vietnam War." — USAF Major General (ret.) Don Shepperd, MS

Combat Fighter Pilot (F-100) during SEA Air Wars with 247 combat missions; Author of several books including "Bury Us Upside Down," the story of the "Misty" Fast FACs over the Ho Chi Minh Trail in Laos. He was awarded numerous decorations for bravery and competence including the Silver Star, Legion of Merit and three Distinguished Flying Crosses (DFC). General Shepperd was the CNN military analyst from 1994 through 1998. He was also head of the United States Air National Guard during the same time period.

"The author, Russ Goodenough, working with the USAF Historical Research Center staff, assisted my Southeast Asia Declassification Team by identifying specific documents for declassification that could potentially provide special insight into the conflict in SEA. Utilizing this wealth of declassified information, the author has gained an exceptional understanding of the conflict, enhancing & enriching his own combat experience.

"A reader should follow this fighter pilot's airborne journey that placed him into benchmark events in the escalating Vietnam conflict. He was one of the first involved. Cockpit experiences combined with research data have created a unique story that portrays this conflict very differently than what we have been told. His detailed portrayal of the massive, clandestine Laotian Air Wars and the CIA involvement deserves to be read by anyone interested in our history. This book should be required reading for all Air Force cadets. Very eye opening!" — USAF Colonel (ret.) James R. Annis, MBA, MS

Combat Electronic Warfare Officer (B-52) in SEA Air Wars; Former Air Force Deputy Director for Intelligence, Pacific, which covered Southeast Asia. Director of the USAF Southeast Asia (SEA) Declassification Team, which was responsible for the declassification of all United States Air Force documents covering Southeast Asia, including Laos, during and before the years of the Vietnam War. In 1996, his team was recognized by then-Vice President Al Gore for, among other things, outstanding public service.

Why Johnny Came Marching Home

Why we lost the Clandestine Air Wars
that engulfed Vietnam and Laos

By Russ Goodenough
Combat Fighter Pilot

To a fellow RTB
Enjoy
Russ Goodenough

Why Johnny Came Marching Home

www.whyjohnnycamemarchinghome.com
www.phantomincombat.com

Copyright © in 2017 by Russ Goodenough
Printed in the United States of America

Published and First Printing in 2017 by:
Create Space, a DBA of On-Demand Publishing, LLC
an Amazon company
www/Createspace.com

U.S. Copyright Office Case Number: 1-444429437(J)1, dated 2-16-2017
Library of Congress Control Number: 2017902863
International Standard Book Number (ISBN): 9781544902333

CONTENT: Declassified maps, certain declassified documents, and selected photos provided courtesy of the United States Air Force. Certain declassified documents provided courtesy of the Central Intelligence Agency, National Security Agency and the Department of Defense. Combat photos provided courtesy of the United States Marine Corps and the United States Army. Cover designed, maps enhanced and photos arranged by Vincent Williams, Anaheim, California. Cover photo provided by Phantom Co-Pilot from the 559th Tactical Fighter Squadron, Cam Ranh Bay, Vietnam. End-of-book maps of Southeast Asia provided courtesy of National Geographic Magazine.

All author's profits from this book will be donated to
the Assistance League® of Conejo Valley (California)
"Enhancing the lives of children."

Special Thanks

To the United States Air Force Academy

Colorado Springs, Colorado,

For providing values, education and mission.

Why Johnny Came Marching Home
Chapter Contents

www.whyjohnnycamemarchinghome.com

continued next page

Why Johnny Came Marching Home
Chapter Contents

(continued)

Support Information

Additional support & relevant information may be found at www.phantomincombat.com

Dedication

This book is dedicated to the intrepid American F-105 Thunderchief fighter-bomber pilots who flew for year after year from bases in Thailand against the toughest targets in all of Southeast Asia in and around the North Vietnamese cities of Hanoi-Haiphong. Those targets were the most heavily defended in the history of aerial warfare.

In addition to MIG fighter planes, they had to brave the barrage-firing of surface-to-air missiles. They had to evade the anti-aircraft artillery massed around their targets. They also had to contend with automatic, rapid-fire, radar-guided weapons and small arms fire concentrated right over their targets.

Their courage and tenacity against almost impossible odds, fighting a war without objective, was a source of inspiration for all the rest of us who participated in that unnecessary and misunderstood war.

Preface

THE AUTHOR:

Russ Goodenough was born in Los Angeles and grew up in the small ranching and oil town of his father's birth, Fillmore, California. His father grew oranges on his family's original homesteaded land that westerners call a ranch.

His introduction to writing started early. While in high school, he wrote weekly stories for the local newspaper, the Fillmore Herald, relating to what had transpired at the high school football games. He would quarterback the team and write about it afterwards.

At eighteen, Russ left home for the then-new United States Air Force Academy in Colorado Springs, Colorado. After four years of Academy education, he went to Air Force pilot training at Laredo Air Base, Texas and graduated with a selection to fly the F-4C Phantom II, which at the time was the hottest and fastest operational fighter in the world.

In his senior year at the Academy, his essay about reforming the immigration system was published by the Air Force and became part of the national dialogue preparatory to a review by Congress.

After Phantom duty stations in Florida and Okinawa, Russ was stationed at Cam Ranh Bay, South Vietnam, where he flew 148 combat missions in Southeast Asia and saw many of the complex aspects of the War. Most of all, he was part of the long-lasting clandestine war in Laos that was shielded from the American public. His disillusionment with how the Vietnamese and Laotian Wars were being fought and the reasons for the wars themselves, led him to leave his Air Force career.

After leaving the Air Force, Russ became a pilot for Continental Airlines. He founded, and for thirty-four years owned, a truck and equipment rental company (Cal U-Rent) in Thousand Oaks, California. While still active in civic affairs, he has retired from both the airline and his business.

He served as Editor and chief writer for the "Conejo Business Times," the publication of the Greater Conejo Valley Chamber of Commerce located in Thousand Oaks. His first book was the "History of Q.B. (Quiet Birdmen) Hangar 99," which was written for internal consumption by that fraternal group of civilian and military pilots and ex-pilots.

Retirement finds him either at home with his wife Carolyn in the Southern California City of Thousand Oaks, or at their vacation home in the Village of Pine in the forested mountains of Central Arizona.

AUTHOR'S INTENT:

Several people have asked the author, "Why write a book about a war that ended over 40 years ago? Why write about stale news?"

There were many events and things associated with the war in Southeast Asia that needed time for clarification and confirmation. Time was needed for classified documents to be de-classified. He did not want to report events based on hearsay.

Another reason for delay was that, after his return from war, emotions were too fresh. The American public was too angry. Time was needed to heal the wounds.

One of the reasons for his intensive research for this book was to find out the truth of the many rumors in Vietnam of the possible involvement of France. He did manage to debunk some, but not all, of the rumors. Other than the indisputable facts of their early involvement, he chose not to include any mention of unconfirmed French action. He found no proof of the much-rumored French handing over their intelligence apparatus in SEA to the Viet Cong. The cause for that widely-reported rumor may have been the obvious United States Air Force enmity against the French. That enmity dates back to French President Charles De Gaulle throwing the Americans off over sixty U.S. built and maintained military installations scattered across France that were part of NATO. Several of those installations were large and expensive Air Force bases that provided Cold War depth to the stationing of our units across Southern Germany. However, he did find proof that French pilots, under the control of De Gaulle, were flying MIGs out of Cambodia and training Cambodian pilots to fly them.

As for SEA, many of the events that he witnessed and were rumored were confirmed by documents from many agencies including: The Department of Defense, the US Air Force, the US Navy, the National Security Agency, the Central Intelligence Agency and others. Each agency had its own story to tell. When all the stories are heard, a comprehensive picture emerges of the overall events.

He was fortunate to have been in the right place at the right time on numerous occasions regarding SEA. It had nothing necessarily to do with his efforts or abilities, but had everything to do with timing.

This book is a history. His participation allowed this history to be documented, but his participation is also included as a representation of what was happening to many other fighter-bomber pilots. His story is the story of many.

The history that we read is sometimes inaccurate due to the author's agenda or his reporting events of which he or she was not witness. The events and people mentioned in this book are all accurate and real. Many of the events were things that the author had participated in or had witnessed. The rest were verified.

It has oft been said that history that is not learned will repeat itself. Our mistakes need to be properly identified and learned so that they will not be repeated in current or future wars. War is a very serious business and, if at all possible, we need to avoid it. It should be entered into only as the very last resort, if other means have been exhausted and only if our nation is imperiled.

In SEA, the Rules of Engagement that hamstrung our air battles denied us the ability to win that mistaken war. The misguided reliance on a policy of "gradualism" was another, as were the continual violations by our political leaders of the time-tested military Principles of War.

In future wars, our national political leaders must allow our military leaders to fight to attain the war objectives as defined by our politicians. If we must fight, we should fight to win and minimize the destruction and loss-of-life for ourselves, our allies and our perceived enemy.

Americans seem much more inclined to read about or watch documentaries about our successful military operations than about failed exercises like our Southeast Asian War. Yet it is the failures that need our attention and understanding. Knowledge of history must be learned, understood, and acted upon.

It is essential that Americans understand what really happened in Southeast Asia. In SEA, the ignorance and cowardice at the highest levels of our government caused a huge loss of national treasure, loss of human life, loss of national self-respect and loss of national honor. Additionally, we destroyed much of SEA and killed a great many people, both military and civilian. It was the hubris that came out of our World War II victory that nurtured the mistakes that happened later in SEA. We thought we were invincible.

America cannot again afford to replace common sense with unreasonable decision-making that was evidenced in our handling of SEA. It is with regret that our national leaders seem to be now making the same mistakes and acting with the same arrogance that caused such tragedy in the past. The mistakes recorded in this and other books of its kind are bound to be repeated if the lessons are not understood and corrected.

What is very troubling to the author is that the mistakes made in SEA were corrected forcefully in the 1st Iraqi War, but since have seemingly been forgotten. The field-grade officers of the SEA War became the Generals who led the 1st Iraq War. They managed to complete the job and terminate the ground action in only 100 hours. President George H.W. Bush had been a naval fighter pilot in World War II and understood that the military has to be allowed to do its job. He made the overall political decisions and assembled the coalition, then gave the military portion of the job to General Colin Powell and his staff.

Part of our current problem is that our modern communications have advanced to the extent that they are interfering with a proper allocation of authority. When the author sees the President of the United States and other prominent leaders watching a live visual transmission of a military event, such as the killing of Osama Bin Laden, we have to ask ourselves why they are doing it. It would be understandable for our military leaders to visually monitor an operation, but only to the extent that they could assist in the event something went wrong. Otherwise, the military is spending a lot of money and effort to provide theater for our national leaders.

When the Pentagon and White House are both in constant visual contact with a military operation as it unfolds, the temptation is great to interfere or issue orders. In most cases, that does not help, takes needless time and complicates the matter.

Our military has a visceral enmity for limitations in the conduct of our wars. But, due to the changing nature of conflict and relations between nations, our military future will surely be ruled by adherence to limitations. Primarily, past limitations have dealt with geographical objectives and weaponry used. Yet limitations come in many colors and include intensity, personnel, equipment and duration as well as geographic. Those limitations must be decided in advance of the initiation of combat. After the initiation of hostilities, it is no time to "wing it." The intent of this book is to show the political and military mistakes made in the planning, preparation and conduct of our actions in Southeast Asia. Those mistakes led to the first military defeat in any war for the United States. But it is more than that. The author has attempted to show how history conspired to create the conditions for war.

Finally, his intent is to show how the air war was experienced by one fighter pilot. It is to show the intensity, boredom, and the trauma of war. It is to show the cause of frustration and the evolution of attitude. His combat diary did relate what was happening elsewhere in the combat theater and how that affected morale and enthusiasm. This book answers the question of why he and so many other military men left the service after Vietnam.

Where the author has included portions of his combat diary, it may seem repetitious where he continued to show bomb loads and weaponry utilized. But that is also a part of what he is attempting to show through this book. From a military viewpoint, shortages of bombs, rockets, 20mm ammunition and the externally-mounted Gattling cannon also contributed.

Of importance is that he does not consider himself a hero in what he is relating to you. He was doing his job as were all of those tasked with fighting the Air War. If there were heroes, they would be the F-105 pilots who flew against impossible odds, in a little understood war, with no clear military objective and with no governmental desire to take the risks necessary to insure victory.

In spite of the conditions, the F-105 pilots still kept flying and fighting with most being shot down and either killed or captured. While stationed at Naha Air Base in Okinawa, the author witnessed the F-105s flying south to the Thai bases. They were on three-month temporary duty (TDY) out of Kadena Air Force Base in Okinawa. The F-105 squadrons would consistently return to Okinawa with only 40% of the pilots and planes with which they left. In other words, they each lost 60% of their aircraft and pilots, who were either killed or captured. They did this year-after-year until almost half of the constructed F-105 airframes were destroyed. It is to those intrepid aviators that we owe our recognition of their intense courage and many sacrifices.

As related from his combat diary, the author's war was filled with danger and adventure as well as conflict relating to the policies dictating how we were waging the war. To varying degrees, other fighter pilots also had their stories of individual courage and sacrifice. It is for all the above-mentioned reasons that he wrote this long-delayed story.

THE AUTHOR'S PERSONAL COMMENTS:

Having said all of the above, there is another, more personal, reason for writing this story. When I left the Air Force, I was unaware that I left my heart behind.

My subsequent forays into the civilian world were gratifying and interesting. They were challenging and offered a measure of success. But, I never ever found the level of dedication to a common cause or the feeling of camaraderie that I experienced in the Air Force.

My associates in the Air Force were an extraordinary group of men. As much as they tried not to admit it by sentiments or actions, they were at heart true patriots.

As an aging ex-pilot, I feel it is my duty and mission to leave for others what I learned under very trying circumstances. Call it adding to the overall institutional memory, but I do want to give back to the Air Force. My heart tells me that I never really left the military. I have lived as a military man even when I held civilian jobs. I will die as a military man.

When I returned from Vietnam, my strong urge was to bury the memories. Most of us that returned seemed to have similar sentiments. But my obligation to a war that we lost and to the country I served is to revive those memories. If we are to survive and prosper as a nation, it is our collective obligation to learn from Southeast Asia. Learn what went wrong and determine what we need to do to correct future actions and policies.

My intent is to become part of that institutional memory by recording part of the history of that far-off conflict so that we will not forget.

Introduction

Marching Home
From Confederacy to Confrontation

> *"Every attempt to make war easy or safe will result in humiliation and disaster."*
>
> Union General William T. Sherman

In the American history of its wars, its Civil War had more combat deaths than the combined totals of all our other wars. It was a tragedy of historic proportions. When the defeated troops of the Confederacy began to return to their homes after the Southern surrender, they found devastation and ruin. The Southern population was dispirited after four years of conflict and the deprivation caused by war.

Many of the returning soldiers found their properties destroyed and their communities torn asunder. They found that many of their friends and associates would never return. They found many of those who had been their neighbors before the war were now looking at them as sad reminders of what had been and the defeat that was.

The returning Northern troops came back to parades and jubilation. They also returned to communities that had lost many of their youth who had marched off with such enthusiasm, never to return. For the soldiers of the North, the marching home was a time of relief and a cause for celebration. They also returned to lives that were forever changed. But, the troops of the Union Armies returned home with honor and glory. The soldiers of the South received no such celebration. There was no honor and no glory. Such is the difference between victory and defeat.

In 1863, during the height of the Civil War, a song was composed looking for an end to the bloody conflict. It was filled with hope and high spirit, but also contained a strong desire for the cessation of the war and an ending to the bloodshed, maiming, killing and destruction. Its theme was the envisioned homecoming of the soldiers. The song, "When Johnny Comes Marching Home" was written by a Northerner.

By 1865, the high spirit had turned from hope to intense Southern fatigue and sadness, for by the end of the war the song was identified with the South. For the South, it was a time of sorrow as the defeated soldiers returned to shattered lives. The song seemed a mockingly sad lament of their return.

The Southern men took up the yoke and began the long process of rebuilding the homes, farms and communities that had been neglected or broken by years of deprivation and Sherman's Army. They may have returned as defeated soldiers, but there was no questioning their honor or valor. They may have lost, but they had served their nation well.

Exactly a century later, in 1965, the first numbers of soldiers, sailors and airmen from another war began to trickle back to their homes and communities. This time, the soldiers returned to an indifferent nation that seemed at first not to realize or care we were even in a war. Later, that indifference turned to anger at the war, confusion as to its purpose and antagonism against the men who fought.

The conflict in Southeast Asia (SEA) would eventually lead to the third highest toll of military deaths of any American conflict, save the Civil War and World War II. After WWII's VE (Victory in Europe) and VJ (Victory in Japan) Days, the military men of our victorious armies, navies and air forces returned to joy and the respect of a grateful nation. They returned to parades and returned in honor.

Those returning from Vietnam and the rest of Southeast Asia did not return to parades or honor or tales of their valor. Instead, they returned to a divided nation. Many experienced confrontations. Few spoke of their honor.

The fighter pilots and other airmen who arrived back had largely fought a secret, clandestine war against frightening odds in the skies over North Vietnam and Laos. The nation was not told by their leaders what our airmen were doing or where they were flying and fighting. They returned after having fought against the heaviest defenses in the history of aerial warfare only to find that they were scorned and reviled by many. That they had been honoring the Constitution by obeying the orders of their political leaders seems to have been lost on those who scorned. The airmen and the many soldiers and sailors who would return from that far-off land had done the same as the returning soldiers of both the Union and Confederate Armies had done during the Civil War. They had served their nation well.

The story contained herein is about Southeast Asia and the war that consumed it. In particular, it is about the region that was once known as French Indochina. The Indochinese countries of Vietnam, Laos and Cambodia are all part of the story, but so are Thailand, China, Russia and even France. The Vietnamese War was a much larger conflict than just involving the nations of Vietnam and should have been called the Southeast Asian War.

Actually, there were four wars being fought simultaneously in SEA. The first was the known conflict in South Vietnam that pitted the forces of the United States, South Vietnam and their allies against those of the Viet Cong and the North Vietnamese Army.

The second was the less-known air war against North Vietnam, which consisted of interdiction air strikes against their command and control, air defenses, industrial base, communications, transportation and their endless supplies and equipment. From the standpoint of the United States, this was largely an air war against, not only the forces of North Vietnam, but those of North Korea, China and the Soviet Union.

The third was support for the Royal Lao Army and other tribal forces in their civil war against the forces of the Communist Pathet Lao and their ally, North Vietnam. That war was largely fought in the North Central highlands of Laos and, from the standpoint of the United States, it was a combined air and ground war.

The last of the secret wars was being waged against the forces of the North Vietnamese Army as it tried to protect its avenue of re-supply for the Communistic forces operating in South Vietnam. This war was mainly waged in Southern Laos and, from the standpoint of the U.S., it was largely an air war, but also involved clandestine ground troops of varying nationalities who were inserted into the jungle corridor known to many as the Ho Chi Minh Trail.

The initial conflict, known as the First Indochinese War, started when the Vietnamese portion of Indochina rose up against their foreign oppressor, France. That initial Vietnamese rebellion against foreign domination actually started against the Chinese. Later it was against the French, was continued against Japan, was revived against the Chinese and finally culminated in a victory against the French. The enmity against foreign control and domination continued against the United States in what is considered the Second Indochinese War. To the Vietnamese the war is called the American War and to the Americans it is known as the Vietnam War.

This story is told from the perspective and experience of an American fighter pilot who flew and fought and eventually returned. By almost any measure of evaluation, SEA was the most confusing and misunderstood war in which we have ever fought.

In 1966, the author became one of those F-4 Phantom fighter-bomber pilots flying out of South Vietnam. Vietnam was one of those wars that Americans would like to forget. The stories out of that war are not what Americans like to hear. Americans are used to stories of our heroic wars of creation. We like to read of battles across unblemished frontiers and of valorous troops storming far-away beaches. We want stories of wars fought for honor and purpose and to save the world for democracy. We want to vanquish evil nations and to ride to the rescue of others by defeating tyrannical dictators. We don't want to hear about a war that the United States lost. It is painfully troubling to our collective notion of who we are as Americans to realize that we are not always virtuous or right.

During his year's stay at Cam Ranh Bay, South Vietnam, the author flew missions of every description throughout all of Southeast Asia. What he saw, participated in and learned about in SEA caused him to question who we were and what we were doing. The war was a lot larger than what Americans were told or what our history books might tell us.

To most Americans, the Vietnam War started out with the Gulf of Tonkin incident in August of 1964. The "Incident" was supposedly an attack by North Vietnamese fast patrol boats against U.S. Navy destroyers. It was the precipitator of the Gulf of Tonkin Resolution by Congress that gave President Johnson the authorization to strike back against North Vietnam. That we had been "striking back" against Laos, the Viet Cong and the forces of North Vietnam for years before the Gulf Incident was unknown.

Our newspapers told us that the War really did not get started much earlier than November or December of 1965. Reported casualty figures were low. The nightly news did not show the grisly carnage of real war until later.

Statistics are boring to most of us. However, those cold numbers can tell a very honest and effective story. Much more recent than Vietnam is the 2nd Iraq War. During that entire Iraqi War from invasion in 2003 through 2010, the United States lost 14 fixed-wing fighter planes to hostile fire. During the entire ongoing Afghan War our loss rate has been similar.

Compare that to Southeast Asia. It is of great interest to know when, where and how many we lost. Those numbers alone tell a story that we have not been told.

From 1961 through 1973, the United States lost the staggering total of 3,322 fixed-wing aircraft due to combat or operations. Another thousand were lost when the conquering armies of North Vietnam overran the South in 1975 and the American-gifted South Vietnamese aircraft fell into enemy hands.

If rotary-winged aircraft (helicopters) are thrown in, we lost almost 10,000 aircraft, which compares to the over 41,000 aircraft lost in World War II combat. While the SEA conflict was spread over a much larger time-frame than WWII, the fact that World War II was fought over much of the entire globe signifies the intensity of the Southeast Asia conflict that was confined to a much smaller geographical area.

We had 3,265 fatalities in the air and had 497 Prisoners of War. The pilot fatalities began in 1961. Prior to the purported August, 1964 Gulf of Tonkin Incidents, we lost close to 100 pilots killed. It is apparent that our nation lied to us. By 1964, we lost over 300 pilots in that year alone.

The bulk of the author's combat missions in Southeast Asia were against North Vietnam and Laos. Most of those missions required the use of high-performance fighter-bombers due to the nature of the air defenses in the North. For the Air Force, those high performance fighter-bombers were the F-105 Thunderchief and the F-4 Phantom.

The Thunderchief, with only a single pilot, was flown exclusively by the Air Force out of two bases located in Thailand. They lost 397 F-105s with 150 pilot fatalities and 103 taken prisoner. That means that 253 pilots were lost out of 397 aircraft downed. Only 1/3rd of the F-105 pilots shot down were rescued.

The Phantom, with a crew of two, was flown by the Air Force, Navy and Marines. The Marine F-4s flew out of Danang and Chu Lai in South Vietnam. The Navy flew combat exclusively off ships.

The Air Force flew the Phantoms primarily from two bases in Thailand and two bases in South Vietnam. The Thai bases were Udorn and Ubon. The South Vietnamese primary attack bases were Danang and Cam Ranh Bay. The Air Force Phantom missions ranged from close-air-support of Army and Marine combat to interdiction, MIG cover and MIG screen flights against Laos and North Vietnam.

The Marines flew in close-air-support of Marine combat troops in South Vietnam, while the Navy was attacking interdiction targets in Laos and North Vietnam. The Navy claims that over half of the airborne attacks against North Vietnam were flown by the Navy, which would be hotly disputed by the Air Force. The Marines lost 98 F-4s with 55 fatalities and 4 POWs. The Navy lost 128 F-4s with 65 fatalities and 42 POWs.

The Air Force, on the other hand, lost 443 F-4s with 321 fatalities and had 135 POWs. Additional losses occurred in the recce or reconnaissance version of the Phantom. The author's squadron, the 559th Tactical Fighter Squadron (TFS), lost 18 F-4C aircraft during the war, with six losses coming in 1966 when the author flew his missions, with several fatalities and six POWs, one of who died in captivity.

The location and number of losses can tell a story of how widespread the war was and where it was most intense. The locations of Air Force Phantom losses were as follows: South Vietnam, 97; North Vietnam, 193; Laos, 111 (88 in the civil war in the central highlands and 23 in the Ho Chi Minh Trail area); Cambodia, 8; Other Regions, 36. These are statistical stories derived from official military records. Due to the sensitivity of the situation in Thailand, our military referred to our losses there as "other regions."

Most Americans are unaware of the intensity and duration of our air war in Laos. It may come as a surprise to some that of all the Phantom fighter-bombers lost in Laos and North Vietnam, fully 32% came in Laos.

This story is written to include the author's own military journey through the tragedy that was Southeast Asia. Not because he was an exceptional pilot. He considered himself a good pilot. The Air Force is filled with some exceptional pilots and many of those served in SEA.

The timing of his presence also involved a lot of luck. His being at the right place at the right time certainly helped. His curiosity played a part. But the greatest reason for seeing the "big picture" was the timing of his arrival in Vietnam. His involvement in air actions took him from the initial combat missions against the Delta, through the Central Highlands to the DMZ (Demilitarized Zone). It took him through the "Tiger Hound" region of Laos to the "Tally Ho" region of the North Vietnamese Panhandle. It took him to bombing and rocketry missions against Vinh and Thanh Hoa on the North Vietnamese (NVN) central coast. It finally took him to MIG-cover protecting air strikes against Hanoi/ Haiphong, MIG-cover of airborne intelligence missions up to the Chinese border, and MIG-screen missions all across the North from the Red River Valley to the Gulf of Tonkin and finally to China's large Hainan Island.

The results of many interviews that are included in this story show a much larger conflict than what the American public was told or shown. To Americans in the 1960s, the war was about South Vietnam with only a vague knowledge of the Air War against the North. The knowledge of Thailand and Laos was kept secret.

The author not only talked with many fellow pilots, but many others involved in different aspects of the War. In this, he included a great deal in this book, but feels it was necessary to show a complete picture.

While it may sound strange, being a fighter-bomber pilot in SEA was not only dangerous, but exciting. To pilots trained for combat, it is the ultimate challenge to test their skills and courage in warfare. He was blessed to have had the opportunity to participate. Life itself is an adventure and this story was his ultimate adventure.

Sadly, his individual return was, like the Confederate troops a century before, filled with lament. The trickle of men returning became more of a flood when the author returned home in January of 1967.

There were no parades of honor for the men returning. Instead, those were replaced with looks of hatred and words of condemnation. In that, he was one of many. The soldiers, sailors and airmen marched home to rejection and confrontation.

> *"We have a responsibility to confront the past with honesty and transparency."*
> President Barack Obama

INTRODUCTION

BOOK ONE
History

CHAPTER ONE
The French Connection
Indochina: 1787 to 1954

> *"You can kill 10 of my men for every one I kill of yours,*
> *but even at those odds, you will lose and I will win."*
>
> Ho Chi Minh to the French at the start of the First Vietnam War

As a combat pilot faced with the reality of a very determined and patriotic enemy, I often wondered how they became who they were. Any meaningful assessment of the war that engulfed all of Southeast Asia needs an understanding of the background and motivations of the Vietnamese. Who are the Vietnamese? How did their history create the fiercely independent people faced by the United States? How did they become such an integrated people with a desire for a common destiny? That fierce independence has manifested itself against China, Japan, France and, most recently, America.

Ho's above quote proved prophetic. In their war with France, the Vietnamese lost more than ten men for each French Foreign Legion soldier lost. In the final tally of what became known to the world as the Vietnam War, the Viet Cong/North Vietnamese Regular forces lost more than ten soldiers to each American killed, yet they ended up victorious just as they were victorious in their rebellion against the French.[1]

Before the involvement of America, France used religion to propel the forces of its spreading empire to subjugate the Vietnamese. The Vietnamese reacted against such subjugation and that reaction was against the Catholic Church as well as the forces of the French military.

The story of the American involvement and confrontation in Vietnam starts with that imposition by France of its will against the nations that later became colonial French Indochina.

Vietnam was not always called Vietnam, but it was always fighting for union and independence as though there was a manifest destiny that it should occupy and control the same slender slice of land that borders the South China Sea. The French flirtation with Vietnam has been a part of that history that reaches back as early as the 17th century.

It was a French Jesuit priest, Father Alexander de Rhodes, who envisioned a beachhead for the Catholic Church on the far-off shores of Southeast Asia. In the early 1600s, he chose to start his Jesuit mission by

---

Author's Note: *1. The French Foreign Legion is no more. But during its existence, it gained a reputation that became romantic legend. It was composed of a motley group of soldiers from every walk-of-life and from many of the countries of the world. Many were escaping the law. The common thread was that they represented France in wars on foreign soil.*

settling in the sparsely-occupied Mekong River Delta. The Vietnamese, who at the time called themselves Annamese, were also interested in expanding their nascent empire into the fertile Delta, which showed such promise for growing their food staple, rice. The Mekong River Delta was then populated by the non-Annamese Cochins. The Cochins are an ancient people, reportedly of Chinese origin, and the Delta area where they settled would be later-known as Cochinchina. For France, Rhodes was following in familiar footsteps that had propelled the Church to reach out worldwide to convert the heathen for God and empire.

What later became known as Annam got its start in the northern area called Tonkin. A dynasty was created in 1009 that took in much of the area that later became North Vietnam. Additional territory was added to the Tonkin Dynasty after 1407 and again after the Siamese-Annamese War of 1834, until the borders of Tonkin became almost identical to that of North Vietnam, created in 1954.

In the 13th Century, prior to the annexation of Tonkin, Annam itself developed further to the south in the coastal area centered around the modern City of Danang. Two hundred years before de Rhodes embarked on his journey, in 1428, the first of a long line of Annamese military leaders, General Le Loi, took control of the developing nation and created an independent dynasty similar to that to the north. His influence eventually reached into Tonkin where he extended his Loi Dynasty.

The separate parts of what much later became Vietnam were in a continual state of flux. In 1568, the southern portion of Annam formed a separate principality under what was called the Nguyen Dynasty. South of Nguyen control, Cochinchina was centered in the more heavily populated areas around present-day Ho Chi Minh City (Saigon) but also encompassed all of the Delta land. To the north of Annam, Tonkin was controlled by the same Loi Dynasty that allowed administrative control by the Trinh Dynasty. At the time, the Trinh Dynasty was also very influential in northern Annam. This confusing condition continued for a considerable period of time, but did result in bringing the separate dynasties closer together. Just as propelled the United States, the spreading of a common language slowly created a united people with a common destiny.

In the latter-half of the 17th Century, The Catholic Church was expanding its influence in Annam that had been started by de Rhodes. The Church was closely associated with the French government and both had a keen interest in spreading Christianity and French Colonialism to far-off lands.

By the start of the 18th Century, Annam had spread south to encompass the coastal regions all the way to a point south of Cam Ranh Bay. The French influence also continued to spread and by the late 18th century, France was vying with England for worldwide colonial dominance. By 1787, the French were fresh from a successful alliance with the 13 English colonies in America that had recently won a rebellion and had split from English dominance. What would later be called the First British Empire had been crippled and Catholic France wanted to replace Protestant England by establishing its own empire and spreading its religious, political, military and commercial interests throughout North Africa and the Pacific region, including Southeast Asia.

France saw its chance for worldwide empire develop in a seemingly obscure event. Pigneau de Behaine, another French Catholic priest living in northern Annam, petitioned the French government to aid a follower named Nguyen Anh who had lost family land in the so-called Tay Son Rebellion. The reasons for the rebellion are murky and it seemed a thinly-veiled pretext to involve the French government and allow an intervention.

The Tay Son Rebellion was instigated by three brothers from the Annamese village of the same name in what later became North Vietnam. By 1787, the low-key rebellion had lasted for 17 years without any resolution. The rebels, while they apparently had ample grievance, did not seem interested in territorial acquisition. Their issue involved what they considered improper treatment of locals. Nonetheless, the rebellion served the interests of the French quite well. They were able to use the excuse of the rebellion and the Annamese request for French military assistance.

Acting on the Church petition, the French government, under King Louis XVI, landed military volunteers in support of de Behaine and immediately came to the aid of the Nguyen Dynasty in its attempt to put down the rebellion. These French troops that landed in 1787 are believed to be the first French soldiers to fight in Southeast Asia.

With the presence of their strongly-armed French allies, the Nguyen Dynasty was able to extinguish the fire of the Tay Son uprising, although it still smoldered until it was finally and totally extinguished in 1802. The French ruse was successful and the influence of the Church increased with the continued presence of the French Army.

Apparently, the Nguyen Dynasty was so grateful to the French for their help at Tay Son, that the Nguyen Emperor, Gia Long, signed a treaty with French King Louis XVI in the same year, 1787. In the treaty, Gia Long ceded the Annam areas of Tourane and Pulo Condore to France in return for continued French military support. This treaty marked the beginning of formal French influence in Southeast Asia. Pulo Condore is a group of islands off the coast of Vietnam near the city of Can Tho. Tourane is another name for the City of Danang and the Tourane Protectorate also included the region surrounding the city. This Port became a valuable point of embarkation for French troops and supplies, plus priests and Annamese-speaking operatives.

In 1801, Gia Long cashed in on the French support promised in the 1787 treaty and acquired control over Cochinchina. The French military also toppled the Loi and Trinh Dynasties, operating in Tonkin. After his competition was vanquished, Gia Long and his French allies turned their guns on what was left of the rebels at Tay Son. With the surrender of the last of the Tay Son rebels, the Nguyen Dynasty held total control over all of what was then called Annam, which stretched from China to the Gulf of Siam.

Since the fifteenth century, it had been a dream of various Annamese leaders to unite all of the Annamese-speaking regions under one government. Under the Nguyens, that dream was realized and Annam was finally united. However, union meant one thing to the Annamese while it meant something quite different to the French. In its own dream of conquest, France now had only one entity with which to deal.

During the early 1800s, France was heavily involved in Annam protecting the work of the Paris Foreign Missions Society, which was affiliated with the Catholic Church. At least that is the reason French history uses as justification for their continued involvement.

The early 1800s also saw the rise of the French General Napoleon Bonaparte in Continental France. To reinforce his army and to fuel his European conquests, Napoleon withdrew the French military from Annam sometime after establishing Gia Long as emperor over the entire Annamese-speaking region. In spite of the loss of their military protectors, the Catholic missionaries continued their stay and continued to expand their influence. The French were apparently following the Spanish model in having the Church subjugate the native peoples before the actual establishment of a colonial system of government. However, they underestimated the Annamese who, in the absence of the French military, began acting against the subtle

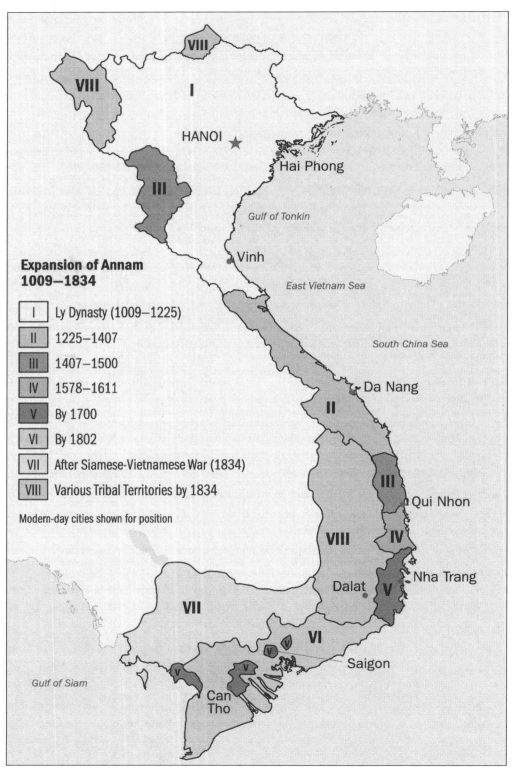

**Expansion of Annam
1009–1834**

I	Ly Dynasty (1009–1225)
II	1225–1407
III	1407–1500
IV	1578–1611
V	By 1700
VI	By 1802
VII	After Siamese-Vietnamese War (1834)
VIII	Various Tribal Territories by 1834

Modern-day cities shown for position

French plan of subjugation. This would not be the only time that France would underestimate the Annamese.

The Nguyens increasingly saw these Jesuit missionaries of the Foreign Missions Society as a political threat. They began to consider that the Jesuits were acting in behalf of more than just the Church. Courtesans were an influential factor in the dynastic system and the Nguyens feared the influence of the Society and the Church due to the church's insistence on monogamy. Courtesans were concubines who were important and integral parts of the dynastic courts of the emperors. The emperors used the concubines as sources of intelligence and as a means of influence and control. If the Church was able to prevail on monogamy, the dynasties would have been thrown into confusion and instability. Monogamy was thus a major threat to the entire dynastic order.

Relations between the Nguyens and France continued to deteriorate until the French military again decided to land troops in Annam. Sometime prior to or during the time of the fall of Napoleon in 1815, the French had relinquished control of Tourane. As France began to rebuild after the disaster of Napoleon, the French military worked to reinstall it influence around the world.[2]

In 1858, in what amounted to an invasion, the French Navy, under orders from Napoleon III, landed French Army troops and began to invest the City of Danang and the important Port of Tourane. Once the Port was under their control, the French were able to land additional forces and supplies and began waging a military and political campaign to topple the dynasties.

For the next five years, the French used a combination of guile, diplomacy and military prowess to increase their influence over the entire region. In 1863, the Cambodian King Norodom requested the establishment of a French protectorate over his country. Siam (now Thailand) had suzerainty over Cambodia but renounced it in 1867 in favor of France in return for certain guarantees by France.

The French campaign for control of Annam lasted until 1874, when France finally seized all of Annam by military force. They installed a dual system of administration along with the Nguyen Dynasty. In effect, the Nguyen's administered and the French controlled.

Ten years later, France militarily attacked mainland China. The Sino-French War of 1884 and 1885 ended in a French victory and resulted in France expanding its territory in Southeast Asia by obtaining control of the extreme north of Annam, the ancient land of Tonkin.

In 1887, an even hundred years after France had first landed troops in Annam, it formally formed the colony of French Indochina, which initially included Annam, Tonkin, Cochinchina and the Kingdom of Cambodia. Annam, Tonkin and Cochinchina are all part of what is now Vietnam.

France continued its military conquests by attacking Siam. In 1893, Laos was added to the French colonial territory after the conclusion of the Franco-Siamese War with what is now Thailand. The small territory of Kouang-Tcheou-Wan was added to Indochina in 1900. An accompanying map shows the development of Annam, while a second map shows the creation of Indochina by the French through land acquisitions.

France continued pressuring Siam for additional lands and territory. From 1904 through 1907, under pretexts of entitlement, they were able to acquire territory on the west bank of the Mekong near the city of Luang Prabang and around Champasak in southern Laos as well as additional territory in western Cambodia.

Author's Note: *2. One hundred and thirty years after the fall of Napoleon, France would again work to reinstate French troops in Vietnam after another French defeat.*

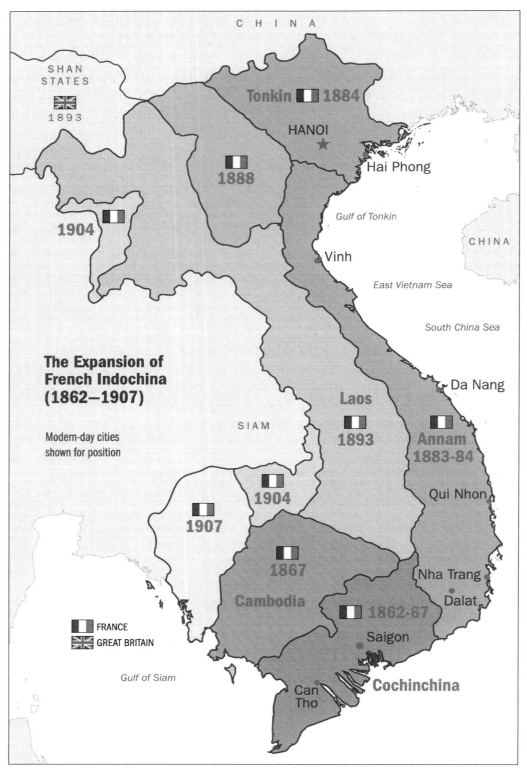

CHINA

SHAN
STATES

1893

Tonkin 1884

HANOI

Hai Phong

1888

Gulf of Tonkin

1904

CHINA

Vinh

East Vietnam Sea

South China Sea

**The Expansion of
French Indochina
(1862–1907)**

Modern-day cities
shown for position

SIAM

Da Nang

Laos

1893

Annam
1883-84

Qui Nhon

1904

1907

1867

Nha Trang

Cambodia

Dalat

1862-67

Saigon

FRANCE
GREAT BRITAIN

Gulf of Siam

Can
Tho

Cochinchina

From then until 1938, they exchanged territory with Siam until the borders of Indochina were finally determined. These borders did not last long due to the swift advance of Imperial Japanese troops with the advent of WWII. In a bit of irony, the treaty between France and Siam securing the borders of Siam and Indochina was signed in Tokyo in 1938, well after the Japanese had attacked China and initiated the Pacific portion of World War II.

When Germany overran France in WWII and established the puppet government in Vichy, the Colonial French soldiers and administrators in Indochina transferred their allegiance to the control of Vichy, which then continued the administration and occupation of the colony. Since Vichy France was under the control of and allied with the German Nazis and the Nazis were allied with Japan, the Japanese shared administration and control of all of Indochina with Vichy France, starting in 1940. Both Vichy French soldiers and Imperial Japanese soldiers together patrolled the streets of Hanoi and Saigon.

THE MAKING OF A REVOLUTIONARY:

Nguyen Sinh Cung was born in 1890, the son of a teacher in French-dominated Annam. In 1912, at the age of 22, he worked as a helper to a ship's cook and traveled by boat to the United States. He lived in Harlem working for a time at menial labor. In 1913, he moved to Boston and continued working at menial jobs, but eventually was hired as a line manager for General Motors.

During his stay in the United States, Nguyen reportedly became familiar with the history of the American revolt against their British overlords and the ideals embodied in the American Declaration of Independence and Constitution.

At various times, Nguyen traveled to England and worked at odd jobs there, including as a waiter at a hotel and reportedly as a pastry chef. In 1918, he was back in Boston working as a helper for a wealthy family.

Nguyen was an intellectual, as was his father, and before leaving Annam he had become fluent in French. In 1919, Nguyen left the United States and traveled to France, where he stayed until his 1923 move to Moscow. It was in the Russian capital that he was first acquainted with Communist doctrine.

In 1924, he moved to Canton, China to continue his studies. Nationalist Chinese General Chiang Kai-shek interrupted those studies in 1927 by fomenting an Anti-Communist military action, which forced Nguyen and some of his associates to leave China and begin a series of journeys. Nguyen's journeys and studies took him to various European countries and eventually back to China in 1938. From then until 1941, he worked as an advisor to the Communist Chinese Army under General Mao Tse Tung (Zedong), then operating against General Chiang Kai-shek and his Nationalist Chinese Army.

REBELLION:

The history of Annamese rebellion against French rule started in 1885, two years before the formal establishment of French Indochina in 1887. The rebellions were fomented by various groups and continued off and on until the advent of WWII. The motivations of those who rebelled were the same as motivated Americans in their desire to live free of foreign oppression in the form of the British monarchy. Those motivations go back to the ancient Annamese "dream of unity" free from outside or foreign influence.

In the mid-1920s, Annam changed its name to become Vietnam. When WWII arrived in the form of Japanese troops, they found the Vietnamese in open rebellion against the French. The elusive Vietnamese guerrilla force of black-clad rebels called itself the "men in black." The more formal name for the rebel force was the Viet Minh.

In 1941, Nguyen returned to a very changed Annam. It was now called Vietnam and he was a Vietnamese instead of being an Annamese. The French troops and administrators were the same, although under a different, now Fascist, government. Japanese troops now patrolled the cities and countryside along with the French.

Nguyen had also changed. He had left Annam as a 22-year-old student who longed for adventure. He returned as a Communist revolutionary with patriotic ideals, largely fostered by the United States. He returned with knowledge of military requirements and organization from his time in China. He returned with a flaming desire to rid his country of foreign domination. He also returned with a new name: Ho Chi Minh.

Nguyen now Ho, took over the political arm of the fledgling Viet Minh and, with the help of his long-time associate, General Vo Nguyen Giap, led a force of 10,000 "men in black" in their battle against the Vichy French, which later became known as the start of the First Indochina War. The Viet Minh also recognized Japan as the occupiers that they were and declared an unofficial war against the military forces of Japan. The Viet Minh actually had three foreign enemies: The Vichy French administrators, the Imperial Japanese occupiers and the Nationalist Chinese military who was making inroads into northern Vietnam to counter the Japanese. The Nationalist Chinese were fully aware that Ho had been working with the Chinese Communist Army under their leader General Mao Zedong, also known as Mao Tse-Tung. The Nationalists briefly imprisoned Ho in 1943, but then they released him with the knowledge that Ho was fighting their common enemy, Japan.

The American government was also involved and allied itself with the Viet Minh. The clandestine OSS, predecessor of the CIA, supported Ho and smuggled weapons and other supplies to the Viet Minh in their battles against the Japanese. Actually, Ho worked very closely with the United States as represented by the OSS. In late 1944, he was successfully treated by OSS doctors for malaria and dysentery.

In March of 1945, with Continental France liberated by the Allied armies and the collapse of the government of Vichy France, the French troops, who had maintained control of Indochina with the Japanese, began to leave. Japan then decided to take complete control of all of Indochina. The Viet Minh resisted, but the stronger Japanese military forces kept power for five more months until the news of their government's surrender to the Americans came through in August of 1945. With that announcement, Japanese forces began a general withdrawal from its occupied territories including Indochina. That left the Viet Minh with the only military force of any consequence.

During August, when the Japanese forces were withdrawing and the Vichy French military forces were long gone, the Viet Minh proclaimed Ho Chi Minh to be Chairman of the Provisional Government and Ho proclaimed the Declaration of Independence of Vietnam. With this declaration, the Democratic Republic of Vietnam (DRV) was born.

The opening lines of the Vietnamese Declaration of Independence read: **"All men are created equal; they are endowed by their Creator with certain inalienable Rights; among these are Life, Liberty and the pursuit of Happiness."** Thus, the exact words of our own American Declaration of Independence were used at the birth of an independent Vietnam. It appears that some of the same common values that motivated the Viet Minh under Ho also motivated the creators of our own government. Readers are left to wonder just how dedicated a Communist Ho was with his obviously strongly-instilled American values of independence.

After the end of WWII, the major powers had something different than independence in mind when it came to Vietnam. The United States, Britain and the Soviet Union had already met regarding the aftermath of the defeat of Germany and Japan. The last meeting between Churchill, Roosevelt and Stalin dealt with the disposition of a post-war world. The then-insignificant war being fought by Vietnamese partisans against French rule was lost in the considerations for a new world order being created by the victorious powers.

President Roosevelt actually offered Indochina to the Nationalist Chinese for their control after the end of WWII. The Nationalists refused. Roosevelt then worked a deal with Stalin to share hegemony in Vietnam after the war, with the Communists taking the northern part and the British taking the southern. This cavalier attitude of playing God with the lives of those in Southeast Asia had unforeseen consequences. With Roosevelt's death and Harry Truman's ascent, the attitude of the United States towards Russia and, indirectly, Indochina took a turn.

In 1946, the United States was beginning to view its wartime ally, the Soviet Union, with a different eye. The Soviets were ignoring verbal agreements they had made with the British and Americans and had established Communist regimes in those eastern European countries that they had overrun in their military drive toward Nazi Germany.

With the Japanese defeated, Nationalist Chinese General Chiang Kai-shek turned his attention to his Communist foe, General Mao Zedong. In September, 1946, Chiang Kai-shek sent an army of 200,000 men to Hanoi to force the dissolution of the Communist Party of the Democratic Republic of Vietnam. Facing such an overwhelming military force, the Viet Minh had to capitulate. Ho formed a coalition government with the Chinese and renounced the Communists. While professing allegiance to world Communism throughout his career, his actions often showed him to be more of a nationalist patriot rather than an internationalist.

With the end of WWII, the Free French under General Charles de Gaulle were influencing the victorious allied nations to reinstall French control over its former colonial empire, including Indochina. De Gaulle would later repay the United States for its support by opposing American action in Southeast Asia. In the mid-1960s, he visited the Cambodian capital and demanded that America leave Southeast Asia. He also sent trainers to the Cambodian military and French instructors were involved in the MIG training of Cambodian pilots.

After the end to the WWII hostilities in Europe and, with the support of the United States, France began to make plans to retake control of Algeria, Indochina and the rest of its pre-war colonial empire. France was faced with a de-facto Viet Minh/ Nationalist Chinese government backed by a Chinese army of 200,000 soldiers. At the time, France had commercial and territorial interests in Shanghai, China. France reached agreement with the Nationalists that their troops would depart Indochina in return for France ceding its interests in Shanghai. Before they departed, perhaps recognizing that a future conflict with the Communists was looming, the Nationalists forced Ho to sign an agreement with the French in which Vietnam would be an autonomous state within the French Indochinese Federation. The French then landed troops and reestablished control over Indochina.

Prior to WWII, the Indochinese Federation was comprised of four protectorates controlled by France, but administered by the Emperors of Vietnam and the Kings of Cambodia and Luang Prabang. Luang Prabang was the former name of Laos and also is the name of its ancient capital. After WWII, the Indochinese Federation consisted of Cambodia, Vietnam and Laos. The territory of what used to be the Federation is geographically a major part of what is now considered Southeast Asia (SEA).

While the French formally left the local rulers in control, they gathered all power in their hands with the local rulers acting only as figureheads. Ho's agreement with the French was just a ploy by Ho to get the Chinese Army out of Hanoi. When the Chinese left, the agreement with the French broke down. The Viet Minh reinstated the Communist Party and again proclaimed independence. Ho is reported to have said, "The last time the Chinese came, they stayed a thousand years. The French are foreigners. Colonialism is dying. The white man is finished in Asia. But if the Chinese stay now, they will never go. As for me, I prefer to sniff French shit for five years than to eat Chinese shit for the rest of my life."

In retrospect, it is a shame that the government of the United States did not have better knowledge of the enmity between China and Vietnam. If it had, the history of SEA might have turned out very differently.[3]

While the Nationalist Chinese army had gone, the forces of the De Gaulle Free French, that had recently arrived, were in its place. Fighting soon broke out between the Viet Minh and the French. This time Ho's enemy was the same that had established Indochina and not the Vichy imposter.

Ho was under no illusion regarding the upcoming battle with the French. Ho stated that, "Our resistance will be long and painful, but whatever the sacrifices, however long the struggle, we shall fight to the end until Vietnam is fully independent and unified."

The fighting continued for eight long years, until 1954, when the Indochinese Federation dissolved in the ashes of the French military defeat at Dien Bien Phu, a northwest Vietnamese outpost on the Laotian border.

Prior to the arrival of the Chinese, in February 1946, Ho had sent a telegram to the Truman Administration in the United States. The telegram stated: "I therefore most earnestly appeal to you personally and to the American people to interfere urgently in support of our independence and help making the negotiations more in keeping with the principles of the Atlantic and San Francisco Charters."

The newly liberated French had been requesting American assistance for at least a year prior to the receipt of the telegram. Clark Clifford, the former Special Assistant to President Truman, recalls that there was a strong push from the French to support the French effort to re-impose its domination over Indochina now that WWII was over. He felt that there was not much of a push inside the US to support the Vietnamese. Very few meetings took place between the Americans and the North Vietnamese. The entire issue was considered minor.

Clifford later recalled that the general feeling in the administration about Indochina was: "It was more the attitude that now that the Second World War was over, we would attempt to help the nations of Western Europe to reconstruct. France had owned Indochina. The reason they'd lost it was due to Japanese aggression. We were, I believe, attempting to take those steps which would tend to return areas of that kind to the status quo. I don't recall taking part in any kind of discussion or policy debate about whether we should assist the French in their colonial or imperialist attitude. I would be rather surprised if there was much of a debate in that regard because it seemed to me to be the rather settled policy that we were attempting to return conditions to those that had existed prior to the changes that had taken place in the Second World War as the result of Japanese aggression."

Author's Note: *3. A short four years after the surrender of South Vietnam to the Northern Communists and only ten years after Chinese Communist MIGs, pilots, AAA batteries and military units left North Vietnam, there was an intense border war fought between Vietnam and China. That war will be more fully described in a later chapter.*

Several things acted against the Vietnamese request: The administration felt that the North Vietnamese situation with Ho Chi Minh was contemporary with the Chinese situation with Mao Tse-Tung and that many of the timing issues were germane to both. The Truman Administration apparently did not have adequate information about the importance of Vietnamese independence and it was concerned about Communist expansion. If there had been knowledge about the Vietnamese long hatred of the Chinese, the issue might have ended differently. However, no such appreciation or knowledge apparently existed and the result was that the well-intentioned telegram from Ho Chi Minh remained unanswered.

One is left to wonder how our American history would have changed if someone back in 1946 would have had the interest to dig deeper into the events happening in Indochina; find out about the history of the area and had had the courtesy to at least answer the telegram.

THE CHARTERS:

In his telegram to Truman, Ho mentions the Atlantic and San Francisco Charters. To what was he referring?

Most Americans would like to believe we, as a country, stand for a strong set of specific principles. It is those principles for which most of us believe that ours is an exceptional country.

Author's Note: *The following information comes from the website of the United Nations (www.un.org under Atlantic and United Nations Charters). It also includes information from our own Department of State's Office of the Historian (https:history.state.gov/milestones):*

In August of 1941, the United States had been supplying the British with war equipment and munitions for over two years. The gathering storm of the ever-widening war threatened to engulf America. It was looking more and more that we would soon join Great Britain in its attempt to stop the Fascist countries in their threat to dominate the world.

The Atlantic Charter was a statement of the unified principles for which the United States and Great Britain stood as America faced imminent war. It was signed by President Franklin Roosevelt aboard the USS Augusta on August 14, 1941 along with the Prime Minister of Great Britain, Winston Churchill.

The Charter was later signed by the following countries in London, England on September 24, 1941: USSR, Belgium, Czechoslovakia, Greece, Luxembourg, Holland, Norway, Poland, Yugoslavia and France as represented by General Charles de Gaulle of the Free French forces. Since many of the signatory nations were occupied by the Nazi's, the document was signed by the occupied nation's legitimate governments in exile.

The United Nations interprets that the Atlantic Charter includes "the right of every people to choose their own form of government." The United States Department of State agrees that the Charter means that "the United States and Great Britain would be committed to supporting the restoration of self-governments for all countries that had been occupied during the War (WWII) and allowing all peoples to choose their own form of government."

The San Francisco Charter, to which Ho refers, was actually the United Nations Charter signed on June 26, 1945 in Veteran's Memorial Hall in San Francisco, California.

Chapter XI, Article 73 of the U.N. Charter requires "countries administering those colonies (pre-war Colonial systems) to develop self-government, to take due account of the political aspirations of the peoples, and to assist them in the progressive development of their free political institutions."

This document was signed by more than 50 countries, including the United States and France. Now hear the words of President Truman as he spoke to those United Nations delegates on the day of their signing of the Charter: "The Charter of the United Nations, which you have just signed, is a solid structure upon which you can build a better world. With this, the world can begin to look forward to the time when all worthy beings may be permitted to live decently as free people. If we fail to use it, we shall betray all those who have died so that we might meet here in freedom and safety to create it. If we seek to use it selfishly for the advantage of any one nation or any small group of nations, we shall be equally guilty of that betrayal."

Ho's request to Truman was a representation of a people who had been under a colonial yoke and were even then fighting French forces to gain the freedom mentioned in both Charters. Clifford stated that the Truman administration was attempting to reset the colonial structure that was in effect prior to World War II. Yet the U.N. Charter, which Truman signed, specifically states that pre-war colonial governments would develop self-government for the peoples that they had colonized.

Truman's lack of action and implicit support of the re-imposition of the colonial domination of France over the peoples of Vietnam represents a repudiation of the American and UN principles for which he had previously spoken. In Truman's words "we shall be equally guilty of that betrayal."

In 1950, the Soviet Union recognized the Democratic Republic of Vietnam, which included all of Vietnam. That year the Chinese, now under a Communist government, also recognized Vietnam. Both the Soviets and Chinese assisted the Viet Minh with supplies and training in their war against the French.

The Communists had only taken over China the year before, in 1949, after having defeated Chiang Kai-shek's forces and driven them offshore to the island of Formosa, now called Taiwan. Part of the agreement between the Soviets, the Chinese and the Vietnamese was that China would act as a protector for Vietnam in its own war of independence. With the addition of Chinese support and Chinese and Russian supplies, the war against the French started to take a turn.

The French were at a disadvantage in Southeast Asia. For the Viet Minh, their lines of supply were short and they were operating in a familiar area. Many of their fighters were operating near their places of birth. The French, however, had long and cumbersome supply lines. They were continually besieged by guerrilla forces and were continually subject to sabotage.

After 1950, it was only a matter of time before the forces of the Viet Minh were victorious. Ho's military commander, General Vo Nguyen Giap, proved to be a genius in planning and fighting a guerrilla war. The French, represented by the French Foreign Legion, were out of their element. By the start of 1954, the situation was getting precarious for the French. Their forces had been driven into small pockets. Their national leaders were tiring of the long wars to keep their former colonial territories under control. Their armies in Southeast Asia were exhausted.

The culmination of eight years of warfare was the battle of Dien Bien Phu. On March 13, 1954, the "men in black" started their offensive surge. For 56 days, the French were forced back and back until they only occupied a small enclave in a militarily precarious position surrounded by high hills dominated by the Viet Minh. On May 7th, the French capitulated.

The following day the French announced that they were withdrawing from Vietnam and the rest of Southeast Asia. French Indochina was no more. The French had suffered 7,000 casualties and a further 11,000 were taken prisoner. Twelve years later, a gang of 300 of these same French prisoners would be forced to repair road and railroad damage caused by the interdiction efforts of US Air Force and US Navy planes bombing the Northeast and Northwest rail lines in North Vietnam.

In 1954, following the French defeat, an Accord was signed in Geneva, Switzerland that split Vietnam into two parts, North and South, with the North under the control of Ho Chi Minh and his Viet Minh Army.

The same victorious Viet Minh General Vo Nguyen Giap, who vanquished the French at Dien Bien Phu, would later guide the formerly Viet Minh North Vietnamese Army and the South Vietnamese Viet Cong military forces to their eventual ouster of a second Western power from Indochina.

"History does not long entrust the care of freedom to the weak or the timid."

General of the Army Dwight D. Eisenhower

VIỆT-NAM DÂN CHỦ CỘNG HÒA

CHÍNH PHỦ LÂM THỜI

BO NGOAI GIAO

*

YKB-3735-1

HANOI FEBRUARY 28 1946

TELEGRAM

MAR 11 REC

PRESIDENT HOCHIMINH VIETNAM DEMOCRATIC REPUBLIC HANOI

TO THE PRESIDENT OF THE UNITED STATES OF AMERICA WASHINGTON D.C.

ON BEHALF OF VIETNAM GOVERNMENT AND PEOPLE I BEG TO INFORM YOU

THAT IN COURSE OF CONVERSATIONS BETWEEN VIETNAM GOVERNMENT AND FRENCH

REPRESENTATIVES THE LATTER REQUIRE THE SECESSION OF COCHINCHINA AND THE

RETURN OF FRENCH TROOPS IN HANOI STOP MEANWHILE FRENCH POPULATION AND

TROOPS ARE MAKING ACTIVE PREPARATIONS FOR A COUP DE MAIN IN HANOI AND

FOR MILITARY AGGRESSION STOP I THEREFORE MOST EARNESTLY APPEAL TO YOU

PERSONALLY AND TO THE AMERICAN PEOPLE TO INTERFERE URGENTLY IN SUPPORT

OF OUR INDEPENDENCE AND HELP MAKING THE NEGOTIATIONS MORE IN KEEPING WITH

THE PRINCIPLES OF THE ATLANTIC AND SAN FRANCISCO CHARTERS

RESPECTFULLY

HOCHIMINH

Dated February 28th, 1946, this telegram was sent from Ho Chi Minh to President Harry S. Truman, requesting the assistance of the United States government in the negotiations with France. Source: (National Archives Identifier 305263); Joint Chiefs of Staff. Office of Strategic Services. (06/13/1942 - 10/01/1945); Records of the Office of Strategic Services, 1919-1948; Record Group 226; National Archives.

CHAPTER TWO

A New Foreign Legion
Southeast Asia: 1955 to 1965

"The first casualty, when war comes, is truth."

California Senator Hiram Johnson, 1918

While the French defeat at Dien Bien Phu is well known, what is less known was that the Eisenhower Administration tried to reverse the inevitable. The United States Air Force flew 1,800 airlift sorties comprising 13,000 flying hours from the start of 1954 until the end of the battle on May 7th. Operating out of Gia Lam airfield near Hanoi, the USAF dropped tons of American supplies to the surrounded French Foreign Legion troops in a vain effort.

Gia Lam eventually gained notoriety as a primary MIG (fighter) base for the North Vietnamese in its defensive actions against attacking American aircraft during the Vietnam War. Gia Lam was also the departure point for the American Prisoners of War (POWs) in their flights to freedom from long captivity under their Cuban overlords in the North Vietnamese prison sardonically-known to the POWs as the "Hanoi Hilton." [4]

THE ALLEGED START OF THE VIETNAMESE WAR:

The Gulf of Tonkin Incidents that were used as a pretext for the Gulf of Tonkin Resolution by Congress, which authorized Vietnamese combat operations, were reported on August 2 and August 4, 1964. The Incidents, and a declassified National Security Agency report on them, is the subject of another chapter. Both purported attacks cannot be confirmed.

The Gulf incidents that precipitated action involved North Vietnamese coastal patrol boats that supposedly attacked US Navy destroyers. In retaliation, American President Lyndon Johnson later stated that our first offensive action in Southeast Asia was a US Navy fighter-bomber attack on four patrol boat facilities located near the North Vietnamese coastal city of Vinh on August 5th, 1964. That statement was a fabrication.

What can be confirmed is that the Congressional authorization for war against North Vietnam and the Viet Cong in South Vietnam came on August 7, 1964 in the form of the Gulf of Tonkin Resolution. From our government's stated perspective, the Vietnam War started with that Resolution. That is also a fabrication.

Author's Notes: *4. Long after their return, the author attended a reunion of the POW Wing and the Red River Valley Fighter Pilots Association, also known as the "River Rats." The Rats, comprised of those who flew and fought against the Hanoi/ Haiphong targeting complex, and POWs were guests of Ross Perot. The author was present when the POWs, at a seminar, told of their torture at the hands of the two Co-Commanders of the Hanoi Hilton, both soldiers from the Cuban military.*

THE REALITY:

Over four years before the Gulf of Tonkin Resolution, first President Eisenhower and later President Kennedy authorized the movement of military units to Southeast Asia. In 1960, Eisenhower committed the first American military units in the form of Special Forces to the Republic of Vietnam (RVN), better known as South Vietnam. Eisenhower's commitment came only six years after he also committed air combat units to help France in its defense of Dien Bien Phu, as mentioned above.

In 1960, a slow buildup of Allied forces began in Laos. Air units were deployed and on December 23, 1960, the first American Air Force aircraft was fired upon. It was an AC-47 carrying the American Air Attaché to Laos and it sustained hits. On March 23, 1961, the Pathet Lao shot down an American C-47. In April, the USAF 6010th TAC Group was moved to Don Muang airfield near Bangkok, Thailand. Also in April, 1961, F-102s from the 509th Fighter Interceptor Squadron (FIS) were moved to Don Muang. On April 29th, the Joint Chiefs of Staff authorized CINCPAC to move 5,000 troops to Ubon Air Base in Thailand and Danang Air Base in South Vietnam. That was followed up in November, 1961, with an RF-101C reconnaissance (recce) unit moved from Misawa Air Base in Japan. The Thai government actually gave the USAF the keys to five Thai bases in 1961. Further south, on November 14, 1961, the American Joint Chiefs of Staff (JCS) directed air units to be deployed to the Republic of Vietnam from the First Air Commando Group based at Eglin Air Force Base near Fort Walton Beach in Florida.

The units were part of an operation called "Jungle Jim." This was a covert training and reconnaissance operation to be flown by American pilots using Vietnamese markings on their aircraft. Jungle Jim was replaced one month later in December, 1961 by "Operation Farm Gate." Farm Gate flew covert strike, not training, missions. The overt mission of Farm Gate was supposed to be flown by Vietnamese Air Force pilots trained by USAF pilots. Instead, American military pilots were flying actual combat missions in South Vietnam in December, 1961.

What is even less known is that American military and contracted civilian pilots were flying combat in Laos at an even earlier date. These flights were conducted by a variety of aircraft and forces. Some were observation flights flown by U.S. Army light aircraft. Some were Forward Air Controllers or observation flights flown by USAF pilots. Others were transport missions moving troops and supplies for allied tribes and armies. Still others were training flights.

As described in a later chapter, there were many so-called airlines that had aviation divisions devoted to combat flying using civilian pilots from various countries, but mostly from America. While cargo and search-and-rescue were flown, actual bombing missions were also flown by forces in Thailand and Laos under contract with the Central Intelligence Agency (CIA) and the U.S. Agency for International Development (USAID). These missions were the start of two clandestine air wars that involved all of Southeast Asia.

On May 31, 1962, the Australian Air Force joined the nascent fight and moved a squadron of F-86 Sabre fighter jets to Ubon Air Base in Thailand.

Prior to 1962, clandestine air forces soon began operations out of remote SEA bases using the A-1H and T-28 propeller-driven aircraft for combat as well as numerous transport aircraft for cargo. The clandestine air forces were primarily contracted for airlift of people and supplies by the CIA, although some actual combat was flown. The headquarters for these clandestine units was Udorn Royal Thai Air Base in the jungles of northeastern Thailand. These units were primarily used in Laos, but some operations were performed in

North Vietnam and some in Cambodia.[5]

These documents were declassified in the 1990s. Excerpts are included in this chapter and also in Chapter 24. *Direct quotes from those documents are included in italics.*

The SEA War was the largest use of paramilitary forces by the CIA in their history, before or since. The clandestine air forces, including that of the CIA, Air America, Continental Air Services (CAS) and other contracted air forces, will be described in another chapter entitled "Spook Heaven." Additionally, clandestine USAF air units called the Air Commandos were moved to Southeast Asia, initially operating out of Bien Hoa Air Base located near Saigon.

In 1965, I attended AGOS (Air-Ground Operations School). This was a joint Army-Air Force school based at jungle-shrouded Eglin Air Force Base just outside of Fort Walton Beach, Florida. Eglin is a huge base with lots of auxiliary fields. Hurlburt Field is designated Eglin Auxiliary Field Number 10 and was the headquarters of the Air Commandos. While at AGOS, I visited Hurlburt and talked two Commando pilots into allowing me to fly with them on range missions.

It was slow flying as co-pilot on the lumbering A-1Hs. Pattern speed was 160 knots and while in a bombing dive, the speed stayed at 160. The large engine nacelle and propeller acted as a giant speed brake. One of the two pilots that I flew with at Hurlburt was later killed flying strikes for the Commandos in SEA.

The Air Commando units operating in SEA were initially flying both training and operational flights within South Vietnam. Later, they were moved to a clandestine base in Thailand called Nakhon Phanom (NKP) that housed a variety of aircraft including those of the CIA, CIA-contracted airlines, and the USAF "Nail" and "Raven" FACs (Forward Air Controllers flying observation aircraft) that played such a significant part in the air war in Laos.

The primary air base for clandestine operations was Udorn, also in northeastern Thailand. From Udorn, CIA and USAF air units were based at a multitude of airstrips located throughout northern Laos and specifically in the north central portion that included the strategic Plain of Jars.

This twin subterfuge of the Kennedy Administration that the American forces were not engaged in SEA combat operations and the secret natures of the civilian and military covert operations in Laos were continued into the Administration of Lyndon Johnson after Kennedy's assassination.

THE PATHET LAO ATTACK:

The Pathet Lao was one of three Laotian armies operating in Laos at the start of 1964. The Pathet Lao was the Communist military force engaged against the Royal Lao Army in what was essentially a civil war. A third force was the independent Neutralist Army. The Pathet Lao was created in 1954 with the help of the Chinese and North Vietnamese and was supplied and supported by both the Viet Minh in North Vietnam and the Chinese Communists, although the primary support came from North Vietnam.

During the SEA War, the Laotian political and military situation was very confusing. While American and Royal Lao aircraft were operating in the panhandle and central Laos, the Chinese Air Force had unopposed

---

Author's Notes: 5. *Two declassified Air Force documents detailed the history of our actions in Southeast Asia as well as the Rules of Engagement that defined how we were to fight the war. The two Air Force documents that dealt with our Rules are: "Evolution of the Rules of Engagement for SEA – 1960-1965" and "Rules of Engagement – January 1, 1966-November 1, 1969." Both of these documents were classified TOP SECRET NOFORN. This meant that no foreign nationals were allowed access.*

control of the skies over the far northern part of Laos. China was protecting its road system through the mountains that connected it with Laos, North Vietnam, Burma and, indirectly, Thailand.

The presence of North Vietnamese troops in Laos had a dual purpose. They had been located there since the fall of the French Foreign Legion forces at Dien Bien Phu. Their primary purpose was to protect their supply lines into South Vietnam over a Southern Laotian (panhandle) road system that became known as the Ho Chi Minh Trial or the HCMT. The HCMT supported the Communist rebel army of South Vietnam popularly known as the Viet Cong.

A secondary purpose for the large presence of North Vietnamese troops in Laos was the support for the Communist rebellion against the forces of the Royal Family of Laos. This rebellion was instigated by a significant Communist army called the Pathet Lao. The Pathet Lao were entirely dependent on the support given them by the North Vietnamese

On the ground, the North Vietnamese Army had battalion and then division-sized units protecting their supply lines to the South. On the opposing side, special operations forces included Cambodes, Hmung tribesmen, Philippinos, the Americans and later South Vietnamese Regular Army units operating against the Ho Chi Minh Trail areas of infiltration that snaked through Southern Laos as well as Cambodia.

The covert air war in the HCMT area was flown primarily by USAF high-performance jet aircraft flying out of bases in South Vietnam and Thailand as well as US Navy attack aircraft flying off a multitude of aircraft carriers located in the Gulf of Tonkin and occasionally the South China Sea further south of the Gulf.

In the north-central part of Laos, the ground war was being fought against the Pathet Lao by the Royal Laotian Army and the clandestine tribal forces allied with them and supported by the CIA. These forces were primarily the Mao, Lao and Hmung tribesmen. In the air, the Royal Laotian Air Force was supplemented by units of CIA pilots flying propeller-driven aircraft and other air forces referred to as airlines, which were on contract to the CIA and the United States Agency for International Development.

The second of the three independent armies operating in Laos, primarily in the Plaines des Jarres (Plain of Jars), was the Royal Laotian Army. The Royal Lao Army was the official protector of the King of Laos and was created in 1954, with the help of France, after the fall of Dien Bien Phu.

The third military force operating in Laos was the Neutralist Army, which was not supporting the King nor were they supporting the Communist insurgency allied with the Viet Minh in North Vietnam. In early 1964, the Pathet Lao was not fighting the Neutralist forces, instead concentrating their own forces against the Royalists.

In what can be considered the first day of what became the enlarged SEA War, *on May 17, 1964, the Pathet Lao turned against the Neutralists who were co-located with them on the central Laotian Plaines des Jarres. An overt intervention decision was made by the United States to bolster the Neutralists and to serve notice on the Communists that the U.S. was determined to back the legal government decided by the Geneva Accords, signed in 1954. It was decided that a reconnaissance effort might provide a means of proving that the Viet Minh and the Chinese Communists were illegally* (according to the Geneva Accords) *assisting the indigenous Pathet Lao.*

On the same day, May 17, the American Ambassador to Laos, Leonard Unger, authorized the use of 100- and 500-pound bombs against the attacking forces. The naval commander of the Pacific alerted the Navy to *be prepared to conduct a show of force and reconnaissance over Laos.*

20

United States Air Force units were already pre-positioned in SEA. A recce task force, nicknamed "Able Mable," was in place at Tan Son Nhut Air Base outside of Saigon. F-100 Supersabre fighter-bombers were located at Clark Air Base in the Philippines and Takhli Air Base in Thailand as well as at Tan Son Nhut.

The first combat missions against the Pathet Lao positions in the Plaines des Jarres (PDJ) were the first effective use of jet aircraft on combat missions in the widening SEA war. They occurred on May 18, 1964, and were flown by armed US Navy aircraft. *The USAir Force flew its first mission "during the daylight hours" of the next day. The joint USN-USAF forces were designated the "Yankee Team"* under the command of Air Force *Major General Joseph Moore,* who acted as *coordinator between the Air Force and Navy. Unfortunately, General Moore was only given authority to "suggest" but not to compel Navy actions,* thus creating divided command which was a hallmark of many of our actions throughout the war.

On May 29, General Moore sent a message to Pacific Air Forces (PACAF) requesting that he be given authority to employ U.S. aircraft and crews for search and rescue (SAR) as he "deemed necessary in the event U.S. aircraft were downed over Laos. He did not receive a reply until June 6, 1964 when a Navy aircraft was shot down. The photo-recce pilot ejected successfully.

The USAF Air Attaché in Vientiane Laos, Colonel Robert F. Tyrell, requested Air America (CIA) helicopters be used to rescue the Navy pilot, Lieutenant Charles "Chuck" Klussman. Three requests were forwarded to the Ambassador asking for planes to fly close-air-support for the Air America rescue choppers. By the time authorization came through, both rescue choppers had been shot up and Lieutenant Klussman was a prisoner of the Pathet Lao.[6]

The following is an account of the Navy action, described above on June 6th, taken from the unpublished book, "Sundowner Days—Recollections of a Fighter Pilot" by former Navy F-8 Fighter Pilot Lieutenant Freeman Marcy:

"In late May 1964, we (Carrier Kitty Hawk) arrived off the coast of Vietnam and the photo birds began their missions over the Plaines des Jarres of central Laos, where the Pathet Lao, aided by the North Vietnamese, threatened to take over Laos. The rest of the wing flew normal training-type flights off shore. However, the photo planes were coming back with battle damage and it was obvious a rescue plan was needed. Soon after the photos launched, June 6th, skipper Ray and I as his wingman went down to the ships intelligence room for a RESCAP (rescue combat air patrol) briefing. After a rather long briefing, the skipper and I manned our aircraft on the port and starboard catapults. Meanwhile the next two pilots began the second briefing. It was a short watch, and not long after we manned up, the news came that Lt. Chuck Klussman (flying one of the photo birds) had been shot down over Laos and we started our engines, my war had begun. Hooked to the catapult, ship into the wind, I saw CAG (Navy-Commander Air Group) signaling me to open my canopy. He climbed up on the side of the aircraft (F-8) and gave me a last-minute briefing on the "Rules of Engagement:" basically, don't fire unless fired upon, or as directed by the on-scene commander. He climbed down and we launched.

Author's Notes: 6. *Klussman, one of over 600 American Navy and Air Force pilots to be downed in Laos, later became one of only two pilots to escape from the Pathet Lao. He made his way back by foot to Vietnam and freedom. American naval pilot Dieter Dengler also successfully escaped and was picked up by a helicopter. No pilot or prisoner ever successfully escaped from North Vietnamese captivity.*

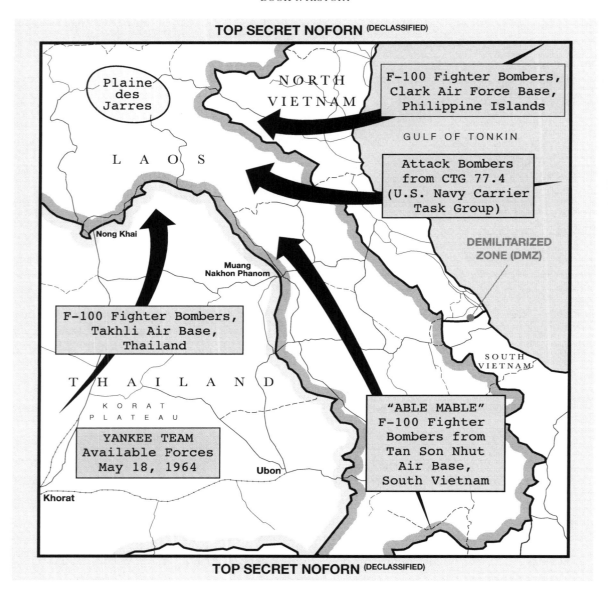

Plaine des Jarres

NORTH VIETNAM

F-100 Fighter Bombers, Clark Air Force Base, Philippine Islands

GULF OF TONKIN

LAOS

Attack Bombers from CTG 77.4 (U.S. Navy Carrier Task Group)

Nong Khai

DEMILITARIZED ZONE (DMZ)

Muang Nakhon Phanom

F-100 Fighter Bombers, Takhli Air Base, Thailand

SOUTH VIETNAM

THAILAND

KORAT PLATEAU

"ABLE MABLE" F-100 Fighter Bombers from Tan Son Nhut Air Base, South Vietnam

YANKEE TEAM Available Forces May 18, 1964

Ubon

Khorat

May and June 1964 American Air Action against the Pathet Lao (originally classified Top Secret NOFORN) — *The map depicts the availability of American air units on May 18, 1964. The shooting down of U.S. Navy fighter-bombers in early June, 1964 over the Central Laotian "Plaine des Jarres" (Plain of Jars) by Communistic Pathet Lao forces, created an immediate air response and a widening of the "Secret" Laotian Air War. These American air attacks occurred over two months prior to the purported Gulf of Tonkin Incidents.*

The air units ordered by the Joint Chief of Staff to attack consisted of both United States Air Force and United States Navy air assets, collectively called the "Yankee Team." Yankee Team forces included Air Force F-100 Super Sabers based at both Clark Air Base in the Philippines and Takhli Air Base in Thailand. The Naval air units flew off aircraft carriers based in the Gulf of Tonkin designated Carrier Task Group 77.4.

Photo reconnaissance for bomb damage assessment (BDA) was flown out of Tan Son Nhut Air Base near Saigon (now Ho Chi Minh City) in South Vietnam. The photo recce birds were RF-101 Voodoos which were part of operation "Able Mable."

"We headed west for Danang, about 150 miles distant. Just before Danang was a large thunderstorm and Commander Ray tried to climb over it in afterburner. At about 48,000 feet it became obvious that we were not going to top it and we went around it. However, we used a lot of fuel that I could have used later on. Over Danang, the skipper lost his utility hydraulic system and, after radioing the ship, he returned to the Kitty Hawk while I was ordered to circle Danang and join the second section which had launched 20 minutes behind us.

"I joined Dick Cavicke and Terry Appelgate over Danang and we headed west across Vietnam and up the Laotian Panhandle. Cavicke was doing the navigating and I remember trying to keep track of where we were and making mental notes of our headings in the event I had to make my way back alone. For a while we were in range of the Danang TACAN (Tactical Air Navigation), but eventually we were beyond range. We were dodging towering thunderstorms, but I could see the jungle below and finally the Mekong River.

"Nearing the Plaines des Jarres, we were on frequency with Air America T-28s at Klussman's SAR site and in fact used ADF (Automatic Direction Finder) direction finding to locate their position from the radio chatter. Arriving overhead, Dick reported to one of the call signs (Air America) we had been listening to, that we were a flight of (3) F8s with 400 rounds of 20MM each and asked if they could use us? The answer was negative, and it was getting too dark and the Air America pilots were breaking off their own contact with the downed Navy pilot from the Kitty Hawk.

"We were all low on fuel, with me the lowest and I didn't even have enough to make it back to Danang. As we left the scene of the failed rescue, we switched from the SAR frequency to the tanker frequency. It was a big relief that the A3 had followed us up the Laotian Panhandle a considerable distance and we soon joined up to take on some gas. He didn't have enough to get us back to the ship, but did give us enough to go "feet wet" (cross the shoreline), and he assured us there would be another tanker with plenty of gas to get us home.

"We rendezvoused with the other tanker after crossing the shore and made a night landing on the Kitty Hawk. On the evening of the 6th of June, Gene Gollahan signed my logbook and credited me with a 2.9-hour flight with .5 hours' night with a flight code of IP for survivor search including combat. I note this because, apparently, the flight was scratched from the record. Gene was later killed on a North Vietnamese strike mission.

"In an article in the July 1999 edition of the Naval Institute magazine, "Proceedings," by Commander Glenn Tierney, US Navy (retired); Commander Tierney writes of an order concocted by Secretary Dean Rusk and Secretary Robert McNamara that there would be "no round-eye rescue" (American) efforts made for downed US pilots. CINCPAC Admiral Felt went to President Johnson to have the order rescinded. However, Admiral Felt said that a RESCAP (rescue combat air patrol) from the Kitty Hawk was launched but was recalled and never showed up at Klussman's location. This was obviously incorrect and the flight flown by us on the 6th was erased from the records.

"The next day, June 7th, when armed escorts did accompany the photos, our squadron XO, Commander Bud Day was shot down. The DOD (Department of Defense) news release of Day's flight stated that he was another photo pilot instead of the armed escort that he was."

According to the Air Force classified report, on June 6, the JCS (Joint Chiefs of Staff) directed CINCPAC (Commander in Chief–Pacific) to *"be prepared to fly two low-level reconnaissance sorties as a single flight over Laos on the Plaines des Jarres area on 7 June* with *eight fighter-bomber escorts with optimum mix of weapons for AAA suppression. Escort aircraft are authorized to employ appropriate retaliatory fire against any source of anti-aircraft fire against recce or escort aircraft. Suggest Kitty Hawk resources be employed if operationally feasible. Mission should not overfly Khang Khay or Xieng Khouang.* It was one of these escort aircraft which was shot down and the pilot recovered.

The JCS did direct that the US was going to conduct this reconnaissance program and use force if necessary. On June 9, a strike force of eight F-100s staging out of Tan Son Nhut was directed to strike the AAA (Anti-Aircraft Artillery) installations at Xieng Khouang. After the strike, pilots reported direct hits on the target.

This June 9th, 1964 mission was the first actual use of USAF fighter jets in an offensive strike mission in the SEA War. The air war had begun for the United States with the implementation of Air Commando propeller equipment back in 1961. Thus, the USAF Air War in SEA lasted thirteen years, until the last mission was flown in 1974. These missions were also well before the Gulf Incidents.

The escalation continued on June 18 as *General Moore directed that the 33rd Tactical Fighter Wing element located at Danang place two F-100s on immediate alert, two more on 15-minute alert and four on one-hour alert. PACAF allowed that Thai based USAF assets could be used for Search and Rescue (SAR). On June 22, the Pacific Air Rescue Center (PARC) at Tan Son Nhut informed PACAF that the procedures for coordinated rescue between Air America (CIA) and USAF resources had been established.* Later, the Pacific Air Rescue Center (PARC) would move its headquarters to Nakhon Phanom Royal Thai Air Force Base right across the Mekong River from Laos and better positioned to rescue pilots who ejected over Laos and the North.

In July of 1964, the military command *in Saigon had two missions that were pressing it for time and effort: the stepping up of American activities in SEA and the pacification efforts in South Vietnam. On July 12, General William Westmoreland urgently requested a TDY (temporary duty) augmentation which would permit manning of an operations war room 24 hours a day.*

Initial air assets that were being used in Laos had severe restrictions on their activities. As June became July and then August, the air war intensified and restrictions began to relax.

The losses in the air war go a long way back to when we lost our first aircraft to hostile action on March 23rd, 1961. That loss was a C-47B with seven KIA (Killed in Action) and one POW who was kept in the South. Up until the June 6th, 1964 shoot-down, a total of 36 American aircraft were downed with 71 fatalities recorded in SEA from 1961 through June 64. Almost all of the losses were aircraft flown from Bien Hoa Airfield, located near Saigon. What is not known is the number, if any, of pilots and aircraft lost in Laos and Thailand by the several clandestine air forces operating as airlines. Also, the U.S. Army had spotter planes flying early in that action.

The day after Klussman was shot down; an F-8D from the Kitty Hawk was also shot down. All of these losses occurred before the Gulf of Tonkin Incident. The Gulf of Tonkin incidents in August, and the subsequent congressional resolution, signaled a significant change in the American participation in the civil war that was gripping South Vietnam and had enlarged into the civil war being waged in central Laos.

There was a sudden upsurge of air activity. The day after the purported attack on the American Destroyer C. Turner Joy in the Gulf of Tonkin Incident, the USN attacked four NVN coastal installations on August 5th. President Johnson committed Navy fighter-bombers to retaliatory action and an A-1H and an A-4C were shot down off the Carrier Constellation. Lt. (Jg.) Everett Alvarez was one of those pilots and became the longest held captive of the North Vietnamese. Johnson called the August 5th retaliation our "first" offensive air action of the war, which was another fabrication.

Subsequent to the Tonkin Incident, *the Thai government approved the use of its bases for out-of-country operations and a system for U.S. control of air defense and the employment of air in out-of-country operations got approval from the South Vietnamese Government.*

For the USAF, the Tonkin Gulf incidents were the start of a new emphasis on air power in the counterinsurgency struggle. Of more significance than the retaliatory strikes being authorized and flown, was that the deployment of Air Force units to SEA increased dramatically. *PACAF was alerted to dispatch two squadrons of B-57s from Clark AFB in the Philippines; one F-105 squadron from Japan; plus, F-100s, F-101s and additional tanker support.*

Other units, primarily in Okinawa, received deployment alert orders involving the Marines and the Army's 173rd Airborne Brigade. The 173rd and the 1st Marine Division were both based in Okinawa as well as the 18th Tactical Fighter Wing flying the F-105s, which was located at Kadena Air Base.

South Vietnamese *General Khanh, in a meeting with General Westmoreland, agreed to allow American B-57s and F-102s into the RVN. On August 6th, just two days after the events on the Gulf, photo recce flights were allowed at mid and low-level over the North Vietnamese entries* to Laos and South Vietnam through the Mu Gia Pass or *into South Vietnam across the 17th Parallel (DMZ).* At the time of the F-102 approvals, a unit was flying air defense out of Naha on Okinawa. The 102s were moved from Okinawa to SEA to participate in "Silver Dawn" and they were replaced by F-4Cs operating TDY out of MacDill AFB in Tampa, Florida.

On August 7th, in a meeting with the Thai Minister of Defense Marshal Dawee, the U.S. Ambassador Graham A. Martin signed an agreement allowing for the launch of combat sorties out of Thailand. The authority was granted reluctantly, but it was unlimited and included strikes against North Vietnam.

The situation, although it was unfolding with amazing rapidity, was complex. Since it involved multiple militaries from both the Communist side and the Allied side, multiple SEA countries and multiple agencies, rules had to be developed that would satisfy everyone involved. Sometimes these "rules" created problems with command and control and with timely deployment of assets. *The Commander in Chief–Pacific told his subordinates that missions required approval by State, Defense and the JCS. Missions had to be flown exactly as planned and if deviations were desired they had to be submitted and could not be flown without approval.*

Near the end of September 1964, the Royal Laotian Air Force (RLAF) gave approval for use of its T-28s in the proposed interdiction strikes along Route 7 (of the Ho Chi Minh Trail). *These aircraft were authorized for use in high-cover support, flak-suppression roles and SAR (search and rescue) operations. Armed Yankee Team recon missions were also authorized to strike targets beyond the capabilities of the RLAFs T-28s.*

In an embassy telecom from the Ambassador in Bangkok to the State Department on October 5th, the Ambassador summarized guidelines for using Thai-based USAF assets. Briefly, they included photo reconnaissance over Laos; armed escort for photo reconnaissance over Laos; SAR (Search and Rescue) operations in Laos; armed escort and suppressive fire for Laotian SAR; air defense of Thai airspace with hot pursuit over neighboring borders authorized; and, in the event of direct Chinese Communist intervention, any use of Thai-based air power as needed.

The above quote from the declassified report on the Rules of Engagement that stated criteria for use of assets (F-100s and F-105s) out of Thailand against Laos was in 1964, six years before the American statement that it was starting to fly Laotian operations. The approved "use of assets" against Laos from 1964 through 1966 would also include those by clandestine air forces, other American assets out of Thailand, plus assets out of the South Vietnamese bases.

There seems to be a misconception about CIA operations in Laos. The fact that Air America was doing contract work for the CIA was one of the "worse kept secrets." However, their primary combat role was to transport cargo and personnel. After 1964, they picked up an important rescue mission, but prior to that much of what they did was supply the CIA-affiliated armies of the Meo, Hmung and Lao tribesmen. As I was to learn on a visit to the CIA Flightline at Udorn, Thailand, the CIA had its own fighter pilots and aircraft in addition to its contracted "airline" pilots and craft.

While the Air Commandos fought their clandestine war in South Vietnam prior to the Gulf of Tonkin Resolution, CIA combat aircraft were also fighting in Laos and had been since late 1961 and early 1962. Thus the "Secret Laotian Air War" using American aircraft and fighter pilots lasted from 1961 until the secret was finally admitted in 1970. This period of American involvement is the longest period of combat that the United States had ever been involved in up until that time and it was all done without the knowledge of the American public.

INTERDICTION OF THE HO CHI MINH TRAIL (HCMT):

The Viet Cong forces operating in rebellion against the government of South Vietnam needed supplies. Most of those supplies came from China and Russia by way of North Vietnam. The hub of incoming and outgoing supplies was Hanoi. The Northeast and Northwest Rail Lines brought the Chinese, Russian and Warsaw Pact supplies to Hanoi and various routes moved this to the South.

The three major North Vietnamese seaports, especially Haiphong, were also conduits feeding supplies to the route south. The ports accepted supplies from Russia and other Communist countries in addition to certain Free World countries. From Haiphong Harbor, the transports or lighters first went to Hanoi via ground or Red River routes to where the North Viets marshaled the supplies for loading on trucks and any other form of transport, including bicycles. The trains of supplies moved almost due south out of Hanoi.

Those supplies then moved through the Mu Gia and two other passes in the Annamite Mountain Range into Laos. The several routes down the Panhandle of Laos from the Mu Gia and the other passes became known as the Ho Chi Minh Trail. These supplies continued south and then took various routes of infiltration into South Vietnam. Some direct routes into the South came from Laos and others from Cambodia. The North Viets also moved battalion sized units of the North Vietnamese Army into the Trail area to protect those routes. Later the NVN Army increased these protective units to division size.

American War Planners recognized early in the SEA conflict that, to win the war in the South, we had to interdict those supply trains coming from the North. In 1964, the political situation in Laos needed changing to mount an effective effort from the air against those supplies.

A final planning meeting for air strikes against targets in the Laotian Panhandle was held at MACV

(Military Advisory Chief–Vietnam) Headquarters in Saigon on October 9, 1964. Representatives from 2nd Air Division, MACV, U.S. Embassy Vientiane, and the 7th Fleet attended. At this meeting, the Air Attaché, Vientiane (Laos), said that the RLAF would go against certain targets, including the Mu Gia Pass, on October 14, 1964. This would be done whether or not the U.S. provided CAP (Combat Air Patrol) for Yankee Team strikes. If authority was not granted for CAP aircraft to fly over Laos, such cover could be provided by aircraft orbiting over RVN or Thailand.

The issue of automatic strikes using American jets from Thailand or South Vietnam was not questioned in support of SAR operations or air defense.

The Navy reported that the U.S. close air support for RLAF (Royal Laotian Air Force) operations in Laos was authorized using forces based in Vietnam or aboard aircraft carriers. The Ambassador to Laos approved Yankee Team operations in Panhandle areas.

In late October, approval for Yankee Team strikes against Route 7 (of the Trail) *were approved and flown.* Yankee Team assets were based in the Philippines, Saigon, Thailand and aboard the U.S. Navy 7th Fleet Aircraft Carrier Task Group.

The Yankee Team aircraft strikes cut down enemy daylight activity and increased night movements, which created a need for night recce aircraft. From October through December, needed photo and electronic recce aircraft were deployed.

The Laotian combat strikes also created political problems with the Ambassador to Laos. He was critical of strike mission results and seemed to consider himself an expert on military matters and capabilities.

In spite of the political and operational problems, the first of the "Barrel Roll" missions were flown on December 14, 1964. Barrel Roll was the designated strike area for central and north-central Laos. The Barrel Roll area of December 14th changed by the following month, signaling a confused situation with many of the participating parties, both political and military, with competing agendas. This situation demanded unity of command, which was not forthcoming from Washington. Apparently, President Johnson was either unaware of the situation or did not care if we had divided command.

In January of 1965, the Barrel Roll area was again changed and comprised the north-central and eastern portion of Laos north of the Plaines des Jarres. The southern portion of Barrel Roll was renamed "Steel Tiger" and was extended south to the southern terminus of the Laotian border with South Vietnam to cover the entire area of the Ho Chi Minh Trail system north of Cambodia.

<u>*Several restrictions were placed on Barrel Roll missions commencing February 12, 1965, which no doubt served to offset the effectiveness of the program.*</u> *Early Barrel Roll missions were limited to small numbers of strike aircraft and were sparsely spaced. A period of 72 hours was initially required between armed reconnaissance missions (later reduced to 48), and the use of napalm as a weapon was prohibited, although there were advocates for its use. Overflight of NVN was not permitted and a two-mile buffer zone was established along the Laos/ North Vietnam border.*

General Ma, the Royal Laotian Air Force (RLAF) Commander, insisted that Barrel Roll operations be under the exclusive preserve of the RLAF. The American forces were to attack targets *restricted to vehicles and troop movements spotted on or near authorized recon routes.*

Under the then-prevailing "rules of engagement" the deputy commander in Thailand was authorized to use available resources to engage and destroy hostile aircraft overflying the country. Hot pursuit of the enemy into North Vietnam, Laos, and Cambodia and over international waters was also authorized. Crossing into Communist Chinese territory was not.

It is understandably apparent that early considerations in war planning were heavily weighted toward the possible use of Chinese ground troops and the use of hostile aircraft being used offensively by the enemy. This did not happen. At least the offensive use of the many Chinese troops in North Vietnam did not happen.

The hostile MIGs that were flown by the North Vietnamese, North Koreans and the Chinese were flown defensively and never got anywhere near Thai territory. The only concentrations of MIGs noted during the entire war were usually around the Red River Valley and north to the Chinese border. In early 1965, MIGs were reported by Navy pilots as being between Vinh and Vinh Linh in Route Pack 1. They soon pulled them back. MIGs were never more than a nuisance compared to AAA and AW defenses, although those shot down by MIGs might disagree.

The sterile interval required between missions in the early months resulted in mission delays and created scheduling problems. The requirement that the JCS give final approval of all Barrel Roll missions also limited the scope of the early Barrel Roll program. Fleeting or mobile targets, pinpointed by such intelligence sources as Laotian ground forces and Meo tribesmen, road watch teams and Air America pilots, had to be left to the RLAF T-28s until the establishment of the *Bango/Whiplash missions in mid-1965.* Bango/Whiplash referred to the heart of the American air attack against North Vietnam that employed F-105 and F-4C fighter-bombers out of Thailand. Bango/Whiplash was also used against the "Steel Tiger" area of infiltration in Southern Laos.

A lack of low-level recon photography over Laos was another example of early restrictions affecting air operations. The Navy considered low-level oblique and vertical photography essential in locating and confirming dispersed and concealed targets. They recommended low-level recon by Yankee Team aircraft to obtain the required intelligence. Reflights by Steel Tiger/Barrel Roll aircraft, merely to obtain BDA (Bomb Damage Assessment), also had to be approved by higher authority. MACV (Military Advisory Chief–Vietnam) felt that the three-day waiting period for approval of reflights gave the enemy ample time to remove the evidence, especially where mobile targets were concerned. MACV wanted provisions made in the original operations order to allow reflights to obtain BDA when necessary, without the necessity of obtaining further approval.

The long-awaited approval for the use of napalm in North Vietnam was finally granted and used in the March 15, 1965 strike against the Phu Qui Ammunition Depot. The following day, to provide operational flexibility on future strikes, the JCS authorized strike missions against the NVN on a weekly basis, with strikes to be executed at any time during a seven-day period. Those targets not struck during a seven-day period could be carried over into subsequent weeks. This was another example of piecemeal and sometimes halting conflict escalation, a destructive policy of the Johnson Administration known as "gradualism."

CINCPAC (Commander in Chief–Pacific) further relaxed the ground rules for the four-week Rolling Thunder program from March 17 to April 13, 1965. "Rolling Thunder" was the code name for the USAF and USN bombing campaign against North Vietnam. *Thai-based planes could now be used. U.S. forces could fill out Vietnamese Air Force requirements. Enough aircraft could be used to achieve a high-damage-level. Random armed-recce missions employing 4-8 aircraft plus suitable CAP and flak support were authorized. U.S. strikes were not required in association with VNAF missions. Armed-recce of highways and railways to strike rolling stock was authorized after strikes. Flak and CAP aircraft could expend on rolling stock and military vehicles. Low-level and medium altitude BDA recce was also authorized.*

In late March, according to CINCPAC, the U.S. was transiting between a situation where the U.S. was not involved in a large war with the NVN and/or Chicoms (Chinese Communists) and a situation where large U.S. forces were actually engaged in combat.

By mid-1965, the Bango/Whiplash missions were begun. This was the first heavy use of American airpower against the Ho Chi Minh Trail system. Bango stood for the newly arrived F-4Cs and Whiplash referred to the F-105s. Bango came out of Ubon Air Base in Thailand and Whiplash flew out of Korat and Takhli Air Bases in Thailand with "Barrel Roll," "Steel Tiger" and "Rolling Thunder" as its target areas. "Barrel Roll" and "Steel Tiger" were Laotian targeting areas while "Rolling Thunder" comprised all of the non-restricted use areas of North Vietnam.

When the 45th Tactical Fighter Squadron arrived on temporary duty at Ubon in early April of 1965, it became the first USAF F-4 unit of the SEA War. In June, the 45th lost its first crew that was downed in North Vietnam on "Rolling Thunder." The 45th TFS had deployed from MacDill Air Force Base, Florida to Ubon, Thailand on April 4, 1965, two months before my unit, the 559th TFS, deployed from MacDill to Naha AB in Okinawa. Within two weeks of the 559th deployment, I flew the replacement aircraft for the first F-4C downed in the War. Our trip was to Ubon, Thailand from Okinawa. After that delivery to the 45th, on July 10 two of the 45th pilots became the first Air Force pilots of the rapidly expanding war to shoot down enemy aircraft. The two MIGs destroyed were MIG-17s.

The shoot downs were actually lucky kills. After the 45th swapped squadron designations with the 559th, I joined the 45th PCS (Permanent Change of Station) at Cam Ranh Bay. The two victorious pilots told me that they were being chased by the MIG 17s and they were very surprised at the MIGs climb capability. The F-4s, hung in the climb with the MIGs on their tails until the F-4s stalled. When the F-4s dropped down in the stall, they found that the 17s had also stalled and dropped down before them and were thus located dead ahead. Since the C-model Phantom has no internally mounted gun, they used the heat-seeking Sidewinders and shot them down.

The two high-performance fighter-bombers utilized by the Air Force in its offensive actions against North Vietnam were the F-105 and the F-4. The F-105 had been designed for low-level, high speed (Mach +) penetration of a highly-defended enemy area for nuclear delivery. The F-4 had been designed for multiple roles including air-to-air, air-to-ground and nuclear delivery. Neither of these aircraft was contemplated for the types of targets we faced in Steel Tiger or South Vietnam. If we had it at the time, the A-10 Warthog would have been a far better weapon system for this use. The Phantom (F-4) and Thunderchief (F-105) use against low-grade targets in much of SEA is an example of misuse of resources and an unacceptable loss of high-cost equipment.

By mid-1965, many of the restraints and restrictions placed on Barrel Roll had been gradually removed or modified to provide daily missions; larger numbers of aircraft were assigned to individual targets; the use of napalm (was) permitted when approved by the American Ambassador to Laos; removal of the two-mile buffer zone; low-level photography and more flexible target assignments were provided for. However, many old limitations were replaced with new ones and political restraints were a never-ending problem in the Laos interdiction operations.

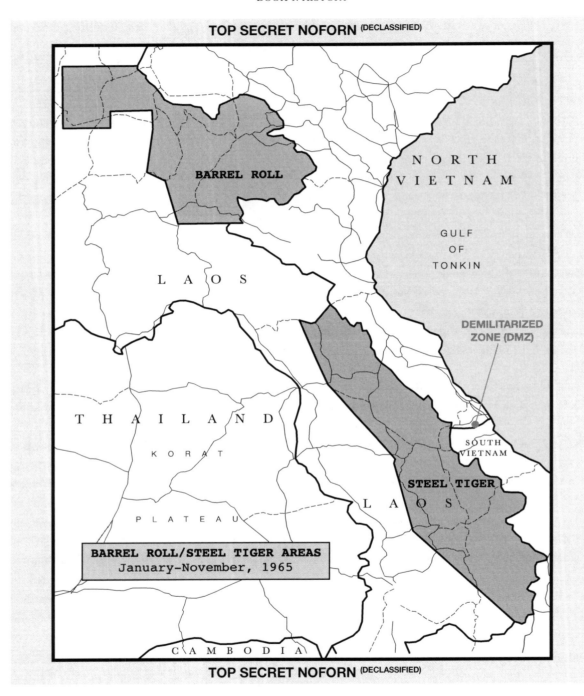

Laotian Operating Areas in 1965 — *(Original classification - Top Secret NOFORN). The Laotian "Barrel Roll" and "Steel Tiger" areas through November in 1965: "Barrel Roll" was primarily an air operation in support of the Royal Laotian Army and the Neutralist Army against the forces of the Communistic Pathet Lao. The "Steel Tiger" air missions were primarily to suppress infiltration from North Vietnam into South Vietnam. While both operations were part of the "Secret War" and utilized some of the same attack and reconnaissance aircraft, the operations were very different.*

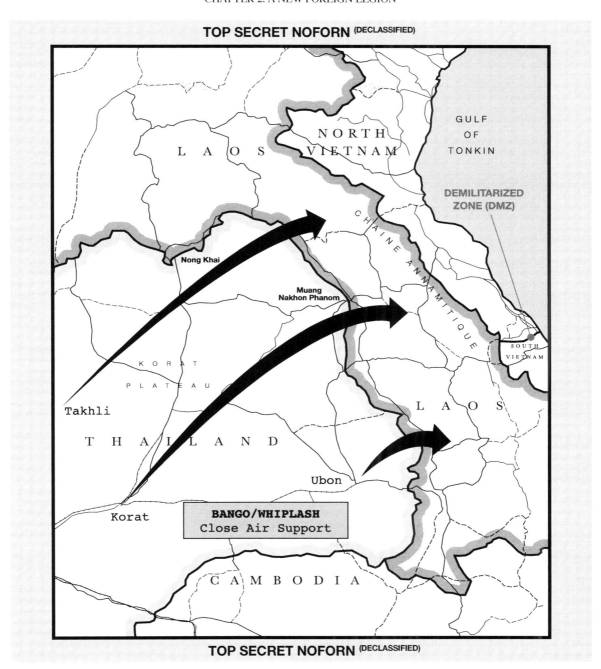

TOP SECRET NOFORN (DECLASSIFIED)

Fighter-Bomber Strikes against Laos and North Vietnam in 1965 — *(Original classification - Top Secret NOFORN). The Bango/Whiplash missions against Central and Southern Laos were flown out of Thai bases beginning in 1965. Bango referred to the F-4C Phantom II flying out of Ubon in the far northeast of Thailand and Whiplash referred to the F-105 Thunderchief flying out of Korat and Takhli.*

The Central Laotian operating area was referred to as "Barrel Roll" and the Southern Laotian area was "Steel Tiger." The missions against North Vietnam were called "Rolling Thunder." The southern half of "Steel Tiger" was later named "Tiger Hound."

The effect of all the countries and agencies being involved resulted in a very slow escalation of the level of violence, which violated many of the long-standing Principles of War and allowed our enemies to continually change their methods and recover from damage. Long-range goals of the interdiction campaigns were almost impossible to attain with this level of gradualism.

In May of 1965, Thailand gave permission for the U.S. to station 12 RF-101s and a Recce (reconnaissance) Task Force at Udorn. The RF-101 addition at Udorn raised to four the number of Thai bases housing American jets that were operating against the NVN routes to the South as well as against NVN itself. In September, 1966, I was to visit this same RF-101 outfit as a representative of the 12th Tactical Fighter Wing.

By June 1965, there were three Thai bases launching strike missions against North Vietnam: Korat, Takhli and Ubon. Korat and Takhli were using F-105s on TDY (temporary duty) from the 18th TFW in Kadena AB in Okinawa. By December, that picture would change with a rapid introduction of additional units.

When I was flying with the 559th out of Naha in Okinawa, our mission was air defense and we shot hot intercepts on Red Chinese "Beagle" bombers and the Russian's high-flying "Mandrake" (the Soviet U-2). While airborne, we watched the 18th TFW "Thuds" fly south toward their Thai bases. Each time a squadron returned from a three-month TDY at Korat or Takhli, they had lost 60% of their pilots and planes to shoot downs. The men were all dead or prisoners due to the intense anti-aircraft defenses of their targets in North Vietnam. Few pilots were rescued.

Continual restrictions plagued operations "Barrel Roll" and "Steel Tiger" against North Vietnam (NVN). While the USAF continued to press for freedom in applying suppressive fire ahead of recce flights into heavily defended areas, it wasn't until September, 1965 that it was authorized, but still had to have approval of the American Ambassador in Vientiane as well as CINCPAC (Commander in Chief–Pacific).

Yankee Team aircraft continued to have a restriction against use of napalm on escort missions. Second Air Division considered napalm an outstanding weapon against Anti-Aircraft Artillery (AAA) positions, but its use was specifically disapproved. Use of CBU-2A (Cluster Bomb Units) munitions was authorized by JCS (Joint Chiefs of Staff) in August of 1964.

My personal experiences have shown that napalm is a highly and universally effective weapon. We were able to destroy many AAA and AW (Automatic Weapons) weapons with its use. The CBU (Cluster Bomb Units) were also outstanding weapons, especially against AAA because it is an anti-personnel weapon of unexceeded capability. In my 1966 trip to visit the Thai bases in behalf of the 12th Wing, I discussed which aircraft in a dive-bomb attack of four aircraft should be armed with CBUs. The F-105 pilots were using them and our base was just about to receive shipments.

We carried cans of napalm that were filled with a substance called incendagel. It would ignite shortly after drop. The incendagel spread on impact and caused widespread devastation in any target area. Incendagel is a highly-flammable, jelly-like substance that sticks and burns. Depending on the type of target, we sometimes would mix ordnance. The first planes in would drop the iron bombs and blow targets open. The second wave would drop napalm to burn what was opened up.

Cluster Bomb Units (CBUs) were also devastating. The largest iron bombs we used on the F-4 in SEA during my war were the 750s (750 pounds). Later, much heavier bombs were carried centerline. In our CBUs, 600 tiny bomblets were placed inside a 750-bomb casing. When dropped, the 750 casing would break apart in the air causing the bomblets to spread over an oval-shaped area. When the bomblets hit the air, they started spinning and would spin-arm. On impact the bomblets would explode and spread a deadly spray of ball bearings in every direction.

We used CBUs on flak suppression missions with outstanding results. As an anti-personnel weapon, it was unbeatable. Within the oval shape of its impact area, we figured it had a 100% kill-ratio.

The above observations are strictly military considerations. The long-term aftereffects of the usage of weapons-of-war, while relevant, were not part of our equation or consideration. We needed these weapons-of-war to accomplish our mission and to survive.

While anti-personnel weapons may be abhorrent to some, one should not forget that the personnel we were targeting were bent on killing us pilots and destroying our planes which were purchased with American tax dollars.

In November 1965, SAR operations were permitted to use suppressive fire if the rescuers felt that the downed airman was endangered by ground activity. Authority was also given to suppress AAA in the rescue area.

Also in November, "Steel Tiger" was reconstituted by renaming the southern half of Steel Tiger as "Tiger Hound." Tiger Hound aircraft were allowed to perform unlimited armed recce along the roads and motorable trails within the TAOR (Tactical Area of Responsibility). They could not hit villages or built-up areas regardless of military value, without having the target validated by Vientiane or the RLAF (Royal Laotian Air Force). Even with the elaborate communications equipment aboard the ABCCC (C-130 Airborne Command and Control Center), including the single side-band radio, target validation took an agonizingly long time.

On November 6, 1965, an advanced party of the 12th TF Wing deployed from MacDill AFB in Tampa, Florida to the First Air Force Expeditionary Field at Cam Ranh Bay in South Vietnam. The establishment of "Tiger Hound" coincided with the introduction of the F-4Cs of the 12th to the SEA War. During the first three months of 1966, Cam Ranh F-4s flew over 9,000 sorties against Tiger Hound in Laos.

In early December, 1965, when Cam Ranh Bay was receiving its first F-4s, it was proposed to streamline the system for authorization of targets. Authority was obtained to have two Royal Laotian Air Force officers attached to the Tiger Hound task force, to ride in the C-130 ABCCC and act as observers with on-the-spot approval authority for any targets detected. This turned out to be highly successful.

On December 8, 1965, the 8th TFW was deployed from George AFB in Southern California to Ubon. The 8th eventually became the "MIG Killers" with the only Air Force pilots to become Aces in the entire SEA War. The 12th Tactical Fighter Wing's 555th Tactical Fighter Squadron joined the 8th at Ubon in June, 1966, and by December of 1967 the "Triple Nickel" had shot down 18 MIGs.[7]

The tarmac at Hickam AFB in Hawaii was crowded on December 8. Some F-4 units of the 12th TFW were parked preparatory to their second leg to be flown on December 9 to Cam Ranh Bay. The 8th TFW was also parked after flying a Trans Pac from George AFB in Southern California. It awaited its second leg to Ubon, Thailand. Our 559th TFS was also parked as we prepared for our second leg, but going the other way to MacDill in Florida. The two Phantom Wings were the first Air Force units to be moved PCS (Permanent Change of Station) to the rapidly-expanding war and they were doing it at the same time.

The 8th was soon to be commanded by new arrivals to Ubon from RAF Bentwaters in England. The

---

Author's Note: 7. *Pilots become aces by shooting down at least five enemy aircraft.*

commanders of the 81st TFW at Bentwaters were transferred to take up the same duties for the 8th at Ubon. Wing Commander Colonel Robin Olds and his deputy, Colonel Daniel "Chappie" James were combat-tested veterans from the Korean War and World War II.

Robin Olds was what we considered a fighter pilot's fighter pilot. He led by example and had a total of 16 kills to his credit in three wars: WWII, Korea and SEA. Olds was one of the highest decorated officers in the history of the United States Air Force. His face was easily recognizable by us. When he later greeted me in the latrine of the Ubon Officer's Club, I had no doubt to whom I was talking.

Colonel Olds was later promoted to Brigadier General. His sidekick, Colonel James, later became a four-star General. James was an African-American and the two affectionately became known in the pilot fraternity as "Black Man and Robin."

Unknown to those of us overnighting in the Hickam VOQ, we would soon become the 45th Tactical Fighter Squadron. The original 45th had returned from Ubon to MacDill on August 10, 1965 for a short stay as it then turned around and returned to SEA on New Year's Day, 1966, only this time to join the 12th at Cam Ranh.

In March 1966, the 366th Tactical Fighter Wing, mainly comprised of F-100s, was moved to Danang Air Base in South Vietnam. It was incorrectly determined that the F-100s could not operate in the low altitude, high speed environment of the Tiger Hound close-air-support area, so the 100s were initially confined to missions in the South (South Vietnam). Later, the 366th at Danang would be entirely comprised of F-4s.

By this time, the Air War was really heating up. In June 1965, when the 45th was TDY at Ubon, it was the only F-4C unit in all of SEA. That single SEA USAF Phantom combat squadron in June 1965 expanded to ten F-4C combat squadrons by January, 1966.

Two of these squadrons located at Cam Ranh Bay were from the 12th TFW at MacDill with another 12th squadron located at Ubon. A third Cam Ranh squadron came from Holloman AFB in New Mexico and a 4th, the original 45th from the 15th TFW, arrived in January from MacDill. Three other squadrons at Ubon were from the 8th TFW out of George AFB in Southern California. Eventually an F-4C unit was also assigned to Udorn. Phantom units out of Holloman AFB in New Mexico were assigned to Danang AFB located in the northern region of South Vietnam. Phantoms were positioned everywhere.

By January, 1966, the Phantom table was set for the expanding war that was to come. The three formerly George AFB Phantom squadrons at Ubon started 1966 as the primary F-4 attack forces in "Rolling Thunder." The four Phantom squadrons at Cam Ranh Bay were the primary F-4 attack forces against "Tiger Hound" in Laos with the Danang F-4s covering the South, "Tiger Hound" and "Tally Ho" in the Panhandle of North Vietnam. Phan Rang, located south of Cam Ranh, accepted F-4s later and also flew against the South.

In the summer and fall of 1966, the "Trail" was sufficiently subdued of visible activity that Military Advisory Chief-Vietnam (MAC-V) shifted the priority of the 12th TFW from "Tiger Hound" to "Tally Ho," which was in what was called Route Pack 1 of North Vietnam (NVN), or the southern panhandle.

Tally Ho was split into five working areas: Peter, Paul, Mary, Ford and Banjo. Each of our missions was targeted against one of those areas. Later in the fall, the 12th was used more and more in MIG Screens to protect Gulf ELINT (electronic and communications intelligence) aircraft plus the aircraft carriers in the Gulf and in MIG Cover missions that flew top-cover for the F-105 bombing strikes, usually in the Hanoi-Haiphong area. Other MIG Cover missions protected the RB-66 (later re-designated the EB-66) electronic reconnaissance planes that were flown all the way to the Chinese border.

Our multi-capable Cam Ranh Bay Phantoms were used to: fly MIG protection for F-105 bombing strikes against North Vietnam; fly MIG protection for the EB-66 standoff electronic jamming aircraft flying over North Vietnam; fly our own interdiction bombing missions deep into North Vietnam; carry much of the high-performance air war against supply, equipment and personnel infiltration down the Ho Chi Minh Trail in Laos; sit Close-Air-Support Alert for quick, scramble missions to aid US Army and US Marine ground forces engaged in fire-fights; provide MIG Screen of the Gulf of Tonkin to protect our aircraft carriers and to protect our ELINT aircraft from similar air attacks; fly regular interdiction missions against South Vietnam and, finally, to protect the Special Forces Camps during attack by the Viet Cong.

We considered ourselves the air vanguard for the New Foreign Legion.

> *"Such will be a great lesson of peace—teaching*
> *all the folly of being the beginners of war."*
>
> President Abraham Lincoln

CHAPTER THREE
Illusions and Provocations
Gulf of Tonkin Incidents

> *"If history is deprived of the truth, we are left with nothing but an idle, unprofitable tale."*
>
> Polybius

JUSTIFICATIONS:

American government administrations usually extoll justifications for any initiated military action. Some of our stated justifications are legitimate and others not.

A case can be made that war itself cannot be justified. The carnage of war is inhumane, brutally stupid and the act itself has absolutely no beneficial aspects. It has been my observation that those American leaders who are the most sanguine about going to war, have usually never experienced the brutality themselves.

There have also been arguments about an economic justification for every war we Americans have fought, yet there are no justifiable economic reasons for any war. Although the losses of life, injuries and destruction are tragic, my argument is not just from a moralistic standpoint. The Earth has finite resources and mankind is destroying them needlessly.

As a species, we cannot continue to squander those resources. Just a portion of the worldwide money expended on war-making equipment, personnel and ancillary costs would make a profoundly positive impact on expenses for the benefit, and not the wastage, of mankind.

This does not argue that we should not be prepared for war. We just should be overly cautious about the making of war and the usage of the weapons of war. The making of war should only be considered as a very last resort and only if all diplomatic and political methods have failed in the protection of our nation, its values, its organization, its facilities and its people.

In World War II, the Japanese and Germans were our enemies and we killed them in the millions. Yet now we are friends of both the Germans and Japanese. Does this make any sense at all? Did the Germans and Japanese suddenly turn from being bad to being good? They were always good people. Their leadership needed to be changed and war was necessary to foster that change.

The Chinese and Russians were our allies and friends during WWII and now they are potential enemies. Did they suddenly go from being good guys to bad? As with the Japanese and Germans, they are good people who have a history of living under brutally totalitarian regimes.

The reality is that mankind is not yet civilized. It is still in a tribal stage. To make the necessary steps to becoming truly civilized, individual Americans need to cast aside our provincial viewpoints and look at the world from an international standpoint. However, we are not there yet. Unfortunately, in today's world, there is no alternative to war as a last resort if we are to protect our country and our way of life.

If we include the collective Indian Wars, the United States has fought 13 wars in its history. To varying degrees, each war has had a justification used by affected administrations as an excuse to initiate military action. While the Mexican and Spanish-American Wars were obviously fought for territorial acquisition, most of our purported American justifications for our other wars were indeed just. The war in Southeast Asia, unfortunately, had no legitimate justification and thus cannot be considered a just war.

GULF OF TONKIN:

During the SEA war, the US Armed Forces treated the Gulf of Tonkin almost as an American Lake. It is a landlocked area surrounded on the east by the Chinese Hainan Island and the Luichow Peninsula. Mainland China lies to the north and North Vietnam to its west and southwest.

Halfway between Hainan and Haiphong is a small island named Bach Long Vy. This island, for some unknown reason, was bristling with anti-aircraft guns. Those of us in the front seats of Phantoms would try to avoid Bach Long, but our backseaters liked it. It was an entity with known coordinates that could be used to update our internal Inertial Navigation Systems (INSs). Our backseaters called it "Update Island."

Protective air operations over the Gulf were shared between the US Air Force and the US Navy. Coordination for this shared air effort was much higher than at simple base level.

Coordination on ground targets between the services was also done at a higher level. That didn't always work out too well. More than once we experienced Navy and Air Force air units mixing it up over targets. When that occurred, it caused scary moments when fighters from both services struck targets located so close together that our approach patterns to the targets would mix and we then would experience multiple, high-speed near-misses. On one target against the North, my flight of four arrived only to find Navy aircraft bombing the same target.

Over the Gulf, the inter-service coordination worked very well. The "Big Eye" missions flown by our F-4Cs were strictly Air Force. We were tasked to protect the "Silver Dawn" intelligence gathering and radar aircraft plus the naval aircraft carriers operating out of Yankee Station in the middle of the Gulf. The Navy F-4B units that flew "Big Look" also provided a MIG Screen function, but they did it elsewhere over the northern part of the Gulf. The Air Force and Navy Gulf radar operators kept our flights separated. Only once can I recall seeing any of the Big Look aircraft and that was at a distance.

In the second half of my war, I was tasked to fly many "Big Eye" missions. Our task was to prevent the enemy MIG fighters from entering the skies over the Gulf of Tonkin and to shoot down any that posed a threat.

IDENTITY OF ENEMY FIGHTER AIRCRAFT (MIGS):

Our operations that were necessary to properly protect the carriers were a provocation to China. We were not officially at war with China, although there were seven confirmed Americans who were shot down by Chinese fighters. Since the identity of the MIGs we were fighting against could not be confirmed, it is highly probable that we lost a much greater number to China than reported and also some to the North Korean MIGs fighting us out of North Vietnamese and Chinese bases.

Except for intelligence-gathering aircraft, it was almost impossible for the rest of us to identify the origin of a MIG. To get close enough to identify an insignia was too close. When the post-war reports that came out of China about their MIG support of North Vietnam were studied, it appears that our actual loss rates to the Chinese were much higher than reported. Also, the statement made to me by the pilots of the Gulf "Silver Dawn" ELINT flights that their monitoring of the North Vietnamese "Strike" frequency showed the only language being spoken was Chinese was ample evidence that China was much more deeply involved than thought. While the issue of Russian participation in the Air Wars has not been cause for much discussion, post-war reports of the "honoring" by Russia of one of its "instructor" pilots for shooting down six Americans over North Vietnam does indicate their participation.

The identification of the national origin of enemy fighters was also very difficult for the intelligence-gathering aircraft. If an American fighter was squawking on his IFF "parrot," he could easily be identified. If the pilot had failed to turn on the IFF, then identification became difficult. The particular airfield that a fighter may have used for takeoff also did not identify his national origin. As will be shown later in this book, the initial MIG fighters that attacked our aircraft were flown out of North Vietnamese bases. Those initial pilots and aircraft were from North Vietnam and China. As the Air War continued, the North Koreans sent pilots and aircraft to join the fray. As the American F-4 Phantoms began to clear the North Vietnamese skies of MIGs, the Russians began sending piloted aircraft to fight. It is unknown if the Russians retreated to the sanctuary of the Chinese fighter bases, but the North Vietnamese (NVN), North Korean and Chinese MIGs all began using the six fighter bases lying north of the NVN-China border.

The vast majority of fighter aircraft operating in both the North Vietnamese and Chinese Air Forces were either MIG 17s or MIG 21s. Because we never got close enough to identify insignia, we could not differentiate between North Vietnamese, North Korean, Russian and Chinese MIGs. Our mission criteria stated that, for defensive reasons, we would not allow North Viet MIGs to enter the Gulf. This meant that we would also not allow Chinese or Korean MIGs to enter the Gulf, even though the waters of the Gulf were contiguous to China and they were not contiguous to the United States.

The United States would never allow that situation to exist if it were reversed. Even though our position was somewhat unfair, it was still essential for the proper protection of our fleet and our intelligence monitoring aircraft.

Intelligence gathering and monitoring can take many forms. Our USAF "Silver Dawn" aircraft that operated over the Gulf served several purposes. Prior to our arrival in SEA, "Silver Dawn" was known as "Queen Bee" and after we left, it changed its name in 1967 to "Commando Lance." Their missions were "passive" in that they did no radar or communication jamming. They did no photo reconnaissance. Their tracks were entirely over water and their purpose was to monitor radar and communications. They monitored air-to-air and ground-to-air communication and had linguistic experts aboard that translated Chinese. They monitored flights of friendly and enemy aircraft over North Vietnam as well as the coastal areas of China's Kwangsi Province and Hainan Island. Operators "read" the IFF emanations coming from American aircraft as well as performing other "classified" functions to aid our efforts.

The one "Big Eye" mission I flew where I encountered a Chinese MIG is illustrative. He was at a distance and I had no way to identify him by country, other than to know he was a MIG. The radar operator told me he was hostile and that was all I needed. I plugged in afterburner to close the distance between my aircraft and the MIG. I was equipped with a full load of air-to-air missiles including four radar-guided Sparrow IIIs and four heat-seeking Sidewinders. As I closed the distance, he fled and I chased him all the way to China's Hainan Island, where I broke off just before crossing over land.

THE AMERICAN PUBLIC'S VIEW OF THE VIETNAM WAR:

When American participation in the Vietnam War became known to the public, televised news stories began transmitting to American homes. From that point to the end of the war, those words and images were almost exclusively of and about South Vietnam. To the ordinary American, the Vietnam War meant South Vietnam. That it was, in reality, a much larger war covering much of Southeast Asia would never be known to most.

The public's perception of the ground action in South Vietnam mixed the North Vietnamese troops in with the Viet Cong as though they were all Viet Cong, when the reality was that the North Vietnamese Army regulars were supporting the Viet Cong by participating in combat, but that they were very distinct and different organizations. To the public, the American Air War against North Vietnam was rarely mentioned.

Likewise, the fact that Chinese and North Koreans were manning many of the anti-aircraft artillery guns in the North was never mentioned, as was the fact that the surface-to-air missile batteries (SAMs) battling our fighter aircraft were entirely manned by Russians. Nor was there mention of Chinese and North Korean fighter pilots manning many of the MIGs flown against our forces. Those aircraft launched from Chinese military airfields as well as those in North Vietnam.

The public's geographic knowledge was also limited and the independent country of Laos was almost unknown, even though it had been one of the three countries that comprised what was known as French Indochina. The significant air and ground wars being fought in Laos were also never mentioned. The fact that Thailand was the location of the air bases that launched fighter-bomber strikes against both Laos and North Vietnam was largely unknown throughout much of the war. For the United States Air Force, the initial air action against North Vietnam was flown exclusively out of the Thai air bases. For the United States Navy, its attack bombers launched off the several aircraft carriers operating out of "Yankee Station" in the middle of the Gulf of Tonkin.

American media were not allowed in Laos or Thailand, nor were they embedded in any of the fighter plane attacks against Laos and North Vietnam. No newsmen flew in the backseats of those fighter aircraft that had back seats. Due to the intensity of the Air War, professional eyes were needed in those back seats.

The United States didn't admit to fighting in Laos until 1970. Even then, it was spoken as though we had just started operations in that year, when the truth was that offensive air operations went back to 1961 and possibly even as early as 1960. CIA contracts with "airlines" operating in Laos go back to 1957. Those initial contracts were for personnel and cargo transport, which later took on an SAR (Search and Rescue) function as well as direct combat.

Our Air Force was also involved in Laotian efforts beyond what even those of us who flew were aware. On March 10, 1968, the USAF 1st Combat Evaluation Group fought the Battle of Phou Pha Thi, which was an effort to protect Lima Site 85, located a short distance west of Sam Neua, the Pathet Lao Capital of Laos. This Air Force ground force joined elements of the Royal Laotian Army, elements of the CIA-controlled Hmung Army, plus units of the Royal Thai Border Police. The result was a defeat and a loss of Site 85, which was a radar, aircraft-support, bomb-control site assisting bombing raids over the North. In the ground battle, the United States Air Force lost more combatants than any other engagement of the entire war.

For the American public, the unfortunate reality of Southeast Asia was that it comprised a series of secret wars. It is ironic that the war most Americans thought existed only in South Vietnam had its provocation in the North.

GULF OF TONKIN RESOLUTION:

On August 2 and August 4, 1964 there were two incidents that precipitated an August 7 vote in the United States Congress giving constitutional authority to the Johnson Administration to wage war against the Viet Cong and the Democratic Republic of Vietnam, more commonly referred to as North Vietnam.

The Gulf of Tonkin Resolution, also known as the Tonkin Gulf Resolution, passed overwhelmingly in the House of Representatives by a vote of 414-0, and the Senate by a vote of 88-2.

The two incidents were both attacks by North Vietnamese PT boats against the much-larger American destroyers. The first was against the USS Maddox on August 2 and the second was against the USS C. Turner Joy on August 4.

The official war lasted from that initial vote in August of 1964 until the Fall of Saigon on April 30, 1975. The unofficial war started when clandestine American units first arrived in SEA in 1960. Actually, as will be shown in the concluding chapter, the war started for the United States in June, 1956 when an American airman was killed. The end of the war was also not when our helicopters evacuated so many from Saigon as the North Vietnamese tanks entered the outskirts of Saigon. That too will be described in the last chapter.

GULF OF TONKIN INCIDENTS:

In 2005, the National Security Agency (NSA) declassified a document pertaining to the Gulf of Tonkin Incidents that had formed the basis for the Gulf of Tonkin Resolution. In that document, NSA Historian Robert Hanyok states that the purported attack against the C. Turner Joy on August 4th did not happen.[8]

As reported in the book "Fog of War," Robert S. McNamara, the Secretary of Defense during the initial war years, also admitted that the August 4 incident did not happen. Thus, one-half of the purported provocation for the Vietnam War admittedly never occurred.

Let's look at the other half:

In 1936 the French government was in charge of administration for all of French Indochina. At that time the French imposed a territorial limit on adjacent waters out to twelve nautical miles or 13.8 statute miles.[9]

Those territorial waters pertained to all of Vietnam, including what was later known as North Vietnam. Adjacent (territorial) waters include a country's mainland and its legitimate islands. When Ho declared the independent Democratic People's Republic, North Vietnam adopted the French determination of the claimed 12 nautical mile territorial limit. There is no known instance of a complaint by the United States against the French that the 12 nautical mile limit that they had established for Indochina was unjust or illegal.

Department of Defense (DOD) Contract-Historian Edward Drea, in his article "Gulf of Tonkin Incident: Reappraisal 40 Years Later" claims that the prelude to the Incidents started in January, 1964, when President

---

Author's Notes: 8. *For verification, the NSA has an official website with an electronic document search capability. The internet access for the CIA, NSA and other governmental agencies is listed in this book's Bibliography.*
9. A statute mile is 5,280 feet. A nautical mile (NM) has maritime origins and is the measurement of one minute of arc along any meridian. By international agreement, it is exactly 1,852 meters or 6,076'.

Johnson ordered operations to discourage NVN support of the Viet Cong. DOD OPLAN-34A authorized raids along the North Vietnamese (NVN) coast by high-speed patrol boats. Those raids were stepped up in March by Secretary McNamara's National Security Action Memorandum #288. The PT boats were supposedly operated by South Vietnamese Commando boat crews, but were American boats operating as part of an American plan. The Desoto and OPLAN 34 missions were confirmed by McNamara in his book "In Retrospect."

Daniel Ellsberg, in his book "Secrets—A Memoir of Vietnam and the Pentagon Papers" claims that the OPLAN 34 operation was under joint control of the CIA and MACV, which was the overall American military commander in Saigon. He also states that the crews were recruited by the CIA, used American operational assets and included nationals from several different countries. The OPLAN-34 missions were directed to physically attack North Vietnam shoreline installations.

In response to these raids, on July 6, 1964, the North Vietnamese Navy went on wartime status and established a forward headquarters under Nguyen Ba Phat, Deputy Commander of the North Vietnamese Navy, at Quang Khe PT Base, located between Vinh and Dong Hoi. The NVN Navy ordered the 135th Torpedo Boat Squadron, stationed at Ben Thuy and Quang Khe, to attack any (military) vessel invading NVN territorial waters, which included their islands.

On July 31, four OPLAN 34 vessels shelled the nearby North Vietnamese-owned islands of Hon Me and Hon Nieu, north of Vinh. These attack vessels routinely violated NVN territorial waters. On the same day, ships from the US Navy's Pacific Fleet, operating as part of intelligence-gathering American Operation Desoto, entered the Gulf. Two destroyers and several support ships made up the Task Group under the command of Navy Captain John J. Herrick.

The OPLAN 34 and DESOTO missions were quite different, but those differences would not have been known to North Vietnamese Navy defensive units. To the North Vietnamese, both missions operated with American warships under American command, control and communication.

According to the Pentagon, Captain Herrick, commander of the Desoto Task Force, was unaware of the OPLAN 34 missions. According to Ellsberg, this was not the case. He further states that Herrick was aware of the OPLAN 34 strikes against Hon Me Island and asked that his mission be terminated due to the risk of retaliation by the NVN Navy. That request was denied.

Ellsberg also states that the purpose of the Desoto mission was "to provoke them (NVN) into turning on coastal defense radar so that our destroyers could plot their defenses."

This was a common and useful American practice. My next duty station after Vietnam was England flying for NATO. Every week we would fly low-level over Germany and make penetration runs against the Iron Curtain, which was the name given by Winston Churchill to the boundary between the Warsaw Pact countries under Communist control and the free-world countries in Europe during the Cold War.

Over Germany, our altitude was 200 feet and our speed was in excess of 500 knots. The purpose was to make the enemy tracking installations activate their radars. This way we could identify the radar and communications frequencies, but we could also triangulate to identify their location. To facilitate their triangulation, some of us would actually penetrate Czechoslovakia ten to fifteen miles deep.

According to NSA, on August 2, 1964, the Maddox had been "frequently" located just 8 miles from the NVN mainland and 4 miles from their islands before the purported attack by the NVN PT boats. This was well within the North Vietnamese territorial waters. Ellsberg further states that the Maddox was just ten miles offshore, when the warning of attack by the Task Force was received. Hon Me Island, as other North Vietnamese-owned islands, is subject to the same 12 nautical mile territorial protection as the mainland. Thus, the Desoto warships were in North Vietnamese territorial waters when they claim to have been attacked.

International law states that sovereign nations have the right to defend themselves if warships violate their territorial waters.

Ellsberg was new to the Department of Defense and his first full day of Pentagon duty happened to coincide with the August 2 Gulf Incident. He was given the first teletype report that came into the Pentagon alerting it to the Incident. As the "Officer in Charge" he read all the following reports from the destroyers and the Aircraft Carrier Ticonderoga as they arrived. He states that the public statements issued by our government on the Incident varied considerably from what he was reading in the confidential reports.

The two-destroyer, intelligence-gathering Task Group operating under Operation Desoto consisted of the USS Maddox and the USS C. Turner Joy. According to a recently declassified National Security Agency report, President Johnson ordered the Maddox and the Turner Joy to stage daylight runs into (North Vietnamese) territorial waters to "test the resolve" of the North Vietnamese government. NSA also claims that following those orders, the Maddox apparently moved to a position three to four miles inside the twelve nautical mile territorial limit around the North Vietnamese-owned Hon Me Island.

On August 2, the NVN Navy reinforced Hon Me with three P-4 torpedo boats and ordered preparation for battle. The P-4s were Soviet-made motor torpedo boats with a crew of eleven sailors and equipped with two torpedoes with a range of 4,500 yards. The P-4s had a speed in excess of fifty knots. McNamara has claimed that the American Desoto destroyers were in International Waters, yet he also admits that they were eight nautical miles from Hon Me, which is part of the territory of North Vietnam. How did he not consider Hon Me part of North Vietnam?

This action, ordered by Johnson, was a clear violation of international law and a clear provocation to the North Vietnamese government, since the OPLAN 34 PT boats had routinely violated the territorial waters and had attacked installations on the North Vietnamese islands. How was Hanoi to differentiate between the Desoto and OPLAN 34 vessels? Why was there even a need to differentiate? To the North Vietnamese, they were all American boats or ships and the action was a clear attack and a territorial provocation.

The August 2 incident claimed by Johnson stated that the North Vietnamese PT boats had fired first against the Maddox. The NSA disputes that claim by stating that Captain John J. Herrick, commander of the two-destroyer task group who was using the Maddox as his flag ship, "may have opened fire first" when the Vietnamese PT boats came within 10,000 yards of the Maddox. The captain of the Maddox was Commander Herbert Ogier.

According to Drea of the DOD, the following transpired on the night of August 2: "In the dark, moonless night in the Gulf of Tonkin, low clouds and thunderstorms further restricted visibility, leaving the Maddox dependent on its radar and sonar arrays for data throughout the action that followed. Maddox had relayed a message to the (aircraft carrier) Ticonderoga about radar contacts with unidentified boats and the carrier launched fighters to protect the Maddox from attack. At 10:08 Saigon time, the Maddox reported that certain radar blips were maintaining a 27-mile distance. At 10:34 Rear Admiral Robert B. Moore, commander of the Carrier Task Force, signaled that the blips had receded to 40 miles, but that three new "skunks" had appeared and had closed to 11 miles. At 10:40 Saigon time, the Maddox flashed "Commenced fire on closing PT boats." Nowhere in those transmissions did it state that the Maddox was fired upon, just that they had opened fire on the PT boats. If there had been an attack and had the Task Group been first fired upon, that would have been the first item reported.

When Johnson announced the first Gulf of Tonkin Incident, he claimed that the Maddox was in International Waters and that North Vietnamese boats had first fired upon the Maddox. Both claims were false.

Did McNamara (and the DOD) deliberately disregard the waters of Hon Me when he insisted that the Maddox was in International Waters? The NSA claims that the Maddox was eight miles from Hon Me while McNamara claims it was 65 miles from NVN. Additionally, North Vietnamese General Phung The Tai claimed that the Maddox had attacked fishing boats inside their territorial waters. If this is correct, was this also part of President Johnson's aggressive actions in "testing the resolve" of North Vietnam?

At the time of the alleged Gulf of Tonkin Incidents, nothing was mentioned to the public about the classified OPLAN 34 missions. While Johnson claimed that the American ships were operating legally and were merely responding in defense, the opposite seems to have been the case. American-controlled and owned PT boats had physically attacked NVN soil and violated NVN territorial waters. The Task Group destroyers were following up that offensive action with a further violation of the NVN territorial waters, only this time with much larger ships.

As retaliation for the purported raid on the Maddox, on August 5, 1964, USN carrier-based fighter planes attacked 4 torpedo boat bases and oil storage facilities at Vinh, on the North Vietnamese coast.

Assuming the above is true, the Executive Branch of the US Government was guilty of illegal acts and lying to Congress in order to affect a constitutional legality for its subsequent military actions.

Going back to the unanswered telegram from Ho Chi Minh: Considering the clandestine introduction of air and ground forces in 1960, and all the other provocations of the United States against Indochina, is it any wonder that North Vietnam reacted the way that they did?

What provocation against the property, government and people of the United States could justify these acts against a sovereign nation?

Since it is apparent that Ho and the Vietnamese held great hatred for the Chinese, what was the purpose of involving ourselves in what appeared to be an internal civil war?

To further complicate the issue: according to Robert McNamara in his book "Argument Without End — In Search of Answers to the Vietnam Tragedy," President Johnson on May 27, 1964, in a discussion with his advisor MacGeorge Bundy, stated, "I believe the Chinese Communists are coming into it (the war). I don't think we can fight them (the Chinese) 10,000 miles from home — I don't think it's worth fighting for and I don't think we can get out of it. It's just the biggest damned mess I ever saw."

This discussion happened more than two months before the Gulf Incidents. There are two questions worth asking: Why did Johnson continue a war if he did not think it was worth fighting for? Why did Johnson feel compelled to fabricate the Gulf of Tonkin Incidents if he didn't think he was doing something wrong? Johnson could not claim that it was Kennedy's war, for the huge military buildups occurred after Johnson became President.

There has been a lot written about the Gulf of Tonkin Incidents in a great number of books and articles. It is confusing with several conflicting accounts. Even with all the varying "memories," there may be an even different scenario.

Almost 40 years ago, I had discussions with two former Navy fighter pilots who were involved in SEA. Freeman Marcy was involved in flying an F-8 on Rescap for the Klussman mission mentioned elsewhere in this book. Freeman stated that he felt that the Gulf of Tonkin Incident had been "fabricated" by the Navy. A second Navy pilot stated that he had participated in a "dress rehearsal" of the Gulf of Tonkin Incidents three weeks prior to the August 2nd date. Additionally, the American Special Operations Group (SOG) reported, as part of a listing of all its SEA operations, that it was involved in the Gulf Incidents. How is it that a combined CIA and MACV operational group was itself involved in what was a reported attack on a United States Navy task force? If the attack did in fact happen, how could any group pre-position itself for a supposedly surprise hostile attack? That group was operational and not involved in post-mortems.

More than 50 years has passed since the incident. Memories can fade and events can be blurred with the passage of time. In 2015, in preparation of this book, I asked the "dress rehearsal" pilot to confirm his recollection of events. For obvious reasons, I will not divulge his identity. There is no confirmation of his story from a second source, which does not mean it did not happen as he reported. Confirmation of events of that nature would be very, very difficult to obtain.

According to him, the mission was a "daylight" flight in support of Operation Desoto. The significance of a "daylight" action is that both Gulf incidents occurred at night. Was he inferring that the "daylight" portion was the dress rehearsal?

He did share the following in an e-letter to me:

"I was involved with an operation in the Gulf of Tonkin with two guided missile frigates, as I recall. The operation took place on a sunny day, not at night.

"A high-speed boat was in attack profile coming southeast in a confrontational nature towards the destroyers (Maddox & Turner Joy). We were the watchdogs out in front of the ships.

"The PT-style boat was making a good 50 knots plus, when it was struck by a missile from the lead naval vessel (frigate). The PT-style boat disintegrated instantly with no known or observed survivors. I could clearly see the outline of the former boat and what appeared to be three engines prior to (the boat) sinking completely.

"There was a lot more to this event than I can go into for various reasons. Lots of photos were taken (by) both Navy and others. I suppose they exist in some warehouse?"

What I do recall from the 1970 discussions was that the "dress rehearsal" pilot stated that the PT boats were loaded with explosives that were remotely detonated by the American Navy. Could this have been the action reported by and possibly controlled by the Special Operations Group? Again, this information has not been confirmed.

If the above "rehearsal" is true, I cannot imagine the US Navy instigating anything of this nature or magnitude. The orders had to have come directly from the White House. Whatever is the truth regarding the "Incident," at the very least it was a deliberate provocation of North Vietnam.

What I find difficult to understand is the purpose of Johnson's Gulf actions? Were there resources in SEA that we could not live without? Did America consider that Cam Ranh Bay would be a viable substitute for the naval refurbishment, refueling and resupply port of Singapore, lost by the British in WW II? Did the Vietnamese pose a threat to us?

The only plausible reason to go to war in SEA was if Communist China had an aggressive intent against our national interests. If our actions were against China, then why didn't we have the courage to stand up to them? Why fight a war against a considered proxy of China, if we were not willing to fight China itself? When Johnson stated that: "it was not worth fighting for," then he should have had the courage to pull out of the war. It appears we had a President who did not have the courage to fight the war properly, and conversely did not have the courage to leave.

Prior to my leaving the Air Academy, I read a book supposedly written by Mao Tse Tung, leader of China. It was titled "Blueprint for World Conquest." In it, Mao proposed the first thrust in a military conquest of the world would be through Southeast Asia. That was enough to convince me of the viability of a war in SEA. I mistakenly also believed that any decision to involve ourselves in SEA had to have been backed up with credible intelligence information. Both possible justifications are now questionable.

In research for this book, I did not find any reference to a book entitled "Blueprint for World Conquest" written by Mao. Instead, I found a "Blueprint for World Conquest" as a product of the First Communist International held in Moscow in 1920. The Moscow "Blueprint" is a collection of documents which, while they do propose military conquest to achieve world Communism, do not propose specific geographic areas.

Perhaps the title of the book written by Mao had been changed? Whatever the circumstances, our intelligence-gathering agencies should have had evidence of Chinese intent regarding SEA. If it didn't, then the entire reasoning for any military action in SEA comes into question.

While these discussions may seem academic to some, to those of us who were tasked to fight the war, it was a matter of life or death. To the families of the more than 58,000 who were lost, it was a matter of death.

The reasons why I and many others opted to defend this country had everything to do with what this country represents. Does it represent adherence to principles? Does it stand for the truth? Does it stand for fairness in dealings with other countries? If not, then many of our citizens will have second thoughts about any future willingness to defend the United States.

> *"History teaches that wars begin when governments*
> *believe the price of aggression is cheap."*
>
> President Ronald Reagan

CHAPTER FOUR

China Prepares for War
Reaction to the Gulf Resolution

> *"If you are afraid—don't do it.*
> *If you're doing it—don't be afraid."*
>
> Mongolian Conqueror of China Genghis Khan

Dean Rusk, Secretary of State during the majority of the war years, 1961 to 1969, stated that the reason for the imposition of the extremely severe Rules of Engagements, which critically limited the American military in SEA, was a direct result of President Johnson's fear of starting World War III.

Rusk was a member of President Johnson's unofficial Tuesday lunch "War Planning Council" and was thus privy to both Johnson's and McNamara's thoughts and reasons.

The Rules of Engagement differed from country to country in SEA and also, in many cases, from region to region. There were "Rules" for each of our military services. The Air War against the North was subject to its own Rules of Engagement, which included the U.S. Navy air arm and the U.S. Air Force. There were "Rules" governing actions by our ground forces. Laos, for example, was split into districts by American planners. North Vietnam was split into seven "Route Packs" that necessitated differing "Rules." South Vietnam was split into four Corp areas, again often subject to differing "Rules." A later chapter will deal with the effect of the extremely restrictive Rules of Engagement (ROE) on the conduct of our Air Wars against North Vietnam and Laos.

One has to wonder why Johnson would fabricate the Gulf of Tonkin Incidents if he was fearful about the involvement of the major Communist powers, China and the USSR, in the creation of another world war. If he was truly fearful of starting another world war, why risk it by fabricating a subterfuge to widen an existing war? Did his fear of their involvement come later? If so, on what did he base his fears?

There is strong evidence that Johnson's reason for creating the subterfuge had to do with domestic consumption back home. He wanted to galvanize the American people behind a widening war and also wanted the American Congress to vote on an authorization giving his administration the power to make future military moves that he may have deemed necessary and appropriate. That much is obvious. Indeed, many of President Johnson's comments and actions throughout the war seemed totally for domestic consumption and had little positive to do with the actual conduct of the war.

Perhaps he was unaware of how the Gulf Resolution would impact the rest of the Communist World, especially China? Part of the Chinese response to the Resolution had to have been subsequently known to American Intelligence. If so, his fears of Chinese intervention may have been well-founded.

CHINESE-AMERICAN MILITARY HISTORY: THE KOREAN WAR:

The Chinese Communist Army, under its leader General Mao Tse Tung, had finally defeated the Chinese Nationalist Army in 1949 and had driven the remnants to the offshore island of Formosa, now called Taiwan. A second Nationalist army was marooned in Burma, now called Myanmar. That army fought subsequent actions right up to and including our time in SEA.

The map of Asia in 1950 included three Communist countries: China, USSR and North Korea. A Communistic insurgency had also been brewing in French Indochina for four years as the Viet Minh forces fought to free Vietnam from colonial domination.

Perhaps sensing American vacillant resilience five years after its demobilization following the end of WWII, the industrial, Chinese-Communist-allied-state of North Korea launched an invasion of the agrarian and unprepared South Korea in 1950, thus starting what became known as the Korean War. When the American troops occupying Japan were shifted to Pusan in the extreme south of South Korea to counter the threat, the North Korean invaders were themselves caught unaware.

The relatively green American troops were able to halt the North Korean advance and, with the help of additional troops from the States, they reversed the North Korean advance and began their own advance back up the Korean Peninsula. As American forces approached the Yalu River, separating North Korea from China, the Chinese became very concerned.

There is no confirmation that China knew of the North Korean invasion in advance, but they did react when American forces actually stood overlooking the Yalu and American warplanes flew strike missions right on the border itself.

Surreptitiously, Chinese troops began in infiltrate North Korea by the thousands. They surrounded and fought American Army and Marine divisions, who retreated to the south. The Chinese Air Force sent MIG-15s into air combat against the United Nations air forces, largely comprised of United States Air Force aircraft and pilots.

China was only a year away from fighting its own civil war. This proved a benefit as they had hundreds of thousands of battle-tested troops at their disposal. These tested Chinese troops were successful in driving back the U.S. Army and U.S. Marine Corp troops. The Korean War ended in stalemate in 1953, with the opposing armies facing each other across a no-man's land which approximated the original line of demarcation that separated the two Koreas. No formal treaty ended the war and opposing sides still face off against each other across a demilitarized zone.

HISTORY: THE FIRST INDOCHINA WAR:

While Vietnam might have had a long-standing enmity against China, like its North Korean brethren, it welcomed Chinese support of its own revolution. As mentioned, Ho Chi Minh had studied in China under the Communists and had been a military observer, along with Vo Nguyen Giap, of the Communist war against the Chinese Nationalist forces.

In 1950, the same year as the start of the Korean War, Newly-Communistic China became one of the first countries to recognize an independent Vietnam.

Even before it defeated the Nationalists, Communist China supported Vietnam with munitions. After 1950, when it conquered all of China, the Communists started supporting Vietnam in earnest in its own battle for independence. In 1950, Vietnam was one of three countries, including Laos and Cambodia that made up the colony of French Indochina.

Vietnam was not split into North and South until the 1954 Geneva Accords. The Accords were formulated after the French surrender to the forces of the Viet Minh at Dien Bien Phu, thus ending the First Indochina War.

Under the terms of the 1954 Geneva Agreements regarding SEA, North Vietnam could not augment its military forces. However, that agreement soon was violated as China continued to supply significant quantities of arms and ammunition to North Vietnam, as it had to Vietnam prior to partition.

Between the end of French Indochina in 1954 and the Gulf Resolution in 1964, China provided the Democratic Republic of Vietnam (North Vietnam) with 2,730 artillery guns, 15 military aircraft, 28 naval vessels and enough weapons to equip 230 infantry battalions.

CHINESE REACTION TO THE GULF FABRICATION:

The Gulf of Tonkin Incidents and the following Congressional Resolution occurred just eleven short years after the cessation of hostilities in the Korean War.

Chinese memories were still fresh of what it considered America's imperial response to an internal civil war on the Korean Peninsula. Memories were still fresh of the brilliant Inchon Beach Landing of American troops behind enemy lines that enabled General Douglas MacArthur's forces to turn the tide against the North Koreans.

With American military history in mind, China would have been justified to fear an American seaborne invasion of North Vietnam. North Vietnam was China's southern neighbor and bordered China's gateway to the South China Sea and the rest of Southeast Asia. Recent history has shown that China highly values the South China Sea with its strategic location and its petroleum resources.

The United States is history's foremost nation in both the experience and equipping for a seaborne invasion. World War Two's seaborne invasion of France and the Korean Inchon landing aside, the Pacific Theater of WWII provided for the world's first sustained military advance against enemy defenses by repeated seaborne invasions.

During WWII, General MacArthur led the U.S. Army, along with significant elements of the U.S. Navy, in an advance by multiple seaborne invasions from New Guinea through the Philippine Islands. Under Admiral Chester Nimitz, the U.S. Marines, supported by U.S. Navy sea and air power, advanced from island to island across the Central Pacific.

At the time of the Vietnam War, a Chinese perception of the tide of history favoring Communism would have been justified. With the aid of Soviet military forces, Communism prevailed over the European nations of: Poland, Czechoslovakia, East Germany, Bulgaria, Hungary, Romania, Albania and Yugoslavia. Communism threatened the African Congo under Patrice Lumumba. Fidel Castro's Communist Cuban troops were making inroads in other Caribbean Islands, Central America and Southern Africa. Ernesto Che Guevara was galvanizing others in South America. Red advancements were everywhere.

To the Chinese, the North Korean invasion of South Korea was just another civil war of an oppressed people fighting to overthrow the puppets of an imperialistic foreign power. To them, Russia's and China's revolutions were just the beginnings of a worldwide movement to free subjugated peoples from the yoke of colonial-like imperialistic powers. In China's eyes, the Americans had just replaced the French, Dutch,

Spanish and British as imperialists in Asia.

To the North Vietnamese and Chinese, the faking of the Gulf of Tonkin Incidents must have been a great cause of alarm. Johnson's reasons may have been for domestic consumption, but the falsification must have alerted China to the danger (in their opinion) of another aggressive, imperialistic move to subjugate Asian peoples. It would have been understandable for China to conclude that the falsification was directed against them and not to mollify the American people. The Chinese leadership had to have been worried about possible American intentions toward China.

Whatever the internal Chinese thinking, the Chinese military was galvanized to quick reaction by the Gulf Incidents. The Chinese Air Force's response was immediate. The day before the American Congress voted on the Gulf Resolution, August 6, the Commander of the Chinese Air Force, General Liu Yalou, moved the 7th Air Corps Headquarters to a fighter base outside Nanning, located just north of the Gulf of Tonkin in Kwangsi Province, which includes the Luichow (Leichou, Leizhou) Peninsular Area. He also moved the Chinese 12th Fighter Division and the 3rd Anti-Aircraft Artillery (AAA) Division to Kunming, in Yunnan Province, located due north of North Vietnam.

Mao immediately approved the movement as well as moving a Chinese Navy fighter division to Hainan Island, which borders the Gulf. Construction was immediately started on airfields and radar installations in three Chinese provinces bordering Laos and North Vietnam.

In 1965, China had four airfields on Hainan Island and an additional two on the Luichow Peninsula. Currently, the Chinese Air Force stations two fighter divisions on Luichow and another two on Hainan.

The August, 1964 movements continued with the 17th Fighter Division first moving to Kunming from bases further to the north and then to Mengzi (Mengtzu) just north of the border and on a direct rail line to Hanoi, later-known to the USAF as the Northwest Railroad.

Later in this book I mention watching Chinese MIGs taking off from Chinese airfields and climbing to the visible contrails levels before initiating their flights south to engage and attack our American fighter units. It is from Mengtzu that I saw the planes reaching the altitudes that clearly showed the condensations, called contrails, left in their wakes.

The 17th, the 26th Fighter Division at Suixi and the 9th Fighter Division stationed at Guangzhou were ordered to get ready for action. Clearly, the Chinese were anticipating the possibility of an immediate attack on their homeland. Backing up the three front-line fighter divisions, eight other air divisions plus an all-weather fighter regiment were assigned second echelon (backup) support.

In Guangxi (Kwangsi) Province, one of the three Provinces mentioned above, three new airfields were constructed and another located just north of the Laotian border at Simao (Ssumao) had its runways lengthened and facilities upgraded to support the deployment of MIG jet-fighter aircraft. A fifth airfield just north of Burma (Myanmar) was also expanded to accommodate MIGs.

New, long-range ground-control intercept radar systems were installed, including one at Ningming, just 12 miles NE of the Chinese-North Vietnamese border and on a direct rail line to Hanoi, later-known to the USAF as the Northeast Railroad.

"The most significant development was the deployment to Phuc Yen Airfield near Hanoi of a (Chinese) fighter regiment with 36 MIGs." The permanent movement of Chinese MIGs into North Vietnam was a two-day operation that concluded on August 7, the day that the U.S. Congress passed the Tonkin Resolution and just three days after the second of the purported Gulf of Tonkin Incidents. To anyone familiar with the logistics and complexity of a movement of aircraft from one country to another, such a movement was amazingly fast and stark evidence of the seriousness of the situation in Chinese eyes. It appears that the movement had been pre-planned as a contingency. Planning involves support equipment and personnel in addition to the aircraft and pilots. Provisions for fuel, food, spare parts and other necessities is also included in any planned move.

A month later, the Chinese equivalent of our Joint Chiefs of Staff sent a delegation to Hanoi to discuss military cooperation against the perceived American threat.

China's concern for possible aggressive American military action against its own soil was seemingly justified, if we are to believe the accuracy of Chinese reports? China reported that during the remainder of 1964 and early 1965, Chinese Air Force and Navy aviation units intercepted and shot down unmanned American spy aircraft over its soil. The Chinese refer to them as spy, while the Americans refer to them as reconnaissance. Special MIG-19 and MIG-21 combat units were organized and deployed to airfields in Nanning, Suixi, Kunming, Mengzi and Hainan. Their missions were to shoot down the drones and they were partially successful.

While the Chinese support of NVN in its airborne defense was significant, the support on the ground was even more so. In January, 1965, Chinese Air Force engineers constructed a new fighter airfield, including hangars and parking aprons, well within North Vietnam in mountain caves at Yen Bai, 140 KM northwest of Hanoi and on the Northwest Railroad lines running from Kunming, China along the Red River.

At the same time, Mao authorized Chinese engineering units to build or repair 12 roads important to Ho Chi Minh for the movements of his troops and supplies into South Vietnam.

The Chinese Navy shipped supplies to several Vietnamese off-shore islands where Vietnamese junks and sampans transshipped the supplies to Viet Cong-controlled regions in South Vietnam.

On April 27, 1965, the Chinese and North Vietnamese governments signed an agreement in Beijing that stipulated China would undertake over 100 projects designed to increase the capacity of the rail lines connecting China to NVN. This was significant and the projects were not small. It gave evidence of the seriousness of the perceived threat. The older means of transportation used against the French would not suffice against the vastly improved capabilities of the Americans. The importance of both the NE and NW railroads to the USAF and US Navy will become apparent later in this book.

While China and the Soviet Union were not on good terms at the time of the Vietnam War, China did allow usage of its rail lines by other countries, including Russia, to support North Vietnam. The NW Railroad lines allowed more direct supply shipments from Warsaw Pact countries such as East Germany, Hungary, Poland, Czechoslovakia, Romania, Bulgaria and Russia. The lines went directly to the marshaling and storage yards in Hanoi. Those supplies were essential to NVN since, at the time, it was a very poor country and its industrial base was not initially geared for war.

The Chinese work on the rail lines included installation of all new rail tracks, new rail yards, new and wider railroad bridges, and the conversion of the track size from meter gauge to the more standard dual gauge. The work was assigned to the Chinese 2nd Railway Engineering Division based at Changsha. The PLAs (People's Liberation Army) 63rd AAA Division was deployed on June 23rd, along with the engineers, to provide protection in case of American air attack.

By May, 1965, only six short months after the Gulf Incidents, according to the Chinese, there were over 80,000 Chinese troops in North Vietnam doing road building and repair work. Beijing then decided to send another 80,000 troops to build an additional seven military roads.

By June, in response to "Rolling Thunder," the American air offensive against North Vietnam that started in March, China created the Road Construction (Company) with its headquarters located in the Red River Valley. The headquarters commanded three engineering divisions of the Chinese Army (PLA) and additional AAA divisions to guard the roadwork from air attack.

On August 1, 1965, another two Chinese Anti-Aircraft (AAA) divisions plus four AAA regiments crossed the border into North Vietnam. Since by then thousands of Chinese troops were manning the anti-aircraft artillery, Hanoi was able to free up thousands of its own men to infiltrate down into the South and escalate the conflict there.

The presence of Chinese Army troops doing the road building and repair work served a dual purpose. In the event of an American invasion of North Vietnam, combat-equipped Chinese troops were already in position to offer immediate military assistance to the North Vietnamese. The Chinese Army and Air Force units assigned to AAA divisions were also available.

On August 9, 1965, Chinese Air Defense units fought their first battle against American combat aircraft operating against North Vietnam, supposedly downing an F-4C in an attack against the Yen Bai area, which included a fighter airfield and extensive railroad facilities. The airfield itself was off-limits to attack as evidenced by the Rules of Engagement.

By August, the Chinese defense system in North Vietnam was formidable. Units of AAA were supplied by both the Chinese Army and Chinese Air Force. While the Chinese Army's 61st AAA Division operated at Yen Bai, the Air Force's 7th AAA Division operated 24 batteries around the Kep Railway Yards. Kep also had a MIG base, which along with Phuc Yen, Yen Bai, Hoa Lac and Gia Lam, was instrumental in the MIG defenses of Hanoi. The Kep Airfield would later house North Korean MIGs flown by North Korean pilots.

In September, U.S. strategy was shifted in earnest into interdiction of supplies on the rail lines connecting the Chinese border with Hanoi. Chinese troops were called upon to repair the 554 km of rail lines, between the Hanoi marshaling yards and China damaged by American air strikes. U.S. air attacks on the North Viet transportation system produced significant damage. Even though Hanoi and Haiphong were off-limits to attack, NVN leaders admitted that the bombing destroyed much of the transportation and communications facilities built after 1954.

During my combat assignment in 1966, Air Force Intelligence repeatedly reported the existence of over 500,000 Chinese troops repairing road and rail line damage in the North. I would daily read the intelligence reports inside the "vault" located at Base Operations. Also, the reports never failed to mention the 300 French Foreign Legion prisoners from Dien Bien Phu that were employed in road-repair work.

China, on the other hand, claims that between 1965 and 1969, a total of 320,000 Chinese troops served in North Vietnam, with the greatest number at any one time being 170,000. This is at significant odds with the USAF Intelligence estimates.

Late in 1966, China added a third AAA division, the 62nd, and placed it in defense of the Thai Nguyen Iron and Steel Complex. Again, according to the Chinese, on March 10 and 11 of 1967, the American Air Force attacked Thai Nguyen and flew 33 flights totaling 107 fighter-bombers. The Chinese claim that they shot down 18 of the attacking planes, while damaging five. They also claim to have captured 10 American pilots. How they can claim damages to aircraft escapes me. Some of the time we pilots returned from missions not even aware of our own combat damage.

China dictated much of what went on with the NVN defenses. For example, they told the North Viets where Chinese AAA units were to be positioned. Apparently, they were cautious of stronger American reaction by insisting that their AAA units would stay north of the 21st Parallel, while the North Viets asked for the 19th Parallel. Hanoi is located on the 21st.

China also reprogrammed some of its industrial base by creating 20mm AAA weapons specifically designed for the troublesome U.S. Army helicopters used extensively in the South.

After President Johnson announced that he would not seek reelection, denied the US Army another 200,000 troops and terminated "Rolling Thunder" in November of 1968, China began to slowly withdraw its troops and equipment. Chinese forces were completely withdrawn by March of 1969.

The huge contributions of China to the defensive effort in the air war that we fought in the North cannot be overestimated. By their own admission, a total of 16 AAA divisions, involving a total of 150,000 troops, had served in air defense of North Vietnam on a six to eight-month rotational basis.

From August of 1964 through March of 1969, China was prepared and ready for war with the United States. As time went by, it became even more prepared. If we are to judge their intentions by their actions, it seems the Chinese were indeed ready for a much larger entry into the war. However, the "triggers" that might have caused their full-scale entry into SEA are still cause for conjecture. Strong American military action against China itself would most certainly have caused a Chinese reaction. What is unknown is what, if any, actions by the United States against North Vietnam would have triggered a much-stronger Chinese military intervention below their border.

> *"Communism is not love. Communism is a hammer which we use to crush the enemy."*
>
> Chairman of the Chinese Communist Party and Commanding General of the Chinese Communist Army during the Chinese Civil War, Mao Zedong

BOOK 1: HISTORY

BOOK TWO
Prologue

BOOK 2: PROLOGUE

CHAPTER FIVE

Fighter Pilot
The Road to Combat

"It is error alone which needs the support of government. Truth can stand by itself."

President Thomas Jefferson

My personal preparations for war and connection to Southeast Asia began as a young boy in a Southern California ranching and oil town. It started in a movie theater in the little town of Fillmore, California. In 1949, at the age of nine, I paid my 10-cent ticket fee to see a movie called "Fighter Squadron" at the tiny Fillmore Theater. I still remember my seat, which was on the left side of the balcony in the "loge" section.

"Fighter Squadron" turned out to be a heroic tale showing World War II-style combat attacks by fighter aircraft against European targets. Much of the story included actual gun-camera footage of the aircraft dropping bombs and shooting their cannon. There were "enemy" railroads, factories and tanks. The pilots would roll their aircraft in, dive at the enemy and destroy their targets. I was hooked. The fighter pilots were heroes in my eyes. I wanted to be just like them.

THE ACADEMY:

In 1955, the United States Air Force opened its brand-new Air Force Academy in temporary quarters at Lowry Air Force Base in Denver, Colorado. Their new campus north of Colorado Springs would not be ready until the fall of 1958. Even then, the landscaping would not be complete for another year and many of their facilities would not be complete until after my class graduated in 1962.

In 1956, when a sophomore in High School, I contacted the Academy and began a series of tests which included mental, physical and psychological as well as other evaluations. That all led to acceptance in 1958 and a trip to Colorado almost immediately after graduation from High School.

The Academy wanted me to participate in Summer Training at Lowry, which turned out to be filled with nothing that had anything to do with a University. It included obstacle courses, bayonet training and bivouac. It meant doing everything at attention and learning the meaning of "yes sir, no sir and no excuse sir." It meant adhering to a very strict Honor Code which stated: "I will not lie, cheat or steal, nor will I tolerate anyone who does."

If we could not hack summer training, we were gone. If we violated the Honor Code during our entire stay, we were gone. It was a non-forgiving life. It created a bond among all of us who were in the Class of 1962. Life Magazine recorded the event as we marched 10 miles from bivouac to waiting buses in Denver that transported us to the gates of the new Air Academy a then-seventeen miles north of Colorado Springs. Life showed us in photos marching with our M-1 rifles uphill 7 miles to participate in opening the dust-covered, marble and glass structure that would be our home for four years.

My notions of flying during "college" were dispelled. Other than summers, the only flying we would do at the Academy had us sitting at tables in training aircraft learning to navigate. This was definitely not sitting in a cockpit and challenging the enemy.

During the late summer of that first year, we were sent to various training bases throughout the South and Southwest. I was assigned to Moore Field near McAllen, Texas. Our instructors were veteran civilian pilots and our aircraft were the ancient T-28s with propellers instead of the more-sexy jets. It was our first taste.

My memories of Moore Field are filled with fighting the torque of the prop fighter-trainers on takeoff and visiting the nearby Mexican border towns. The Flightline bore the scent of aviation with a mixture of leather and petroleum and all the rest that made us think of gallant aviators waiting to launch against attacking enemy aircraft.

Academy life was tough, but most of us in our Class of 1962 would agree that the discipline received made better men and officers out of us.

After four years, graduation from the Academy featured a ceremony where we received our Air Force Commissions from Air Force Chief of Staff General Curtis Lemay, and our diplomas from then-Vice President Lyndon Johnson. We threw our hats into the air and spread out to varying destinations, with most of us heading for one of the eight pilot training bases located in the areas of the country that experienced the best flying weather.

In 1963, a little over a year after our graduation ceremony, Lyndon Johnson was elevated to the American Presidency after the assassination of President John F. Kennedy. Little did we know how Johnson would negatively affect many of our lives in a few short years.

Colonel Curtis Lemay was the commanding officer of the 8th Air Force, which launched the bombers that attacked Nazi Germany from England during World War II. After the Nazi capitulation, he led the B-29 strikes against Japan. Later, Four-Star General Lemay created and led the Strategic Air Command (SAC), the force that kept the Communist World at bay during the Cold War.

THE AIR ACADEMY CLASS OF 1962:

The Class of 1962 became known as the RTBs or the original Red Tag Bastards, since our class colors, bathrobes and name tags were all red. The name was initially a derogatory one given us by our upper classmen. The RTBs would eventually create an enviable record and the Red Tag Bastard name eventually came to represent achievement.

Of the 297 commissioned officers, a total of 221 became military pilots. In addition to all types of combat and non-combat pilots, class members became test pilots, physicians, lawyers, college professors, ministers, astronauts, politicians, business owners and participated in a wide range of disciplines and activities both in and out of the military. A huge number became airline pilots. A few became Marine, Army and Navy pilots in addition to the Regular Air Force while many served in the nation's Air Force Reserve and Air National Guard.

Educationally, it would be hard to find any class in our nation's history that can boast over 1% of graduates who became Rhodes Scholars. Of the 298 total graduates, 3 went on to Oxford, 37 received their doctorates and there were 182 Masters Degrees awarded. While the military decorations listed below were confirmed by the USAFA AOG, the number of doctorates and masters were single-source and not verified by a second confirmation.

Militarily, the Class of 1962 was the most combat-tested class in the history of the Air Academy, with more combat deaths as a percentage of graduates than any other class. Three members became Prisoners of War (POWs) and 29 were awarded the Purple Heart. Three members of our class flew the F-105 and two were killed in combat. Seven out of twelve members of my graduating Academy Squadron flew in combat and two were killed. As shown below, the awarding of medals for combat valor and merit was almost unequaled, in spite of the small number of graduates.

It was and is an exceptional class.

An unofficial tally of the achievements of the Class of 1962: Rhodes Scholars, 3; PhD's, 37; other Master's Degrees, 182; Generals, 17; Full Colonels, 72; Lieutenant Colonels, 70; White House Fellows, 3; military pilots, 221; military navigators, 23; flight surgeons, 1. According to the Academy Association of Graduates, the following military decorations were awarded the Class: Air Force Cross, 1; Silver Stars, 27; Bronze Stars, 47; Purple Hearts, 29; Legions of Merit, 95; Defense Distinguished Service Medals, 4; Distinguished Service Medals, 15; Defense Superior Service Medals, 30; Airmen's Medals, 2; Distinguished Flying Crosses, 207; Defense Meritorious Service Medals, 19; Meritorious Service Medals, 292; Aerial Achievement Medal, 1; Joint Services Commendation Medals, 27; Air Force Commendation Medals, 253; Air Force Achievement Medal, 1; and the astounding number of 1,786 Air Medals. Other significant awards were given, some by foreign governments, but no tally of those was made.

During my tour in Vietnam, my squadron received two Air Force Distinguished Unit Citations and the award of "The Palm" from the Vietnamese Air Force. Many other graduates were members of military units that also received unit citations. Additionally, the many graduates who earned their law or medical degrees were not evaluated.

PILOT TRAINING—LAREDO AIR BASE, TEXAS:

Graduation from the Academy gave me 77 days of vacation before reporting to Undergraduate Pilot Training (UPT) at Laredo Air Base located right on the Mexican border. Five weeks of those vacation days were spent with three Academy classmates running the bulls in Pamplona and traveling through much of the rest of Spain.

Laredo turned out to be a great place to learn. The weather was hot, but it was clear. The mornings would find us in school learning about engines, weather, physiology plus other flying-related courses. In the afternoons, we would fly.

Thirteen months later, we were ready to graduate and challenge the world. At least we thought we were ready. The attitude was, "Chuck Yeager, here we come."

Graduation order-of-merit determined what aircraft the fledgling pilots would start flying in the real Air Force. The usual choices included flight instructor, transport pilot, tanker pilot, bomber pilot or fighter pilot. The tankers and bombers were going to the Strategic Air Command (SAC). The transport guys were going to

USAF Undergraduate Pilot Training's Laredo Air Force Base Operations in 1963.

Military Air Transport Service (MATS). The instructors were going to Air Training Command (ATC), while the fighter guys would end up either in Air Defense Command (ADC) or Tactical Air Command (TAC). Further operational training would come after the newly-winged pilots checked into their assigned bases.

While SAC had a higher rate of promotion, it was undesired because most of us were not interested in bombers or tankers. We wanted to be like Yeager. SAC had the notion that it would take as many Academy guys as it could get and targeted the A and B classes out of pilot training.

The Air Force had pilot training classes graduating every 6 weeks and numbered them with the year and class letter. The year coincided with the year of graduation from "advanced" training and not "basic" training. Pilot training at Laredo, as it was at other bases, was "primary" and "basic," not "advanced." Advanced training was done at the base and in the aircraft of assignment. While I was due to graduate from Laredo in 1963, I was assigned class 64-B. The classes were numbered 64-A, 64-B and so forth. All the Academy guys were in the A or B classes, no matter to which pilot training base they were assigned.

What type of aircraft you ended up flying also was determined by what plane and base assignments were handed down to each class from Air Training Command. When I got close to graduation, Laredo had never been given a fighter assignment in over two years.

Years ago, I read a flying story called "Fate is the Hunter." The story was about how experience and talent may not be the determiners of how things turn out. A pilot can do all the right things but still lose his aircraft and possibly his life. Other pilots can do everything wrong and still survive. It is fate.

As fate would have it, I suffered serious facial fractures and injuries in an automobile accident several months prior to graduation. It took time to recover and get back on flying status. It was the most fortunate auto accident any pilot could have. It gave me a bus trip back to California and I got washed-back to Class 64-C. Over 80% of Class 64-B were given assignments to SAC with none of the coveted fighter assignments. At Laredo, Class 64-C was given 5 slots for the newest and fastest fighter in the world, the F-4H. The aircraft designation would soon change to F-4C. The base where I was assigned to fly the F-4 was MacDill Air Force Base in Tampa, Florida.

"TORTURE" SCHOOL:

I used the short time between graduation from Pilot Training and reporting for duty at MacDill by driving to California and seeing my family. I also attended the so-called "Torture School" at Stead Air Force Base, north of Reno, Nevada. Officially it was called Survival Training.

Survival training in December in the High Sierras north of Reno was extremely cold. For the first two weeks, we sat in a classroom. Then they took us out to a parking lot next to our "schoolhouse." It was there that we received our weekly "ration" for the coming trek through the mountains. Each of us was given a roll of life-savers, one onion, one potato and a small handful of beef jerky. That was all we got and was to last us for the entire week in the Sierras.

Part of our classroom training consisted of our learning how to set traps for animals. During our week in the mountains, we never saw any animals or even tracks of animals. They were smarter than us and kept out of the cold. The only animal we were to see was one lonely rabbit. He didn't stand a chance as a couple of starved airmen ran after him through the snow wielding clubs.

We also signed for a web belt, a canteen, a sleeping bag, and a small tent that was supposed to provide shelter for several of us at a time in case we ran into any "inclement" weather. They gave us one of those baseball hats with lots of fur inside. It had furry flaps on each side that could be dropped down over our ears when "chilly." A pair of snow shoes completed our assigned equipment for our upcoming venture.

Since there was 4 feet of fresh snow on the ground, we did manage to learn how to travel with snowshoes and that made for interesting trekking. Somehow, I was designated as "point" man and that meant I had the "privilege" of being the first in line through the snow. I got to tamp down the powder and establish the track. We traveled over 10 miles each day through that snow.

The December nights were chilly in our sleeping bags with below-zero temperatures. Ken Pastore, one of my hiking mates who later joined me flying Phantoms at MacDill, had the bright idea of warming a water bottle and taking it to bed with him. During the night, the bottle broke. In the morning, he climbed out of his bag with a sheet of ice clinging to his body. He might not have been smiling, but the rest of us doubled up in laughter at the sight of the look on his face.

Our training was based on World War II-style escape and evasion, which often worked in a country full of Caucasians. The idea was to trek by day between "safe" houses or areas. In Europe, it was between houses. In the northern Sierras, it was a trek between marked trees that were about ten miles apart.

In the evenings, we cut additional slices from our personal potatoes and onions. With the slices and some melted snow, we made potato soup over a fire. With the addition of that rabbit, we had wonderful rabbit stew. It is amazing how good food can taste when you don't have much of it. With a week of trudging through snow for mile after mile with little to eat, I lost seventeen pounds.

The leaders of the "torture school" had something in store for us other than a welcome-back meal. On return, our trek took us into an area that was bordered by what is called concertina wire. Concertina wire is rolled like razor wire and it cuts just the same. The wire effectively kept all of us contained in an ever-narrowing funnel of landscape. We were practicing evasion as we met and conquered various obstacles. We were supposed to remain invisible as we stealthily moved as Indians through the forest.

We ended up this "escape and evasion" drill by entering a shallow valley with concertina wire on either side, as well as abundantly located in the middle areas. Our plan was to keep a low profile and keep the "enemy" from catching us. It was dusk and the lighting was subdued. As we crawled from obstacle to obstacle we got closer to the "mouth" of the funnel in which we were moving. The sides of the valley were getting closer and closer. Their plan was to capture us all and it worked.

From there they took us to a simulated Prisoner of War (POW) encampment. The overseers of the camp were refugees from Communist Hungary and were very serious about their business. They meant to make our experience as real as possible. They wanted to prepare us in case we were shot down and taken prisoner. I was interrogated and beaten. They eventually threw me into a watery hole in the ground that was covered with a heavy wooden door. I lay in total darkness in the muck and nursed my wounds. Eventually they dragged me out and beat me again. They placed all of us inside very tight wooden boxes. I was crammed in like a sardine and the outside temperature was below zero. They began to beat on my box with what sounded like baseball bats and this continued for what seemed an eternity.

The morning found us all inside a frigid stockade. Since we were all starved from the trek through the mountains, we did not mind eating the grasshoppers, ants and other insects they provided for our meals.

It was interesting to see the reactions of my fellow "inmates." A few tried to escape time and time again.

Second Lieutenants Russ Goodenough (top left) and Ken Pastore (top right) at the end of their trek through the Northern Sierra Nevada mountains. They both were training at the infamous Stead AFB "Torture School" in 1963. Pastore and Goodenough were enroute to their first Air Force duty assignment at MacDill Air Force Base in Tampa, Florida.

They were caught each time, beaten and thrown back into the stockade. Me? I tried to make myself invisible. It was all very real.

FIRST DUTY ASSIGNMENT—FLORIDA:

After Stead, it was back on the road for an interim stop in New Mexico and a very long leg back to Laredo to say goodbye to friends. Finally, it was off on the last leg of my journey to Florida.

The excitement mounted as I drove through the Florida Panhandle and made the turn to the south at the entrance to the peninsula, heading for Tampa. Ocala is located about half way down the Florida peninsula to Tampa. When I reached the outskirts of Ocala, I knew that I was getting close to MacDill.

It was raining heavily. The car radio interrupted its regular program to report on an F-84 from MacDill that had just crashed in a thunderstorm immediately outside of Ocala. I had not even reported for duty, but this would spark a series of events that would hasten my departure to war more than two years later.

The pilot of the F-84 was reported to have been killed in the crash. Actually, he survived the parachute descent but did sustain an injury to his leg. He propped himself up against a tree while awaiting rescue in the rain. Javalinas, smelling the blood, attacked the pilot and there was not much of him left to rescue.

By the time of my arrival, they had re-designated the F-4H to the F-4C. However, there were no "C" models in the Air Force. They were still to be delivered from the McDonnell factory in Saint Louis. The base was somewhat in turmoil as new pilots were reporting daily. The future F-4 Aircraft Commanders were still flying the venerable, single-seat F-84s, as evidenced by their recent loss near Ocala. Earlier arriving pilots were already assigned squadrons starting with the 557th Tactical Fighter Squadron, followed by the 558th TFS. By the time of my arrival, both squadrons had their full complement of pilots, so I was assigned to the 559th.

When we were assigned the F-4 in Pilot Training, our instructors had no idea what our assignment meant. We were unsure if we were to be assigned in the front or back seat of the two-seat aircraft. Our new Wing, the 12th Tactical Fighter Wing (TFW), cleared that up immediately. All newly arriving pilots reporting directly from Pilot Training were assigned to the back seat and were designated Pilot System Operators or PSOs. They had already dubbed us "Pasos." We felt insulted. Many of us had been tops in flying at the pilot training bases. To be "demoted" so soon after having earned our pilot's wings was a great disappointment.

Even though I was not overjoyed to be labeled a PSO, I was overjoyed to find that a very good friend from the Academy, Alex Harwick, would be flying with me in the 559th. Somehow Alex had also managed to get back to 64-C.

While we waited for arrival of the F-4s, those of us from the pilot training bases were given T-33s to fly for proficiency and we took them frequently on joy rides over the Everglades, where we could scare the numerous flocks of egrets into flight. As mentioned, we had flown the T-33 in the "basic" portion of pilot training. During the dead time waiting for our aircraft commanders to receive training in the F-4, we back seaters studied our Phantom manuals to learn about avionics, aircraft systems, emergency procedures and anything related to F-4 flying.

We "back seaters" did not like the position nor did we like the name "Paso." We were pilots and wanted to fly with an unobstructed view dead ahead instead of a view of the Aircraft Commander's ejection seat.

Years later, in 1967, the Air Force was rushing to create an all-weather aircraft for the air war against North Vietnam. They wanted to match the Navy's A-6 night-fighter and have an all-weather capability. The

A-6As carried a crew of two, which included a radar bombardier-navigator in addition to the pilot.

In its race to get the converted F-105F "up to speed," the Air Force determined it had no time to recruit and train radar bombardier-navigators of the type manning the A-6As and SACs B-52s and B-58s. So, the Air Force placed combat veteran F-105 pilots in place of the bombardier-navigators. The name of the operation was "Commando Nail" and the crews were given the nickname of Ryan's Raiders.

It was similar to our situation at MacDill but worse, and the morale among these pilot back-seaters, who were used to a single-seat fighter, was bad. So bad that they created an appropriate mission-patch to be sewn on their flight suits. The design shows a large golden screw piercing the rear cockpit of an F-105F.

In those early months at MacDill, as we waited for the arrival of our aircraft, we back seaters would sit around squadron operations and chat. We decided that we needed a new name other than Paso. Alex came up with the name GIB, meaning Guy in Back. The name stuck so effectively that, when I later left the Air Force and started out as a pilot for Continental Airlines, my first seat in the cockpit was as a Flight Engineer and I was called a GIB.

Finally, the F-4s began to arrive at MacDill, only it was the Navy's "B" model instead of the Air Force's "C" model. McDonnell-Douglas, manufacturer of the Phantom, was still in initial production of the "C" model and none had come off the assembly line.

The Navy likes to do things differently. That also applied to their version of the Phantom. Instead of a pilot in the back seat, they had a guy that they called the RIO or Radar Interceptor Officer. We GIBs thought it was a great idea to have all pilots fly in front. Not so great was their oxygen system.

The Navy has to contend with planes that don't make it successfully off an aircraft carrier on takeoff due to a soft cat (catapult) shot or some other malfunction. If an F-4B crashed into the water after an attempted takeoff, their pilots needed oxygen underwater while getting out of the cockpit. Their system was called force-feed, which is reverse of the Air Force system of diluter-demand. The meaning of it all is that in normal breathing we use strength to inhale and relax that strength to exhale. That is the way that the diluter-demand system works. The Navy, on the other hand, forces the oxygen into the pilot's lungs and the pilot is left to force it out. The Air Force system is on-demand while the Navy's is continuous flow. Doesn't sound like much, but it did cause us to learn how to breathe again.

The Navy sent their F-4Bs with Naval Instructor Pilots (IPs) and maintenance guys. They helped make the transition fairly easy. The "B"s arrived with retrofitted back seats, where they had installed control sticks similar to those in the front seats.

The Navy developed the Phantom II. Those of us Air Force pilots were very grateful to the Navy for providing an outstanding aircraft, both the "B" and "C" models. In addition to being a brute, the Navy provided it with very strong landing gear for the hard landings on carriers and with a strong tail hook, for normal cable-arrested landings on carriers. We Air Force guys inherited both.

Normally transition into a new aircraft requires two-seat trainer aircraft. Since the Phantom was already a two-seater, all our aircraft were trainer versions. The Navy IPs (instructor pilots) quickly trained a group of Air Force IPs and together they quickly checked out the F-4 Aircraft Commanders. On the ground, the GIBs learned the differences between the F-4Bs and Cs. In the air, we received our training with our regular Aircraft Commanders flying in the front seats.

When we received our F-4Bs, they were assigned to our squadrons just like the pilots had been. After our squadron, the 559th, got its aircraft, the final squadron to receive was the 555th even then called "Triple Nickel." The Triple Nickel would later receive fame as a MIG-Killer squadron when it attacked North Vietnam out of Thailand.

We flew the B model for several months until McDonnell Douglas finally started sending us the C models. The differences between the two aircraft were remarkable for a back seater. Normal B models do not have control sticks in the back and ours did. "B" models have vertical side-panels and our Cs had the more comfortable horizontal. The C model also was the first American military aircraft to be equipped with the Litton Inertial Navigation System, which allowed entirely internal navigation. The only difference that I noted in the "B"'s favor was a slightly better radar system, although we all judged the "C"'s radar to be excellent.

MacDill was home to the 12th and 15th Tactical Fighter Wings. No other American base in the entire world housed two complete Air Force fighter wings. Each Air Force full-strength wing consisted of four squadrons. Each squadron consisted of four administrative flights of usually six crews each. This meant that we had 24 crews, 48 pilots and 18 aircraft per squadron. Some augmented squadrons had 24 aircraft.

The four squadron "Flights" are for administrative purposes. While a crew of two pilots would almost always fly together, the makeup of an airborne flight of two, three or four aircraft might be crewed from anyone in the squadron, but often from the same administrative Flight.

After we got all our squadron aircraft and had completed our training, we felt ready and we were excited. We were "Combat Ready" and we felt ready for war.

FIRST LIEUTENANT LENNY WILSON & CAPTAIN JOHN ROBERTSON:

My assigned Aircraft Commander was First Lieutenant Lenny Wilson, who turned out to be a superb pilot. Lenny was married with three children. He had graduated from Purdue University, where he was named All-Big Ten halfback (tailback) in football. Lenny played professional football in Canada before joining the Air Force out of Reserve Officer Training (AFROTC) from Purdue.

When I was assigned to Lenny, he was the youngest Aircraft Commander in the entire Wing. He was the youngest and the best and had been the Top Gun in the Wing while flying the F-84. He would continue that mastery in the F-4.

Since the F-84 was a single-seat fighter, Lenny and the other F-84 pilots were unsure how to take having another pilot sitting behind them. By the time each of us "Pasos" had arrived from Pilot Training, we had been promoted to First Lieutenant. In an aircraft, the Aircraft Commander is in charge no matter what the rank of other crew members. With my promotion, we were both 1st Lieutenants. Lenny was a Type-A personality and so was I. We did not hit it off. He was resentful of having to share a cockpit and had little in the way of people skills when it came to dealing with his co-pilot. We were both prideful and stubborn and often had arguments. Occasionally he would end up shouting at me as we flew. When that happened, I would turn off the intercom and not have to listen to him. That further infuriated him.

In the F-4, the Aircraft Commander was primarily responsible for conventional warfare with dive bombs, skip bombs (simulating napalm delivery), rockets and gunnery. The GIB was primarily responsible for practice nuclear delivery, but we also controlled the Inertial Navigation System (INS) and the radar used for ground-mapping and airborne intercepts of other aircraft. Together, in spite of our lack of rapport, we were able to earn Top Gun for the 12th Wing.

12th Tactical Fighter Wing's Top Gun crew of First Lieutenants Lenny Wilson and Russ Goodenough in front of an F-4C at MacDill Air Force Base in Tampa, Florida in 1965.

At MacDill, Lenny was considered the "ace of the base." In 1967, Lenny was killed teaching pilots to fly in Morocco as part of an Air Force Military Air Advisory Group (MAAG). A young Moroccan trainee flew their aircraft into a mountain. Four years after his death, I married his widow, Mary Wilson, and adopted his children. The marriage did not last. Mary and her children reside in Southern California.

My assigned administrative Flight Commander was Captain John Robertson. John and I got along very well and I ended up flying with him on numerous occasions. He understood what I was going through with Lenny and provided balance. He was also a good pilot with a lot of enthusiasm for life and the Air Force.

The following year, John acted as my Aircraft Commander and gave me the instruction needed to upgrade to Aircraft Commander in Okinawa. Within two years, John was killed as he was shot out of the skies by a MIG near Hanoi.

Lenny and I were involved in an aircraft accident in 1965, shortly before our squadron rotated to Okinawa. Lenny was unfairly blamed for the accident and was permanently grounded from flying the F-4. John and I became a team later in Okinawa and flew together on the single-ship flights that introduced the F-4C to Japan and also delivered the first replacement Phantom of the War to a base in Thailand. The ship replaced an F-4C downed on an attack mission over North Vietnam.

Lenny's flying talents could not be denied and he eventually ended up flying the F-5 in South Vietnam for Operation "Skoshi Tiger." Lenny was pictured on front of the Pacific Stars and Stripes showing USO entertainer Bob Hope around Bien Hoa Air Base, which is located outside of Saigon (now Ho Chi Minh City), Vietnam.

Once the 559th Tactical Fighter Squadron got up and running, we started to fill our "squares" to gain

559th Tactical Fighter Squadron Jump FACs (paratrooper-qualified Forward Air Controllers) at MacDill AFB in 1965. Lenny Wilson is third from right-rear on right side; Scotty Wilson is at right-rear on right side; and John Roberson is third from right-front on right side. On Robertson's right is Kenny Thomas and on Kenny's right is Alex Harwick. Dell Dyer, killed in Okinawa, is on the left floor. His back seater, also killed, is behind Harwick. Two years later, almost half of these pilots were dead. Scotty Wilson was shot down by a SAM and John Robertson, a MIG, both over North Vietnam.

combat-ready status. Being combat-ready meant that we were considered proficient in conventional dive bombing, napalm (or skip) bombing, rocketry (2.75" Mighty Mouse rockets) and gunnery (20 millimeter Gattling Cannon), nuclear bomb delivery, air-to-air radar missile firing (Sparrow III missile), air-to-ground missile firing (Bullpup missile), air-to-air heat-seeking missile firing (Sidewinder), air-to-air intercepts, air refueling, low-level navigation, formation flying, air combat tactics (dog fighting), etc. "Squares" refer to the squares on our Plexiglas scoring charts mounted on our squadron walls and marked with black grease pencils. Being proficient meant that we had to successfully accomplish each of the above on a regular basis and we could mark an "X" in the appropriate Plexiglas "squares."

JACK STARKEY:

On May 2, 1965, I was visited by an Academy classmate and Pilot Training squadron mate, Jack Starkey. Jack stayed with me in St. Pete for two nights, leaving on the 4th. Jack had left the Air Force and was then working for an aircraft transport company.

He had been assigned to fly a C-47 (DC-3) from the United States to Spain. While visiting, he asked me to fly as his co-pilot. It was a very tempting offer. I considered it, but decided that it was taking too much of a chance. I had vacation time that I could have used, but I was scheduled to fly to Okinawa on rotation with the 559th early in the following month. I reluctantly told Jack, "I can't take the chance of being delayed on our trip to Spain."

I bade Jack good bye and good luck on the 4th. The next day, I had a training mission over northern Florida. We were to offload fuel from a tanker aircraft and then practice ACT or Air Combat Tactics. In World War II, it was called "dog fighting."

During the mission, Lenny and I were forced to eject from the Phantom as it screamed at high speed, straight toward the ground. It was a close brush with death for me. Five weeks later our squadron was rotated to Okinawa.

Prior to our departure for Asia, I received word that Jack Starkey had been killed on his way to Spain. The DC-3 he was flying had exploded over Labrador, Canada. It was the second brush with death for me in five weeks. Fate is truly the hunter.

HIGH SPEED EJECTION:

We were in a flight of two and our mission was to intercept a tanker aircraft and offload 10,000 pounds of fuel. After the air-to-air refueling, we separated from the tanker track and began ACT (air combat tactics) practice. Our practice was to simulate trying to get advantage over an enemy aircraft to make a missile or gun shoot.

The ACT portion started out uneventfully with slow-speed, horizontal "scissors" maneuvers. Our altitude was 20,000 feet. The horizontal fighting method learned initially during WWI and continued in WWII and Korea, was also practiced by our Aircraft Commanders who had previously flown the F-84. Later, when we back seaters graduated to the front, we studied the energy maneuverability charts for the Phantom. The result was that we began to fight vertically. Optimum altitudes for vertical fighting were between 15,000 and 35,000 feet with lots of rudder flying and speeds cycling in and out of supersonic.

In the skies over Ocala, Florida, we encountered trouble during one of our horizontal, slow-speed maneuvers. Our aircraft nosed over to the right and started a nose-low right corkscrew turn. I asked Lenny what was wrong and he said, "I don't know." The corkscrew tightened and we started to increase our speed. Lenny was "washing" the cockpit with the control stick and nothing happened. He said, "I can't control it." Our dive increased and our airspeed got faster and faster. Soon we were going straight down. Lenny popped the drogue chute and I could see in my rear-view mirror that it had shredded. He popped the speed brake and nothing happened. As a last resort, he dropped the landing gear and—nothing.

By then, my altimeter was unwinding so fast that I could not read any altitude. It was in full spin. We entered a cloud and I knew we were low.

There are two methods of ejection using the Martin Baker ejection seat on the Phantom. The primary system requires the pilot to reach over his head for the lanyard handles and pull them down over his body. The secondary system had never been used. We were told that it was a much faster system, but would probably break our backs if used. The secondary system required us to simply reach down to pull a lanyard between our legs. I had already determined that, if I had to punch out, I would use the faster secondary system no matter what might happen.

Without saying anything to Lenny, I reached down and pulled the lanyard. It all happened fast, but I was aware of blasting out into the wind and feeling the massive jolt. My head crashed back into the ejection seat, causing a hole in the helmet. I was unaware of seat separation, but I felt another, smaller blow as the canopy deployed. Remembering my parachute training with the Army at Fort Benning, I reached up and grabbed the risers. My lateral movement was fast, indicating a high wind. I pulled the risers on the side away from the direction of drift. It slowed down the side motion and gave me time to look around. We were out of the clouds. Lenny was floating below me and I could see the wreckage of the Phantom burning to my right with the smoke drifting up from the forested floor. Below me, my survival kit dangled on a lanyard at about fifteen feet. We were probably 500 to 600 feet in the air.

Below us was a sparse forested area that was part of the jungles of northern Florida. I could see lots of stumps of trees that had been cut. The chute of the Martin Baker was only 20-foot wide and they were non-steerable, which meant we dropped fast without much control. I was descending backwards due to the strong winds. My lateral motion increased and I prayed I would not hit a stump. I hit on my back in a small meadow, surrounded by trees and the stumps of trees. I immediately hit my parachute release allowing the canopy to fly away and deflate in the strong winds. I left the survival kit on the ground and grabbed my helmet with its oxygen mask dangling from it.

I looked around and shouted for Lenny. He answered with a shout and I started out in the direction of the sound. He was hung up in a tree with his risers having caught the upper branches of a pine. I helped him down and we assessed our situation. My buddy John Brennan was in the back seat of the F-4 circling us. I knew he was busy giving directions to the rescuers so that we would not have long to wait. We gathered up our chutes and sat down on a couple of stumps next to a nice, clear landing area and waited for the arrival of the anticipated helicopter.

We heard the helicopter long before we could see it. The pilot of the chopper let me fly it for part of the trip back and the experience was both unique and fun. The controls of a chopper are very different than a fighter.

Rescue flew us to a base about 30 minutes to the east of the crash site. After arrival, I went to their helicopter operations and placed a call to the MacDill Command Post. Major General Al Shintz quickly got on the phone. Shintz was commanding officer of our Air Division, which comprised the 12th and 15th fighter wings. He asked me what happened and I told him that we were in a high-speed spiral and could not control the plane. Shintz was a little guy and very sure of himself. He corrected me and said that we were in a spin. I corrected him a second time, "Sir, we definitely were not in a spin. It started as a high-speed spiral and ended up going straight down." Spins are low-speed and deployment of the drogue chute should have taken us out of it. It was not a spin, but Shintz had already made up his mind and did not buy my description. Because of his inability to listen to reason, Lenny was permanently grounded and never again flew the F-4.

After we arrived back at MacDill, the base told me that we had ejected at about 4500 feet. They said that, with the tremendous downward speed of the aircraft, if I had waited two seconds longer we would have been killed.

Over the years after the accident, I followed the accident reports from the Air Force, Navy and Marines who flew the F-4. I was looking for similar entries to our "situation." I counted 21 planes, including ours, that were lost in the same mysterious way. The first indication was the dropping off of the nose to the right side, followed by a high-speed spiral and the inevitable crash. Three years after the accident and while I was flying F-4s in England, someone discovered what had happened and they grounded all the F-4s worldwide until the design problem was fixed.

The Phantom has six fuel tanks that are located in the fuselage. The rest are in the wings. Open manifolds allowed fuel to shift from one to another of the fuselage tanks as the fuel flows from the higher, forward tank towards the lower, rear tank. At heavy fuel weights and low airspeed, the aircraft angle of attack is higher and gravity forces more fuel toward the rear of the plane. Our slow-speed "scissors" maneuver created the high angle-of-attack.

Stability of an aircraft is predicated on the distance between the center of pressure and center of gravity. The greater the distance between the two points, the more stable an aircraft. The center of gravity is the point where the aircraft would balance if you placed a stand at the exact center. The center of pressure, on the other hand, is the point where the pressure exerted by the control surfaces acts on the plane itself. Control surfaces are things like ailerons, elevons and elevators that are part of the wings and tail and make the plane climb or descend or turn when directed by the pilot.

What had happened in all 21 aircraft was that the fuel surged back in the manifold toward the rear fuel tanks and caused the center of gravity to shift past the center of pressure. Trying to regain control with the control surfaces had no affect since they were neutralized.

The Air Force, in all its wisdom, refused to go back and exonerate any of the pilots who were found guilty of losing an aircraft due to a design defect. Lenny had been found guilty according to General Shintz and that was it.

After our arrival back at MacDill and after having been debriefed by Shintz and the rest, we were finally allowed to go home. To some, it might have seemed a debrief. To me, it was more of a grilling.

Ironically, the area that we landed in Northern Florida was the same area as the F-84 pilot that had crashed the year before as I drove to MacDill. At the time of my accident, I was dating Elsie Gibson, the widow of the dead pilot. For her, it was an agonizing revisit to Ocala.

FIREPOWER DEMONSTRATIONS:

When the 12th became operational, the Air Force wanted us to represent our aircraft to others. The usual form of that representation was in firepower demonstrations, which took place in North Carolina. Firepower demonstrations were for various groups which the Air Force wanted to impress. Our squadron was tasked to fly two during my time at MacDill and I got to fly both. Once it was for journalists and the other was for visiting African dignitaries.

For the pilots, this demonstration was a form of preparation for war. Instead of the small, practice bombs used in normal training flights, the firepower demonstrations allowed us to carry and drop actual napalm, combat bombs and real rockets.

The usual demo procedure was to have a flight of four F-4s fly to Seymour Johnson AFB in North Carolina. We would stage out of Seymour, which was an F-105 fighter base and we would drop our bombs at Fort Bragg.

One of the demonstrations had Lenny and I carrying seventeen 750# bombs for a drop. That was the maximum load for the F-4. While we might have been able to carry them and they made one hell of a bang when dropped in "ripple," with almost 13,000 pounds of bombs hanging from our wings the Phantom was very sluggish. Our fuel consumption was also very high, which meant our combat radius carrying those bombs would have been very short. It was not a recommended combat load.

A second demo flight out of Seymour had us fully loaded with rocket pods. In the dive, we fired them in "ripple" starting at 4,000 feet in the dive and there were so many rockets (almost 300) that they didn't stop firing until we reached 2,500 feet. Each of the 300 fired individually.

For the demonstrations, we would orbit at a distance from the show as we waited for our turn. Timing had to be precise and to the second. When it was our time to go in, we would break out of orbit and fly directly to a pre-determined Initial Point. From the Initial-Point we would fly directly to our "target." The timing was worked out when we practiced for the event. The result was that whoever was announcing the show could know to the second when we would be there and with what ordnance. It always worked out.

However, once it didn't work as planned. I was part of a four-ship orbiting about four miles from another four-ship flying F-84s. The 84s were to be the first in. The F-84 lead aircraft broke as planned from orbit and then called for the rest of his flight to check in on the radio. Number four did not reply. Lead was intent on the demonstration and did not follow up. My A/C (Aircraft Commander) and I were worried and looked intently at their orbit area. We saw black smoke and informed our lead that we were breaking off from our orbit and that they could fly the planned drop without us, if necessary.

We quickly flew the four miles over and looked down. Barely visible was the hole in the trees left by the crashing aircraft. It had gone in almost vertically. Later we were told that the engines were all that was left and they were buried 17 feet down. The pilot, who we had spent the prior evening with, was killed.

On the other demonstration, we were returning to Seymour when a plane crashed on the runway. We diverted to a Marine F-4 base in South Carolina named Cherry Point. We landed and gassed up and waited for word that the runway had been cleared so that we could fly back. When that word finally came, we started our engines. At least we tried to start our engines.

When starting jet engines, we first hit ignition to get the spark and then hit fuel. Ignition usually fires up instantaneously. Not at Cherry Point. Lenny hit ignition then fuel and—nothing. We tried it again, and again. Still there was nothing. Finally, on probably the fourth or fifth time, it fired. During all of those attempted starts, fuel had pooled at the bottom of the engine bay. When it did fire, it exploded. Smoke and flames shot out at least 20 feet from the rear of our F-4. We were totally engulfed in smoke. Those J-79 engines are tough and we had no damage. Later we learned that the Marines use JP-5 for fuel. The Air Force uses JP-4. The JP-5 requires a higher ignition temperature and our engine igniters were set for lower.

BOMBING PRACTICE:

Winter Park was our bombing and gunnery range, which was located across the Florida peninsula from MacDill. Winter Park provided the combat training that we would later utilize while flying and fighting in Southeast Asia. It also had an excellent nuclear bombing range. Since the Phantom had a nuclear bomb delivery capability and mission, this training assumed an importance.

When simulating nuclear drops, we would carry a 2,000-pound "bullet" of concrete mounted centerline. We had two different methods of dropping nukes. One method was to come in at low level (200 feet Actual Ground Level-AGL) and then commence a 45-degree climb and drop the bomb in a "loft" maneuver. The bomb would continue climbing on the same trajectory as we were flying. The bomb's parachute would deploy and as it slowed down; it would reach its maximum height and then slowly turn down as it started its descent.

Most combat planes have two altimeters. The Phantom had the usual barometric altimeter that showed our elevation measured from Sea Level. Of more importance is our elevation above the actual ground level (AGL) and we had a second altimeter that did show us a radar-determined AGL.

On our simulated nuclear runs, detonation was predicated on the arming of several electrical and barometric relays. Detonation would occur at a pre-selected altitude as long as the relays had been satisfied. On the Phantom, the GIB had a nuclear consent switch that had to be moved to the "on" position. Several other relays also had to be satisfied in an actual drop for detonation to occur. In fact, there were so many relays necessary that we pilots questioned whether the things would ever go off, if required.

The chunk of concrete we carried centerline had the chute with a barometric relay, so the simulation was realistic. After dropping the practice weapon, we would pull back in an Immelman Maneuver. After drop, the Immelman was completed by continuing to pull back on the stick until we went past vertical and on our way to heading in the opposite direction, only upside down. Then we would execute an aileron roll and get the "hell out of Dodge." [10]

In an actual nuclear drop, the trick would be to get as much distance away from the area as possible before the blast occurred. We had no way to outrun the blast wave, which would cause us to tumble wildly out of control. It was a recoverable situation. At least they said it was.

The second method of bomb deployment was to drop when aimed straight up into the sky in a so-called "over the shoulder" maneuver. This would give us a longer "escape" time, but the maneuver was tricky. Our gyro-stabilized horizon indicator in the cockpit was not reliable when flying straight up. It would tumble wildly. The completion of the "over the shoulder" drop was the same Immelman.

The first F-4C aircraft lost out of MacDill was on the range at Winter Park and the crew was executing an "over the shoulder" maneuver when they became disoriented and crashed. Both pilots were killed.

NUCLEAR BOMBS FOR CUBA:

Our practice nuclear drops took more of a feeling of reality during 1964. While the Cuban Missile Crisis of 1962 riveted the nation, the confrontation of 1964 took us closer to nuclear war.

Years later, when I "sat" nuke alert in England, I was the designated "Nuclear Bomb Commander" of an initial four bombs that was later increased to five. We were living in the alert shack at the end of the runway and practiced the two-man concept of bomb security. Whenever any pilot got close to a nuclear-loaded aircraft, there had to be at least one other reliable person with him. The base would park fire engines in front of the hangar that housed our nuclear-loaded aircraft anytime any of us got near the plane.

Not so in 1964. We had no tactical alert shack at MacDill. We had no safeguards. We did not practice the two-man concept. What we had were nuclear targets in Cuba. My target was Matanzas Bay.

The Air Force moved hundreds of fighters into Florida in '64. We were right on the edge of going to nuclear war. The 559th had fourteen F-4s loaded with nukes that were sitting side-by-side on a taxiway. Our crews were all at operations, prepared to run to our aircraft and launch. It was no drill.

Years later I was on an ocean cruise in the Caribbean. As the ship cruised down the coast of Cuba within

---

Author's Notes: *10. The Immelman was invented by a German WWI pilot of the same name.*

sight of land, I could barely make out Matanzas Bay through the mist. I felt a chillingly eerie feeling as I watched my former target and wondered what might have been.

ALPHA SQUADRON—FIRST STRIKE:

The Air Force designates a single squadron to be poised to deploy at a moment's notice to some "hot spot" in the world. It is called the "Alpha" Squadron and it is sort of on a worldwide alert. During our stay at MacDill, the 559th was designated "Alpha."

It has been speculated that 95% of what is really going on in the world never gets into the press. The press is just unaware what we are doing and that became evident during our alpha alert.

We were tasked to stand by for deployment to Tibet. Years prior to that assignment Tibet had been overrun and made part of Communist China. We pilots were all wondering what was really going on. Were we getting ready for war with China?

When we were given our briefing on Tibet, I asked what the altitude was where they were planning to send us. The reply was that it was slightly above 10,000 feet. I then asked the briefing officer if consideration had been given to the fact that our barometric parachute release activated at 10,000 feet. In other words, if we ejected, our parachutes would not deploy.

The situation was similar to that encountered later when stationed in England. Ejection over the North Sea was futile because rescue could never get to us in time due to the freezing water temperatures. The answer for both predicaments was...don't eject.

> *"The power of making war often prevents it."*
> President Thomas Jefferson

South-East Asia, with Okinawa and Guam highlighted and boxed.

CHAPTER SIX
Phantoms in Asia
Okinawa, Thailand and Japan

*"It is one thing to show a man that he is in error,
and another to put him in possession of the truth."*

John Locke

TRANS PAC (TRANS PACIFIC):

The first time that the Air Force stationed Phantoms in Asia was on December 9, 1964, when the 557th deployed to Okinawa. The 557th was one of our sister squadrons that was based at MacDill Air Force Base in Tampa, Florida.

The two-day "Trans Pac" deployment was what we called a "ball buster." Each day saw the aircrews strapped into a very cramped cockpit for nine hours of overwater flying.

Cockpits of any fighter-bomber are cramped. On entering the cockpit of an F-4, a pilot plugs his G suit into the ship's pneumatic system, straps his parachute harness into the seat-mounted parachute and then plugs his helmet into the ships oxygen and communication systems. The sides of the cockpit have panels on which are mounted easily accessible and necessary items or instruments. On the left side is the hand-held throttle. On the right are the control switches for the aircraft's munitions.

Instead of a yoke that is used to guide a transport plane or a commercial airliner, the flight controls are "controlled" by use of a "stick." On the stick are a trim button, the trigger for the gun or missile and a bomb release button. Movement of the stick is in the desired direction of flight. Push left for a left turn, pull back to climb and so forth. The trim button is used to trim up or align the ailerons, which are the wing-mounted control surfaces that enable turns. All-in-all the cockpit of the Phantom was tight with very little room to move around. There was no standing or even half-standing. Once we were in the cockpit, we were told to just sit there and be good boys. The Air Force kindly supplied a zip-locked bag with a sponge inside that was used in place of a toilet. Hence, we developed what has been referred to as a "fighter pilot's bladder."

The mission of the 557th was to be the air defense of Okinawa. The F-4C was replacing the aging F-102 Delta Dagger, which was strictly an air defense interceptor. The 102s were being sent to Southeast Asia to give fighter protection to the "Silver Dawn" missions. The Phantom, however, was a multipurpose fighter that could not only fly air defense with a very effective air-to-air radar intercept system utilizing the Sparrow III intercept missile, but could also fly air-to-ground bombing, rocketry or gunnery missions as it did in SEA or sit nuclear alert as it did in Europe.

While flying the F-4 in SEA, we sat close-air-support Alert in the mobile homes located at the end of the runways. We slept in our flight suits, ready to jump in our Phantoms, cart (cartridge) start the engines and be airborne within two to three minutes of the alarm sounding. We often would strap in after takeoff.

While flying air defense in Okinawa, we also sat alert in our flight suits, ready for a two-minute launch if an actual intruder invaded the airspace controlled by the air defense "blockhouse" housing all the ground-based radar.

My assignment after SEA took me to RAF Woodbridge in England flying for NATO. A third of our English lives were spent on nuclear alert in the alert "shack" at the end of the runway. Our Phantoms, in this case, were equipped with a centerline-mounted thermonuclear bomb.

The Phantom was truly a versatile weapons system.

The "cart start" method of spooling up our engines is very different than a normal start. In a normal start, an air compressor drives air through the turbine section of the engine and starts the rotors moving so that air is sucked into the engine and into the combustion section to allow ignition. This usually takes some time.

To save lots of time, the Air Force would mount a cartridge directly aimed at the engine inlet. The cartridge or cart was like a large munition without shrapnel. Firing it would create a rush of air (and smoke) through the engine and start the rotors moving. The upside was that it was very fast and great for Alert situations. The downside was that it was extremely hard on engines.

The arrival of the first Air Force F-4 in Asia caused some unexpected fireworks. Since this was the first time that the F-4C had arrived in Asia, there was a certain level of excitement. The landings attracted the curious, base personnel, local Okinawan officials and military officers from the Air Force, Army and Navy. The large crowd watched intently as the lead F-4 banked as it turned on final approach for landing after an extremely long non-stop from Hawaii. The lead pilot made a beautiful landing however he forgot one thing—his landing gear. The first Air Force Phantom to land in Asia landed with his wheels up.

He slid down the runway with sparks flying as the metal of the aircraft undercarriage ground into the concrete of the runway. He was obviously unable to taxi to the waiting dignitaries ready to greet the 557th. The fatigue that caused the pilot to forget his landing gear caused the Air Force to order what were called "Go" pills to be taken one hour prior to landing on subsequent Trans Pac flights. The Go pill was Dexedrine.

On that first Trans Pac, my aircraft commander Lenny Wilson and I were assigned support duty. In case the 557th needed a replacement crew, we were pre-positioned in Hawaii. It seemed that the 12th Wing was rewarding us for winning Top Gun.

The military has long owned a stretch of the beach at Waikiki known as Fort DeRussy. Before they remodeled the beach section, they had a rather primitive Officer's Club located right on the sand. Next to the "O" Club stood a bungalow type, two-story barracks that was used for transient military. In back of the "hotel" was a wide grassy area of the type that used to abound in Hawaii. The meadow was surrounded by the colorful Royal Poinciana or Flame Tree.

In Hawaii, direction is not like on the mainland. Americans are used to a grid pattern with a north, south, east and west alignment. Not so Hawaii. They describe directions as either mauka or makai. Mauka means towards the mountains or inland. Makai means toward the ocean. It makes sense in an area of islands.

To the mauka side of the grassy meadow at DeRussy stood another accommodation for visiting officers. We had a choice: either pay $1.25 a night for the mauka rooms or pay $1.75 per night for the makai rooms. We, of course, paid the extra 50 cents and settled into the makai.

Our "duty" required us to call MacDill operations once a day. Otherwise we were free to do what we wished. Since the beach at DeRussy was reserved for military, we spent a lot of time there between the sand and the Club and those mai tais. We stayed a week and were not needed by the Trans Pac. It was rough duty.

On March 9, 1965, the 558th replaced the 557th. The 557th had stayed the entire three-month TDY period and so did the 558th before returning to MacDill. While in Okinawa, the 558th lost a plane and crew. The back-seater, Quentin Lusby, was one of the five of us who were assigned to MacDill out of Laredo. They flew into the water about nine miles from the runway. The visibility was not bad and there was no distress call. They just flew into the water and that was it. Flying fighters is dangerous duty and operational losses are common. At the end of their TDY, the 558th flew back with seventeen of their original eighteen planes.

On June 9, 1965, the 559th replaced the 558th. The 558th was returned to the Continental U.S. at the same time that we deployed. Our squadron was on TDY status, which means the married guys were unaccompanied by their wives. When we reached Hawaii after our first leg of the two-legged journey, we passed the 558th flying the other way.

The start of our Trans Pac took us from takeoff at MacDill Air Force Base in Tampa, Florida to a radar join-up with the KC-135 aerial tankers. For the journey, we were uploaded with three external fuel tanks. One was larger and was mounted centerline, while the other two were smaller wing tanks.

The KC-135 was the military version of the civilian Boeing 707. Our tanker buddies escorted us for an hour or so. We gassed up just before they departed and that fuel lasted us until we had another radar join-up with tankers orbiting above Santa Barbara, California. The tankers fed us over Santa Barbara and stayed with us (buddy tanked) to a point a little more than halfway to Hawaii.

At the midpoint between California and Hawaii, we took another drink of gas. Since this was the most critical fueling point of our journey, the tankers stayed with us for another twenty minutes. Anytime we take long overwater journeys with fighters, we always needed enough fuel to carry us to land in event of a critical malfunction. The most critical at that point was a malfunction of our refueling receptacle. So, twenty minutes after the mid-point fueling, we again topped off with JP-4 fuel. The 2200 miles from the California coast to Hawaii is the longest stretch of water in the world without any land of any kind and thus no chance of landing. We needed those tankers.

One hour out from Hickam Field, Hawaii, we took one of the pills supplied to us by our Flight Surgeon. Hickam is the Air Force Base lying next to Honolulu International Airport, with whom it shares runways. The pills were attached to a wood "wafer" that looked identical to the old Popsicle sticks. The Dexedrine prepared us for landing by making us extremely alert. The commanders did not want a repeat of the Naha fiasco.

Years later, I would land many times at Honolulu while flying South Pacific for Continental Airlines. Those landings were usually all controlled, straight-in approaches. In fighters, we would land by flights-of-four flying in echelon off the lead aircraft's outside wing. On those occasions, like at Hickam, we would fly the downwind portion of the approach in echelon and make our turn to final by each plane singly banking sharply to land with only seconds separating each plane as it touched down. Very occasionally, we might fly straight in approaches and land by element. That means an element lead and his wingman would touch down together in formation. However, at Hickam we landed from our standard approach.

After landing we were still "alert" and decided to go out on the town. Several hours later the effects of the pill wore off quite suddenly. I was walking along a sidewalk in Waikiki and my legs just stopped working.

The 559th Tactical Fighter Squadron joining the KC-135 tanker in its racetrack track over the Gulf of Mexico on the first leg of the fighter Trans Pac flight to Hawaii.

They felt rubbery and it was all I could do to get back to the base where I just passed out.

The next morning, we were given a briefing by the Commander of PACAF Intelligence himself, which we were told was quite unusual. PACAF (Pacific Air Force) apparently thought we would be the second squadron of F-4s to fight in the War and briefed accordingly. During the brief, we were shown photos of Surface-to-Air Missile (SAM) sites being constructed in North Vietnam by the Russians. At the time, there were only eight. Our aircrews were told that attacking the sites was forbidden. After the briefing, we went immediately to our aircraft parked in rows on the tarmac and were quickly airborne on the last leg of our journey.

The prohibition against attacking the SAMs continued until the Russians had constructed over 100 missile sites before we were finally allowed to defend ourselves by attacking the sites. The presence of the missile sites did not mean that they were all manned with personnel or missiles. The mobile SAM batteries would rotate between constructed sites and occasionally would locate to unprepared sites at remote jungle clearings.

During much of the duration of the Southeast Asia War against North Vietnam, Russian crews manned the SAM sites that downed so many of our aircraft. In 1965, the Soviet Union sent 17,000 missile technicians and operator/instructors to North Vietnam. During 1965 and continuing through the end of my SEA stay in December, 1966, 48 fighters were downed to SAMS. All of the fighters were shot down by Soviet technicians manning the missile sites. In the latter part of 1967, North Viet technicians were also used. The final tally was 205 fighters downed to surface-to-air missiles during the duration of the SEA War.

Reportedly, 7,658 missiles were sent from the Soviet Union to North Vietnam and those were used in 5,800 launches. Those figures are suspect because so many of the missile attacks, especially later in the war, used the highly successful barrage-fire techniques that fired multiple missiles per launch.

USAF's late retaliation against the sites was designated operation "Iron Hand." Specially equipped "Wild Weasel" aircraft armed with Shrike Missiles attacked the sites, which consisted of a missile battery surrounding a central control radar shack. The Shrikes homed in on the emissions from the control radar. The Iran Hand strikes are described in Book Three- Combat.

We met the tankers after takeoff from Hawaii and they accompanied us for the first several hours of our trip to Okinawa. Then they left. Anyone who has flown over the Pacific knows what a huge ocean it is, covering over a third of the earth's surface. We were left to our own navigation from that point until our radar picked up the telltale blips of more tankers orbiting above Guam. Other than a stationary ship along our route called Ocean Station November, we had no other external navigation aids that could help guide us.

The distance from Hawaii to Guam is enormous. At least it seemed enormous to our butts as we sat for hour after hour, unable to move around. On a great-circle direct flight from Hawaii, Guam is almost twice the distance from Hawaii that Hawaii is from California. If it wasn't for the large external fuel tanks that we uploaded for the trip, we would have run out of fuel halfway to Guam.

GUAM:

After WWII, the United States was given the task of governing and supporting several island chains that were involved in the fighting, many of which had been in the Japanese Empire. The Micronesian Islands were administered by the U.S. and included the Marshall's, the Caroline's, Yap and the islands of Palau. The island groups lie approximately 400 miles north of the equator and due east of the Philippines.

Guam was inherited from the Spanish after the Spanish-American War of 1898. It is a territory of the United States and thus American soil and is the largest island in the Mariana's chain. After the dissolution of Micronesia as a protectorate, all of the island groups, other than the Marianas, became independent island nations affiliated with the United States. The Northern Marianas opted to become a territory of the United States. For the other island groups, there are still some support functions done by the United States including using the Sea Bees (CBs- Naval Construction Battalions) for road maintenance. Over twenty of our federal agencies are still affiliated with the Federated States of Micronesia (FSM), which comprises the islands of Yap and the Caroline Islands. An agreement with the FSM obliges the United States to be its military protector.

The Northern Marianas consist of fifteen islands, five of which are occupied, with a total population of less than 60,000. The inhabitants are legally American citizens. The main islands of Saipan, Tinian and Rota are joined by Guam to form our Mariana Island Group. Guam has a population of 183,000 and has a lively tourist trade with Japan, whose citizens like the 1500-mile distance to travel to American soil. There were many Japanese marriages on Guam.

Guam is also home to Andersen AFB, which had tanker units stationed there in 1965. It was from Andersen that our tanker friends were orbiting, waiting for us to contact them over the pre-assigned radio frequency. Within weeks, we were to find that Andersen also housed the B-52s used in their assault on Southeast Asia.

Andersen has a 13,000-foot runway, which is one of the longest in aviation. Much later, I flew cargo flights for Continental Airlines between Hawaii, Guam, Taipai and Hong Kong. On a night takeoff from Andersen flying a DC-10, we used all of the 13,000 feet and had to yank the aircraft off the runway before staggering just above the water for miles until we had gained enough speed to climb.

Our aircraft had been mistakenly loaded with 50,000 pounds of cargo over maximum allowed weight for takeoff from Andersen. We had no way of knowing. We had to trust the weight written on the outside of the cargo cartons by the shippers themselves. It was a primitive system that was soon changed as more sophisticated equipment became operational.

After offloading our needed fuel from the Anderson tankers, we turned from the tankers a little more to the north and aimed for Okinawa across the Philippines Sea, which is separated from the rest of the Northern Pacific by a chain of islands that stretch nearly from Tokyo all the way to Indonesia.

Our tanker buddies only stayed with us as long as was necessary and then were off on their return to Anderson. Our squadron landings at Naha Air Base on southern Okinawa were without incident. All our aircraft landed with wheels down.

While in the pattern for landing, we could see black tunnel entrances spread over a wide area next to the base at Naha. We found out later that those tunnels were part of the famous Shuri Defenses built by the Japanese prior to our WWII invasion of Okinawa. The Shuri Defenses rank as the toughest we have ever faced in any war. Happening very late in the Pacific War, the Battle of Okinawa did not gain the notoriety of other American battles waged over our long history, but it was the bloodiest we have ever fought in any war.

AN ARMED CAMP:

Okinawa is the largest island in the Ryukyu Group that stretches from Japan almost down to Taiwan. It is 60 miles long and boasts a current population of 1,378,000, which is larger than the combined populations of all of the Hawaiian Islands. One third of their pre-WWII population of 450,000 died during the bloody battle for Okinawa. In that battle, we killed over 100,000 Japanese soldiers and shot down over 7,900 Japanese planes in the huge and far-flung battle that took our Navy all the way to the entrance of Tokyo Bay. Before the invasion, we marshaled more ships, men and supplies than we did for D-Day in Europe. Much of the marshaling was in the Caroline Islands atoll of Ulithi. The pre-invasion inventory of ships anchored in Ulithi was 722. This battle marked the high-point of the Japanese use of the Kamikaze suicide planes. It was a massive battle and ranks as the greatest in all of American history.

Okinawa itself was the most concentrated military area that America possessed at the time. All four major American military forces were represented multiple times. The Air Force utilized two bases: Naha AB and Kadena AFB. Naha was actually controlled by the US Navy, with the USAF represented by numerous units including the C-130s of the Military Air Transport Service (MATS), and our detachment of air defense fighters (F-4C) and a half-squadron of Marine F-4Bs that had rotated down from Iwakuni AB on Honshu, Japan. Kadena Air Force Base, further north on the island, housed the 18th Tac Fighter Wing flying the F-105s.

The US Army was represented with numerous installations including Fort Buckner with units including the Special Forces and the 173rd Airborne Brigade. The First Marine Division was headquartered farther up the island and they had a helicopter detachment at the old Japanese landing strip named Futima. The Marines also had a guerrilla training center where I, as squadron intelligence officer, later took our pilots for familiarization. The US Navy had all the port facilities located at Buckner Bay named after General Simon

The island of Okinawa in 1965. Naha Bay is on the left and Buckner Bay on right. Note seven different aircraft runway complexes, one of which is abandoned and five housing American military. The U.S. Navy-controlled Naha Air Base is the large complex on the left side below Naha Bay. The American-controlled Ryukyu Islands capital city of Naha is on the northeast side of Naha Air Base, while the USAF's Kadena AFB is the large complex north of the Bay and due north of Naha City. Two Japanese Zero (fighter) strips from World War II are visible at Yontan and at Marine Corp Air Station Futima (Futenma). Airlines, such as Continental Airlines affiliate Air Micronesia, utilize the compacted-coral Zero runways throughout the islands of the Central Pacific, such as the Mariana's, Palau, Yap, the Caroline's and the Marshall's.

Bolivar Buckner who was the commander of the invasion forces during the Battle of Okinawa. He was killed in the battle as was the commander of the Japanese forces.

The Army was also represented by their defensive missile forces which were armed with the nuclear-tipped Hercules Missiles. Okinawa was the central nuclear weapons storage facility for all United States installations and ships located throughout the Western Pacific. There were literally hundreds of the nukes sheltered in the many island bunkers.

Before we left Florida, those of us who were jump (parachute) qualified were told that we needed our quarterly jumps to maintain currency in our status as Jump Qualified Forward Air Controllers. We knew that Okinawa had organizations and facilities for us to stay current. My experience with jumping went back to my first few months with the 559th and a scheduled trip to the US Army's Parachute Training facility at Fort Benning, Georgia.

JUMP TRAINING:

In the spring of 1964, after my January arrival at MacDill AFB in Florida, I was asked if I wanted to go to Army Parachute School at Fort Benning, Georgia. Our commanding officers informed us that after graduation from Jump Training, those of us selected would become Jump FACs, which would be further combat preparation.

The idea sounded good to me so I agreed and a time was scheduled. Since Jump School was strenuous, I self-imposed a rigorous training schedule to prepare myself for Benning. Within a week of my scheduled departure for Georgia, our squadron Operations Officer came to me and asked if I would participate in a medical evaluation program being held in Texas. The Air Force wanted to set evaluation standards for the Project Apollo astronauts. Since all the astronauts were fighter pilots, NASA wanted to develop performance norms from the fighter pilot community and they tested 200 fighter-pilot volunteers to set those standards. The problem was that, if I went, I would have to reschedule jump school. The squadron wanted me to go and was very persuasive, so I went.

The worst result for me was that the squadron rescheduled me for Georgia in June. Fort Benning in June is very, very hot and humid. I had been in great shape for the Apollo evaluation and was judged "superior" in the endurance part of their testing. As a result of the testing, I was medically cleared for Space Pilot duties. However, for Jump School, I was not in great shape and far from superior.

The jump trainers showed a little kindness by placing the Air Force officers at the end of an Air Force Academy cadet platoon for the runs. Reveille was at 5:00 AM and we immediately were out of our barracks for calisthenics. Before breakfast, we had a five-mile run with our M-1 rifles held at high port. During the day, there was more of the same. Several of us were "dying" and were glad that the cadets did not see the pain. After weeks of heat alerts and broken heat records, we finally had our five jumps and the coveted jump wings.

JUMPING AT YONTAN:

Prior to our stay in Okinawa, I had jumped with the Army's 82nd and 101st Airborne Divisions and with the Marines. In Okinawa, there was an old Japanese Zero base called Yontan. The Zero was the primary Japanese fighter plane of WWII. Other than the bare runway, there was nothing to Yontan other than flat areas of gravel, coral, and rocks interrupted by ravines.

During my stay in Okinawa, I had one jump with the Special Forces (Green Berets). It was from a helicopter and was the nicest jump I ever had. The chopper was stationary so we had no air blast that we usually had when exiting a flying aircraft. After we jumped, the downwash from the rotors caused the chute to slowly billow, which eliminated the opening shock. It was all very gentle and then we landed on soft grass.

A second jump turned out to be my last "regularly scheduled" jump in the Air Force. Four of us were scheduled for an individual jump over Yontan with the Air Force. Two of us were Lieutenants and the other two were Captains, one of whom was designated in charge of the mission. The measured winds were eight knots above maximum allowable by Air Force standards. The Captain-Commander said he would jump in spite of the strong winds and that got the rest of us to agree. But at the last minute he bowed out, quickly followed by the other Captain. He ordered the other Lieutenant, Kenny Thomas, and me to jump.

We "tailgated" out of a C-130, which entailed running off the horizontal cargo tailgate. The chute was connected to the aircraft by a static line as was usual for any of our jumps. That meant that the chute was automatically deployed without us having to pull any "D" ring. The jump was enjoyable because, as we ran off the tailgate, we could view the very visible shoreline and blue waters in the distance. We were facing away from the wind, which lessened the initial blast. Everything was normal until I hit the ground. Due to the strong winds, when I got close to the ground my lateral motion increased. I landed in a ravine and slammed hard into the far side. The impact stunned me.

Normally when we land, our chute collapses and we just have to gather it up. This time my chute remained inflated due to the very strong winds. Those winds carrying my chute lifted me out of the ravine and dragged me along the gravel and coral strewn ground. Under our chute harnesses we wore water wings in case we experienced a water landing. As the wind dragged me across the surface, I was being cut and bruised on the rocks. My inflation lanyard for the water wings also dragged and pulled, inflating the wings. With the wings inflated, I could not reach my chute release. As the wind kept dragging me, Kenny saw what was happening and ran to catch up with my dragging body. He slashed the wings with a knife and ran to grab the chute and deflate it. I was then able to hit the chute release. His actions saved me from more severe consequences.

When we returned to Naha from Yontan, both Kenny and I were incensed. The entire side of my left thigh was yellow, blue, purple and every other color in the rainbow. It was rock hard and without any feeling. Both of us walked into our "Captains" and demanded to know why they ordered us to jump in illegal conditions. The Captain-Commander could see the condition of my leg and my ripped and tattered flight suit. I told them that "I will never jump again." And except for one more unscheduled parachute descent, I never did.

THE PHANTOM IN THE PHILIPPINES:

On the same day, June 9th, that we arrived on Okinawa, the first Air Force Phantom was downed in Southeast Asia. That F-4 was assigned to the 45th Tactical Fighter Squadron then based on TDY (Temporary Duty) at a base in Northeast Thailand called Ubon. The 45th was part of the 15th Tactical Fighter Wing, also permanently based with the 12th TFW at MacDill. The pilot actually ran out of gas during a combat mission against North Vietnam. Eleven days later, a squadron mate of his was downed over the North, but this time it was to a MIG-17.

I was asked to fly a replacement plane for that downed aircraft for what would be my first contact with

Southeast Asia. My task was to work the radar and navigation for my aircraft commander Captain John Robertson, who was also my Flight Commander. Our Ubon Royal Thai Air Force Base destination was 60 miles from the panhandle portion of Laos, one of the three countries that comprised the old French colony of Indochina. Ubon turned out to be a rather primitive facility hacked out of the jungle. The base housing was a series of bamboo, thatch and chicken wire "hooches" that housed our flight crews. The pathways connecting various parts of the base were raised boardwalks that kept everyone from trudging through the continual mud created by the monsoonal rains.

We took off the morning of June 18, 1965, only nine days after arrival in Okinawa. The trip down from Okinawa to Ubon was unlike what we were used to in the States. We were on our own. There was no air traffic control system to monitor and control our destiny. The Phantom ground-mapping radar was highly accurate. Flying down the Chinese coast toward Taiwan was precise with the radar screen presentation showing the coast as if looking at a map. Taiwan rose up ahead of us and we motored past it on our way to the Philippines. Our pre-flight briefing had informed us not to overfly the northern island of Luzon. When I asked the reason for the diversion, the briefing officer told me that headhunters were operating in Northern Luzon. It was one of those "yes sir" moments and we definitely honored their admonishment not to overfly.

As we approached Clark AFB in Central Luzon, we also had to avoid a Communist village ten miles north of the base. At Clark, we landed, refueled and were given the weather over the South China Sea. We prepared our aircraft for the next leg of our journey. Since most of the trip was over water, there were no navigation aids along the way. We would be doing our own navigating by dead reckoning (DR). We did have the INS (Inertial Navigation System), but considered it unreliable.

As we taxied to the departure runway, all hell started to break loose. The radio crackled with myriad aircraft declaring "minimum fuel" or "emergency fuel" and we could see several lined up on approach to land on our same runway. The nearest one was a SAC tanker about eight miles out. We could see the rest lined up after the tanker and we asked tower to "let us get the hell out of here" and the tower willingly complied. We departed into a very dark thundercloud.

Normally, when crossing the South China Sea, any assistance required could be received on the common radio frequency called "Stargazer." This time, it was useless. There was too much chatter and we could not even transmit. As we overflew their position and listened to what was happening on Stargazer, we learned that two B-52s had run into each other and crashed into the sea. SAC was doing its best to fish the crews out. We later found out that all crew members had perished.

This was the first mission in SEA for the B-52s. They were operating out of Andersen AFB on Guam, the same base that gave us tanker support on our Trans Pac less than two weeks before. During the War, the Buffs (B-52s) operated out of Andersen in Guam, Kadena in Okinawa and U-Tapao Royal Thai Air Base, located near Bangkok.

THE PHANTOM IN THAILAND:

We set a DR course and just flew over the South China Sea without navigation aids or traffic control until we picked up the Danang TACAN (Tactical Air Navigation Station). We crossed onto land at Danang and looked down at the airbase that housed Air Force and Marine fighters. Later, Danang would house both Air Force and Marine Phantom units. We continued heading west and overflew the southern panhandle of Laos, navigating to Ubon via TACAN and found it to be a spot in an immense landscape of very green jungle.

For the next few days, we stayed with the rest of the 45th pilots in their "hooch" and partied with them at their rudimentary Officer's Club. The 45th had been the first Phantom squadron in combat after arriving at Ubon on April 4th. John was itching for a combat mission and that is why we didn't immediately return to Naha. Two days after our arrival, on the 20th, another of the 45th Phantoms was shot down over the North. The first downed plane was manned by Captains C.D. Keeter and Gary L. Getman. I knew Gary but did not know Keeter. The flight that was shot down on the 20th was crewed with guys we knew pretty well: Captains Paul Kari and Curt Briggs. It turned out that they had been shot down by a North Vietnamese or Chinese MIG-17.

We joined the rest of the 45th in the crowded Flight Operations. The rescue mission for the two downed pilots was well underway and we were receiving reports of their progress. The ejection beepers for the downed aircraft had been heard and Rescap had been in radio contact with both downed pilots. Helicopters had been sent from Udorn Royal Thai Air Base, located to the north of Ubon and near the Laotian border. As we were to find out later, Udorn was entirely manned by the CIA, Air America, Continental Air Services, USAF reconnaissance and other types of aircraft. We correctly presumed the rescue choppers were from the CIA-contracted Air America.

We ended up staying a week at Ubon, hoping for permission to fly combat. On June 22, it became evident to me that it was not to be. I left John at Flight Ops and jumped on board one of the military transports that flew down to Don Muang Airport, outside of Bangkok, spending the rest of the week in Bangkok, exploring the city.

When John and I arrived at Ubon, we had no civilian clothing. Before I got on the transport aircraft, I went over to the Australian side. The Aussie's were flying F-86 Sabres in defense of Ubon and on selected combat missions. They had the only Base Exchange (BX) at Ubon. I purchased a shirt and a pair of slacks. On short notice, there was nobody to tailor the slacks, so I took them without cuffs or sewn pant bottoms. I just tucked them inside my combat boots and off I flew.

After landing at Don Muang Airport, I caught a bus into Bangkok. My arrival must have provoked a lot of curiosity among the Thais. Since the F-105s at both Korat and Takhli were on TDY, they flew seven-day weeks and never got off base. The same was true of the F-4s at Ubon. To the best of my knowledge, I must have been among the first, if not the first fighter pilot to visit Bangkok from the fighter-bomber bases.

When I got off the bus, I had on a civilian shirt and pants with shiny black flying boots. Hanging from my arms was: my "G" suit, my parachute harness and my flight helmet. Base Operations at Ubon had advised me that I should take my stuff with me since I did not know what might happen on my journey. On my helmet was painted the silhouette of a Phantom in dark blue against a powder blue background. There should have been no doubt to my identity as a Phantom pilot. This was no stealth mission.

THE THAI BASES:

Several times during the six months that we stayed in Okinawa, I visited all the Thai fighter-bomber bases manned by the Americans. The tours were in behalf of the 559th and were for the purpose of finding out intelligence information.

The Thai bases in 1965 and 1966 were an interesting mix of forces. There were six principal USAF bases in Thailand, all Royal Thai Air Force Bases: Don Muang, Korat, Takhli, Ubon, Udorn, and Nakhon

Phanom, usually just called NKP. It was from Korat, Takhli and Ubon that the main air battle against the North was waged. These were the bases from which the F-105s and F-4s attacked North Vietnam. The rest of the fighter-bombers involved against the North were from the aircraft carriers stationed in the center of the Gulf of Tonkin.

The transport aircraft that brought me to Bangkok was part of a regular transport system in operation between the American bases in Thailand. This trip was my first introduction to the Thai base system that became so important in the USAF operations against North Vietnam. Before I left SEA, I traveled in this transport system many times.

While in Bangkok, I called back to Ubon on a daily basis to see what was happening and to see if I was needed or wanted. When John finally decided that a combat mission out of Ubon was not to be, he told me to catch a hop, return to Ubon and that we would then catch transport back to Okinawa.

I jumped aboard a C-130 headed for Ubon. The planned trip to Ubon had us landing at Korat, which was almost directly enroute from Don Muang to Ubon. When we arrived at Korat, the flight was diverted to Udorn, which was way up north near the Laotian border. The reason we were diverted was that we were reassigned as a medevac (medical evacuation) flight for a Laotian Colonel who had been, we were told, wounded in an attack against the North.

Recently declassified CIA documents mention an event that was significant in the escalation of the Laotian conflict. The report mentions that in June of 1965, a Laotian Army Colonel was killed on a clandestine mission with the CIA inside of North Vietnam. The CIA was then flying missions out of Udorn and dirt landing strips in Laos that landed on North Vietnamese hilltops to establish temporary way-stations to support the Thud (F-105) airstrikes.

It turned out that the mission, during which the Colonel was wounded, was an Air America rescue to pick up Kari and Briggs. The two pilots had somehow gotten separated and Kari was captured and became a POW, but Curt Briggs managed to evade capture and was picked up by Air America. During the rescue, the Air America chopper was shot up and the Laotian Army Colonel riding in the chopper was fatally wounded.

When we arrived at Udorn, we were told to stay on board while the Laotian Colonel was loaded aboard and the C-130 took off quickly on a direct return flight to Don Muang that bypassed Korat. The Colonel, headed for a Bangkok hospital, was unconscious and was being medicated intravenously. Information that I received revealed was that he later died of his wounds.

Udorn, then-headquarters for the CIA in SEA, is also called Udon Thani and is only 40 miles south of Vientiane, the capital of Laos. Udorn was, like Ubon, in the middle of the jungle and was also headquarters for other American clandestine air forces operating there, including Air America and CIA and USAID-contracted Continental Air Services. Another CIA-used base of consequence was Nakhon Phanom (NKP), due east of Udorn at about 100 miles and situated right on the Mekong River.

After landing in Bangkok, the Colonel was swiftly carried off to a hospital. The C-130 then refueled and we were off again, this time we flew the schedule and landed at Ubon without further incident. On landing I heard the welcome news that Curt, a friend, had been rescued. The next morning John and I said good-bye to our new 45th TFS friends and returned by transport to Danang and then further east to Clark in the Philippines before heading north to Naha in Okinawa. At the time, I had no idea that within eleven months, I would rejoin the 45th as one of their fighter pilots.

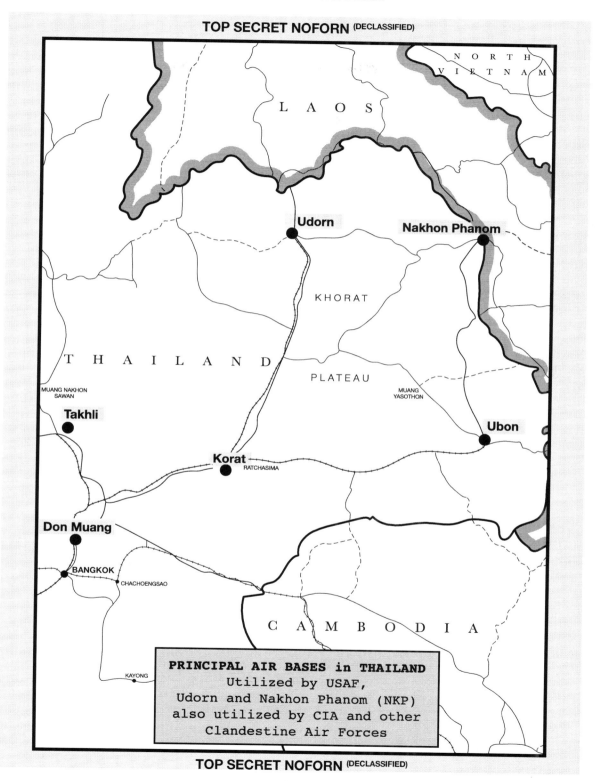

PRINCIPAL AIR BASES in THAILAND
Utilized by USAF,
Udorn and Nakhon Phanom (NKP)
also utilized by CIA and other
Clandestine Air Forces

OKINAWA:

The American Far Eastern military shield built at the end of WWII had a lot of parts. By 1965, American forces were in South Korea, Japan, Formosa (Taiwan), the Northern Marianas, Guam, Okinawa, the Philippines, Thailand, Laos and Vietnam, plus the 7th Fleet at sea. It was a formidable force. The island of Okinawa was at the heart of that military shield.

For those of us who were there at the time, Okinawa was special. Today Okinawa is part of Japan, but to say that the inhabitants are Japanese is a mistake. They are a distinct people who speak a dialect of Japanese and are only Part-Japanese by blood. Their ancestors include an indigenous population that preceded the Japanese occupation. Ancient tribes occupied Japan, Taiwan, the Philippines, Guam, Okinawa and many of the Pacific Islands long before the current inhabitants arrived.

I got to be friends with several Okinawans and their story is far different than is generally known. Prior to WWII, the Japanese government treated the Okinawans horribly. The infrastructure over the entire island was in disrepair. At the start of WWII, there were only seven miles of paved highways throughout the island. The Japanese treated the natives as poor relatives at best and at times could be outright barbaric. The Japanese authorities would cut off a native's hand if he was caught stealing. They considered the population inferior.

It is a shame that our postwar administrators did not have a better understanding of the culture, history and attitudes of many of the peoples of Asia. In the case of Okinawa, if we had shown them equality and dignity and given them identity, the recent history of Okinawa might have taken a very different road. We could have turned the Ryukyu Islands into an American State and thus made permanent the expensive island military installations.

On Okinawa, our social calendar was usually always filled. We dated the school teachers that taught the children of the military. I drove an "island car" that I had purchased sight-unseen for $50 from a departing pilot from the 558th. It was a Dodge sedan and, while it didn't turn heads, it got us around. Nobody needed a car around the base because everything we needed was within walking distance. We did use the Dodge to often drive to downtown Naha and occasionally to a beach resort on the extreme northern part of the island. Most of the roads in the southern part of the island were paved, but not in the north. We drove to the resort over a packed coral road that served as the major highway going north.

The school teachers at Naha were part of a Pentagon program that sent them to all of our overseas bases with dependents, including Naha. The following year I ran into several while on holiday in Hong Kong and the year after that met many of the same girls again when I was stationed in England.

THE OFFICER'S CLUB @ NAHA:

The center of our social world was the same as it was at any Air Force base, the Officer's Club. Even though the Air Force was a tenant of the Navy, who owned the base, the USAF had most of the major assets, which in this case were F-4s and C-130s.

Most of our free time would find us at the Club or down in Naha. Occasionally we might drive to one of the many military facilities spread throughout the island. Occasionally, I would drive over to the Club at Kadena to share MIG-25s or French-75s (cocktails) with the F-105 drivers stationed there. At Marine Corp Futima, they had a room filled with Akai reel-to-reel recorders, which they used to record whatever selection of music was wanted by customers. All it cost was 25 cents per filled reel and the only requirement for purchase was that you had to be military.

Our parties at the "O" Club sometimes got to be a bit rowdy. After all, when you send 48 unaccompanied pilots overseas, they have to let off steam someplace. For us, it was the Club. The Navy, being more of a straight-laced service, often complained about our actions. It all came to a head one night when a party really got wild. We ended up dancing on the top of the cherished Navy piano. For that, our Squadron Commander, Colonel Hollingsworth, was permanently banned from the Club for the duration of our stay. The rest of us were only temporarily banned.

We ate most of our meals at the Club, which were served by two hostesses who were always there to serve us. One was a half-American girl, who was the only really beautiful Asian woman that I saw on Okinawa. I had seen many, many beautiful women in Bangkok and would later see a whole lot of beautiful Asian women in Tokyo and Hong Kong, but not in Okinawa.

The other hostess was a shy, sweet girl of Japanese descent named Suchiko. She was the favorite of almost all of us.

The Club is a real treasure for the Air Force. It serves multiple uses including creating lasting bonds between the pilots. We ate, drank and caroused at the Club. It also served as a gathering place for the unattached American women who might be in the area.

The usual squadron TDY stay of the type we were on was three months. Both previous squadrons only had to stay for three. The Air Force decided to extend our stay for another TDY, then another and then another which left us there for six months. This didn't mean much to those of us who were unmarried. For the married guys, it was tough.

Our Club in Okinawa left many lasting memories. Before arrival, I had never ever drunk a White Russian. While there, I drank nothing else. After leaving, I never had another. Mental images have Suchiko serving me the sweet and sour pork that was my introduction. A final memory was of a gracious Naval Commanding Officer inviting me to take a cruise the following morning on his Nuclear Attack Submarine. The chance of a lifetime was lost when I slept through my alarm.

NAHA CITY:

Many Americans have heard of "The Teahouse of the August Moon." If asked, most might say it is in Japan or they might be more specific and name Tokyo. They would be wrong. The Teahouse is in Naha City. I have driven and walked by it many times, but have never been inside. The military had made it off-limits to all military personnel. It is a refuge for Japanese and Okinawans and it was quite proper for our military to show its respect.

Naha City sits on the edge of Naha Bay. It was Naha Bay where I got my first inkling that SEA was building up to a much larger war. In mid-1965, most Americans thought that Vietnam was only a small battle and that our troops would probably take care of the "black clad" guerrilla forces of the Viet Cong in short order. The military must have thought otherwise for there were cargo ships anchored for weeks off the coast of Naha Bay, waiting for an opening on one of the docks for either on-loading or off-loading of supplies. The ships were everywhere and we had a good view from the air. The port facilities at Naha served as a major supply hub, where supplies arrived from all over the world and were then loaded on other ships heading south. Buckner Bay, on the far side of the island, served the same purpose for the Navy.

Naha had a "red light" district. But it was not like most red-light districts. At least it does not resemble the common notion of what a red-light district should be in the Western World. The Teahouse is in the district, called Nama Nui. The tradition of the Geisha has placed most such establishments in a different light. Nama Nui has prostitution—yes. But the houses of prostitution often have the flavor of culture. Many of the houses in Nama Nui did have significant culture and prostitution was not allowed and frowned upon. It is similar to the massage industry. Many massage houses front for prostitution, but many don't.

Nama Nui also was where you went if you wanted a Hotsi Bath. There was a favorite Hotsi Bath house in Nama Nui that I often frequented. It was not a front for prostitution or anything else. It was a legitimate form of entertainment like the Baths during the Roman period.

In 1965, this is what my Hotsi Bath offered: An Okinawan lady placed you in an enclosed wooden steam box and then placed towels around your neck. She would serve you a cocktail as you sat with your arms inside. She would also place the cocktail glass to your lips when requested. The steam bath lasted for as long as you wished. After stepping out, the attendant would wash and soap your body down and then offer for you to step into a pre-drawn bath. You were also free to sit in the bath for as long as you wished. After stepping out, she dried and then powdered your entire body prior to having you lay on a massage table. The massage lasted for close to an hour. The full price for this evening of luxury, including cocktail, was $1.75.

The Hotsi baths offered an option for our massages. For the same price, we could have an Okinawan maiden walk on our backs. They usually selected the fattest hostess to do the walking. During the agony, I wondered if it was a form of Japanese revenge.

OUR MISSION—AIR DEFENSE:

Our mission on Okinawa was the air defense of the entire island. When airborne, we were controlled by "the blockhouse" which was Navy and housed all the radar and intercept controllers. The intercepts were not practice. This was the height of the Cold War and our intercepts were hot.

Early on, the Navy radar blockhouse controllers would give us turn directions in "Navy Talk." Our Air Force fighters would often "shudder" as their drivers tried to figure out the difference between "starboard" and "port."

We sat air defense alert and usually were airborne within two minutes of the sound of the blaring alert claxon. Most of our intercepts were against the Chinese "Beagle" light-bomber. We also occasionally intercepted a Russian "Bear" propeller driven bomber that was monitoring the Chinese nuclear bomb testing.

The Russians also had a high-altitude recce aircraft very similar to the American U-2. The NATO designation for this aircraft was the "Mandrake." We had to do extreme "snap up" maneuvers to try to reach near their altitudes. Each of our cockpits was "armed" with Nikon cameras so that we could "shoot" them with the Nikon.

Each week, we usually had a war-game day. On those days, an "enemy" squadron would launch an attack against Okinawa. Since these attackers would try to sneak under our radar coverage by flying close to the water, we would have planes orbiting. The Phantom has a great radar with ground mapping capability and a 200-mile range on its sweep radar. The airborne target acquisition radar had a lock-on range of 50 miles, which was terrific at the time. Lock-ons mean that we pin-point the radar blip recorded on the sweep radar and electronically lock on to the blip, after which we could continuously monitor his position. By flying orbits at low-level, we could differentiate the "blips" of a possible target from radar ground clutter. The entire day was a challenging experience and we would meet the "enemy" pilots at the Club after the event to trade lies about our exploits.

The Army also had an air defense mission on Okinawa. Only theirs was manning the nuclear-tipped, ground-to-air Hercules Missile. The Hercules could reach out over a 100 miles to stop any intruding aircraft in the "event of war." The value of a nuclear-tipped missile in air defense is that it is a proximity weapon. That means that the missile can explode in the proximity of the enemy aircraft and still kill it.

The Soviet SAMs used in SEA were also proximity weapons. However, they had a conventional warhead and their lethal range was up to 300 yards from the point of detonation. Since it was nuclear, the Hercules could detonate and kill all aircraft within an unspecified, but much larger area.

Early, during the initial indoctrination to our air defense job, the pilots met with the Army Hercules launch crews. Their missiles were obviously radar controlled and the Hercules had internal radar as well. When fired, the Hercules was controlled by the launch radar until the missile closed on the target. During the flight, the missile radar was synched with the launch radar. That meant that when the missile took over control as it neared the target, that their internally mounted radar was already "up-to-speed" and could easily finish the shoot with target destruction.

During our briefing, I asked the launch controllers if they had IFF recognition equipment on their launch radars. The IFF is a cockpit-mounted box in the F-4 and all other fighter- bomber aircraft that emits a pulse that can be read by ground radar. It is for the purpose of identification and is called Identification Friend or Foe (IFF). Depending on what number is entered in the IFF by the pilot, the ground radar can "read" an aircraft. In civilian airliners, the IFF is also used to tell the ground based air traffic controllers if they are being skyjacked or if they have an emergency. All radar in the free world commercial air traffic control systems have IFF recognition equipment. The Hercules launch controllers revealed that they did not.

Our job as fighter- interceptor pilots in an air attack was to fly out to meet the enemy with a full load of 4 Sparrow radar missiles and 4 Sidewinder infrared, heat-seeking missiles. We were to engage an attack force and do what we could to stop them. The obvious problem with the Hercules radar was that they would be firing nuclear missiles at all of the planes in the sky without concern of friend or foe. The defensive Phantoms would be vaporized as we fought.

RUSSIAN "WAR GAMES":

In 1965, the Russians had a reported fleet of over 12,000 trawlers that plied all of the world's oceans. A few were actual fishing boats, but a majority of them were military with a multitude of missions. Many of those missions were intelligence gathering and the trawlers were often top-heavy with antenna towers.

In the East China Sea, some trawlers contained false-target identifiers. The identifiers could shoot an electronic signature above the trawlers that would paint as a blip on the Okinawan defense radars. The blip to the radar controllers would constitute an unidentified aircraft of unknown origin.

Once, our Okinawan defense radar operators sent me on an intercept of an unknown target. With our 200-mile search radar in the Phantom, we easily picked up the bogey blip. The weather that day was what we pilots called CAVU, which stands for Clear Air Visibility Unlimited. The weather allowed us to fly by visual rules (VFR). By this time, I was flying the front seat as a new Aircraft Commander with a regular back seater and was at the altitude identified by the controllers. I actually flew through the blip without seeing anything. As soon as we flew through it, I waited about ten seconds and executed a split S maneuver.

In a Split S, the pilot rolls the aircraft inverted and pulls down and through to end up heading in the opposite direction. It is the opposite of an Immelman maneuver. The difference being that in an Immelman, the roll is at the end of the maneuver and it is aimed up instead of down, as in a Split S.

This time I flew a loose Split S and ended up right off the water. As I dove inverted, I identified a Russian trawler dead ahead. After leveling, I lifted up and increased speed, passing over the trawler antennas with a good twenty feet to spare. The blast of my speed to the sailors on deck sent a very clear message: "we know what you are doing and don't mess with us."

While we were in Okinawa, the Russians occasionally flew the TU-95 "Bear" Bomber across the East China Sea. The usual mission was monitoring, by taking air samples of, the Red Chinese nuclear tests. The swept-wing Bear had four turboprop engines with two variable-pitch, counter-rotating props for each engine. It could really move if it wanted. The Bear had a rear gunner located under the tail.

On every flight of the TU-95s into Okinawan airspace, our Phantoms would intercept. It was the same for the Russian "Mandrake" U-2-type, Yak-25s that overflew Okinawa at very high altitude.

On one such TU-95 intercept, the rear gunner sat behind his bubble canopy. The F-4s flew very close formation with the Bear and the Phantoms had a very clear image of the gunner up close. He was probably no more than 20- 30 feet from the fighters. He smiled, gave the guys a thumbs-up signal and spread a Playboy centerfold out for all to see. He then motioned for the F-4s to fly up beside the Bear cockpit and indicated that the Bear pilots wanted to take photos. For some reason, our guys did not comply and that upset the gunner. He then gave our guys a signal, which created the strange situation of the "bird" being sent from their bird to our birds. Flipping the "bird" seems to be an international signal.

A story made the rounds of the pilots about a fighter base located in Central Japan that played games with the Soviets. It was common Air Force knowledge in Okinawa. In those days, Russian fighter pilots had, at best, a reported 20 hours of training every year as contrasted to American fighter pilots who flew 20 training hours per month. We felt very confident that, if we had to engage Soviet MIGs, that American pilots would prevail. Even in Russian-controlled airspace, they still had the same identification problems that we do.

Twenty hours of training a year meant that they had to be very "rusty." The American fighter squadrons in Japan would wait until the weather over Vladivostok was close to zero-zero, which means really lousy. Zero-zero actually means the low clouds were zero altitude above the ground and visibility was also zero. The usual cause was the prevalent fog. When zero-zero conditions were encountered at the air defense interceptor base located near Vladivostok, the American squadron would launch. It would fly at altitude toward the Russian mainland to ensure that they were painted by the Russian radar and until they got word that the Russian defense interceptors had launched. Then they would dive to the deck (just above the ocean and under Russian radar visibility) and fly back to Japan.

The Russians were left to recover their planes in zero-zero conditions. Invariably, they would have losses for the returning planes that crashed in the fog. These operations were unknown to our military and to our government. To American fighter pilots, they were "Russian War Games."

The "Games" were not all one-sided. Once when I was flying an F-4 single-ship enroute from England to North Africa, I received a call while I was near Malta. The caller spoke perfect American-accented English.

He informed me that he was Wheelus Air Base Air Traffic Control. He gave me a vector and requested that I turn to that heading. Since Wheelus at that time, had no Air Traffic Control, I ignored the caller and flew the rest of the way direct to Wheelus Air Base in Libya. When we flew non-stop from England, we usually had nothing but gas fumes on landing. The caller was later identified as Russian who was attempting to run me out of fuel.

In 1967 and 1968, I flew NATO as part of the European War Plan. This was a very classified plan of nuclear attack against the Warsaw Pact countries, including Russia. In England, we sat alert with 500-pound nukes loaded centerline on the F-4. That nuke was what we called a "dial-a-bomb." There was a small access panel with a wafer switch very similar to those on your home washing machine. Our choices were not whether we wanted cotton, towels, delicate or speed wash. The four choices were all about "yield." The 4th or highest choice, gave us a yield 100 times more powerful than the Hiroshima bomb.

One of the great problems in the War Plan was eye protection for pilots. The planned attack against the Communist World was what was called a carpet attack. That meant that the exploding nuclear bombs would literally "walk" across the land as they went eastward toward Moscow as if unrolling a carpet. All of our weapons would be employed. That included ICBMs, IRBMs, heavy bombers, tactical missiles, fighter-bombers and sea-launched missiles. The path ahead of attacking Phantoms, as they crossed the Iron Curtain, would be filled with nuclear detonations. The War Plan had us flying close enough to many of the detonations that, if our gaze was directly at a detonation, we would be permanently blinded.

The Air Force answer to the problem was to supply Phantom crews standing nuclear alert in Europe with eye patches. The two-man crews were to wear the patches with only one pilot eye used to fly. As each eye was permanently blinded, we were to uncover another eye. We had four eyes to reach the target. What a comforting thought.

My nuclear target in Europe was in Poland. On the return from an attack, we would run out of gas somewhere over Germany. The Air Force solution, land on an autobahn. You really have to love the Air Force. Actually, it made no difference. If it got to that point, it was all over. The Russians had four nuclear missiles aimed at my base, RAF Woodbridge. We would be vaporized long before we entered the cockpits, well before launch.

ONE "DARK AND STORMY" OKINAWAN NIGHT:

One evening, six of our squadron planes were scheduled to fly night missions. I was flying one of four, as Aircraft Commander, who were to meet up with airborne tankers on radar and offload gas. This was part of my Aircraft Commander checkout in night tanker hookups. Air-to-air refueling practice was required training, both day and night, for all crews. Two other planes were scheduled to fly low-level night intercepts. This meant that they would use their radar to practice intercepts against each other.

Captain Gary Smith, our Naval Academy grad who would later die in an air crash, was the briefing officer. Gary said that he did not like the weather and thought we should not fly. But, we had to "fill the squares" and pilots with higher rank than Gary decided to go ahead and fly.

The weather was okay for our tanker mission. It helped us prepare for later combat missions over Laos when we intercepted the tankers on radar and in the clouds with no more than ten feet of visibility between aircraft.

That night, the weather was terrible for low-level intercept training. The interceptors were to fly at 3,000 feet and run at each other to get a radar pickup out of the radar clutter of a choppy sea. Halfway through our tanker mission, we heard the "blockhouse" controller calling out for number two. He received no answer. The radar controller must have lost him off his radar screen.

It did not take us long to figure out what was happening. Sometimes the cause is radio failure. But we had heard that type of call before. The situation and conditions shouted out the answer. We all knew.

At the end of our mission on that dark and stormy night, we all quietly took off our flight gear and assembled in the operations room. We worked out the fuel figures and estimated how long they could remain airborne until fuel exhaustion. The AC of the aircraft was Captain Dell Dyer, who lived with me at the Bennett Apartments in Tampa.

We walked outside and stood quietly in the light rain while we waited. When the time came and passed, we all looked at each other and nobody said a thing. Their fuel was exhausted. If they hadn't crashed before, they would now.

We slowly walked up to the VOQ and started knocking on the doors. Everyone assembled at the Club and we started to party. Halfway through the evening one of the "schoolies" (schoolteachers) found out what had happened. She berated the heck out of us for being so callous. We just looked at her and again nobody said a thing. She just did not understand.

No evidence of the crash was ever found.

THE PHANTOM IN JAPAN:

After our ferry mission to Ubon, John Robertson and I would have one more adventure before I was selected as the first Lieutenant in the Air Force to begin upgrading from being Systems Operator (PSO) in the backseat to be Aircraft Commander (AC) in the front seat. John and I were given the task of introducing the American Air Force bases in Japan to the Phantom.

It was shortly after this trip that I began training in earnest at Naha for AC. Up until that time, I was given more or less equal time between the front and back seats. Since we had no bombing range within reach of Okinawa, I was unable to complete training until return to the Continental U.S. (CONUS) and thus I ended up second (by a week) in the Air Force to actually complete upgrading.

The Phantom was the hottest operational aircraft in the world at that time and none of the bases in Japan had ever seen one. The Air Force asked us to show them.

John and I flew all the way north to a base near Hakodate on the southern tip of Hokkaido Island. The trip up the Island of Honshu had been on the west side and we landed at several American installations. When we departed Hakodate, we flew down the east side of Honshu, the largest of the Japanese Islands.

All the free world's traffic control systems speak English. At least that is what they are expected to do. Reality sometimes is a different story. Occasionally, John and I would have no idea what the Japanese traffic control operators were asking us to do. It was a mystery. However, it was a beautifully clear day and we were not worried about enroute problems with other aircraft. The snow-clad Mount Fuji was a focal point that we could see almost the entire journey over Japanese soil.

One of the installations where we landed was Misawa Air Force Base, located on the northeast coast of Honshu. After we landed and parked the aircraft, we were swarmed with military personnel wanting their first glimpse of the Phantom. We stayed as long as we could to answer their many questions and sign autographs, but had other bases to hit before we flew back to Okinawa. The entire "show and tell" demonstration flight was a daylight event. By evening, we were expected to land back "home" in Okinawa. Each base that we visited refueled us with a minimum load for the next stage of our journey.

After we were refueled, on taxi-out the Misawa tower asked us to give them a max (maximum) performance take off. The tower operator asked us to "show them what we can do." It was a challenge that we could not ignore. The Phantom has two Pratt and Whitney J-79 engines, each with a thrust of 17,000 pounds. The afterburner has four different stages. Each stage gave us further power fueled by raw JP-4 gas being shot directly into the engine combustion chambers.

The thrust of the two-engine Phantom was so great that we could accelerate flying vertical with a fuel load of less than 3,000 pounds. We, of course, had a partial load of fuel that was enough to get us to the next base. A max-takeoff using all four stages of AB (afterburner) meant that we would give the Misawa tower, and all of those watching from the ground, a great show.

John gave me the stick as we lifted off and I saw a hole in the cirrus cloud deck high above us. I aimed for that hole and we just rocketed. Our gyro tumbled and we had no instrument position reference. Our eyes were outside the cockpit and we shot through the hole at an altitude of 20,000 feet. As I rolled the aircraft over and looking down, we could see that we had not reached the end of the runway. In other words, after liftoff, we had reached the end of the runway at an altitude in excess of 20,000 feet. The Misawa guys were suitably impressed.

AIRCRAFT COMMANDER:

My "official" upgrade to Aircraft Commander occurred shortly after John and I returned from Japan. It consisted of navigation missions, intercept training, day and night air-to-air refueling training, and formation flying but not a lot else. We did not have a bombing and gunnery range on Okinawa and we were too far from Japan to get there with a load of bombs, practice and then return to Okinawa. So, I flew simulated dive bomb passes without bombs against the volcanic rocks sticking out of the sea. Okinawa is part of the Ryukyu Island Chain, which stretch almost from the southern tip of Japan proper to 75 miles from Taiwan. There are a lot of small, rock islands, steaming sulphur, that lie north of the main Ryukyu island of Okinawa.

The result of my abbreviated upgrade training was that I felt comfortable sitting in the front cockpit, but I was not sure if I was prepared for what was to come.

FLORIDA REVISITED:

When I returned to MacDill after our six month TDY on Okinawa, our squadron changed its mission and became a CCTS (Combat Crew Training Squadron). Our task was to train pilots for Vietnam. The base asked me to be a flight instructor in the Phantom. Since I had just upgraded to AC (Aircraft Commander), I thought this idea was ridiculous and I told them so. How could I effectively train aircraft commanders for war when I had been an AC for such a short time, had not had range training and had not even been to war? They then asked me to be a ground instructor and I again refused. I wanted to fly and not be stuck to a desk.

ORDERS TO WAR:

Previously, I volunteered for Vietnam in the Phantom and any number of propeller-driven aircraft, including the T-28. Major Davis, our Squadron Director of Operations, put my requests in his desk and did not forward them. I had actually volunteered for Vietnam in whatever I could fly.

When they finally acceded to my wishes, it was in a manner entirely unexpected. My arrival back at MacDill was in December. In February, I got orders to Vietnam in the Phantom. I suspected that my immediate orders had something to do with my ending my relationship with Elsie Gibson and starting one with Judy Spencer. Elsie was a favorite of the Officer's Wives Club.

It turned out that my first encounters with MIGs in combat situations were without my having had any air combat training, other than with radar missiles. The lack of a gun at MacDill meant that the first time I fired the gun was in combat. What we called "the gun" was really a six-barreled Gattling Cannon. It fired 20mm shells at a rate of 100 rounds a second.

Since I had been volunteering for Vietnam and was willing to fly anything, the orders to Vietnam in F-4s made me joyful. I would be rejoining the 12th TFW, which had left for Cam Ranh Bay in December, 1965. The only problem with the orders was that they had me moving very quickly. It turned out that the assigned base, Cam Ranh Bay, had no idea I was coming. They also had no need for me to replace combat losses. That would change.

The orders to Vietnam also had me again ordered to participate in Jungle Survival, but this time it would be in the Philippines and not Panama.

> *"There never was a good war, or a bad peace."*
> Benjamin Franklin

CHAPTER SEVEN

Jungle Survival
Panama & the Philippines

> *"Battle is an orgy of disorder."*
>
> General George S. Patton

FLYING TO WAR:

My mid-February combat orders gave me little time to make arrangements. My Port Call was March 4, which meant that I had to be catching a flight out of the airport of Los Angeles on that date. The shortness of time also meant I had to make arrangements to sell my car and take a loss.

I loaded my few possessions and boarded a military transport out of MacDill to Southern California, where my stereo and my new color television were left with my parents. Since my March 4 Port Call was almost upon me, I had little time to visit with my family.

In a short time, I was back at Los Angeles International Airport and boarding another military cargo plane. We lifted off from the LAX runway heading due west along the coast of Southern California. At Point Conception in Santa Barbara County, we left the coast on our great circle route heading directly for Hawaii. The cargo plane belonged to the Air Force Military Airlift Command (MAC), which was the same command as the older Military Air Transport Service (MATS).

During our trip across the Pacific, we landed at Hickam Air Base in Hawaii. While there, they didn't even let us get off the plane. We parked for as long as they needed to gas up the plane and off we went on the continuation of our journey. Our destination was Clark Air Force Base in the Philippines Island of Luzon.

The Air Force has three fighter commands worldwide. In earlier and simpler times, when ocean-going vessels crossed the equator, they held an on-board ceremony to commemorate their crossing of that imaginary line. For us, there was no ceremony when we crossed a similar imaginary line. The 140th Meridian marked the boundary line between two different fighter commands. All Air Force fighters that were stationed in what is called the CONUS (Continental United States) were assigned to Tactical Air Command, more commonly called TAC. The TAC area of influence extended to the 140th meridian. West of the 140th was PACAF, or Pacific Air Forces, territory.

When my war was complete and I left Southeast Asia for my next Air Force duty assignment, I was assigned to fly out of England and Libya. While in Europe, I was assigned to USAFE, the United States Air Force in Europe, which was a fighter command similar to TAC.

After crossing the 140th, I was owned by PACAF. Hickam Air Force Base, Hawaii was PACAF headquarters. The Commanding General for PACAF was known in AF jargon as CINCPACAF, which obviously means Commander in Chief- PACAF. His Admiral buddy, who controls the 7th Fleet in the Pacific, was in Hawaii too. He was called CINCPACFLT. Obviously, he was Commander in Chief for the Pacific Fleet. In the military, the higher your rank, the more letters they award you. The overall boss of CINCPACAF and CINCPACFLT is CINCPAC (Commander in Chief- Pacific). He is also stationed in Hawaii.

My flying friends on the long overwater journey were all military guys going to war. Later while flying with Continental, one of the flight attendants, who had flown MAC, told me that the trips to Southeast Asia were sad. The soldiers, sailors and airmen were mostly young and enlisted. They were quiet as they each contemplated what might be in store for them in Vietnam, or wherever else in SEA they were headed. This trip was no exception.

My status was a little different. I was a professional military officer who had volunteered. Being professional, I wanted to see how I measured up. I had been a member of the most experienced Phantom Wing in the Air Force. Now I was flying to rejoin them.

Two of my flying friends were wearing different uniforms than all the rest of us. I was in my standard-issue greenish fatigues with highly-polished black flying boots. My canvas military duffle bag, which was part of the load lashed down in the middle of our cargo compartment, held my flight gear and other uniforms.

I wanted a pair of the highly-desired combat boots, but was told I would have to wait until I was actually in combat to wear them. The combat boots were lighter than our flying boots. They were made of leather and a green canvas that would have matched my fatigues. They had breathing holes which might prove invaluable in the heat and humidity of Vietnam. They had rubber soles with good tread that could give the wearer a good grip in the ever-present mud. Flying boots had slick leather soles. The combat boots had one further advantage, they looked sexy. I figured that I would look good to the girls in my fatigues wearing my pilot wings, my jump wings and, of course, my combat boots.

I never did get those combat boots. During my stay, none of the Air Force issue combat boots ever got out of Saigon. They were worn by senior Air Force wienies who would only fly a desk and never see combat. Within six weeks of that Trans Pacific cruise, I would greatly regret the loss of those treaded boots as I desperately tried to climb a muddy hillside toward a rescue chopper as North Vietnamese gunners fired over my head.

My two buddies who wore the blue uniforms of the South Vietnamese Air Force turned out to be good companions on the trip. They offered me intelligent discussion covering a wide range of subjects. While we had the usual webbed canvas-seats lining the sides of the cargo compartment, many of us stood and chatted as we flew. Of course, discussion eventually turned to the War. They seemed to feel that they needed to convince me of the wisdom of my choice to fight for their country. They actually buoyed my spirits. They believed in the righteousness of their cause.

Strangely, it turned out to be the last time I would discuss the War or any subject with a South Vietnamese officer. I later met their leader, General Nguyen Cao Ky, when I commanded the Cam Ranh Command Post, but he was the only other Vietnamese Air Force Officer that I ever encountered. In Vietnam, we rarely met any Viet civilians. Our squadron decided we would not allow any Viets into our Quonset hut to clean. We cleaned it ourselves, which meant that it stayed dirty.

The 12th Tactical Fighter Wing had been permanently transferred from MacDill to Vietnam in November of 1965. The fighters themselves flew west to join their initial squadron contingents in December. When the

559th returned to MacDill from Naha, we passed the 12th fighters at Hickam on December 8. We saw their F-4s on the tarmac from a distance. Most of us felt a sense of remorse as they were going to war and we were flying in the other direction.

My squadron in Okinawa had belonged to the 12th. Now it belonged to a Combat Crew Training Wing (CCTW) at MacDill. MacDill itself was no longer a fighter base, it was a training base. The eight full-strength fighter squadrons that had been at MacDill in 1965 were now spread all over the map of Asia. The 15th TFW squadrons had also been moved from MacDill to Vietnam.

In 1965, the 12th was at Cam Ranh Bay on the coast of central South Vietnam. There were MacDill F-4s at Danang in Vietnam and Ubon in Thailand. There was a squadron in Okinawa. In 1966, an F-4 squadron from MacDill was at Udorn in the extreme north of Thailand. They were everywhere.

The 12th at Cam Ranh was not the same as the 12th in Florida. My old squadron, the 559th, was now back at MacDill. It had been replaced by the 45th squadron. It was the same 45th that accepted the replacement Phantom that I had delivered in 1965. Then it had been at Ubon in Thailand. Now it was at Cam Ranh.

The 12th had also lost the 555th, which had gone to Ubon. The 555th was nicknamed the "Triple Nickel" and would later win fame as one of the MIG Killer squadrons. At this early time in their deployment, they were flying night missions nicknamed "Night Owl."

Replacing the 555th at Cam Ranh was the 391st TFS, out of Holloman AFB in New Mexico. So, as I flew across the Pacific that March day in 1966, the 12th at Cam Ranh was composed of the 557th, the 558th, the 45th, and the 391st.

To confuse the matter further, while I was staying in the Philippines preparing for combat, the Air Force decided to make numbers match. In their wisdom, they decided that the 45th at Cam Ranh would change squadron numbers with the 559th, my old squadron. But, while over the Pacific, I was ignorant of all of that. My interest and thoughts were on what lay ahead of me: Jungle Survival at Clark Air Force Base in the Philippines.

CLARK AIR FORCE BASE:

My return to the Philippines was not as dramatic as my first visit. On that one, I was flying the plane and narrowly averted an extended stay by outrunning the SAC (Strategic Air Command) planes that were all heading our way and crying emergency as they came.

This time, I was just a passenger.

Clark Air Force Base, now closed, was located on the northern Philippine Island of Luzon and north of Manila, the capitol. Clark was a huge base, the largest Air Force base in the world at that time. The population of Clark was more than 100,000 and it was the principal USAF operational base west of the Hawaiian Islands. Clark was also the headquarters for the 13th Air Force.

PACAF controlled all Air Force units or personnel stationed anywhere in the Western Pacific. In 1966, we had units and/or personnel in Australia, Vietnam, Laos, Thailand, South Korea, Japan, Taiwan, Guam, the Northern Marianas and Okinawa. The southern portion of the Western Pacific was originally controlled by the 13th Air Force. When the buildup of forces in Vietnam and Thailand got to a certain point, command and control from Clark got cumbersome. The Air Force created 7th Air Force and then also stationed it at Clark. The wisdom of correcting a distance problem with another distance problem from the same base confused me. They ended up calling the new command 7th/13th Air Force. Perhaps their thinking was that they would split 7th Air off and send it to Saigon, which is what they eventually did.

LEADERSHIP IN TIME OF WAR:

Control of their operational area by the 13th Air Force was minimal as that was seemingly concentrated in Washington. This lack of control so early on in the SEA War carried throughout the War. One of the reasons that World War II was so successfully fought by the United States had to do with command and control. President Roosevelt gave the broad guidelines to the military leadership and then let the military run the operation. The Joint Chiefs of Staff, under Admiral King and General Marshall, also realized that on-site military leaders were better able to run a theater operation. They realized that specifics should be left to area commanders who are better able to control because of on-site experience and observation. General Eisenhower, General MacArthur and Admiral Nimitz were given broad guidelines and then were given control of their theaters. There was unity of command and it was based on respect for the structure and the participants.

In Southeast Asia, President Johnson was no Roosevelt. His structuring of command seemed to indicate he was comfortable with divided command. His thinking also seemed to have filtered down to the leaders, both civilian and military, in the Pentagon.

One of the tenants of good leadership is creating respect. Unfortunately, President Johnson was not well respected. Johnson served during World War II as a Navy Reserve Officer. As an officer, he served in Australia and New Zealand. In 1942, Lyndon Johnson participated as a passenger during a WWII air combat mission flown out of Australia. He later stated he was acting as "an observer" and pressured the US Army Air Force to give him a combat decoration. Photographs of President Johnson, taken when he took the oath of office as President on board Air Force One after Kennedy's death, show him wearing the Silver Star ribbon on his lapel.

During my year flying out of Cam Ranh, not one pilot was given a Silver Star, awarded for courage in combat. Seventh Air Force in Saigon forbade it. The Distinguished Flying Cross was the highest decoration allowed to be earned at Cam Ranh. A Silver Star is a higher award and given for courage and performance in combat. Yet our leader, President Johnson, received one for sitting as a passenger and "observing." Such was the character of the leader of the Free World who presided over the first war that America ever lost. This was the man who later would turn cowardly when faced with a possible Chinese intervention in Vietnam.

WATER SURVIVAL & JUNGLE SURVIVAL ONE:

The Air Force kept sending those of us at MacDill to different survival schools. After "torture school" at Stead, I supplemented my survival knowledge by taking a vacation to the Chesapeake Bay, outside Washington DC. I learned how to survive in the water in what was appropriately called Water Survival. This school was run by the Navy.

Quentin Lusby, another of the five of us from Laredo that had been assigned the F-4, was with me and we became Chesapeake raft mates. Quentin and I also got to sit in single-man rubber rafts floating out on the Bay, just soaking up the morning sun. For me, this was by far the best of my survival schools.

When NASA (National Aeronautics and Space Administration) was training the future Apollo astronauts, they sent them through water survival at indoor pools. It was part of their preparation for landing in the ocean on their return, which was part of their plan. NASA also thought of the possibility that they might land unexpectedly in the tropics. So, they included jungle survival in their training. NASA sent them to Albrook Air Force Base in what was then the United States administered Panama Canal Zone. Albrook was also where they sent me for what turned out to be the first of two jungle survival courses.

The curricula and routine at Albrook was similar to Stead. The first two weeks were spent in the classroom. The chairs in the small room were from some old schoolhouse. They were wood with metal frames similar to what we had in grade school. To keep us alert, the Air Force had provided a classmate. We would find him wrapped around one of the metal frames each morning. We never knew which student would be the lucky one to share his seat with a boa constrictor.

During the third week, they loaded us on a helicopter and we headed for a jungle clearing where the chopper landed and offloaded us. Just as I stepped down, an iguana lizard measuring about three-feet long scampered across our makeshift landing pad. It was an introduction to what lay ahead.

I hooked up with another fighter pilot, Hal Alston, and we decided to sling our hammocks between trees down along a jungle stream, away from the other guys. They were all senior reservists who flew big aircraft. We were junior regulars who flew small aircraft.

In Panama, we didn't go hungry. We managed to shoot a couple of coatimundies for dinner. Coatimundies are members of the raccoon family, but are a bit larger. We left nothing to waste, even consuming their eyes and brains. In a survival situation, one eats what is available. I would not recommend the eyes, but with a bit of salt, the brains are quite tasty.

One late evening as Hal and I lay in our hammocks, we heard a terrible commotion. We both froze and remained frozen as the noises lasted far into the night. During the entire night, I did not sleep and did not move. Even in the tropical heat, I was frozen. Hal had the same reaction. The next morning our Panamanian guide and instructor came to visit. He examined the tracks of the many animals who had visited their watering hole the previous night.

Not 10 feet from where we had slung our hammocks lay a muddy entry area to the watering hole. It was filled with fresh animal tracks, some of which were large cats and others belonged to even larger jaguars. It was a school and we were there to learn.

The jungles of Panama were not the same as those in the Philippines. After signing into the Clark Jungle Survival Course and completing the introductory first day, we were then introduced to another bout of jungle education and training, but this time with the specter of the oncoming war.

JUNGLE SURVIVAL TWO:

From March 5 to 29, 1966, I participated in my second jungle survival school. The location was in the heavy jungle area lying to the west of the gigantic Clark Air Force Base on northern Luzon.

Throughout Asia, there are peoples who migrated to their current countries only to find them occupied. Long ago, the Japanese crossed the Korea Strait to settle Japan. They found a very primitive, indigenous people who are considered Caucasian and look very Russian. Recent DNA testing may prove them to be of Polynesian origin. Today the Ainu number about 5,000 and are on reservations.

The Taiwanese Chinese landed on the shores of Formosa to find it occupied with native tribes. They have also placed these indigenous people on reservations. The same happened on islands all over the Pacific. The Philippines was no exception.

When the current Philippinos migrated to the islands, they encountered black pygmies they later called Negritos. Around Clark, the Negritos were civilized. To the north, they were not. When we flew the replacement Phantom to Ubon, we were advised not to overfly Northern Luzon. For lying underneath the jungle canopies of the north were headhunters, who were cousins to the Clark Negritos. Several years before I arrived at Clark, two airmen who were visiting the northern resort community of Baguio were found beheaded, so the threat was real.

At Clark, the now familiar pattern of classroom work followed by living in the jungle was followed in the Philippines. As we had in Panama, a native served as guide. Our guide was Angel, a very civilized Negrito. Angel was no ordinary man. He was credited with rescuing 27 American pilots from the Philippine wilderness during WWII. When they were shot down, he went in after them and returned them to safety. He proved that extraordinary men can come in all sizes.

The khaki-clad Angel took care of us in the jungle. It was to be our home for longer than the usual week and Angel taught us that the jungle could be our friend.

Instead of a classroom with wood and iron seats, our Philippine classroom consisted of the jungle surrounding Clark. We learned which trees harbored succulent berries and which ones could be tapped as a source of fresh-tasting water. One type of tree could be tapped like the syrup maples in Vermont. Overnight we would harvest three to four gallons of fresh-tasting water per tree.

We learned to fashion eating plates and cookware from the ever- present giant bamboo. As in Panama, we learned which animals were the tastiest. We learned which plants contained poisons. We learned the good and the bad of jungle living.

The Negritos around Clark were actually a mixed group. Most had adopted the ways of the Philippinos; some had not. The natives who had not adopted and adapted were living an essentially stone-age existence. They were very primitive and were suspicious of strangers. They traveled through the jungles north and west of Clark.

Angel and the rest of the helpful Negritos let us travel alone through the jungle. For well over a week, after we initially entered the jungle, we encountered Iguana lizards hanging dead by their tails next to the trails on which we traveled. It was apparent that they had been hung up to dry for later harvesting by the hunters. The method used was to split a branch and slide the tail into the cut.

One day during training, I was trekking on one of the jungle trails with another pilot. I was leading and saw a Negrito coming down the trail toward us. We both seemed to see each other at the same time. He was dressed in a loin cloth and nothing else, while carrying a blowgun and a lethal-looking bow and arrow. He was larger than the pygmies we had seen and had a much lighter complexion. It seemed he might have had other blood.

His height was probably a little over five feet, which was a giant among the others. Both of us stopped dead still, each staring warily at the other. My mind was on the headhunters and I was not armed. He was obviously heavily armed.

We stood about 15 feet from one another. With very deliberate caution, we both moved at about the same time and left the trail very slowly. In a circular motion, I moved counterclockwise and so did he. My trail partner stayed in-trail behind me. Still watching one another, we finally regained the trail about the same place as the other had left. He turned his head and was quickly gone. So was I.

To the west of Clark lay a shallow valley. At the end of the valley rose a small mountain, probably 4,000 to 5,000 feet tall. Our "graduation" from jungle survival consisted of another escape and evasion course, this time trekking the valley. Since the eruption of the Pinatubo volcano, I have often wondered if that was the small mountain which overlooked the valley?

The rules for the evasion were to have the students start out down the valley to be followed in an hour by the Negritos, who were tasked to find us. We were to spread out anywhere in the valley and hide. Much of the shallow valley was open country and offered a chance for rapid movement.

We partnered up for the exercise. My colleague was another young fighter pilot heading for war like myself. Both of us were in great shape. Our hunters, the Negritos, had been promised a sack of rice for each of us that they found. It might not sound like much, but to the Negrito families, it was important.

When given the okay to start, we headed out at a run, wanting to put as much space between us and the hunters within that first hour as possible. The sparse vegetation soon became thicker. After about 20 minutes, we met a huge stand of elephant grass and crawled underneath for a long way, eventually arriving at a meadow area covered with large trees. The vegetation was denser here and we were encouraged.

We passed through the heavily-treed area and came upon a multitude of small streams cascading off the mountain. As we crossed the streams, we climbed higher up the side of the mountain, eventually coming to a small streambed lying deep within a wooded area. The streambed was dry and led up into a higher elevation. We carefully masked our entry point and started walking up the streambed, climbing higher. We stepped on the rocks so as to hide our trail and leave nothing resembling footprints or scrape marks. In addition, we would carefully wipe our trail with branches after we had passed. It seemed we had left nothing to chance and that it would be extremely difficult for any tracker to see any evidence of our passage. How wrong we were. After about 15 more minutes of climbing, we left the streambed, while again making every attempt to mask our exit.

We traveled perpendicular to the stream and hiked maybe 50 to 75 yards higher up the slope. On the slope were several shallow cavities in the soil which held water. We stopped at one and covered our arms and faces with mud. We retraced our steps to a shallow depression filled with leaves that was below an outcropping of rocks on the hillside. The depression gave us a good view of the streambed through the trees and we felt that our position was obscured from the stream while offering a sheltered place to hide and observe. We both covered ourselves with leaves, only allowing our mudded faces to protrude. Then we settled down to wait.

In about 20 minutes we saw a small Negrito boy of approximately eight or nine years old who was walking slowly up the steam bed with his head down, studying the ground. The Negrito families employed everyone in the search, no matter what the age. The boy appeared from the same direction from which we had initially climbed the hill. He searched over the rocks of the streambed and kept walking slowly until out of sight as he traveled up the mountain. We breathed easier and thought we had possibly fooled the boy.

We had been lying there for another 10 minutes when suddenly we saw the boy slowly walking toward us down the streambed. Again, he disappeared from our sightline. This time it was in the direction down the mountain. We did not have long to wait. He reappeared in about 5 minutes and thereafter never left our sights.

His head was always bowed as he searched and studied the ground. The boy stayed in the streambed as he slowly climbed back up, toward the mountain. Then he stopped and closely studied the bed. With his head still down, he returned to the exact point where we had left the stream. His eyes swept back and forth.

The small, black, barefooted figure dressed in red shorts and a white T shirt, slowly turned in our direction, exited the steam and started walking up the wooded incline. His eyes were staring at the leaf-covered jungle floor. About 20 feet from our hideout, he stopped. Then he lifted his head. His eyes swept from right to left, looking all around us. Finally, his eyes met mine. Slowly a warm smile spread across the young face with twinkling eyes. It was so genuine that I had to smile back. My thought at that moment was: If the Viet Cong are half as good as this boy, all was lost.

Looking back, we had learned a lot in the short time we were there. We had learned how to cook, what to cook and where to find it. We knew that, if downed, we could live comfortably off the jungle. I felt that I could live indefinitely in that environment. I actually relished the chance. It was a confidence builder.

Our release from survival was a little earlier than our scheduled date of March 29. It gave us a chance to see what Clark was all about, sample some of the local delights and make purchases for our families back home. It also gave us a chance to eat hamburgers and fries.

The "feel" of Clark was one of immensity. The base still had the colonial feel to it and the traditions and structures of a much smaller military were still evident. In the center of the base stood MacArthur Park, which was large and had the green, tropical look of Hawaii. MacArthur Park was named after General Douglas MacArthur's father Arthur, who was Chief of Staff of the US Army and, prior to that, had been based in the Philippines. General Douglas MacArthur, who was born in an Arizona fort created to fight the Apaches, spent part of his later childhood in the Philippines where his father was in charge of the military.

Looking around the base, it was evident that the expansion of the SEA War was having an explosive affect. A hodge-podge of structures had greatly expanded the facility. A frontier military existed alongside the old colonial military.

Clark was a hub of air activity and the major supply depot for the rapidly expanding air presence in the entire SEA theatre.

Outside of the base, the Philippines do not leave a very good impression on a visitor. Angeles City, located just outside of Clark, was a sleazy place of bars, thievery and prostitution. Many of the locals worked at Clark and had developed the art of theft to a high degree. We were warned that we had to be extremely careful of our belongings.

One story became a legend. Angeles City needed a fire engine. So they sent representatives to Clark and "borrowed" a military one. Riding the engine, they came roaring through the front gate of the base with their sirens screaming. The Air Police manning the gate thought that the base was responding to a local fire and let them through. Angeles City soon had a new fire engine that had a familiar look.

With the additional time allowed with our early departure from Jungle Survival School, I traveled to Manila, the capitol, which is about 60 miles to the SSE of Clark. My parents had friends there, the Cancions, who were invested in the fledgling movie industry. They proved to be wonderful hosts and showed me around the "studio" district followed by lunch at a café located on an upper floor in the fashionable business district.

The café was frequented by American Embassy staff as well as a large contingent of well-dressed Philippinos. Everyone seemed to know one another. During lunch, a lovely lady sat down with us at our table to share our meal and good conversation. She was gracious and unpretentious. My host later told me that she was the sister of the then-President of the Philippines, Magapagal. Three years earlier, I had seen her brother sitting with the Spanish dictator Francisco Franco in the royal box, together viewing a bull fight, in the Plaza de Toros in Madrid.

Back at Clark after my brief stay in Manila, I had glimpses of the growing war as I had at Okinawa. Vietnam would cast its shadow over much of the worldwide military. At the base swimming pool, I met a Navy pilot who was recovering from a broken back suffered in a hard carrier- landing of his F-4B after a mission against North Vietnam.

Hard landings can sometimes be necessary. Later, when flying for Continental, I often would fly up the West Coast of the U.S. with a takeoff from Ontario and then on to Burbank, San Jose, Portland and eventually Seattle. Burbank has a very short runway. A good landing at Burbank is a very hard landing to kill off as much forward momentum as possible for our trip down the runway.

The Navy also has very short runways on their carriers. Added to the shortness, is the up and down movement as the big ships ride the waves. Hard landings for the Navy were good landings. However, his landing might have been overkill.

Clark was very much like Wheelus Air Base in Libya. It acted as a gathering place for pilots from throughout the theater. Their "O" Club was hopping. One evening the cause of the activity was apparent. The Continental stewardesses had arrived. They were surrounded by so many horny pilots that those of us on the "outskirts" could barely see the girls. The attention given them seemed obscene and many of us didn't want to be part of the spectacle.

While at the Club, I ran into several guys I knew from MacDill. They were TDY from the 12th Wing at Cam Ranh and very surprised to see me. They said that nobody knew I was coming. I was the first of what would later be called "replacement pilots" and MacDill had failed to inform Cam Ranh.

My friends told me just to stay at Clark and take my time getting to Cam Ranh. I should have listened to them, but I was anxious to get to the war and grabbed the first flight out of Clark heading to Cam Ranh Bay. The date was March 29, 1966.

The flight from Clark to Vietnam was relatively short, but it was not in a comfortable civilian airliner with seats facing forward. It was in a MAC C-130 transport with canvas, hammock-like seats which lined the sides of the fuselage. To get to our seats, we had to step around the cargo stacked on pallets that were lashed to the floor in the center of the cargo compartment.

I had flown in many C-130s. The feeling of the canvas seats was familiar. The aircraft was military. Its direction was west. I was going to war.

> *"Military glory—that attractive rainbow*
> *that rises in showers of blood."*
>
> President Abraham Lincoln

CHAPTER EIGHT

Cam Ranh Bay
South Vietnam

> *"I hate war as only a soldier who has lived it can, only as one who has seen its brutality, its futility, its stupidity."*
>
> General of the Army Dwight D. Eisenhower

Cam Ranh Bay is considered the fourth best natural harbor in the world and certainly the best in Southeast Asia. When I landed there on March 29, 1966, Cam Ranh was just a bay with potential. On a map, Cam Ranh Bay is located on the Central Coast, just below the 12th Parallel and between Nha Trang to the north and Phan Rang, to the south.

Four months before, in late November of 1965, the first contingents of the squadrons of the 12th Tactical Fighter Wing arrived on the barren Cam Ranh Peninsula at the newly constructed Cam Ranh Bay Air Base (CRB). The aircraft and pilots would follow in early December. When an area is selected for construction of an Air Force base, it is considered a "bare base" until construction is complete and it has been properly manned. The bare base had been secured, prior to the arrival of the 12th, by the forces of the Republic of Korea (ROK). The Koreans had taught the Viet Cong a lesson that was to make Cam Ranh one of the safest bases in all of Vietnam.

The ROK Imperial White Horse Division and the ROK Tiger Division provided our base security for most of my time in SEA. The White Horse was one of the most storied in the entire Korean Army. They resoundingly put to rest images of small Asian fighting men created prior to World War II. All 10,000 soldiers in this Division were over six feet tall and had learned hand-to-hand combat and the art of killing with their bare hands. These were tough soldiers. I never worried about our base perimeter security with these men present. Not once in the entire time I was stationed at Cam Ranh was there ever a shot fired in anger or any enemy military activity on the perimeter. Toward the end of my war, a train was blown up nearby, but it was not on our perimeter. The Tiger and White Horse would eventually be replaced by the American 101st Airborne Division

The Koreans also provided our nightly entertainment at the Officer's Club. There was a Korean four-man band that was surprisingly good. I got to know one of the entertainers and he was the one who informed me about their division's preference for hand-to-hand combat.

When I stepped down from the aircraft onto the tarmac of Cam Ranh, I was standing on PSP metal planking instead of the usual concrete. My visual introduction to my new base was of a huge, but raw, canvas, with the sights, sounds, smells and flavors of war.

Six months before, Cam Ranh had been a field of sand and coral dust. During the following year, the base and Peninsula would undergo a profound change, but the sand and coral would always remain a part of our lives. The PSP (pierced steel planking) surface was made of heavy iron, built like a mesh with air spaces that allowed rainwater to penetrate. In a corner of the world subject to intense monsoon storms, this would prove to be beneficial. The PSP was capable of bearing the weight of heavy transport and fighter-bomber aircraft. It could be laid on level coral sand and interlocked. The PSP was almost as strong as concrete.

As I gazed around at what would be my home for the next year, I was surprised at how barren this tropical setting looked. It was virtually a large sand-bar with hills in the distance. The surrounding areas were almost devoid of vegetation. I soon learned that those distant hills were Viet Cong territory.

The lesson that the Koreans had shown to the VC became legend at Cam Ranh. The advanced detachment of Korean soldiers had landed on the uninhabited sandbar and proceeded to establish a base perimeter. The first night that the detachment slept, VC guerrillas crept into the center of the sleeping soldiers and cut the throats of two officers. During the month that followed, the Koreans went into the hills, operating day and night. During the night hours, the hills were bathed in air-dropped flares. During that month, they scoured the hills and managed to capture hundreds and hundreds of VC guerrilla soldiers.

What happened next created a fear of anything Korean. One by one the ROKs slowly killed off their VC prisoners. One method was to take the VC up in choppers to about 500 feet and ask them questions. If the Koreans did not get satisfactory answers, they pushed them out. Another method was to put hoses into the stomachs of the Viet Cong soldiers and then turning on the water. Each death was witnessed by the other VC.

Out of the hundreds of prisoners taken, the Koreans allowed only one to survive. The ROKs told the final prisoner that he was to take a message back to his VC officers. He was to tell them that if they ever killed

Cam Ranh Bay runway complex with the Bay just to the west and the Viet Cong-controlled mountains farther west. The mountains due west of Cam Ranh rise to 7,096 feet, while those west of Nha Trang, fifteen miles north, rise to 7,890.

any more Korean officers, the Koreans would kill 10 times the number of VC in the same manner as he had witnessed. The ROKs then cut off the prisoner's genitals, sewed them into his mouth and sent him back into the hills. After that, not once did the VC ever approach Cam Ranh and the ROKs again. Those Koreans were very tough soldiers.

Cam Ranh Peninsula was teeming with people. Over 50,000 lived on the finger of land and none of them was Vietnamese. We were located near the top of the peninsula and the closest Viets were in Cam Ranh Village, ten miles north of our base. Between our base and Cam Ranh Village lay a small U.S. Army airfield that flew the smaller Army transport planes. I assumed that it was located there to facilitate the flying of cargo to remote Army encampments and Special Forces Camps. To the south of us at the extreme tip of the peninsula and adjacent to the entrance to the Bay, lay Cam Ranh Navy.

When I landed, the American Navy was constructing an extensive series of docks, warehouses and port facilities. This would become the entry point for seaborne supplies for all of our forces in SEA. The United States shipped in food, clothing, fuel, ammunition, bombs, potato chips, toilet paper, everything.

Between Cam Ranh Navy and our base, lay Cam Ranh Army. It was a huge supply facility with massive warehousing, which was continually being increased. During my entire stay in SEA, the Army was relentless in its construction of warehousing to hold all its supplies.

To the west of us and down along the Bay was located the housing and equipment facilities for RMK. RMK was a huge construction consortium and the initials were short for Raymond, Morrison and Knudsen, which was responsible for much of the military construction for Vietnam and throughout SEA. RMK deemed the Viets too small for the tough construction work, so they imported Korean workers. There were more than 5,000 Korean living in the RMK barracks. With their two ROK divisions, there were over 25,000 South Koreans on our peninsula.

Cam Ranh Army was amazing. To say it was the major supply depot for all of SEA does not begin to tell the story. It consisted of acres and acres of supplies, some that were left on the sand dunes and others stored in the many warehouses that were constantly under construction. It was almost like a city with streets made of sand. The same sands of these "streets" also fronted our squadron Quonset hut. The vehicles constantly roaming these streets were forklifts instead of cars.

One part of this supply city, which occupied so much of the central part of our common peninsula, was what our pilots affectionately called "Beer City." Actually, when we visited Cam Ranh Army, this was usually our destination. "Beer City" occupied more than two acres and had skyscrapers. Each skyscraper consisted of stacks of beer cartons, five to six high. Each carton held 69 cases of beer. Occasionally, the forklifts would collide with the cartons and beer cans would spill out onto the sand. Whenever we had free time, which was seldom, we would grab a jeep and drive down to Beer City. They allowed us to pay one dollar for stuffing a gunny sack full of as much beer as it would hold, which was usually 22 or 23 cans. This was used to restock our four squadron refrigerators back in the Quonset.

Cam Ranh Army (CRA) also had stored choice meats and marine delicacies. Occasionally we had barbeques for our squadron. Several times, we had a shared barbeque with the 558th. For those special occasions, we would visit Cam Ranh Army and bum steaks and shrimp. Who said war is hell?

The land at our Air Force Base at Cam Ranh was the only military real property purchased by the United States Government in all of SEA. All the rest of our bases were leased from the host country involved:

Thailand, Laos or South Vietnam. Not only had we purchased the base at Cam Ranh, but we had purchased the entire Bay. The land on the far side of the Bay was for a planned indigenous city of 300,000 to be built after conclusion of the war. That led to consideration on what exactly was the purpose of the United States in Cam Ranh. After World War II, Britain had lost Singapore, which was the best naval repair, resupply and refueling depot in all of Asia, west of Pearl Harbor. What were the motives of America with Cam Ranh Bay? Were we trying to replace Singapore with a similar facility on the Central Coast of South Vietnam?

After I left the Flightline, I casually wandered around some of the vast base. After all, the guys at Clark had said to take my time and that nobody even knew I was coming. My new home that greeted me on that warm and sunny March day reminded me of photographs I had seen of other wars. The operations buildings that lined the Flightline were Quonset-style huts of WWII vintage. Aircraft of every description covered the tarmac parking areas. Haphazardly planted poles, with their power and phone lines attached, gave a somewhat congested look to the "town." Just as described at Beer City, the street system was laid out in a grid pattern with no paving other than coral sand. Everywhere one looked was sand.

A wide variety of structures dotted the sides of the streets in a far-reaching landscape. Modular and mobile units of both modern and ancient design formed a kind of hodge-podge military city. The base was huge and had the taste of a frontier town. It was a tropical wild west. Only it was tropical in name and weather only. The sand-dune topography reminded me of some of the few remaining barren and sand-duned, undeveloped coastlines in Southern California.

My canvas duffle bag was heavy and caused me to look for a place to drop it. My destination of choice was 12th Wing operations. Asking around, I soon found it. Walking into ops, the eyes that greeted me were familiar, yet they looked at me like I had just arrived from Mars. What I had heard at Clark was true. Nobody had forewarned them. These pilots had arrived in in early December and it was now March. No new pilot had joined them since their arrival. My greeting was "Hi Russ, what the hell are you doing here"?

Since they didn't know I was coming, I had no assigned squadron and they seemed very confused as to where to put me. Base Operations had some comfortable lounging seats, so I left my duffle on the ground and waited for them to make a decision. The wait lasted much longer than I anticipated. I assumed that squadron commanders had to be located and consulted.

Up to my arrival, the Air Force Phantoms in all of Southeast Asia had lost just six aircraft to combat. Cam Ranh had only lost one of those when Jack Gagen, who had been with me in the 559th back at MacDill, was shot down. Both he and his back seater had been rescued, so Cam Ranh was not short of pilots that I might replace.

After more waiting, I decided that the front desk was not going to find the keys to my hotel room. They needed more time, but I needed a place to drop my gear.

My greenish, standard-issue, Air Force duffle bag was filled with uniforms, toiletries, flight suits, "G" suit, parachute harness and my flight helmet: Everything for a year's stay in paradise.

My need was to find a home for my duffle, which seemed to be getting heavier, even if it was just for a night. One of the guys that I knew at Ops told me to grab a bunk that belonged to one of the pilots on R&R (Rest & Recuperation). He said that guys who left on R&R may be gone for weeks and then pointed me in the direction of the Squadron Quonset Huts that would be my home for the coming year. Browsing through the partially empty huts, I managed to find an empty bunk with clean sheets and it was where I left my belongings.

The next day, the 12th finally assigned me to a squadron. Ironically, I was assigned to the same 45th Tactical Fighter Squadron that had taken delivery of the replacement F-4 that I had flown down from Okinawa. They had been reassigned from TDY (temporary) status at Ubon to PCS (permanent) status at Cam Ranh and had transferred from the 15th TFW to the 12th. They were also the first Air Force MIG-killer squadron, having shot down two MIG-17s before leaving Ubon.

The 45th turned out to be Gagen's squadron. Jack had somehow gotten assigned to combat while the rest of us visited Okinawa. Jack was a Marine transfer pilot who had been assigned to the 559th back at MacDill, as part of an exchange program between the Air Force and Marine Corps.

Squadron Patches: 45th Tactical Fighter Squadron

Jack was a great guy and a very good pilot. It would be fun to have familiar faces and former squadron mates with me. He and his back seater, Frank Malagarie, had apparently arrived at Cam Ranh within some time after the 45th was transferred from Florida. Frank was another of the good guys.

The 45th guys were not strangers. We had shared drinks together at the little thatch, bamboo and chicken wire hooch that served as the Ubon Officer's Club. But Jack, Frank and I had flown together. They had been part of the 559th from the start.

My assignment created an irony. The old wing of the 45th was the 15th Tactical Fighter Wing and that Wing had been reassigned to MacDill. Only it was now a Combat Crew Training Wing. It was the 15th to which the 559th was assigned when it arrived back at MacDill from its TDY on Okinawa. Since the 45th was now part of the 12th and the 559th was now part of the 15th, the Air Force decided to swap squadron numbers. The 45th would now be the new 559th and the old 559th was now the new 45th. I didn't even have to swap squadron patches. The 559th "Ram" patches on the shoulders of my flight suits would remain. Gagen and Malagarie had the same good fortune.

Squadron Patches: 559th "Goat" Squadron Patch

The actual movement of the 45th from Thailand to Cam Ranh was somewhat convoluted. The 47th TFS arrived at Ubon on July 25, 1965 as replacements for the 45th. They were then trained in combat by the 45th up to its departure for MacDill on August 10. After over three months of combat, the 47th left Ubon to return to MacDill in November, but only the pilots returned. Their aircraft were left at Ubon and 100 of their enlisted men transferred to Cam Ranh. After the return of the 47th to MacDill, the 45th turned around and returned to SEA, but this time to Cam Ranh where they joined the enlisted men from the 47th.

From that first day filled with so much uncertainty, I kept a regular diary of events and descriptions of my missions and life at Cam Ranh. This documentation allowed me to reconstruct my war years later. I kept this diary religiously from April through October.

The first few months of flying were a good introduction to war. I was fortunate to have easy missions in the beginning. The missions were mainly against targets in South Vietnam with increased targeting against the infiltration routes in Southern Laos known as the Ho Chi Minh Trail. Our Wing target area in Laos was called "Tiger Hound" and missions against Tiger Hound had started several months before I arrived. My first combat mission would be against Laos.

On those missions, we would fly four-ship formations the 300 miles north to Tiger Hound and mount our attacks. "Tiger Hound" was officially the southern half of "Steel Tiger" and located in the Southern Laotian Panhandle region. We would fly against truck parks, vehicular convoys, storage areas and just about anything they wanted to destroy. The missions were controlled by airborne Forward Air Controllers (FACs) who flew light planes above the target and identified where we were to drop our fragmentation bombs, lay our napalm, fire our rockets or shoot our guns.

The missions in the South (South Vietnam) were considered "Piece of Cake" missions they were so easy. We would hit a variety of targets including villages, of which I will write about later. The Viet Cong might have been shooting at us, but they were not very good shots when it came to hitting an aircraft that flew at speeds faster than the bullets fired at them. Most of our losses in the South turned out to be operational and not combat losses. Actually, flying combat in South Vietnam was fun flying. There were very few restrictions on how we flew and they actually let pilots think for themselves.

In September, the missions began to take on a different look. We were being tasked more and more against North Vietnam. The first month that our Wing attacked the North, August, we suffered only light losses. The North was unprepared for low-level attacks coming off the ocean and they took time to react. Like a football team changing its defense against a new offense, the North Viets soon learned how to respond.

By September, our mounting losses and depleted inventory of pilots and aircraft created a sort of breakdown of order. We were all under a tremendous strain and my regular entries to my diary began to suffer. Much of my documentation of my later missions was kept on scraps of paper and written notes. But my memory of those events remains vivid, even to this day.

One of the observations that I made toward the end of my tour of duty at Cam Ranh was that almost all of the pilots lost were either shot down during their first month of combat or their last. The reasons for the first month's losses are fairly obvious. They were new pilots in a new and hostile environment who were unfamiliar with the correct method of operation. The last month's reasons for losses were less apparent.

Using the football analogy again: the team with the lead that plays defensively at the end often loses the game. During the last month in combat, some pilots began to focus on leaving and became too cautious. The aggressive behavior that was so successful for them early-on was lost in their later hesitation. Success in air combat relies much on being fast, being aggressive and being relentless.

We have to attack aggressively, but also prudently. We cannot afford to hesitate, even for a moment. He who hesitates in air combat may indeed be lost. The Phantom flies too fast and too close to the ground in attack missions to allow any hesitation. The factors of enemy defenses and harsh terrain can combine for disastrous consequences for a pilot who changes his method of operation. This is what often happened to those guys who were waiting for their ticket home.

My first month of combat was no different for me than others, except that I was new to the front seat and, as it later appeared, to be inadequately trained. When I received my upgrade to the front seat in Okinawa, I was the first Pilot Systems Operator or co-pilot to begin upgrading in the entire Air Force. As mentioned, I could not complete my training without a bombing range. The other pilot beat me to the front cockpit by a week and ended up assigned to training other pilots. My assignment was war.

When they upgraded me, they were in a hurry. I was to have OJT (on the job training). It really didn't matter to me. I thought I was invincible and the fact that I had never fired the gun from the front before, either in or out of combat was inconsequential. My first mission strafing a target with the gun resulted in my bullets hitting far to the left of where I was aiming. After landing I found out about bore-sighting a gun for accuracy.

My first mission, where I actually saw and maneuvered against an enemy fighter plane, was my first taste of air combat. In training, it is called ACT (Air Combat Tactics). The Air Force was in such a rush to get me to Vietnam that they forgot to give me ACT training. In combat, one learns fast and that is what happened. US Navy radar control let me loose against a MIG flying over Haiphong and that was my introduction to "dog fighting."

That was my introduction to war.

LETTERS HOME:

In hindsight, memories of emotions and thoughts change over time. How was I really feeling back then and what were my thoughts? To answer those questions regarding my time in SEA, I turned to letters that I had sent home from Cam Ranh.

My inclusion of personal information is a representation. My experiences were not necessarily unusual, but they did represent what many of us saw, felt and did. All of us in SEA were going through similar experiences and emotions. My combat diary describes the routine of war interrupted by those missions that were extraordinary. It also is a narrative of what was happening at the time to individuals and institutions.

The letters supplement those descriptions of the war and the environment in which we all lived. These letters are thus an extension of that diary in that they further describe the senses of that far-away place and that specific period of time.

April 5, 1966:

"Dear Folks,

"When I arrived, the heat and humidity were very oppressive, but I guess I have gotten used to it. We have been told that we are entering the "hot" season, so the biggest heat is yet to come.

"The base here is well situated defense-wise. We are on a peninsula with all the naval and army areas

to the south of us. Our base forms a defensive block for their areas as we cover the peninsula from beach to beach. The base is surrounded and laid out internally with a great deal of concertina wire. We have sand-bagged bunkers and fox holes all over the place.

"To the north, blocking the isthmus and patrolling all the beaches and also controlling a large area of the mainland, is the Republic of Korea Army. They are greatly feared by the VC because they are just as barbarous. Our base is the only one in Vietnam, except the new one at Phan Rang (30 miles to the south), that has not been attacked or mortared."

After the end of the Vietnamese War, Cam Ranh underwent a transformation. In 1979 the Soviet Union moved its Navy into Cam Ranh Bay, the best deep-water port in all of Southeast Asia. The Soviets lasted until a withdrawal in 1990 that coincided with the dissolution of the Soviet Union. Vietnam signed a new lease with Russia for less money and that did not include aircraft or naval vessels. From 1990 until 2002, Cam Ranh was a Russian intelligence base monitoring the Chinese. They lowered their flag in 2002, but on October 7, 2016, Russia announced a possible naval return to Cam Ranh Bay.

From 2007 until 2010, Vietnam refurbished the port facilities at Cam Ranh. They opened the port to foreign navies and on October 2, 2010, the USS John S. McCain visited Cam Ranh. Could it be possible that Russia and America might establish some sort of joint naval use of Cam Ranh?

Currently, Cam Ranh is the largest of the five Vietnamese naval ports. Frigates, submarines, corvettes and coastal patrol boats call it home. On the airfield that became so familiar to me and my fellow pilots, may be seen the 377th Vietnamese Air Defense Division, flying MIG 21 fighters. The former MIG-fighting base now houses them.

"No event in American history is more misunderstood than the Vietnam War. It was misrepresented then, and it is misremembered now."

President Richard M. Nixon

BOOK THREE
Combat

CHAPTER NINE
Trauma on the Trail
Evading Capture

> *"I am tired and sick of war. It is only those who have neither fired a shot nor heard the shrieks and groans of the wounded, who cry aloud for blood, for vengeance, for desolation. War is hell."*
>
> Union General William T. Sherman

After almost 50 years, memories of specific events tend to fade a bit from memory. Fortunately, my combat diary recorded the specifics.

Within two days of my acceptance by the new 559th and my finding a permanent bunk in which to sleep, I flew my first mission.

COMBAT DIARY:

April Fool's Day, 1966:

This is no joke. Today I flew my first combat mission. My new Flight Commander is Bill Sorrick and he had me fly in his back seat today for an indoctrination flight. Our target was an area near a river bend east of Attapu, in Laos.

We encountered no ground fire although 37MM, 57MM and 85MM AAA (anti-aircraft artillery guns) were reported by intelligence as part of our pre-flight briefing. Bomb damage assessment (BDA) by the FAC (Forward Air Controller) was reported as two structures destroyed and all ordnance on target. We all carried loads of six 500-pound bombs each and our gun. (The 20mm cannon attached centerline under the aircraft). We did not use the gun, sometimes referred to as the pistol.[11]

Attapu (Attapeu) was one of the heaviest defended areas in the entire Ho Chi Minh Trail system in Laos. It was a major crossroads where the trail split with one branch leading to Cambodia and the other branch going due east to an entry point into South Vietnam. The Cambodian routes of the HCMT (Ho Chi Minh Trail) either led to major VC supply depots in the sanctuary of Cambodia or they led directly to VC units or supply areas deeper into the southern portion of South Vietnam.

Author's Note: *11. Laos was part of the "Secret War." The fact of our missions would not be admitted or known for four more years.*

April 3, 1966:

Mission #2 and my first so-called in-country mission. (In-country means within South Vietnam). Sorrick flew in my backseat and this was my first combat mission as an Aircraft Commander. We carried four cans of napalm with the gun. The target was a VC supply area about 35 miles SSE of Saigon that was on a tree-covered hill. All ordnance was on target, but no BDA (bomb damage assessment) due to heavy target foliage. Hell of a lot of choppers in the air. The FAC (forward air controller- airborne) was doing convoy work prior to the hit. The target is the same type as we had day before yesterday. Again, we did not use the gun.

April 4, 1966:

Mission #3 and again we hit Laos. The target was a divert mission (a divert mission is when the primary target is aborted and airborne control diverts the flight to another target of opportunity) and we hit a truck area north of Chevane in our "Tiger Hound" area. One low pass in ripple mode dropped the two napalm cans and my bombs, being the second on the target, destroyed the truck that the FAC was aiming at. Three and four aircraft (in our flight) made it overkill. On the strafe pass, my gun did not operate due to the RAT (ram air turbine) not being extended. The RAT powers the externally-mounted gun. On the second pass it was the same story, but #3, Plotnitsky, who came in right after me, took a hit through his left engine. The FAC had been calling moderate to heavy ground fire.

With "Plots" (Plotnitsky) having combat damage, we diverted to Ubon Air Base in Thailand to recover. Number three stayed several days to have his engine replaced while it turned out that #4 had taken FOD (Foreign Object Damage) through the right engine. The FAC reported that the truck was destroyed. (Several things, including small-arms fire and shrapnel from exploding munitions in the truck, could have caused the FOD).

The return flight to CRB (Cam Ranh Bay) was flown at above Mach (speed of sound) and it was counted as a combat mission. Paul Busch flew in Plot's back seat.[12]

April 6, 1966:

Mission #5 is a banner day as it was my first ride with a regular back seat pilot. Again, we were carrying two napalm cans. The mission was scheduled to the north (Laos) but Peacock Control (Pleiku) diverted us enroute because of bad weather in the target area. We hit east of Pleiku near Tuy Hoa. The target was a village and we plastered it. Dropping the incendagel in singles, we made three passes. The first pass was to spot the village under the trees and the rest to rip it.

Next we rip in with strafe using the 20 mike-mike (mm) ball ammunition. It was a blast and I shot my guns out (of ammo). The gun holds between 1150 and 1200 rounds. FAC Report: Eleven hooches destroyed and three seriously damaged. My napalm cans were both where the FAC wanted them but both had malfunctions. Number 1 flew apart when it dropped and #2 was a dud. Better luck next time. At least the FAC called the 20mm on target and walking the rudder really spread the stuff around. The napalm, which flew apart, was set on fire by the next pass through.

Author's Note: *12. It turned out that Plotnitsky, in #3, had shot out his own engine with a ricochet. We flew our strafe attacks at speeds in excess of those of the bullets we fired. What we were taught for strafe was that we should pull first and then bank and that the bank has to come quickly. The idea is that we must be in a climb before we bank, but we must bank quickly so that we get away from our own flight path. If we didn't divert from the strafe path, the bullets we had fired could catch up to us as we slowed on climb out. We could literally shoot ourselves down.*

April 7, 1966:

Another Laotian strike with two napalm cans and the gun. This time the gas worked and both hit on target. No BDA (bomb damage assessment) due to bomb damage shielded by heavy tree growth. We were hitting just SE of Tchepone, where the heavy flak has been reported. The past three days' intelligence reports have also indicated that our run in to the target from Pleiku is being covered by (enemy) AAA (anti-aircraft artillery).

This was my first day with Paul Busch, my new back seater. Mission went well and we fired 1140 rounds of 20 mike-mike. The first burst was on the napalm run-in and had HEI (high explosive incendiary) shells in it. Sure looked pretty going off. We fired bursts from the pistol to keep the heads of the gunners down. Anyone firing at us when we're skimming the trees would be in trouble. Upon arrival at the target, the area was still suffering "secondary explosions" from a previous hit. The FAC advised us, but we hit low anyway. The Flight Commander said it was a "good mission." The drive up to the target area showed fires all over the place. Looks like they may be having a disagreement down there.

Walked down by the Flightline this evening. The place is sure jumping. Many C-130s were unloading ammo. Even saw a Pan Am plane coming in to use our runway. I guess we must be safe if they are bringing their stews (flight attendants) in here.

April 8, 1966:

Sat alert today and was not launched. My Flight Commander, Bill Sorrick, hit a tree on this morning's missions.[13]

When he hit the trees, Sorrick tore the plane up pretty badly. Lost a wing tank, pylon and tore holes in the wing and rudder. It was a bad target to hit with napalm. Yesterday one of the other squadrons took an AAA hit and suffered severed right-wing damage. Thank God for the F-4. Marv Gradert and Turk Thompson also hit trees. Three in one day makes me think we ought to join the woodchopper's union.

April 9, 1966:

Today we were given another Laotian target. It was a bastard. Just one lousy shack on the upslope of a box canyon. A high ridge was directly in back of the target. Flight Lead (Larry Dahle) rolled in for his first low-level attack. We were again loaded with two napalm cans. Fifteen-hundred pounds of gas in all. Stupid to have us fly 330 miles and have us risk our asses to drop two lousy napes (napalm). As it turned out, Larry Dahle had to pull so hard to miss the (top of) ridge that he stalled and fell over the other side. Fortunately, it was not a plateau.

As the loyal number-two man in the flight, I followed my lead's run-in and managed to skim the trees at the top of the ridge fairly closely, so closely that I hit one of them. I never realized it until I happened to look at the right wing on the way home. What a sinking sensation. Guess they've got to expect it if they keep diverting us with low-level ordnance against such lousy targets. Those hills come up pretty fast. Even after

---

Author's Note: *13. Alert is a mobile unit sitting at the end of the runway. It is for immediate launch in case a Marine or Army unit came under heavy attack and needed close-air-support. Crews live, eat and sleep in their uniforms. When the alert horn sounds, all the crews run to the planes, jump in and have assistance in strapping in from ground crews while the engines are cart-started. Usual time between horn and launch was two to three minutes.*

all the close calls, we only burned part of the building. BDA: One structure damaged. No strafing done.

Analysis: The FAC had no business targeting us against such a target with napalm. I saw no damage to the structure prior to my drop and I know that I did not hit anywhere near it. The building was on the upslope all right, but it was toward the end of a box canyon that gave no option to turn around. When I approached, I was looking at the target, but my attention became more and more riveted on the sheer wall looking ahead. Even today as I write this book, I can see that wall and how it dominated the small canyon in which I was flying. The wall was enormous.

I saw Dahle's aircraft profiled against the face of the wall as he was in full burner and climbing rapidly. It looked like a painting with his twin pillars of flame shooting out from the rear as he rose in afterburner against the wall.

When I saw Larry climbing in burner, I dropped my can of napalm and was not even sure where I was aiming. I had not looked at the warehouse target for the last minute of run in. I plugged in burner and followed Larry in the climb. The wall was very high with a line of conifers on the top. I was climbing on the edge of a stall because the wall was getting so close. I chose to take the trees at the top rather than pulling back on the stick any further and losing control.

From the view of a retired commercial airline pilot, I can say that I cannot recall any other time when I was closer to dying, even when I was downed in Laos. I just rode the stall all the way to the top and barely escaped from crashing into the wall. Even today, the image is as vivid as it was while flying the mission.

When we got back on the ground, Larry came up to Paul and me with Jack Kelly, his back seater. His face was white and he was full of apologies. Larry said that he stalled out at the top of the wall and stumbled over the top in burner. As he stated, "it was the closest I've come to buying the farm (dying) in 3800 hours of jet fighter time."

I didn't blame Larry. He realized the problem and made his decision in enough time that we both survived. If he had not plugged in burner when he did, we would not have made it. My anger was directed against the airborne FAC who targeted us against the building. He was a pilot and should have checked out our run-in and escape situation. He should have looked at that sheer wall that rose to the heavens and realized that this was not good in a box canyon. Other than the wall, there was no other way out.

Larry was a great pilot. He had been part of the National Guard pilots who were activated to the regular Air Force at the time of the 1961 Berlin Crisis. Most of our Aircraft Commanders at MacDill had been National Guard pilots and they turned out to be great pilots and good Aircraft Commanders.

Maintenance reported that my right wing that returned with all the vegetables, had sustained only mild damage.

LETTERS HOME:
April 12, 1966:

"I am presently grounded for two weeks for hitting a tree. It really wasn't serious. They just gave us a target at the bottom of a ravine and we had a high ridge right behind it with a row of trees at the top. I didn't quite make it over the trees. Four of us hit trees in two days, so they are worried.

"The base has really grown considering that there was nothing here but sand last September. I don't think the VC will be able to mount a large-scale attack against us.

"It will only take me about $60 per month to live over here, if that. There isn't anything to spend it on.

"My days have settled into somewhat of a routine. I usually fly once and the rest of the time is free. Two meals a day is all the appetite this heat allows. I usually try to get some sun during the day and nights are spent in our outdoor theater or working on weights.

"Don't worry, I'll be careful."

April 14, 1966:

"The war seems more unreal here than it did back home. We are in a heavily protected area and I have yet to see anyone shooting at us on our missions, even though we know that they are. It seems so peaceful and ordinary to go in and obliterate a village. Strange war.

"Two of our guys went to a Special Forces camp to study their situation and terrain as we are responsible for their protection should the VC attack. Well, the VC have the camp surrounded. The guys went to the nearby town of Quang Ngai and got shot at while driving in a jeep so they came home as quickly as possible."

COMBAT DIARY:
April 15, 1966:

Our Wing Commander was incensed that we had four planes hit trees in two days. All four of us were grounded for several days. Today I flew with Sorrick in my back seat. He was supposed to check me out for hitting the tree, which made a lot of sense. One tree-chopper checking out another. I suppose, like all things, a Lieutenant must be more responsible than a Captain? If I was Sorrick, I would think that flying in someone else's back seat was punishment itself. Me, I still got to fly the front. Sorrick and I laughed at the situation. He is a good guy.

The two-week grounding lasted less than a week.

We carried four 500-pound bombs and ended up doing no strafing. The weather in the target area, Laos, was lousy. Heavily clouded and visibility was very poor over the target. I almost lost lead several times. It was so bad that lead dropped his bombs in ripple over the wrong area and I followed in with a ripple and hit the same spot. So did number three. So there we were, probably hitting one kilometer away from the real target and the FAC gives us one building destroyed and one damaged. I'll bet. Probably all we damaged was the slumber of a few monkeys.[14]

One of the options available to us on the bomb control panel was called "ripple." This would enable the Aircraft Commander to hit the bomb release button, located on the control stick, only once and all of the bombs would automatically release sequentially. This would allow a single-pass option on the target with the aim point in front of the target and a "walk" of the bombs through the target. "Pairs" is another option that was available to the pilot. In this mode, two of the munitions carried under the wings would drop with each hit of the bomb release button.

Author's Note: *14. This is an example of how the reporting of BDA was so wrong. BDA, or bomb damage assessment, was an integral part of an air-to-ground operation. To show commanders the results of the missions, they needed to know the BDA. On Forward Air Controller (FAC) controlled targets, the FAC gave the BDA. On targets without FAC assistance, reconnaissance planes were usually sent to record the damage with cameras.*

April 16, 1966:

Just over two weeks into combat and I am almost feeling like a veteran. Another good target for mission number nine. They called us in on an area target with a lot of hooches (houses). What a great target if we would have had more than just our two cans of napalm. We were flying a three-ship and lead had four 500s and a jammed gun. So it was left up to my two cans and gun plus Plotnitsky's as number three. At the last minute on my first run, I spotted the main hooch in the village and banked to hit it. Dropping in the bank, I learned a valuable lesson. Napalm doesn't quite drop like the practice skip-bombs. I kicked the damned thing over into a rice paddy. One consolation, the nape didn't ignite well. Second pass was ok. The damage came in my strafe passes. Loaded with 800 HEI and 400 TP (target practice- ball ammo); we did low-angle passes because of the negative ground fire. Really ripped them up. Disappointing BDA due to the target type. We destroyed six buildings and damaged six. At least I made sure I got the central house of the village. Fired 1100 rounds out of the pistol. They're still worried about me banking and pulling instead of pulling and banking off target. Afraid I'll grab another tree. They have a point and I'll have to work on it. Another problem I have is not pulling immediately after I pickle (drop the bomb). This will all come with concentration.

April 17, 1966:

I pulled taxi pilot this morning with two jobs and spent all afternoon in the mobile jeep at the end of the runway. Being a taxi pilot only means that I taxi a plane after completion of repair at the Maintenance hangars back to the Flightline in front of our Operations. There is a lot of blowing sand out there, while they run up engines for maintenance.

April 19, 1966:

Today we had an "in country" (South Vietnam) against another village. Weather was beautiful and we encountered no ground fire. Load was two cans of "incendagel" and 20mm. Dropped in pairs and both of mine scored a direct hit. The BDA was four buildings destroyed. "Plots" must have missed by 400 feet due to cockpit fogging. Today my mission number was updated to 11 to account for a previous ferry mission.

April 21, 1966: The following words were written the day after the event.

Yesterday was a day to be etched in my memory like March 4, 1965 and aircraft 483. Today I came close to death and the bird was 531. The target was a truck park in Laos and we were worked by two "Hound Dog" FACs (21 & 24). Two-four (24) took immediate control and said that the trucks looked loaded. I was loaded with two cans and went in as #2 behind Sorrick.

Over the target, I heard two thumps and we were jolted twice. The force of deceleration threw both of us forward sharply against the straps and I felt like we had hit a wall. I immediately went to instruments. Fuel flow was fluctuating and the RPM on both engines was dropping rapidly. As they went through 80%, I tried ignition to no avail. The engines stabilized at 70-71% and I stopped cocked (shut down) the right engine to gain a relight. I hit the transmission button and transmitted, "Hammer lead, this is two, I have engine failure." After stop cocking and back to 100% on the throttle, I was still unable to get engine reaction. We couldn't have been more than 100 feet in the air at the time. I climbed and traded airspeed for altitude. The engines stuck at 70% provided very little thrust.

Sorrick called and asked "which engine flamed out" and I replied "both." "Where are you?" he asked and I replied, "turning to 140 degrees." It was all I could do to keep my finger on the transmission key to talk. All I could figure was that I had ingested part of the load of the truck. It had been burning at the time I had gotten to the truck in my pass. Sorrick had done his job well. As a last resort, I plugged in burner without any luck.

The right turn to 140 degrees was from an initial pass vector of west to east. The right turn was to avoid a fast-approaching hill and during the terrain avoidance turn I had used up most of my available altitude. I was nursing the aircraft down on the stall and that was just by stick feel. My eyes were glued to the instruments. What had happened?

We were close to the stall when Paul shouted "Let's get out." I lifted my gaze from the instruments and stared right at a fast-approaching hill at the same altitude as our cockpit. We were very low. I gently pulled back on the stick. The terrain appeared as a blur.

Aircraft speed was now 155-160 knots from an initial pass speed of 460-470 knots. Pedal shaker began activation indicating impending stall and I looked down at the secondary ejection handle between my legs, reached down and pulled. I was conscious of the seat firing and the windblast. My head snapped back and the facemask and helmet were torn off. Altitude of ejection was about 100-150 feet after clearing the hill. The aircraft immediately slammed into the following hill. We were that close.

My first recollection after ejection was that I was falling into the flames of my own aircraft as they were

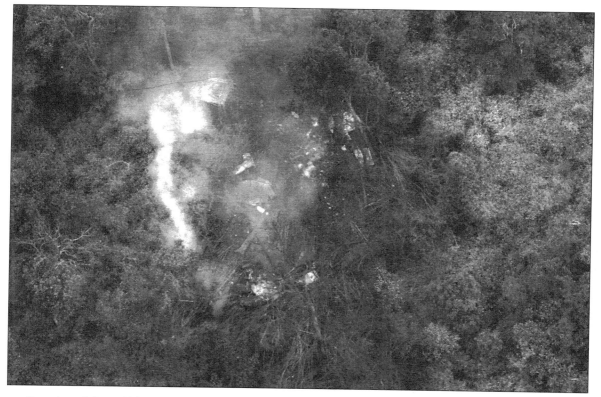

Remains of the still-burning Phantom in Laotian jungle. Pilots Goodenough and Busch ejected seconds before the crash. Several bamboo structures are visible.

licking at my boots. My instantaneous thought was of the story of the pilot who had successfully ejected only to fall into the flames and die. I reached up quickly for my risers and slipped the chute to the side to avoid the flames that were all around me.

I landed on my right side on a sloping hill. I could not have been in the air more than four or five seconds. As later events would prove, that was very fortunate. I was on a burned off hillside and the aircraft was about 10 to 15 feet away, or rather what was left of the burning wreckage. Paul landed about 20 to 30 feet from me and didn't even see me as he struggled and tried to run with his gear still on. As he later told me, he had seen two soldiers running down a ridge toward us when we hit the ground.

Without looking around, Paul bolted toward the foliage. I called out to him but he was gone, disappeared into the undergrowth of the jungle-like terrain. A hissing sound captured my attention and I looked down to see my crash helmet still hooked to me through the oxygen hose. The emergency oxygen system was being force-fed through the hose into the mask and that was what I was hearing.

I picked up the helmet and threw it hard back into the soft soil of the hillside—"Shit." The knowledge that I had lost a second Phantom in less than a year was hard for me to comprehend. However, comprehension of a different sort soon came to me that I had no time for anger. I was in a very dangerous part of Laos. The truck park that we hit was only about two kilometers from Route Nine of the Ho Chi Minh Trail and we could not have crashed very far from it.

This was situational awareness of the first order. Quickly I started throwing things off: my oxygen mask and helmet, my survival vest, my chute and chute straps, my seat survival kit which had been under my seat but which was now lying attached to me by a lanyard. They all were cast aside. My main concern was to throw off as much weight as possible to be able to run. When I had first seen Paul try to run away from the wreckage, he struggled with his connections to the parachute and the rest of his paraphernalia.

As soon as I was free, I started to run up the cleared side of the ridge on which we had hit. My immediate destination was a clump of trees that I had spotted about a quarter mile away. This was part of the Laotian slash-and-burn agricultural land and areas of the jungle were separated by areas of barren earth. My route took me up the burned-off ridge. I did not see the North Viet troops seen and later told to me by Paul. He told me that as soon as he hit the side of the hill after ejection, he had seen two soldiers coming down the ridge directly toward us. His explanation to me indicated that they had to have been coming down the same ridge on which I was escaping, but this was unknown to me at the time.

Thoughts kept running through my mind about keeping my run to the military ridgeline, which is to keep my head below the top of the ridgeline so as not to show my silhouette against the sky. This had been learned at survival training. It is surprising how many things cross your mind when in a situation like this. When airborne in my chute, my instinctive reaction had been learned at the Army Paratrooper Training School at Fort Benning, Georgia. All of these things were coming back to me now.

Reaching my destination in the clump of trees, I quickly hid. Using my hand-held radio, I contacted the FAC in the aircraft circling above, stating who I was, where I was in relation to the aircraft and that I was okay. The sky was already full of aircraft circling to give cover to Paul and me. It was a good sight. The Rescap (rescue combat air patrol) consisted of B-57s, A1Es, F-4Cs, A-4Ds plus the O-1Es.

When I initially contacted the FAC on my belt-mounted survival radio, there was some confusion. Our call sign was Hammer 32, as we were flying on a 391st TFS mission. Hammer was the general call sign for the 391st. If I had been flying a 559th TFS mission, my call sign would have been Phantom. If I was scheduled on a 12th TFW mission, my call sign would have been Boxer. On this mission, I was Hammer 32. The problem was that my GIB, Paul Busch, was also Hammer 32. Apparently Paul had already been in radio contact with Rescap. Our attempted rescue had initially been controlled by our FAC, but control had passed to Hillsboro Control flying the C-130 that controlled Tiger Hound air strikes.[15]

When Rescap finally figured out who I was and that both pilots were still alive and on the run, they sounded relieved. My hiding place was a depression near a log where I could raise the radio antenna and still only be seen from a short distance. The radio made a lot of noise even when I was on "listening-watch" and not talking. I eventually said "to hell with it" and turned the thing off, left the depression and went to the edge of the forested area.

I sat down next to an old burned-out log and just took a look at the countryside and watched the planes flying overhead. The solid jungle line, about two miles away, looked very inviting and I had an urge to just strike out for it to see how things would be living and traveling through the jungle on my way back to South

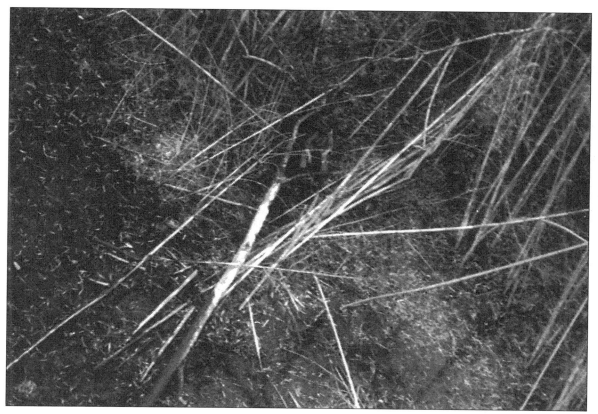

Goodenough hiding on forested Laotian hillside. Photo taken at moment he looked over his shoulder at sounds from North Vietnamese troops behind him.

Author's Note: *15. I learned years later that Hillsboro Control that day had been piloted by "Stinky" Steinbrink, a fellow Academy graduate and later, a fellow Continental Airlines pilot. Stinky and I were in the same Continental Airlines Training class of 30 pilots.*

Vietnam. It presented a challenge, but it was an escape from the reality of war and I could not do it, even though both jungle survival courses had prepared me. There were a whole lot of guys flying above that were risking their butts to get me out.

Farther down and on the far side of the ridge on which I had run, there was a steady drum-beat of firing guns. Pressing the transmit button, "this is Hammer 32, be careful since it seems you are receiving AAA or AW fire." The FAC felt that "it is probably your ammo exploding from your downed aircraft." "I don't think so. The fire seems much too regular."

The FAC warned me to "Be careful. In the ravine on the far side of your ridge there are a bunch of gun bunkers." Curious, I crawled through the trees in the direction he had mentioned and started inching down the other side in an attempt to see. Suddenly, I froze. I had crawled on to the top of a gun bunker. The top was dirt with thatch underneath, but the sides were bamboo. I had no idea it was there until I had crawled on top. It would be almost impossible to see the bunkers from the air, unless one was a FAC familiar with the area. The entire side of the ravine seemed to be covered with them. I listened but did not hear any conversation coming from under me. It was silent, except for the sounds of aircraft circling overhead. It might have been manned, but I couldn't be sure.

I slowly inched my way back off of the roof and crawled up the same way that I had come. When I got to the depression, I covered myself with leaves and just lay there, deciding that I would not do anything foolish like that again.

Soon, I heard people walking through the leaves near where I was lying. They stopped to talk and were speaking Vietnamese. Their voices soon faded as they seemed to move away. Later as I thought back on the event, I was sure that the enemy knew where I was all the time and was staking out gun positions all around me.

If I was going to be shot, it was not going to be defenseless under a pile of leaves, since I still had my 38 revolver at my side. I returned to the burned log so that I could see if anyone was coming, then called the FAC and told him my position. He spotted me and made a pass. An Army spotter plane also made a pass. And he made another and another and another. He was taking pictures. I could have killed him. His passes were giving my position away as if he had spotted it with a flare. I counted at least 10 passes and they rocked their wings in greeting. I don't think they realized that I had guests nearby. They could not have been more than several hundred feet above me—too far to throw a rock, but I was tempted. Anyway, their intentions were good.[16]

A second Army plane took pictures from higher up which also are include herein. The final pictures were taken by a Marine rescue chopper. I was unsure who took the Marine photos because both door gunners were busy firing at the bad guys.

After a long delay, I again checked in on the radio and I heard them saying something about a rescue chopper. At first, I did not know that the chopper was for me, but I finally spotted the rotors of the chopper just above the ridgeline which was above my position. All I could see were the rotor blades. It was on the opposite side of the ridge on which I sat and had landed without me hearing it.

Author's Note: *16. It seems that three different aircraft were taking photos of me on the ground and of the later-arriving rescue choppers. The Army spotter plane took some that are included in this book that shows me sitting by that burned log. I recall hearing a noise behind me as I sat and the spotter managed to shoot one photo at the same time that I turned around to listen. An Army Major in the lower spotter plane took the photos from the back seat.*

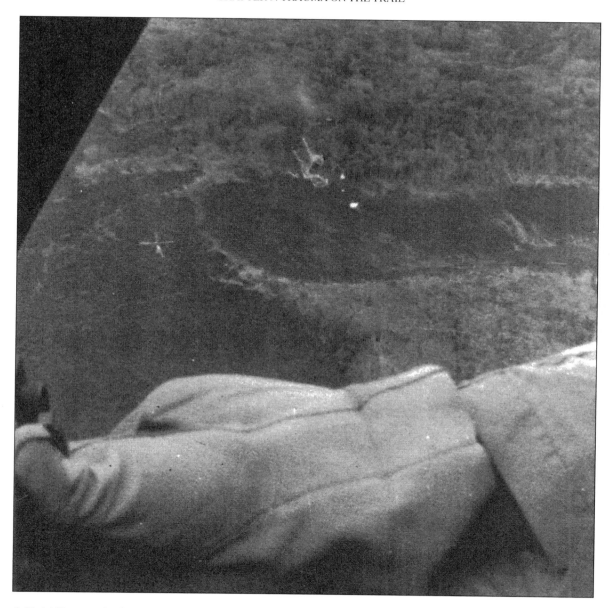

Still drifting smoke from the Phantom crash with Goodenough's white parachute visible on Laotian hillside. Photo taken from an Army spotter plane just before first rescue chopper was shot by a North Vietnamese ground gunner and pilot wounded. Lieutenant Goodenough was approaching the helicopter at the time this photo was taken. Note Laotian slash-and-burn agriculture clearings.

Again taking the military ridgeline, I ran up and over the top of the ridge until I could see the entire chopper and not just the rotors. I kept running until I was about 30 yards away from the chopper and then I made the mistake of slowing down to a fast walk. My walk consumed only about 10 more yards before my whole world seemed to erupt. The sound was deafening. A North Vietnamese gunner opened up from my

Shot up instrument panel of first Marine rescue helicopter. Wounded pilot was flown to hospital at Danang Air Base.

right side. I glanced to my right but could not see him since he was just over a low rise. By the sounds of his gun, he could not have been more than 20 to 30 feet away and probably lying on the other side of the rise.

What I heard was a sickening sound. I glanced back at the chopper and the bullets were ripping into it from right to left. The impact of the bullets into the chopper skin reminded me of the sound I used to make when I was shooting tin cans with a rifle. It was the same puncturing sound. The gunner must have had a machine gun or an AK-47 on automatic, since the rate of fire was so rapid. I was actually looking into the eyes of the pilot when he was shot.

The gunner had come from the same side of the ridge as the gun bunkers that I had been investigating. Just after the pilot was shot, the co-pilot of the chopper lifted off and quickly left the area. I learned later that the pilot was flown to the hospital at Danang and that he was not badly wounded.

As I watched my rescue recede into the sky, I had a brief sinking feeling and I remember being pissed at myself for slowing to a walk. However, even if I had continued running, I would not have made the chopper before the gunner opened fire.

What does one do in a situation like that? I had a momentary urge to go over the rise to my right and surprise the gunner with my 38-caliber revolver. That was a really stupid thought. To my left was the edge of what looked like a cliff. I was standing no more than six or seven feet from its edge.

Without another thought, I dove off the ridge, which turned out not to be sheer but was very steep. As I rolled, slid and fell for a long way, I could still hear firing as I fell and felt that it was directed at me. I felt my arm suddenly go numb as I was tumbling and was sure that I had been shot.

All of a sudden, I was at the bottom and lying in a small, flat area. The gunner's position was far above my own and was no longer a concern. I stood up and took stock of my situation.

I looked at my left arm and it had a hole in it that was spurting blood to the beat of my heart, so I knew it must have nicked an artery. After I investigated it, I was not so sure that I had been shot.

My attention was diverted to an approaching sound in the sky. Above me the blue was swarming with aircraft and a flight of Marine A-4s was rolling in for an attack on the guns located on the ridge above me that had just fired on the chopper. The target of the Marine's attack was on the same ridge that I had just left.

All I could do was stand in awe at the spectacle of their rocket attack. From the angle of their attack, I felt and it looked as though they were coming right at me. The roar of the 5-inch Zuni rockets was loud and distinct as the rockets were individually fired and impacting on the same ridge I had been standing on just a few minutes before. I could feel the ground shaking beneath my feet. Everything seemed to have stopped and held in suspension as those large flaming poles rapidly dove at the ground. I now know what the enemy feels while under our air attack.

Taking stock: My arm was still losing blood and my radio was gone; apparently somewhere up on the side of the slope, lost in my headlong tumble down the hillside. So, communication with the planes above was gone. I still had my G suit with my small personal survival kit in one of its leg pockets and I had my long, heavy knife which could be used for chopping as well as cutting. Also lost in my tumble down the slope was my hip-mounted 38 revolver. The two boxes of ammo in my other G suit leg pocket were thus useless.

I spotted two likely landing spots for another chopper and started running toward the nearest one, even before the end of the A-4 attack. The entire area around me was devoid of cover. It was also wet and slippery from the rains. This time I was running at a very fast clip and happened right into a cluster of three gun bunkers. They were much larger than the first I had seen but also didn't seem to be occupied. The bunkers were well built and camouflaged to blend into the hillside. They also blocked my path toward what I thought would be an ideal second landing site for rescue.

So, I figured it had to be Option B. I turned around from the bunkers and began running in the opposite direction. As I ran I again examined my arm. The flow of blood had slowed. Even though I had heard them, I still had not seen any enemy soldiers and considered myself fortunate in that regard. My stamina still seemed good so I increased my running speed as I launched myself down the canyon toward the other likely landing site that I had spotted, although it was a long way away.

My estimate of the distance to the second site was at least two miles away. So, I continued to run down the canyon and along its associated ridgelines. My situation had deteriorated, but I still had options. I seemingly ran for miles. For some reason, the blood had started to flow from my arm again. Every time my heart would beat a "pulse" of blood shot out.

I was still running down the ravines. The bunkers were far to my rear and I had passed the ridge where the gunner was positioned when he shot the chopper. Ahead and slightly to the right and still a long distance away was the landing site on a cleared hilltop. To my right was the bottom of the ravine and to the right of that was a wooded area.

Although he had no way of knowing where I was or whether I was still alive, one of the circling planes shot a purple flair directly in front of my path, but still at a distance. The purple smoke drifted up from the left side of my ravine. I figured that they were trying to direct me so I continued to run straight for it. Eventually, I ran through the smoke and continued to run past it. Fortunately, an Army Major flying in the back seat of one of the prop planes did spot me.

Then I saw a second chopper land on the place I thought would be the only other likely landing spot, which was at the top of the hill. I again figured that it would take me maybe ten more minutes to make the bottom of the hill. The more I ran down the ravine, the more the wooded area ahead and to my right looked suspicious. I was still running in the open, but I had no options other than to continue running.

The chopper guys later told me that if I had not been spotted in the purple smoke, they would have gone. They would have left because they had received no communication from me for some time. They would have left because they had no idea where I was and thought I was dead.

Since the chopper had already picked up Paul and had been sitting on the ground for several minutes, they had started to pick up fire from North Vietnamese ground troops on the far side of the chopper. As I continued my run, I could hear the muted sound of the battle.

By running through the purple smoke, I placed what I thought was a machine gun position to my back. Just before I hit the smoke, I glanced to my right toward the green reeds of the forested area and I was sure

Second Marine rescue helicopter waiting to pick up Goodenough. Chopper door-gunners firing out of both sides against North Vietnamese Army troops.

that I spotted a gun barrel in addition to some movement. In that moment, I was certain that I would get shot in the back as I ran toward the base of the hill on top of which sat my rescue helicopter. By that time, I was totally exhausted and was so tired that I didn't care if I was shot. I just didn't give a damn.

The Rescap had notified the chopper that I was close and to hold on if possible. I started up the hillside toward the chopper, which I could now clearly see. My legs were beginning to buckle below me and I told them to keep running but they did not cooperate. You would think that they would have run on sheer adrenaline due to my situation, but they didn't.

The hill was steep, wet and slick from the rains and the limit of my endurance had almost been reached. The slick leather soles of my flying boots kept slipping as they had no tread and no traction on the slope. A very brief thought of those sexy combat boots with tread that graced the feet of those Air Force types flying desks in Saigon and then I was back to mentally begging my legs to move faster, but they had the same

Goodenough, assisted by Marine door gunner, running up Laotian hillside on April 21, 1966. North Vietnamese troops are firing from background trees at second Marine rescue chopper. Photo taken by helicopter co-pilot.

lack of response.

Sounds of gunfire erupted all around me. The wooded area to my rear did have a machine gun, or several automatic guns. They were trading shots with the near-side door gunner and I could hear the steady stream of bullets whizzing closely over my head. The chatter of gunfire also was again coming from the far side of the chopper as that gunner was involved in a fight of his own.

The end to my endurance had seemingly been reached when I dropped to my knees and started to crawl. I had managed to crawl maybe ten feet when the chopper gunner on my side came out and helped me by half-running and half-dragging me up the hill. The bullets were still coming close, but they didn't seem aimed at us. Instead they seemed aimed at the chopper.

The gunner dragged me to the chopper door and literally lifted me and threw me inside. I lay at the feet of the other gunner who was firing and under the din of that sound, Paul and I greeted one another. I was so totally exhausted that I could barely move and my eyesight narrowed down to tunnel vision for a short while. I had forgotten about my arm, but now saw that it was making the floor of the chopper red and slippery. All I could say to the gunner who helped me was "thanks." Paul told me that he had been in the chopper no more than five to six minutes while they waited for me. That must have been an excruciatingly long five minutes.

After liftoff, we headed for the chopper's home at Khe Sanh, which was just across the border into South Vietnam. From my position lying on the floor, I could see armed A-1Hs flying cover. Since my head was on the floor, I was looking at things sideways. At least one of the A-1Hs was level with us and I could see him. The A1's turned out to be from Udorn, Thailand, but were Air Force and not CIA. One of our cover pilots was an Air Academy classmate, Butch Vicellio, who later made four-star General.

Even before landing I could hear the constant drumming of the 105 MM howitzers blasting away from Khe Sanh against nearby hills. On landing, we each were handed a beer and greeted with a lot of smiles. By then I was sufficiently recovered that I could sit up and hold a decent conversation. The crew could finally relax and we could look at each other. Thanks could hardly convey my feelings.

After some comments about how close the rescue had been, they quickly led me down a dirt slope. Everywhere I looked I saw sandbags. The walls were built of sandbags. Khe Sanh seemed one big sandbag. We arrived at an underground hospital, which had filtered light streaming down from ground level. The doctor treating my arm said that it was a clean wound and that whatever had caused the hole in my arm was not a bullet, since there was no exit wound. He surmised it might have been a stick or some sharp object that was on the hill when I plunged down the nearly vertical drop. The military doctor worked fast and soon had my arm in a white wrapping from elbow to my wrist. He placed a green bandana around the arm and tied it behind my neck before he walked me back to ground level. It was not a critical injury, but he advised me to check with base hospital at Cam Ranh when I made it back there.

Once I was at ground level I took a better look around. The landing strip used by our chopper was also the only one around and any incoming plane would need to be able to stop pretty quickly. We were to wait for a promised cargo plane, which was reported to be inbound.

The steady pulsation of the howitzers seemed part of the landscape. To Paul and I, Khe Sanh seemed like heaven, but a green-brown heaven. It was remote and sitting in an area of undulating hills, carpeted with dense, deep-green jungle. It was also made of sand bags. Cam Ranh also had lots of sandbags, especially around the mortar shelters dotting that landscape, but Khe Sanh had that look of ready preparation for an immediate attack. The old Special Forces camp adopted by the Marines was all underground, except for those howitzers.

Soon we both saw and heard the C-123 come dropping in from a very high angle. Everyone's actions seemed designed to get the 123 in and out as quickly as possible to avoid any more exposure to the North Viet troops that the Marines told us were surrounding this outpost right next to the Laotian border.

We paid our rescuers a very heartfelt goodbye as we boarded the C-123 with its engines still running. We both waved from the boarding ramp and then we were quickly airborne on a high-angle climb-out. Later I sent the chopper crew a case of scotch for both Paul and me. How inadequate was that? Nothing could really thank them adequately for what they had done.

It was only after I returned to Cam Ranh that I learned it was only by sheer luck that the Marines had stationed two choppers on strip alert at Khe Sanh that day, instead of their usual one. It was this second chopper that picked me up as no other chopper was within range of where I went down. The area was called Tang Hune Nord, which was about 20 miles north of Saravane in Laos.

As we relaxed on the slow flight back to Danang, Paul told me what he had encountered while I was running from the enemy. The Rescap guys had a better idea of his whereabouts and had been tracking him since he still had his radio. He was on the far side of the hilltop on which the second chopper landed. After hiding for a while, the chopper landed and he left his cover. His trip toward rescue saw him evade Vietnamese ground troops dressed in brown uniforms. As he approached the chopper from the far side, he was caught in a cross fire between the Viets and the chopper gunners and had thrown himself on the ground to avoid the bullets. A North Vietnamese soldier, who was later identified as belonging to the 25th North Vietnamese Division, came within 20 feet of Paul's position but did not see him. Paul made a dash for the chopper and was almost killed by the door gunner who mistook him for the enemy. The door gunner's bullets had barely missed Paul before the gunner recognized the flight suit.[17]

The trip over the jungle from Khe Sanh to Danang went very quickly. Still, Paul and I had time to ponder what might have been. The C-123 landed at Danang where we were transferred to a waiting C-47 which flew us on to Cam Ranh. The 12th had planned it well and we were never left waiting.

On landing at Cam Ranh, we were greeted by several pilots and higher ranking staff officers who took us to the base cafeteria for something to eat. They obviously knew some of what we had been through and were seemingly embarrassed and unsure how to treat us. Everyone stood around like they wanted to help but were unsure what to do.

It embarrassed me to see the looks of my fellow pilots. They knew what we had been through because 12th Phantoms had been flying cap for the rescue. It didn't help matters when I tried to carry my tray with my one good hand and the tray dropped on the floor. Pilots are proud people and they knew I would not want any help. Yet when that tray dropped, a bunch of them jumped in to try to help out.

After Paul and I finished our "dinner" we were told that Colonel McClelland wanted to see us in the trailer that served as his living quarters. By now it was dark and several pilots guided us to his trailer, which was surrounded by additional trailers used to house the senior officers.

Author's Note: *17. Much later, the Marines reportedly made a movie of our rescue. I was told that they used it at a Training Center of theirs in Denver, Colorado. Also much later, I was told by an Academy buddy, Steve Mettler, who had transited through the PI, that the Air Force used our rescue as part of their Jungle Survival Training Course back at Clark in the Philippines. That was the same course that I had graduated from less than a month before.*

Colonel McClelland was gracious but also concerned for our well-being. I had known him to be a seemingly gruff man, especially when we had all hit the trees only 12 days earlier. This time the Colonel, who would prove to be a good wartime Wing Commander, showed he had heart. Over a scotch, Paul and I told our stories.

When I was finally alone that evening, I walked outside our Quonset, alone among the stars. Cam Ranh was never very light at night. What exterior lighting we had was always subdued. Even at sea level, the lack of light attenuation made the sky seemingly overflow with millions of stars. The Milky Way was vivid.

My thoughts were filled with what had happened and my usually subdued emotions were begging to be heard. I returned to the privacy of my bunk and released the pent-up emotions by writing several poems.

When very young, my father had taught me that it was not manly to cry. He was only a young boy himself at the very end of the frontier in California and that frontier spirit stayed part of him throughout his life. Men had to be tough to survive in the west of those times. That seems so distant in present day California with its freeways and endless housing tracts. But back in the small town of Fillmore, it was very real.

Those poems were my release. I am not a natural writer and certainly not a poet, but it seemed the proper thing to do at the time. I had never done it before, which shows. With apologies to true poets, I have included my thoughts written on that night:

THIS DAY:

Today, I've challenged the devil and demons to battle.

And from my very depths have surged, life forever lasting.

Today, I've scanned the dark horizons and have seen it…black.

My soul, it beckons me to run, for death it is not fasting.

Tonight, the moon seems brighter than the sun,

And the stars are spotlights painting truth upon the earth.

The breeze is like a breath of newfound life because,

I've met the devil face-to-face…and won.

The devil's face is ugly to behold

For his eyes in deep reflection told

Me that life is vital, ever-present, dear

And death is finality itself, and gone from here.

HOPE:

Years gained and ages viewed,

In but a few short hours.

Guts crying out and scorning loud,

The single falter of a step.

Jungles sound the sickly saber's rattle

Of enemy encroaching.

It's now, it's now or nevermore

For the enemy's approaching.

But from the breeze and on it lightly,

> Comes hope and with it strength, oh strength.

Machines with angel's wings come tread their way,

> Through hail in wrong direction winding.

Hope, hope the savior of those with it ever,

> You guide me and your destiny I'm finding.

Part of my reflection was concerning the incredible heroism of the chopper crews. Paul and I did not choose to be where we were. The chopper guys chose to come in and get us. They were encountering strong resistance and having firefights yet they continued to come in to get us and waited for me to make my appearance.

They first tried to position near me, and then a position nearer to Paul. Knowing that their pilot buddy had been shot and wounded, they still came in and waited some four to five minutes for me, after they had picked up Paul. During those minutes, they were engaged in gun battles out of both chopper doors. What would have happened to them if the enemy firing had disabled their chopper? There was nobody left to rescue them. How can you properly reward that kind of heroism and dedication? I owe my life to those brave Marines. What would have happened if the Army Major had not seen me run through the purple smoke? While downed, Paul and I were surrounded by North Vietnamese regulars and that might have meant a trip to Hanoi. But, one never knows.

Paul and I became two of the 600 United States pilots shot down in Laos and our aircraft was one of 500. When we were briefed by the Crown/Sandy guys at Cam Ranh, they told us that the Laotian civilians usually used machetes on downed pilots and left nothing for the rescue crews to find. Again, one never knows. What I do know is that I owe my life to their courage. It is performance against such odds that is truly awesome.

The FACs seemed to gauge their performance on ours, which placed a strong emphasis on results. That emphasis on results resulted in overinflating BDA. In my case, the FAC wanted to show results for the missions they controlled and that even included those with planes shot down. I can't blame the FACs, because they were trying their best to be good to all concerned and to be successful. The system designed to forward FAC information was bound to overinflate results. I do blame those responsible for setting up the criteria.

The Department of Defense exerted lots of pressure on the Pacific commands to show positive results. The SEA War was totally unlike conditions in a manufacturing company like Ford Motor Company. Yet McNamara demanded results to be reported just as he did at Ford. Yet he could cross-check the findings at Ford. There was no way that anyone could cross-check results in SEA. It was a totally different situation and McNamara should have realized that military results are not the same as the counting of widgets produced. A large part of the blame for what eventually happened in SEA was McNamara's.

The FAC actually gave us BDA for the flight. He reported four structures destroyed when my aircraft hit the ground. Hell of a way to get BDA. The FAC actually was owed strong thanks from Paul and me. Everyone involved in our rescue deserved thanks. They did an extraordinary job and were responsible for a rescue that probably should not have been attempted.

Two days after the event, the Wing told me that I was not of much use to them with a bad wing, so they suggested I pick a place for R&R and I chose Okinawa. While there, I was able to visit some of the friendly

Aircraft Commander Goodenough and Pilot Paul "Stub" Busch back at Cam Ranh after rescue. Pilots flown to Khe Sanh Hospital, then Danang before returning to Cam Ranh. Both members of "B" Flight "Zorro's Bastards" led by Captain Bill Sorrick.

school teachers who had remained from our squadron's rotational stay in 1965. It was a welcome break, but I soon longed to get back into the cockpit and fly again.

ANALYSIS: The cause of the loss of my Phantom has given me concern for a long time. To lose a plane is always hard for any pilot. It feels like failure, no matter what the cause. To say that I was "shot down" was too simplistic. The FAC did report 50 caliber guns firing in the area. What I saw and heard was ample evidence on the ground of AAA fire. Yet there may be another answer.

My reports to Colonel McClelland, Colonel Allen and to Wing de-briefers were what I had witnessed inside the cockpit. There were no cockpit indications that we had received hostile fire. Our Wing Director of Operations, Colonel James Allen, was contemplative when he heard my explanation. He wondered if the J-79 engine was subject to compressor stall. During our initial training in the F-4, the Air Force was so unconcerned that they did not even include information on compressor stalls. At the time of our downing in Laos, I did not even know what a compressor stall was.

One of my fellow pilots from the 559th came up to me in May after I was back on flying status. Dave Warren said that my squadron briefing to the pilots after our mishap made him mentally prepared for compressor stalls and that he had the same problem flying through smoke from a napalm drop. He stopcocked (shut the engine down) and was able to relight. Not sure if he meant it or that he was trying to make me feel better. What he did do was convince me that compressor stall must have been the culprit.

When Bill Sorrick first hit the truck on our two-ship attack, he set it on fire. By the time I took my run-in to drop my napalm, the truck was billowing smoke. I had to fly through that smoke to make a direct hit. The smoke may have starved my engines from the needed oxygen? It probably did.

When the engines unspooled, the deceleration was intense. I was at a height of no more than 50 feet, if that, and I had just released my napalm. The truck was reported by the FAC to be loaded with supplies and the usual supplies heading south on the HCMT included ammo boxes. I had just started my turn off target when we felt the hits. Were they compressor stalls instead of hits from their guns? In retrospect, I think they were.

Compressor stalls are caused by oxygen deprivation to the engine inlets. I was in a slight turn therefore I would have thought that only one of the inlets would have been blocked instead of two. Flying through the smoke was the probable cause of the oxygen loss.

My reaction immediately after the deceleration was to trade altitude for airspeed and to try to get the thing going again. When I climbed without power, my airspeed bled down very rapidly. There was not a lot of time available. While I had my head in the cockpit trying things, I was nursing the aircraft down on the stick feel of where we were in relation to the stall. If Paul had not suggested ejection, I would not have reacted in time to miss the hill. As I mentioned, the deceleration was so fast that our time in the cockpit after being hit was very short and I had little time to look around the cockpit.

While I remain unsure of what really happened, the stabilizing of both engines at 70 to 71% RPM meant that they both had the same identical problem. After reading up on compressor stalls, I am positive that we had them in both engines. My "try anything" approach of stopcocking the right engine should have eliminated the stall on that engine, but I did not realize that at the time. Why it didn't give us restart on the right engine I will never know. Perhaps in my haste I made a mistake?

What I did know was that I had lost two aircraft within 11 months and my introduction to war was not going very smoothly.

The aftermath for me was that the 12th Wing declared our bird as a combat loss and I was put in for a Purple Heart. Martin-Baker, manufacturer of the ejection seats used in the Phantom, later informed me that I had the dubious distinction of being the only pilot in the world to have ejected from both the front and back seats.

The official Air Force report, that was later published, stated:

F-4C 63-7531 of the 559th TFS, 12th TFW, USAF, Cam Ranh Bay Air Base, RVN
— First Lieutenant R.E. Goodenough (survived)
— First Lieutenant P.A. Busch (survived)
"During a Steel Tiger strike a Phantom was hit by ground fire near Tang Hune Nord in southern Laos. The A/C flew SE toward S. Vietnam, but the crew was forced to eject and were picked up by two Marine Corps UH-34Ds of HMM-161, although one of the helicopters was damaged by ground fire and its pilot wounded."

"The object of war is not to die for your country,
but to make the other bastard die for his."
General George S. Patton

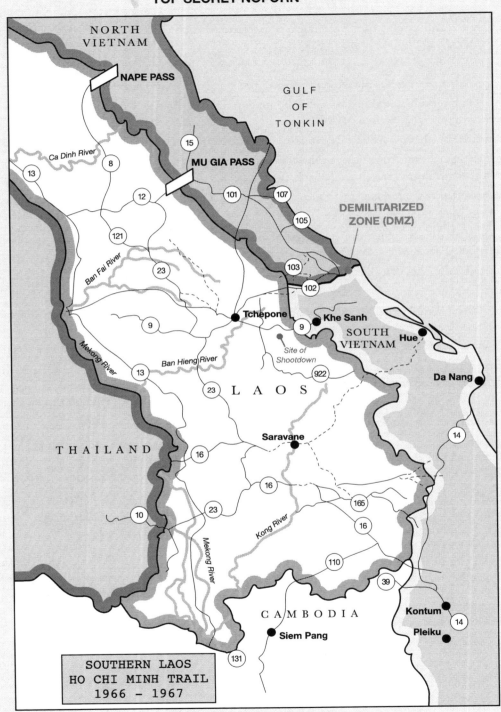

SOUTHERN LAOS
HO CHI MINH TRAIL
1966 – 1967

CHAPTER TEN

"Tiger Hound"

Southern Laos

> *"What a cruel thing war is… to fill our hearts with hatred instead of love for our neighbors."*
>
> Confederate General Robert E. Lee

OPERATION "TIGER HOUND":

Purpose: Elimination of transport and infiltration on the Ho Chi Minh Trail (HCMT)

Started: December 5, 1965

Ended: November 11, 1968

Combat Missions Flown: 103,148 tactical sorties; 1,718 "Arc Light" B-52 strikes

When the base offered to write orders for me to go wherever I wanted while my arm mended, I chose the familiar Okinawa. Grabbing flights out of Cam Ranh was pretty easy since it was such a large transport base. Destinations were all over the map of the Western Pacific where America then had a presence.

As the military often likes to do, the command given the duty to transport military cargo and personnel changed its name. The venerable Military Air Transportation Service (MATS) was formed in 1948 with the merger of the USAF Air Transport Command with the USN Naval Air Transport Service. In January 1966, just a few short months before I jumped on board, MATS again changed its name to the Military Airlift Command (MAC).

MAC operated similarly to today's airlines when it came to destinations. There were some non-stops and some "milk runs." Cam Ranh acted as a hub for Southeast Asia as did Tan Son Nhut Airport outside Saigon. Trips to the west either landed at Tan Son Nhut for Saigon, or they flew directly to Don Muang for Bangkok. Trips to the east went to Clark in the Philippines, to Anderson on Guam or directly to Hickam in Hawaii. Those that headed north often went through Clark, but also went directly to Taiwan, Okinawa, South Korea or Japan proper.

Cam Ranh had a permanent C-130 presence that was augmented from units based in Taiwan. For the 130 pilots "based" at CRB, the Air Force did them no favors. The rules for combat pay in 1966 provided pay for pilots who were considered PCS (permanent change of station) in a combat area. For those who were on TDY status, they received no combat pay. To comply with PCS rules, pilots had to be "in country" for 30 consecutive days or more. The "permanent" presence of the C-130s was provided by temporary pilots who were rotated every 29 days back to Taiwan, only to be turned around to immediately fly back to Cam Ranh.

So the continuing schedule for the C-130 guys was 29 days in the combat area and one day outside. They received no combat pay yet effectively served a year in a combat zone delivering supplies under combat conditions. Those C-130 guys were as permanent as our fighter squadrons at CRB. They used Kung Kuan AB on Taiwan as a turn-around base.

When I caught the C-130 flight going north from Cam Ranh, the pilots were on one of those turnarounds. We flew to Kung Kuan as a stop enroute to Naha.

Kung Kuan Air Base had a combined military and civilian usage. They both used the very long 12,000-foot runway. This was the same setup as currently exists at Honolulu. Honolulu International Airport shares its runway complex with Hickam Air Force Base.

The Republic of China (Taiwan) Air Force shared use of the runway with the civilian Taichung Airport. At about the time of my flight through Kung Kuan, the Taiwanese changed the name of the Air Base to Ching Chuan Kang or more commonly known as CCK. Landing aircraft at CCK either taxied to the civilian terminal or to the military ramps.

To help those pilots who may be unfamiliar with how a base is laid out, military vehicles with a "Follow Me" sign, prominently placed, meet a military aircraft after they depart the landing runways. When we taxied off the runway, I was up in the cockpit. The first vehicles to greet us were not the expected Follow Me truck, but military pickups and stakebed trucks filled with soldiers with rifles pointed directly at our aircraft.

Our C-130 pilots were used to the drill and completely stopped the plane, waiting for the eventual arrival of the Follow Me. Then we followed it to the military ramp with all the Taiwanese Army trucks, bristling with weapons, tagging along behind. It was a good show. Never in my flying career have I seen such air base security.

The USAF had a physical presence at CCK that went beyond a mere tenant status. Reportedly the U.S. Navy Construction Battalion (CB), commonly known as the Sea Bees, constructed facilities there in the spring of 1965. Those facilities were used by a large contingent of USAF personnel that made CCK a de-facto American base.

The remainder of our trip to Okinawa was uneventful. The transport ramps at Naha were south of the fighter ramps and I trudged north, by the fighters, and up the hill, dragging my military duffel bag to the familiar Visiting Officer's Quarters (VOQ). The VOQ was conveniently placed a short distance from the Officer's Club with a commanding view of Naha Air Base, Naha City in the distance and the black, volcanic rocks of the shoreline not so far below. During my TDY stay in 1965, Naha had become like home and it was good to be back.

RETURN TO COMBAT:

Even though Naha was a nice respite from the humidity of Vietnam, my combat experience had hardly started when it was so rudely interrupted by my escapade in Laos. I yearned to return, not only to Cam Ranh, but to the cockpit.

After return to Cam Ranh, I visited the Flight Surgeon, Doc Simmons. He checked out my arm and gave me a clean bill of health. I was cleared to resume flying. While there, he checked my height. During my first ejection in Florida, I had lost half an inch. During the Laotian ejection, I had again lost another half-inch. I thought, "If this keeps up, I will have to get a shorter flight suit."

LETTERS HOME:
May 9, 1966:

"Weather here and in the target areas has been bad lately so we've been doing very little flying. Matter of fact, we have more free time than we know what to do with. As a consequence, we all sleep a lot, play hearts, poker, gin rummy, checkers, chess and acey ducey.

"Our quarters are coming along okay. We live in Quonset huts and are in a sea of sand. The peninsula here is all sand. The Quonsets were originally just shells with bunks in them, but we've done a bit of "remodeling." Some guys have even built complete rooms with roofs within the Quonsets. I'm living with two other guys in our section, which will soon be a room. We decided to leave it open to allow the air to be properly circulated by the fans, which we brought in. Civil Engineering did come along with 2-ton air conditioners for each room, which are already installed. However, we need 220V wiring and circuit breakers before we can cut into the newly-installed base generating system.

"Of late, I've been keeping busy building an upper berth to my side of the room. The lower section will eventually be a shelf and storage space. Day before yesterday I paneled much of my area and yesterday built a ladder to help in my morning "controlled fall" to ground level. Thus, we keep ourselves busy.

"I have not seen one mosquito. The cross-peninsula breeze and lack of breeding grounds keeps to nil any threat of malaria, although "we all just take our pills."

"By the way, of the 11 MIGs downed so far in the war, seven have been by former 12th Wing pilots from MacDill. As you know, I'm now back with the 559th. The 559th has two MIG kills to its credit and the 555th has five. One squadron at Danang has one and the Navy has three, two by Naval Phantoms. So, 10 of the 11 have been killed by Phantoms.

"To calm any worries that may produce, I've never seen a MIG and the Wing down here has not had one engagement with MIGs. That isn't to say we won't, but we aren't and we haven't. By the way, no Phantoms have been shot down by enemy aircraft. (other than the one lost by the 45th in 1965) Phantoms rule the skies.

"About McNamara's statement (and Dirksen's too) concerning any bomb shortage, they are either lying or convincingly fooled by the military, anxious to give the picture that everything is rosy. Well, we have had very few bombs on base and not one rocket. Even our napalm has been curtailed and we're sending aircraft against targets with minimum loads. The forecast for the future looks dim indeed.

"We're doing a fine job against our targets. The enemy has to really be hurting because we have just been pounding the hell out of them in our particular sector. The bombing has been very accurate and getting better all the time as the crews are staying here longer. I haven't been doing badly for a newcomer. I'm holding my own.

"All the bases are hurting for maintenance. Our targets are also being questioned. To risk a two-million-dollar aircraft and two pilots against shacks with not enough ordnance to do the job is hardly my idea of being cost-effective.

"I know exactly what happens on those congressional inquiries (you mentioned). They all seem to go the same. The Congressman may write to the base, but the base would counter with statements, facts and figures to show that we are in good shape. CRB has a complete section at personnel designed to answer Congressional inquiries.

"When the VIPs come to Vietnam, they usually have their photos taken in fatigues for the press back home. They are given briefings on how well the war is going and often are taken to "special" areas to view the war.

"Even we here don't know how the war is going, just our little part of it. You get news quicker and know more of the overall situation than we do. It's all rather unreal.

"When I sent you the card, I was in Okinawa. I stayed there and in Taiwan for about 10 days. Nice vacation.

"I got a letter from Major John Robertson in Virginia. He's one of my partners with Bob Lynn. Robbie asked me if I wanted to join him. (He will be flying against the North out of Ubon). I just may.

"Fifty-seven days gone, 307 left. It's going fast. If you want to send me something, try clothespins and maybe some of those plastic liquid containers for the refrigerator. If you send a parcel that is less than five pounds by surface mail, it will come to Vietnam by air. Everything is OK here."

HO CHI MINH TRAIL (HCMT):

The reason for creating "Tiger Hound" was the Ho Chi Minh Trail used for transport of equipment, supplies and troops from North Vietnam to South Vietnam. The Trail, which started out in 1964 as a trail and road complex over 3,000 miles in length, ended with over 12,000 miles of transport routing, which included trails and roads.

The North Vietnamese created the 559th Transport Group to handle and control the usage of the Trail. In the process, they created over 20 major way stations or "Binh Trams" responsible for air and land defense, delivery of supplies and replacement troops, and liaison units that provided food, shelter, medical support and trail guides.

The 559th camouflaged over 2,000 miles of the trail; built underwater bridges; provided kerosene lamps and even gasoline-soaked rags for illumination; "floating barrels" for later pick up on rivers; and had over 100,000 porters, drivers, mechanics and AAA troops.

The American program called "Igloo White" attempted to counter this transport by using high-tech equipment. Electronic and chemical sensors were dropped on the Trail and the sensors were linked to processing computers in Thailand. The ingenious Vietnamese confounded American efforts by doing such "low-tech" counter-measures as driving herds of cattle over the areas to destroy the sensors; removing the batteries or relocating sensors; broadcasting tapes that sounded like trucks and paying locals to reveal Special Operations Force Teams that had been infiltrated by the United States.

To neutralize our chemical sensors, they even did such things as hanging bags of urine in trees. There was no end to the clever and terribly "cost-effective" methods employed successfully to counter American technology and equipment.

COMBAT DIARY:
May 11, 1966:

I'm back in the air on my first mission since being shot down. And it is the day after my 26th birthday. It is such a good feeling to get back in the cockpit and perhaps regain the confidence that I had lost. Flying fighters is my profession. It is what I have chosen to do and to fly again is a thrill.

Loaded with four "snake-eye" Mark 82 high-drag bombs, we flew in support of the Army's operation Birmingham near the Cambodian border and west of Saigon. The target was a river ford, on the Mekong, among some trees. It was my first drop of the high drags and my second dive bomb with live ordnance. I was still nervous, as it was my first post-crash flight. Net result was one bomb inadvertently dropped while

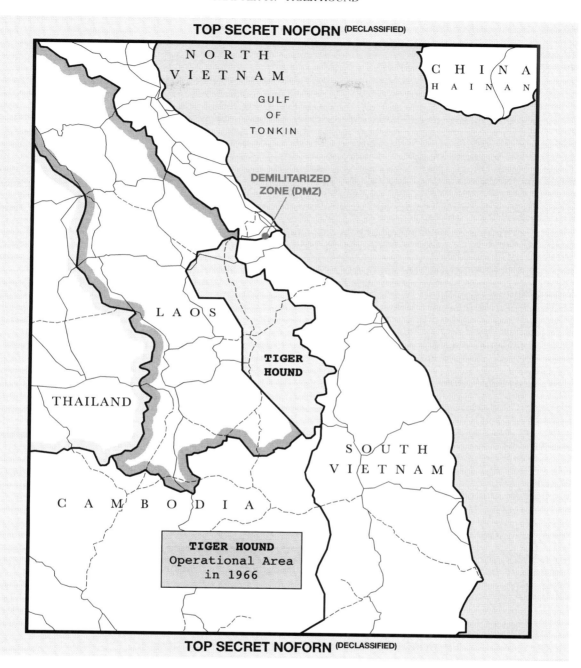

"Tiger Hound" Operational Area at time of Author's Fighter-Bomber Missions — *"Tiger Hound" was formed from the southern half of "Steel Tiger." The areas of attack, by the 12th Tactical Fighter Wing based at Cam Ranh Bay (CRB), were, on average, 300 miles from CRB.*

"Tiger Hound" roughly comprised the boundaries of the main infiltration arteries from the Ho Chi Minh Trail (HCMT) System. While HCMT roads lay outside of Tiger Hound, the attacks concentrated in the areas of closer proximity to South Vietnam. After the author left the combat theater, Steel Tiger was expanded to include all of southern Laos.

in orbit over the target area.

What a dumb thing. Number three saw the bomb drop in the safe mode and thankfully did not tell anyone except me on the ground. I dropped it by selecting the bomb on the weapons control panel and thereby arming the drop mechanism, but not arming the bomb itself. With the bomb mechanism armed, the pickle button on the control stick was hot and I reached across the stick to set another switch and brushed the button. I felt the bump associated with a drop and could only guess what must have happened. At this rate, I'll never win the war for us.

With my remaining bombs, I succeeded in getting closer to the target than the rest, but we only chopped wood.

May 12, 1966:

Again I fly as number two. Sorrick was lead and Phil Cline was number three. Most of our flights have been three-ship. The target was a truck park area in the mountainous region of the HCMT. Weather was lousy and getting worse. Sorrick zeroed in on the FAC and I don't know how he found him, but he did. He is a great flight lead.

We were again loaded with four snake-eyes and made five passes over the target. It was really a bitch. One-thousand-foot overcast in a mountainous area. We were dive-bombing and the bombs were frag, which posed a threat to our aircraft if we flew too close to the bird in front. We had to get good spacing; otherwise our bomb explosions could down us. This eliminated the short, in-trail spacing where we could keep track of the other flight members, especially in the low visibility. Whipping down through holes in the clouds and trying to determine the proper valley to attack at high speed was difficult. We dropped all ordnance and I even hit on one. Cline got the best bombs. We got scattered on the final run and didn't rejoin until reaching Pleiku, far to the south. The BDA was one truck destroyed, two damaged and one road cut. A road cut is what they give you when you miss and they don't know what else to give you.

May 14, 1966:

It was an ineffective strike today against a troop area. The mission was fragged against the VC in support of Operation Austin VI. We orbited near Cambodia for one to one and a quarter hours before returning home with the bombs. I think we even crossed the Cambodian border at one time.

The FAC didn't get off the ground on time due to weather, which was low scud. When he did get off, he directed a medical chopper to another area to care for a wounded troop. They used a Stokes litter to bring him up while the doctor worked on the patient. The medevac chopper pilot was concerned with the defensive perimeter and made sure they extended it for 200 yards away from the chopper position.

On the return, we heard a Mayday call for a downed chopper 15 miles north of Nha Trang. The chopper pilot successfully auto-rotated it onto a road. That is good work.[18]

This is the second Mayday I've heard. The first was for a downed pilot in North Vietnam.

Author's Note: *18. Whatever the circumstances, the chopper had no power and made a successful landing without power. Auto rotation is when a chopper pilot aims his powerless aircraft directly at the ground and gains speed through gravity. The speed causes the rotor blades to rotate. At the last second, the pilot pulls his chopper nose up to a landing configuration and the lift generated by the rotating blades can cushion it for a proper landing. I have been on a chopper when the pilot practiced auto rotation and it requires a good deal of piloting skills. His landing was soft.*

Laotian operations are getting to be hairy with the low-level work, but the AAA and AW (automatic weapons) has slacked off. The day after I went in, a Marine F-4B hit the trees not far from where I went down and he exploded. The bird was loaded with napalm, but both guys made it out okay. That same day, a B-57 was lost on a Laotian hill when the pilot didn't make it over and he was killed.

May 15, 1966:

Today I worked as taxi pilot, desk officer and mobile control officer. Actually, I wasn't called to taxi, only stayed on desk for a half-hour and sat in the operations shack, which is air-conditioned, during mobile due to a weather-hold on the birds.

Weather has really held us down lately. If it keeps going at this rate, we'll never get the war won. And then there are the monsoons. We lost a bird in the Bay two weeks ago due to the weather and we may have more of that? The four-ship flight came in during a heavy monsoon downpour and one of them ran off the slippery runway, another took the barrier at the end of the runway, one flamed out in the fuel pits and the last one ran out of gas and the pilots jumped out over the Bay. Jim Knock was in the back seat. That's number two for him over here. Looks like he has lost weight.

Politically speaking:

Intelligence reports that Danang is having some troubles. All the phone lines in and out of there are out, possibly due to a coup? Sketchy reports but Danang is definitely out as an alternate airfield. There was a report of gunfire on the fringes and possibly on the base itself. This damned war.

May 16, 1966:

Flew from the alert pad today on two "in-country" missions. Ordnance was four cans of napalm on each bird. This was my first close-air-support scramble and the first napalm attack since the shoot down. Missions went okay.

This base is getting to be more chicken. They find something to bitch about just about every day. Today, they complained about one of the guys not signing in from a flight. Then they complained about a small incident in the arming area where a bird rolled a foot and scared some de-armorers. And they got on my tail for landing too shallow. Good Lord, back at pilot training again.

Missions today were both against positions along the Cambodian border. First was against some pinned-down VC on an island in the river itself. We hit them with 1040 rounds of HEI (High-Explosive Incendiary) and napalm. One napalm can of mine flew across the river into Cambodia. The rest of the flight did good work. The strafe was also against a "school" area within Cambodia. The FAC said the border "had been moved." Saw none of the Cambode (Cambodian) MIGs or any of the VC.

After the mission, I asked my flight mates what happened on my long drop. They laughed and Dave Warren said that I had to have been at least 500 feet high. A normal napalm drop altitude for me was about 20-25 feet. I couldn't believe it and must have looked incredulous, for they all laughed again. The look in the eyes of the guys I am flying with indicates that they know what I had been through and there seems to be a respect and maybe even a little affection. It feels good to feel accepted.

The second mission was against a bridge near the border. Dropped in ripple (mode). Lead had a fuel tank malfunction and we had to leave early. The weather going and coming was rough, with some of the thickest clouds I have seen. We almost lost him (lead) at one point. My reflexes and senses are getting faster and more alert in this combat environment. I have more tension now than before. Maybe it is for the better.

We had a good discussion in the alert trailer about the war. Larry Dahle claims that the United States is in reality the aggressor in this war. He also stated that Ho Chi Minh went to Washington in 1946 to try to persuade Truman to support their cause for independence. I am starting to agree. We need a complete reevaluation of our foreign policy.

The FAC was unable to give us any KBA (Killed by Air) or BDA.

May 17, 1966:

Mission #18 just completed and another in-country. We hit about 35 miles west of Qui Nhon against VC emplacements. Number-four saw ground fire coming at us from a ridge. I didn't see it, but I really raked the ridge with cannon fire. Spotted some clear areas, which I aimed at and worked the shells out from there. We were supposed to have HEI, but it looked like TP (target practice-ball ammo). Have to aim the shock (heat) waves of the bullets because we have no flash marks when the stuff hits the ground. The first two passes were with 2.75 inch rockets. We fired the rockets in singles (each rocket pod holds 19 rockets). Both of them went where I aimed them, which made me happy. One cannon pass was long, but it probably did as much good as any. Aimed at a riverbank and raked the hell out of it. On one of my final passes, I intentionally dropped my empty rocket pods. The FAC said to "hit them on the head" with them. He didn't have any info about the damage, but did say that we had 60% target coverage. Hard to say what he was talking about when he said target.

My second mission of the day was against a VC storage area in-country. We hit a clump of trees with a beautiful French-style villa in the middle. We didn't destroy the villa, but did destroy the four storage buildings we set out to hit. Carried two rocket pods, which didn't do a hell of a lot of good unless there were tunnels. The gun wiped everything out. The biggest storage shed was hit by my gun and really burned and was still burning heavily when we left. Only fired 442 shells, but they did the job. I tore hell out of the other buildings too. BDA was four buildings totally destroyed. It was a good flight. One of the guys took battle damage in one of the other squadrons and had to land at Pleiku. Our flight really barreled down the coast after the rest of the flight dropped their rocket pods over water.

Lead was in error since the flight had to go-around due to a drag chute still lying on the runway. Lead had forced us to burn too much JP-4 when we came down the coast in burner.

Number three landed and shut his engines down with only 100 gallons of fuel showing. Number four shut down with 3-400 pounds. That's flameout on final approach fuel figures due to the unreliability of the fuel counter below 500 pounds. Too damned close. We've got other things to worry about than dinging ourselves in.

Politically Speaking:

The political situation in Vietnam looks grim. Hue fell today to anti-government troops (not VC) and Danang is in a state of siege. What a war and we just keep killing and destroying. Guess that is our job.

146

May 18, 1966:

Good mission today. I feel more and more like I'm one and the same with the aircraft and the mission. It is not an unknown environment anymore and the missions are getting a small touch of the routine with confidence as a possible factor. I've gained it back after the experience of last month and it hardly seems possible that it happened less than a month ago.

We went against a storage and truck park area in Laos. It was 145/ 65 off of TACAN 72 near Saravane. Fairly good weather, at least in the target area. Yesterday another CRB bird got shot up so badly he almost punched out, but stumbled back to Pleiku.[19]

We carried 2 LAU pods today, 38 rockets total. The load was 12 high explosive anti-tank (HEAT) and seven high explosive anti-personnel (HEAP) rockets. My rocket passes were good, but they didn't cause any momentous events. Of course, when you're hitting a ground area with no visible target, it doesn't really matter. You hit his (FACs) designated area and trust that you hit something under the trees. Dave Warren came in on strafe and caused good-sized secondary explosions. The rest of the BDA was two trucks destroyed. On the way to hit the target area (a divert), we heard the beepers of ejection. SAR (search and rescue) procedures were underway when we were on target.

Returning to the field, we just beat a storm in. It was raining before we reached the end of the runway after landing. Lead called that he was taking the barrier but didn't. I was number two and didn't have problems. I think his (leads) anti-skid system was off. At the target, leads gun RAT (Ram Air Turbine, which is positioned into the wind for power when shooting the gun) broke and when he was on the runway after landing, 20 mm ammo and chain links littered the runway. Dave had his gun jam at the target.

One flight today caught a whole VC company, or larger, in a set-up situation. It was a three-ship and all three guns malfunctioned. That's almost as bad as what happened to the guys up North. An Ubon flight had a perfect radar set-up on a MIG and fired three Sparrows missiles and all three went ballistic. There goes a (lost) MIG 21. We often refer to going out-of-control like that as going Able Sugar, which means ape shit.

Politically speaking:

The political situation down here is getting so confusing it is humorous. Premier Ky (Nguyen Cao) heads the national government, which controls (some of) Saigon. General Thi and the Buddhists are allied in the north and control the Danang area. Fighting has broken out on the (Danang) base. The intellectuals are also anti-government and control the northern city of Hue. And then there are the Viet Cong.

In Laos, you have the Pathet Lao and the North Vietnamese troops who are at two-division strength. The North Vietnamese are in the South allied with the VC and fighting alongside both the VC regulars and the VC militia. The Laotian neutralists are actually allied with the Laotian Royalists. Over Laos fly US combat, transport and recce planes, North Viet supply planes at night, and Red Chinese MIGs controlling the airspace in the northern part of Laos. Thai pilots are flying in Laos as well as the civilian CIA groups: Air America, Bird and Sons (at this time it was CAS), plus one other airline.

We have the regular Red Chinese troops in northern Laos and the Chinese advisors in South Vietnam (a

Author's Note: *19. I have to wonder why the Laotian War is kept secret. It certainly is no secret to the Laotians. It is no secret to North Vietnam or the entire Communist World that seems to be helping the North Viets. The only apparent advantage to classifying our involvement would be to keep the information from the American public. This is NOT what the classification program is supposed to do. The American public should scream about this lack of transparency.*

Chinese Major General was reported by Intelligence to have been killed at A Shau). We have both American and South Vietnamese guerrillas fighting in North Vietnam. Cambodian mercenaries are employed by the Thai, South Vietnamese and American forces. Cambodians are fighting alongside the VC. There are troop concentrations and territorial violations on both the eastern and western borders of Cambodia—by both sides.

Vietnamese emigrants are reported to be fighting the Thais in northeastern Thailand. The South Vietnamese troops cross into southern Laos to fight the Pathet Lao and the North Viets.

The daily Intelligence reports mention 500,000 Red Chinese soldiers repairing the destroyed rail and road lines in the North that were hit by both the VNAF and US pilots. The reports also often include reference to the 300 French prisoners from Dien Bien Phu who were conscripted into their road-repair gangs. Red Chinese and American planes battle each other in the North while American jets and Cambodian MIGs play games with each other along the Mekong. Montagnard tribesman fight under American advisors in the Central Highlands and the US builds supply areas in Thailand for troop buildups. Burma slumbers along while various tribes are in dissent and both Nationalist and Red Chinese armies fight against each other.[20]

The Malaysians are not on good terms with Indonesia or the Philippines, but Malaysia and the PI are both close American allies. The Indonesians are reportedly infiltrating into Malaysia, which has just split with Singapore. Meanwhile, in Indonesia a reported million Chinese have been exterminated and Bung Karno may not be alive anymore. The PI troops are going to South Vietnam to join 45,000 South Koreans, 255,000 Americans, and 4,500 Australian and New Zealand (ANZAC) troops.

American planes use Thai bases as well as do Australian pilots flying Sabres. The real war that the Pentagon seems to be fighting is the Sortie War between the USN and USAF. Chinese Nationalist propagandists are in South Vietnam. Red Chinese technicians and Russian missile men are in North Vietnam.

The Red Chinese and North Vietnamese use Cambodian territory for sanctuary, rest, travel and transportation, plus supply storage. American aircraft and artillery are striking inside the supposedly neutral Cambodia. The French are reportedly involved against the American's intelligence. The French reportedly are flying missions for the Cambodians. The French are sheltering and training the VC. American planes are actually flying into Red China to strike airfields.

It all equates to ONE BIG CONFUSED MESS.[21]

Some of the above is undoubtedly in error as to accuracy. I include it because it was part of my diary and indicative of the state of mind of our pilots at that time.[22]

Author's Notes: *20. A Nationalist Chinese Army was caught in Burma after their compatriots retreated to Formosa (Taiwan) during the Communist triumph in 1949.*

21. The political comments above were written in the author's combat diary after each mission in 1966. In SEA in 1966, there was not the proliferation of sources for news that we have today. There was no television, no commercial newspapers except when we went on R&R. There was also no internet or radio. The sources of our news and information in SEA came from Intelligence, and in the case of the foreign nations mentioned above, the Pacific Stars and Stripes.

22. The reference above to American planes hitting Red Chinese airfields came from a comment to me from one of the Thai-based F-105 pilots. He claimed he was on one such mission. He also claimed that other missions hit the airfields, which was a violation of the Rules of Engagement. It may have been like the F-105 planes that hit the Russian and British ships that were offloading supplies at Haiphong. Those were unauthorized strikes initiated by the pilots themselves. In the case of the strike against the British ship, I heard an audio recording taken from the deck of the British ship while it was being strafed by the 105s. Reportedly, nineteen British sailors were injured.

If the pilots did generate the strikes against the Chinese bases, it is certainly understandable. When I was flying MIG cover for the RB-66s, we were close to the North Vietnamese border with China. I did see Chinese MIGs climbing out of their airfields at Mengtzu and near Chinghsi, just north of their border. The MIGs hit the contrails level and became visible as they then turned south toward our formations. Scenes such as I witnessed, could have generated the anger necessary for the Thai-based pilots to stage unauthorized attacks against the airfields.[23]

What can be confirmed is that the French company Michelin harbored Viet Cong within their vast rubber plantations north of Saigon. I know that because I led two, two-ship flights off Alert on consecutive days where we bombed VC schools lying within the rubber trees.

LETTERS HOME:
May 19, 1966:

"For God's sake, don't worry so much. What happened to me won't happen again. The base still hasn't experienced many combat losses and I surely won't do it again.

"As for my arm, it is completely healed and there are no after-affects except a small scar. The tendons are okay and it healed amazingly fast. I went to Okinawa to get rested, gather my thoughts and my courage again, not to go to a hospital.

"We don't know much of what is happening. We are told about various Army operations in case we might have to go help them, but not how the operations are doing. Otherwise, we just have our little corner of the war. Even on missions, the war seems unreal. We don't have the problems that the guys up North do. They have to watch for MIGs, SAMs, flak, automatic fire and small arms fire near the ground. Of the first three, we have no need to worry. I have yet to see a MIG and I conceivably could go the whole war without. (This reference to not seeing any MIGs was meant to calm my mother's nerves.)

"We now have air conditioning and it makes a lot of difference. The base continues to expand at a rapid rate and should have 10,000 airmen by the end of the year. It has 6,000 now. The peninsula will have 50,000, which won't be counting defensive forces on the mainland perimeter. I understand that this is the only US base in SEA. All of the other bases are owned by the host country, but Cam Ranh peninsula has been bought by the US government.

"Living conditions are getting better all the time. Morale is high and the food is just great. Food cost $1.17 per day. Billeting costs $2.00 per month. Aside from a few occasional drinks at the Club, items bought at the Base Exchange and a few beers or cokes bought from the squadron fund, all the rest is gravy.

"Yesterday I earned an Air Medal for number of missions flown. It's rather automatic. The missions are going smoothly and I'm not getting down as low off the ground as I used to.

"We get wood this afternoon to finish our room. "Plots" is getting matting from the Philippines to put in our rooms. We have paneling to put on the inside and I've already built a bunk and ladder. We'll put a ceiling in and a door, panel the inside and build a desk. Things are looking up.

Author's Note: *23. The activities of the French have always been a big question mark regarding their knowledge of and participation in events in SEA. The fact of French pilots training Cambodian pilots in Cambodia to fly MIGs has been confirmed. The reported French-piloted MIG flights into Vietnam have not been confirmed. The rumor that the first Air Academy graduate to be killed in SEA, Val Bourque, was killed by French MIGs is definitely false.*

"I got accepted to the Air Force Institute of Technology to do graduate work in Systems Management, with is a type of engineering management. I don't think I'll take it. They also sent a test for business administration.

"I've seen quite a few Academy buddies who've come through here. There are a lot of us over here. Butch Vicellio, remember him from George AFB, flew cover for me when the choppers came in and picked me up.

"In about three weeks, I'll go either to Clark AFB or Nha Trang for a few days' rest. It's a good chance to go shopping and just lounging around over cocktails. Our work day here is every day and we don't have weekends to reference, so we don't know which day of the week it is. Actually, it is better this way, since we have something to do when we fly.

"I'll close for now. Keep rooting those Dodger's along. They're going to win the pennant this year. I can feel it in my bones."

COMBAT DIARY:
May 20, 1966:
We hit a Viet Cong Base Camp area eleven miles from Saigon right on the river (Mekong). All I think we hit were enemy trees. Dropped two 500-pound high-drags and didn't shoot. My first two passes were in "singles" and I had no drops. They were my best approaches yet. The third pass I went ripple and had one dud. The other was a good hit, but the pass wasn't as good. Those 500 HD are really accurate. The FAC said it was an Intelligence target and that he didn't think we hit a thing because there wasn't anything there, just trees. The VC has heavily infiltrated ARVN (Army of the Republic of Vietnam) Intelligence and often send false target messages.

Last night we had curfew because of a possible mortar attack. The guards fired flares and even some mortars or artillery of their own, but nothing came of it. Tonight 18 aircraft are sitting alert because of a possible attack against Duc Co Special Forces Camp on the Cambodian border. Reportedly, several other camps are also ripe for the plucking. Last night one (Special Forces Camp) was taken by the VC, but this morning we took it back.

Politically speaking:

It looks like Premier Ky is going to be overthrown by either the Buddhists or a Buddhist supported military figure. How are we to win without a stable government to win confidence, lasting support and create a decent intelligence and secret police organization able to reach into the back country? As it stands now, the only organization of consequence, outside of the big cities, is the National Liberation Front (Viet Cong).

Only 297 days left to go. Sixty-seven days already gone and 226 days spent in the Far East since June 9, 1965. This was my 21st mission.

May 24, 1966:
Today we hit a VC concentration north of Saigon near Bien Hoa. With four retards (bombs), it was another example of killing enemy trees. No BDA due to foliage, but we had 60% ordnance on target. It rained again this afternoon.

May 25, 1966:
A North Vietnamese truck park in Laos was again the subject of our bombing. The target was on Route 92

of the Ho Chi Minh Trail (HCMT), ten miles south of Route 9. Hound Dog 66 was the FAC and we gave him a rather poor exhibition of bombing with six retards apiece. My first was way long and the rest were in the wooded area. Buck was having a rough time of it and threw quite a few out of the ballpark. Vic Chance had a few bad passes also. We were aiming at a truck and only managed to blow the camouflage off. However, we did get four secondary explosions, which gave us a damned good BDA. We hit something down there.

On the way back, we relayed a Mayday transmission from an Army helicopter "Alligator 851" which was going down in the Duc Co area. One alert flight was vectored in to give cover support. Duc Co and Plei Mi plus one other Special Forces camp are expecting an attack at any time. It could be tonight.

We've been running about 4,000 troops in Operation Paul Revere. They were introduced into the area to keep the more than 10,000-strong enemy off balance. The enemy came from rest areas in Cambodia in two regimental sized groups.

I'm standing alert now for Sky Spot where they can direct us in with MSQ radar to pinpoint bomb areas during marginal-to-poor weather conditions. The radar specialists use highly accurate ranging and azimuth instruments plus a great amount of geodetical (positioning with regard to the varying magnetic field) knowledge. We drop from 15,000 feet and our average miss distance (CEA) is 300 feet and improving. This will greatly aid the defense of Special Forces camps during "socked in" conditions.

This afternoon, I sat waiting for a regular (not alert) Sky Spot mission but the weather again came in and this afternoon was bad. This waiting for flights that never happen is getting old.

Cam Ranh is getting more and more the appearance of permanency. I'll lay a bet to myself that the "permanent" base never gets built as is now planned. Maybe some facilities over there (across the field) but here will be the main post.

They brought in more dirt for the Officer's Club parking lot. That's fine when it is dry, but now instead of six inches of mud, we have 12. When it's wet, the sand is also easy to walk on and when dry, hard to walk on.

Only 292 days left. Time is rapidly going by. And this stupid war goes on.

Politically Speaking:

Today I read where Dr. Brown, Secretary of the Air Force, had said we had enough (tactical) aircraft in Vietnam. His tone sounded like we had enough to hold our own, so why rock the boat? [24]

The Danang birds are still flying out of Chu Lai (Marine base) and some other base. With this crazy, mixed-up situation over here, we can't use Danang as an alternate or battle-damage- recovery base. The Buddhists are rioting in both Danang and Saigon and the dissident ARVN troops are fighting the Viet Marines. When you don't know which outfit attacks your base, it is high time to reevaluate how the War is being fought. These demonstrations and the street fighting have heavy anti-American overtones.

Perhaps we should keep the base here at Cam Ranh as an American Singapore and pull back to Thailand. Either that or go full blast in the war. This halfway routine is no good.

May 27, 1966:

Two missions today for a total of 25, with one an "out-country" (Laos) for a total of 10 Tiger Hound.

It is now in the Laotian monsoon season and the first flight was vectored back in to South Vietnam after

Author's Note: *24. This is another example of our political leaders projecting a lack of will to win, or the appearance of, to both the public and our military. Additionally, it sends a clear message to our enemy.*

we couldn't get on-target. We (flight of 4) each carried six of the 500-pound retards. This is the heaviest flight load that we have had. Our divert target was near Ban Me Thiet and was a complex of three VC buildings that the FAC had been trying to get for three days. He told us the Demon Flight (F-100s out of Phan Rang) wasn't able to touch them and he wondered whether the Phantom flight could do it. We went in and really plastered it. (The psychology of competition works). We've cut down the number of passes over the target in the squadron to three maximum. This is smart. So we pickle (hit the bomb release button) twice on each pass. I've been using a 10-degree dive with a 1200-foot AGL release and it is dead on. The mil setting, which controls the red pipper (aiming point) displayed on the windscreen, is max plus. The FAC reported all three buildings demolished and 100% ordnance on target.

Yesterday I awoke to bad news: Terry Griffey, an Academy classmate, had been killed along with his backseater on an early morning mission out of CRB. They blew up on a low-level run on a coastal city near Qui Nhon. Terry was a good friend whom I was getting to know better over here. He played first-string guard for us on the Falcon Football Team. He was also one of five front-seat Lieutenants over here along with me. He and I were the only Academy men of 62 to make the front seat (so far). It is a sad loss.

During our Laotian missions, we are required to have line-up cards, maps and often photos of the target with us. The pre-target brief includes weather, intelligence and the flight lead's brief on flight procedures, 21A route information, Hawk missile orbit codes (Hawk is an anti-aircraft missile), GCI (Ground Controlled Intercept) info on frequencies, aircraft and start engine, take off and TOT (time over Target) times. The TOT has to coincide with the FACs time so that it will be a coordinated attack. These orders come out of 7th Air Force HQ in Saigon. Additional items included on the line-up cards are mission numbers, bingo and joker fuels (caution and emergency fuel states), emergency procedures, target description, weather and elevation, target defenses and terrain, recent activity, release parameters, TACAN (Tactical Air Navigation Station) radials and DME (Distance Measuring Equipment) info plus bail-out areas and headings. Search and Rescue (SAR) frequencies and locations are also included. Examples of SAR available are the H-43 helicopters available at the Special Forces camps. These call signs are varied, but will either be Northbrook, Pedro, Powerglide, or Market Time. Crown is the airborne rescue craft.

Examples of code words used are the ones we used today: Execute- Koufax; Wx Cnx (Weather Cancel)- Grant; Cnx- Drysdale; Recall- Gibson; Success- Mandrill; Unsuccessful- Knothole; Total Change- Pitcher; MIG Alert- Ice House; SAM Alert- Hurdy Gurdy; Border- Litter Carrier. (Pretty boring isn't it.)

Today we were warned about two operations in Tiger Hound, which we should consider forbidden areas. The forbidden areas can be the result of any of several different types of missions. One type are the B-52 raids called "Arc Light" that are being run against Trail areas. Another is Operation "Shiny Brass," which is the use of indigenous personnel from Laos, along with Viet troops, to cross into Tiger Hound and gain intelligence information or secure certain areas. These areas are called no-bomb zones for specific lengths of time (usually a day or two).

The powers seem to feel that Plei Djerang will be hit pretty soon. The North Viets have possibly three regiments in the area and it looks grim. Mortars are being fired into the camp. I don't know why we don't launch 30-40,000 troops into these areas that are so infested. Plei Djerang is one of the smaller camps on the Cambodian border.

While this morning's mission was fragged against a staging complex on the Sihanouk Road, this afternoon's flight was a direct air support mission against a Viet Cong training camp. The area was 100 miles to the north of CRB along the coast, near Qui Nhon. After takeoff, we contacted Airpatch (CRB Command Post) and then went to Peacock Control (Pleiku GCI). Peacock gave us flight following and relayed us to Panama Control at Danang prior to the hand off to "Baron 35" our FAC on the FAC frequency.

Lead carried four retards and the rest of us carried two each. The target turned out to be the most lucrative yet. We caught the VC sleeping. The target was a VC training area containing numerous dwellings. We couldn't see the buildings, as is often the case, but our bombs went true. I got one beautiful secondary explosion, which looked like holiday fireworks going off. This morning I also got a secondary. The flight total was two secondaries.

Final BDA was 10 buildings destroyed, eight damaged, one secondary, one VC killed and 5 probable. If we had used the gun, it would have been much better. However, the visibility was bad and we didn't know about the VC until we were given the BDA by the FAC on our climb-out. The Wing has limited us to only fire at "hot" or fleeting targets with the gun. It seems we have some shortages of ammo. We can use the Target Practice (TP) ball ammo though. This is a dangerous sport due to the likelihood of getting hit by our own ricochets. Plotnitsky did.

Ball ammo ricochets; HEI explodes and starts fires. HEI is far better than Target Practice ammo.
Politically Speaking:

Our strategy has been to kill them and kill their desire. While I don't agree with this base and limited objective, we should stick to it once it has been formulated. Now we push just enough men into the area to keep the enemy off balance. As my Missouri-born barber back home, Olen Core, once said, "Either shit of get off the pot."

May 29, 1966:
This was the worst mission since coming here to CRB. We never dropped anything. I was loaded with two retards and the other two had cans. The western Tiger Hound weather was bad. We tried to let down through the stuff and it was a no-go. Plotnitsky had a bad day with two dangerous overshoots.

The target was a truck park on Route 185 and it was about 2000' overcast with the stuff reaching up. Bill tried to get down through it, but couldn't chance running into a granite cloud. The weather was thick and it was hell trying to stay on his wing and I about lost him a few times.

May 30, 1966:
A fragged target today that got diverted to another target. It was another panhandle mission against a truck. Just one single, lousy truck. Buck got him with the first of his two napalm cans. Mine were both long. Still a little jumpy about dropping napalm, I guess. We didn't use any strafe. Left the truck burning beautifully.

May 31, 1966:
Scramble off of 15-minute-alert status to hit another truck. Again we were loaded against a single truck with two cans. We got the truck right away and then were diverted to a target a short distance away. I don't know what was in the area, but I threw 614 shells into it. We're back with the old TP ammo again. We got one hundred percent of ordnance on target. My first can was long again but my second was right in there. I

153

might have been the one to get the truck.

Pulled 7.5 Gs off the target, which meant they were firing at us, and for this I bent one of my stabilator wiper blades back and I had to shoot a straight-in approach. Dave Warren thought it was battle damage and called it over the radio. Six birds are down right now for battle damage.

Dave himself had trouble with one of his cans. He was pulling off target when it released and it must have gone for miles. Investigation after we landed showed that part of his TER (Triple Ejection Rack) had been ripped off and there was dried napalm on the rest. The TER is now a DER (Double Ejection Rack).

In missions such as this, I wonder as to the wisdom of this kind of change-off. We send a flight of four to another country for one lousy truck. The operating costs seem to more than offset the cost of one truck. And we may not even get the truck.

Costs of a typical Phantom mission (1966 Dollars):

    F-4 Unit cost: Two million dollars

    Sparrow missile: $25,000 each

    Sidewinder missile: $5,000 each

    Gattling Cannon: $300 per second

    Fuel: $1,400 per hour to operate (2,390 gallons used in a typical combat mission)

We are risking two-million-dollar aircraft and crew members every time we send them over enemy territory. The Russians, Czechs, Chinese, and others can keep giving aid in the form of trucks and other goods to the North Viets. And it just increases the cost of war to us. It looks like a prolonged conflict with us standing to lose a lot. The Viets don't want us here. We're tearing their country apart and for what? Supposedly for them. There have been some great errors of judgment here.

At least half the workers here on base are VC. We know it and the government knows it. Yet we don't press demands that our base be staffed only with American personnel. We'll feel it someday. When they get a thorough knowledge of the interior workings and layout of Cam Ranh, we'll get hit in some way.

Also going against a single truck means that we'll someday get (hurt). Someday they'll (North Viets) set up a flak-trap with a truck and then—zap!

June 1, 1966:

Very short mission today. About five-minute's worth. It is still an out-country mission because that is what the frag order said. I had full nose-down trim on takeoff. This is the first time I've heard of it in the F-4. The gauge read full-down while I was taxiing out. I wasn't sure whether it was a bad gauge or not, so I monitored it on take-off. The gauge was right and I shot a straight-in approach carrying full fuel and two napalm cans. Final airspeed read 170 knots, about 35K above normal, with the on-speed light on. Tomorrow, two more missions.

LETTERS HOME:

June 1, 1966:

"Well, into June and the time is flying by. Seventy-nine days gone and 285 left. This is my 238th day in the Far East this year. It's almost like home except for the reconstituted milk and all. I am really looking forward to a vanilla shake or a glass of real milk.

"I flew my 29th combat mission today and have two more tomorrow. Since the 11th of May, I've flown 17. The flying is getting very easy. I've noticed that I've picked up a great deal of ability to alertly keep track of many things at once in my missions. Of the 29 missions, 14 have been at the same distance from the base and flying to the target is a relaxing time. However, a couple of minutes prior to diving on the target, we become alert to many things. This constant observance of things is itself becoming rather habit-forming. The necessity of war and an enemy that is firing at you greatly increases proficiency. I'd never fired a gun from an aircraft before doing it down here for real. Our strikes are hurting the enemy bad. Many of the reports you read about the ground troops killing so many of the enemy with light losses to themselves is the result of our hits. The ground forces claim the kills for themselves. It's a case of the ground troops looking for the enemy, making initial contact, and then calling us in. With the 20mm cannon and napalm we can do a great deal of damage.

"Another weapon has entered our inventory within the last month. It is a 500-pound bomb with a retard capability. Upon release from the aircraft, fins break open. Accuracy in dive attacks with this has been amazing. The FACs have been doing amazing work spotting the enemy concentrations, trucks, etc. They are the ones winning this war for us. They are doing a great job. Now, if they would only let us loose on good targets, we could start mopping up their supply capability and start concentrating on reduction of their forces.

"Sometimes I get very discouraged when I see the Vietnamese and wonder whether they are worth expending American lives on. For them, I don't think so, but we are in no position now to quit. We have to continue. I once wrote you a letter and detailed the reasons why we should fight. The reasons are still valid, but from what I've seen of the Viets, they don't treat us as friends and allies. The people who work here on base are brought in by truck. They are in a pathetic position. The real losers in this war are not the opposing armies, but the poor peasants caught in the middle. I've gone in and shot up many villages, bombed and napalmed them. It's a pity, but that's the way the war must be fought.

"The innocents that we are forced to kill are the unfortunate byproduct of war in their country. That's the real tragedy. There is very little actual land mass within South Vietnam that we control. Yes, we can move our armies with immediate swiftness, unknown in previous wars, through the land as though it were our own. We are on the offense. However, when our forces leave an area, the VC return and control it. It is difficult for a villager, because he cannot afford to offend any side.

"The Koreans handle the situation a little differently than we do. Going into a village area north of Saigon, the Koreans asked each village chief if there were any VC in the villages. Each said "no" and the Koreans left a detachment of six in each village. Next day, they returned and found the detachment killed in one village. The Koreans killed everyone in the village: men, women and children. Then they went to the other village chiefs and told them what they had done. Again, they asked if there were VC in the villages and in one they got 57. Very effective the Koreans.

"The VC are the most vicious. I'd hate to tell you what they've done to some of our troops and to village chiefs, etc. This is something that you don't see much of back home.[25]

Author's Note: 25. According to USAF Intelligence, by the time I had left SEA, the VC had killed one-third of the chiefs in the 15,000 villages of South Vietnam. Their preferred method of killing was to disembowel the chief in front of his villagers and family and then behead him.

"The VC shot down an Intelligence Mohawk out of Nha Trang and captured the crew. They then proceeded to skin the crew. When we got to them, the crew was still alive but all died shortly thereafter.

"The US has adopted a few methods, which might turn your stomach and make you wonder what has happened to us. This is the type of war we are fighting down here. One method of interrogation is to tie the hands of men behind their backs and take them for a helicopter ride. We then ask the men information. If they do not talk, we push them out @500 feet. Then we ask the next man. This tends to loosen their tongues.

"Militarily, the war can be won, but it will be a useless victory. This area is very backward. The villages are all thatched huts. Laos is a landlocked nothing. The only machinery they seem to have is of a military nature.

"The country worth protecting down here is Thailand. The Thais are a great and friendly people. Our efforts there are growing daily.

"While we may have 250,000 troops in S. Vietnam, the US has 350,000 in SEA and growing. So you see, the war is not localized. You'd be amazed at what is going on down here. So many wars and sides it's hard for us to keep track.

"Our 'great allies' the French are here too, only they're at the other end of the barrel this time. I don't know what they hope to accomplish, but this is a hell of a way to repay us for digging them out of their own hole in several wars.

"When I was shot down, I was possibly hit by small arms or automatic fire from the ground troops or else received damage from the target exploding. They were loaded trucks and I was 25 to 50 feet off the deck. I had no fire, but didn't have much time either. Ejection was none too soon."

COMBAT DIARY:

June 2, 1966:

Two missions within South Vietnam today and both with two 500# retard bombs and the usual cannon.

The first was in support of the 1st Air Cavalry Operation Crazy Horse. It was against VC bunkers in preparation for creation of a landing zone for the choppers. The Cavalry push was in a valley area near Vinh Thanh to the north of here. The target area was alive with fire, according to the rest of the flight members. I didn't see it, but there were 50-caliber and small-arms fire at us from the target area on a jungle-covered ridge. Dave Warren said that it looked like my second bomb wiped out the 50-caliber-gun position. My gun jammed on the strafe, so I didn't get in on it and had to fly high. Both my bombs hit right on the VC. I felt my heart beating awfully fast on the passes. My head tells me one thing and my heart tells me another. BDA: 1 AW site and 5 KBA (probable)

The second mission was just plain lousy. We hit peasants working in the fields in a VC area. We are supposed to attack working peasants as though they are the enemy just because they are in a VC controlled area? This is just plain stupid.[26]

Fired 316 rounds of HEI. We're back on restricted ammo use. BDA: 400 meters of crop destroyed. Can you believe that?

Aircraft losses:

Author's Note: *26. Whenever we were tasked to bomb or shoot peasants, all of us seemed to miss them by significant distances. Nobody would ever say a thing. We just tossed our bombs, making sure they did not bother the peasants.*

Rosato and Ogle got hit north of Pleiku this afternoon on an alert scramble. They went against three machine-gun positions with napalm and got plastered. Ogle made it out and was reported picked up. Rosato, an old head, didn't make it out. Seat or canopy must have jammed. (Fate is the hunter.) [27]

My roommate George Larson had another front seat ride today and encountered heavy ground fire. It's starting to get rough. It turned out that when Griffey and Glandon got killed, Major Solis, who was in his flight, picked up three hits. It looks like Griffey and Glandon were hit with a burst instead of having the retards explode on release, as was suspected. [28]

So far, since the 12th has moved to Vietnam, we've been amazingly lucky. Only seven planes downed (to combat) and six pilots gone. First plane downed was Jim Sala and Wranosky from the 557th. They either spun in or got hit? Both were killed. Then Conlon from the 557th was and is still missing on the FAC exchange program. Jack Gagen and Frank Malagarie got hit and punched out over Laos. Both are okay. They are from our squadron, the 559th. Conlon went down in an O-1 and is probably dead.

Jim Knock and Captain Street, from the 557th, got shot down near Pleiku. Both came through in good shape. The fourth plane was Paul's and mine. Fifth was Giere and Jim Knock again, when they went in the Bay (operational loss). The sixth was Terry's and the seventh was Rosato's today.

The area north of Pleiku is hot. The Plei Mrong Special Forces Camp was evacuated yesterday and everyone went to Duc To.

Politically Speaking:

I can't see why we are sent against these people, just because it is a VC area. This is like hitting the French during WWII simply because they were occupied by the Germans at the time. Poor peasants. I really didn't give a damn where my bombs fell.

June 3, 1966:

Sat spare this afternoon after a morning spent on mobile control. The first flight had a bird lose brakes and they had to use the emergency system to keep from running into the fuel pits. I was scrambled in his place.

The target was a ridge just north of the Special Forces camp at A Shau. A Shau was the camp completely overrun by the enemy and its landing strip is officially termed "closed" on all the flight maps. Supposedly there were 12 structures on the ridge. The bomb-damage assessment gave us two structures destroyed and one damaged.

On the way back, we heard a Navy A-4 get hit and go straight-in at Pleiku. No need for rescue on that one. Ground fire has really been picking up.

June 4, 1966:

Close air support today for the 1st Air Cavalry in Operation Crazy Horse to the north of here. The target was a VC-held mountain ridge with supplies in the way of the 1st Cavs' advance. The incidence of ground fire has been increasing lately and this mission was no exception. The FAC was hit twice prior to our arrival and they

Author's Note: *27. "Old heads" are the guys who have been around for a while. It has nothing to do with age.*
28. During the time I was there, Cam Ranh lost two flights of two aircraft each on Sky Spot missions over North Vietnam. The flights just disappeared from the Sky Spot radar screens immediately after the retards were released. It had been determined that a retard had prematurely exploded just after release on both flights. Those malfunctions in new bombs cost us four Phantoms and eight pilots lost.

were firing heavily on the ground. The load was napalm. Contacted Top Sail Foxtrot on the tactical frequency and about four FACs were talking to us at the same time. I dropped my load in a one-shot ripple delivery and they were long. The BDA was three buildings destroyed—all by my long napalm. They burned pretty.

June 6, 1966:

Two in-country strikes in support of Operation Fillmore, to the south of Tuy Hoa. We hit the village of Hoa Son in a valley just off the coast. The first mission was napalm and I carried two cans. The FAC directed me against the target by distance and direction from his Willy Pete (white phosphorus flare) smoke. I couldn't help myself and changed course at the last minute to hit a French-style home to the right of run-in. It was a beautiful two-story concrete building with a red tile roof, larger than the other homes in the area. My first can went over the house into some other houses. The second pass was with the cannon and I was flying about the height of the top of the home. Exploding tiles were bouncing off my canopy. The third pass saw my napalm knocking at his front door. We bent it around and resumed strafing passes. The load was half and half, ball and HEI ammo. I expended 785 shells into the village and we were credited with nine buildings destroyed, 10 damaged.[29]

The afternoon's flight sent us to the same area to bomb a VC base camp. Our flight loads have been split lately between 500-pound retards and napalm. I was loaded with 2X500s and one was a dud. The other was right on and we succeeded in destroying three buildings in the VC camp. The FAC was Ragged Scooper 89 who'd stayed with us for a week down here (at CRB).

He (the FAC) sent us to the village again and we shot it up for seven more buildings destroyed and two damaged. The rounds fired numbered 722.

The duds that we drop are a cause for concern. The retards are relatively newly built ones, but the straight iron bombs are sometimes left over from WWII. We drop either 250s, 500s or 750s that are dumb, iron bombs. All of them do damage, but we drop the 250s when we don't have any of the rest.

If we carry any of the dumb ones, they are usually the 500s or 750s, both of which are big weapons. When they hit, their shock waves can easily be seen spreading out from the blast point. That concussive effect will also kill.

Missions Recap To-Date:

The following is my "score card" of missions flown to-date in SEA:

Structures destroyed, 69; Structures damaged, 32; Trucks destroyed, 6; Trucks damaged, 2; Road cuts, 1; Secondary explosions, 8; KBA: Confirmed, 1; Probable, 10; Automatic Weapon Sites destroyed, 1; Crop Damage, 400 meters.

The following is what ordnance I had to expend to score the damage above:

Bombs: 750s, 4; 500s, 4; Retards, 38; Napalm, 36 cans; Total 51,000 pounds of bombs; Rocket pods, 6 with 105 rockets; Cannon, 8325 rounds.

Looking at the destruction compared to the risk and ordnance expended, it does not seem we are getting our money's worth.

Author's Note: *29. This was an example of how the fangs can come out in an attack. To this day, some of my missions still stand out in my mind as vividly as they did at the time of the attack. This mission with the red-tile roof and the tiles continually bouncing off my canopy was one of those vivid strikes. On one of the strikes against a beautiful multi-storied, red-tiled building, I asked the FAC who had built it and he said it was USAID (Agency for International Development). This is a case of the United States using taxpayer's dollars to build a structure and I am using taxpayer's dollars to destroy it. Made about as much sense as the War.*

July 7, 1966:

Scrambled off alert today. Target was two companies of VC near Can Tho, south of Saigon. On the way down, we saw the smoke of an F-4 that crashed and burned on take-off from Phan Rang. The pilots made it out okay. They jumped and ran.

I carried 4 napalm cans, which did good work on the area. Lead had six high-drags (HD). The BDA was 4 buildings destroyed and six damaged. I think it was more than that, but the FAC never flew too low so he couldn't get good BDA. My gun jammed after the first pass. I had used it to keep the VC heads down on the napalm run-in.

Run-ins on napalm drops make the aircraft vulnerable to the defenses because the run-in is flown level. If the attack is a dive, the enemy gunner has to figure altitude as well as azimuth. On a nape attack, he does not have to worry about the altitude changing.

Total rounds-fired was 60. We didn't get a head count and won't until possibly later.

Lead was going to go in for strafe, but we were called to go down to fly cover for a VNAF plane that had just been shot down in the Delta area. We couldn't find the plane while we were down there and neither did anyone else. The Delta areas are much more open than many of our target areas. It is very flat with sparse tree growth and is a large rice-growing region, which needs open space.

After looking for the downed pilot, Flight Control sent us back to the original target area because of some hot target that had been spotted. It turned out to be either a false alarm or another flight got it. We were low on fuel so we landed at Bien Hoa, near Saigon.

The Army, on one of their patrols, found Rosato still in the aircraft and buried him on the spot. The flight back was logged as my 37th combat mission.

June 8, 1966:

Observation: The morale around here seems to be going down. Perhaps it is due to this being the in-between period for most of the troops. That period where they've been here a long time and they still have a long time to go. Some in our squadron are beginning to see glimpses of the end and this gives them a little hope, which is bad at this time. I can't be permitted that luxury.

While most of the Aircraft Commanders in this squadron, and some of the backseaters, flew missions against North Vietnam from Thailand (as members of the 45th out of Ubon), the rest of us still have a long way to go. Many in the 559th will be leaving in August. Major Wells, our Squadron Commander, leaves in two weeks. These will be hard times for those of us who stay. July should see an influx of new blood into the Wing. Two men leave today from the 557th to go to various stateside assignments. Tomorrow, I'll be eligible to take a few days off and get away from here.

Perhaps another reason for the sinking morale is the increased intensity of the war during the last few weeks. That is, the war as we see it, with the ground fire, etc. Perhaps it is due to friends that we've recently lost here at Cam Ranh. It is probably all these things with the rumor of impending northern missions thrown in. Sparrow and Sidewinder missiles are reportedly on base and we may be flying MIG top-cover to the North in a few weeks. This will probably be an intensification of the overall war against the North. The threat of SAM and the heavy anti-aircraft artillery fire will present us with an entirely new outlook on the war. The tension and sweat will be there. The consolation of one-month off our tour for every 20 Northern missions will help.

The F-105s have suffered terrible losses up North. The fellows back from the morning missions say that a Buick bird from Takhli was downed in the North. Many days they lose two birds. Sooner or later they'll run out of Thunderchiefs with that attrition rate. We didn't produce that many. They are vulnerable and I have a sneaking suspicion that our country is utilizing the F-105 against the toughest targets because their loss and subsequent replacement with more modern aircraft, like the Phantom, would serve to modernize the force. It makes it hell on the F-105 Thud drivers.

One ever-present danger is going against targets that have guns at the point of attack or are located where you are aiming. It is a simplification of the gunners tracking problem. When a gunner fires from a vantage point away from the line-of-flight, he has the problem of proper azimuth, target speed and vertical angle. The distance to lead an aircraft is something a gunner must learn with experience. When an aircraft is approaching directly at the gunner, if the gunner has the nerve to stay and fire with the airborne cannon approaching, he can fire directly at the aircraft and only be concerned with distance, vertical angle, and bullet drop due to gravity. Those are small problems to consider.

The probability is greatly increased of the gunners putting bullets down our engine intake and exploding the engine. We are at a disadvantage in this environment, if we take these things into consideration. The airborne platform seldom can see the ground gunner, unless we see the muzzle flashes in the jungle below. An answer would be to put a cannon-burst in on the target as we are going in on each bomb run. However, the F-4 gun has been failing while we are in on target due to a theorized electrical transient in the system for the Bomb Arm, Nose-Tail switch being armed. Se we just decided to forego this method unless it is critical situation.

Conversely, the ground gunners have a problem with the jungle canopy. They have to be able to directly see the aircraft to fire at it and this is often hampered by foliage. This is one great reason to fly very low and very fast. To fire at the FAC spotter plane would disclose the gunner's location and invite rapid retaliation from the fighter-bombers orbiting above. Ground troops often get around this by barrage-fire at a point in space where they think the plane will fly over. Thus, it is advantageous for us to vary our run-in headings, unless precluded by terrain. We also have to keep in mind the smoke and shrapnel debris thrown up by the bomb from the preceding aircraft. With the high-drag bombs, this requires plenty of spacing.

Back to the tactic of barrage-fire: The only place the ground troops can be assured of hitting an aircraft with the barrage fire, considering the varied run-in headings, is at the probable target position itself. This is rather hazardous considering the frying effects of napalm and the shock effects of bombs, which can jelly a man's brain without ever subjecting him to shrapnel. This shock action can be readily seen from the air as it fans out after a bomb detonates. It is like the shock visibly seen on a wing when the aircraft reaches compressibility at Mach .92 and when some of the airflow over the fuselage and wing borders on the supersonic.

Even the target position is varied when we hit area targets. A napalm attack followed up with cannon fire can be devastating to troops caught in an unprotected area. The enemy has been suffering enormous casualties with this type of attack. Unless the target is completely socked in by weather for many days, they'll never be able to launch another Dien Bien Phu. Any massing of troops and machinery only gives us a lucrative target to hit. Our Army now possesses a mobility it never had before. The French never had any of the mobility we have, nor did they have the air strength that we have that can come off both solid and floating fields.

Today's mission was a two-can napalm attack against "one" hooch. The presence of a VC Battalion, which was supposed to be around it, was never verified. Sometimes it is hard to see anything down there in the jungle. I have yet to see anybody on the ground in an air strike.

We destroyed the hooch, but again were given no further BDA due to foliage. The target was on a mountain just above a valley and rather difficult to hit with napalm. We dove the cans in. Napalm is pretty easy as far as sight-settings are concerned. With airspeeds from 450 to 500 knots, a MIL setting of 40 will pretty well do the job from most angles. Have to wait sometimes until it feels "right" though.

One final note on the day's mission: Dave Warren only dropped one can and that was from pretty high up. He had pre-ignition on it. The other can didn't drop and he landed still loaded with it. As the aircraft touched, the can released and bounced end-over-end down the runway alongside his aircraft. The release was probably caused by the jolt of the landing. There was neither can ignition nor any aircraft damage as it followed him down the runway. Those witnessing said it was a funny sight. Only in wartime.

Memorial services for Joe Rosato were held this morning.

LETTERS HOME:
June 10, 1966:

"Just a short note to let you know all is well. The calendar says that I have 277 days left and have already been over here for 87 days. Tomorrow I leave for Okinawa on a little "ostensible" TDY just to get away. I'll be gone five days. When I get back, 1/4th of my time will have been over.

"Missions have been going well and I haven't picked up any hits on my aircraft. The war here is the South has picked up and we don't fly so far away for most of our missions. The Wing here has been dealing some tough blows to the VC. When they get massed, all we have to do is go in and pour napalm and cannon fire on them and we not only kill a lot of them, but destroy their offensive punch.

"In Thailand, tanks, trucks, ammo and other supplies are being stockpiled and we already have enough to support a division. We already are operating fighters out of Ubon, Udorn, Takhli, Korat and Nakhon Phanom (NKP). Vicellio is at Nakhon Phanom, on the Laotian border and it is primarily props there as well as Udorn.

"Cambodia is being used increasingly as a sanctuary by the VC, but they really aren't so safe there. We've wrecked over a 1,000 trucks on the Ho Chi Minh Trail and this is bound to have hurt them.

"There is a question I have been pondering. The question of getting out: pro or con. A further note on my career question: I'll have to forecast within about two months for my next duty station and job. It all hinges on several things. First is the war. If it lasts and it looks like it will, I'll be subject to recall back to the fighting at some future date. They are now starting to move pilots out of non-primary flying jobs into primary flying jobs in preparation for a tour of duty over here. Also, the movement out of bombers is freeing a lot of pilots for fighter-bomber and transport duty. However, many of the bomber pilots are older men. The average age of an Aircraft Commander in SAC is 40 years old and they have not taken well to flying fighters. The increase in those wishing to get out is and will continue to be a factor. Therefore, if I stay in I'll have to consider the possible redeployment back here after say two to three years. It all, of course, hinges on the extent of our commitment in the future. If they would open up more lucrative targets, we could make shorter work of it.

"If I do stay in, my move directly out of Vietnam will be to graduate school, then possibly to a joint planning staff or Academy instruction. As I have always contemplated my career, I must get out of primary flying and get some place where I can use my head. It is better to get a balance career-wise. Therefore, if I

stay, it will be graduate school. That is if the Air Force Fighter Branch lets me go? The Air Force Institute of Technology has already accepted me for grad training and will send me to a civilian school. I will have my choice out of three universities. If the Air Force decides to send me non-voluntarily to a school, that will give me an additional service commitment. They can do this by regulations. I have to serve one year at my next duty station, but I can't afford to do anything which will give me an additional commitment. Therefore, I won't go to Europe because of the commitment.

"Three days ago, I went on another longevity step in the Air Force. Four years of active duty, which means a $16.00 raise (whew) and a service ribbon. Within the last six weeks, I've earned: the Vietnamese Service Medal, the Purple Heart and the National Defense Service Medal and almost a second Air Medal. They give them for missions flown. So these all may have a bearing on my career, if I stay in.

"It's getting near dinner so I'll close for now. I've given up poker for a while. I lost more than $50 last night to almost balance the $80 that I won at craps while at Clark.

"Was sitting at the 'O' Club having a coke this afternoon when a freak 'dust devil' hit a part of the roof and it fell in. Wonder if that was the part that the pilots built? Didn't know what the hell happened. I think it is safer flying.

"Off to Okie."

COMBAT DIARY:

June 17, 1966:

Another trip to Okinawa: It has been nine days since my last flight. Part of the gap was caused by another bombing halt to "convince" the North Viets to bargain.[30]

Several of us took advantage of the break to take a little TDY (R&R) to Okinawa. Enjoyable stay and I picked up a lot of goodies. Came back by way of Tan Son Nhut Airport at Saigon. I was with Jack Gagen and Jack Kelley and we stayed at a VOQ in downtown Saigon.

To say the situation in Saigon is confusing is only putting it mildly. Tan Son Nhut may have started out as a VNAF base, but it is in reality an American Air Base that is loaded with troops. The base is laid out as though there was no plan. Buildings stuck here and there. Barbed wire and bunkers all over.

The night we landed, the Buddhists were demonstrating downtown with tear gas and burnings. Quite a mess. The VOQ was just a little Oriental-French style apartment with pull-chain plumbing. It had no telephone and the clerk didn't speak English. The VOQ had one guard at the gate in a sandbagged bunker.

The morning we left, we had to jump an MP jeep and go about a half-mile to a telephone to call transport at the base. It was a hectic two hours trying to get picked up because the Buddhists were demonstrating very near and shooting up American cars, jeeps and then burning them. This seems an easy way for the VC to damage our military without retaliation. They can claim that they are Buddhists or whoever they want to be.

On the way to the base, we picked up an American military driver whose truck was on the side of the road with a flat. The Buddhists had covered the road with nails. I got out and picked up a few and they were

---

Author's Note: *30. We stood-down many times for these so-called bombing halts. They often changed their names to things like "bombing pauses," or "stand downs," etc. but the effect was the same. Long after my return to the States, I could find no record of the multiple halts we were subjected to. The results were very counter-productive to our campaign of supplies, equipment and personnel interdiction in the North.*

constructed so that they could be thrown (not placed) and every one would be effective as they were shaped like a pyramid with spikes. It is a good design. These guys are organized.

Tan Son Nhut has RF-4Cs and RF-101s for the RVN recce work. The rest of the base is full of transports. The other day, when we went to Bien Hoa (which is close by Saigon), they had the 3rd TFW with F-100s plus a squadron of F-5s. Only eleven F-5s left however. The F-5s are part of a special Air Force program called "Skoshi Tiger."

All the F-4s at Udorn, Thailand are being moved to Ubon for Night Owl (night flights) work. The F-104s are being moved in to go against the MIGs. The 555th Triple Nickel Squadron, from the old 12th TFW at MacDill, shot down a total of five MIGs at Ubon.

The F-104s are just an engine with stub wings. It was another one of Kelly Johnson's creations out of the Lockheed "Skunk Works" at Burbank Airport. It is a great air-defense interceptor, but does not have much fuel capacity. We have heard that the Air Force is equipping them with bomb racks on either side of the fuselage and not under the tiny wings as the rest of the fighter-bombers. This seems lousy aircraft utilization, because the F-104 is definitely not an attack aircraft.

Upon return to Cam Ranh, I found out that our (B) Flight was still doing well. Larry Dahle hit a big tree and had Class 26ed (totaled) the aircraft. The same day Dave Warren caught fire on takeoff and flew all the way around the pattern and landed.

At Kadena Air Base, I picked up a lot of items such as towel racks, door handles, etc. for my room in the Quonset. I also ate a steak at just about every meal. It was just tremendous food.

The mission today was about my best and also my longest in distance. We flew up to Tchepone, Laos, which is about 340 miles from Cam Ranh. Tchepone is a very dangerous location with heavy defenses. It is at a very important Trail crossroads. On the way up, Hillsboro Control (call sign John Austin) diverted us up to the target. We were a flight of three aircraft. I carried four cans of napalm and the other guys two each. No gun however.

The target was a self-propelled anti-aircraft artillery piece supported by automatic weapons (AW) positions. It sounded like suicide with napalm and I never did as much jigging of the aircraft. My first pass was nerve-racking. I swung very wide to insure a stable approach and also to ensure that I got my desired approach vector. The gun was on tracks like a large tank. The FAC reported that the huge gun barrel was slowly swinging in my direction. He kept giving me flight updates on the position of the gun barrel as it swung. The long inbound run-in seemed to take forever, but I wanted to make it right. It was a race between the gun barrel and me and he almost had it pointed at me when I hit him. My napalm destroyed the big gun, which made the FAC ecstatic. He told us that it was the biggest gun he had ever seen.

On my second pass, I dropped the third of my four napes and destroyed a few of the AW positions near the big gun. On my third pass, I dropped the remaining one and the FAC went ballistic. Apparently the gas took out an AAA site along with another couple of Automatic Weapons positions. He was terrifically elated. I felt good.[31]

Hillsboro was listening in and personally congratulated me on the way home. This was the only time I could ever recall Hillsboro doing this for any flight. I felt it was quite an honor, especially for a wingman.

Author's Notes: *31. I was awarded the Distinguished Flying Cross for this mission.*

June 20, 1966:

Flew a night flight under the control of Sky Spot against a target south of Pleiku. Pleiku is located in the Central Highlands and is the location of one of our smaller airfields. We just dropped two clean 500-pound bombs from a level 20,000 feet with no BDA.

Learned last night that a C-130 flight flying from here to Okinawa, carrying 14 people, was downed in the water and all lost. No idea what happened. Two of the pilots from the 391st were in the aircraft going R&R. I had flown on that same flight to Okinawa.[32]

Two FACs who slept with us in the Quonset have been killed in the last month. One slept in Sorrick's rack for a week. Miller was his name and he was ready to go home.

June 23, 1966:

This was the first mission of our new commitment. The base has been getting committed more and more and our free time has been getting less and less. First of all, General Moore said that our base had the highest abort rate of the theater. So, Colonel Chase, our new Wing Commander, has one crew sitting spare beside an aircraft for each flight. This not only commits more of the pilot's time, but also is putting an increased burden on maintenance.

Then 7th Air Force told us to increase the crews on Alert from two to four. And finally, we are committed to about 10 or 11 hours of MIG Screen over the Gulf every day. For this they cut three in-country missions. They make up for the three cuts by scrambling the alert birds all the time, some of them on pre-selected targets. That is not how we are supposed to use Alert. The maintenance guys are really hurting.

The new commitment, "Big Eye," lasted 4:50 hours and was rather uneventful, if very confusing. We fly our mission and then fly south to gas up with a tanker located in the southern portion of the Gulf of Tonkin. The screen is about 20-50 miles off the coast and up and down off Haiphong. We flew between 20-25,000 feet and could see both the North Vietnamese mainland and Hainan Island off Red China.[33]

Made a total of four hookups with the tanker and offloaded about 28,000 pounds of fuel. Only one ID pass made. Saw the aircraft carriers Hancock and Ranger, with their destroyers and destroyer escorts, in the middle of the Gulf on Yankee Station. The Gulf was really hopping with aircraft. We seem to consider the water our territory and will shoot anything down that comes off the mainland, either Vietnamese or Chinese. This seems a strange position for us to take, but we are at war.[34]

Author's Notes: *32. It was later determined that the VC had placed a bomb, probably in the form of a satchel charge, inside before takeoff.*
33. Several months later, after the original 12th pilots left, I started leading some of the Big Eye flights. At those times, I would not use the Air Force "Connie" and its airborne radar. Instead, I contacted Navy radar aboard their destroyers. The naval radars were much better than the Air Force and I just operated with them and moved the flight right over Haiphong or just off the coast for better contact.
34. If we got close enough to see the aircraft markings of the MIGs, we were too close. Thus, the nationality of any MIG could not be determined. Our duty was to protect the Navy carriers and their Task Forces as well as our own reconnaissance aircraft. Any foreign aircraft that approached our fleet was a potential threat and would either be chased away or shot down. On one Big Eye, I chased a MIG back over Hainan, however I did not venture over land. I figured he must have been Chinese since he seemed to come from Hainan and escaped back to their territory.

June 25, 1966:

After quite a few days of ground aborts and no available aircraft when scheduled, I fly again. I did today what I meant never to do: flying after I'd had a "night" at the Club. It was with my new Squadron Commander, Major Stockman. The flight was lousy.

My four rocket pods were all shot on target, but I ingested part of the rocket fins and some part of the malfunctioning rockets and got FOD in the engines. The commander got mad at me for screwing up radio channel changes.

The area was a VC assembly area and we were given 100% ordnance on target with one VC killed. Maintenance is still hurting badly.

Militarily Speaking:

I'd like to comment on a conversation I had with an U.S. Army Captain who flies a chopper for the Korean troops up at Tuy Hoa. The following are bits of information gained from our conversations and are highlighted by italics:

Within South Vietnam are Chinese Hmung and Philippino mercenaries who are periodically dropped into Laos in unmarked Air America choppers. The Chinese Hmung soldiers are indigenous to SEA, but of Chinese origin.

The mercenaries are required to seek out and find units infiltrating down the Trail. They are charged to follow the movement of the troops into either Cambodia or Vietnam, and to keep contact with them. Cambodia is harboring many NVN regiments. American 1st Air Cav Division troops have moved 20 miles deep into Cambodia to destroy the battalions that were using the sanctuary after they had struck the Cavalry units.

During several operations with ROKs and the 101st, prisoners were pushed out of the chopper doors during interrogation and even one out of his own chopper.

During shifts of troops into landing zones (sticks of choppers), the choppers would find ground fire developing on the second and third lifts into the drop zones. The fire would develop from the ARVN themselves who would move out and establish a perimeter and then turn the perimeter inward and fire on the choppers that had just delivered them. One of his chopper gunners found a grenade with the pin pulled under the seats where the ARVN soldiers had been seated.

His chopper gunners have standing orders to gun down any ARVN soldiers who turn and face the choppers after offloading. The reason for this is to keep them from firing at the choppers as previously mentioned.

What a war and these are our ARVN brothers? The Korean interrogation techniques must be SOP for them. I was told the same story when I arrived at CRB by the old 45th guys about the Korean cleansing of the bare base before arrival of our planes.

The ROKs are a little unhappy that their job here is primarily security and that they are not used as offensive units. They want to get out and fight.

Operations that are presently underway in II Corp areas are: (1) Ethan Allen, (2) Paul Revere, (3) Hooker

---

Author's Notes: *35 (next page). A "stick" of choppers is what they refer to a line of helicopters moving across the landscape on a mission. They often posed problems for us. Flying low over the jungle canopy to avoid enemy gunners, we would occasionally come upon a "stick" of choppers traversing an area. Sometimes we would only have a few seconds to avoid them and that would be by "hopping" over the stick with just a few feet to spare, which I am sure would surprise the choppers.*

and (4) Hawthorne. Two Corp is the hottest at the present time and this is Cam Ranh Bay's prime area of operations.[35]

Another problem we would sometimes encounter on low-level flights just above the jungle canopy would be dead trees. Occasionally very tall trees would grow above the rest of the canopy and be exposed. For some reason, those trees would invariably die and their gray-colored, dead trucks would be hard to see. More than one Cam Ranh plane hit these hard-to-see, lonely sentinels.

Politically Speaking:

We had a strange brief from a guy from Saigon on the "Silver Dawn" missions in the Gulf. He mentioned the Rules of Engagement under which we operate. He stated that after we had hit within 10 miles of Hanoi on one strike, Hanoi complained to Washington that we had broken the "rule." He said that Washington's answer was that they had changed the rules. The briefing officer was highly critical of the way the war is being run and rightly stated that it is a political war.

There must be some element of truth in what he says and the concept of Hanoi-Washington correspondence is rather hard to believe. To be having a conversation with the enemy about an issue of how we are fighting the war, sounds like our government is treating this as a negotiation rather than the carnage that it has inflicted upon us.

June 26, 1966:

I'm now sitting alert at the trailers. This is one phase of my job that I dislike. Not knowing whether we will go or not, is unsettling. We are just sitting here waiting for the bell to go off for 12 hours. Sometimes it feels as though it is a sort of "bell to hell."

We sat air defense alert in Okinawa, but that was a controlled situation and this isn't. Today we started at 5 a.m., so it will be about 13.5 hours on. We 'll get scrambled for sure, maybe twice, but the waiting for the bell is what gets me.

We launched off the pad against a VC assembly area and it turned out to be one of the best BDA flights yet flown from Cam Ranh Bay. At the time, it seemed as though it was just another mission against the trees, but it turned out to be a little more. I was carrying four cans of napalm.

We passed over a Special Forces Camp during the attack and bent around the camp as we approached the target, which was beside a village. The village lay by a river and the camp was on top of a high hill next to it. A lot of the Special Forces guys on the hill were out looking at the fireworks. We rocked our wings in "hello" to them and they waved back.

I flew the usual racetrack pattern and hit the area with lots of gun and napes. On each pass, I flew downwind over the Special Forces camp and rocked my wings. Then I flew base leg and my final was with a lot of fire.

We were not given any BDA off the target, but learned after we got back that the Army had moved in after our two aircraft and four A-1Es had hit the area. The Army counted 78 VC bodies. They sent our base a congratulatory telegram and we were given a letter of appreciation from Colonel Allen, who is the Wing DO (Director of Operations).

June 28, 1966:

To follow up the fine last mission of yesterday, today we have a lousy mission. I carried two cans of nape to an area in Laos on the 005 radial at 46 miles from TACAN Channel 72 near Saravane. It was a camouflaged and partially damaged truck. The target was down a shallow canyon, which had trees of the same color as the earth. The truck was just off the road and was hidden by trees as we approached. Number two bird had camera pods and was photographing the whole affair while dropping napalm. I couldn't see the truck and we all missed it. It was raining and the clouds were overcast with low visibility. Keeping the flight members in sight was a job in itself. I didn't like the looks of the situation and had my eyes more on what was going on around me rather than on the target.

We didn't have any BDA. I fired 75 rounds in a short burst from my pistol to try to mark the target.

June 29, 1966:

This was a mission with four napes against a canal and the huts and sampans along its banks. Everything went as per usual only we encountered scattered sniper fire. No one hit. The BDA was five structures destroyed, four damaged and one sampan destroyed.

June 30, 1966:

We scrambled only five minutes after going on alert as Boxer 05 flight. The target was a VC unit near Tuy Hoa that was pinned down. We each carried four napalm cans apiece.

Plotnitsky was lead and had utility hydraulic failure as we reached the target. He should have passed the lead to his element lead, but didn't. As a result, we wasted our napalm. We dumped the cans in the South China Sea and headed in. I landed out of a straight–in approach due to my heavy fuel load. Plot's tail hook skipped over the emergency barrier and he hit burner and went around for another try.

Took a walk this evening and was amazed at how much the base has grown. It's getting to be a good-sized city. It's rather exciting to be in the ground floor of what may one day be a huge facility.

I, of course, had no way of realizing the significance of that evening for me. That night I was a combat veteran with 46 missions behind me. I did not know that my experience had only been a preparation for what was to come. There was no announcement. There was no specific day when we shifted from the South and Laos to the North. It just happened.

Our commanders never said a thing. They just got the missiles stored on base and waited. Over 100 missions still lay ahead of me and the next day would mark the beginning of a four-month period that would change my life. The month started out innocently enough, but we soon saw a significant increase in the number of missions flown over the Gulf. It remained to the last week of July for me to experience my first bombing mission against the North. It would not be my last.

In 1967 and 1968, the Air Force started the operational development of the later-called "smart bombs." There were multiple "Pave" programs that featured the introduction of newly-developed television and laser-guided bombs. The Phantom acted as a test-launch-platform and Laos acted as a test-bed of sorts. We mounted and dropped 2,000-pound smart bombs of varying descriptions. The bombs were too heavy for our

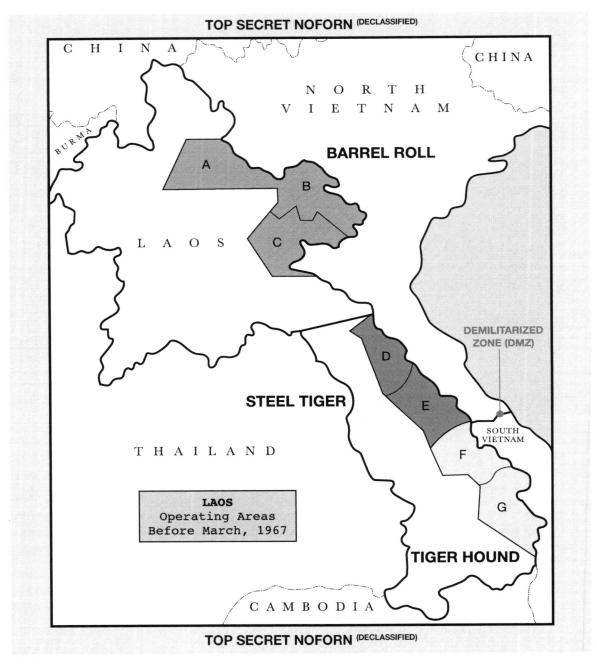

Laos Operating Areas Prior to March, 1967 — *"Barrel Roll" operations were against the Communists in the Laotian Civil War. The three operating areas of "Barrel Roll" are depicted in orange (A, B, and C). The four operating areas of "Steel Tiger" are depicted in green (D and E) and yellow (F and G), with the yellow portion being "Tiger Hound."*

The Thai bases operated against the orange and green areas and while Cam Ranh and Danang operated against the yellow area, which was the most intense area of interdiction for supplies, equipment and troops coming to South Vietnam from the North on the Ho Chi Minh Trail.

wings so they were placed on our bomb ejection racks mounted centerline under our fuselage.

Among those delivery and guidance methods developed in Laos was one where a Phantom circling over the target would pinpoint the target with a laser beam and the smart bombs dropped by his flight would then follow the beam down to the target. Another method had the dropping pilot pinpoint the target via laser and then the information was transmitted internally to the bomb so that it could complete its trajectory to impact. A third had the dropping pilot illuminate the target from bomb release to impact. This method proved very harmful to the pilot's health.

The utilization of Laos was to determine which method was the most effective when dropping against defended targets and the pilots had to also contend with evading those defensive guns while still illuminating the target with the lasers. Obviously, the less time spent by the pilot getting the bomb on its correct path the better.

A bomb was not a rocket and thus did not have any internal propulsive power.

Thus, the pilot still had to drop the weapon so that gravity would propel it and the laser would only guide it. The drop speed, altitude and placement were still important to a successful attack.

While SEA "dumb bomb" average CEAs were hovering in the 280-foot range, reported results of the "smart bomb" average CEAs was close to just 30 feet. With the huge impact craters resulting from the 2000-pounders, target destruction was almost assured.

The development program was similar to the German utilization of the Spanish Civil War in the 1930s as an excuse to develop the equipment and tactics later used in its hugely-successful initial military operations during World War II.

When these Laotian-developed "smart bombs" were utilized in the deserts of the Middle East, the U.S. Navy did not have any and "borrowed" the technology from the Air Force when the Navy saw the bomb effectiveness.

Enemy transport using the HCMT carried a majority of their cargo by truck. Interdiction of the Trail was effective enough that, by 1968, 85% of the truck traffic used the cover of darkness to move.

An evaluation of the data on tactical sorties flown, especially at the height of the tactical air war against North Vietnam in 1966 and 1967, shows that over half of the SEA fighter-bomber sorties flown during the author's year in SEA were flown against North Vietnam and Laos.

Tactical Fighter-Bomber Sorties Flown in SEA in 1966:

Country:	Sorties Flown:	Percentage of SEA:	Sorties/ Square Mile:
South Vietnam	124,686	49%	1.85 (67,108 Sq. Mi.)
North Vietnam	81,131	31.9%	1.32 (61,293 Sq. Mi.)
Laos	48,469	19.1%	.53 (91,400 Sq. miles)

The sorties flown per square mile figure is included to show intensity. The sorties flown during the entire bombing period from 1965-1968 shown in the Support Section might lead one to question the BBC claim that Laos was the most bombed nation in history. When one considers that the full fury of the United States Air Force, the United States Navy, the United States Marine Corps, the Royal Laotian Air Force, the CIA Air Force and the other clandestine air forces was focused on Laos after Johnson's Northern Cease Fire, then the validity to the claim makes more sense. That focus made Laos much more heavily bombed than South Vietnam from 1968 through 1973 with fully 60% of the overall effort against Laos.

The secrets from the "Secret War" in Laos has made it difficult to ascertain bombing levels. There are many "estimates" of total tonnage dropped in Laos. The one estimate that is widely claimed is 2.5 million tons of bombs dropped from 1965 through 1973. If this is correct, it does not exceed WWII bombing as far as overall tonnage. However, if it is considered on a per capita basis, then the claim has credibility. The current population of Laos is almost 7 million. In 1966, it was 2,437,000 and in 1973, it was 2,915,000. The United Nations states that .84 tons of explosives were dropped per person in the decade starting in 1965. That estimate is very close to the 2.5 million-ton figure and, on a per capita basis, does make Laos the most bombed nation in history.

From a historical perspective, the massive bombing of Laos achieved none of the goals of the multiple campaigns. This is a stark example of why a war cannot be won entirely from the air, unless one would consider the use of thermonuclear bombs (this is not an advocacy for their use). It seems self-evident, but under almost any circumstance, it is necessary to have a sufficient and capable force on the ground to occupy if a war is to be won through geographical control.

> *"War is mainly a catalog of blunders."*
> Prime Minister Winston Churchill

CHAPTER ELEVEN
"Rolling Thunder"
North Vietnam

> *"We will either find a way, or make one."*
> Carthaginian General Hannibal Barca

OPERATION "ROLLING THUNDER":

<u>Purpose:</u> American Air War of interdiction against North Vietnam

<u>Started:</u> On March 2, 1965 with 100-plane attack against North Vietnam

<u>Partially Ended:</u> On March 31, 1968, President Johnson ordered the military to cease bombing north of the 19th Parallel.

<u>Totally Ended:</u> Total cease-fire ordered on November 1, 1968 by President Johnson

<u>Combat Missions Flown:</u> 304,000 tactical sorties; 2,382 "Arc Light" B-52 strikes; 922 American aircraft shot down.

<u>Results:</u> 77% of ammunition depots destroyed; 60% of POL storage destroyed; 60% of power plants destroyed; 50% of major bridges destroyed; 40% of railroad shops destroyed; 12,000 naval vessels destroyed; 10,000 vehicles destroyed; 2,000 railroad cars and engines destroyed

<u>Reasons for failure:</u> Overly restrictive Rules of Engagement, political interference in military operations, failure to follow the time-tested Principles of War and the lack of a <u>sustained</u> interdiction campaign due to multiple bombing halts and pauses.

TARGET ASSIGNMENTS:

The Pentagon separated North Vietnam into seven targeting areas. They assigned each to one of the three military services that were conducting bombing strikes. The US Navy was assigned Route Packs 2, 3, 4 and 6B. The Air Force was assigned 1, 5 and 6A. The Marines backed up the Air Force in Route Pack 1, just north of the DMZ and within easy reach of their fighter bases at Danang and Chu Lai.

Starting in July, 1966 and continuing until Johnson ceased bombing of the North in the fall of 1968, all of the Phantom and Thud bases suffered severe and mounting loss rates in the air wars against North Vietnam and Laos. During December of 1966, I received promotion to Captain. My attitude toward the war continued to deteriorate and during my final months at Cam Ranh I put in my papers leading to separation from the Air Force. I gave up my chosen career due to the disillusionment with how and why our government seemed to be fighting the war. Actually, I was disgusted with the government, the military, and our populace. I was disgusted with our government for its betrayal of our fighting men and our military structure. I was disgusted with the military for lying to the government about our bomb, bullet and rocket shortages and for the absurd and destructive "sortie war" being fought between the Navy and Air Force. And I was disgusted with our populace for its treatment of those pledged to defend the United States. That disgust had permeated much of the Air Force officer corps in Southeast Asia.

The results of "Rolling Thunder," shown above, are impressive. But they should be viewed in the light that destruction of targets must be sustained to maximize the objective. The bombing pauses, halts and stand-downs only allowed the enemy to resupply and repair. The destruction listed came at an exceedingly high price in terms of aircraft destroyed and lives lost.

As stated, the American air war against North Vietnam was and still is the most intense air war in the history of aerial warfare. It was also largely misunderstood. It was one of several secret wars then being fought in Southeast Asia. As a consequence, the American public never got to know the true nature of our involvement and the deadly nature of the conflict.

Route Pack Five and Route Pack Six A&B were the Pentagon designated areas that defined the Hanoi-Haiphong target complex. Both cities are located in the Red River Valley. USAF Intelligence reported that it was home to over 10,000 anti-aircraft artillery weapons. Recent research brings that number into question. A more likely number was 7,000 to 8,000. The Nazi's never had anywhere near that concentration of AAA for protection anywhere in Germany during all of World War II.

When it came to its aerial defenses during the SEA War, North Vietnam was truly an international effort. North Koreans and Chinese manned many of the Anti-Aircraft Artillery weapons as did other Warsaw Pact soldiers. Chinese, Vietnamese and Korean MIGs roamed the skies over northern Laos and northern North Vietnam, attacking the intruding American fighter-bomber formations.

During the Korean War, it was reported that many Soviet fighter pilots became aces by each shooting down five or more American aircraft. The American public was never told of this huge Soviet involvement in Korea. It was the same in SEA. Vadim Petrovic Sechbakov, an "instructor," shot down six American fighter-bombers over North Vietnam. Boris Mazajev was also given credit for shooting down five Americans as part of the Soviet Missile Forces. Iliinyh Fyodor, another Russian missile man, was the ace of aces and was honored by the Soviet Union for shooting down 24 confirmed American planes with even more probable kills.

The SAM sites were located all over North Vietnam and in the northern portion of Laos at the time I was over there. Later, they moved into southern Laos and the northern part of South Vietnam.

One point of confusion when referencing the number of SAM sites was the actual number of SAM batteries. While the North Viets and Russians had a large number of constructed sites, not all of them were manned. Their units were mobile and they continued to move them from site to site. They were moving SAMs south into our operating areas of Laos by the time I left the combat theater. It was widely known in the USAF forces that, at the time I was over there, all Surface to Air (SAM) missile batteries in SEA were totally manned by Russians, yet that fact was kept secret.

COMBAT DIARY:

July 1, 1966:

Took a truck today and went across the pontoon bridge to the mainland. We left the Air Police defensive area and drove right into the Korean defensive sector. The hill area looked tough to crack. Just bristling with

Korean machine guns and bunkered positions. We went down to Bangoi. I was very surprised to see so many friendly people among the Vietnamese. They seem to like Americans. Had a few beers with some Koreans and came on back.

July 2, 1966:

A very bad day for maintenance: four barrier engagements, 10 MNDs (maintenance non-deliveries) and one mid-air collision. The mid-air was with a Sharkbait flight (557th TFS) hitting a FAC flying a "Bird Dog" aircraft. The FAC went in (crashed) and was killed. The F-4 flew to Danang with major damage.

July 3, 1966:

General Westmoreland and Admiral Sharp visited us today. On the first of July the Thuds from the Thai bases hit Hanoi and Haiphong petroleum storage areas. Our flights flying the "Big Eye" escort missions to the North saw the huge black clouds from the burning petroleum. The smoke went as high as 20,000 feet and must have been quite a sight.

Jack Gagen took a good-sized shell through his vari-ramp today. He seems to have all the luck. (The vari-ramp is part of the engine inlets that optimize the volume of entry airflow.)

On our mission, the target was an area with a few storage sheds near A Shau Special Forces Camp, which was overrun by the VC. I carried four pods of rockets. The second element carried napalm.

LETTERS HOME:
July 3, 1966:

"Enclosed you will find a photograph taken of Paul Busch and myself after our little "incident." My arm was in a cast at the time, but the injury was in no way serious. It could have been if the doctor at Khe Sanh hadn't gone in and cut away some of the stuff inside. However, no infection and it healed beautifully. I have only one small scar. The only reason that they put my arm in a cast was due to the tendons. Whatever went into my arm penetrated through the tendons and past the bone. It was blunt and just pushed the tendons aside. Again, very fortunate. They immobilized the arm to let the tendons heal. So, don't let the picture worry you.

"I flew my 47th mission today. Tomorrow, I fly my 48th and it will be a long one. They're all going well. I have yet to bring an aircraft back with bullet holes in it.

"Also enclosed you'll find a joke that I thought was too good not to send along. Mom, the joke's for Dad.

"Koufax is doing a good job. He should win 30. And the Dodger's will take the pennant. Their hitting has been doing very well and Tommy Davis is back at it.

"Tonight we had a hamburger fry with shrimp for an after-thought. Dessert was ice cream. This was out on our little patio. Can't say we're not eating well.

"Last night they hooked up a new power supply to the air conditioners so they're all working well. And our hot water is back on after being off for two months, so things are looking great. The Base is expanding at a fantastic pace. What we have here is real strength and the Koreans have made us impregnable.

"I put some more paneling in the room at the Quonset and wired it for additional plugs. By the time I leave here, the place should be a palace."

COMBAT DIARY:

July 4, 1966:

We celebrated the 4th with another Gulf of Tonkin mission. Nothing really exciting happened, other than we flew a lot of hours searching for the bad guys.

As mentioned yesterday, the bombing missions to the North have begun hitting POL storage facilities. I understand it is getting big play back in the States. The Air Force did good work, but the Navy didn't get as good results.

The Air Force hit the Hanoi POL Complex and out of 36 tanks, destroyed 23 and heavily damaged the rest. The Navy hit Haiphong and only destroyed 7 storage tanks. Of course, this was from an Air Force report.

July 6, 1966:

An aborted mission today. To start out, we got out of the aircraft and the crew chief told me that the bird had blown a new tire the day before. Since it was new, this indicated to me that we probably had an anti-skid problem. The anti-skid was checked and found okay, so we proceeded with caution. After we taxied out to the arming area, the arming chief plugged into the aircraft intercom system and told me that my right wheel strut was down, but that he would clear me "conditionally."

After takeoff, I noted both the fuel counter and fuel tape were spinning, giving me no indication of fuselage fuel, wing fuel or backup indication of external tank feed. I notified lead and he made the decision that I return to base. I trapped the wing tank fuel for dumping and held over water to the east of the field, with speed boards down and in afterburner to burn my external tank fuel. In the hold, I got a flickering BLC (Boundary Layer Control) light indicating another compounding problem, this time with serious possibilities. This also meant I should land immediately. With my two bombs on board and the extra fuel, I was landing awfully heavy. Only I had to get the gear and flaps down ASAP so that no hot air could damage the interior of the wings.

I opened the dump to drop my wing fuel and then came on in and landed. I had to shoot a low-angle approach to insure adequate power for a go-around in case of a blown tire due to the possible anti-skid problem and also to avoid heavy impact forces against the bottomed out strut. I landed hot, but okay.

Anyone who has flown military or commercial aircraft is aware that it is flights such as this that have a real danger. Most of the time single malfunctions can be dealt with properly. It is when multiple, often seemingly unconnected, problems start to mushroom that aircraft have a greater likelihood of being killed.

LETTERS HOME:

July 6, 1966:

"So ends another day at Cam Ranh Bay. Days seem to be going by very quickly due to our flying quite a bit. The squadron has also expanded to include the 198 enlisted members in Maintenance, so we are now 250+ strong.

"I have been given the job of selecting men to be decorated and going through all the paperwork of their missions. Or if a request originates elsewhere, I'll take care of the matter for them. I have been busy these last few weeks setting up a system and creating files and records that were non-existent. The background work is almost done for the expeditious processing of decorations.

"I don't know if I told you, but I was flying in a two-ship alert flight launched to help ground troops in trouble. Our two planes and four prop planes killed 78 Viet Cong by Army body count. For this flight, they said we would probably get decorated.

"During FAC Bill Carpenter's fight as part of the 101st Airborne, he called napalm in on his own position. The planes that dropped it were from Cam Ranh.

"Our squadron has been getting outstanding results, the best, by far at Cam Ranh. In June, we were credited with 126 VC confirmed killed, 12 estimated, 43 VC wounded, six vehicles destroyed, six guns and gun-sites destroyed, 9 sampans destroyed, 487 structures destroyed and 182 damaged, 201,000 pounds of rice destroyed or damaged, plus all sorts of odds and ends. The large anti-aircraft gun I destroyed with a low-level napalm attack was self-propelled, like a tank, and I dropped two cans of napalm right on it.

"Next month most of the squadron returns to the States. On top of that, Jack Gagen is being recalled by the Marines and one more Aircraft Commander is being pulled out to be made Officer Club Officer. So, that leaves us with four Aircraft Commanders left in the squadron. Three more Majors make up the Command Section and with the addition of one of them from Wing, we'll have five, line fighter pilots, three of which are upgraded (from the back seat) and one who was recently upgraded. They'd better start pumping replacements over from the States. What this probably means is that I'll be leading flights of four aircraft within two months. Experience counts.

"Tomorrow I fly my 50th mission. Brief is at 5 in the morning. I hardly have one eye open by then, let alone two. Enclosed I've included our little "paper" from here at Cam Ranh."

COMBAT DIARY:
July 7, 1966:

I can now legally wear a 50-mission crush in my flight cap. Our mission was a scheduled Sky Spot against Laos, but Penlight Control did not know we were coming, so we contacted Hillsboro and he directed us to attack an area of hooches and storage bunkers. We were only carrying two 500-pound slick bombs. My first was good but my second was really bad. I should have aborted the pass. It was only the second time that I've done high-angle delivery since coming over here. Our BDA was three storage bunkers destroyed. Sky Spot is the name given to ground based radar control of bombing attacks against different types of targets including lots of SAM sites. Most of the SAM sites are in North Vietnam, but Laos is starting to get its share. Sky Spots are good for bombing when the weather in a target area is reported to be bad. It allows us to bomb through an under cast, but does pose dangers due to us flying a set altitude, set direction and set airspeed. Against the SAM sites, the Sky Spots are scary missions since they would know our parameters before firing SAMs against us.

July 9, 1966:

Flew back seat with George Larson today. The squadron asked me to see how he is doing. George is one of our new front seaters and he has been having problems. For the first time I think I really felt like I'd had the course (was killed). One of George's strafe passes was real low and I thought he had target fixation. We were about to the treetop level and I know that there was a hill right in front of us. I pulled back on the stick and pushed the throttle forward. I thought I was dead. Larson never ever said anything about my actions.

We had the only gun today and I think it will probably be the last time I'll carry the gun, other than off alert, for a long time. The USAF managed to buy the guns without spare parts and no replacement guns have come over. So, we can only fly with them on alert from now on. Our most effective weapon has thus been neutralized.

Along with the gun, we dropped 2X250 pound bombs. The weather was poor so we dropped level. The 250s don't make much of a bang. Total BDA was five structures destroyed and three damaged. We fired 600 rounds of ammo.

July 15, 1966:

Flew two missions today.

The first was with two 500-pound retard bombs against a widely-spaced village. Lane led the mission and didn't even come close. He dropped his napalm in the middle of the biggest clear space in the village area. My bombs were good and helped destroy four structures and damage two.

Politically Speaking:

It is these missions targeted against villages here in the South that has me concerned. I have to wonder, just what are we doing? We were sent to South Vietnam ostensibly to protect its citizens from the VC and the North Vietnamese Army regulars. And here we are killing the very villagers we are tasked to protect. What kind of war is this?

We are told that the targeted villages have shown hostile intent against friendly troops. What does this mean? Does it mean that someone from the village shot at friendlies? If so, that would be a nice way for the VC to get a village to go against the Americans. The VC would only have to sneak into a village, fire at us, and then wait for the expected retaliation.

We pilots are forced to rely on reports from some US or ARVN Army troop who made a judgment. Our weapons kill these defenseless villagers based on those judgments. Since the ARVN is notoriously infiltrated with VC sympathizers, the whole concept of village elimination does not make sense.

With napalm and the gun firing high-explosive, incendiary 20 mm shells, it does not take any of us very long to totally destroy a village. The longer I fight this war, the more troubling this action becomes.

My second mission was the most screwed-up one that I have ever been on. It was Ken Cordier's first mission in which he led the flight and none of the screw-ups were his fault. What a way to start.

The flight was a scheduled Sky Spot and when we took off we contacted Peacock (PK) Control at Pleiku. On contact we were told that their weapon was bent, which meant their radar was not working. I should have told him that I had been over here long enough that my weapon was bent too.

We then tried to contact Penlight and they couldn't handle us. Contacted Panama Control for a target and they gave us three frequencies to find a FAC. The FAC we were able to contact gave us a target that was too far north for our fuel load, so we orbited south of Danang and tried to contact a FAC handling a nearby strike. He wouldn't talk to us on any frequency.

We then told Panama we were going back to Peacock Control. Peacock told us they would try to find us a target. Meanwhile we had flown to Pleiku and orbited there. PK found us a target and gave us the FAC frequency, but the friendly troops had just overrun the hill we were supposed to hit so we left the FAC and went back to Peacock. He told us to fly on to An Khe and orbit there for another FAC. One finally came up on the frequency and directed us against an area of trees (what is new). Our fuel was very low.

We dropped in pairs and, as I pulled off target, I lost another bomb (number three bomb) that just disconnected from the TER. I called it over the air and another aircraft joined on me to look me over. I thought I had dropped my bombs, but they had not released and I still had them. Lead (Cordier) transmitted that two still had his bombs and should go back in and drop. I thought it was three who had joined on me, but it was lead. Lead thought that I was two instead of four. Two went back to the target to drop when he actually was clean (without bombs). We never did rejoin with #2. (Who's on first?)

The BDA was a possible KBA (Killed by Air) with the area left burning.

We are getting a lot of new guys. Most of them were part of the rotating squadrons that flew TDY out of Ubon and they are on TDY status over here and will soon return to Europe. It seems everyone who is coming in and new to Cam Ranh will be returning before I do because I am PCS (Permanent Change of Station) and they are TDY (Temporary Duty). All of my buddies from MacDill and the old 559th are arriving and flying "out-country" missions at a rapid rate. They'll all be gone before I leave. Oh well, I have been here 130 days and have 289 days in the Far East this year with only 234 days left to go. "Asi es la vida" and it could have been a two-year tour.

July 16, 1966:

Flew two rocket missions today. The first was near Ban Houie Sane, which is our Laotian "safe" haven in case we needed to bail out. We shot all the rockets and dropped all the napalm within 20 meters of the target. My load was four rocket pods of 19 rockets each on both missions. The Pathet Lao bad guys were on a hill about four miles from Ban Houie.

The weather was a low overcast and they were firing heavily at us with automatic weapons (AW). At the end of our passes we silenced their guns. Our BDA was one secondary explosion, one stores fire and an estimated five Pathet Lao troops killed. The Pearl Safe Area is now considered non-secure.

The afternoon mission was down near Saigon and it was another tree shoot-em-up with no damage assessment. I wasn't as accurate on my afternoon shooting.

LETTERS HOME:
July 22, 1966:

"This is an answer for your past letters. All the packages that you sent arrived and I thank you for them. The candy is good but a little rich, so maybe you could stop sending it. Thanks much for it. It was delicious.

"It sounds as if you've both been doing excellent work on the links. Nice work Dad. You're winning lots of tournaments. Congratulations to you both.

"There is no chance I will come back with the 559th, because it's not leaving Vietnam. The unit stays and the personnel are changed.

"Our stupid government has us down to dropping two 250# bombs per aircraft. We don't have any more guns because the government forgot to buy spare parts with the guns so our best weapon is neutralized.

"On notifying the military about home-town press releases, this is the least of my worries. If the military desires to release information they will. Some items are of sensitive nature and therefore are not released.

I'm not greatly interested in the press.

"Who's this guy who's a test pilot and wants to talk to me when I get back? Sounds interesting.

"I've got a big mission tomorrow so I must go."

COMBAT DIARY:

July 23, 1966:

Another MIG-screen mission to the Gulf in Fox 1 through 4 sectors. We came close to the Chinese border today. It's easy to see Hainan Island, the Chinese mainland and the coast of North Vietnam at the same time. We are patrolling the area heavily and we consider anything over the Gulf as our territory and any MIG that ventures out is fair game.

The mission started out with an abort due to a modulator failure in the missile tuning circuitry in one of the birds. I launched as backup after we had an air abort. Tom Bennison lost his utility hydraulic system and had to land at Danang with an emergency. I flew up and joined the rest of the flight on the tanker to assure that we had the "Silver Dawn" aircraft covered by a flight of two at all times. While we were up there, we were treated to an hour-long drama on Guard Channel that described the rescue of a downed pilot. The rescue pilot had to swing his manned tree penetrator under the tree canopy to reach the pilot, whose chute had been tangled and caught up in a tree. They got him out.

July 24, 1966:

A bad weather day today. I flew in the squadron's COs (Stockman) back seat. I felt like an IP (Instructor Pilot). The aluminum planking we use for a runway is worn away in so many places that very little abrasive surface is left. When it rains, it is like ice.

Before Major Stockman and I ever got off the ground my roommate George Larson went off the end of the runway. He was flying one of the missile birds on early takeoff and was aborting for a low gear-strut. The tower told him to expedite down the runway and he misjudged the stopping power of the 55,000-pound beast on a slick runway, with the Phantom having a full load of fuel and missiles.

He lowered his tail hook, but it was too late. George busted his nose-wheel off, ruined the radome, ruined both engines from dirt ingestion, crushed all three external fuel tanks and broke the main landing gear off. It was a major accident, but both pilots were unhurt.

The aftermath was that George was grounded and kicked off the base. Major Stockman and our Operations Officer, the second in command, were fired. Such is life under Colonel Chase, our Wing Commander. I must be bad news for COs, since I had been sitting in the cockpit with Stockman when George took his doomsday ride.[36]

July 26, 1966:

Today we hit North Vietnamese Route Pack One in the operational area they call "Tally Ho." We have

Author's Note: *36. During my stay in Vietnam, I had a total of five different squadron commanders. It was all a case of timing. COs were rotated in and out. Several, like Stockman, were fired. From my perspective, Major Stockman did nothing wrong. What happened was beyond his control. He was a decent commander and good pilot. The Air Force can be unforgiving and looks for someone to blame for almost every accident or incident. I am not saying that approach is wrong. It is just difficult for those in the wrong place at the wrong time.*

Goodenough (far right) returning from a combat mission over North Vietnam. The flight, above the South China Sea, was just about to turn right to downwind for a south landing. Looking northwest, the entrance to the Bay and the sandy peninsula are barely visible at the top of the tail of the middle Phantom.

effectively eliminated the infiltration down the Ho Chi Minh Trail and the "Hound Dog" FACS have shifted us to the area just north of the DMZ to continue operations against a more lucrative target area.

My right engine flamed out twice during starting operations. However, I was going to take it, whether it had two engines or one. We carried 6X250s and the bombing was high-angle. The results were very accurate with excellent area coverage.

The afternoon's mission carried 3XBLUs and the drops accounted for 75 meters of trenches knocked out. I don't know what good napalm does against trenches, but maybe they contained a few Viet Cong?

We received no morning BDA because the FACs usually don't get too close in Tally Ho. It is a heavily defended region and to fly close to any target can be risky in those slow FAC planes.

July 27, 1966:

I had an aborted Big Eye mission to the Gulf of Tonkin. This time, I had a fire warning light caused by three defective fire-warning loops in the engine bay. Maintenance has really been bad. We're getting new replacements who know next to nothing about the birds.

July 28, 1966:

Another "counter" up North today. We were fragged to hit about 900 meters north of the DMZ line, but bad weather forced us to find a target to the east. We dropped our 4X500s on a North Vietnamese storage area and again the FAC did not go in to investigate. I really don't blame them. We did have full coverage with a 6,500-foot release altitude while dropping in ripple mode.

My mission total is now 62 with two counters, which means either an attack or MIG mission over land in North Vietnam. The Gulf missions do not count. Even the times that I have ventured over Haiphong on our Big Eye missions do not count.

July 29, 1966:

Took a bird up to Danang to have some missiles uploaded and bring them back. Al Bernal rode in my back seat. He is a former F-106 pilot, who isn't completely checked out in the F-4. Saw a lot of guys that I know. John Brennan is up there along with Greg Smith. John was the backseater who called in the emergency helicopter, when I crashed near Ocala, Florida the year before. Joe Latham and Wayne Bechler are also at Danang.[37]

The story of Joe's later victory against the MIG-21 is informative. The 21s got accustomed to sitting up on high station and flying parallel to inbound flights of Phantoms. They knew that we are helpless within a mile of an airborne target, because that distance was required for the heat-seeking Sidewinder Infrared Missiles to swivel their missile heat-seeker heads and lock-on to an aircraft engine kicking out heat.

The 21s were in a habit of sitting high up and then having one of their flight drop down directly in front of a Phantom. They were correct in figuring that the pilot of the F-4 would be concentrating on getting that mile back so he could shoot his Sidewinders. The intent Phantom pilot and his wingman often would not notice the other MIGs diving in from high station and we lost some Phantoms that way.

Joe's squadron at Ubon decided to trick the MIGs. Joe was flying with one of the Vulcan Gattling Cannons mounted externally centerline. When the 21 dropped in front of Joe, he did not have to back off for the Sidewinders. The gun requires no such maneuver. Once the 21 was in place just ahead of him, Joe squeezed off some bursts of the cannon and the 21 just blew apart. Joe didn't have to do any fancy flying or pull a lot of Gs in a dog fight. All he had to do was sit there and pull the trigger.

July 30, 1966:

Sat alert this morning and they scrambled the two bomb-loaded birds to drop Sky Spot with Penlight Control. We each carried 4X500s and held below a thunderstorm. We flew around and around in it prior to the drop. "Plots" was in about a 20-degree banked turn to the left, when the controller called a right break. Plots seemed to forget he had a man on his wing (which was me) and immediately broke to a 45-degree turn to the right making a total of 65 degrees of bank turn. Since I was flying his wing, it was all I could do to avoid hitting him as he suddenly banked into me. It is tough on a wingman, to say the least.

We didn't get any BDA, which we seldom ever do on Sky Spot as we are dropping from 20,000 feet and level. The accuracy of the MSQ Radar controlling the Sky Spots is down to 283 feet CEA, which is terrific for the Dong Ha based radar operators. The wind factor alone on a drop from 20,000 would be substantial.[38, 39]

On many of the Sky Spot missions in which I dropped, the altitude was from 24,000 feet. The controllers had us flying straight and level at a set speed just prior to the drops. Since our Phantoms had no sensors

---

Author's Notes: *37. Joe later was one of the first to shoot down a MIG-21. Air Force Intelligence reported that all MIG-21s were manned by Russians.*

38. The term CEA was widely used in the AF at the time I was flying. It was used to show miss distances when we were on the bombing ranges. It means Circular Error Actual or average miss distance.

39. Cam Ranh lost four Phantoms and 8 pilots on Sky Spot missions. The losses were not due to enemy action, but resulted from the premature explosions of the bombs right after they left the aircraft bomb-carrying racks. The bombs were called retards, because they had four fins that deploy on ejection from the carrying racks and, on a drop, the fins retard the forward speed of the bomb. The 500-pounders are amazingly accurate. The bombs have an arming relay on release from the dropping plane and also a spin-arm device designed to allow it proper separation from the aircraft before that relay was armed. The radar operators controlling the drops saw the radar blips of the two-shippers just disappear from their screens right after they gave the order to drop the bombs. It has been speculated that the second arming relay somehow malfunctioned.

telling us if we were being locked on by the SAM radars or when a SAM had been fired at us from the missile sites we were hitting, it was pucker time when we had no eyes looking down. At the time of many of the Sky Spot missions, I was flight leader and always had the planes in my flights "jink" and roll right and left to keep sight of the ground and any missile that might be launched. At the last second, I would call the guys to "tuck it in" in time for the drop command. After the drop, the wingmen would immediately roll over to check for MIGs, SAMs or anything else the North Viets might send to greet us.

For the second combat mission of the day, we carried 4X500 high drag or the same "Snake Eye" retard bombs we use for the Sky Spots. My drop was long and it was not a really good day for me. Our BDA was seven structures destroyed, two damaged and one secondary explosion with 40 meters of trenches destroyed. The target was a VC company involved in Operations Hastings.

Secondary explosions are welcome sights. They usually occur after we have pulled off the target and have expended all our munitions. They are almost always the result of explosive war supplies blowing up after our attack. Sometimes the secondaries would last a while and it was always pretty to a pilot.

Politically Speaking:

It has become obvious to us that the war is not being pushed by our government. Added to that, some missions are against worthless hooches. This is ridiculous.

July 31, 1966:

Another bird was downed while we were on station with Big Eye today and the Jolly Green Giants (helicopters) were called in to get the guy out.

We shot two ID (identification) passes on blips that the Connie was curious about. Then we plugged in burner and headed from the Gulf home to Cam Ranh. Our new squadron Commanding Officer, Major Jack Barnes, was the lead and he often did not pay attention to the fuel state of his wingmen. I decided to teach him a lesson. He has to listen up and know the flight status of his guys.

We have what we call Bingo fuel status, which alerts the flight lead when we are low on fuel. When we really get low, it is minimum fuel status and it can be critical. As we motored back to CRB in burner, I called Bingo fuel, which should have caused him to get out of burner and throttle back. It didn't and I knew Barnes was not paying attention. When I finally called minimum fuel, Barnes almost shit. I was minimum at 80 miles out, which meant I only had 1500 pounds of fuel left. We shut down with only 500 pounds of gas, which is not much in a two-engine fighter jet. That gave no margin for any problem on the runway before we arrived, which might have caused us to go to an alternate field. In this case I did not have enough to go to any alternate. Barnes had no business keeping us in burner for such a long distance.

August 1, 1966:

The morning mission was about the most fearful one I've been on, not counting the April missions. The ordnance was four pods of LAU (rockets). Two birds ground aborted before takeoff and our four-ship flight became a two-ship. Sorrick and I pressed on to the target, which consisted of three warehouses and two small buildings in the Tuat Son Warehouse area. The area was covered with automatic weapons and AAA positions. We penetrated well to the north and found our target heading south. The bad weather was again a factor.

One of the jobs of lead is to visually locate the Bird Dog FAC, flying an O1E-type aircraft and sometimes this presents a considerable problem from 20,000 feet, especially if the O1 is camouflaged. With bad weather reducing visibility and clouds obscuring the target, his problem is compounded. This NVN target was in Tally Ho and thus still had a FAC controller.

We spotted two FAC birds and they reported that the ground fire was so intense that all other birds should stay out of the area. After letting down, we rolled in at 13,000 feet. Then the flak hit. It burst all around us at our altitude and followed us down in the dive. It was the 37 mm AAA variety with an orange flash and white smoke. It was hitting all around us and CLOSE. So close it rocked our plane as we rolled in and continued to rock it as we rocketed down in the dive. Bill Sorrick's bird took one hit just above the left wing. I was "jinking" the aircraft frantically to keep from getting hit. The shrapnel from the blasts was so close it repeatedly bounced off my canopy with the telltale "ping." I pickled all four rocket pods at 8,500 feet and pulled so hard that I registered 8 Gs on pull out. We just had that one pass at the bottom of which the FAC pilot controlling the strike called out that they had shot off part of one of his wings. He barely got back to land at Dong Ha, just across the DMZ.

On the return, I flew over and checked for battle damage on both our birds and Sorrick was the only one that got hits. I had several rivets popped from the large G load and oil was leaking on the fuselage.

The afternoon mission was in the South and against a Viet Cong company. I carried two napalm cans as well as the Wing Director of Operations, Colonel McGlothlin, who was also in our flight. The other birds had bombs. The napalm birds went in low and Col Mac picked up two VC 30-caliber shells that went through his radome. We got credit for killing five of the VC.

Prior to the attack, while we were in orbit waiting for the go-ahead, an F-101 recce bird passed right through our formation and right between #3 and my own position at #4, very nearly hitting me. It's a crowded sky up here. The 101 was undoubtedly on a low-level photo mission to assess bomb damage from our strikes. Sure wish that there was a little more coordination. It scared the hell out of me.

August 3, 1966:
Used 1150 rounds of HEI (High Explosive Incendiary) today. Also dropped two high- drags as we got one building destroyed and four damaged. The air was filled with A-1Es, a Caribou, choppers and a flight of F-100s also hitting targets in the immediate target area.

August 4, 1966:
Flew as Lightning 14 today as we went North on an early morning mission. I lost my right generator and flew the mission on my left. Returning from Pink Anchor (KC-135 refueling tanker track) from Danang, we heard Panama call out a radial and distance shouting for "the flight bombing the village to cease immediately as it is friendly."

Twenty minutes later, we again heard a frantic call on Guard (frequency) for the gunships (choppers) that were hosing down the area to cease fire, as they were shooting friendly troops. Confusing or what?

Losing a generator on a mission was not critical. Any jet aircraft has a generator on each engine and we had two. Recalling a specific mission, I have searched through my diary and, apparently, it was flown after I stopped making diary entries.

On this particular mission, I was flying at night and was leading the flight on a return to Cam Ranh.

My entire electrical system failed and I was "in the dark." Since I had no radios, it was difficult to get my wingman to notice. I eventually was able to alert him to my problem and I grabbed his wing. Without power I was without speed reference for final approach. I needed his help. He went to GCA control and I flew his wing on a radar-controlled straight-in approach and we landed as an element of two.

Compounding the problem was the bad weather. I got vertigo as I concentrated on flying his wing in the clouds and the red glow from his belly light was mesmerizing as it illuminated the underside of his plane and glowed off the surrounding clouds. As we turned and banked, I had to continually focus on position in the bad weather.

The results of the strikes against the North on the 2nd are back and we lost five aircraft. I now have more than 100 combat hours and 71 total missions.

August 5, 1966:

Flew in a C-130 to Ubon, Thailand today to pick up a bird. They are utilizing one squadron of aircraft for a two-squadron operation, both day and night flying. Danang and Cam Ranh are getting the suddenly "excess" aircraft. The project is called "Rapid Roger" and will fall on its face. They just can't turn an aircraft around that fast and there is very little consideration for discrepancies. Maintenance will be a disaster.

August 6, 1966:

I am still at Ubon and the bird isn't ready for the return flight, so I will just wait. Ubon is a beautiful base and makes CRB really look grim. Cam Ranh lost a bird today. They were on a return from Big Eye and one of the engines blew up and caught fire. They ejected 35 miles north of the Bay and Bavausett broke three vertebrae in his back. It was another 557th plane.

Talking to the guys in the Club here at night and finding out all sorts of good stories. They tell of the F-105 jocks pulling off targets up North and strafing Russian and British ships docked in Haiphong Harbor. They naturally don't like them supplying all those goods. Our government, of course, denies we did it because they don't know it. Neither does our military. Just the pilots.[41]

Last night, here at Ubon, Bob Walmsley crashed on GCA approach after calling out a fire warning light about 8 miles from the Ubon runway. He was in the weather. The back seater ejected, but didn't make it out of the seat and was killed. Bob stayed with it and the whole front of the plane was broken off. He is mighty lucky.

Also out of Ubon, Major Hamblett was attacked by MIGs who shot out his right engine. He dove for the deck, while his wingman fired a Sparrow missile at his pursuers. Hamblett made the coast and hit Brown Anchor tanker with 150 pounds of fuel remaining. Way too close.

August 7, 1966:

Still up here at Ubon waiting for their maintenance to check out the Rapid Roger bird. While I was waiting, Ubon Wing Operations had me fly a test hop for one of their downed birds and I flew it without

---

Author's Notes: *41. As previously mentioned, I heard an audio recording of the British sailors on board the ship that was strafed by the 105s. The recording covered the duration of the attack, which I was told wounded 19 Brit sailors. There was a lot of yelling by the Brits and the roaring sounds of the F-105 engines and shooting sounds of their cannons could clearly be heard.*

a back seater over Laos. These test hops are routine unless the maintenance repair did not fix the original malfunction, then it can sometimes be hairy.

Today was a grim day for the Air War. We lost seven fighters today and five were the F-105s out of either Tahkli or Korat over to the west of us here in Thailand. The other two were F-4s. Two of the Iron Hand F model birds got it and only one man was rescued. Iron Hand is the SAM site attack mission call sign. The Iron Hand missions must be the toughest of the War and they are currently only flown by the Thuds. They attack the SAM sites that are well-defended and the SAM sites have started barrage-firing their missiles. Instead of a single missile aimed at you flying at four times the speed of sound, our guys up here have six to eight fired at once. Evade one and run into another. It is only a short time before our CRB Phantoms will be encountering the same thing.

Seventeen missiles were fired at us in the morning. Ray Salzarulo said he was in the flight right behind the Thud flights in on a Route Package Six target. Just like a circus. Four of our birds shot down in less than 20 minutes with more calling emergencies with battle damage. The flak is terrible. All types of AAA up to 85mm.

During my stay at Ubon, I had the opportunity to share drinks at the Ubon Officer's Club with Ray Salzarulo, a 1964 grad of the Air Academy, and his AC Spike Nasmyth, who was a buddy from MacDill who stayed in my room in Saint Petersburg while I was in Okinawa. I actually spent the entire night talking with Ray and Spike, mainly about the types of missions they were flying.

Three weeks after I left, Spike and Ray were shot down. They were hit by the sixth SAM in a barrage-fire of eight missiles. As he rolled away from the 5th, he rolled right into the 6th that blew right above his cockpit. Ray was killed, but Spike made it out and ended up captured and spent six years as a guest of Hanoi. He told me on his return that he had endured torture until September of 1969, when the enemy probably decided that they were better off keeping the prisoners at least looking healthy.

Specific tortures Spike mentioned included tying his hands together behind his back and then lifting him by rope off the ground. That torture was done on almost all the POWs and often resulted in dislocated shoulders. Since Hanoi usually didn't offer medical help, the agonies inflicted by their cruel torturers lasted. Another favorite of the North Viets was putting out cigarettes on Spike's skin.

Senator John McCain endured the same type tortures while a POW and he still has an arm that will not work correctly.

Spike was the focus of a very well-publicized campaign by his family to have him released. It involved billboards in the Los Angeles area, where they lived, and a book entitled "Hanoi- Release John Nasmyth."

"Hanoi Jane" Fonda specifically mentioned Spike after repatriation and called him a liar and a TAC-trained killer. She claimed he lied about the tortures that he had endured. She might have had the best of intentions with her comments, but she had no idea about the nature of our enemy and did irreparable harm to our cause. Her wartime visits to North Vietnam and her intense criticisms of our efforts led to further pilot losses. She was guilty of the same thing as many Americans, and that was aiming much of her criticisms against our military instead of against our civilian leaders who ordered our military actions.

While I agree with some of her criticism of the war, I will never ever be able to forgive her for what she did and how she did it. How can she explain Senator McCain's torture-created disfigurement? While our country made mistakes in SEA, that did not mean that our enemy was right while we were wrong.

Statements made by the North Vietnamese leaders in their discussions with McNamara after the war indicated that the actions of Fonda and Ramsey Clark gave them added incentive to continue the war, especially after the catastrophic military defeat suffered by the VC and North Viets during TET in 1968.

August 8, 1966:

Finally returned from Ubon today and it was another grim one. Larry Goldberg and Pat Wynne were shot down and missing in Route Pack Six. They are friends flying the Phantom out of Ubon. Two F-105s were also lost. Maybe more in the afternoon? It's grim.

This afternoon the 557th lost another plane. Walling and Ado Kommandant were killed when their plane hit about two miles at 12 o'clock from their target in the South. Reason unknown but ground fire suspected. That makes two 557th Phantoms killed in three days.[42]

August 9, 1966:

Two-thirty get up for a very early morning Sky Spot against a target right on the Cambodian border. Sky Spots are now being targeted against non-SAM targets, which is fine with me. The drop was in support of Operation Paul Revere. We dropped 2X500s and were followed by two scramble birds plus a flight from Phan Rang. There must have been some action, because we could see flashes underneath the overcast, which we assumed was artillery.

August 10, 1966:

Carried 4X250s against a VC base camp area near Saigon. It was 100% of ordnance on target, but no BDA due to trees (as usual). It was a good bombing for me after several mediocre flights. It seems that bombing is similar to pitchers on a baseball team. Sometimes the pitchers are on and pitch a good game and sometimes they are off and pitch a lousy game. Same with the aircrews. Don't quite know why, but it happens to all of us.

All my bombs spotted where I wanted them to and the run-ins themselves were good. Saigon is getting to be a high-threat area for flights with much ground fire being reported.

August 11, 1966:

Diverted from an I Corp target to the southern edge of the DMZ. The 324th PAVN (North Vietnamese) Division is in the area and the B-52s have hit it hard. The evidence of their attacks was present in the carpet-bombing areas. I carried four high-drag bombs and we attacked some gun bunkers on top of a ridgeline.

I have to assume that they were firing back at us. It is very difficult for aircrews in high performance aircraft to tell sometimes if they are being fired at. We can't see the bullets or hear them. When AAA is fired at us, we can tell by the "sparkler" look coming from a round clearing. That means it is a triple A gun and if we can see the sparkles, it means that they are firing at us.

High drag bombs are highly accurate, but make the bomber vulnerable. The best delivery is in a 10-degree dive and the approach makes a pilot a little uneasy due to its duration and stable run. However, the bombs

---

Author's Notes: 42: *Much later we found out that Larry Goldberg was killed on his mission. That ended up to be four Ubon friends killed on the day I left Ubon.*

all went on top of the ridge, with no BDA received due to the FAC being too far away from the target to see anything. My first pass was aborted because I had set up for a 30-degree approach and the clouds were obscuring the target. On the second pass, I dove below the broken cloud deck and leveled off, then dove in again.

The northern missions are showing we can make it a long way with only two external fuel tanks.

August 12, 1966:
Morning mission went above the DMZ into the North on a divert. Flight carried four napalm and four 500s with one gun. I carried two napalm cans. Number two man aborted because he didn't get one afterburner on takeoff and had subsequent nose-wheel steering problems, also while on takeoff.

The target was a suspected storage area under some trees at the end of a canyon, a bad place to carry napalm and a very bad place to go low-level if there are any defenses. The FAC reported no defensive fire, so we proceeded.

Communist gunners sometimes wait for a certain pass or set-up before they start firing and then they open up with everything. It's a bad situation. Anyway, the clouds were low and broken and lead found a hole and dove two of his bombs right on target. With a mix such as ours, it's best to get the bomb birds in first to uncover any supplies, etc. and then move the napalm-armed birds in to drop.

Learned of additional MIAs and KIAs from up North: Bill Andrews, Ron Bliss (from the Academy) and Kellems. Seems Bill Andrews, who was a friend from MacDill, was on the ground talking with the guys overhead and the bad guys came up on him. He chose to use his gun and the guys flying cover for him think he was shot dead on the spot.[43]

August 13, 1966:
Scramble off the alert pad today as Boxer 03 Flight. The Army was fighting near the Mekong River fairly close to the Saigon area. I carried 4X500s and dropped them all on-target from 3,000 and 5,000-foot altitudes. The high altitudes are really unusual for attacks against the South, but they were necessary due to the bad guys firing at us. We hit some houses down there. I'm happy with my bombing again, as it has been better than ever the last few weeks with no misses.

There was a lot of confusion on the ground as the FAC didn't quite know where the Army wanted us. I dropped one bomb and they halted bombing while they called in the choppers and their load of troops. The choppers came in formation and the troops spread out. We originally had to wait for a flight of F-100s to hit before we went in and had a low orbit while waiting. It was raining. The return to Cam Ranh was nip and tuck as they had run us low on fuel.

August 14, 1966:
One note on yesterday's mission: During my first bomb run, I was pulling out and had to dodge to miss both the FAC O1E and a chopper. It is a crowded sky. I went so close to the FAC, that he ruddered to the right to miss me. He was in the wrong position and was talking to me about my bomb at the time.

A further note about the missions on the 12th: The mission in the morning was carrying two napalm and we opened up a supply area. Ray Seal threw his napalm over a hill from the target and got a nice secondary

---

Author's Notes: *43. He never came home with the other prisoner's, so that assumption was probably right.*

explosion. His first nape also got a secondary. We left the area with two large POL fires that were spreading. The fires looked like the Hanoi POL raids in miniature. We didn't experience any ground fire.

The afternoon mission on the 12th was actually a night mission. We Sky Spotted against a VC plantation. It was in the weather or just below it and Polar Bear Sky Spot had trouble even picking up our skin paint on radar. It was another III Corp target. Bombs (2X500) got off well and made quite a night flash.

This morning's mission was a Tiger Hound divert to the Tally Ho area. Tally Ho is now split into five working areas: (1) Peter, (2) Paul, (3) Mary, (4) Ford, and (5) Banjo. We hit north of Banjo (DMZ) area in Ford. My load was three napes and we left two target areas blazing.

The buildings must have been loaded, because the second target area burned like a son-of-a-gun. They were big hooches and easily seen from the air. FAC gave us 13 super hooches destroyed and 29 more probable. That is a huge BDA. The smoke and flames made an accurate count impossible.

This was one of the largest destructions that I have participated with in this war. The North Viets did not seem prepared for the 12th coming off the water at low level to hit them with napalm. They are used to the 5,000-foot minimum altitude for pull out that is required of every other fighter force fighting the North. Instead, we hit them at 50 feet.

Our attack started off low over the water and we popped up and then dove down. I was a little uneasy as we orbited in a flak area. I dove my napalm in with a low pull off of 150 feet. All my napes hit buildings and the splattering gas ignited a lot of others. I've never seen hooches burn like those. It was just a billowing fire seen for many miles. The automatic weapons opened up on us on the last pass. It was too late for us to go in and hit their gun positions.

Lead never called off target and I took an extra orbit. I was high because I had no gun and the rest were strafing. As the rest of the flight left the target, I locked on to them in-trail with radar and caught them not too far north of Pleiku.

August 15, 1966:

Today's mission was against another supply area under that tree canopy in Tally Ho. It was the western portion of Tally Ho and my load was four rocket pods and the gun. Major Lane, Colonel Ellis and Captain Plotnitsky were the others in the flight and did a lousy job of bombing. My rockets were okay and I fired out 1150 rounds of 20 mike-mike into the area and into some guns showing ground fire that we spotted. That is about max for bullets expended from the gun.

An Army message, one of only three or four that have arrived on base, congratulated the flight and informed us we had destroyed seven trucks and damaged five others. I guess it was not so lousy bombing after all.

August 17, 1966:

Flew as a test pilot today. Maintenance had fixed a trim malfunction and wanted me to check out its airworthiness. As I rotated the nose on takeoff, my windscreen shattered. It did not come apart, but totally delaminated and had spider cracks all over. It was a little disconcerting and I had trouble seeing. I landed without incident. Fuel loads on test missions are usually light and allow for an immediate landing, if necessary.

Recently, General Pearson, from 7th Air in Saigon, wanted to have a firepower demonstration of the attack performance of the F-4. He could have easily flown in one of our backseats to do the evaluation.

Instead, during the height of the Air War against the North, we divert F-4s to satisfy this guy's desire to see a combat drop, but without the danger involved in being shot at. This is the type of political General that we do not need.

August 22, 1966:

Sky Spot against the Tchepone Airfield in Laos. Tchepone is a heavily defended area, but we dropped from altitude through the clouds so that nothing came up against us. We were carrying 4X500s and we missed the airfield. Taxicab (GCI) estimated that we were only off by 100 feet, but the FAC only gave us holes in the ground for BDA. We were dropping on their command and could not see the ground.

August 23, 1966:

Big Eye today for 6 hours and 15 minutes. Really tires the ole rear end. The only significant occurrence was the interception of some Navy F-4Bs and A-4Ds that weren't squawking on their "parrot." The parrot is what we called the IFF (Identification Friend or Foe), which is the electrical gizmo that commercial airliners also carry. Whatever number it is squawking on the IFF can be read on the radars. But first, the IFF must be turned on.

It really sounded like the blips were MIGs and we dropped down to low level to hit them. My radar went out on the run-in so I switched to heat for a Sidewinder kill. We flew over a bunch of North Viet sampans right off the beach at Thanh Hoa and then pulled off after the pass and ID and almost went over the beach and their SAM emplacement. The Navy guys did not know how close they were to being shot down and all because they had forgotten to turn on their IFFs.

What was ironic is that I had switched from the Connie and was using the radar on the Navy destroyers out in the Gulf. So it was Navy guys who gave me the go-ahead to shoot down their own planes. After, of course, we had made the proper ID passes.

The idiot military planners who decided not to include the Vulcan gun internally in the Phantom did not think the problem through. I have been told that the planners envisioned an entirely missile war being fought at a distance. So they disregarded the fact that we had no offensive weapons within a mile of the airborne target. The problem is that any of us will always make an ID pass to ensure that we are not shooting our own guys. The problem then became that when we are close enough to ID, we are too close to shoot.

August 24, 1966:

Attacked a suspected POL storage area in the western part of the southern panhandle of the North. I carried 4X500 high drags and the bombing was just okay. I pulled in behind Ray Seal and we ran repeated strafe runs across the target. I thought I saw a brown secondary out of it. The cannon fired out of bullets and all we got was one road cut. A "road cut" is next to nothing.

August 25, 1966:

I was sitting as spare and someone had a ground abort so I was called on to fly. We flew to IV Corp and the Delta south of Saigon. My load was three napalm cans. We hit a VC position, where they were fighting some of our troops in the area. Choppers were moving and we had to vary our run-in headings to avoid them.

The Delta is very flat and we were hitting houses relatively in the open. I dropped all my napalm right on the hooches and the FAC was very happy. We left the area burning and he gave us 10 destroyed and five damaged.

LETTER HOME:
August 26, 1966:

"Today I only have 199 days left with 165 gone by. Time is rapidly slipping away, yet I feel that I've been here a lifetime already.

"Got back about a week ago from Okinawa, where I had a break. Stayed with a friend who flies C-130s and had a ball. All of the school teachers are back from last year. The Club was jumping and I got a lot of good relaxation. I also bought another tape recorder and a pre-amplifier for recording. It's a lot nicer than my Sony.

"Have a favor to ask. Could you please send over my blue uniform and my light blue shirt to go with it. I think I am going to need it on the return journey home. It looks for sure like I'll be getting one month off early and will be leaving here around the first week in February. I've got some friends over here who are looking after me.

"The squadron has had a complete changeover in the last two weeks. Almost all the Aircraft Commanders have left for the States and that leaves only a few of us left plus replacements. They've all done a good job and deserve to go home with a lot of missions flown."

COMBAT DIARY:
August 28, 1966:

We struck a village this morning in support of a big operation. Carried four BLUs. Colonel Quinn led it and it's the first time I've been in the burble in orbit over the target. The burble indicates you are close to stall.

It was a good target and my hits were good. Two of my napes hung up and I had to ripple them. My left throttle stuck in idle over the target and I could not break it free with my arm. I tried my left leg and still it would not budge. There seemed to be a mechanical blockage somewhere in the throttle linkage. I informed the back seater of our problem and asked his left leg for assistance. With both our left legs operating in unison, we were able to break it free, but not without a lot of effort. I was starting to have visions of losing a third aircraft because of the malfunction. It was really STUCK.

Our BDA was 11 buildings destroyed and five probable VC KBA. The afternoon's mission was scrubbed due to a cut tire.

This mission marked a turning point in my war. From here on, almost all the missions were against the North. Only two "in country" missions remained and two more against Tiger Hound. All the rest were either air-to-ground strike missions or MIG cover against the North.

> *"In war, haste can be folly, but I have never seen delay that was wise."*
>
> Sun Tzu

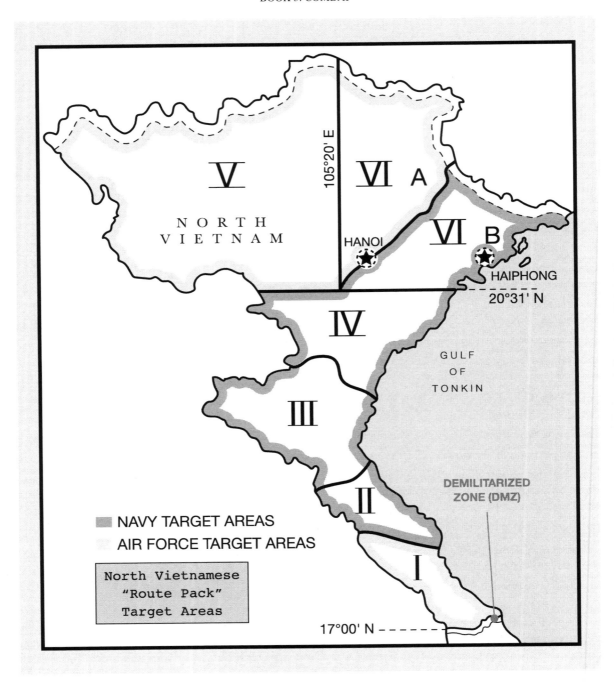

Department of Defense designated "Route Packs" — *This map depicts the seven "Route Packs" or attack areas as designated by the Department of Defense. "Tally Ho," an area hit heavily by the 12th TFW out of Cam Ranh Bay is located in the southern portion of Route Pack I. Hanoi is in Route Pack VI-A and Haiphong is VI-B.*

The Hanoi-Haiphong Target Complex was by far the most heavily defended areas of the SEA War.

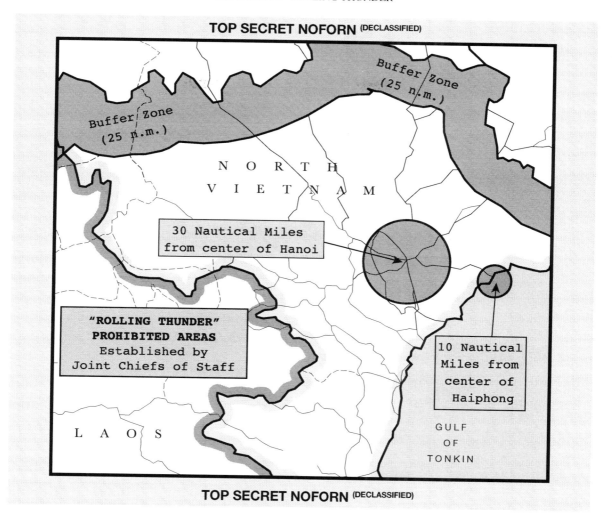

"Rolling Thunder" Strike Areas and Prohibited Areas in North Vietnam — *The area highlighted in yellow is North Vietnam. The orange (darker) are the areas that were prohibited from any air strikes until the Linebacker II missions in 1972. The orange area along the north (buffer zone) is a prohibited area next to the Chinese border with North Vietnam. The small circular area is around Haiphong Harbor and the larger one is around Hanoi.*

These prohibited areas constituted a sanctuary for the North Viets. In the circular areas around Hanoi-Haiphong, they placed their MIG fighter airfields, major supply warehouses, Anti-Aircraft Artillery (AAA) gun positions, railway yards, air-defense radar installations, Surface to Air Missile (SAM) sites, truck parts, troop barracks, military industrial plants, plus other military uses. The negative ramifications of this prohibition to the Air Force and Navy air wars of interdiction against North Vietnam cannot be overstated.

The "Rolling Thunder" missions were restricted to below the 20th parallel until June 11, 1965 and then expanded north of it to include all areas other than that shaded in orange. That target area was again changed by President Johnson in the fall of 1968; he increased the prohibition to include all of North Vietnam and that held until President Nixon attacked Hanoi-Haiphong in December of 1972.

The purpose of the massive Christmas raids of December, 1972, that utilized heavy bombers, was not to win the war but to force the North Vietnamese to the bargaining table so that Nixon could extricate the United States from the SEA war with a measure of dignity.

BOOK 3: COMBAT

CHAPTER TWELVE
Mounting Losses
Perilous Defenses

> *"Great is the guilt of an unnecessary war."*
>
> President John Adams

COMBAT DIARY:

August 30, 1966: **(ELINT, MIG Cover Mission)**

We flew the Wing's first flight on our new escort mission for the electronic intelligence or "ELINT" RB-66s. The flights are over Western North Vietnam, between Hanoi and the Chinese border. The flight takes about four hours and it's a 500-mile trip up. Major Barnes, our Squadron CO, was the flight lead and he had a bad radio so I took over the lead midway through the mission. The takeoff was at night with a wet runway. We all had full loads of missiles with 4 Sparrow and 4 Sidewinders each. The mission went fine until I landed. The Runway Condition Rating (RCR) was 8 and very slick due to rains. I landed on the slow light, as I should have with the conditions, but something went wrong and I started to side-skid with my nose to the right and the skid to the left. Nose-wheel steering and differential braking did no good. It started to straighten out and then I hit a patch of abrasive stuff on the aluminum runway. I felt the rough bumping of a blown tire. The anti-skid system had failed.

I fought the aircraft, trying to keep it on the runway. At about 60 knots, I lost it. It jacked to the left. The aircraft (610) skidded off and did a 150-degree turn before digging directly into a sand dune. The impact threw us both forward against our straps. I quickly shut the engines off and we both got out fast, ending up standing around for someone to arrive with wheels back to Operations. The right gear and wing spar were damaged, but not badly.[44]

August 31, 1966: **(ELINT, MIG Cover Mission)**

The same RB-66 MIG cover mission with a 5:30 takeoff. The same wet conditions and same souped-in weather up to and in the refueling track area. Major Barnes had a problem and I led again.

Refueling was in a thunderstorm on the Red Anchor track up in Thailand. My training in the back seat helped as I located the blip on radar, slowly rising up to merge with the blip as we were in heavy, souped-in weather and nobody could see the tanker. We were 10 feet away in the soup, when we finally saw his flashing belly light.

We didn't see any MIGs.

Author's Note: *44. Subsequent investigation found that the anti-skid system had failed and that the engines had been shut off in-time with no damage to either engine from ingestion. The base had to use a crane to lift the aircraft out of the sand.*

September 1, 1966:

Everything socked in by weather today. We went north and Tiger Hound was down. Called Tally Ho FACs and it was also down. I Corp in the South was down, so we ended up bombing some hooches under the trees near Phan Thiet, 70 miles to the south of Cam Ranh. Fifty percent ordnance on target with no hooches destroyed. Bombing was okay considering the FACs directions, but it was very turbulent around the bombing pattern. Load was 6X500s.

September 2, 1966: (ELINT, MIG Cover Mission)

Another flight covering the same mission as on the 30th and 31st. An armed escort of the Electronic Countermeasures (ECM) bird as MIG Cover. Barnes had another problem and I ended up as lead again. This is starting to get, old and I had better start preparing to lead it before the flight.

About the only significant thing that happened was hearing the Thuds go in and locate a downed pilot in the North who was shot down two days earlier. During our flight on the 31st, we heard Fresno Lead get hit and go down on the last mission up North, but they didn't get a response from him at the time. Today they went back in and this time they received a beeper response from him and initiated rescue procedures. It is a very good story.

September 3, 1966:

Carried four napalm cans against a storage area on the coast of Route Pack One. The air was filled with aircraft as we hit from various angles. The area was defended by 12 automatic weapons (AW) sites, 92 AAA guns of the 37 & 57 mm variety, and one of the 85 mm size. All told, we had 105 defensive guns. With all the guns, I didn't want to go down low, so I dove my cans in with a 30-degree dive angle and released at 4,000 feet AGL. Even from that altitude, the unstable cans went right on target. We spotted four warehouses burning as we left. The FAC called out three secondary explosions. I fired out 350 rounds from my gun on two strafe passes prior to the final pull off.

Our approach was from the water and very low (probably 50 feet) and fast. We rippled all the cans off on one pass and got out quickly. We saw no defensive reaction, although the automatic weapons were undoubtedly firing.

September 4, 1966:

Don Martin got sick on Big Eye today and we had to launch as spare to relieve him after 2.5 hours. He is still in the hospital with some type of problem involving loss of his sense of balance. By the time we got up to the Gulf to replace the lead's wingman, his time "on-station" was over, so we just turned around and flew back to Cam Ranh after refueling with the tankers south of Hainan.

September 5, 1966: (ELINT, MIG Cover Mission)

We had another early morning briefing as we have had for over a week now with a 3:30 get-up time. The morning ECM mission was about the most tiring I've ever flown. We flew for five hours with a full hour of it over western North Vietnam. It had me really jumping and straining to be sure that all the aircraft were covered from MIGs and that SAMs couldn't get us undetected. I again became de facto lead because Barnes called that he had a sick bird.

With the tension caused by the constant vigilance for missiles and the constant weave behind the RB-66 to give him fighter protection, it is very exhausting. Part of our problem is that we are the only Wing in all of SEA that does not have the electronic warning devices in our birds. The sensors warn pilots of the MIG Atoll missiles, MIG airborne radar, and SAM and AAA radar. If we had them, we could at least be forewarned. We don't even have the computers for bomb drops. It is all manual and that means FAST thinking in the dive.

The afternoon mission was against a truck park and storage area along the NVN coastal plain. Again the defenses were heavy with 28 AW sites, 57 AAA sites containing the 37 and 57 mm guns. Three of the sites contained the 85 mms that Intelligence tells us can reach up to 80,000 feet.

I dove in fast as we had no FAC and target recognition was from a photograph. I registered 7 "G"s pulling off, so I must have been receiving heavy fire. We were away in short order. We did not strafe and our drop load was 4X250s. The 250s are too small to drag all the way up to the North. We attribute these loads to the "Sortie War" being fought against the Navy. There was no BDA, but again my bombs were the most accurate and were all in the center of the target area.

Yesterday we lost a bird from Cam Ranh with our flight surgeon, Doc Simmons, in the back seat and Cliff Heathcote in the front. Cliff was a good friend and I knew his wife Pam when we worked together back at MacDill. Together we organized the homecoming celebration for the return of the 557th from Okinawa. She is beautiful with an English accent, striking blue eyes and black hair. She is also Cornish, having been born in Cornwall, which is where some of the ancient Bretons were driven by the Romans. Cliff was a good and gentle man.

Cliff and Doc were lost in a thunderstorm. It's another sad loss.

We got word today that Spike Nasmyth and Ray Salzarulo from Ubon took a direct SAM hit and both were killed. Spike was in my PSO class and lived two doors down from me at the Bennett Apartments in Tampa. Prior to that, he stayed in my St. Pete home when I was in Okinawa. After we came back from Okinawa, Pete Lappin and I gave up the St. Pete house and I moved to the Bennett. Ray was from the Academy and trained with us in the 45th at MacDill. I was with both of them at Ubon last month.

We also got word that Pat Sealey's plane got a hard-over up at Danang and went off the runway. The back seater got out okay but Pat's canopy was stuck. His plane was on fire and the only way he got out was when his canopy melted. The cockpit consoles were on fire and he was badly burned.

We also got word that Ken Robinson, from the old 43rd Squadron, was killed with his back seater at Route Package One, northwest of Dong Hoi, when they were hit on a roll-in and went straight in. The grim reaper is striking heavily these last two days.

September 6, 1966: (ELINT, MIG Cover Mission)

Two more missions against the North today. One was one of the most confusing and dangerous missions I've ever flown. We were confused from the start, when the frag orders were in error. We took off 17 minutes late and this time it was to fly the Gulf of Tonkin side of North Viet. Captain Owen, the flight lead, did a miserable job of joining us with the RB-66 after we had fed off the tanker. Just prior to join, I came the closest to a mid-air that I have ever had. The flight that almost hit us was our "Big Eye" flight with two planes that flew between me in 3 and Major Barnes in 4. Fifteen to 20 more feet and it would have been all over.

To top it off, Barnes had a gutless aircraft, which means we were continually behind lead and the 66. Barnes was my wingman and it was all I could do to keep sight of the 66 and also my wingman to the rear. We flew right over SAM sites at Thanh Hoa and near Vinh. With my situation, I was giving all my attention to keeping Barnes in sight and also the front runners. We were sitting ducks for the MIGs and SAMs. Barnes may be my CO, but he sure pissed me off. He can't fly worth shit. To top it off still further, lead again had radio problems.

The afternoon's mission was another Tally Ho with me leading and Barnes on my wing. My gun jammed as we went in after a storage area in the western part. No defensive reaction and the area was heavily rain-forested. The target was almost inaccessible, but my four napalm cans went off where they were aimed. BDA was obscured by trees and smoke.

September 7, 1966:

Two more missions against the North today. They were easy Tally Ho targets. On the morning mission, I carried 6X500s and I took over as lead again had radio problems. I took one pass and my bombs were "right on" as the FAC put it. I immediately headed south and the rest of the flight joined on. No BDA due to smoke. It was another storage area near a road.

The afternoon mission carried 4X250s (Sortie War) and the gun. My gun again jammed after about one or two bursts. The bombs were again good, but the FAC had no BDA for us. The FACs were flying high and couldn't see the storage area for all the bomb smoke. Again, lead had radio problems, so I took over after we rejoined halfway down to the base. After that, it was a merry trip through a thunderstorm.

The tally came through on aircraft losses. Last month (August) we lost 18 F-105s, a high for them. We also lost seven F-4Cs, which is a high for us as well. On the 4th of this month, we lost 2 F-105s and on the fifth, we lost one F-105 s well as an F-4E. The Thuds are slowly going into the horizon.

September 8, 1966:

Two more missions against the North today. And I flew my 100th combat mission as well.

This was another Sortie War mission with only 4X250s as a load. This morning's strike was against a storage area with a shed easily visible from attack altitude. The weather was broken and it was moving across the target area making variable-angle passes necessary. My bombs were the best of the lot, but we never got the building. I kick myself for not taking 10 mils off the bombsight. With the steeper dive bomb deliveries, I should have taken it out. I think I would have gotten it. The BDA was 75% ordnance in the target area.

The afternoon mission was my 100th and again I carried 4X250s up to North Viet. The target was gained visually without a FAC. It wasn't hard to spot because the target was located at a turn in the river. A road crossed the river and we hit truck parks on both sides of the road. I was number 2 in a flight of 2. Lead threw his bombs as he pickled and pulled off. I made two passes in "singles" and pickled twice per pass. It was an area target with all bombs hitting in the area with one partial road cut. A road cut is worth nothing as their manpower can quickly fill it.

September 9, 1966:

One more mission against the North today. My 20th NVN mission and one month off the time I have to stay in Vietnam. We hit two Tally Ho targets on this mission. We got part of a river ford (easily bypassed) on the first drop and I dropped a lousy napalm delivery in ripple the second. The first BDA went as a road cut and my pass was "forgiven" as obscured by smoke and foliage. I came in on a bad heading with my four napalms and didn't see the FACs second marking smoke until too late and I hesitated. He who hesitates is LOST and I dropped them all long. My fault.

LETTERS HOME:
September 9, 1966:

"190 days "in country" and 146 to go.

"I'm due home on the 14th of February, which means I'll leave here the first week of February. I've just been assigned to the Command Post as Controller, so I'll really have my hands full. This month is already my best flying month for time I've ever had and it is only the 20th. (55 hours this month so far). Being Controller means that I will be taking the shift with two others, which will cover the full 24 hours each day. Therefore, along with Awards and Decorations and being a flight leader, I'll have few free minutes. I didn't have any choice about the Command Post, but I did when they asked me to be a test pilot and I said "no." Experience is the key factor and it is all relative.

"When I arrived here six months ago, I was just the green guy from the States who had recently upgraded to the front seat and who was the first replacement pilot at Cam Ranh Bay. Now all the "old heads" are gone or are going home. So, what do I suddenly become, but the experienced "old head." It's a funny world.

"I'd rather not be a flight leader because that means I'm going to have to think and direct four aircraft in an attack and make the right decisions in case of emergency, which we are always on the edge of. It's a responsibility I'd rather not have at this stage.

"Send my uniform alone, no cap. I don't know if I told you, but I've been promoted and will become a Captain in December.

"I'll be home soon."

COMBAT DIARY:
September 12, 1966:

Dean Cook, a pilot with the 557th, was shot in the butt yesterday while flying in an Army chopper looking for the crash site of Cliff and the Doc. He was in great pain and they fished two pieces of lead out of him. It's a million-dollar wound though, because he now returns AIREVAC to the States.[45]

I flew a scramble mission off the PAD today and it was not too red hot. I carried 4 napalms and we hit our target heavy on fuel. I made good passes on the first two, but missed horribly on the last two. On the last two, the FAC gave us hooches in a rice paddy in a valley that was submerged in water. With the bird so heavy, I didn't want to risk not making the hill on the far side. I guess I was more concerned with the fast-approaching hill than with the accurate delivery of ordnance. However, I started a good fire on the hill. He gave us 75% on target.

Jim Grier got a BLC malfunction on the way home and we had to fly back at 190 Knots with the flaps

Author's Notes: *45. Dean later almost died flying to the States when the Air Evac aircraft shifted in flight and the movement caused a piece of imbedded shrapnel to cut an artery and he almost bled to death.*

down. After I landed and taxied off the runway, I got a flat. I waited for them to come pick the plane off the taxiway and carry it in. While I waited, I watched the takeoffs and landings. I was watching as a C-46 took off and caught fire. He had to quickly bend it around and return to the field.

September 14, 1966:

This was my first chance at leading a flight against the North from briefing all the way through and I blew it due to an aircraft malfunction that caused me to abort. Just after I taxied out to the arming area, they changed the runways on me and a thunderstorm hit the field. I sat out there for 20 minutes in the rain while they recovered aircraft on the other runway. Then we taxied the length of the runway and turned a 180. I got a CNI Cooling OFF light on engine run-up and that was supposed to abort the mission. I took off anyway. Seven attempts at shutting it off failed, even after turning off the radar and Tacan. So, I burned down fuel and landed without further incident.

I read in the Intelligence vaults today that North Koreans are manning the AAA sites up North. It is also suspected that the Cubans are helping. With all of the reports we have been getting, it sounds like the entire Communistic World is involved.[46]

September 15, 1966:

Bad news comes thick and fast. Ubon lost a bird on the 11th when a SAM hit Doug Peterson and his back seater at night. Both are missing and presumed dead. On the 12th, Kritzberg and Knutson (Academy) crashed on takeoff from Phan Rang and Knutson was killed when he ejected into the ground. Kritzberg was badly injured when his chute didn't fully deploy. I went through Jump School right behind Kritzberg and knew Knutson. On the 13th, John Stackhouse (Academy) and his back seater were killed at Ubon when they had flight control problems similar to Kritzberg and crashed on takeoff.

Yesterday, Hobo 27, a FAC friend who had controlled many of the strikes that I have flown, was shot down in the DMZ and was captured by the black pajama boys. I was scheduled to fly the strike mission that covered for him, but was taken off at the last minute.

He must have been in the process of being overrun by the North Viets because he called the cover flight to drop the napalm in on his own position. They may have killed him, but if they did they took lot of bad guys with him. It was probably a better end than prison anyway.

Today's mission was another ball buster with 6.5 hours on Big Eye followed with a night burner return to the base.

Author's Notes: *46. Years later, as a member of the Red River Valley Fighter Pilots Association, also known as the "River Rats," Ross Perot invited the Rats and the POW Wing to his ranch outside of Fort Worth, Texas. When we arrived at the event, he managed to shake the hand of each of us, Rat and POW alike. He is a very gracious man. Perot was also very hospitable and he invited all the Dallas Cowboys Cheerleaders to entertain us as we shared a barbeque. We also viewed an airshow, while we ate Texas-sized ribs. Lockheed Martin allowed us to tour their plant in Fort Worth. They also provided a detailed briefing on the F-35, for which they had started tooling up their factory. I even had a chance to lift the entire F-35 wing, it was so light. While the skin composition and internal design is still classified, it certainly presented a contrast to the very heavy Phantom. Many of the guys in charge of the Lockheed Martin presentations were Rats themselves, so we were treated to some TOP SECRET briefs about the F-35. Lockheed Martin treated us very well. While at the River Rat Reunion, the POW Wing presented a seminar. The POWs confirmed that the two Co-Commanders of the POW camp, called by the POWs the Hanoi Hilton, were Cuban military men.*

September 16, 1966:

I finally did manage to lead a flight from brief all the way through to landing and it was screwed up. We were fragged for Tiger Hound and the FAC, Covey 54, decided to hit another target so we orbited over the divert target for the FAC to arrive. He got there and decided we couldn't hit it because of the bad weather. Well, we contacted Hillsboro Control and they had no target in Tally Ho. We then went to Waterboy Control and they had no target except Sky Spot. We told them twice that we could not use our ordnance (slick bombs and napalm) on Sky Spot and they still kept trying.

We then went to Peacock Control at Pleiku and they got us an immediate target, since we were then low on fuel. We broke through the overcast and immediately found the FAC and had him mark. One half-circle and I hit it with my 4X500s and Jerry Shilt hit it with his napalm. Ray Seal had to make several passes before he discovered that he was trying to drop on the wrong station, which is controlled by the weapons delivery panel located on the cockpit console. The BDA was five hooches destroyed and the area left burning and under heavy smoke. The FAC, Cagey 82, said he would pass on further BDA later on.

Today a Special Forces troop was trying to get into Cliff and Doc's crash site and fell out of the chopper at 80 feet into the wreckage of the F-4. He had a compound fracture of his leg, plus a dislocated shoulder. He was lucky to be alive. The crash site indicated that both guys stayed with the aircraft and tried to pull it out before they hit in dense jungle on the upslope of a mountain.

Giere and Jim Knock were shot down over the DMZ today and were picked up within 15 minutes. It's Giere's second time and Jim's third. Knock looks like he has lost even more weight. They had one engine on fire and the other one cut off. They both will get to go home.

My former Flight Commander and co-owner of my Florida property, Major John Robertson and his back seater were flying a strike mission this morning out of Ubon for the Triple Nickel. A MIG 17 jumped his flight about 15 miles from the MIG base at Kep, near Hanoi. John was shot down and presumed killed. A friend of mine, Jerry Jamison, was able to shoot down the MIG 17.

John and I flew together when we showed the Phantom to Japan last year and also ferried the first replacement plane of the War down to Ubon from Naha. He was my Flight Commander both at MacDill and Naha. We owned real property together in Sarasota, Florida. He was always so hot to get a MIG. This loss hurts more than most and I worry about his wife Barbara. They were a close couple. It is a sad war.[47]

One of the problems with the long MIA status was that our property in Florida had a "cloud" on its title and Barbara and I were unable to sell it. Just another consequence of such a long, terrible war.

A positive in a very negative situation was that the Air Force continued to promote John while he was MIA. Upon the declaration of his KIA status, he was a full Colonel and his wife, then widow, was paid accordingly. The Air Force did help its own.

September 17, 1966:

No flying, but I sat mobile control and did awards and decorations today. We lost another bird up in Tally Ho, but we don't know which base owns it. The fighting is getting worse. I learned that my former Assistant Operations Officer for the new 45th (old 559th) at MacDill, Major Pat Patterson, had to eject at Ubon three

Author's Notes: *47. John was listed as MIA (Missing in Action) for nineteen years until the Air Force finally declared him KIA (Killed in Action). Barbara was left in a kind of limbo.*

days ago. He did it over their ordnance jettison area. The rear bolting on one of the TERs (triple bomb ejection racks) held up and it tore off, hit the tail section and started a fire. It happened less than an hour before John Stackhouse was killed. They suspect sabotage. That made two Ubon F-4s that went down in the same area within an hour of each other.

Politically speaking:

I'm getting fed up with our leadership and the way that it is running the war. I want out of the Air Force and out of Vietnam. This war is still basically a Sortie War against the Navy and Marine Corp. with the pilots used as cannon fodder. The Navy pilots are dealing with the same issue. The politicians could do so many things to make our position better.

Letter From Home:

This evening, I went down to the Flightline to do some paperwork and write a letter in answer to my brother's critical letter to me. Dave had written asking me "what the hell is going on?" He managed to criticize us as though we had something to do with us losing. Since we have our hands tied behind our backs in fighting the war, it is very frustrating to have to defend something that is indefensible, especially to a brother.

I could not tell him about the greatly restrictive "Rule of Engagement" that so hampered our ability to damage the enemy. I could not tell him that we were going against Chinese aircraft and that the Russians had been reported flying green-tailed MIGs up north. It was all very frustrating that my own brother did not support me. We could take the questioning from the public, but we relied on the support of our friends and family. That we were not allowed to fight to win made it all the more frustrating.[48]

Flaming Disaster at Cam Ranh:

At about 2100, as I continued to write my answering letter to my brother down at Flt Ops, I heard a tremendous explosion. The building, not that well-constructed, shook violently. My initial thought was that our base fuel storage tanks had somehow exploded. Rushing to the outside, my eyes took in the surreal sight of two planes falling in flames and making slow, silent circles in the night sky. The flames licked high into the sky above their craft as they slowly dropped to impact the water of the Bay. For some reason, the sound was muffled and I heard nothing of the impact. It was just so odd seeing everything as in slow motion and eerily silent.

Tonight was the weekly movie night at the theater. I was later told by one watching that they saw the same eerie descent of the twin torches, only their view was of the twin flaming spirals slowly dropping directly over the movie screen. The watchers could do nothing but stare in silent shock.

After watching the impact of the flaming aircraft with the water, I went back inside the flight shack and finished writing the letter to my brother. In it, I explained to him that I was not responsible for the war, other than my small part of it. I could not explain where and who we had been fighting, since it was classified. I did explain how many of my friends from the various bases had died in just this month of September. We were being decimated.

I finished the letter with a grim description of what I had just witnessed. Then I took the letter and quickly

---

Author's Notes: *48. The reports we received about the possible Russian MIG- involvement in the air war could not be confirmed. However, the Russians did later honor one of their "instructor" pilots who shot down six American fighters over North Vietnam.*

drove over to the base hospital to visit any possible survivors. Lying in his hospital bed, Captain Browning, the one guy who had survived the flaming Phantoms, told me what had happened.

It was a 558th combat flight that involved air support for a night recovery rescue for a downed helicopter. The flight of two had overstayed their cover mission and had to land at Danang to refuel before coming back to Cam Ranh.

As Browning explained to me, his wingman was joining on him for a tighter formation turn to their approach to the runway. The backseat guy in the wing aircraft had been given the job of flying the plane down from Danang. The GIB overshot his approach to the lead aircraft and slammed into him, killing himself and his aircraft commander plus the GIB in Browning's backseat. Bob Rocky and Mike Surwald were in the wing aircraft and Ed McCann was flying in Browning's back seat. Browning had been badly burned, but was able to talk and explain what had happened. He did not seem in pain, was surprisingly calm and did a good job of explaining.[49]

Rejoins at night have to be much slower than daytime in order to keep the other aircraft continually in sight by use of a much shallower slowing bank. Night visibility can also play tricks with depth perception and with properly ascertaining closure speed.

LETTERS HOME:
September 17, 1966:

"This is just a short note to let you know that all is well over here. I've flown 106 missions so far and am definitely coming home in February, possibly sooner.

"I am presently sitting out at the end of the runway in Mobile Control observing runway operations and watching for any emergencies. Our days are taken up with this and sitting alert at the end of the runway; or going to meetings; or sitting in the cockpit as spare aircrew for any plane or crew which may abort either on the ground or in the air; or planning and briefing for flights; or flying them and debriefing them.

"Many of our missions are now 6-7 hours long and these are tremendously tiring Northern missions. We are always flying the plane because I never use the autopilot. The autopilot has been known to malfunction and aircraft have been lost because of it. The missions consist of looking for the tankers, often in the weather; or refueling off them; or looking for MIGs; or keeping track of the other guys in the flight; or looking for SAMs. When we arrive back here from those missions, we are just exhausted. The actual strike missions are the best because they last only 1+45 to 1+55 hours long.

"We are presently entering the monsoon season and we still have one more month to fly off the aluminum runway. It's just like ice during the rains. They've made me a flight leader, which means I'm probably the only Lieutenant flying Phantoms in this miserable war that's leading flights on combat strikes. It's an added responsibility, which means I have the responsibility of eight pilots instead of two.

"During any "free" time I have, I devote to writing recommendations for decorations, which is the hardest and most frustrating job I've ever experienced. It actually requires a full-time man. It wouldn't be so

---

Author's Notes: 49. *Rejoining another aircraft at night is a tricky maneuver. The trick is to properly judge the rate of closure between the two aircraft. One can rejoin quickly and stop abruptly, when close to the other aircraft, by banking sharply and pulling back sharply on the stick. That is best done during daylight hours. The problem with a faster closure is that the bank has to be steeper than usual and that blanks out visibility of the other aircraft.*

bad, if they would leave well enough alone and just accept the damned documentation, but we now have a new Commander of the 7th Air Force and the policies keep changing down in Saigon and our own paperwork mill is long and laborious to such an extent that the write-ups get out-of-date before we can get them up to 7th Air, so the whole process starts all over again.

"With the rapid changeover in personnel, added requirements from 7th Air, and the increased knit-picking attitude of our own ground-pounders who think pilots have time to burn in going through the extensive administrative machinery, and the added administrative burden of 193 enlisted men just dumped in our laps, it makes for a very frustrating time indeed.

"I've about decided to start working nights to make it up. Once I get caught up, then only time will make the difference and no sweat. But we had 30 write-ups that had been sent down to 7th Air when General Momyer took over. I had to do all the typing and they had to be perfect with no typos or corrections or they would be returned to Cam Ranh.

"Momyer kicked all 30 recommendations for awards back down on "form." The forms that I submitted were the forms desired by the outgoing General Moore and Momyer's actions added up to the negation of countless hours of work. We have to start all over again. Do these guys know that there is a war going on and we are terribly short-handed to even fly, notwithstanding the stupid paperwork? [50]

"As for our quarters, they've gone through them and torn everything out that we had built and started all over again. Well, they didn't plan ahead and ran out of lumber so we live in the biggest mess you ever saw. Nobody knows where any of their stuff is located.

"The "third" man in charge decides to inspect our quarters. Imagine inspecting the homes of grown officers! Well, he decides that the place isn't fit for a visiting General, who may or may not look through the Quonset. He had everybody's stuff thrown into boxes and nobody knows where their stuff is and everybody's stuff is mixed up in all those boxes. So, I have no way of knowing where my other hats are and only have the one on my head.

"This morning somebody in the Quonset borrowed or moved the hat that belonged on my head, so I walked down to Operations without my hat and some Colonel makes a wise comment about me not having a hat on. I felt like jamming my fist down his throat. He's worried about inspecting quarters while at the same time he has a plane shot down over North Vietnam and should be worrying about whether we got the pilots out or not. This is the type of leadership we have over here and one of the reasons I have definitely decided to get out of the military and the sooner the better.

Author's Notes: *50. This action by General Momyer had adverse effects on the careers of some of our deserving pilots. The re-submissions of those 30 denied submissions would never be received back at Cam Ranh before I left for the States. When I was flying out of England, I met one of the 30 denied pilots at an Officer's Club in Germany. He confronted me with the fact that he had not received the DFC that he richly deserved. I was embarrassed and mortified. Thus a "power" act by Momyer was detrimental to the careers of those affected by not receiving the decorations that they earned.*

51 (next page). After leaving Vietnam and enroute to England, I stopped by Washington D.C. While there, I met with Congressman Charles Teague and told him of my concerns. He scheduled a meeting with me, Congressman Charles Gubser and another member of the House Armed Forces Committee. The Committee was scheduled to leave the following week for a "fact finding" trip to SEA. I told them of my concern with the quality of targets and that we were not winning the war. I also told them that we were already fighting China because the only language spoken on the North Vietnamese MIG Strike Frequency was Chinese. The Congressmen thanked me for my input and then proceeded to visit Vietnam where they were told the "true" story by our military briefers. There was no action taken on my statements.

"The whole operation of running this war is terrible. The stupidity of our national planners and leaders is amazing. I doubt if even they realize what's going on in this war. [51]

"I've been hitting North Vietnam, but it's a relatively lightly defended area and nothing to be overly concerned with. But the other Phantom bases have been hitting the heavily defended areas and the defenses are intense and growing moreso. Yet, our great leaders refuse to let us hit "obvious" targets. Why not hit their airfields and catch the MIGs on the ground? Why not hit the Red River dike systems and flood the lands so that their anti-aircraft system is flooded? A byproduct would be destruction of much of their agriculture production. Why not hit Haiphong Harbor and the river transport system carrying the bullets that shoot at us and the supplies we are supposed to be interdicting?

"Now we are sitting and watching the North Viets build an anti-aircraft defensive network. We aren't winning the war yet either."

COMBAT DIARY:
September 18, 1966: (ELINT, MIG Cover Mission)

An Electronic Counter Measures (ECM) escort mission today over the Gulf of Tonkin. We wandered over the Gulf islands on the east side of North Vietnam. This time I saw a MIG.

While flying over Haiphong and covering the 66, I had a plane fly alongside us for a way, but he was at a distance and initially I could not tell if he was a MIG. The Navy radar guys said that they had been following him for an hour and that he was not squawking. They also felt that, based on his actions, he was a MIG. Radar

Just before a bombing attack against the Hanoi area, a California airman, A2C Michael R. Ravenscroft of Tarzana, presented Goodenough with a flag to be carried on the mission.

gave us the okay to attack. I turned toward him and pulled. In response, he turned away and dove toward the ground. I followed him down and kept turning him. He was evading me and I felt by his profile that he was not one of ours.

But, my job was to protect the RB-66. We were over land and it was a MIG Cover and not a MIG Screen mission, so the chance of being followed by MIGs was increased. The MIGs had a habit of following the ELINT planes and not those of either "Big Eye" or "Big Look."

The reaction of the pilot confirmed to me he was a MIG, but I did not want to follow him all the way down as I suspected that was what he wanted me to do. My mission was to protect the 66 and keep it from being shot down by a MIG. Of the RB-66s that had been shot down, they had managed to lure protecting Phantoms away before attacking.

Today they found the remains of the three pilots killed last night. They also got to the crash site today and determined that Cliff and Doc are both dead. Due to the extent of the search for the aircraft and the great flare activity for the last night of the search for the crash site, over 250 VC have surrendered to the Special Forces team going into the crash site. More are coming in all the time. Guess they think we will launch a major assault.

September 19, 1966:
Another Big Eye and another six and a half hours. It is really a "butt buster."

September 20, 1966:
Carried 4X500s in a ripple pass against a storage area in North Vietnam today. I was flight lead and the flight went very well. The weather in the target area was bad and I had to immediately pick up the FAC aircraft against the green background and deliver the ordnance. It went very fast. First we motored in and immediately picked up the FAC and he immediately marked the target and we immediately dropped our bombs in ripple and immediately left the target area. The entire attack probably took less than two minutes. That is how I love to attack. It usually means that you beat the defensive gunners and get away without combat damage.

September 29, 1966:
After a long combat pause, I Flew as #2 in a flight with Colonel Quinn. It was against Tally Ho again with six 500s dropped. No BDA given.

We were ordered to fire the gun with only target practice ammo and not the more effective HEI. Cam Ranh has no explosive ammo for us to use.

September 30, 1966:
Four napalms carried against a storage area in Laos. We were directed against 55-gallon oil storage drums. What a stupid target. The drums were painted red, which leads me to believe that they must have been dummies to draw us in on them. Why on earth would the enemy paint them red if they didn't want them hit? They must have been empty because I fired 350 rounds into them with no ensuing fire. What a waste of gasoline (JP-4) and munitions. We were credited with destroying seven 55-gallon drums and getting one

secondary explosion. Those results only paid for a little of our mission cost.

October 2, 1966:

My 25th mission against NVN was my stupidest mission. It was an early morning get-up for a two-ship attack against Tally Ho. I flew Ray Seal's wing.

My stupidity was staying up, drinking and partying the entire night before. I must have hit the sack about 5 for a 5:30 get-up. Several of the guys had to drag me out of bed. I was still smashed when we took off to the North. I was "drinking" in the 100% oxygen. Drinking and driving do not mix and drinking and flying is stupid suicide.

Sometimes I wonder why I wasn't killed long ago. It must be the nature of fighter pilots to try everything once, sometimes twice. Bad enough that I add another factor to an already ticklish situation up North, but there are other people that I have to consider and the mission entrusted to me. I guess maybe the tension has been getting to us all lately. We've been losing a lot of planes and guys, especially friends up north, but that is no excuse.

The mission itself was challenging. The target area in the NVN panhandle was covered with a low cloud cover and we punched down underneath to find the targeted storage area. Ray and I each carried 4X500 pound bombs. The visibility was low due to rain and we leveled at about 800 feet. All North Vietnamese strike missions were supposed to have a minimum altitude of 5,000 feet, but there was no way we could observe that altitude with the clouds covering the target.

When we were at 800 feet, we both started searching for the target that had been shown to us in the pre-flight photos. Sometimes it is quite difficult to tell if we are picking up fire from the defensive guns. This was compounded by the rain. We were set up and in a very vulnerable position and obviously were picking up heavy AAA fire as a later inspection of battle damage revealed.

We finally spotted our target and maneuvered for the attack. Due to the clouds, the attack had to be level. One pass with four quick releases put my bombs right on target. It was a beautiful pass. After release, I banked around so that the backseater could get a visual damage assessment. He related to me that two of my bombs actually bounced off the bridge, but did not explode.

My first thought was that my drop altitude had been too low to allow for the four-second free fall arming fuse to fully arm prior to impact. The drop in all probability was too low. However, my post-strike de-arming check revealed that I had failed to arm the bombs before drop. What a stupid waste and it was my entire fault. All the way to NVN, brave the guns and then forget to arm. My backseater must have been disgusted. Maybe I hit somebody on the head.

On the way home, I flew over to Ray's plane and gave him a once-over. He had sustained severe battle damage. I spotted a big hole in Ray's tail caused by one of the unseen AAA shells being fired at us. The hole was at least a yard to four-feet wide.[52]

I don't exactly know when it happened, but it was sometime in October that I started to change. Some of

Author's Notes: *52. It was about this time that I started to call the prior month the September Blitz. It was in September that Phantom losses reached 13, which would not be matched until 1972 during the invasion of the South by the North. By October, our squadrons were terribly short manned. And the bases tasked against North Vietnam were suffering horrific casualties.*

my humanity was lost. My outlook was different and I am not sure that I liked what I eventually became. I also noticed that, starting in the latter part of September, my combat diary entries were getting shorter and shorter. By the end of October, I stopped making entries altogether.

We were overwhelmed. I was still working the Command Post and would until mid-December. Our squadron lost two aircraft in November to automatic weapons fire on a single pass and by the end of November our squadron was down to 14 pilots from a start of 48. Many of those missing pilots had left to fly back to the States.

In the first week of December, my squadron lost another two aircraft, one in the North to a SAM, and we were then down to 10 pilots total. That is hardly enough to man a Flight much less a Squadron. After that first week of December, I was serving as Summary Court Officer for the eight pilots downed from our squadron. We had two pilots killed when they were vectored by GCI into a hill and six were taken prisoner by the North Vietnamese. One of the pilots subsequently died in captivity, but five were eventually returned in "Operation Homecoming."

This might seem a lot of pilots and aircraft lost, but our losses paled in comparison to the F-105s out of the Thai bases.

October 6, 1966:
Led an in-country mission today using 4X500 HD (high drag) bombs. One of the guys had battle damage on the mission and had to abort early. The flight lasted an hour and a half.

October 7, 1966:
Ken Cordier led the flight against a POL storage area in Tally Ho. The area was located in the usual dense foliage and assessment of damage was impossible. However, 100% of the ordnance fell in the designated target area. We diverted to Ubon to gas up and returned to CRB uneventfully.[53]

The night that Kenny went down, I visited the Officer's Club at Cam Ranh and deliberately wore my hat into the bar, which indebted me to buy all of those in the bar a round of drinks. Then I squeezed the horn on the wall and that cost me another round of drinks. The entire bar hoisted our glasses and toasted Ken and his backseater.

October 8, 1966:
Another Tally Ho attack against a truck park and storage area. Dropped all five 500- pounders on target.

LETTERS HOME:
October 10, 1966:
"Before I get started, I would like to assure you of something: If any bird would ever go down, or anything would happen, you would be the first to know, before the newspapers, or anyone. So, if you hear nothing, rest assured that things are well.

Author's Notes: 53. *Within the month we would lose Ken in a shoot-down to a surface- to-air missile. It was later confirmed that he had been taken prisoner in the North. He served six long years in Hanoi. On repatriation, the POWs formed a POW Wing and Ken served as its commander.*

"Did you see the story in Life Magazine; it was in the Sept. 9th issue, about Cam Ranh that shows all the pictures? Some great pictures that showed a Phantom in a rocket run. It was Gene Fischer.

"Can you send me some bleach and laundry soap? We can't get them here.

"Major John Robertson, my former Flight Commander and co-owner of the property in Florida, was shot down and killed by a MIG and is listed as MIA. He may be alive, but the conjecture among pilots is that he's dead. A friend of mine, Jerry Jamison, shot down the MIG that got John. Tell Bob Lynn that John is probably dead.

"As of today, I have 129 days left. Almost assuredly, I will get a month knocked off, so as of today it's probably 99 days left. I am shooting for two months off and I have a good chance of doing it, so I am counting 69 days left.

"The base is flying almost entirely against North Vietnam. I have flown 25 missions against the North and only need 35 more to get out around the first part of December. I have a total of 115 combat missions-to-date.

"A lot of the pilots are leaving and going back home, which leaves few of us "old heads" left. We aren't getting many replacement pilots in and I don't know when we will. The pilot situation is critical. It all stems from the wide range of commitments we have made and the use by the AF of 2 pilots per aircraft.

"The pilots in Thailand are leaving after 4-5 months and 100 missions against the North, which means that the turnover is fast. Therefore, I am going to be careful how I play my cards or I'm going to be pulled back for another tour before I can get out. The dissatisfaction among the new pilots is great.

"The AF has no feelings for personnel or the individual. Their actions are purely for the service and its needs. You can't run a system without people. When the great numbers of us come up for resignation at the ends of our commitments, then the powers will suddenly be concerned and try to "correct" past errors and give some carrot to attract the pilots. What the AF doesn't quite realize is that too many will say, "You wanted pilot officers with college degrees to man your aircraft. Those degrees and skills will assist us in getting other jobs. We don't need you and therefore you can "go to hell."

"The Air Force these days is a bad place for married pilots. As a bachelor, the Air Force life is great. But separation is the name of the game in the Air Force and that's no type of life for marrieds. In Tactical Air Command, prior to the war, pilots spent about three-fourths of their time away from home once they became combat ready. Now we have this war and it's a war that isn't being fought to win. To hell with them if they expect me to be their cannon fodder in a war such as this.

"Missions have been slow of late due to the monsoons. They are here to stay a while. I've been very busy in the Command Post. I rather like the Post now that I'm into it because I can name when I want to fly and what missions and don't have to sit alert. I don't like alert.

"Dad, I don't know if I've said it before, but congrats on the fine shooting with the clubs. Two recent holes-in-one is quite an accomplishment. You both have done quite well.

"I read that the star of Rawhide, Eric Fleming, drowned and also that he was from Santa Paula.

"Looks like the Dodgers did it again and USC and UCLA look tough. Air Force beat Washington and Navy, so things are looking up.

"You needn't worry about my being careful. Longevity is spelled with a capital C for caution. Thanks for the vote of confidence and the offer of backing for finances on any additional schooling. Remember the GI Bill of Rights? I'll be able to get 36 months of schooling for about $150 per month. By the way, I'm not

Squadron Commander, just a leader of flights.

"Could you send me some shower thongs? And an additional favor: I can't get out to do it, since there are no florist shops here, so: please wire Judy a dozen long-stemmed red roses and time it to arrive on the 17th of October, her birthday. And just add a little something from me. Take the cost out of my account."

COMBAT DIARY:
October 11, 1966:
Tally Ho again only this time against the DMZ and just north of it. We carried four napes on one of the strangest missions I have flown. Our target was—a mule train. A mule train carrying supplies for troops in the South. The terrain was a gently rolling plateau with dry meadows and sparse tree growth. We could plainly see the mules and my napes were all on target. We were credited with six pack animals destroyed. Believe it or not, we got two secondary explosions out of them. They must have been loaded with ammo.

October 12, 1966:
Tally Ho carrying 4X500 pounders and destroyed two trenches. Ray Seal was with me and we also hit a VC Command Center.

October 13, 1966:
Tally Ho carrying 4X500 pounders with no BDA.

This afternoon, Wing Director of Operations Colonel Allen asked me to come down early to the Command Post. On my arrival, he asked me if I would like to fly to Thailand and be the representative of the 12th Wing in finding out how the F-105s were employing their CBUs.[54]

The pattern of the bomblets was oval shaped and extended farther than a football field. The CBUs are an anti-personnel weapon designed to kill the gun operators. The Air Force considered that the kill ratio for them was 100% in the oval impact area.[55]

October 17, 1966:
Of course my answer to Col. Allen was yes. The 12th Wing was just starting to get CBUs on base and we had already flown our first missions with them.[56]

Going to Thailand was a very familiar trip for me. This would be my fourth trip after the 1965 replacement

Author's Notes: *54. CBUs are Cluster Bomb Units and were a devastating weapon used in SEA. They were used for flak-suppression against AAA that was protecting targets. The CBUs were housed in 750-pound bomb canisters that contained 600 small hand-grenade-like bomblets that would explode on contact. After being dropped, the 750 canisters would blow open and the bomblets would spin-arm in the air. The bomblets, or cluster bombs, were filled with ball-bearing-like projectiles which would be thrown out 360 degrees with devastating effect.*
55. A tragic aftermath of the war in Laos was the great number of unexploded bombs that killed so many long after cessation of hostilities. Estimates of remaining unexploded bombs hover around 30 million and most are CBU bomblets.
56. In retrospect, I think Col. Allen was being kind to his Command Post Nocturnal Commander. He was fully aware of how we had been buried with pilot losses that included those returning to the States and those who had been either killed or taken prisoner. He was also aware that I worked nights on Awards and Decs for the Wing as well as for the Squadron. He was also aware that I was spending my days flying the missions and what free time I had was spent as Summary Court. I figured that he just wanted me to get away and he knew that I loved Thailand.

flight and the two Intelligence trips I took that summer. The Thai F-105 bases had employed the CBUs for months. What method had those guys found to be most effective? They had the experience and we wanted to find out.

Armed with orders from the 12th Wing, I jumped on a C-130 heading for Don Muang Air Base just outside of Bangkok. At Don Muang, I found another C-130 heading "up-country" and I jumped aboard. The plane stopped at Korat RTAFB, which stands for Royal Thai AF Base. It might have been owned by the Thais, but it was manned exclusively with F-105 crews, maintenance, administrative and support personnel. Korat resembled Ubon in its primitive look, but the surrounding countryside was much less dense than Ubon. Ubon was literally created out of the jungle. The Thud drivers had been located at Korat longer than the outfits at Ubon. Korat had that "lived-in" look.

The reception that I received in the 105 squadron I visited was not really cold, but they had more important things to do than talking with a Lieutenant from Cam Ranh. At the time, Cam Ranh had limited experience in the North. Most of our air-to-ground missions had been against Tally Ho, which was in the extreme south of North Vietnam. Cam Ranh did not carry the reputation that it later would. Of the Phantom bases, Ubon and Udorn had the rep.

The F-105 guys did warm up when they found out the reason for my visit. That meant that the Phantoms from Vietnam would be joining those out of Thailand in the bombing strikes against the more heavily defended targets in Route Packs Five and Six, which meant Hanoi and Haiphong. They did need help. The Thai bases of Korat and Takhli had carried most of the load for a long time. They were, of course, augmented by the US Navy and the F-4s at Ubon.

While at Korat, I talked to the Commander of one of the squadrons. He told me that he found arming the second plane with the CBUs was effective. The theory was that the first plane in on the target would get the gunners out of their protective bunkers and manning the guns. This was when they were the most vulnerable. But the crews were wondering the same things that we were. Which bird would be the most effective?

One of the other squadrons was arming the 4th plane with CBUs. The enemy was certainly resourceful and would change their strategy to match ours. If the second plane expended its CBUs, then the gunners would know that the flight was empty of CBUs and would then open up with intense flak. Perhaps the answer was to arm the 2nd and 4th planes with them. But that also meant that the defenses had managed to cut the entire bomb load of the flight in half. If we armed the 4th plane, then the gunners might be in action before his dive. Such were the considerations.

The tactics meetings were rather short. This gave me time to wander around, talk to the pilots and see the base. What I saw was disturbing. The pilots were like zombies. There were no smiles. They earned a ticket home with 100 "counter" missions against the North. They rarely flew Laotian missions and never flew South Vietnamese missions. Laotian bombing strikes were not counters, although our Cam Ranh strikes encountered defenses in Laos that were much stiffer than those in the South and approaching the North in difficulty.

The attitude of the pilots at Korat was that 100 missions against the Red River Valley was almost a ticket to death. Their chances of achieving their goal were a lot less than 50%. I could see it in their eyes. They seemed to think that it was not a question of whether they would be shot down and either die or be taken prisoner, but when. Even with the extensive and courageous rescue attempts, most of the Thuds that were downed were not rescued. It was sad.

It is the nature of fighter pilots to think that they are invincible. The instantaneous transition from the cockpit to a parachute in an ejection can cure that bit of overconfidence. I had been cured twice. All of us who had ejected knew just how quickly the cockpit cocoon could be lost. The pilots at Cam Ranh never did lose that feeling of invincibility, but the guys at Korat had lost it. They thought that they were dead men and behaved accordingly.

After the flight brief for a Route Pack Six mission, I walked to the tarmac with one of the pilots. The Thuds were single-engine and single-pilot weapon systems as opposed to the Phantom, which had two men and two engines.

The Thud guy did his pre-flight on the fighter and on its bomb load, then turned around and went to the edge of the parking apron and puked. He apologized and then mounted the boarding ladder. There was no crew chief to send him off. He would rejoin his flight mates in a trip down the taxiway to the runway. It was truly a single-man operation.

These guys had lost it and they had every reason to lose it. Never before had aircrews been asked to attack targets that were protected by such heavy defenses. Our Cam Ranh missions seldom sent us to Route Packs Five and Six. These guys went there every day. They knew they were dead and they still launched. How do you measure that kind of courage?

October 18, 1966:

I got on another C-130 that was on a "milk run" and landed at Takhli. I got out, stretched and looked around. The few fighter pilots that I saw convinced me that these guys had lost it too. Takhli was flying the same stuff as Korat. They didn't need to puke in front of a guy from Cam Ranh. My trip to Korat was enough. I didn't need to talk tactics with these guys. I got back into the Hercules.

On each of my previous trips to Thailand, I had spent time at Ubon. I knew the bamboo, thatch and chicken wire hooches that the pilots called home. I had slept in them. I had walked enough times on the wooden boardwalks to keep my feet out of the constant monsoon-filled mud holes. At Ubon, we walked on board planking between our home hooches, the "O" Club and the Flightline. The F-4 drivers out of Ubon had also been hitting tough targets. Their losses in pilots and equipment were horrific and approached that of the Thud bases. They did not need me to remind them that they were flying much tougher missions than Cam Ranh. Many of my buddies that I had drunk with not much more than a month before were now gone with many shot down. With their loss rate, much of the camaraderie would probably be gone. I then decided that I would also bypass Ubon and go where the C-130 would carry me.

The Hercules carried me to Udorn and a visit to the CIA. That visit is detailed in another chapter entitled "Spook Heaven" about clandestine combat and the CIAs participation.

October 19, 1966:

I arrived home to news that two more F-4s had been shot down. One was from Ubon, but the other was a night mission being flown by the 480th TFS out of Danang. Murray Borden was aircraft commander of that flight. Murray was one of the backseaters with me in the 559th when we first started out at MacDill. He flew as my backseater on my first navigation mission after returning to MacDill from Okinawa. I was a guest for dinner in his home when we flew to Seymour Johnson for a firepower demonstration. Both he and his backseater were killed. Tonight, I didn't feel like celebrating at the Club and, instead, drank beer alone from our squadron reefers.

My subsequent report to Colonel Allen was that there was no set policy at either of the Thai bases about which plane in a flight to arm with the lethal load. That much I had gleaned from my few chats that I had with wandering pilots at the second Thud base, Tahkli.

While there was no set policy, there was a consensus that either #2 or #4 in a flight should be loaded. But there was no consensus among the Thud drivers about which method would kill more gunners. My choice was #2 and that is what I reported to Col. Allen. I also reported that it might be wise to consider varying which plane had the CBUs. That way the enemy would be constantly left wondering.

CONQUEST OF FEAR:

Fear is ever-present in combat. It is a normal emotion and those experiencing it should feel no shame. Fear can elicit beneficial qualities, but can also pose a problem for a participant. Fear needs to be confronted and conquered.

I recall as a small boy being left alone at night in our ranchhome. Often, my parents would attend social gatherings and felt that I was responsible enough to be left alone. At the time, my fear was of the dark. It took time, but eventually I was able to develop the courage to descend the stairs into our very dark basement. Once I was able to do it, my attitude greatly changed. Instead of being afraid, I became part of the darkness. The simple act of doing what I feared to do cured me of the fear and I began to relish the dark.

In Vietnam, dangerous missions into well-defended areas were conquered in the same manner as the dark. They became challenges and I began to relish them.

EXPERIENCING DANGER AND GRIEF:

The night of my return from Ubon was one of introspection regarding the continual and escalating number of planes and crews being lost. The introspection was filled with sadness for those who were gone. It had become apparent to me that men and women, both individual and collectively, handle grief in different ways.

My father was born in 1902. The Frontier in California is said to have lasted until 1910, meaning that my father was a child of the Frontier. In those days, part of what fathers taught sons was how to shoot weapons and practice safe hunting; to show them how to properly treat and behave as a gentleman toward women; to show strength and be able to shoulder grief. It was not considered manly for a man or boy to cry. As a consequence of my father's guidance, the last time I had ever cried was when I was in the 7th grade.

While I do think it is important for a father to raise his boy-children to be strong, I envy the ability of a woman to cry. It is an emotional release and allows a woman to get the emotional poison out of her system.

It is hard for a military man to try to convey the thoughts and feelings of being under the constant threat of imminent death. For a woman that has not experienced combat to equate, I suppose one would have to go back to the 1800s when the instance of the death of a mother during childbirth was so great. Emotionally, for a pregnant woman of the 1800s to go into labor must have been a terrible two-edged sword. Part of the emotional peak must have been elation at having a child and the other part must have been dread at what might happen. In the instance of grief, the ability of having a pressure-release in the form of tears would help get the grief out in the open where it could be dealt with. For a man like me and so many of us that

211

experienced intense war, the grief is internalized. When grief is piled on grief, then the stress can manifest itself in unfortunate ways.

The rainy Okinawan night when we lost Dell Dyer and his backseater during low-level intercept practice over the East China Sea, was a night of grief for many of us. Inside, we all were bleeding. Outside, we covered it up by having a party and partially drowning our sorrow in drink. Drink is no cure for grief, but it does cover up the symptoms. The school teacher who berated us for our insensitivity, showed her own level of insensitivity. As men, we could not show our sorrow. Part of the equation was our thought that it could have been any of the rest of us who had crashed that night. The school teacher could not understand and none of us was about to teach a teacher.

The morning at Cam Ranh when I went down to the Club for breakfast and found out that Terry Griffey had been killed, I mourned inside but could not let the rest of the guys notice. Terry and I had shared similar roles. We both were Academy classmates and both had been upgraded to Aircraft Commander. We were two of only five guys at Cam Ranh who had been upgraded from the back seat and we both were still Lieutenants. Those common circumstances threw us together and we would spend quality time at the Club getting to know each other. Terry was one of the real good guys and it hurt greatly to lose him. Many of us mourned and mine was significant, but it was also internal.

The greatest war loss for me was Scotty Wilson. Scotty was another Academy classmate. We had been together in the old 559th at MacDill and he had also been upgraded. We had grown close in Florida. Scotty had been transferred to Danang and on the morning of his death, he was on a mission over North Vietnam. There was an undercast layer of white clouds. It was determined that he had been downed by a SAM missile launch and it was speculated that the white missile could not be visually picked up against the white background of the undercast. At four times the speed of sound, the SAM would not take long to reach the aircraft. I loved Scotty Wilson and my internal pain was severe.

It was those and other early losses that caused a defensive mechanism to develop within. I am sure it also occurred in others. When the losses of guys that I knew kept getting more and more frequent, I started to shut it all out. I pushed my emotions down deeper and deeper with each loss.

By the time I left SEA, I had managed to cover over most of the pain. It might have seemed that I and others like me did not care about the losses of our combat-brothers. That was not the case. We cared very deeply.

The process of burying emotions did manage to lessen the stress. But the blunting of emotions regarding the other pilot losses also had a downside risk. My feelings for other people were affected. However, the loss of Scotty managed to break through the outer shell I was building. His death was one of those times that greatly affected me. The mechanism of dulling my emotional response and pushing the feelings to some remote part of me, led me to my return home feeling as a lesser man. But, at least I returned alive and with a rational mind, albeit with an emotional deficit.

> "In peace, sons bury their fathers.
> In war, fathers bury their sons."
>
> Herodotus

CHAPTER THIRTEEN
"Flaming Skies"
Missiles, MIGs & Guns

> *"The only way human beings can win a war is to prevent it."*
>
> General of the Army George C. Marshall

For fighter-bomber pilots, missions targeting the North were filled with trepidation. The farther north we flew, the greater the chance that death might await our arrival. Will we be greeted with the seemingly-innocent puffs of fire that rained destruction? Will the missile-driven expanding fireballs-of-fate determine our destiny? Sometimes, the blue that canopied our targets turned a fiery red and orange as if the earth below had erupted.

Radar and heat-seeking missiles were quietly waiting for us on ground-mounted SAM launchers and the airborne underwing-rails of MIG fighters. Cannon shells were loaded in automatic weapons and the deadly anti-aircraft artillery barrels were pointed skyward. As our flights flew north from Cam Ranh and Danang, east from the Thai bases, or west from the aircraft carriers, we wondered what the enemy might unleash. The weapons at the disposal of those defending North Vietnam were fearsome.

"The North Vietnamese mounted the most sophisticated and effective anti-aircraft defense in the history of warfare." The dreaded defenses of the German Reich, that posed such a threat to our incoming bombers, paled in comparison. No other aerial combat comes remotely close to the intensity of the defensive system that awaited us in the North. The Vietnamese built it well, but they did not build it alone.

THE NORTH VIETNAMESE AIR DEFENSIVE SYSTEM:

The defensive system devised by the North Vietnamese was complete. It offered no major weaknesses. They completely covered all the altitudes that attacking aircraft could utilize, which included both our tactical fighter-bombers and strategic bombers such as the massive B-52s.

Their system relied on many different sources of information regarding the probable destination of our attack formations. These included: Russian trawlers at sea; Vietnamese and Thai "spotters" located outside all of our tactical fighter bases; Chinese area radar that covered the northern parts of Laos, North Vietnam and the Gulf of Tonkin; Vietnamese offshore "spotter" sampans; the incomprehensible State Department notifications, which presumably applied only to Northern targets; Laotian track spotters; operatives located on Okinawa and Guam monitoring B-52 takeoffs; prior Vietnamese knowledge of our restrictive "attack corridors" and their comprehensive, long-range radar installations which formed the basis for the entire system.

The nerve center that coordinated this intelligence and then acted on it by notifying and positioning its defensive components was located in the Rules of Engagement (ROE)-protected Hanoi area. Their radar "blockhouses" not only followed incoming American attack aircraft, but they also directed their MIGs to aerial pre-positioning or ground pre-positioning at one of their many area bases and then directed the MIGs on intercepts.

Given enough advanced warning, the nerve center would direct mobile SAMs to pre-position at any of the more than 150 available SAM sites located strategically throughout their country and even more in Laos. Much later in the war, SAMs were even located in South Vietnam. Each SAM site had at least three trucks capable of moving the missiles. Some of the missiles were mounted on trailers that could be towed. Many of the Defensive System's AAA units were also mobile and could be pre-positioned to cover the anticipated tracks of incoming aircraft.

OUR FIGHTER-BOMBER RESPONSE:

Many of our initial tactical-bomber approaches utilized by the F-4s and F-105s were low-level attacks using the terrain to mask the approach. When Cam Ranh started regular attacks against the North, we hit them hard at very low altitude. Many of our initial approaches came off the sea at 50 feet or less. This also afforded us great accuracy, especially on napalm drops.

The napalm cans were inherently not very aerodynamic. When they released from our carrying racks, they would tumble end-over-end, sometimes wildly. To counter their tumbling, in the South we dropped from very low and very level. We could hardly miss. Our aircraft would be scraping the treetops.

The North Viets were creative and flexible in their defensive system and this tactic of ours of attacking at such low levels was lucrative for about a month. The Viets countered with concentrations of low-level fire that caused us a lot of aircraft damage. Instead of aiming at individual attacking aircraft as targets, they threw up a barrage of fire from all kinds of weapons to form a "curtain of steel" through which we often had to fly to reach our targets. They used the same tactics against "terrain-following" low-level attacks over land, with the same successful results.

Once we arrived at a target, the defenders would protect our approaches to the target with these curtains of steel and waited until we had to fly through them. This negated the need for them to figure how far to lead us when firing, which was a very difficult task due to our speeds.

The combination of fire-power created with the use of quad-mounted, 50-caliber guns, small arms, other forms of automatic weapons, and even AAA firing at low altitudes, caused us to designate a "floor" of 5,000-feet AGL below which we were not supposed to fly. After I left SEA, the Soviets started supplying the low-altitude SA-7 "Strela" Missile to the arsenal of the North. The NATO designation for the Strela was the "Grail" and it further complicated the situation for our attacking fighter-bombers at low altitude.

The World War II and Korean War tactics used in low-level approaches to targets utilized terrain features like hills to visually mask the approach. On sunny days, we would use the sun at our backs as we attacked. In SEA, these tactics still worked, but the widespread use of radar for all their defenses: artillery, aircraft and missiles, further complicated our problems. Their gunners and missile men were looking at scopes instead of looking into the sun.

Normally, we would come in very low and pop-up to a higher altitude to identify the target before plunging back down to the deck to bomb. In the South, our attacks with napalm drops utilized level approaches, which allowed us to set up and deliver very accurate drops. For the retard bombs, our approaches were very shallow but equally accurate. In the North, many of our initial attacks used level approaches, but we soon devised aiming criteria for diving the napalm cans in on the targets. Many of us were surprised at the results. Against targets heavily defended by AAA, I used steep dive-angles and dropped the cans from as high as 4,500 to 5,000 feet above actual-ground-level. On those attacks, we still approached the target area at low level and then popped-up. To avoid the "curtains of steel," we would start our climbs to set-up for the bombing attacks well away from the targets. We also employed the "fan" attacks by having each pilot approach the target from different directions.

The results of diving in napalm amazed me. "Shacking" a fragmentation bomb in a dive resulted in the target exploding apart in all directions. "Shacking" a napalm can in a dive meant that the target was enveloped in flames. Both were visually gratifying to a pilot, but the cans took gratification to a new level. Because of the unpredictable nature of napalm, I found it hard to believe when I saw them hit dead-center from high altitudes.

Those initial NVN attacks were against warehouse complexes. Using the words from the movie "Top Gun," they were "target-rich environments." We plastered them, often leaving them totally blazing with all the warehouses destroyed or being destroyed by the intense fires.

The combined fire-power of the North Viets at low altitude forced us up to altitudes where their other defenses could harass us: the deadly trio of SAMs, MIGs and AAA. Each of these "higher altitude" threats extensively used radar. The MIGs relied on ground-based, theater-radar more powerful than airborne radar because they didn't need to worry about weight or size. Once the ground-based radar operators gave the MIGs intercept vectors, the MIGs internal radar would then take over for their approach to our fighters. The surface-to-air missiles also relied on radar to detect our aircraft and guide their missiles after launch. The most effective weapon in their arsenal, the AAA, also relied on radar. What we called their AW or automatic weapons were also a form of AAA, only of smaller caliber. These deadly weapons were their low-altitude protection and were all automatically driven by van-mounted radar.

LOW-LEVEL SIGHT PICTURE:

Pilots develop "sight pictures" that then tend to come naturally when needed. I personally learned that commercial pilots have sight pictures that they develop for when to rotate the aircraft up just prior to touch down on a landing. When I flew for Continental, the sight picture developed for landing a 727 was quite different from landing a DC-10. Rotating for landing a 10 initially made me feel like I was several stories above the runway because the sight picture for the 727 required a much lower rotation elevation.

It was the same for a fighter pilot in combat. The sight picture developed for dropping napalm carried over to my subsequent duty station. After leaving SEA, I was stationed in England and would drop bombs on several ranges in East Anglia. Our practice bombs were either dropped level against upright, rectangular canvas targets or dive-bombed against concentric circles marked on the ground.

For the level drops in England, my Vietnam sight picture had me coming in so low that, when I would rotate for the climb after dropping the practice bomb, I would invariably blow down the canvas targets with my jet exhaust. This meant that I was between 15 to 20 feet off the deck when I rotated. Not once did any of my commanding officers complain about or suggest changing my approach. This continued for months until I was finally able to readjust my "sight picture" to conform to the realities of peacetime. Probably the greatest reasons for an adjustment to my approach altitude were the backseaters. It was rumored that I was scaring the hell out of them when I dropped.

ANTI-AIRCRAFT ARTILLERY (AAA):

From a fighter pilot's viewpoint, those of us who attacked the North in Southeast Asia had the advantage that bomber pilots in WWII did not have, and that was the ability to "jink." Jinking is the quick movement of an aircraft vertically and horizontally to evade flying through the defensive radar tracks that aimed the AAA guns. We also avoided flying across the track of any of the aircraft ahead of us in an attack. We didn't want a bullet aimed at one of those flying ahead of us to shoot us. So we were constantly changing direction and jinking. Even though we were larger than many World War II era bombers, the F-4s were incredibly maneuverable.

For the F-4C, operational altitudes rarely exceeded 40,000 feet. For cruising or fighting, performance and fuel consumption were optimized between 33,000 and 37,000 feet. Lower altitudes were used for attack missions or for defensive evasion of fighter aircraft or missiles.

This meant that the enemy's altitude problem in defense was simplified. Attacking formations of American aircraft were vulnerable to most sizes of enemy anti-aircraft artillery employed. The 85mm and 100mm artillery weapons were able to hit at altitudes far higher than what we (F-4Cs) could feasibly fly, which was slightly in excess of 40,000 feet. The B-52s usually dropped at altitudes less than 40,000. The Linebacker B-52 attacks against Hanoi were flown at 36,000 feet. The extensive 52 attacks against the Annamite Mountain Passes in 1968 and 1969 often resulted in flak damage created by the 100 mm AAA.

For a comparative analysis of how the North Vietnamese aerial defenses fared in history, one must go back to World War II. In 1940, the year that Germany invaded Denmark, Norway, the Netherlands and Belgium, the Luftwaffe controlled the air defenses of the Reich and employed 791 AAA defensive guns. These covered all of their cities and heavy industrial areas, such as the Ruhr.

In 1964, the year of the purported Gulf of Tonkin Incidents, North Vietnam had a reported 700 AAA guns, which was very similar to the number employed by Germany in 1940. The Soviet Union was reported to be the source for most of their artillery.

On December 22, 1964, a Soviet ship carrying anti-aircraft artillery guns and ammunition landed at Haiphong Harbor. This first shipment was barely four months after the Gulf of Tonkin Incidents and much later than the initial Chinese reactions, but portended a much stronger response. That first shipment started a continual string of such supply ships and by February, 1965, the number of defensive guns protecting the North had risen from 700 to over 2100 and included the 14.5mm, 37, 57, 85 and 100mm varieties. Those weapons were also almost exclusively supplied by the Soviet Union.

Also in February, 1965, Soviet Premier Alexsei Kosygin visited Hanoi. At the time, the ruling party in Hanoi was called the Lao Dong or Vietnam Workers' Party. Kosygin met with the Lao Dong Politburo to work out the timing and conditions for aid from the USSR to North Vietnam (DRV). He signed a defense treaty that promised aid. This was after North Vietnam had already become one of the most aerially-protected nations in history. As the war progressed, that aid continued to increase. It seemed that the Communist behemoths,

China and the Soviet Union, continually tried to best each other in showering the North Vietnamese with weapons and ammunition.

According to Russian Sergei Blagov writing for the English language "Asia Times," during the course of the war the USSR gave North Vietnam, on average, $2 million dollars per day in military supplies. Blagov also said that the Soviet aid came in the form of aid and not loans. He claims that the Chinese demanded deferred-payments on the equipment that it supplied. Blagov stated the Soviets demanded no such repayment. According to the "Russia and India Report," by the late 1960s, more than three-fourths of the technical and military equipment received in NVN was supplied by Moscow. Much of that aid involved equipment for the aerial defenses of the North and the majority of that aid was AAA guns and ammo.

Additionally, the numbers of Chinese AAA divisions supplied to NVN were significant. The difference between Chinese and Korean aid and that supplied by the Soviets was that Chinese and Korean AAA units came manned by their own soldiers, while Russian AAA supplies just included equipment and ammunition.

As mentioned in another chapter, the Chinese initially restricted their AAA divisions to north of the 21st Parallel. Hanoi sits right on the 21st. When I participated in attacking Vinh, located between the 18th and 19th Parallels, Intelligence reported more than 600 AAA guns in defense and they all seemed to be shooting on our arrival. It was suspected that some of that AAA was supplied by nations other than NVN. When I was involved in an air-to-ground attack on Thanh Hoa, located between the 19th and 20th Parallels, Intelligence reported more than 900 AAA guns.

For those of us attacking the North in 1966, the presence of 150,000 Chinese troops sent to NVN to operate the AAA guns meant that many of our planes were downed by Chinese AAA manned by their own troops.

During the "Rolling Thunder" operations, the AAA defensive fire continued to increase. It was, without a doubt, the most effective weapon in the substantial defensive arsenal of the North Vietnamese. By November 1, 1968, the date of cessation of Rolling Thunder, North Vietnam had amassed a reported 8,050 AAA guns and 400 radar systems to go along with and direct them.

During my year in SEA, our Air Force Intelligence repeatedly mentioned that the Red River Valley held more than 10,000 AAA weapons. From my research, it is certain that those reported numbers were inaccurate. While there may not have been 10,000 AAA guns, the Red River Valley still held significant numbers in excess of anything ever seen. With consideration of the post-war reports coming from enemy combatants, it seems that the numbers of AAA varied between 7,000 and 8,000 from 1967 until the Chinese withdrew in 1969. By WWII comparison, at the height of their ground defensive capabilities "in the summer of 1943, the Germans had 2,132 flak guns."

Tactics used by the North Viets varied with the type of AA guns employed. They felt the 37s and 57s were inferior to American fighter-bombers and they used varying tactics to equalize. I saw no personal evidence that the 37s they were using in Tally Ho were inferior. The 57s employed at Vinh and Thanh Hoa were also effective. In Tiger Hound, the North Viets would triangulate AAA around a target, utilizing the tops of the many hills. In the North, they would radar-direct multiple AAA guns against singular targets with high rates of success. The Vietnamese were inventive and tried several different approaches to AAA defense. In addition to the triangles, they used diamonds and even pentagon formations of guns to provide complete coverage of a target area. In this, they were also successful.

They also shifted positions from day-to-day. With the Johnson-imposed specific air attack corridors, the Chinese Triple A adopted a "fire and move to ambush" tactic.

Chinese statistics from nine AAA divisions show that they shot down 125 U.S. planes or 20% of their total claims during their move and ambush operations. This tactic could not have been possible without Johnson's insistence on specific attack corridors where the Chinese Triple A could ambush incoming aircraft.

During my year in SEA, the North Viets reorganized their AAA air defenses in May and June of 1966. They created the 361st AAA Division, which was employed in the defense of Hanoi. The 363rd operated in the defense of Haiphong; the 365th and 367th in the defense of other areas, including Vinh and Thanh Hoa, and the 369th, which was a mobile AAA Division which took advantage of the pre-attack targeting information supplied by the Americans. These units were Soviet equipment manned by North Vietnamese soldiers. Adding the North Korean and Chinese AAA Divisions, which arrived with ammunition and soldiers to man them, the AAA defensive forces were more than formidable.

While the combination of small arms, SAMs and MIGs posed multiple problems, the most effective and deadly weapon in the arsenal of the North was the Triple-A or AAA weapons, which included the small-caliber, low-level AAA mentioned earlier. "Fully 80% of United States aircraft losses in North Vietnam were attributed to AAA."

AAA ATTRITION RATES: Consideration has to be given to the attrition rates for enemy AAA weapons. We pilots destroyed a lot of guns. I can't answer for other pilots, but I can attest to my personal destruction of at least three anti-aircraft artillery guns plus multiple automatic weapons. If the statements of other pilots in my flights can be counted, several other AAA guns can be credited to me and I was just one of many pilots operating against their AAA weapons.

While one artillery piece and the AW guns were included in bomb damage assessments included in my mission reports, two other artillery guns were destroyed by me on my personal initiative. Other pilot reports that my bombs had eliminated multiple AW sites were not included in post-strike reports because they could not be corroborated. I did not report either of the two AAA that I destroyed because it might have been construed as an unnecessary risk for my aircraft.

My experience had to have been multiplied many times by others making the same evaluations and taking the same actions. Unreported attacks had to have resulted in significant artillery loss rates for the Chinese, Koreans and North Vietnamese.

To destroy AAA guns on our F-4 missions against the North required a certain confluence of events. First, a mission had to be targeted against the North, where the bulk of the AAA were located. Some AAA guns were not located near any known targets. Secondly, the targets had to be heavily defended by artillery. Additionally, the guns had to have been supplied with ample ammunition. Often our interdiction bombing severely interrupted the enemy distribution network and the guns were not supplied.

Thirdly, we had to have our aircraft uploaded with one of the dwindling supply of 20 mm Gattling cannons. Finally, they should be loaded with the high-explosive, incendiary bullets instead of the "ball" target ammo. Ball ammo was just bullets, while the HEI would explode on impact and cause an incendiary reaction. From the pilot standpoint, we could see the HEI hit but could not see the ball ammo. We had to direct the target ammo by the shock waves from the bullets, which we could see. For safety and accuracy reasons, we needed HEI ammo.

Both artillery pieces that I destroyed were discovered on climb-out after hitting our bombing targets. The cleared circles in the jungles were a dead give-away. No way of hiding them. When I attacked, I would send the rest of my flight south and would try to catch up to them later on radar.

In retrospect, attacking the guns might have been stupid, but I figured that my attack method would give me the time I needed. By quickly rolling in and lining up on a gun, I solved his tracking problem. Both guns were firing at me at the time I rolled in and I had to assume that their artillery barrels were swinging in the direction that I was flying.

By my solving the gunners tracking problem, he did not have to worry about ranging or azimuth. He did not have to lead my aircraft at all, which meant that my speed no longer was a factor in his planning. All he had to do was to aim slightly above my cockpit to compensate for bullet drop due to gravity.

However, I had the advantage of surprise. I quickly set up my arming switches as I rolled in. He was busy moving his gun to fire ahead of the track my aircraft was flying. With a quick roll-in, I was able to line up my gun directly at the circle in the jungle where his artillery piece was located. He would have to stop the swing of his barrel and reverse direction to line up with my aircraft. By the time he managed to do that, he was dead.

I also aimed just above the gun, which I could see flickering like a July 4th sparkler indicating he was firing at me. The steeper my dive angle at his position, the closer I could aim directly at him. Gravity was all I had to contend. Accuracy was assured due to my being able to see where my bullets struck.

Going gun-to-gun was thrilling. It was him or me, but I figured I had the advantage and it was not nearly as dangerous as it might sound. He might have larger bullets to fire at me, but I had a gun that fired 100 rounds of 20mm cannon shells every second. As soon as I had the gun dead-ahead of me, I started firing and adjusted fire as I saw the HEI explode. As I dove, I would gently "walk" my rudders to effectively spray the entire clearing and even some of the nearby areas under the jungle canopy, where support people should have been standing and support equipment parked. Both times that I did it, I was certain that no gun or operators could have survived the attack. I am sure that the guys flying out of the Thai bases probably did the same time-after-time. If so, we had to have their air defenses reeling and in constant need of replacements.

ENEMY MISSILES:

While the Soviets declined to supply personnel for their AAA units supplied to North Vietnam, they compensated by totally manning their Surface to Air Missile (SAM) sites, at least for the time that I was in SEA.

In 1965, more than 17,000 Soviet missile technicians and operators flooded into North Vietnam. They took over the construction of the missile sites and the eventual manning of them throughout 1966 and well into 1967.

They eventually built over 150 SAM launch sites. Not all of them were continually manned because the Soviets, and later the North Viets, would continually move their units from site to site. When the North Viets eventually took over control, it was the PAVN or People's Army of Vietnam who operated them.

Each manned SAM site was home to a missile battalion. The site configuration consisted of six missiles and missile launchers surrounding a central core of command and radar vans. On the perimeter of the site rested the "Spoon Rest" radar, associated generators and communications vans. The Spoon Rest would acquire and monitor incoming aircraft. Also around the perimeter were located at least three transloaders for moving the missiles quickly, if necessary.

In the central core of the site sat the "Fan Song" engagement radar vans as well as a command van and six missile-control vans. Often the vans, missile launchers, radars and transloaders were protected by bunkers or revetments.

When the Spoon Rest radar picked up a likely target, the Fan Song radar would activate, lock on to the approaching target and prepare to launch the two-stage SA-2 missile. After launch, the Fan Song would initially guide the SA-2 until the internal missile radar would take over and complete the shoot.

The SA-2 was called the "Dvina" by the Soviets and "Guideline" by NATO. A later, updated version called the Volkov also was used in SEA. It carried a proximity warhead weighing 434 pounds and had a range of 30 km with a reported ceiling of 60,000 feet.

Apparently, the SA-2 could be effective at heights above 60-thousand feet as evidenced by the shooting down of Francis Gary Powers over the USSR. In 1960, three SA-2s were fired at the intruding Powers flying his U-2 high-altitude photo reconnaissance plane in excess of 70,000 feet altitude.

During the entire war, the Soviets reported that they contributed 7,658 of the radar-directed SA-2s to the defense of the North. Of these, over 5800 were launched, often in groups of three. After analysis of Linebacker II, it is suspected that almost all of the SA-2s on hand were used, and that the 5,800 figure was significantly low.

When I talked to Spike Nasmyth, who spent six years as a POW, he said his Phantom had been downed by the barrage-firing of six SA-2s. In the first part of the war, all the SA-2s were fired individually. When the enemy learned that we could out-maneuver the SA-2 by out-turning them in dives, the North Viets changed their tactics and began to do multiple (barrage) firings to overwhelm the fighters. That is what happened to Spike, who managed to outmaneuver the first five, but was downed by the sixth.

The later-introduced SA-7 "Strela" or "Grail" low-altitude, anti-aircraft missile was guided by infrared. It would lock on to the heat generated by an aircraft engine. The SA-7 had a range of 14,750 feet and a speed of 1260 mph. Both the SA-2 and SA-7 were used extensively in other wars or confrontations. Operators generally gave the SA-2 good marks, but rated the SA-7 poorly due to its habit of locking on to the sun.

The SAM-2s were fairly primitive compared to later versions. They had a separate operator for altitude, azimuth and range and required coordination between the three. Each missile in a battery thus had its own control van.

The Russians have to be credited with designing and producing very effective and competitive weapons systems, including guns, missiles, aircraft and spacecraft. However, there is one area where American know-how is clearly superior. That is in the area of miniaturization. The Russians went big and we went small. Our choice was better.

The USAF countered the SAM threat by creating the "Wild Weasels," which initially were modified F-100s, replaced by the two-seat F-105s and later were the two-seat F-4s. The Weasels would attack the SAM sites armed with missiles that homed in on the emanations from the Fan Song radars. Often the Weasels were armed with bombs and rockets instead of anti-radiation missiles. The initial Wild Weasels carried the Shrike air-to-ground missile. The Shrike suffered from a too small warhead, limited range and a poor guidance system. The Russians used a tactic against the Shrikes of turning-off the Fan Songs until 10 to 15 seconds prior to firing the SA-2s. This allowed them to fire the missiles and then turn the radar off before the Shrikes could lock on. However, this also degraded the SAM performance because the Fan Songs did not have enough time to properly prepare their attack and guide the missiles after launch.

The Air Force and Navy countered with a replacement for the Shrikes called the "Starm" (AGM 78 Standard ARM), which was carried by the F-4G version of the "Wild Weasel" Phantom. The AGM 78 was introduced in 1968 and circumvented the Russian tactic of shutting down their Fan Songs. The 78 had memories and continued to home in on the Fan Songs after initial acquisition, whether the unit was turned on or off. This countered the Russian trick of turning the unit on and off and on and off. The Russians then countered by turning on a nearby Fan Song simultaneously with shutting down the targeted Fan Song. This often resulted in the memory chip not being activated and, instead, the Starm would acquire the new Fan Song, turn toward its radar signature and then the Russians would immediately turn that Fan Song off. Thus, the game of "cat and mouse" continued.

Under the conditions, our attack Weasels would have been better off using continual loads of iron bombs and napalm with the assist of the cannon, instead of reliance on anti-radiation missiles. We would have had a higher incidence of battery destruction with bombs.

Cam Ranh Bay was tasked to hit the SAM sites in all-weather conditions. The Thai-based F-111s also had all-weather capability as well as a terrain-following feature. They were utilized against the SAMs as well as Cam Ranh. I led quite a few of these two-ship missions that bombed from altitude through the clouds under "Sky Spot" control.

While most SAMs were stationary at pre-built SAM sites, all the SAM batteries were built to be mobile. When the Soviets moved from permanent site to permanent site, they thus became mobile. With the introduction of actual mobile SAM batteries that continually moved, sometimes to areas that were not constructed sites, they became a real headache for planners.

When the United States began their insane advance notification of targets, the mobile SAM concept really came into its own. They were thus able to move many SAM batteries to the designated areas in time for the American strike aircraft. They moved the mobile SAMs daily to meet our threat. They could set up in a new location in a manner of hours and that new location could be anywhere, since they were self-contained. One truck towed the Fan Song trailer, another towed the SAM mounted on a track launcher while others towed the support vans including Spoon Rest, generators and replacement missiles.

The first actual use of Russian-manned SAM sites was in July of 1965, when a Soviet SAM battery fired at a flight of F-4Cs and they claimed that they shot down three of the four aircraft. This claim was false as only one of the F-4s was downed. This flight will be detailed in a following chapter.

The Soviets did not get around to training the North Viets in the operation of the SAMs until sometime in 1966. Since the training of North Vietnamese SAM operators took close to nine months, all aircraft shot down by SAMs in 1966 were shot down by Russian operators. It was not until late 1967 that some NVN missile operators took control of some missile batteries. With the advent of the first of the Johnson-ordered Rolling Thunder stand downs, the air war in the North barely had six months of operation against the mixed Russian and North Viet crews before Rolling Thunder started to close down.

To the attacking aircraft like our Phantoms, the triple threat of MIGs, SAMs and AAA often forced us down to less-than-optimum flying altitudes. I have already mentioned how their "curtain of steel" tactics forced us up. Sometimes we felt like yo-yos.

When Surface to Air Missiles (SAMs) were fired, bomb-laden planes often dropped their loads to evade and thus nullified the effectiveness of bombing missions. Sometimes a pilot would call out "SAM Break" over the common strike frequency without identifying where he was and all hell would break loose as pilots throughout the theater, all monitoring the frequency, heard his call. Since time was critical if a missile was flying at you, the tendency was to drop your bomb load and look to locate the missile and then evade. This could be disastrous to the plan of attack. It could mean that multiple attacks were ruined because any attack flights within range of the voice of the pilot calling the break might all drop their bombs.

If these triple threats did manage to force us back down, the closer we got to the ground, the closer we got to deadly territory. The flooring altitude mentioned previously provided a means to avoid part of the damaging fire, but not all of it. This "flooring" altitude was to avoid the automatic weapons (AW) and small arms fire that was so thick at those lower altitudes. There really was no "safe" altitude for us to fly.

The MIGs seldom forced anyone down. The SAMs were a different story. While the MIGs approached us at subsonic speeds, the SAMs flew at four times the speed-of-sound. This often did not give us much time to react if fired upon. However, we learned to dive and out-turn the SAMs fired against us. The barrage-firing technique partially nullified our defensive tactics against their missiles.

During my war, we only had the SA-2 to contend with, which did not have a good turning radius. However, we had to visually pick up the SAMs before we could start evasion tactics. Since it was painted white, the color made it difficult to discern against cloudy backgrounds. A benefit to us was that the SAM-2 was not good at lower altitudes. The later-introduced SA-7 corrected this difficulty for the Northern defenses.

For the 5,800 SAMs reportedly fired against us, we lost 205 aircraft. But the longer the war lasted, the fewer kills were made. In addition to our flying tactics and the Wild Weasels, we worked on the technical end. It was a deadly game of punch and counter-punch. In that exchange, we won. When the SAMs were first introduced in 1965, they scored a kill for every 15 missiles fired. By 1972 when Linebacker I and II were initiated, they scored one kill for every 50 launches.

Linebacker I was earlier than the Christmas attacks of Linebacker II and utilized tactical bombers like the Phantom. Linebacker II used the huge B-52s as well as tactical bombers. In one of the initial B-52 raids, three were shot down by the SA-2s. That enemy success caused a flurry of activity in Strategic Air Command (SAC). They successfully countered, but did lose a total of seventeen B-52s to the SAMs.

The methods used by SAC included the increased use of chaff and a different use of electronic counter-measures. The North Viets were clever. When the SAC moves disabled the effectiveness of the North Vietnamese defensive radars, they used manual methods of tracking.

The 52s had a habit of not varying the physical parameters of an attack. They flew the same routes at the same altitudes. They also flew the same headings and turn points as past missions. The Viets took note. They barrage-fired their SAMs without activating their radar. Instead, they aimed their missiles at presumed positions and scored almost as well as when they had the use of radar for tracking. When will we ever learn?

SAM MISSILEER COMMENTS:

The following is taken from an interview of retired North Vietnamese Lieutenant General Nguyen Van Phiet who, as a young military man, served on one of the SA-2 missile batteries:

"My introduction to the Dvina missile was when I was selected in 1965, along with 1,000 others, to attend a Soviet missile school in Moscow. Our training took a rigorous nine months of working 14 hour days and seven days a week.

"We learned that the SA-2 was 10.67 meters long, its range was 33.8 kilometers, we could fire it at aircraft flying up to 27,400 meters and it had a proximity warhead effective to 300 meters.

"After training, I was assigned to a missile battery located outside Hanoi. There were five of us that controlled each missile launcher: three operators, one controller and the battery commander. Others provided maintenance and support functions. While we had vans to protect us during the day, we slept on the ground outside our missile control van at night.

"One of our nearby Dvina sites downed the famous American John McCain by shooting off the right wing of his Navy A-4 Skyhawk. My battery was responsible for shooting down several Phantoms and, when I was battery commander, we shot down four B-52s.

"The Americans were technologically clever and managed to reduce the effectiveness of our missiles. In 1967, they started using an air-to-ground missile against our (Fan Song) radars and it was very effective. In 1968, the enemy planes started carrying anti-missile wing pods that further reduced the number of our victories.

"Our missileers started to use a "cat and mouse" game with the American pilots. The (Fan Song) would operate until the planes were 40 kilometers out and we would turn it off. Then we would calculate speed, direction and distance to determine when it was within 2 kilometers. We would turn the (Fan Song) back on, quickly swivel our missiles and fire. This allowed us limited success."

ENEMY FIGHTER-INTERCEPTORS (MIGS):

The surface-to-air missiles were not the only missiles with which we had to contend. The MIGs were equipped with an air-to-air, infrared, heat-seeking missile we called the Atoll, which was similar to our Sidewinder. The Atolls would home-in on the heat signature created by our aircraft engines. Since the Phantom had two engines, it made a vulnerable target for the Atolls.

Enemy MIG fighters operated at the same altitudes in which we were operating. We felt very capable of holding our own against the MIGs, even in their own radar-controlled airspace.

For those of our planes shot down by MIGs, the piloting could have been done by North Vietnamese, Chinese or North Korean pilots. There were unconfirmed reports, told to us at Cam Ranh, of Russian pilots flying MIGs with green tails, but those reports were never verified. One report was verified by F-105 pilot Harry Paddon of the 34th TFS based at Korat. He stated that a fellow squadron-mate saw a blond-haired pilot falling in his parachute after his MIG-21 was shot down over the North. Additionally, he reported that several months later a "Wild Weasel" pilot at Korat also saw a blonde-haired pilot who had ejected after his MIG-21 had been shot down. USAF Intelligence at Korat confided that the Russians were thought to be flying all the MIG-21s.

The Soviets did credit one of their "instructor" pilots in North Vietnam with shooting down six American fighters. There were many confirmed kills of Americans by Chinese MIGs and, as mentioned previously, the actual figures are probably much higher. There were no confirmed reports of the Cambodian MIGs flown by Cambodians and French pilots having shot down any of our aircraft.

Encounters with MIGs were rare, but that was not due to the quality of the pilots or the aircraft. The MIGs, even the MIG-17, were very maneuverable and surprisingly good. Their pilots were also good. They were just no match for our Phantoms.

The top North Viet Ace was Nguyen Van Coc who had nine kills to his credit that were confirmed by US records. Seven of his kills were manned American fighters and two were unmanned drones. In addition to Van Coc, the North Vietnamese Air Force has 15 other pilots who qualified as aces by shooting down at least five American aircraft.[57]

With apologies to Radar Intercept Officers (RIOs) and Weapons System Officers (WSOs) who rode the back seats, there were only two American pilots (front seat) that became SEA War aces: Randy "Duke" Cunningham from the US Navy and Steve Ritchie from the US Air Force. Robin Olds, the famous leader of the 8th Fighter Wing at Ubon, had four kills to add to the 12 he achieved in other wars.

The U.S. Navy flew substantial missions from its aircraft carriers stationed in the middle of the Gulf of Tonkin, as well as elsewhere in the South China Sea. A total of 25 aircraft carriers served in SEA during the war.

ENEMY AIRCRAFT & UNINTENDED CONSEQUENCES:

The enemy MIGs were never much of a threat, unless you happened to be one of our planes shot down. To most of us, they were more of a nuisance. Early in the conflict (late 1964 and early 1965) there were MIGs reported by naval fighter pilots to be based as far south as Vinh, which is about two-thirds the way up the NVN coast to Thanh Hoa. Navy fighter pilots reported that a MIG attacked them just north of the DMZ. However, after that incident, the North Vietnamese pulled their aircraft back to bases closer to Haiphong and Hanoi.

One unfortunate result of the purported MIG threat was a decision by the Pentagon, during my tour in Vietnam, to paint participating aircraft in camouflaged colors. This was very expensive and counter-productive. It also degraded our capabilities.

The initial, factory paint job on the F-4Cs was a light gray color. It blended in with the skies, which was beneficial when we rolled in on a target and contended with the Anti-Aircraft Artillery (AAA) gunners aiming from the ground up at us in our dives. When the Pentagon, in its wisdom, painted us in browns and greens, we stood out and made easier targets for the gunners.

Since we had total control of the air, we never had any enemy aircraft above us that posed a problem. That would have been the only justification for painting our Phantoms in camouflage colors. Ironically, when we were given a brown and green overcoat, we started to encounter problems from above, but with our own aircraft and not any enemy.

Probably the starkest evidence of what could happen involved our Wing Commander, Colonel McClelland. He was a fighter jock and often led missions. In this particular mission, his flight was going north to hit an NVN target. All of a sudden, the pilots witnessed sticks of bombs falling through their flight of four aircraft. Looking up, they spotted the B-52s on a bombing mission against the South. The camouflaged Phantoms were invisible to the 52 pilots against the jungle below. The Colonel's flight happened to escape any mishap, but it could have been tragic. It indicated both the ill-advised decision of the Air Force to paint the planes and the lack of proper coordination between SAC and the PACAF (Pacific Air Force) fighter-bomber forces represented by 7th Air.

Author's Notes: *57. The infamous Colonel Toon was the subject of a Life Magazine article concerning his air-to-air engagement with the F-4B flown by Randy Cunningham. Colonel Toon was a figment of someone's imagination. He never existed.*

Another example of the lack of proper planning in the painting fiasco involved our C-130 Hercules aircraft. McNamara's Pentagon Whiz Kids decided to paint all the rest of the aircraft operating in the combat theater. It took over 2,000 pounds of paint to cover each C-130. The paint managed to degrade performance. The 2,000 pounds was just additional weight that had to be lifted by the same engines. Added to that, the paint managed to partially disrupt the laminar flow over the fuselage and wings and the pilots reported that their speed actually dropped 10 knots. So, McNamara managed to spend a lot of money degrading our aircraft and making them more vulnerable to both enemy gunners and friendly aircraft.

When Lenny and I were still at MacDill, the Wing asked us to brief McNamara's chosen Whiz Kid fighter expert, Robert Comer, on the capabilities of the Phantom II. Comer obviously had an encyclopedic memory. His questions caused me momentary confusion. Instead of asking questions about the "real" properties and capabilities of the F-4C, he seemed intent on showing us how much knowledge he had accumulated about the plane. Problem with that approach is that the performance charts and graphs compiled by the manufacturer were derived from testing on totally new, partially stripped-down aircraft. Operational fighters, especially those with a lot of hours, don't behave in the same manner. One has to fly them to find out how they really perform. Comer also did not ask the questions of us that he should have. Instead of trying to impress us with his knowledge, he should have been down there to find out what we knew. Comer's trip to MacDill was useless.

Comer later went to Saigon as President Johnson's personal representative to the SEA War. This represents another answer to the question, "what went wrong in Vietnam."

CONCLUSION:

Three other Communist countries were responsible for the formidable defenses created by North Vietnam: the USSR, China and North Korea.

The nation that gave the most help was the Soviet Union. They provided the vast bulk of the AAA guns and ammunition used throughout the war. They provided the surface-to-air missiles used to down a reported 205 American aircraft. They provided the technicians to keep the missiles flying. They provided the missile operators that killed many American aircraft and pilots. They built the MIG aircraft that were provided by all three of the contributing, fighting nations. The Soviets also designed, built and gave the Atoll air-to-air heat-seeking missiles fired from the MIGs. In short, to paraphrase President Roosevelt, they were the "arsenal of the Communist World."

The Soviets helped NVN in other ways as well. They placed monitoring ships in the South China Sea and gave early warnings to the Viet Cong by picking up the B-52s when they flew out of Guam, Thailand and Okinawa. To the VC, the 52s were the most feared weapon in the American arsenal and the Soviets helped them by plotting trajectories and figured possible target areas.

The official DRV (NVN) claim is that their defenses shot down 4,154 U.S. aircraft over North Vietnam. This is significantly at odds with the 1,096 claimed by the United States and also at odds with Hobson's figures.[58]

Author's Notes: *58. Chris Hobson's book "Vietnam Air Losses" is a must-have for any student of air warfare. His excellent and well-documented research has yielded a treasure. Much of the data and statistical analysis located on the website of this book has utilized his information. Readers will also be pleasantly surprised by his written material that tells a complete story covering the many aspects of our air wars in SEA.*

The Chinese claims may also be exaggerated. They state that all Chinese AAA divisions operating in NVN, plus units assigned to protect engineering troops, fought 2,153 engagements. They claim that they shot down 1,707 U.S. planes and damaged 1,608, while capturing 42 American pilots. These seem wildly inaccurate. Discrepancies could occur when Russian SAM units, Chinese AAA units and North Vietnamese, Korean or Chinese MIGs might claim the same downed aircraft. Again, how would they accurately ascertain if fighter-bombers have been damaged if we pilots were sometimes unaware of battle damage to our own aircraft until after landing?

Aircraft damage can come in many forms. Bullets can go through an aircraft without hitting vital lines or equipment. If system lines, such as electrical or hydraulic, are severed, we would see indicator lights in our cockpits alerting us to the problem. Many times we would not see or feel anything and only discover damage after we landed. Once, I was shot by small arms in South Vietnam and did not know it until a maintenance guy came to me after the mission and told me. I could not see the hole, even on post-flight walk-around.

While the various claims for aircraft shot down are wildly inconsistent, what does not change is the fact that American fighter-bombers faced cruel odds in the skies over North Vietnam. While defenses were heavy throughout much of the North, those around Hanoi-Haiphong were the deadliest. "Rolling Thunder" attacks against those heaviest-defended targets were flown by the Thai-based F-105s, operating out of Takhli and Korat, the U.S. Navy bombers flying off their carriers, the Thai-based F-4Cs operating out of Ubon and occasionally Udorn and the South Vietnamese-based Phantoms stationed at Danang and Cam Ranh Bay.

One hundred missions or sorties against North Vietnam qualified those courageous Thud pilots for a ticket home. According to a May, 1967 Department of Defense (DOD) report: "The air campaign against heavily defended areas (Hanoi-Haiphong) cost us one pilot in every 40 sorties." The Thai bases normally only hit Hanoi-Haiphong, which are both part of Route Packs Five and Six.

Those of us at other bases who attacked the North had reasonable confidence in our abilities to get back home. Since the Thai-based Thuds were shot down once in every 40 sorties and they could not go home until flying 100 sorties, those pilots operating out of the Thai bases justifiably considered themselves "dead men flying."

"War does not determine who is right—
only who is left."
Bertramd Russell

CHINA

NORTH VIETNAM

BURMA

HANOI

LAOS

GULF OF TONKIN

VIENTIANE

DEMILITARIZED ZONE (DMZ)

Udorn

Nakhon Phanom

Phu Bai

Da Nang

THAILAND

Chu Lai

Ubon

Phu Cat

Takhli

Pleiku

Korat

Qui Nhon

Don Muang

CAMBODIA

SOUTH VIETNAM

BANGKOK

Tuy Hoa

U-Tapao

Nha Trang

Cam Ranh Bay

PHNOM PENH

Phan Rang

Tan Son Nhut

Bien Hoa

GULF OF THAILAND

SAIGON

SOUTH CHINA SEA

Binh Thuy

SOUTHEAST ASIA

★ National Capital

● U.S. Air Base

○ Principal Bases in Air War against North Vietnam (highlighted)

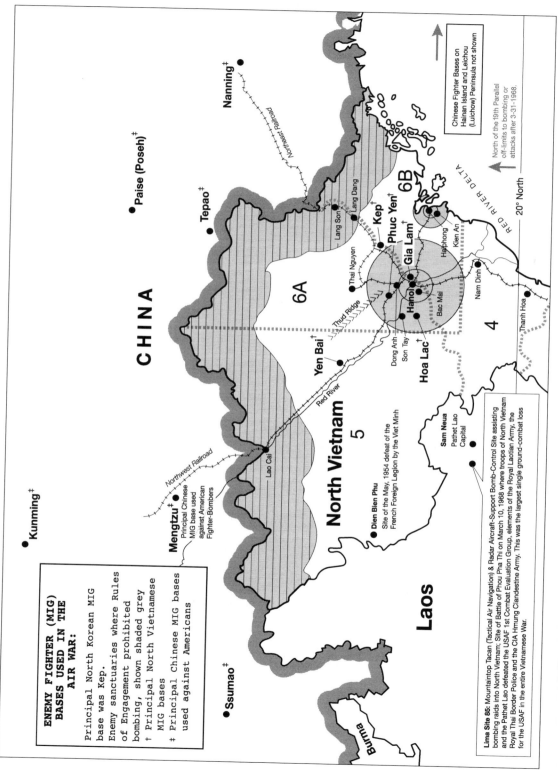

ENEMY FIGHTER (MIG) BASES USED IN THE AIR WAR:

Principal North Korean MIG base was Kep.

Enemy sanctuaries where Rules of Engagement prohibited bombing, shown shaded grey

† Principal North Vietnamese MIG bases

‡ Principal Chinese MIG bases used against Americans

Mengtzu‡
Principal Chinese MIG base used against American Fighter-Bombers

Chinese Fighter Bases on Hainan Island and Leichou (Luichow) Peninsula not shown

North of the 19th Parallel off-limits to bombing or attacks after 3-31-1968.

20° North

RED RIVER DELTA

CHINA

North Vietnam

Laos

Burma

Kunming‡

Ssumao‡

Paise (Poseh)‡

Nanning‡

Tepao‡

Northeast Railroad

Lang Son

Lang Dang

Kep†

Phuc Yen†

Gia Lam†

Kien An

Haiphong

Thai Nguyen

Hanoi

Bac Mai

Nam Dinh

Thanh Hoa

Dong Anh

Son Tay

Hoa Lac†

Thud Ridge

Yen Bai†

Red River

Lao Cai

Northwest Railroad

Dien Bien Phu
Site of the May, 1954 defeat of the French Foreign Legion by the Viet Minh

Sam Neua
Pathet Lao Capital

6B

6A

5

4

Lima Site 85: Mountaintop Tacan (Tactical Air Navigation) & Radar Aircraft-Support Bomb-Control Site assisting bombing raids into North Vietnam; Site of Battle of Phou Pha Thi on March 10, 1968 where troops of North Vietnam and the Pathet Lao defeated the USAF 1st Combat Evaluation Group, elements of the Royal Laotian Army, the Royal Thai Border Police and the CIA Hmung Clandestine Army. This was the largest single ground-combat loss for the USAF in the entire Vietnamese War.

CHAPTER FOURTEEN
The "Deadly Game"
Electronic Warfare

> *"If there is a World War III, the winner will be the side that can best control and manage the electromagnetic spectrum."*
>
> American Admiral Thomas Moorer

Author's Thanks: *To Bernard C. Nalty for his insightful article, "Electronic Countermeasures in the Air War against North Vietnam 1965-1973." Much of the information included below comes from that book-sized article. My thanks also go to the Office of Air Force History for their provision of information. Material included below was provided by: The Albert F. Simpson Historical Research Center and the Air University Library at Maxwell AFB, Alabama; the USAF Security Service in San Antonio, Texas and the defunct USAF Strategic Air Command at Offutt AFB, Nebraska.*

LEOPARD TWO:

As mentioned in a prior chapter, the first actual combat loss of the war for the Phantoms occurred on June 20, 1965, when a 45th Fighter Squadron F-4 was shot down by a MIG. Even though the June 9th loss was on a North Viet mission, it was not lost in combat since it ran out of gas. When the 20th shoot-down happened, John Robertson and I were waiting in Ubon Base Operations for the combat mission that never happened. We left Ubon to return to Naha on June 26, after leaving a replacement F-4 for the June 9 loss.

On July 10, Tom Roberts and Ken Holcombe of the 45th, who later joined me at Cam Ranh, became the first USAF pilots to score victories against the MIGs when they downed two MIG-17s.

Just two weeks later, on July 24, the 45th Squadron's Leopard Flight took off from Ubon on a MIG cover mission to protect F-105s attacking near Hanoi. Leading Leopard on that early morning flight was 45th Squadron Commander Lt. Col William Alden.

At just past eight in the morning, while Leopard was cruising at 23,000 feet just 37 nautical miles west of Hanoi, an RB-66C ELINT aircraft orbiting nearby relayed a warning. They had just picked up at signal from a Russian SA-2 missile battery. This was the second time in as many days that they had intercepted a similar signal, which was the first time such a signal had been detected in the nascent conflict.

Almost simultaneously with the warning, Colonel Alden saw two missiles streaking skyward, closing rapidly from the right and below. Without much time for evasive action, the first missile exploded directly below Leopard 2, flying wing on Alden. Flames erupted from the trailing edge of the F-4 and it rolled inverted before plunging out of sight.

Shrapnel had been flung out in all directions from the explosion of the SAM proximity warheads and the other three Leopards scattered. They managed to evade the second missile and later rejoined before returning to Ubon, where maintenance discovered missile damage to all three remaining Phantoms. The proximity-detonation had involved them all.

The two crewmembers of the stricken Leopard 2, both acquaintances from MacDill, suffered different fates. Dick Keirn managed to eject and ended up a POW who had to wait eight long years before repatriation. Ross Fobair was not so lucky and was killed, either by the missile strike or in the subsequent crash.

The loss of Leopard 2 was our first combat loss to the recently deployed Soviet SA-2 anti-aircraft missile. This followed the announcement by the Commander of PACAF Intelligence to my squadron in Hawaii just 46 days before, that the Soviets had constructed eight SAM sites throughout North Vietnam. We were not allowed to hit the sites until the Soviets had constructed over 100. That number later expanded to a total of over 150 sites.

Wartime Air Force Intelligence disputed that number and quoted numbers far fewer that were primarily concentrated around and in Route Packs Five and Six. They numbered fewer than 50, according to Nalty, but my experience refutes those low numbers. On Sky Spot missions that I led, we attacked SAM sites in Tally Ho and in Tiger Hound, while Nalty says they were then concentrated only around Hanoi-Haiphong.

Within the last three months of 1966, I participated in quite a few "Sky Spot" missions, leading most. Initially, the Combat Sky Spots were all against SAM sites. Later, they expanded Combat Sky Spot to include other targets. The primary reason for establishment of this program was to be able to strike at night and during the monsoonal weather.

The Sky Spot attacks against SAM sites were high-altitude drops usually using altitudes from 15,000 to 24,000. Because they were weather drops, our attacks were "blind" in that we had no visual on the targets, nor did we have any sensors to alert us of eminent or actual launch of the SAMs. We also lacked any stand-off jamming support nor did we carry any jamming pods or internal jamming equipment. They were just normal missions against abnormal targets.

The monsoonal weather was a significant factor in air operations. During the last month of my combat, between December 5 and December 18, 1966, fully 94% of 1310 sorties scheduled for Route Pack 6A were either cancelled or diverted due to weather.

Operation "Combat Sky Spot" utilized the MSQ-77 (Miscue) ground radar located at Dong Ha, near the DMZ. During my first month in combat, the Air Force flew 56 Sky Spot missions. Post-strike BDA of many of the flights showed a roughly 300' CEA with some damage.

The follow-on program, "Combat Proof" added a radar beacon transponder to the bombing aircraft that enhanced the MSQ ability to "skin paint" the attacking aircraft. With "Sky Spot," the maximum control distance from Dong Ha was close to 50 nautical miles. With the addition of the beacon used in "Combat Proof," MSQ could track up to 196 nautical miles, allowing them to control bombing into much of the HCMT area and all the way up to Route Pack Three.

In 1967, Air Force tactical bombers muddied the planned separation of the use of the Route Packs between the Navy and Air Force. During a 19-day period, the Air Force flew 88 sorties against RP- 2; 17 sorties against RP- 3; and 6 sorties against RP-4, all previously exclusive Navy territory.

The times that I participated in "Sky Spot" attacks probably numbered less than fifteen, at the most. Most of the missions were against the NVN Panhandle area, above the Finger Lakes. The rest were against Laos, primarily against the Tchepone Airfield and its AAA defenses. Many of those were against either known or suspected SAM sites, and that included in Laos. We had no way of knowing if the SAM sites were manned or unmanned or if they had any equipment. We were ordered to attack and we attacked. The significance of the missions is that they seem at odds with research to find any information on SAMs and their dissemination. This was early in the SAM war in 1966.

The destruction of Leopard 2 was the symbolic first shot fired in an intense, deadly and continually escalating electronic war waged in the skies above North Vietnam.

TACTICS OF EVASION:

This first actual evidence that the Soviets had entered the war with their fully-manned SAMs caused consternation in Washington, not only from a political standpoint, but also a military one. The President himself took notice and authorized retaliatory measures. Both Air Force and Navy brass were busy trying to figure out methods of reply to the threat, while technicians intensified their work on electronic answers.

For the fighter pilot who had to daily face this new threat, it was not a theoretical exercise. When a pilot finds a flaming telephone pole on his tail bent on death and destruction, he will try anything.

What we found were limitations on the performance of the SA-2 missile systems. The first pilot who behaved against a SAM the same way he would behave against a hostile aircraft, found that diving toward the ground and "turning" the missile was a very good tactic. The second and killing stage of the two-stage SA-2 was itself 26 feet long. With both stages intact, it was 35 feet long. Both the combined stages and the single second-stage did not perform well in a turn. Some actually broke apart in flight while they strained to make a sharp turn in pursuit.

At the time, we had no idea of the actual parameters of the SAM capabilities. But we learned through evasive tactics during our missions. We learned that the SAM sites had distance limitations. That turned out to be 17 nautical miles from the launch site. We learned that when we flew close to the actual launch sites, they did not fire at us. We later learned that their missiles needed to discard the first stage, arm the fuse and engage the internal guidance system before they could kill. That took five nautical miles to accomplish, which created a "SAM dead zone" around the sites. Of course we were unaware of the reasons, we just knew the results.

The most important finding, from a fighter-pilots defensive play book, was that the Fan Song radar was not good at low altitudes against our fast-flying Phantoms, Thunderchiefs and whatever the Navy happened to be flying. We later learned that the Fan Song could not track us below 3,000 feet.

These were all technical considerations. For us, they were "safe harbors" we used when confronted with the threat. However, Leopard 2, combined with the increasingly prevalent AAA, meant that the enemy had the initial advantage.

SAM FAN SONGS:

The target of jamming aircraft and equipment were the transportable "Fan Song" radar vans that controlled the SAMs, and the equally transportable "Fire Can" radar vans that controlled and directed the vast collection of AAA and lower-altitude AW (automatic weapons). We called the lower-altitude guns AW, yet they were actually small caliber AAA guns.

The Fan Songs were mounted on trailers for easy movement from site to site. They employed two antennas which scanned horizontally to determine azimuth and range and vertically to obtain elevation and verify range. Fan Songs were able to track additional targets, while locked-on to a single aircraft for destruction.

To acquire a target, lock onto it, and launch a single missile, took about 75 seconds with 30- 40 seconds required to shift to a second target and launch. If a barrage fire was needed, the crews could salvo their missiles against a single target at 5-second intervals.

The max range to fire the SA-2 "Guideline" missiles was 17 nautical miles. The guidance signal would commence at roughly four seconds after launch and be picked up by the sustainer section mounted on the SAM. When launched at max range, the missile would fly approximately 23 seconds before receiving the arming signal for the warhead.

After second-stage separation, the missile would accelerate to four times the speed of sound, which equates to about 1,116 feet-per-second at normal surface temperatures. As temperatures dropped, this feet-per-second rate would also drop. The automatic arming feature was calculated to occur within 1,000 feet from the estimated point of interception with the intruding aircraft, which means that the signal would reach the SAM less than a second from estimated impact. If the missile missed, it would explode roughly 60 seconds after launch.

The guidance portion was obviously crucial for accuracy, so when the Fan Song radar operators would shut the Fan Song off to fool the anti-radiation missiles fired from the Wild Weasels, they also cut off guidance control. The success rate for SA missile firings dropped accordingly. Thus, one of the evaluation parameters, when considering the effectiveness of the Wild Weasel SAM countermeasures, had to be the success rate of the SAMs fired and not just the SAM units destroyed or damaged.[59]

One of the effective defenses of the SAM battalions was the rapid movement of batteries from site to site, thus often eluding attacking aircraft that arrived at vacated sites. A complete SAM battalion had 25 assigned vehicles and vans. Those included: acquisition radar, a Fan Song set, electrical generators, a fire control computer van, three transshipping trucks and 18 Guideline Missiles, one for each of the launchers and a dozen spares to load after fire. Depending on the location of the next site, a battalion could completely move within six to eight hours, sometimes less.

The advances made in our own technology, as indicated below concerning the continual improvements made on our "self-preservation" jamming pods, was matched by improvements to the enemy capabilities. In this, the North Viets had considerable help from the Soviets and from the Chinese who did their own modifications on Soviet-made equipment.

The Chinese learned quickly and, with the technological start given them with Soviet-made equipment, they have joined the elite of those designing and manufacturing advanced weapon systems. The SAMs of 1965, at the start of the Wild Weasel battles, differed from the missiles fired in 1972, during the "Linebacker" operations. In addition to other changes, in 1972 the NVN techs changed the Fan Song signal from the usual E-band frequency to the seldom used I or India-band, making our defenses of the threat more difficult.

A weakness in the SAM system was its inability to operate effectively at low altitudes. A modification, first introduced in 1968, of the addition of an optical sighting and tracking system enabled missile controllers

---

Author's Notes: 59. *The Wild Weasel countermeasures against the SAM sites are discussed later in this chapter.*

to track aircraft flying as low as 1000 feet. For maximum effectiveness, this modification had to be used in conjunction with radar tracking since the optical equipment was useless during inclement weather.

This modification led to another clever NVN ploy. Fan Song radar would transmit to grab the attention of a fighter flight, while another passively tracked the flight optically and then fired with the SAM coming from an unexpected direction.

At the time of the first "Linebacker II" B-52 raids, they were installing modified Fire Cans for the AAA defenses of the SAM sites. The new Fire Cans, built by the Soviets based on a WWII American design, shifted frequencies from the heavily jammed E & F bands to less vulnerable frequencies. The Fire Cans were essential to the SAMs inner defenses because the SAMs could not fire when fighters came within five miles of the launchers. They were defenseless without the smaller caliber AAA automatic weapons that were automatically controlled by the Fire Can radar vans.

COUNTERMEASURES:

President Johnson ordered an essentially political response in the form of an immediate retaliatory air strike against North Vietnam for the downing of Leopard 2. Three days after the downing, a force of 46 F-105s, 12 F-4Cs and eight F-104 interceptors attacked two SAM sites and related barracks 25 nautical miles west of Hanoi. The strike force was electronically defended by three USAF EB-66C standoff jamming aircraft and six USMC EF-10Bs who also jammed enemy radar. This was our military's first indication of "the difficulty in locating and destroying" SAM complexes.

The strike Thunderchiefs came in on the deck at altitudes between 50 and 100 feet, only to be ripped to pieces by the automatic weapons fire. The attack resulted in six of our attack aircraft destroyed and five pilots killed or captured, victims of the most dreaded of the NVN defenses, the light anti-aircraft guns. Post-strike analysis indicated that one of the SAM sites may have been a decoy to lure the fighter-bombers within range of the guns. This was one of the first examples of the cleverness and cunning of the North Vietnamese. As we were to find out time and time again: only underestimate their ingenuity at our own peril.

The American military's response to the downing of Leopard 2 was the initial creation of a triad of countermeasures. The first was already in place. That was the use of EB-66s "Destroyers" that flew tracks across North Vietnam, Laos and the Gulf lying outside the limits of the SAMs. The Destroyers would jam the radar and communication frequencies employed by the enemy defenses, including the SAM and AAA radar control and the MIG intercept radar and communication control. This was called stand-off jamming.

The second method consisted of utilizing "self-protection" electronic jamming pods. These pods could be carried as "external stores" on the underwing carrying racks and rails of the fighter bombers. These were automatic jammers. With varying success, the services also mounted the equipment internally to the aircraft, either as modifications on two-seat models or as manufactured add-ons. The Air Force found that the ability to take the pod off for other types of missions more than offset the increased drag induced by the pod.

The third response from the military came in the form of "hunter-killer" teams called "Wild Weasels" that would attack the SAM sites and, in particular, their radar control in the form of the Fan Song system. As a secondary target, the teams would attack the related Fire Can towable, radar units used for AAA control. Since these Fire Cans controlled the inner defenses of the SAM sites, they often would be the first target of the Wild Weasels.

Wild Weasel I: The contributions of US Naval Air to the burgeoning air war were considerable. Their three aircraft carriers, sometimes four, cruising at "Yankee Station" in the Gulf were supplemented by others much farther south in the Gulf or at other locations. During the entire Southeast Asian War, fully twenty-five American carriers served in the South China Sea.

The Navy and Air Force formed a joint program called Operation Iron Hand. Simply, the program was designed to reduce the threat from SAMs by overt and offensive action against the SAMs themselves and, to a lesser extent, reduce the effectiveness of the enemy's AAA defensive systems, which were also controlled by radar that was vulnerable to anti-radiation missiles. Anti-radiation means that the missiles fired against the SAMs homed in on the radiation emanating from the Fan Song radar when it "painted" attacking aircraft.

The US Air Force's response, as part of Iron Hand, was to create an airborne force to attack the SAM sites with anti-radiation missiles as well as bombs, rockets and airborne cannon to eliminate or damage their ability to launch missiles against American attack formations. This force was called "Wild Weasel" and the term is used interchangeably with Iron Hand.

The Navy's contributions not only included daytime attack fighters, but they had the only true night fighter in the A-6. They provided the airframes for the EB-66s and also had an existing anti-radiation, air-to-ground missile named the "Shrike."

In August, 1965, one month after the downing of Leopard 2, Wild Weasel I was formed for evaluation at Eglin AFB in Florida. The testing proved that the utilization of the two-seat F-100F fighter-bombers was feasible. The results of the test also showed that the aircraft could pick up Fan Song signals beyond the 17-nautical mile effective range of the SA-2 System. However, the approximate, instead of precise, vector information provided by the on-board equipment forced the pilot to search visually for the SAM site. This proved too costly for the Weasels.

Actual combat tests using the single-seat F-105Ds showed that to operate at very low level in a heavily defended environment, while simultaneously looking for the often-camouflaged missile launchers and radar vans and also keeping all the other members of the flight in sight, was too much for a single pilot. We needed help to pinpoint the SAM sites.

The Wild Weasel crew "consisted of a pilot and, seated behind him, an electronic warfare officer (EWO) with radar homing and warning equipment to locate Fan Song and other transmitters." A panoramic scan receiver showed the overall electronic picture to both crewmembers and a vector homing device showed the direction of the Fan Song radar. Additional visual and audio sensors warned when a missile was about to launch or had been launched against them.

The F-100s joined F-105 units at Korat Air Base in Thailand and formed what would be known as "hunter-killer" teams. The Wild Weasels were the hunters and the Thuds were the killers.

The task force had its debut on December 19, 1965, when it led flights of "Thuds" against the North. No Fan Song signals were detected, however. The following day, in at attack against a SAM site 5 miles SE of Kep Airfield, one of the two F-100Fs was shot down, with one survivor.

On December 22, that loss was avenged by the Weasels adopting a technique where they utilized the valleys of Thud Ridge, a hill complex NW of Hanoi, to "porpoise" up and down from one valley to the next. Only one Weasel led this particular flight. The pilot would climb to an altitude where a strobe indicating a radiation source could be seen on their scopes, then the pilot would dive down to use the "radar-masking" protection of the valleys. This technique allowed the Weasels to get close to the source. Rounding the final hill, he climbed again to 4,500 feet and spotted the SAM site. The radar van was sitting in the center of a village and the launchers were hidden within thatched structures inside the village. The Weasel marked the site with a rocket and then watched the F-105s destroy the target.

The slower speed of the F-100s forced the Thuds to weave behind the Weasels. Depending on the number of attack aircraft being flown, separation was either by individual plane or by elements of two using from 2,000 to 4,000 feet. From the perspective of the "hunter-killer" wolf pack, the team seemed to work with the weaving maneuver having the added advantage of clearing six o'clock for the fighters, which was their most vulnerable location for attacking MIGs. A gentle weave was incorporated in later versions of the "hunter-killer" teams to provide for that defensive coverage and to minimize jamming loss, caused by higher banked angles, from the later, externally-carried jamming pods.

The F-100s weren't the only ones who had trouble keeping up with the Thuds. The F-105 was designed for low-level, high-speed penetration of enemy territory for thermonuclear bomb delivery. Military power is what is called 100% on the throttle without afterburner. When the Thuds cruised in military power on their attacks at lower level, our Phantoms flying MIG cover above them had to cycle in and out of burner to keep up. That burned a lot of gas.

The later-mounted jamming pods had a rigid mount without any gyro-stabilization to keep the unit pointed at the ground during maneuvers. This caused both tactical and heavy bombers to lose much of their jamming protection while in steep turns.

Shortly after the successful SAM site destruction, we lost a second F-100F meaning that our Weasel loss-rate in only a handful of sorties was horrendous. It convinced Second Air Division that the plane (F-100) was too old and slow to survive the hostile skies of the Red River Delta so Wild Weasel I was cancelled beginning in May, 1966 to be replaced with an improved version.

The improved version, called Wild Weasel II, was a modified, two-seat F-105F. This too proved to be unusable due to dangerous aircraft vibrations, which led to the creation of Wild Weasel III.

Wild Weasel III: Wild Weasel II and III were created and tested simultaneously. A modified two-seat "F-105F equipped with the same internally-housed homing and warning equipment as the F-100F was selected after it had passed the Eglin test. This plane reached Thailand in May, 1966 shortly after cancellation of Wild Weasel I and served the rest of Rolling Thunder as the primary weapon used in attacking the SAM sites.

By mid-1968, the Weasels had perfected their attack profile. The body of the main strike force was commanded from the lead ship in one of the first flights of the attacking force. The strike force was given MIG top cover by the missiles-armed F-4Cs, F-4Ds and the newly acquired F-4Es with their internally-mounted gun.

One Iron Hand flight preceded the main strike force by one minute, thus giving it the protection of the F-4 top cover. Another Iron Hand flight was located tight to the strike formation on the side with the perceived major threat.

The Air Force continued to perfect the system and created Wild Weasel IV, which was a modified F-4C, with upgraded equipment. It did not enter service in time to serve in Rolling Thunder. However, this plane, along with the F-105G model were both on hand for Linebacker. The G model "featured an improved radar warning receiver and jamming transmitter mounted in a blister located beneath the fuselage." The "blister" was aerodynamic and significantly reduced the drag that was inherent in a pod carried externally. Both these final variants of the Wild Weasel aircraft proved invaluable, along with the F-111, in the 1972 "Linebacker" campaigns against the SAM & AAA defenses protecting the targets from the tactical and strategic bombers.

An overall evaluation of Wild Weasel was that the flights caused little damage to the SAM sites, which may have been the fault of the anti-radiation missiles. What they did create was a disruption of the SAM protection system and that saved a lot of aircraft and lives. They "showed their fangs without drawing blood."

Stand-Off Jamming:

At the start of Rolling Thunder, the Air Force had acquired the B-66 from the US Navy. The USAF Tactical Air Command had 58 of them ready for combat, although few had been modified for electronic warfare. With the increased need due to Vietnam, three dozen 66s were re-commissioned from storage at Davis-Monthan AFB in Tucson.

The 66 suffered from a common Air Force disease, and that is that the airframe was not constructed for electronic warfare (EW) and the engines were not changed to compensate for the increase weight of all the EW equipment. However, the 66 did manage to perform well. The designation of the B-66 was changed to RB-66 to identify the aircraft as reconnaissance but that was later changed to EB-66 to identify it as an electronic-warfare plane.

The initial deployment of 6, EB-66Bs was to Tahkli Air Base in May, 1965. In September/ October they increased that complement to fourteen. The maximum strength of the EB-66s was achieved in May, 1968 with 37 aircraft.

The first use of the EB-66B was the day before the Leopard 2 shoot-down. These first units concentrated on SAM warning and intelligence gathering. Navy and Marine aircraft did most of the radar signal jamming. Each of three aircraft carriers operating in the Gulf in 1965 carried a 4-plane EW detachment.

The EB-66 enjoyed advantages over their Marine and Navy counterparts. They could refuel while airborne and the floating-forces could not. When modified, they could carry almost twice as many jamming transmitters and had several chaff dispensers when the "others" had only one. Plus, they had extensive intelligence gathering equipment.

The EB-66 jammers entered combat in October, 1965. The 66s operated two orbits over northwestern North Vietnam during Rolling Thunder. An additional orbit was flown just off Haiphong over the Gulf and a fourth was flown over Sam Neua, the Pathet Lao Capital, in northeastern Laos. The tracks varied as the aircraft maneuvered into position to cover the SAMs for attacking fighter-bombers and also to avoid flying too close to the sites and endanger themselves and their MIG cover escort fighters.

The two northwestern tracks were initially over land free of SAM sites. They were then able to do stand-off jamming in defense of the attacks against areas adjacent to Hanoi-Haiphong. The enemy countered this stand-off jamming threat in mid-1966 with the introduction of the first SAM sites in the northwest.

An example of the danger presented to the EB-66 crews: on February 4, 1967, a flight of two EB-66s (call signs Harpoon 1 and Harpoon 22) took off from Takhli Air Base in Thailand and enroute to Laos joined with a flight of two F-4Cs (Sword 1 & 2) that would act as MIG cover. They flew in support of a Thud strike against the Thai Nguyen Army Depot. During the flight the Phantoms identified three fast-closing SAMs and dove away in evasion. They were able to witness one of them strike Harpoon 1 directly and the aircraft broke in half with both halves falling in flames.

The pilot, fellow Southern Californian and Academy classmate John Fer was immediately captured when he and his parachute hit the ground. He and two of his five crewmates were POWs for six years. The crew complement of an EB-66 consisted of a pilot and navigator, plus four EWOs or electronic warfare officers. Three of the six were killed by the SAM or the subsequent crash.

Losses such as this helped the Air Force decide that "the EB-66, unfortunately, was incapable of accompanying strike forces into heavily defended areas and therefore could not effectively assume countermeasures responsibilities."

MIG fighters forced the 66s to move their orbits below the 20th parallel, well south of those previously flown west of Hanoi/ Haiphong. They established one overland orbit south of the DMZ and two in Laos. The final two were located over the Gulf. The introduction of "self-protection" jamming pods carried by the fighter-bombers helped offset the effective loss of this stand-off capability.

In the spring of 1968, the Air Force introduced the EB-66C model which incorporated steerable antennas. This "enabled operators to focus a plane's jamming energy against a specific radar transmitter." In spite of this and other modifications, the EB-66 did "only what the enemy allowed it to do." They had effectively forced the aircraft to operate far enough away from the Red River Valley that stand-off jamming was only marginally effective at best.

When Johnson declared everything north of the 19th as "off limits" in April, 1968, Rolling Thunder continued in the southern panhandle and much of the fighter-bomber capacity was shifted to Laos. On the panhandle missions that lasted seven months, one EB-66 would orbit over Laos and another would orbit just off the coast. Both of these were the newly-modified E models.

The E models, the first of which arrived in Thailand in August of 1967, had 21 jamming devices, two fewer than the B model. What was different was that the transmitters were tunable, allowing the operators to adjust frequency during flight, and that the transmitters were also adjustable to all frequencies and not pre-determined ones. This was "so effective that the enemy received no radar warnings until the attacking aircraft were within 10 to 30 nautical miles from their assigned targets."

After the November total bombing halt, stand-off jamming by the EB-66s was reduced to assisting the fighter-bombers and B-52s operating in Laos in support of Barrel Roll and in support of the manned and unmanned reconnaissance aircraft overflying North Vietnam and China. They were also used in support of the Linebacker raids of 1972, which will be described later in this chapter.

"Self-Protection" Jamming Pods:

The third and final military answer to the downing of Leopard 2 was the introduction of externally mounted "self-protection" pods on the MER/ TER (multiple and triple ejection racks) ejection racks under the wings of the F-105s and F-4Cs. In late 1966, the pods were being flown into NVN. However, Cam Ranh did not receive any pods until after I left. While awaiting this upgrade, we attacked without any sort of protection, which included no radar activation sensors to alert us to SAM, AAA or MIG activity.

It was a trade-off of sorts because we were not targeted against the hardest targets. However, in December my squadron did lose an F-4C to a SAM in the far north, three weeks before I left Vietnam for the States. Ken Cordier was the AC and December was not lucky for him. Three weeks before he was shot down by the SAM, he led a flight of three and lost both the others to AAA over one NVN target within 30 seconds of one another. Both of those planes were manned by pilots who lived with me in our Quonset "Apartment" and were half of my administrative Flight. Unfortunately, Ken rejoined his former wing mates when the North Viets finally united the far-flung POW prisons at the single one that our crews annointed as the "Hanoi Hilton."

The Air Force had begun testing of a jamming pod that could be carried on fighter-bombers in 1963. The original unit was designated the QRC-160. Combat tests in 1965 confirmed the effectiveness of the QRC-160A-1 variant. Pilots still had to fly above 4,000' to evade the murderous fire of the "curtain of steel." The pod was re-designated the ALQ-71 shortly after its introduction to combat.

Stanford University's electronics laboratory was contracted by the Air Force to evaluate the pod. The appropriately-named William R. Rambo, Director of the laboratory, stated: "before the (combat evaluation) the North Vietnamese were averaging one kill for every 35 SAMs launched, but that after (the planes were equipped) the ratio was one plane downed per 60 launchings." So, the pod was effective. Rambo was an expert in jamming, having invented a jammer that was used extensively against Germany during WWII.

The anti-radiation pods did not confer total immunity. The normal load of two pods per aircraft protected fighters up to 8-10 nautical miles from the SAM sites. At that point, "burn through" occurred and the Fan Songs overpowered the jamming signal and allowed a radar lock-on for the missile operators. Also, the jamming antenna on board the fighters lost effectiveness during some aircraft maneuvers such as during steep turns. After burn-through, the attacking aircraft were vulnerable to missile attack outside of five miles, if they were pointed at the SAM site or longer if they were flying tangentially to it.

As they arrived in SEA, the pods were mounted on both the strike and Wild Weasel aircraft, with the weasels getting first shot. By the month that I left SEA, January 1967, Seventh Air Force had equipped most of the 105s and had enough pods and mounting brackets to begin equipping all the F-4Cs as well as the rest of the F-105Ds. The pod was not a large addition. It measured 7.5 feet long and 10 inches wide. The total weight was 200 pound and it did not have to borrow power from the bird, since it had an integral ram-air-turbine to generate electricity from the slip stream of air flowing around the pod.

The Thuds carried two pods, but the Phantoms were only wired for one. By mid-1967 AF electronic technicians had modified the Phantoms and they were equipped with a second pod. Strike forces out of Thailand came to rely on the pods to frustrate gun-laying and missile-control radars guarding "hot" targets in the North.

In November 1967, the SAMs had eight kills within four days, despite the use of the self-protection pods. Analysis discovered that the cunning North Viets were transmitting on a slightly lower frequency and thus escaped the jamming barrage. Part of the problem was that the SAM operators were targeting the jamming "noise" on their scopes, which meant that instead of a radar "blip" to fire against, they targeted the center of the jamming noise. Our answer was to open up our formations so that there wasn't a concentrated jam point to aim against.

While concentrated jamming allowed a "window" for enemy radar operators, they still needed ranging information from triangulation, which they received from widely separated radar sites and linked them through radio or telephone. They also received ranging from ground observers who relayed distance and direction information to the radar sites.

Pod protection initially caused fighter-bomber flights problems when they reached a target. The pod-protection positioning of the fighters had them out of position to set up for dive bomb attacks. We solved this by abandoning the pod formation one minute prior to the strike, which allowed proper set-ups by the individual fighters, but did not allow enemy radar enough time to lock-on and fire.

Air Force evaluations of the effectiveness of the pods determined that the loss rate was only 25% that of the missions flown without pod protection. However, the intensity of combat in the target areas made proper evaluations very difficult. Many factors contributed to losses and coming up with specific figures for evaluation proved an inexact effort.

Other problems also plagued the pod use. The greatest was that the effectiveness of the jamming was greatly reduced in heavy turns using sharp banks. The pods also increased drag, replaced bombs and fuel tanks that might also hang under the wings. Steeply banked turns directed the strongest portion of the jamming signal into space where it was ineffectual. The fighter formations compensated by using shallower turns, and some sort of weaving was necessary to visually protect against MIGs. Approaching our fighters from the rear was the most effective way for MIGs to successfully attack and constant monitoring of "our six o'clock" was necessary.

The North Viets would learn the idiosyncrasies of each pod and cleverly figure out methods of radar pulse transmission to thwart them. They used similar techniques to thwart the air-to-ground missiles employed by the Wild Weasels. Sometimes that meant staying totally passive and waiting for the last minute to energize the acquisition radar. Other times they might turn a Fan Song off at the moment the Weasels launched a missile and then activate another nearby Fan Song, thus confusing the missile internal tracking device.

In late 1967, another pod jammer, the ALQ-87 was introduced to compensate for the deficiencies of prior pods. The 87 could lay "down a continuous jamming barrage and had a sweep modulator, which could simultaneously perform any two of three functions: denying range and azimuth data to the Fire Can (AAA & AW detection and direction radar); depriving the Fan Song of range, altitude and azimuth; and jamming the position beacon (sometimes called the down-link beacon) installed in the sustainer section of the Guideline (SA-2) missile."

"Down-link jamming interfered with the signal used by the SAM controllers to follow the missiles on radar and to correct their trajectories." The effectiveness of down-link jamming would be rediscovered by SAC in 1972.

The utilization of the ALQ-87 on Iron Hand missions could only be evaluated during the four months left before President Johnson stopped bombing north of the 19th Parallel. In those four months, SAM batteries launched 495 missiles at Wild Weasel Thunderchiefs resulting in only three 105s being shot down. Two of those fighters had pods jamming the tracking beam instead of the down-link beam. This is another lesson that SAC had to relearn in December, 1972 in time for Linebacker.

In April of 1968, just after the initial Rolling Thunder cease fire, another pod was introduced to Wild Weasel Phantoms and Thuds that was installed beneath and integral to the fuselage and not hanging under a wing. This was the QRC-335, which had minimal impact on Rolling Thunder due to its exclusive use below the 19th.

The overall success of the self-protection jamming pod program can be attested to by the statements of two leading combat pilots in the war:

Colonel Robin Olds, commander of the Ubon-based, F-4C flying, 8th TFW MIG-killers: "The most significant development in the air war over NVN during my tour was the introduction of the ECM (electronic countermeasures) pod and with it a return to mass formation tactics reminiscent of fighter operations in WWII and Korea."

Brig. General William Chairsell, commander of the 388th TFW flying F-105s out of Korat Air Base in Thailand: "Prior to the pod, our aircraft were required to ingress and egress to and from the target using terrain-masking for protection and employ the "pop-up" maneuver over the target," tactics that brought the planes "well within range of the majority of AW and AAA and made them extremely vulnerable to SA-2 firings and AAA at the peak of their pop-ups." Due to the pod, "our aircraft could now roll into the target from medium altitude (12,000 to 15,000 feet) a change that reduced losses and improved bombing accuracy."

Then- Colonel Chairsell also commanded the "Ryan's Raiders" who flew the dangerous night and all-weather missions against RP 5&6. Four, of the original contingent of 8 pilots to arrive at Korat on April 24, 1967, were shot down by May 15th , which resulted in a 50% loss rate in only three weeks, with the pilots either dead or captured.

AMERICAN RETALIATORY MISSILES:

AGM-12B "Bullpup": The US Air Force had an air-to-ground missile called the AGM-12B "Bullpup" at the start of the SEA War. MacDill pilots were required to be "certified" in firing of the Bullpup annually. That certification was done in a simulator.

The Bullpup was developed as a result of Korean War experiences. Bullpup was used in North Vietnam to attack bridges with limited success. Its warhead, while larger than many air-to-ground missiles at 250 pounds, was unable to knock down concrete structures. The later-developed AGM-12C had a 970-pound warhead, which made it a real warhorse. However, the C model was very expensive, very heavy and was created for nuclear delivery. While it was available for use in SEA, it was seldom used.

The Bullpup required the pilot to continue flying the same track by following a flare on the back of the missile (the C model had two). This was double-jeopardy for pilots. Flying the same track in highly-defended areas is a recipe for disaster. Following the smoke of the flare allowed the ground gunners to aim starting at the flare smoke and just walking the bullets backward to the aircraft. Due to its deficiencies, the Bullpup was not considered for SAM sites.

AGM-45 "Shrike": The missile of choice for the SAMs was the air-to-ground AGM-45 Shrike, developed by the Navy. While it proved marginally effective, it did have several problems.

The primary problem with the "Shrike" was that it had to be fired at a Fan Song while in a 30-degree "loft" maneuver. The usual distance away from the target to fire was 15 miles, which amounted to about 50 seconds of flight time. During the first 10 seconds of flight, the pilot had to stay on the same general course to insure the highest level of accuracy. The aircraft radar could offer assistance to the Shrike for its initial burn, but some 10 seconds after launch, the rocket motor burned out and guidance ceased. This meant that for 40 seconds, the missile would essentially be ballistic. To hit a target, successful launches required flying very precise parameters.

The Shrike did offer the ability to be fired from outside the Fan Song envelope. It could be successfully fired to home on a radar transmitter from a distance of more than the 17-nautical- mile max effective range of the Guideline missile. However, the farther away from the target when fired, the less chance for a successful hit.

The Shrike was first used in combat on April 18, 1966. A "Fire Can" AAA radar unit was attacked near

Dong Hoi in Route Pack 1.

Initial implementation of the Wild Weasels had them preceding the main strike force by 5 minutes. This 5-minute separation proved too far in advance because it deprived them of the protection of the missile-carrying F-4Cs flying MIG top cover which was protecting the main strike force. To add to the danger for the Weasels, the strike aircraft could withdraw from the target area after expending its munitions, while the Weasels had to stick around for as long as 35 minutes while searching for SAMs in an area "bristling" with AAA.

The loss rates were so heavy that by mid-August, 1966, only four of the converted F-105Fs remained flyable. The rest had either been shot down or shot up so badly that extensive maintenance was required to bring an aircraft back to flying status. The Thud 355th TFW had been assigned six of the F models. Four had been shot down and the other two were damaged beyond repair.

In October, replacements arrived. Almost immediately the North Viets had shot down the commander of the entire Wild Weasel detachment. From that point until the end of Rolling Thunder, the Thud Wild Weasel aircraft inventory varied between 4 and 12.

When in a tense, high-threat attack, once an AGM or an ARM missile had been fired, pilots were then concerned with rapidly exiting the area. To watch a Shrike until impact was a luxury most could not afford. Thus, from that first firing until July 15, analysis showed that of 107 Shrikes fired, they scored only one confirmed and 38 probable hits. This may sound as if the missile was a failure, but that is not necessarily the case. Since fighter-pilot focus after firing a missile would have been on evading defenses, a visual confirmation of a kill would not be a high priority. A variety of factors needed to be considered and proper evaluation was complex.

The Fan Song operators found out that they could turn Fan Song off and deprive the Shrikes of a source of radiation. This might have negated a hit, but the consequences were greatly diminished SAM accuracy and attack aircraft that would survive to fight another day.

The enemy found that by relying on acquisition radars and ground observers instead of fire control radars, they could accurately figure track azimuth and range and fire accordingly at a presumed target location.

The Weasels tried various schemes to mask their positions from the radar operators. They sometimes would come in at high altitude and other times low. They often would be close enough to the strike formations that they were assumed by the defenders to be strike aircraft instead of SAM killers. The Weasels usually carried bombs, rockets or 20mm guns for any time that they sighted a SAM battery or whenever a Fan Song or Fire Can was bold enough to transmit. It seemed the motto of the Weasels was "attack, attack, attack."

The Shrike suffered from a small warhead, limited range and a poor guidance system. The Shrike had a blast-fragmentation warhead that weighed 149 pounds. It also required pilots to stay in a loft mode aimed at the target for the first 10 second after launch. It was susceptible to enemy radar operators turning off the Fan Songs, which often caused the missile to miss wildly.

Noting the several deficiencies of the Shrike, Navy planners started development of the Standard ARM. This was a much larger anti-radiation missile and the Wild Weasels had high hopes.

AGM-78B Standard ARM "Starm": The "Starm" B model included a memory circuit allowing it to track a target once it locked on, even if the enemy radar was shut down. This was a large improvement over Shrike, against which expert Fan Song operators used a standard tactic of flipping the radar off and on.

On paper, the Standard ARM was the answer for the Shrike deficiencies. Its warhead was considerably larger at 215 pounds of blast-fragmentation efficiency. The B model featured a broadband seeker, which allowed the missile to be used against a variety of targets without having to pre-select the seeker head before each mission.

"In theory, a pilot could engage a target 60 to 70 miles distant," but operationally that was not feasible. The better homing ability of the Starm allowed a pilot to launch at a Fan Song without having to fly directly at the target.

The first operational uses in SEA of the AGM-78B Standard ARM were in March, 1968, which limited its use due to the bombing halts of Rolling Thunder. Operationally, the Starm suffered from the same NVN tactic of shutting off his radar. Another deficiency was its cost. While the Shrike cost $7,000, each Starm cost $200,000.

Anyone who knows pilots know they love paperwork (right). The Air Force's answer to widespread use of the very expensive Starm was to require using pilots to fill out a great deal of paperwork with each launch. This tactic effectively reduced its use. Another tactic was to stop ordering the weapon. At the end of Linebacker II, the B-52 assault of North Vietnam, the counter-SAM Weasels had only 15 of the Standard ARMs left to fight the war

One result of the reduced use of the expensive Standard ARM was that the Weasels carried a mixed load of both Shrikes and Standard ARMs. A standard load for the F-105G was a 650-gallon fuel tank mounted centerline for extended range and time-over-target, plus two Standard ARMs mounted on inboard pylons and two Shrikes mounted on the outboard. That mix may occasionally have been changed with the addition of jamming pods or Sidewinders, but that was standard.

While the cost and paperwork factors inhibited some to its use, "most F-105G crews preferred the AGM-78 even though its aerodynamic characteristics reduced aircraft performance."

ENEMY GUN DEFENSES:

Wild Weasels not only had to contend with the probability that the SAMs would be fired at them, they also had to consider the gun defenses, which relied heavily on either towed or self-propelled batteries of four to eight 57mm guns. These could be considered the medium-altitude defenses. Lower altitude defenses proved the most-deadly to attacking fighters.

Van-mounted Fire Can radar normally controlled the guns, feeding the data gathered into a fire-control computer. The fire-control computer would then feed firing data out to an entire system of automatic guns. Later, optical tracking and ranging was available.

Radar controlled, the 57mm guns fired 80 rounds per-minute per-gun and could engage an aircraft at 20,000 feet. The later optical guidance weapons had a reduced effective range of 13,000 feet. The 85 mm AAA weapon was effective when it was radar controlled and could be accurate to 27,500 feet while firing 20 rounds per-minute, while the 100 mm was effective at 39,000 feet at 15 rounds per-minute, but like the 85s could shoot much higher.

The "curtain of steel" method of barrage-fire mentioned in the previous chapter used the 37mm and 57mm AAA guns, machine guns, and automatic rifles. The 37s and 57s had a useful, much faster rate-of-fire than the larger 85mm and 100mm AAA weapons. The Weasels faced this wall of fire across their most obvious attack corridors to the Fan Songs. This "curtain of steel" was augmented by hand-held rifles.

According to North Vietnamese Army Manuals, a NVA rifle platoon could fire a barrage of 1,000 rounds within five seconds.

Optical sighting was very effective, especially at low altitudes. When pilots usually referred to the AW or automatic weapons fire, they would be referring to the smallest weapons in the AAA team. Each of these smaller sizes of AAA mounted optical sights. The benefits for this lower-altitude gun mix were that they employed a much higher rate of fire with either radar controlled or optical sighting. This combination was deadly for any low-flying fighter.

The lightest of the AW guns was the 12.7mm machine gun, effective up to 3,000 feet and capable of firing 80 rounds per-minute. The deadly-effective, 14.5mm machine gun boasted an effective range of 4500 feet and a rate of fire of 150 rounds-a-minute. A later-added 23mm also had a high rate of fire. The 37mm gun could fire 80 rounds per-minute and down a fighter at 5,500 feet, but its accuracy dropped with an increase in altitude. This "curtain of steel" was automatically controlled by the Fire Can radar.

An example of how the various components of the gun system worked is the Soviet ZPU-4 (14.5mm) Gun System. This is a carriage-mounted array of four heavy, fully automatic machine guns. Each of the four guns is automatically fed from a 500-round drum mounted on the carriage. The optical control was mounted on the carriage as well. Its operation could be automatically controlled by off-carriage fire control radars, such as the "Fire Can." The Fire Cans would acquire a target and feed firing information to all the guns electronically tied into the individual system.

While individual AAA batteries were important to knock out, the most important element in the NVN AAA and AW gun protection system was the automatic control created by the "Fire Can" radars. These were very important spokes in the smoothly turning wheel that was the AAA defensive Gun System.

In the category of "it might come back to bite you," the Soviet designation for the Fire Can towed-radar was Son-9. The Son-9 is a derivative of the American SCR-584 radar given to the Soviets during WWII Lend-Lease.

The NVN counter-tactic of their "curtain of steel" accounted for over 90% of the fighter-bomber losses from the start of Rolling Thunder in March, 1965, until the end of 1965. That evaluation of the kill rate of the deadly curtain continued throughout the SEA War.

PUNCH & COUNTERPUNCH:

The North Vietnamese had been discovered to be worthy adversaries. Their "defenses improved with stunning speed" and Tactical Air Command (TAC) struggled to keep up. While it was a war for which the United States was very adept, against North Vietnam it became a series of battles of "punch and counterpunch" as each side modified tactics and equipment, as evidenced by the string of upgrades to the "self-protection" pods shown above.

Chaff: The electronic air war waged over North Vietnam had its origins from several important items developed by the British in WWII. The invention of radar was one and the invention of chaff was another.

Chaff is usually thin aluminum strips that are expelled over corridors or areas of the sky to confuse defensive radar sets. It provides a strong radar return that shows up on a screen as a sort of "blanket" of returns often covering a wide area. The effectiveness was that radar operators were not likely to be able to discern individual blips of aircraft in a sky full of returns.

At the start of Rolling Thunder, little thought was given to chaff. Then an innovative F-4C driver, who was flying MIG cover, decided to use chaff. Whether he cut the strips himself, or had them imported is unknown. What is known is that he loaded them inside his speed brake well. Then on a mission he dropped his speed brakes in a vulnerable location. The results could be seen on the screens of the stand-off jammers.

An equally inventive RF-4C pilot got into the act and loaded up his photoflash cartridge dispenser, intended for night photography, and dropped a couple of chaff containers on a mission. The practice spread to the EB-66s, which actually had chaff dispensers.

This became the principal change in the operational tactics employed by jammers after the end of Rolling Thunder. The use of chaff during Rolling Thunder was discouraged by the Navy. Their concern was that the vast screens of chaff dense enough to blanket NVN radar would interfere with electronic equipment on board ships stationed off the coast. Their concerns were alleviated by a tactical change in ship deployment.

Decoy Drones: Drones were used to trick enemy radars into transmitting so that EB-66Cs and EA-3Bs could locate the Fan Songs and their associated batteries. This use was only marginally successful. It did reduce the reaction time for the Weasels induced by manned photo reconnaissance aircraft, but it was not significant. While it sounded good to recce pilots, the use of pilotless drones did not give the Weasels accurate and pinpoint site identification. Upon reaching the supposed site, they often had to search an area of 4 nautical miles in diameter in an attempt to find the site. This was unacceptable and the use of decoy drones was discontinued.

MIG Defensive Fighter-Interceptors: The weakest link in the deadly triad of Vietnamese weapons was the defensive system utilizing the MIG fighter-interceptors. However, any air force that can operate within its own airspace and use its own intercept radars has a significant advantage over intruding strategic or tactical bombers. North Vietnam was no exception.

Additionally, the Chinese, Korean and Vietnamese fighter pilots manning their MIGs could escape to China for sanctuary, if needed. Indeed, while the inventory of MIGs operating in defense of the North climbed as high as 240 MIGs, at one time in 1968, so many were operating out of Chinese airfields that only 15 (8 MIG 21s and 7 MIG 17s) were left at all the North Viet bases. The MIGs then operated against American fighters from their Chinese havens. This element of sanctuary worked well for the enemy in a variety of ways.

As the war progressed, the effectiveness of the MIG contingent became less and less a strong part of the enemy defenses. Their losses to the F-4s constituted a significant part of their entire inventory. While they were very effective against the F-105s and other attack aircraft, the Air Force and Navy Phantoms ruled the skies and shot down many MIGs with both the Sparrow and Sidewinder missiles and even the externally carried Gattling gun. Later F-4 models carried the Gattling internally.

The use of the Chinese sanctuary airfields created "situations." MIGs being chased back across the Chinese border to their sanctuary bases caused inadvertent border crossings by our Phantoms. Our Air Force issued warnings to our pilots against crossings. The pilots sometimes ignored the warnings, which they gauged to be a hindrance to operations. Some turned off their IFFs when nearing the border and others just failed to turn them on during the missions, thus negating their ability to be tracked by American radar.

Discussions that I had with Thud drivers indicated that they were attacking the Chinese airfields that were operating against our forces and they did it without the knowledge of our Air Force. We pilots at other bases didn't blame them and we were glad they did it. The war was becoming so horribly mismanaged that sometimes we had to take things into our own hands. The times that the Thuds strafed the Russian and British supply ships was another example.

By the time of the last air battles of the war in the form of Linebacker I and II, the usefulness of the MIGs was reduced to confirming the altitude of the B-52 bomber streams to the jammed radar operators manning the SAM defenses.

THE "DEAD PERIOD":

During the "dead period" from the total cessation of Rolling Thunder in November, 1968 until the initiation of "Freedom Train" in April, 1972, there was lots of aerial activity. We continued to fly manned and unmanned reconnaissance aircraft over North Vietnam and China and those were provided pod and stand-off jamming protection. We also turned our fighters to bombing Laos and created immense damage.

Reconnaissance Drones: These were flown at low altitude. The Vietnamese defensive system seemed to use the 20/ month, low-level recce drone missions as a means for practice. For three weeks or so, the SAMs would challenge each drone that entered the heavily defended portions of the Red River Valley. During that period the MIGs would not fly. The following three weeks the SAMs would stay silent while the MIGs would fly and intercept. They would then repeat the cycle. While it may have been productive for NVN training, this allowed our EB-66s to concentrate on just one threat at a time.

The importance of voice communication with the MIGs was emphasized on these EB-66 missions. During a MIG attack on a drone on May 16, 1970, the protecting 66 jammed the strike (vocal) channel and the drone escaped. An identical attack on July 3 resulted in no voice jamming and the drone was shot down. Ground controllers were providing necessary vector information.

The leading North Vietnamese ace had two of his nine kills against drones, which also operated over Chinese soil.

During these stand-off missions, the North Vietnamese controllers learned to identify the EB-66s. The characteristic radar returns from the jamming aircraft helped them. The speed, altitude and radio call signs were changed infrequently and that also led to identification. They were able to stereotype our flight profiles.

The ability to identify the type of aircraft to assign to the various blips that enemy radar operators saw on their screens was of significant importance. Once known, the operators would then know the tactics and equipment needed to affect a shoot down.

The final months of Johnson's Presidency also saw a tightening of the Rules of Engagement once again. The recce RF-4Cs had the Weasels flying cover. For a time, "the Weasels were unable to hit a SAM site that was painting the RFs unless the RFs or the Weasels actually had seen a missile hurtling skyward." This again elicited the pilot response, "how can they be so stupid?"

THE LAST AIR BATTLES:

In 1968, Nixon won the Presidency and inherited the war. He took a card from Johnson's playbook and allowed the war to fester for almost his entire first term in office. Actually, Nixon seemed to start out his first term literally with a bang. Within a day of the Nixon Inauguration in January of 1969 and within three months of the total cessation of bombing in North Vietnam, Strategic Air Command launched a 100-plane

B-52 attack against VC sanctuary sites in Cambodia, apparently sensing that Nixon would approve. The attack dropped fifteen miles short of their intended target with the bombs actually hitting in Vietnam. That ineffective attack was shortly followed by another 100-plane attack that was very successful, with the bombs hitting in Cambodia as intended. After those two attacks, air activity seemed to slow down.

"Proud Deep Alpha":

With the two-step cessation of Rolling Thunder (RT) in 1968, the North became more and more emboldened. Their primary fear seems to have been the potential damage that could be inflicted by the B-52s when they carried their loads of 108 of the 750-pound bombs. Toward the end of RT, the North Viets began installing SAM sites just inside their own territory allowing the Guidelines to hit 52s as far as 15 nautical-miles beyond their borders. Their primary aim seemed to be to defend the hugely important Mu Gia and Ban Karai passes into Laos.

The "battle of the passes" continued through much of Nixon's first term. Starting in 1968, the B-52s were used heavily against the three mountain passes through the Annamites. The battles came to a head in December of 1971, when the enemy shifted even more SAMs and MIG interceptors into the NVN panhandle to counter the huge 52 attacks. The Pentagon's response was in the form of operation "Proud Deep Alpha."

On December 26, waves of Air Force and Navy bombers pounded "stoutly defended airfields, petroleum storage tanks, and military barracks" located in the North Vietnamese panhandle between the 17th and 19th Parallels. For five days, a total of 1066 sorties were flown: 935 of them strike; 102 radar suppression and 29 were armed reconnaissance. "The countermeasures gear that had served effectively during Rolling Thunder was returned to action."

December was in the monsoon season and the clouds affected operations. However, both the Air Force and Navy had effectively used the time after cessation of RT by beefing up their all-weather capabilities. The enemy defenses only included SAM and AAA as no MIGs rose to counter the multi-plane formations. The effectiveness of the Phantom in its encounters with MIGs managed to neutralize this portion of the NVN defensive shield. In fact, the actions by the MIGs, after getting their noses bloodied in RT, seemed to show a fear of any engagement with the Sparrow and Sidewinder-equipped Phantoms.

However, the SAMs and AAA were their usual menace as a Navy F-4 and A-6 plus an Air Force F-4 were downed. The SAM sites fired 45 confirmed missiles. Retaliatory radar-suppression Iron Hand flights relied upon the Air Force F-105Gs with the Shrikes and Standard ARMs, plus the 20mm cannon, while the Navy used the A-6As and A-7Es. The radar suppression flights attacked both the Fan Songs, the Spoon Rest surveillance radar, which they found more vulnerable, the gun-laying Fire Cans and ground-control intercept (GCI) radar.

Proud Deep Alpha encountered moderate to heavy fire from every AA gun in the significant enemy arsenal. If anything, the small caliber automatic machine gun fire, supplemented with the newly-arrived 23 mm cannon, was even deadlier. The smaller "weapons fired planned barrages, while the bigger ones were radar controlled."

Enemy response to the Standard ARM had been perfected enough to effectively neutralize it. Their tactic was to use the missiles memory circuit against it. When possible, they would wait for a Starm to be fired and then simultaneously turn the target Fan Song off while beginning transmission from a second, similar Fan Song that stayed on just long enough to divert the missile.

Proud Deep Alpha seemed a dress rehearsal for coming events as both sides were showcasing their latest offensive and defensive equipment and tactics. The lessons learned in that short five-day air war would be on display three months later.

On April 6, Nixon reversed Johnson's sequential stand-down of the war in the north by re-imposing an air war up to the 20th Parallel. Instead of Rolling Thunder, his action was now called Operation "Freedom Train." In his case, his impatience may have been a virtue for just 10 days later; he initiated Operation "Porch Bravo" which took the air war all the way to the Chinese border. The combined actions of Freedom Train and Porch Bravo continued until May 9, when Nixon and company really started to get serious.

Freedom Train included B-52s that struck on April 9, the farthest north of any B-52 strike of the war, when they sent a dozen aircraft to bomb the rail yards and POL storage complex at Vinh. Three days later, the Buffs again struck even further north at the Bai Thuong Airfield, a MIG base just six miles south of the 20th Parallel. This time the 52s beat "Porch Bravo" by a day and pounded a POL depot at Haiphong. These were followed by two Freedom Train B-52 strikes against Thanh Hoa on April 21 and 23.

These Thanh Hoa raids resulted in the SAMs getting involved. The operators were proficient in tracking the jamming source and ended up firing at least 23 SAMs which inflicted damage on one heavy bomber. None of the bombers took evasive action, instead relying on chaff, the Wild Weasels and internal electronic jamming to thwart the defenses.

Post Thanh Hoa, the Buffs concentrated farther north and flew more than 2,300 sorties, which hammered the supply lines that sustained the Viet Cong and its NVN allies in the South. Most of these flown sorties were part of Operation "Linebacker."

"Linebacker": Linebacker was a campaign to sever North Vietnam's overland transport arteries and supply stores. This consisted of the northern roadways and, in particular, the rail lines connecting NVN with China and beyond. These were the infamous NE and NW railroad lines of Rolling Thunder.

The most startling departure from the rules of Rolling Thunder was the political approval to sow aerial mines in the harbors and river mouths that were the avenues of Russian supplies. Thus, we were finally knocking out their supply warehousing and also stopping the re-supply. We were getting serious about resolving the conflict.

While the B-52s were a major part of Linebacker, it was the tactical bombers, including the multi-purpose Phantoms that led the charge and sustained heavy losses. Starting in April, Air Force F-4Cs, F-4Ds and F-4Es conducted raids into the North and by the end of October had sustained the loss of 73 Phantoms, 18 in the month of July alone. This was the largest single-month loss for the F-4s in the entire war. While the Phantom might not have been the size or carried the crew of a B-52, this was a high loss rate for these first-line tactical fighter-bombers. That included 146 pilots and weapons officers downed in hostile territory with the outcome for them usually death or imprisonment. For some, it meant imprisonment and death.

The return of the bombers to the North created a rebirth of importance for both the self-protection pods and chaff as weapons in the electronic war. Four pods were available for use, including two that had been used during Rolling Thunder. The two new ones showed that the military had put the lull from 1968 to 1972 to good use. ALQ-119 and ALQ 101 joined ALQ 71 and 87.

Of interest is that the failed fighter-bomber, the F-111, was successfully introduced as a night bomber. The 111 had been used with mixed results during Rolling Thunder, but was given a more important roll against the North under Nixon. The early missions of the F-111 were plagued with probable malfunctions of the terrain-avoidance radar system. In an area of sharply-rising karsts, this presented a lethal problem.

As with the Thunderchiefs, the 111s had internal jammers installed in its fuselage. Additionally, the major cause for both the USAF and USN to reject the 111 became the cause for its success in SEA. Its elongated fuselage did not fit on many of the Navy aircraft carrier elevators nor did it allow for tight turns in "dog fighting" but it did allow faster speeds at lower altitudes. On top of that, it was equipped with automatic terrain-following radar and flight control. This allowed for night, fast, low-level penetration of enemy territory. The terrain-following feature provided the speed and low-level needed to thwart the SAM Fan Song. The failed fighter became a successful night and all-weather bomber.

"The F-111 jammer pods generated a modulated noise barrage and could also transmit a deceptive radar return. The basic noise barrage compromised the Fan Song ability to determine range, while noise modulation disrupted tracking. When faced with the combined electronic jammers, operators had to resort to optical tracking." The Special or Down-Link jamming feature caused a distorted position signal which frustrated the Fan Song crews from even using optical guidance. Just as the pilots of the 111s finally became confident in the low-level auto pilot feature of terrain-following, fighter-bomber pilots gained respect and confidence in the down-link jammers.

The F-111s, which would be re-designated the B-111 to note its change from a fighter to a bomber role, were used to destroy missile sites and MIG fields protecting Hanoi/ Haiphong. The 111s had a built-in jammer which, when combined with an advanced pod, created complete jamming coverage. Their electronic countermeasures also were effective against Fire Can, which negated the AW portion of low-level retaliation. The North Viet radar men who controlled the AAA consistently underestimated the speed of the 111 and their defenses were thus compromised.

The F-111s did have trouble with radar-controlled AAA batteries that kicked up the "curtain of steel." The 111 pilots changed tactics and did not turn on the SAM and gun-laying radar jammers unless their warning sensors alerted them to SAM or AAA tracking. In Linebacker I, ten SAMs were fired at the low–level speedsters and none scored a hit.

The SAM threat continued at a high level with 2661 fired from the start of "Freedom Train" until the end of "Linebacker." The results were mixed for any effectiveness evaluation. For example: 41 pod-equipped planes were downed by the 2661 SAMs, for a ratio of 65 launchings per aircraft destroyed (**65:1**). During the same seven-months of 1966, 548 missiles shot-down 15 non-pod-carrying planes, for a ratio of 37 to one (**37:1**). That would seem to show the pod-equipped fighter-bombers were twice as safe as non-pod-carrying. Yet, in the same period in 1967, the enemy had to launch 83 SAMs for every non-pod-carrying aircraft destroyed (**83:1**).

Statistics are only as good as the input provided. Variables in weather, types and numbers of defensive weapons, the skill of the defenders, the skill of the attacking pilots, the differences in tactics employed and the ability of the attackers to maintain a pod formation, all combined to subvert a proper statistical analysis. Because of the many variables, the best and truest evaluation is that of the participating pilots. The statements of the combat leaders above attest to the success of the constantly improving pods in SEA.

The MIG threat, which had receded, was reinvigorated when they attacked the fighter-bomber formations relying on the pod array. During May and June, the MIGs shot down 15 American aircraft. This could have meant that the confidence level of our pilots had increased with the effectiveness of the protective pods and the long absence of the MIGs. Some of the pilots may have been lulled into not including visual sweeps to identify the small spots in the sky that might be enemy aircraft.

Technological advancement did not just involve jammers. "On May 10, 1972, Ubon Phantoms severed the highway and railroad spans of the Paul Doumer Bridge at Hanoi, using laser and television-guided bombs. The attackers approached through a chaff corridor 2 nautical miles wide, 4,000-feet deep and 34 nautical miles long," laid by 8 Phantoms 15 minutes prior to the attack. The attack F-4s dove below the chaff corridor to bomb with a release altitude as low as 8,000 feet.

The SAM response was 160 missiles fired with no damage caused, "thanks to the combination of chaff and the ALQ-87 jamming pods."

This attack was significant for several reasons. First, it showed the tech advancements in what would be called "smart bombs" that would be so effective in our later air battles in the deserts of the Middle East. Secondly, it showed the heavier and heavier reliance on the F-4 in carrying both the offensive and defensive loads in an attack. The now dispenser-equipped F-4s were the aircraft of choice for laying chaff. Thirdly and most importantly, that flight became one of many showing that "during the 1972 fighting, chaff earned the reputation of being essential for the survival of the strike force in an SA-2 and radar directed AAA environment."

While accurate statistics are very difficult to come by, from the start of Freedom Train until the end of Linebacker I, the Air Force fired 908 anti-radiation missiles with a total of only 3 confirmed kills. However, 185 active fire-control radars were forced to shut down. The Navy had 1425 launches with 33 confirmed kills. They had "521 instances when the enemy fire-control radar abruptly shut down." Just shutting down the radars resulted in many of our attacking aircraft escaping destruction.

The heavy use of bombers, both tactical and heavy, was starting to show significant results in Linebacker when Nixon again followed Johnson's lead. He called a bombing halt on October 23. With the national election just two weeks away, political considerations may have played a part? Since his political situation at home did not seem to include the escalation of the conflict to a level where victory became a possibility, he also seemed intent on the bargaining table. His options were definitely much more limited than those available to Johnson when he inherited the mess from Kennedy.

"Linebacker II": Less than two months later and after the election, on December 18, three waves comprising 121 B-52s (out of 207 in SEA), converged on seven targets near Hanoi. Nineteen Air Force countermeasures aircraft were in support of each of the first two waves. Three stand-off 66s were joined by eight F-4 chaff birds and eight Weasels. On the third wave, Navy A-7s replaced the Weasels and five EA-3Bs joined the 66s.

This was the start of the massive heavy-bombing campaign, lasting 11 days that would finally re-teach American leaders that the only sure-fire method to achieve goals (in this case the bargaining table) was through strength and not weakness. This massive assault must have shown a resolve on our part that the North Viets had not previously seen. The returned POWs shared with me that they had heard and witnessed the sound and fury of the night attacks from the shelter of their Hanoi prison. They were able to peek out through narrow slits at the entire city of Hanoi burning. The concussive sounds of the 750# bombs lasted well into each night and were thrilling to these long-deprived pilots. They could finally add hope to their miserable conditions. For the first time, they saw fear in the eyes of their captors.

The B-52s carried their own complement of EWOs or electronic warfare officers. While the pilots up front witnessed the bright puffs of exploding flak bursts, they also beheld a scene never before witnessed: that of a full SAM effort as only nighttime can portray.

Onboard the 52s were the SAC ALT-22 and ALT-28 jammers. Both worked effectively together, with the ALT 28s engaging in jamming the down-link beacons aboard the SAMS. As a further defense, the 52s flew the attacks above 35,000 feet, which was beyond the accurate reach of enemy AAA except the 100mm guns. Those were partially neutralized by countermeasures against the Fire Cans.

My close friend, Colonel Jim Annis, was one of those EWOs who sat alone in the bowels of the 52s. While the EB-66s used four EWOs, the 52s only needed one. The D & E models of the B-52s used tail gunners who were actually located in the tail. The G & H models had the gunners sitting with the EWOs while monitoring and firing their guns remotely with radar. Prior to Linebacker II, the EWOs fought a lonely and often boring war. During Linebacker II, it was a different story. When it did heat up, the tension was intense as they fought their own war using electronic swords to cut the tenuous bonds between the enemy defensive weapons and their controllers. Their focus was on the screens depicting the many dances playing between transmitters and jammers.

During the attack, the SAMs remained strangely silent. "All hell broke loose" when the 52s started their turns after dropping their bombs. The Fan Song operators had not forgotten the lesson learned with the tactical bombers: that the jammers became partially ineffective during the sharp, 45-degree turns. Five B-52s were hit that first night by the barrage of 164 missiles fired, with three plunging to the earth.

These were not the first Buffs that had been shot down. Actually, as early as April 9, 1972, a SAM site located near Dong Ha, in South Vietnam, had fired at least three missiles and damaged a B-52 that had to have an emergency landing at Danang. Later in the year, an EB-66 was actually shot down by a barrage firing of three missiles fired by a SAM site located 20 nautical miles south of the DMZ in South Vietnam.

The first of the massive bombers to be shot down was a Thailand-based aircraft attacking near Vinh. The crew of the damaged plane limped to an emergency landing at NKP, but crashed 12 miles short of the runway. This Buff was victim to a patient Fan Song operator who followed the jamming source and hit him on the B-52s turn away when in a 45-degree, banked turn, the most vulnerable position in an attack.

On the second night of Linebacker II, no bombers were lost, but on the 20th, 221 SAMs were fired. Seven bombers were hit and six of them spun to the ground in flames. Four of the six were determined to be carrying an older model of jamming transmitter instead of the newer ALT-22.

The Strategic Air Command ran tests at Eglin while Linebacker was underway and determined that the SAMs were using "a more powerful guidance beacon that was less susceptible to a modulated noise barrage." They then countered with a changed mix of jammers for their December 26th attack.

During Linebacker II, chaff earned the reputation of being "essential for the survival of the strike force in an SA-2 and radar directed AAA environment." The first method of use was the creation of a "corridor" several miles wide, 4,000 deep and over 30 miles long. As the attacks progressed, "area coverage emerged as the standard method of chaff usage."

The aircraft of choice for spreading chaff was the F-4. However, carrying the required load of six chaff "bombs" restricted the Phantoms to a maximum speed of 480 knots and 36,000 feet of altitude. This also restricted the bomber streams to less than 36,000 to utilize the protection. This allowed protection against the 85mm guns, but not the 100s.

Analysis of US Navy fighters who utilized chaff as last-minute protection vs. the US Air Force method of provision of area coverage or corridors up to 30 minutes prior to the attacks, found that the Air Force fliers reported SAM miss distances over 1000 feet greater than reported by Navy pilots, thus chaff area coverage was the superior choice.

In 1972, Wild Weasel tactics for Linebacker I and II changed from those employed earlier. A Weasel modified F-4C or the F-105G acted as the hunter, and F-4Es acted as killers. The Standard ARM was "beset with malfunctions." In many cases, Weasel flights reverted to total use of the older "Shrike."

As the air war against North Vietnam was winding its way toward completion, Weasel flights depended more and more on the F-4. The F-4E model could carry more ordnance than other Wild Weasel aircraft and the F-4 had the ability to drop its load of "hunter-killer" bombs and engage the enemy in case of a MIG attack. By the end of Linebacker II, many of the Weasel flights had reverted back to loads of bombs instead of the less reliable anti-radiation missiles.

During Linebacker II, Weasel pilots determined that a minimum of 8,000 feet was needed above any cloud deck in order to react to SAM launchings. They also determined that the best way to foil the SAM was to outmaneuver it after launch.

"In the 11 nights of Linebacker II, SAMs destroyed a total of 15 B-52s and damaged nine." Two were lost on landings making a total of 17 B-52s lost to SAMs due to outright shoot- downs or mortal damage. "Following the loss of six planes on December 20, missile effectiveness declined rapidly." In the eight nights of raids following December 20, SAMs damaged ten B-52s, six of which spun down in flames.

"As Linebacker II progressed, the enemy's defenses grew weaker. On December 18, 164 missiles soared into the night sky." On December 19, 182 were fired and 221 on the 20th. By the 23rd, just 4 missiles shot into the sky. That rebounded to 73 on the 27th and dropped to 23 the final night of the attack. "Intelligence confirmed that 567 SAMs were fired the first three nights and 315 the remaining eight." "The North Vietnamese were running out of missiles. By mining the harbors, bombing the rail and road network and attacking the SAM support facilities, American airmen had prevented the enemy from stockpiling enough SAMs to replace those expended during the first three nights."

The 11 days of massive and sustained bombing shocked the North Vietnamese and severely damage civilian morale in Hanoi. The bombing was halted by President Nixon after the United States received word that the enemy wanted to finally discuss an armistice.

Bombs had provided what bombing-halts had not and the elusive bargaining table was finally within reach.

THE STRATEGIC AIR COMMAND (SAC):

SAC has been disbanded, but its legacy lives on.

While many fighter pilots did not think very kindly of SAC, I would like to set the record straight. When I graduated from the Air Academy, the Air Force officer who gave my class their Air Force officer commissions was Four-Star General Curtis Lemay, the head of the 8th Air Force in Europe during the bombing campaign against Nazi Germany and the creator of SAC. He was a hell of a good General Officer. He was also a fighter. SAC was the offensive sword that protected the entire Free World during the dark days of the Cold War.

The airborne tanker guys that fed us belonged to SAC and they often performed incredible feats of courage to drive deep into North Vietnam and Laos to give our shot-up and leaking fighters a drink of gas. That critical refueling often was the difference between probable imprisonment and landing back at home base. They saved many aircraft and crewmembers to fight another day.

These guys exposed themselves over an enemy terrain that included a lot of Surface to Air Missile (SAM) sites. We fighters could maneuver against the SAMs, but the large tankers could not and they carried a lot of explosive JP4. More than once, the tankers hooked up with a plane entirely out of gas. The tanker pilots skillfully managed speed and altitude to allow enough gas to flow for a restart of the fighter's engines and a completion of the refueling in a more normal manner. The tanker pilots are real heroes in my book and any other SEA fighter pilot's book.

If any tanker crewmembers from SEA happen to be reading this, I would like to thank you on behalf of all the pilots that you saved, both Air Force and Navy. That thanks goes to the entire crew, not just the tanker pilots. You all risked your asses time and again. Thank you.

For an in-depth and surprisingly objective analysis of the Linebacker II raids, a 38-page Soviet report is archived at Fort Leavenworth for the U.S. Army: "Patterns and Predictability: The Soviet Evaluation of Operation Linebacker II," www.fmso.leavenworth.army.mil

The report by the Soviets stated that the SAC B-52s did not change or vary their attack parameters. From a tactics standpoint, to the North Viets the heavy bomber attacks became predictable. The SAC planners seemed to have on blinders when it came to laying out the attack parameters. The clever North Viets would aim their missiles at predicted points in space as evidenced by SACs predicted attack headings and turn points and they scored almost as high a percentage of hits as they did with accurate radar tracking.

However, the reduced effectiveness of the North Vietnamese air defenses in the latter half of Linebacker II was caused by the immediate and timely upgrading of SAC electronic countermeasures plus the lack of enough SAMs caused by the Navy's effective mining of their harbors which negated restocking of their depleted missile inventory.

The results of the critical electronic battles fought with North Vietnam and its Communist allies on one side and America on the other, could be considered mixed. While it remains the most intense and bitter battle of its kind in military history, the electronic portion of future wars will only get larger and more critical. However, it may be judged, the "deadly game" proved both participants to be extremely clever and competent adversaries.

> *"I know not with what weapons World War III will be fought, but World War IV will be fought with sticks and stones."*
>
> Albert Einstein

well to the southwest of Communist China's Hainan Island.

The tankers would fly a racetrack pattern and we would pick them up on our airborne radar. During the latter part of my war, I would fly at fast speeds to a join up with the tanker and we would echelon off his right wing. With a two-shipper, my wingman would be off my right wing.

We would never make a radio transmission, instead we would rock our wings as we closed and the boom operator, watching us from his perch on the belly of the tanker, would move his boom up and down in hello. When we were in position on his right wing, the boomer would give me the okay and I would then move to an "in trail" position under the belly. I would move up without any transmission and I would open the fueling receptacle located behind the cockpit. The boom operator and I would then be staring at each other from maybe 20 feet away. We would wave our hellos and then the boomer would insert the boom in the fighter refueling receptacle to the lock position.

As we got heavier during off-load, we may have to add additional power to stay connected. After we were full of fuel, I would salute the boomer. He would disconnect the boom and raise it out of the way and then I would move to left echelon off the tanker's left wing. Once all the birds are refueled and in left echelon, I would slowly move the flight off the tanker wing, rock my wings in goodbye and we would rocket off to the North and a rendezvous with the "Connie" or Constellation, which was our electronic, radar and communications intelligence aircraft, and a start to our time "on station."

Our "on station" time usually meant that we would have to go back to the tanker at least one more time to fill up again before we were relieved by the next flight. Toward the end of our scheduled time, we would start to anticipate the arrival of our replacements. There were four separate flights that were scheduled to fill the scheduled times during the day.

On this particular flight, we were the first "on station." During the entire day, each succeeding flight due to relieve us had problems getting green lights on their missiles. As each replacement time came and went, we continued flying back and forth between our own track, just off Haiphong, and the tanker. The flying was very boring. Radar IDs of potential targets on Big Eye were few and very far between. On this record flight, they were non-existent.

We watched the sun rise, linger during the day and then slowly set over the gulf waters. The photo on the cover was taken of a 559th fighter flying the last "shift" of the day over the Gulf.

At the end of this last "shift," we did a final tank and then I plugged in burner just off the tanker and we really rocketed south to Cam Ranh. The weather was fine and no fighter flights were scheduled that night so the danger of a closed runway was small. We were all so tired that the use of burner was a necessary option.

We were in a hurry to get to bed so we went supersonic. The trip back was again in total darkness. The flight time was over fourteen hours strapped into a cramped cockpit with only a plastic Ziploc bag to serve as our in-flight bathroom.

Landing was one of the most satisfying any of us had felt. We were all scrubbed from the following day's flight schedule as we were "basket cases."

IN-FLIGHT FIRE:

On return from a mission, I had an engine-fire-warning light come on in the cockpit while in the landing pattern. Sometimes, those lights only meant a malfunction of the light itself. I asked the tower to check me out and he gave me a clean bill of health. However, after landing, Maintenance told me that I had had a fire.

The J-79 engine normally smoked a lot. We smoked so much that the enemy could see us coming a long way away. If we had a small engine fire, it might be hard to tell visually from the normal smoke.

NIGHT MISSION-POL STORAGE TANKS:

POL stands for Petroleum, Oil and Lubricants.

Majors Kasler and Reisner had led F-105 attacks, along with the Navy, against the Hanoi-Haiphong POL complex earlier in 1966. That has been previously reported in this book. The results were very successful and spectacular. Our attack was on a much smaller scale, but it was also spectacular since it was a night mission and the fires really lit up the sky.

This mission was about a month after the original warehouse attack mentioned in another chapter. By this time, Cam Ranh had made several of the off-the-water attacks and the North Viets were not caught with their pants down on this mission. But this time, instead of napalm, we carried the 500-pound bombs plus the gun loaded with HEI against the complex located just south of Vinh.

We encountered heavy fire from the AAA batteries surrounding the complex. We popped up and did a strong nose-over, aiming at the POL tanks using a high dive-angle. Again, we used a fan attack with each of us coming in from a different direction. We bombed first and then hosed the area over with the cannon. Some of my cannon fire was against the larger sparklers coming from the side which indicated we were being hosed by their AAA guns. I think I might have destroyed a couple of the artillery guns because I really plastered their areas. Each gun pass was not like a regular shallow strafe because we were again diving at a steep angle.

We had no malfunctions on any of the bombs or guns. Everything worked and all our ordnance was on-target. The reason for, as lead, temporarily discarding my rule of "one pass and haul ass" was the lucrative nature of the target and that the tanks were spread out and "one pass" would not be sufficient to knock them all out.

This was not a single target, but a group of targets and we had to cover them with maximum damage. The huge POL tanks were much like the warehouses and had to be singly eliminated with each pass. The decision to attack each tank individually was one made at the target and not during the pre-flight briefing. Sometimes flight leads have to depart from the plan and that is what I did due to the nature of the target that we found. The risks were worth the reward.

Since it was night, we could see the heavy flak shot at us by the anti-aircraft and smaller bored guns. It seemed that some of the guns were small caliber with tracer ammunition. Their arcs were reaching toward us. On most missions, we were unable to tell if we were getting shot at due to daytime attacks. Not this time. It was spectacular, only it was deadly and aimed at us.

As we climbed out and away from the AAA fire that tracked us, we managed to look back at another spectacular sight that was spreading before our eyes. It looked like the Hanoi-Haiphong raids in miniature, but more magnificent since it was at night. The fires reportedly burned for hours after we left and the smoke rose toward the 20,000-foot altitude reached in the Hanoi raids. Tanker aircraft returning from their stations to landings at Danang could see and report the results. To them, it was a sight to be seen out of their front canopies. To us, we viewed it in our rear-view mirrors.

258

CLOSE CALL:

Most enemy aircraft we might encounter on "Big Eye" would launch from Phuc Yen Airfield, located close to Hanoi. This was the largest of the MIG airfields, but by no means the only field. Other MIGs might launch from Gia Lam, Kep or one of the five Chinese fields north of the border.

Every "Big Eye" bogey (unidentified radar blip) needed an Identification Pass. On one mission, while I was under the control of Navy radar on one of their destroyers, the naval controller stated that he had a bogey that was not squawking on the IFF. He classified it as a potential enemy aircraft and cleared me for a hot ID pass.

I dropped from altitude into a four-mile trail behind my wingman as we dove for the deck. Leveling at 200 to 300 feet off the sea, we passed over numerous fishing sampans enroute to the beach somewhere between Thanh Hoa and Thai Bin.

Our Phantom radar had no trouble identifying the radar blip described to us by Navy control as we were looking up from low level and did not have ground-clutter to contend with in our search. Both my wingman and I had radar lock-ons from a distance and my wingman commenced his climb toward the unidentified target. At our speed, I covered the 4 miles in about 30 seconds before I also commenced my climb in-trail behind my wingman.

When firing our radar-controlled interceptor missile, the Sparrow III, the Phantom internal radar "synchs" up with the internal guidance radar of the Sparrow prior to missile launch. Four miles was well within the range of the missile and the automatic guidance indicators in my cockpit were also well within the required parameters. They included a slowly narrowing circle on my radar scope with a meandering steering dot in its center.

The closer we got to the target, the smaller the circle. To consolidate the parameters for the best possible launch, the idea is to keep the small dot in the direct center of the constricting circle. Keeping the dot in the exact center of the circle will provide the best percentage of making a kill once the missile is launched.

The closer I got to the radar blip, the smaller the circle and the aiming dot remained centered and unmoving. My missile switches had been moved to "armed" and Navy radar, convinced that the bogey was a MIG, gave us clearance to shoot. Everything looked perfect. This was far closer to an actual MIG kill on "Big Eye" as any aircraft from Cam Ranh had experienced. The adrenaline was pumping as I was within several seconds of a launch with the firing trigger on my control stick "hot."

At that moment, my wingman flashed by the bogey and peeled off as he transmitted to me and the naval destroyer radar controller that, "he is an A-4," which is a U.S. Navy attack tactical-bomber.

BATTLE DAMAGE:

On a strike mission to North Vietnam, I was leading and was first in on the target. I rippled my bombs and on pull-out I had cockpit lights indicating utility hydraulic failure. The usual cause in that environment was a bullet through a hydraulic line. I passed control of the flight to #3 and headed south. When still over the North, I dropped my hydraulically-operated landing gear before I had total hydraulic failure. I saved dropping my hydraulically-operated wing flaps until later to conserve fuel, since we burn a lot faster with gear and flaps down.

After I got below the DMZ (demilitarized zone) and therefore south of North Vietnam, I dropped my flaps, but it was too late. My hydraulics were too far gone and the wing flaps would not drop. I placed my flap control back in the "up" position and contacted Danang Tower.

I notified Danang that I had possible battle damage and that I had no hydraulics. In addition, I told them that I would be taking a wide base-leg to blow down my flaps by the secondary (emergency) pneumatic system.

When I got to an extended final at Danang, I blew the pneumatic flap backup system and it too malfunctioned.

Two year later, I would also suffer the failure of a pneumatic backup system. Then, it was at Wheelus Air Base in Libya and I had brake failure on landing. With both brake systems malfunctioning, I dropped my tail hook and engaged the departure-end cable barrier.

When I did blow it down, one of my flaps blew completely down and the other stayed up. This created an imbalance in the flight controls. That was okay as long as it was stable, but then the downed flap began to cycle up and down. This was NOT good. It meant that the required aircraft speed on final would vary.

I notified the Tower and requested an extended stay outside their pattern as I investigated the problem. My backseater and I began to pull circuit breakers and do everything we could figure to stop the fluctuations. Finally, we were able to stop the movement, but one of the flaps stayed full down and the other full up. By then, I had meandered around Danang for over an hour. Our condition was not critical. What would have been critical is if we were unable to stop the fluctuations. In that case, our final speed would have been even faster than we eventually flew.

Captain Goodenough just before one of his last combat missions in December, 1966. The F-4C is protected by a revetment in back. Note under-wing fuel tank on this Northern mission with minimal load of ineffective 250-pound bombs loaded under wings.

We lined up on final and began a fast-final approach. Usual final approach speed was about 135 knots. However, with one flap down and another up, I had to fly 170 knots with full stick deflection to the left. Flaps in the down position change the camber or shape of the wing. They allow safe lower speeds when they are extended. In this case, I had greater lift on the wing with the flap that was down. But the wing with the flap up required me to fly a faster final speed because that wing would stall at a faster speed. My full stick deflection was to compensate for the extra lift on the flap that was down.

As I lined up on final, a gunner below shot me through my radome, which is located just in front of the cockpit. It was beginning to appear that this was not my day. I then notified Tower that I would be taking the approach barrier cable since I would not have the hydraulically-activated brakes. I dropped my tail hook.

At the last moment, I kicked rudder to straighten out the bird and align it with the runway and barrier. After touchdown, my hook caught the barrier and we were thrown forward in our straps. After full stop the cable recoil pulled us back a few feet and we then came to a complete stop. All-of-a-sudden a voice came over the Tower frequency, "Welcome to Danang, Russ." It turned out that my buddy John Brennan, who notified rescue a year before when I ejected over Ocala, Florida, was in the mobile control unit at the end of the runway and watched and listened to the whole thing. Apparently, he recognized my voice.

John also asked, "What took you so long?" I stayed a few days for Maintenance to fix my bird, and I joined John and other friends at the Danang Officer Open Mess or the DOOM Club. This is the formal name for their Officer's Club. DOOM seemed prophetic.

While at Danang, I saw for the first time a Continental Airlines flight attendant that was not surrounded by pilots. She was in the distance and I considered her sort of like an endangered bird. Normally, the stews were so surrounded by guys that we could never see them. Little did I know that less than three years later I would be flying the South Pacific with those same hostesses as a Continental pilot.

LETTERS HOME:
November 7, 1966:

"The last two weeks have been filled with change. Each day brings a new change of policy. And with the changes at first came despair and then came hope. Today the word is hope.

"I have now flown about 135 combat missions. Forty of these are against North Vietnam, either MIG cover or bombing strike missions. I think I have about 35 against Laos, but not sure. The missions against the North are even getting boring. We still get shot at all the time, but with everything, a certain exposure brings familiarity and the knowledge that to be shot at a lot is a vast difference from being hit.

"Whenever I lead a flight into a target, I pick the target up visually from altitude and at a distance, then I make a fast roll-in and dive against it. The dive angles can be up to an almost vertical dive. And one of my cardinal rules in hitting targets is: set the target up right at first so that the approach is good and the dive run will place all the bombs on target with one release. A fast approach with constant change of heading, altitude and airspeed and one quick dive and get the hell away. I usually can hit a target this way without the enemy getting to their guns in time and swiveling around to shoot. "One pass and haul ass." The guys who get shot down make multiple passes and lose the element of surprise.

"Yesterday, I flew three combat missions in one day against the North, which set a base record, and I am now coming home on the 14th of January, which means 73 more days. The 14th is what is known as my

DEROS. This means I have to be in the States on the 14th. Therefore, my date of Port Call is the day that I leave Vietnam. And I'll stop fighting several days prior to that so: I should be through with the war the first week of January. This, as you know well by now, is subject to change. But it looks pretty solid. You can probably count on my getting to Travis AFB around the 12-14 of January, which is much better than March.

"I have not been off-base for 2.5 months so I've decided to take leave to go to Bangkok. I'll probably leave around the 8th of this month. And my R&R will be the first of next month.

"I was on duty at the Command Post when President Johnson came in. This type of work is the most challenging and interesting I've ever done. It is a job with responsibility and in this I relish. It was left to me to do the coordination of much pertaining to his visit and many people had a hand in it.

"We didn't know of his visit until about six hours prior to his arrival and then Colonel Allen came to me requesting I work both of the day shifts. I worked ten straight hours in the Post coordinating. We had to cancel flying and get some birds ready for fighter escort of the President's plane, while he was in the combat area. The Army moved in with a thousand troops and the field was covered with machine guns. I was even given control of their movements.

"Keeping track of all the Generals, in a fiasco like this, can be interesting. We work on a command radio net that is connected to all areas of the base, aircraft in the air and relevant agencies and command posts in Saigon. For the President's visit, I stood on the floor of the Command Post with two sergeants. Up on the dais sat the Senior Controller. I have a working arrangement with the Senior Controller where I do all the controlling and he just sits behind the glass and watches. I like this work.

"During the day of the visit, I had occasion to turn around to see Premier Ky watching me. Five minutes later I turned around again to see General Westmoreland and some other Generals and Admirals that were in there watching. Then I step out into the hallway to get a drink and Henry Cabot Lodge comes up and shakes my hand. What a day. I never saw so many stars on shoulders. I also never saw Johnson because I was so busy.

"I've had quite a few officers that are leaving for the Pentagon and elsewhere, tell me "if I can help you out, I will." This somehow makes the sweat, hours, toil and heartaches worthwhile. For better or worse, warfare is a great maturing factor. I don't care how old or poised a person is, the experience of daily facing a hail of tracers and flak bursts is a teacher in itself. I've had several experiences over here which have given me gray hair, mostly having to do with aircraft mechanical failures.

"My attitude has amazingly improved. I am ashamed to admit that it did slip quite a bit. It's bad psychology on the part of the AF to deny a person a definite goal. The goal of the war is not victory, because what is victory? Our push to target is purely pride, duty and professionalism. It is not performed under a sense of high patriotism, because this war is not a patriot's war. This war is a non-war.

"To the airman, this war is a war where the air belongs to us and us alone. And the ground belongs to the enemy. To eject, we have to make the sea. Last night the Cong even blew up a train just across the pontoon bridge on the west side of the Bay, opposite the runway. There are a lot of VC battalions in the area.

"I have been wondering why I get such a feeling of exhilaration in my guts when I attack a target with a gun. Perhaps it is a perverse nature of man to exhilarate in the knowledge that he is exerting the power of life and death and meting out death. Perhaps it is the God-man concept. Perhaps that is why women have the most rational viewpoint toward conflict. The nature of man is not the nature of women and the nature of women is to create, not to destroy.

"I'm starting to look forward to the time I can get back to resume life among the humans. Hope is a wonderful thing."

December 3, 1966:

"I've been assigned to Europe. I asked for the States and another job, but it looks like I fly in Europe. This will mark the end of my commitment to the Air Force. If I go accompanied by a wife, it will be a three years more. If I go without a wife, it is only one year. The country will either be England or Germany."

December 4, 1966:

"I got my assignment and it is Bentwaters RAF Station, England. My job will be flying Phantoms for the 81st Tactical Fighter Wing.

"Sorry I was unable to be with you during Thanksgiving. Missed you all and my thoughts were with you.

"It looks like I will be through with most of my flying on the 21st of December. On the 22nd I go to Hong Kong on R&R and arrive back on the 29th. My Port Call hasn't arrived yet, but it may be the 7th or 8th of January. And on the 31st and 1st, we have another cease-fire.

"I'm getting to think of going home as it gets closer. It will be so good to be home again. I didn't ask for Europe, but have to go there due to the manpower shortages. The war effects the whole military establishment.

"Have to go fly."

December 19, 1966:

"Time has a way of slipping by and my date of departure is coming soon. Today I'll find out when my Port Call will be. In all probability, the Port will be Saigon. However, the authorities are rushing Cam Ranh to become the Port of embarkation and debarkation.

"I'm again sitting out in Mobile watching the earth moving equipment on their daily chore of leveling and spreading. We are without a generator and we have no radios here, so I'm not much good for the Air Force right now. For additional diversion, I can watch the Koreans shell the VC on a hill across the Bay. It's nice to have the ROKs as friends.

"I leave for R&R on the 22nd and it is now the 19th. I don't fly today. Yesterday I had two missions within South Vietnam and they were what can be said as "enjoyable." The weather yesterday and today has been just beautiful. Our usual monsoon conditions have temporarily left us.

"The squadron told me yesterday I wouldn't be flying any more missions against the North, so I end up with a total of 47 up there plus the MIG Screen missions over the Gulf and Haiphong. I've flown the last of those too.

"I finished work in the Command Post on the 14th. My total missions-to-date are 146. Hopefully I'll make 150 before I leave.

"Within the last month, one-quarter of the pilots left in my squadron have either been killed or missing-in-action. This is due to the heavy fighting in the North. But now the squadron has taken me out of that action. The fighting and the losses are among the reasons I haven't written much of late.

"Today, I also should terminate the personal business affairs of one of my good friends and have his things checked, inventoried and all personal effects sent to his wife. This is one of the tragedies of war. When

eight pilots are lost from our squadron in the last three weeks, it has a definite shock effect. Such is war and we are not winning.

"My length of stay in the States is predicated upon whether I can get an extension from England on my February reporting time.

"See you soon."

> *"Older men declare war. But it is the youth that must fight and die."*
> President Herbert Hoover

BOOK FOUR

Aspects of War

265

CHAPTER SIXTEEN

Night Visions

The Command Post

> *"Truth will ultimately prevail if there (are) pains*
> *taken to bring it to light."*
>
> President George Washington

Sometime in the early part of September 1966, the 12th Wing Director of Operations, Colonel James R. Allen, requested that I assume command of the Cam Ranh Bay Command Post for the 12-hour night shift. For a First Lieutenant, I considered it an honor, but had one request. I wanted to fly our Squadron missions during the days. He agreed to that request and immediately assigned me to the dual-authority position. Colonel Allen would be my immediate supervisor at night and my 559th Tactical Fighter Squadron (TFS) commander would have me during the days. There was only one problem. When would they schedule me to sleep? They didn't.

The Command Post was located near the offices of our Wing Commander and right next to the office of his second-in-command, Col. Allen. The Command Post layout had a floor they called the "pit." Essentially, the pit consisted of consoles that faced Plexiglas boards on which were written the flight information for the following day's missions in black grease pencil. The boards stood out away from the walls so that enlisted men could create and update the board information. They stood between the windowless walls and the Plexiglas.

The two NCOs (non-commissioned officers) learned to write backwards so that those at the consoles could see the info correctly from the front. The boards were also backlit since it was dark in the room, both day and night. In the center of the pit stood the consoles, where I sat or stood. Often, I would stand to direct the non-commissioned officers who manned the phones. Occasionally I manned the phones myself, but at night there was little need, especially as the nights wore on. The consoles consisted of banks of phones and radios, which were everything we needed to communicate with anyone on our base, in the air or down at 7th Air Force Headquarters in Saigon.

Off to the side of the room were uncovered tables. It was there that I would work on and type the Squadron, Wing and attached helicopter squadron awards and decorations. It required using the old typewriters for submissions that had to be sent to 7th Air Force in Saigon. Seventh Air, under General Momyer, required submissions to be perfect, without mistakes or corrections. As it turned out, this requirement for officers working under war conditions proved to be onerous. Those were the days of carbon paper for typewritten copies.

Behind the consoles was a glassed enclosure. It was primarily used during daytime operations, since that was when all the action took place. Nighttime in the Command Post was more a caretaking operation where we planned the next day's combat missions. During the days, the glassed enclosure was home to an overall Post Commander who oversaw operations in the pit. At night, it sat empty, which meant I was in charge. During the days, the enclosure also was where visitors came to observe operations. At night, we very rarely had visitors from the Wing. However, we occasionally had outside visitors who used our runways at night. Almost all of the night-landing pilots came to the Post.

After a week or so in the pit, the sergeants were kind enough to set up a cot for me behind the boards. During the day, the cot was stored in a back room, but at night it proved a nice addition. Theoretically, I was supposed to stay awake and alert for my entire shift. Colonel Allen and the rest of the command staff at Wing knew that was impossible and the subject of sleep just did not come up. They realized that I was flying at least one of the missions the following day and sometimes more than one. As my stay in the Command Post stretched into months, it became increasingly likely that I would be leading at least one of the combat missions the following day. However, even with the cot, sleep would only be of short duration. If anything happened or we received any calls, I was always awakened.

When I arrived in the pit at the start of my shift, I was handed a copy of the "frag" order from 7th Air Command Center located in Saigon. The frag or fragmented order listed the targets and TOTs (times over targets). I assumed that "frag" meant that it was the Cam Ranh portion of the overall combat order of the day.

It was my job to assign the targets to the listings of flight crews and aircraft that had been forwarded from the Squadrons. The flights consisted of anywhere from two to four aircraft and crews. I also assigned the munitions to be carried. Actually, Wing Maintenance gave me the flight set-ups, which included aircraft and weapons. Coordination had already been made between the Squadrons, which provided the crews, and Squadron Maintenance, which provided the aircraft, on matching of aircrews with aircraft. What I did was match up the 7th Air targets and TOTs with what the Wing provided in the form of aircraft, crews and loaded munitions. Maintenance was already loading the aircraft for the next day's missions. If maintenance loaded a flight with napalm, I found a 7th Air target where napalm could do the most damage. It was the same for rockets or iron bombs.

There was usually additional information needed from 7th Air. It might be clarification of the orders or to identify the location or nature of the targets to accomplish the job.

There was also a steady stream of teletype information coming in that I needed to evaluate. The teletypes really slowed down as the evening progressed. Most of the messages were routine and only required routine handling or routing. Occasionally, we would get something juicy. On one occasion, I felt the information was of such importance that I had the Wing Commander awakened and notified. That was my job.

After evaluating the frag orders, I invariably placed a call to 7th Air Headquarters at Saigon and talked to the Duty Officer. Each of the operational bases in SEA that were under 7th Air control did the same thing. It not only served to smooth out the operation, it allowed us to communicate on other matters. As the Duty Officer and I got to know each other, our conversations included topics other than the clarifications of the "frags."

There was only one Duty Officer at the 7th Air Command Post at any one time and the same guy had the duty each afternoon when I called. Prior to our talk, the Duty Officer would also talk daily with the White

House, which reportedly had a Command Post in its basement. That "Command Post" might have been the "Situation" Room? The timing of our calls insured that my call was made shortly after the White House had completed its call.

Structurally, wars are designed to be controlled either from the field or from the Pentagon. That was not the case with the Southeast Asian War. President Johnson personally approved the targets in the North, the munitions used and the flight paths used to get to them.

It effectively removed the element of professionalism from the operation. It also was one of the direct causes for the large combat losses of aircraft and crews we experienced in the North. The Duty Officer's everyday conversations with the White House were with President Johnson himself.

THE PRESIDENT AS COMMANDER-IN-CHIEF:

While our Constitutional structure mandates that the President is commanding officer over the military, that was just to insure an elected officer was in the senior position and not a General or Admiral. I am sure that the founders could never have comprehended an untrained President actually acting operationally as a Commanding General, yet that seems to have been the case with Lyndon Johnson.

Other presidents have been military veterans, but our history does not record instances where Presidents actually insinuated themselves in the chain-of-command as Johnson did. Actually, Generals who were elected President all seemed to have honored the military chain.

Of our 44 Presidents, 26 have been military veterans. Of those 26, 12 were General Officers. Several are well-known, but many of the others might surprise the reader. Six of the twelve came out of our Civil War: Andrew Johnson, Ulysses S. Grant, Rutherford B. Hays, James A. Garfield, Chester A. Arthur and Benjamin Harrison.

The Revolutionary War produced George Washington and World War II produced Dwight Eisenhower. The 1812 War against England had two Generals elevated to the Presidency: Andrew Jackson and William Henry Harrison, grandfather of Benjamin. The Mexican-American War saw Zachary Taylor and Franklin Pierce later become President.

The presidencies of Washington and Eisenhower are illustrative. Other than his taking the field during the Whiskey Rebellion, Washington, while president, allowed his military leaders to lead and did not impose his prior position as Commanding General of the Continental Army. Eisenhower, who commanded the European armies of America and its allies and was professional back to his time at West Point, made military suggestions regarding the Korean War, yet allowed the military chain-of-command to control.

Franklin Roosevelt, who was President during most of World War Two, had military experience as a civilian based on his time as Secretary of the Navy, yet he allowed control of the war to remain in the hands of the Joint Chiefs of Staff.

That is a lot of military experience, yet each seemed to allow the military command structure to operate on its own with only policy guidance and not operational guidance from the President. Lyndon Johnson, a man without any military training or experience whatsoever, broke that tradition. Let us hope that he did not set a precedent as world history is replete with those leaders who actually wore uniforms and acted as Generals themselves without experience or training as military officers. In almost all cases, their aggressive military actions led to resounding defeats.

7TH AIR'S ASSIGNED TARGETS:

Our Cam Ranh targets were initially in South Vietnam or Laos. Twice I participated in attacks against Cambodia, but these were not planned strikes authorized by 7th Air. Those missions were usually diverted from another target for some reason and the decisions and control were in the hands of the Forward Air Controllers.

When I first arrived at Cam Ranh, our missions were often targeted in Laos to disrupt the supply trains moving from the North to the South. When August and September came, the targets specified by 7th Air included more and more missions assigned to the North.

The positive effect of helping plan those missions allowed me to have a better picture of the overall effort. That effort did not appear to be following a cohesive plan. Much later, it became apparent that 7th Air was not the cause of the lack of cohesion, it was the Rules of Engagement that controlled our actions.

Helping plan the missions also had the effect of angering me at the lack of creativity or variation in the assignment of the TOTs by 7th Air. For example, the TOTs were always on the hour or half-hour. This allowed the enemy gunners to take breaks until several minutes prior to the usual times. One of the time-honored Principles of War is surprise. Any first-grader can figure that attacks always scheduled on the hour and half-hour do not constitute surprise. Selecting TOTs on the hour and half-hour was habit instilled by our Stateside training. That business-as-usual approach permeated much of what we did in SEA.

VISITORS:

Occasionally, I entertained visitors who would drop in on the base at night. One was an RB-47 crew from SAC, who had to divert to CRB for fuel. The pilot told me of a B-52 mission near the DMZ (demilitarized zone) that was attacked by enemy aircraft. He described in detail the supposed attack by MIGs against the B-52s.

Up to that point, I had listened politely to the full Colonel. However, I did have to correct the SAC misperception. The Wing "visited" the DMZ and into Route Pack 1 repeatedly in the conduct of our strikes. During those strikes, we never saw B-52s operate anywhere near the North. The one time we did, the tail gunner for the B-52, which was flying near the Demilitarized Zone (DMZ), mistook one of our F-4s for a MIG. The curious Phantom pilot had ventured near the Buff since he had never seen one in combat. Our Phantom driver almost got shot down by their counter fire. The "enemy aircraft" which the Colonel was mentioning was a Cam Ranh Phantom.

Another visiting crew was from the "Big Eye" Connie, which operated over the Gulf of Tonkin, near Haiphong. Our Gulf missions to protect the aircraft carriers at "Yankee Station" also included a responsibility to protect the Connies (Constellations- type of aircraft). On Big Eye, what we referred to as the Connie gave us alerts and vectors if they spotted a suspect blip on their radars. Part of the Connie's job was to monitor the North Vietnamese Strike frequency. Their strike frequency is a common one that communicates to all the fighter-interceptor aircraft protecting their vital installations. The Connie crew told me that the only language spoken on the North Vietnamese strike frequency was Chinese.

While flying on one of our Big Eye missions, I confirmed the origin of one of the MIGs when I chased him back over China's Hainan Island. I visually confirmed the Chinese origin of others while flying MIG Cover for the Elint RB-66s that operated between Hanoi and the Chinese border. There are six Chinese fighter airfields just north of their North Vietnamese border. We could easily see the MIGs as they reached the contrails level after taking off and before advancing south toward our formations.

Two other visitors to the Command Post were memorable, but their visit happened at a bad time for me. To describe it, I have to go back to several "scramble" missions off of our end-of-the-runway close-air-support alert.

Twice in as many days, I led a flight of two off the alert pad. We were scrambled against what the flight controllers called Viet Cong training camps, which were located in the middle of the Michelin Rubber Plantations north of Saigon. The fact that the French owners of the plantations cooperated with the Viet Cong is another matter.

The return to base from the second scramble took us into heavy, black, monsoon clouds that covered Cam Ranh. At the time, I was under the control of the Cam Ranh GCA (Ground Controlled Approach) and was asked to drop to 3,000 feet. The ground controller then gave me a vector that would have taken me straight into a hill that rose to 3,012 feet.

Instead of screaming at the controllers and taking them to task for the dangerous heading, I broke off their approach and took my flight on a self-directed approach using our radar mapping that took us up the inlet to the Bay and on into landing in the dense monsoonal weather.

At that time, the Wing was experiencing a lot of pilot attrition. Some were rotating back to the States and others had been shot down. We had a Major Lee Greco who had arrived at our squadron from the States just four days before my aborted GCA approach. He flew a mission the day after my approach with one of our veteran squadron back seaters, John Troyer.

The Major was obviously unfamiliar with the local terrain. GCA gave him the same vector that they had given me the day before. Only this time the results were different. They were both killed as the plane plowed a trench on the hill at 3,000 feet.

Those same GCA operators decided to visit the Command Post a week after the crash. They apparently did not realize that the Command Post night commander was a fighter pilot. When they joked about the tragedy, it was all I could do to control myself. Part of the reason for my subdued reaction was a sense of guilt on my part for not identifying the problem before the tragedy occurred. After they were killed, I was just sick. Immediately after my mission, I should have gone to the GCA shack and created a scene. I should have made them aware on the radio of the nearby terrain and altitudes. It was my responsibility to correct their misconception. It certainly was not their prerogative to joke about the loss of life. However, it seemed that I bore an equal responsibility for their deaths.

The same tragedy happened several months before up at Danang. In that situation, Danang GCA controllers had directed a flight of two Marine Phantoms into Marble Mountain resulting in the loss of both aircraft and crews.

VISITS OF PRESIDENT JOHNSON & DEFENSE SECRETARY McNAMARA:

The high points of my time in the Command Post had to do with the individual visits of President Johnson and Defense Secretary McNamara to Cam Ranh Bay. Colonel Allen asked me if I would run the Post for both day shifts for the two visits. That turned out to be a kick.

The daytime "work" at the Post involved two, six-hour shifts. I was still a Lieutenant waiting for my

Captain's bars and it left me feeling a little nervous and worried that I might screw it up.

It was a heady experience. For the President's visit, the Army gave me 1,000 soldiers to deploy around the base. I asked for and got a flight of four F-4s to fly out to meet the President's aircraft approaching Cam Ranh from the direction of the Philippines. For security reasons, the Air Force had only given us a six-hour notification that he was coming. That really had us scrambling.

For McNamara's visit, I had to keep our pilots away from his entourage. The fighter pilots were in a state of revolt about the lack of munitions on base and the "Sortie War" with the Navy. We had an on-base bomb shortage and were not telling our civilian leaders about it. I had to go against what my gut wanted and keep our pilots separated from the civilian groups.

Cam Ranh was a very safe base and provided our political leaders an ability to "meet the troops" in Vietnam and not take any risk in the process. Both visits were memorable, but the one involving the President was the most. For both missions, I was working the phones and usually had two phones working continually. My job was to coordinate and smooth things out.

During Johnson's visit, I turned around and saw the South Vietnamese President Nguyan Cao Ky, a fellow fighter pilot, dressed in his purple flight suit. He really looked neat with his black boots, black hair, black gloves and flowing purple scarf. Ky was watching me from the glassed enclosure and stayed for a long time.

Other Generals and Admirals were constantly coming and going in and out of the Command Post. As Colonel Allen reminded me later, the senior officers were busy constantly giving advice and orders. The challenge was for me to try to create order out of the constant barrage of often-conflicting orders from our senior ranking guests.

When General Westmoreland arrived, there was hardly any space left in the large room. I had to take a break from all the commotion and went into the adjoining hallway. A smiling Henry Cabot Lodge came up to me and, while introducing himself, shook my hand. For a young Lieutenant, Johnson's visit was possibly the highlight of my Cam Ranh Command Post stay, which terminated on the 14th of December, 1966.

> *"You have to take chances for peace, just as you must take chances in war."*
> John Foster Dulles

CHAPTER SEVENTEEN
Every Day is Wednesday
Life At War

> *"To make no mistakes is not in the power of man, but from their errors and mistakes, the wise and good learn wisdom for the future."*
>
> Plutarch

Everyone's life has its routine and war is no different. Once the excitement and thrill of arrival and first combat are over, the routine sets in. In a wartime setting, weekends are meaningless. For us, time also become somewhat meaningless. There were no calendars on the walls of our barracks or at flight ops. Flying combat on weekends was no different than weekdays. In fact, nobody seemed to know what day it was or even seem to care. If anyone ever asked me what day it was, I would always say "Wednesday." It seemed to satisfy everyone.

For a combat pilot, life revolved around the flight schedule. If we had a flight scheduled for a certain day, then what we did for the rest of that day always was fitted around our flight.

Where we spent our days also became routine. There were three places that became our "homes" for most of our lives in Vietnam: Our squadron "barracks," which initially was a bare Quonset hut; the "Flightline" where we briefed/debriefed and otherwise prepared for combat missions, or the Officer's Club.

THE CAM RANH OFFICER'S CLUB:

One of the best investments made by the military, for either peacetime or wartime, is the Officer's Club. It is at the club where male bonding is accomplished. It is the Club which serves as a casual "debrief" location where fighter pilots discuss the day's missions. It is the same with training pilots, tanker pilots, transport pilots or bomber pilots. It is the social and communications center of an Air Force Base as well as our primary on-base restaurant and recreational destination. Much is learned at the "O" Club.

It is equally important for the wives at permanent CONUS (Continental United States) bases or those overseas bases where officers could be accompanied by their wives. They can feel part of the process and can learn much of what their husbands are doing. Wives can also bond with other squadron wives. The sacrifice of women who are associated with military officers cannot be overemphasized. This is true of all services. Naval wives and girlfriends have to suffer the long absences of their mates, while they are at sea on extended cruises. Whether needed or not, Air Force, Army, Navy and Marine wives welcome the support of others while their husbands are gone on unaccompanied missions and TDYs (temporary duty). The Club serves as a focal point for this support.

When our squadron was stationed at Okinawa, it was an unaccompanied mission. The wives left behind were told we would only be gone three months. It turned out we were gone six. The Club served as our emotional release from the tension of our day's flying missions. The very presence of the Club served as a base for that needed support, especially for those guys who had to leave their wives at home. Overseas rotations can be lonely times.

The Officer's Club at Cam Ranh was no different. It was of immense importance. Almost one-third of our waking lives were spent there. It was where we ate, drank and socialized. It was there that we were able to find relief from combat tensions and to ease the emotional drain of losing our comrades. Occasionally, some of us might go to the Base Cafeteria to relieve the monotony of continually going to the Club to eat, but the food provided at both locations was good and we had no complaints in that department.

Contrary to what Columnist Drew Pearson wrote, the pilots at CRB built our own Officer's Club. My late arrival still allowed me to participate in laying concrete for the outdoor patio, which marked the completion of the facility. Admittedly, the taxpayers paid for the supplies, but the labor was ours during our free time. We volunteered. Everyone from all of the squadrons volunteered. It was a group effort for the entire base. Pearson wrote about how much of a waste of taxpayer's money that the Club represented. How wrong he was and what a disservice he performed by making it look like we were on a "boondoggle."

The Club had only one rule, and that was a requirement to check our guns at the door. We would stash our web belts, with attached pistols, into little wooden slots provided near the entry. That worked well until someone would have a bit too much to drink and would "misidentify" his weapon on leaving. Once we passed the entry, the Club was like the Wild West without a Sheriff.

In August 1966, the base started to hit the North in earnest. By October and November, we had lost a lot of guys to the defenses. Many had also left for home. When their replacements arrived was when the activity at the Club again became livelier.

The nurses from the base hospital partied with us. They were an integral "part of the guys" and a welcomed addition. They did not mind when we used the occasional profanity. They laughed when we danced on the tables or did an impromptu striptease. They seemed to approve when we tested our abilities and swung from the Club rafters. They sang along with the rest of us when we started the raunchy "Twelve Days of Christmas" long before December. Those nurses served the cause of war far more than just their fine efforts and long hours spent repairing the damages of war at the base hospital.

The Club had a large horn attached to the wall next to the bar. Whenever anyone "went in" (was shot down), his friends would go to the bar that night and honk the horn in honor and remembrance. If you honked, you had to buy drinks for the entire bar. Another "bar rule" stated that anyone wearing his hat to the bar also had to buy the bar. The night that Ken Cordier was shot down, I walked into the bar wearing my hat and honked the horn. Not that Ken was a close friend, but he was the last friend.

THE FLIGHTLINE:

Before and after flights, we were at the "Flightline," which is really just the area where we park our aircraft, which includes Flight Operations and Maintenance. It consists of the buildings, the tarmac and our planes.

Normally, we didn't frequent Maintenance except during debrief to tell them about malfunctions or battle damage. The Maintenance Section was our usual contact with the enlisted men. In our squadrons, we never encountered enlisted men because we lived in two different worlds. Our living quarters housed only officers. The Flight Operations building only housed officers. Our usual contact with enlisted guys was when we arrived at our aircraft to fly and they might help us strap in.

The pilots would check out the aircraft prior to entering the cockpit and we might discuss an issue regarding the aircraft with the crew chief. But normally it was just check it out, jump in, light the fires and off we would go. At the arming areas, airmen would pull the safety pins and check out operation of our missiles, if we were going against the MIGs. For bombs and rockets, the crew chiefs would also pull the safety pins from the munitions that had been uploaded to their external carrying racks located under the wings. For all flights, the chiefs would pull the safety pins for the landing gear.

When at the Flightline, we were almost always at Flight Operations, which we referred to as Flight Ops. There were no enlisted who worked there. What non-flying work needed to be done was accomplished by pilots as part of their "additional duties."

Outside of Flight Ops were the aircraft parking ramps. In the States, the ramps were concrete. At Cam Ranh, as well as most of the other bases in SEA, they were PSP. PSP is Pierced Steel Planking, which consists of interlocking metal planks that serve as our aircraft ramps and taxiways. Pierced means that the planking had holes, which was good in areas of intense monsoon storms. Many runways in Vietnam, especially at short runway fields, were also constructed of PSP. At Cam Ranh, we had aluminum runways and later, concrete.

The outside of Flight Ops was just your usual wartime Quonset look of a rounded, corrugated tin-top. Inside, we had attempted to make it look like a stateside ops and it did slightly resemble one. There were a few cubicles where the more senior officers shuffled papers. There was the "lounge" where we could sit on chairs. The walls were largely bare, which we all liked.

Stateside ops had the ubiquitous Plexiglas-covered wall charts. In Vietnam, we pilots loved the bare walls. We were in Vietnam to bomb and not mark charts with grease pencils. Later, after the 12th pilots were gone and I was the only one left, the replacement guys came in. Since I led most of them on their indoctrination flights, I knew that many needed lots of additional work on bombing, but they were good on charts.

Flight Ops also housed our flight gear. We had a room where we could dress for war. Since we entered Flight Ops in flight suits and wearing our 38 revolvers on our hips, dressing for war consisted of strapping on our "G" suits, putting on our parachute harnesses (the parachutes were in the ejection seats) and grabbing our helmets with their oxygen masks and radio plug-ins attached.

Our "G" suits contained our personal stuff, like survival gear, in pockets. My bone-handled chopper knife was in a suit pocket. Ammo for the 38 was in another. The last item we grabbed was our thigh-mounted clipboard. We placed our completed Strike Report Form, filled in during our pre-flight brief, on the clipboard and were ready to go.

The Strike Report included everything needed on a mission. The cards fitted on our little clipboard. In the cockpit, strapping the clipboard onto our thighs was the last thing we did prior to engine start.

THE QUONSET:

The Flightline, containing our squadron flight Quonset, has already been described. That was where we flew. The Officer's Club was where we relaxed, communicated and ate. The third side of our Cam Ranh triangular home was our barracks, or squadron Quonset. We referred to it as the "Quonset."

On arrival at Cam Ranh, a few of the guys from my squadron took me to the Quonset to find a bunk. The Quonset was a WWII vintage structure designed by the British as Nissan Huts, and ours was bare inside. There were very few bunks, so some of the guys bedded down on a very dusty wooden floor. It was just a large, empty room that was home to 48 squadron pilots who were sleeping in Air Force-issue sleeping bags with some placed on cots. Eventually we all got cots.

Early on, I had a squadron commander who decided that we needed to do something to our "house." We did our own carpentry work and I helped build a bunk bed for myself and a flying friend. I got the top bunk of many that were scattered around the room. My top bunk allowed me a measure of quiet privacy with a few books and a place to make entries into my diary. I had wired the bunk for electricity, so we each had lighting.

During my 10 months in Vietnam, I had five different squadron commanders (COs). The first had initiated the Quonset construction, which was done by the pilots. The Air Force provided the supplies. A later one, shortly after his arrival, looked at our scattered bunks and decided to do some major remodeling, only this time it was done with contractors who knew what they were doing. The entire construction project took a month to six weeks. We had to put up with the dust and the result of living in a mess, but the inconvenience was more than worth it.

The results were remarkable. What he created was a building with a central recreation room and six apartments housing eight pilots per apartment. The recreation, or rec room, was large enough for lounging chairs and four refrigerators, which were always loaded with beer. The chairs were scrounged, along with a lot of other stuff, on periodic C-130 supply runs over to the Philippines.

Each apartment had an outside entry door and an inner door that opened to the recreation room. The apartment living rooms were furnished with rattan furniture, matted flooring, a toaster oven and indirect lighting. The pilots assigned to my apartment pooled money for a sound system, the toaster oven and we acquired a hot plate plus other "essentials." We created a bar at one end of the living room. This was for the hard liquor and wine as the lounge was for the beer. We pilots also installed indirect lighting. The bar and counter were both backlit. Standing lamps allowed for reading if we wished.

Doors opened from the living room of each apartment into two bedrooms. Each bedroom housed four pilots in two sets of bunk beds on either side of the room. Each bedroom had a window in which the CO had placed a two-ton air conditioner. It is difficult to describe how comfortable the air-conditioning made us feel in such a hot and humid tropical environment. The bedroom floors were covered with the same Philippino matting that we had in the living rooms. It muffled sounds and made for a cozier feeling.

A final touch to our living arrangement was to place nametags in outside slots beside each apartment door. Our B Flight was assigned to one of the apartments. When I first arrived at Cam Ranh, we had six crews assigned to each of the four administrative Flights. By the time of our construction project, due to those that had been sent back to the States, B Flight had been reduced to a total of four crews instead of the original six. We had to be augmented with pilots assigned to Wing Staff. This actually made a nicer arrangement, because all the B Flight pilots could bunk in one apartment instead of one and a half. Each of the other three flights also had their own apartment. The two other apartments allowed for the Commanding Officer and Director of Operations to have their own apartment. Several of the pilots assigned to Wing Staff decided that they loved the arrangement and bunked with our CO (Commanding Officer) and DO (Squadron Director of Operations). The final apartment was vacant, awaiting reinforcements to cover our losses and get back to full strength. The addition of the Wing Staff pilots had the additional advantage of having them fly missions with us and get us back to a measure of full strength, at least for a while.

After living in the mess of the open Quonset, we were now living in luxury. Our Quonset was the envy of the other squadrons and several tried to emulate our success, to no avail. All of this was the work of our CO and Capt. Lee Plotnitsky, who was our squadron supply officer. "Plots" was responsible for all the furniture and goodies. He commandeered a C-130, flew to Clark and returned with a full load. Nobody asked questions. His performance was magnificent.

The flight surgeon, who had replaced Doc Simmons after his death, and I became friends. After his work and after my "work," we got together in my apartment living room and sat in air-conditioned comfort, while listening to the stereo and sipping Courvoisier. We discussed the war, politics, whatever, far into the night. It was a wonderful escape from war. Our indirect lighting added to the illusion.

In September, after only about six weeks of this comfort, the Wing DO, Colonel Allen, asked me if I would run the Command Post at night. That Command Post assignment rudely interrupted our cozy bit of sanity.

The "rec" room of the Quonset was really something else. In addition to the reefers, it also was air-conditioned. Some sainted pilot had donated his lifetime collection of Playboy centerfolds. One can scarcely imagine that wallpaper. There were many years of beauty decorating our walls. It gave a man hope

The "Quonset" living-quarters for the 559th TFS at Cam Ranh Bay in 1966. The Quonset of the 558th TFS is just beyond the truck. Note the 2-ton air conditioners in the windows, the ever-present coral sand and the ubiquitous power and phone poles.

on what he might expect on his return to America. I had a favorite among the crowd on the walls. She was a beautiful blonde sitting next to a green parrot. In such a tropical setting, I thought it was appropriate. I spent long periods studying that parrot.

Years later, while flying as a pilot for Continental Airlines, I started dating a flight attendant domiciled in Seattle. There was something vaguely familiar about her. Turned out she was the one sitting next to the parrot.

NON-COMMISSIONED OFFICERS (NCOS):

My nocturnal stint at the Command Post meant that I was the only commissioned officer in a crew of three officers manning the Post. The other two were NCOs. That worked out really well. Each of us had our job to do within the structure of the military, but the human side was supportive. We functioned as and felt like a team.

One of the startling revelations to me, when I first started with the Air Force, was the significant representation within the Non-Commissioned Officers (NCOs) of those coming from the South. That section of our country that was defeated in our Civil War became the patriotic provider of a huge portion of those who currently serve our country. In this, we owe a great debt of gratitude to General Robert E. Lee for providing the example and setting the national course for the South during the last month of that distant war.

Even though we had little actual interface with the NCOs, they could make or break an officer. Piss them off at your own peril. Without the NCOs, all of our military services would cease functioning properly. They are the backbone and keep things running. Militaries are structured with rules and sometimes those rules needed to be "adjusted" in order for our militaries to properly function. Our Sergeants provide that necessary reason.

They also could "save the bacon" for some ignorant and untrained junior officer. Case in point: During my first months at CRB, I was often required to taxi aircraft from one place to another. Often it might be from Maintenance to the tarmac or positioning a plane for a boresight check of the gun or a trip to the fuel pits. Boresight checks were to verify the accuracy of the gun.

One of those trips took me down a taxiway near the end of the runway. Crews were positioned there to pick up drogue chutes that had been dropped by the fighters after landing. When fighters land, they cannot slow the aircraft down sufficiently with just braking. They use drogue chutes that are popped open on landing by the pilot. The jet exhausts billow the chutes behind the planes and provides a counter-force to the aircraft runway momentum. Those chutes are then released by the pilot after he slows down and prepares to turn off the runway. The collector-crews would then rush out and grab the chutes off the runway and throw them into little, towed collector-carts.

While taxiing near the end of the runway, my right wing hit one of the stationary carts sitting beside the taxiway. One really feels stupid when things like that occur. The airmen on the crew took pity on the unobservant pilot and made sure that nothing was reported. Those little niceties went both ways and allowed for an efficient operation.

While at Cam Ranh, I once visited the NCO Club to drink beer with our crew chiefs, but normally the officers did not socialize with the enlisted guys. That is not to infer that we considered ourselves elite, better than the enlisted airmen or anything like that. It is just the way things are done in all militaries. I suppose that tradition got its start so that commissioned officers did not have close bonds with those that they had to order into battle and possibly die. In the Air Force, that doesn't make a lot of sense. In our case, it is the commissioned officers that are the ones who have to go to battle and die and not the NCOs or airmen. The airmen and NCOs make up the bulk of support personnel for our mission. Personally, I think more familiarity and association between enlisted and officers would be a good thing. But I was not in Vietnam to try to foster social change. I was there to fight a war and that took all of my energy.

CAM RAHN BAY AIR FORCE BASE:

By the time I left, Cam Ranh Bay Air Force Base had a population of slightly over 8,000 airmen. Of that, about 180 of us were considered combatants. At least in the fighter units, that is the case. The base itself was located on a sandy peninsula about 230 miles northeast of Saigon. The local area population was very sparse. Ten miles to the north of us lay Cam Ranh Village, which was very small.

The base was covered with sandbagged bunkers for our protection in case of attack. When the alert sirens would sound, we were all supposed to run inside the bunkers and wait out any attack. That is what we were supposed to do. The reality of it was whenever we heard a siren, which was quite rare at Cam Ranh; we would all run outside to see the fun. Thanks to the 20,000 men comprising the Imperial White Horse and Tiger divisions of the South Korean Army, our base was very secure.

The surrounding countryside, outside of the Korean security zones, was considered Viet Cong country. However, there was no state of war existing between our two areas. They left us alone and, for the most part, we left them alone. There were occasional attacks against the hills we could see across the Bay, but they were always staged by someone else's artillery or fighter planes. Late in my war, that would change as the Koreans began shelling the hillsides.

None of the Koreans, the Air Police or any of the 50,000 of us stationed on the peninsula went out to fight our VC neighbors, at least in 1966. In 1967, after we left, there were VC attacks against the base perimeter and the nearby POL storage facilities, but none when we were there. By that time, the 101st Army Airborne Division had replaced the Koreans. In 1966, we did our thing and they did their thing and we had our own little peace.

The runway situation was good and for SEA our runways were very good. When I arrived, we were using an aluminum runway that was coated with a non-skid compound. The Pierced Steel Planking (PSP) of the ramps was also coated with the same non-skid treatment. The non-skid surface provided great traction when new, but as it wore it became smooth and, when combined with a little rain and coral dust, became as slippery as ice.

Later in my stay at Cam Ranh, the aluminum runway became very smooth. At least part of it was smooth. The non-skid surface wore unevenly, making overweight or monsoon landings a challenge.

To counter the problem of skidding on the smooth aluminum, the base decided to construct a concrete runway parallel to the aluminum one. Everyone was very enthused to give it a try. We all waited during construction. Take offs and landings were right beside the construction machinery for months and months. Finally, the big day of inauguration arrived. Unfortunately, it rained. All the launches were routine. However, when the flights returned from their missions, four planes skidded off the new concrete into the sand. What had happened was that the ever-present coral dust combined with the rainwater to form a grease-like substance.

We returned to the aluminum runway. It was less risky.

The Bay was really spectacularly beautiful if one took the time to view it without distractions. That part of the Vietnamese coast will someday be a major tourist attraction. It will also someday be the most important port facility in all of Vietnam south of Hanoi/ Haiphong.

Several years after Vietnam finally fell to the Communists, Cam Ranh Bay was leased to the Soviet Union and became the largest Soviet port outside of their country. The outside "occupation" lasted only a short time as the Vietnamese demanded $200 million annual "rent" from the Soviets. The Soviets deemed the price too high and partially pulled out in the early 1980s.

The Bay offers shelter and the surrounding flat land would provide adequate space for the construction of all the warehousing and facilities needed for a world-class port. Much of that construction had been left behind when the United States pulled out of SEA. The American contribution plus what was added by the Soviets would provide a very good start for Vietnam to develop the port.

FLYING @ CAM RAHN:

There were several different types of flying in Southeast Asia. During the latter part of my war, I would take planes up on test flights to ensure that a maintenance fix had been done correctly. These were not considered combat in any way and were not logged. I stayed close to the base and was airborne just long enough to do the test. Once in a while I would get to ferry a flight, either taking an aircraft to another base or bringing one back.

Our missions were divided by type and area flown. The South Vietnamese missions were actually more fun than those experienced back in the States. There were few restrictions, which gave us a sense of freedom and a chance to experiment. Stateside, we had published approaches to airports, which were strictly adhered to. In Vietnam, we were able to fabricate our own approaches to Cam Ranh.

We created approaches to the US Army Special Forces camps we had adopted and who we pledged to protect in the event of an attack. The VC usually attacked them when the weather was lousy in hopes that we would be unable to respond. These adopted Special Forces Camps were all over South Vietnam. Distance was not considered a factor.

We would send pilot crews of two to each of the camps to connect with the Special Forces guys and coordinate radio frequencies; be advised of things to be aware of; study terrain & approach considerations and learn and discuss whatever else might be needed. Special consideration was given to the terrain surrounding the camps. The pilots would then design the safest approaches. While the Phantom had internal Inertial Navigation Systems (INSs), they were not considered reliable enough to be used in bad weather. We had to rely on outside navigation aids. That meant figuring distances and azimuths off known ground-based stations such as Tactical Air Navigation (TACAN) stations. Whatever approach design was adopted, it had to be safely usable in the worst of fog and low-scud conditions because that was what the VC provided us in their attacks.

The runway approach for landing is a pattern flown precisely as to altitude, speed, distance from the airport and the headings we would fly. They are necessary for proper separation from other aircraft and for terrain avoidance. It is not handy to have a granite cloud blocking your flight path.

The enemy defenses in the South were almost exclusively small arms or automatic weapons (AW) fire.

During my war year, the VC and North Viet Army had no SAMs or AAA in the South. Those were up north in Laos and North Vietnam. The high speed of our aircraft almost always insured that we would avoid the gunners in the South. For enemy gunners, it was just too hard to lead us sufficiently, especially if we stayed low.

Our main loss of pilots in the south was on R&R, which is hard to believe. While I was there, six guys were killed flying away from Cam Ranh on Rest and Relaxation missions. Another was killed flying with a FAC on a familiarization ride. Officially, R&R is Rest and Recuperation, but for us it was rest and relaxation.

The C-130 transport planes often flew cargo in and out of Cam Ranh, which was a major air cargo base in addition to housing fighters. Our Wing pilots often jumped aboard the 130s and sat sideways on the canvas seats lashed to the walls of the cargo areas. Three of these C-130s were blown up in the air when VC sappers sabotaged them with satchel charges. On each of these aircraft sat two pilots going on R&R. Thus, we lost six pilots sitting sideways. Those were considered operational and not combat losses.

Often we experienced interesting situations caused by the unpredictability of war. Once, when we were returning from a Northern mission, we decided to take a sightseeing trip along the coast. Actually, this was my call since I was flight lead. The area I chose for sightseeing was the beautiful coastal area south of Danang. As we leisurely strolled down the beach at low-level and flying a very loose, four-ship formation, we were made aware that something was not right. U.S. Navy ships were lying offshore and firing artillery rounds at the beach. Apparently down there in all that beauty were some bad guys. Our problem was that the artillery shells were passing between our planes. We plugged in burner and "got out of Dodge."

Not only were our targets in the South easy to hit with little defensive fire, they often were interesting targets themselves. One of our jobs was to delay or eliminate as much of the enemy transportation capability as possible. Usually that transport was in the form of individual trucks, truck parks and truck convoys that we attacked both in the South and in Laos. They used every means of conveyance known to man including the ample use of bikes. Occasionally, it would be something else. One flight of mine was against a mule train crossing the Demilitarized Zone separating South Vietnam from North Vietnam. We killed lots of Communist mules on that mission. Other missions killed transport buffalos and even elephants. The war in South Vietnam was animalistic in more ways than one.

When we experienced the massive transfer of the old 12th Wing pilots back to the States, their replacements were often in a "take over" mood. This did not sit well with the rest of us who had been there. I found myself in the strange position of leading the flights and training almost all of the incoming guys in our squadron. And all of the Colonels from the other squadrons and Wing were assigned my flights for indoctrination. I was the most experienced pilot left on the base so those responsibilities fell on my shoulders. I taught the guys to fly combat.

As soon as they were "up to speed" in combat, these senior wonders started issuing orders. Apparently none of these newly-experienced combat pilots had experienced a Lieutenant flying as an Aircraft Commander and certainly not as a Flight Leader and Instructor Pilot.

One day, the newly-minted combat Colonels issued a decree: no Lieutenant Aircraft Commanders could fly night missions. There had been no incident to precipitate it. They must have felt that rank had something to do with ability. Those of us affected began to refer to ourselves as "Sunshine Pilots." Our logo was a smiley face.

In the late fall of 1966, I had become somewhat of a crusty veteran and a very wary pilot for a 26-year-old. We had lost so many from all the attack bases and the status of those downed pilots was unknown. Were they dead or had they survived the ejections and become POWs? At that time, very little was known. In the fall, I had more combat experience than anyone else at Cam Ranh. I was the only one left from the old guys from MacDill except for Ken Cordier who was there when I arrived, then went back to the States and then returned. He was soon to be gone again and this time it was for an extended time in Hanoi.

In the fall, we received word that one of the decorated squadrons that had just completed its combat tour had been declared non-combat ready when they crossed the 140th meridian into TAC airspace. We were incredulous. Here was a squadron of F-100s, who had performed admirably and honorably in combat. To be declared not ready for combat, because they had failed to practice nuclear delivery while undergoing combat in SEA, was beyond belief.

There were no bombing ranges within reach of our bases in SEA. We didn't need ranges when we had the entire region in which to bomb. But we had no nuclear bombing practice ranges in SEA and that caused our newly-departed combat buddies to be judged "not ready for combat." This was the kind of thinking that drove us up the wall and was prevalent in some of our newly-arriving replacement officers.

OUR COASTAL NEIGHBOR, NHA TRANG:

All of our missions in the South and Tiger Hound were controlled by FACs. This was primarily due to insure the avoidance of needless civilian deaths. The FACs were flying in aircraft just like the rest of us, only they were small, slow-flying, propeller-driven planes with excellent visibility. They would come to be known as "Slow FACs" flying the 0-1s, 0-2s and OV-10s. The FACs acted as our "eyes in the sky."

The year following my combat, F-100s and later the Phantoms joined the fray as "Fast FACs." The F-100s use as Fast FACs was vividly portrayed in the book "Misty." The book describes a group of outstanding officers and pilots who were selected to fly in selected areas in the clandestine air wars then being fought. Of the 80-some Misty Pilots, two became Air Force Chiefs of Staff, which is the highest-ranking officer in the Air Force. The book is a compilation of stories by individual Misty pilots and is recommended reading by the author. The Editor of the book "Misty" is Major General Don Shepperd (USAFA Class of 1962), a former Misty pilot who served four years as Military Analyst for CNN and was Commanding General for the Air National Guard.

The F-4 Fast FACs operated out of Udorn, Thailand under the call sign "Laredo" and was, for a time, under command of Major (later Colonel) Alex Harwick (USAFA Class of 1962). South Vietnam was split into operating sectors for all the FACs. In Laos, the sector was Tiger Hound and the FACs were "Hound Dogs." In the southern part of the North Vietnamese panhandle, the sector was Tally Ho and the FACs were "Covey." Each FAC was very familiar with his sector. However, there was one group that knew what was going on in all the sectors in South Vietnam. They were the "Special Action FACs."

Fifteen miles up the coast from Cam Ranh is a delightful little coastal village of red-tiled roofs and pristine beaches that lay inside a tiny bay. This is Nha Trang. During their time of rule, the French created it into a coastal resort city. It was a resort before the world knew of resorts. The architecture showed hints of the Spanish Colonial and palatial buildings snuggled against the low-lying hills that surrounded the beach area. It looked deceptively peaceful.

Nha Trang was home to the Army Mohawk aircraft that flew intelligence missions in the interior, Cambodia, North Vietnam and in Laos. It was also home to the Air Force Special Action (SA) FACs. When individual FAC sectors got overloaded, such as during a major operation, or when they needed FACs to fly special missions, they called up the SA FACs. They also had specific missions that were assigned to no other FACs in SEA.

John Flanagan (USAFA Class of 1962) was stationed at Nha Trang and twice visited CRB to share a cup or two of cheer and trade stories with me and a few others. Other SA FACs, Army light-plane pilots and ALOs (Air Liaison Officers) also visited, since we had the nicest and safest club on the Central Coast. The Army's observation planes included a pilot and an ALO observer. Our Air Force FAC planes only had one pilot, who also acted as an observer. One of the Army pilots invited me to visit Nha Trang.[61]

I flew in to Nha Trang for a night on one of our transports and was immediately thrown into a different social climate than I was used to at Cam Ranh. My hosts were the U.S. Army and they were pilots from their Intelligence arm. My Army buddy introduced me to a very pretty girl from the beach area who was half-French and half-Vietnamese. She was very nice, very beautiful, and turned out to be my "date" for the evening. Nothing like that happened at Cam Ranh. I never ever saw a Viet man or woman in our Officer's Club.

The evening did not turn out quite how the lady might have expected. That night, the VC probed the Nha Trang airfield's base perimeter and had infiltrated inside the Nha Trang concertina wire protection. Then they mounted an attack and my anticipated night of camaraderie and leisure was cut woefully short. We had to quickly escort the ladies to safer quarters. It was all a new experience for a Cam Ranh pilot. Through the evening, we could hear the muffled shots and the occasional VC mortar explode. We did not sleep much that night.

One guy from Nha Trang that I really liked was a regular visitor to our Best-on-the-Central Coast "O" Club. Bert Miller was another SA FAC. He always was complimentary to our Club and liked our bar prices.

Over several beers, Bert shared with me that he had been the SA FAC assigned to check out the BDA for the very first Strategic Air Command B-52 attack of the war against the North. Well, it was kind of against the North. Mu Gia Pass was the major pathway for supplies out of the North and into the Ho Chi Minh (HCM) Trail System. The Pass goes through the Annamite Mountains that form the geographical boundary between the panhandle regions of southern Laos and southern North Vietnam. Through Mu Gia passed the supplies, equipment and troops that sustained the Viet Cong military and also those North Vietnamese Army units stationed in southern Laos and in South Vietnam. As the northern terminus for the entire HCMT System, it was an extremely important artery. The Mu Gia also dumped our targets into Tiger Hound.

SAC decided to make their first Northern attack against the Mu Gia. After the strike, headlines throughout the United States proclaimed that the SAC B-52s had pulverized Mu Gia. SAC was exultant.

Bert, however, was confused. He overflew the entire Mu Gia and could find no damage. He dutifully reported his findings. Days later he was motoring over a section of Laos about fifteen miles to the west of Mu Gia. As he looked down, he was amazed to see an entire section of the jungle terrain that had been decimated. The B-52s can each carry a load of 108 of the 750# bombs. They really can unload an awesome amount of damage on any target. This particular target was a bunch of monkeys. Mu Gia was unscathed.

Author's Notes: *61. John Flanagan later became a General Officer and author of the book, "Vietnam above the Treetops."*

RECREATION:

Other than the Officer's Club entertainment, occasionally we might catch a movie at our outdoor "theater" which consisted of a screen and lots of sand to lie on. The base supplied it with a good mix of old and current releases. There was only a weekly showing, but it was free.

Very occasionally we might visit the Koreans or drive down to Cam Ranh Army or go to the beach and fight the undertow, but the rest of our time was spent in that triangle of the Club, the Flightline and the Quonset. We literally beat a path between the three locations.

Going on R&R was one way to avoid combat fatigue. There were other forms of recreation, but not many. When I first arrived at CRB, several of us visited the nearby beach. It was very picturesque, but swimming was a challenge. There were lots of sharks and a very, very strong undertow. We next inquired about swimming at the nearby lake, which was also very scenic. We were told that the deadly Krait snake swam in its cool waters. Swimming was out.

Reading became a favorite pastime, but we had to rely on imports from our parents or friends. There was no base library.

The Air Force did an excellent job attending to the needs of its pilot force at Cam Ranh. If I was to suggest anything that could have improved our situation, it would have been to create a small base library that was open to all military personnel. The cost could be minimal as I am sure families provided books for the pilots as mine had. Those books could then be donated to a library and thus its inventory could be increased at no expense to the taxpayer. To further save expenses, it could be unmanned and the Airmen could be held to the honor system.

Occasionally, Air Force fighter-bombers from some other base would provide our evening entertainment by bombing nearby. They were always from another base, never from our own. When that occurred, we would grab lounge chairs and sit out on our "veranda" to watch the fireworks. Most of the times that happened were near twilight and offered spectacular views of "napalm in the evening." We pilots would drink beer and watch the war, often cheering.

I did meet a very, very nice nurse named Joan Kecer. Joanie and I became close. She and all the nurses were really special. They understood what was going on and partied with us without the "princess attitude" of the later-arriving USO girls. Joanie helped make life at CRB enjoyable. And, dating expenses were minimal. Dinner and drinks at the club and free movies on the sand. What more could a girl ask for?

THE LOCAL VIETNAMESE:

Cam Ranh Village was a place to stay away from. I did visit once, but it was filled with the black plague and ten of the villagers had died the year before from the disease. The Air Force had inoculated all of us against the plaque and a host of other maladies. Many of the local Viets from the village worked at our base doing odd jobs like cleaning the buildings. Our squadron had opted to clean our own Quonsets, both at home and at the Flightline. We didn't want any of them anywhere near us for security purposes.

We had our reasons for excluding them. Vietnamese had worked for months cleaning Quonsets at other Air Force bases in South Vietnam. During that time, they slowly brought in plastic explosives underneath their fingernails. When they had acquired enough, they blew up the Quonsets, often with pilots inside.

The author does not mean to imply that most South Vietnamese were allied with the Viet Cong. It was, after all, a country in the midst of a civil war. According to R. J. Rummel from the Wikipedia report "Vietnam War Casualties," an excess of 36,000 South Vietnamese civilians were executed by the combined forces of the North Vietnamese Army and the Viet Cong between 1967 and 1972.

After my return to the States from SEA, I was often told how beautiful the Viet women must have been. Photos of pretty Viet women were often shown in the States, but that just did not equate with our experiences. We saw none of that and tried to stay away from Saigon. Saigon reportedly did have good looking women, but most of us wanted to stay away from that ugly city filled with sandbags and prostitutes. The only times that I was in Saigon was when I tried to find a VNAF pilot who had been shot down in the Delta and I stayed too long and exhausted my fuel supply; when three of us returned from R&R and had to land at Tan Son Nhut; and when I departed from SEA.

I realize that in many of the larger towns and cities were very pretty Vietnamese women. We just didn't see them around Cam Ranh. My only contacts with Viet women at Cam Ranh were not pretty.

My recollections of Viet women include two who were squatting facing each other in Cam Ranh Village. They were picking lice out of one another's hair and then they ate the lice. Another Vietnamese maiden ran after a cockroach and stepped on it, squashing it. She then proceeded to pick up the roach and eat it.

The local Vietnamese also appeared to have never heard of a dentist.

Please excuse the author's graphic description of such unsavory events. But part of the reason for writing this book is for others to understand what Vietnam was like for those of us who fought. The lice and roaches were part of that reality.

Overall, the Vietnamese seemed very nice. They just wanted to be left alone and given a chance to live their lives. They did not want to be bothered by anybody, including us. They did not want to be bothered by the ARVN troops, who would confiscate food from villages when they passed through. Nor did the villagers want to be bothered by the Viet Cong when they passed through doing the same things.

THE VIET CONG (VC) AND THE NORTH VIETNAMESE ARMY (NVA):

The Viet Cong were not viewed in the villages as much better than the American foreigners. When I was there, it was reported that there were over 15,000 villages in South Vietnam. Sometimes the VC went into the villages and practiced what they considered "indoctrination" of the villagers. To gain proper respect from each village, the VC made a ceremony of the beheading of the leaders of the villages and would do it in front of their families and all the villagers. Often they tortured the village head by impaling him with a bayonet and allowing his intestines to fall out. Before I left, it was reported by Intelligence that they had done this to thousands of the village chiefs. This was VC indoctrination.

For those readers who might still be confused by the enemy we faced in South Vietnam, let me explain how they were organized.

When Vietnam was separated into North and South by the Geneva Accords in 1954, the Communist guerrillas who were fighting the French in Vietnam were called the Viet Minh. With the creation of South Vietnam under Western influence, the Viet Minh of the South became known as the Viet Cong. The Viet Minh of North Vietnam became the initial regular force units of the NVA (North Vietnamese Army).

In time, the Viet Cong split into two different forces. One was the VC main force units, who were regular VC army soldiers. The others were the part-time Viet irregulars who resided in the villages. Both the regulars and the irregulars operated as guerrilla units unless they would mass to fight larger force battles such as Plei Mi, Ia Drang and TET (the Vietnamese Holiday Attack).

Another Vietnamese military organization was the South Vietnamese Army or the ARVN, standing for the Army of Vietnam. Supposedly this was our ally. The ARVN was comprised of some very effective units, but overall it was not too good as a fighting organization. The ARVN were famously infiltrated with Viet Cong sympathizers and our required notifications to them concerning attack targets or ground operations were effective notifications of the VC. This has been dealt with elsewhere in this book.

Of possible consequence is the place of birth for the officers who led the ARVN. Fully 18% of the officers were born in Tonkin, which later became the northern part of North Vietnam. Were they escaping or representing? What is hard to escape is the fact that people have a natural affinity for the place of their birth. One is left to wonder.

North Vietnamese Army units continuously infiltrated the South to augment the Viet Cong. This arrangement lasted until the VC TET Offensive in February 1968. During TET, both the VC regulars and irregulars lost so many men that they were essentially destroyed as a fighting force for the rest of the war. Of over 80,000 VC that came out of the villages and jungles to mass for an offensive, over 45,000 of them were killed in less than two weeks of warfare, largely due to American artillery and air.

Our own Army suffered from the same inhumanity that the VC showed to the heads of their villages. In one operation, a Mohawk Army Intelligence plane was shot down and the pilot was captured. He was forced to construct his own cage, in which the VC paraded him through villages in the South. He would carry the cage during forced marches during the day. At night, he was placed inside the cage. It was a wandering show for the benefit of the interior population. Villagers taunted him and physically abused him.

He was black and the villagers apparently learned the English word for "monkey." He reportedly received other racial taunts and tortures. The Army followed his circuitous trip through the jungles in an attempt to rescue. After four months, reports determined that the pilot-officer was totally insane.

This was the nature of the enemy we faced.

HOLIDAY IN DA LAT:

Any war usually creates its share of strange incidents and SEA was no exception. In January and February of 1966, some of the pilot officers of the 45th decided to take a little local R&R in an area called the Highlands. They visited the town of Da Lat, which is located in the greater Central Highlands directly to the west of Cam Ranh. Da Lat, named for the Highlands "Lat" hill tribe, is now known as a honeymoon mecca and popular vacation spot.

The "City of Eternal Spring" was then, as now, also a resort town and retreat from the pressures of everyday life. The pilots who traveled to Da Lat were not disappointed.

One evening the four of them decided to visit a local restaurant that received high marks from residents. Like most of us in Vietnam, they had nothing to wear other than their Air Force uniforms. The "flight" of four pilots was in uniform as they ate. Seated next to them, also in uniform, were four Viet Cong regular officers.

A DAY AT WAR:

Our squadron Quonset was directly across the sand street from the R&R Center for officers representing every service from all over SEA. This was it. This was where all the officers came to process out and then they would jump aboard transports flying out of Cam Ranh for any points away from the war.

This was a perfect place for a curious guy to live. I interviewed many of the guys who had recently arrived from war zones throughout SEA. We would invite them over to our Quonset and entertain them in our "recreation" room with its picturesque wallpaper and our four reefers full of beer. We let them drink as much as they wished. They had earned it. We found spare bunks for them that had been recently vacated by the guys on R&R. These troops, who had recently escaped the mud, could then sleep in air-conditioned comfort between clean, white sheets.

Over beer, they spilled their guts out about what was really happening. It was a terrific learning experience.

I got this same story from many of the U.S. Army officers from the interior. It is a bizarre description of part-time soldiers:

The irregular troops of the ARVN (Army of the Republic of Vietnam) went to "work" at about 8 in the morning. Being irregular, they lived in the villages. "Going to work" might include hiking down to their trenches to face the Viet Cong irregulars. The VC irregulars would also awaken at the same time and hike down to their trenches to face the ARVN irregulars. During the day, they would trade shots with each other and otherwise make like war.

At four o'clock sharp every afternoon, the ARVN irregulars climbed out of their trenches, hoisted their rifles onto their shoulders and hiked back to their villages. At four o'clock sharp, the VC irregulars would also arise from their own trenches, sling their rifles onto their shoulders and hike back to their villages. Since they often lived in the same village, these weekend warriors from the ARVN and VC often hiked back together. After all, when it is 4 o'clock, it is time to stop work because the day's work is over.

These stories, and there are many from SEA, might be classified under the title, "Absurdities of War."

REST & RECUPERATION (R&R):

Favorite destinations for R&R guys from Cam Ranh were Hong Kong, Japan, Okinawa and Thailand. For me, Japan was too expensive. Okinawa was a return to familiar territory and people, while Hong Kong was the delightfully last R&R of the year for me. But the best of my destinations was Bangkok, Thailand.

Whenever I had a chance to get away, I often tried for Bangkok. Every time I was in Thailand, I could not resist the temptation to catch a flight and visit the Thai Bases. The Thais have a pride that is evident. I am not sure of the source of their pride, which may come from the fact that they have never having been conquered by any foreign power? They are a very gracious and lovely people and their capitol was special. The Bangkok women were also beautiful. Even with the ever-present benjo ditches, it was and is a great city. Benjo Ditches were ever-present in Thai cities in the 1960s. They were open ditches carrying raw sewage.

The fact that Thailand, formerly Siam, had never been conquered by a foreign nation was due to several factors: One of those was that the Thai and Siamese peoples always had very effective armed forces. They were one of the first Asian nations to create an air force.

A second reason is that they have a history of accommodation with potential invaders. When the Japanese forces approached during WWII, the Thais were receptive to Japanese overtures. They allowed Japanese use of then-existing airfields that included Don Muang outside Bangkok. A little-known fact was that Thailand declared war on the United States in WWII. Thai Royal Air Force planes actually fought against American fighter planes on more than one occasion.

The Thais went along with the United States during the Vietnamese War and allowed combat use of their airfields. However, shortly after the end of the war, Thailand asked the U.S. to leave its Thai bases.

Since that time, the Thais have cozied up to the Chinese and with them have even staged joint military exercises. China is now the largest trading partner of Thailand.

On one visit, I had dinner at Bangkok's Imperial Hotel. I spotted a nice looking American woman sitting alone at another table. It turned out that Adda Million worked for the United States Agency for International Development (AID).

On a later visit, I was sitting with Adda on her veranda having coffee and reading the English-language Bangkok Times when my attention was drawn to an article about two Air Force Phantoms that had been shot down on a mission against North Vietnam.

Upon return from Bangkok, as I trudged up to our apartment, I noticed that four of the eight nameplates by the side of the door to our apartment were missing. It turned out that I lost half of my B Flight within 30 seconds on the same pass against a Northern target. The two lost Phantoms mentioned in the Bangkok Times were from my own Flight. It turned out that they had been led on multiple passes. That was insane. Multiple passes against an NVN target was an invitation to the Hanoi Hilton or worse.

The four missing pilots became Prisoners of War. It was not until I was out of the Air Force that I learned that they were POWs and had not been killed. One eventually died in captivity before repatriation.

THE R&R CENTER:

The R&R Center was just an open-sided canopy about 20X40 feet in size. Its floor, like everywhere else, was made of sand on which were placed metal folding-chairs for all the troops being processed. Fortunately, for those of us flying combat at Cam Ranh, we just went on R&R and didn't require processing. That might have been due to the Wing cutting orders for us to accomplish some bogus military mission at some exotic city.

R&R was necessary for us. While those who were processed through the Center were subject to fighting the enemy, they didn't fight every day. The combat pilots flew to find the enemy and fight—every day. I have no way to compare the stress of a soldier in the trenches or on patrol or a sailor residing on a ship, but to those of us who fought every day, the stress levels were very high.

We pilots sometimes wandered over to the Center to chat with some of the guys. It was there that I ran into Hal Allen from the old 559th. Hal was a great guy and one of my favorites. He had an easy smile and an easier Southern charm. When I saw Hal, he was thin and looked very nervous. Being a ground FAC must have been harrowing for him? He was anxious to get away and had been "in country" continuously for eight long months.

Back at MacDill and long before I was assigned to SEA, I was given an assignment as a FAC to the 1st Air Cavalry Division. Actually, eight of us were given the same assignment. The 1st was the first division in the history of the US Army to be equipped entirely with helicopters. They had more than 400 of them.

Our jobs were to be ground FACs for each Division Battalion. None of us wanted the job because of the danger involved and that we would have to control bombing strikes from the ground. If we went to Vietnam, we wanted to fly. Because we had so many pilots, both front and back seat, MacDill was a favorite hunting ground for the Air Force Personnel Department. There had been many previous assignments to Army units for MacDill FACs. Every one of the perhaps eight or nine assigned pilots had returned, either in a body bag or through the Burn Center in San Antonio. None of us wanted that assignment.

Thankfully, very thankfully, one of the other assigned pilots had a father who was a Colonel assigned to Air Force Personnel at the Pentagon. The Colonel didn't want his son to have that assignment. It was rescinded for all of us and we were allowed to eventually go to Vietnam in a cockpit. The Colonel's son even bagged a MIG-17.

Looking at Hal gave me two competing emotions. One was deep gratitude for that Pentagon Colonel and the other was respect and appreciation for what Hal must have gone through.

BOB HOPE & THE "DONUT DOLLIES":

The USO (United Service Organizations) is a wonderful organization that is dedicated to the well-being of American servicemen located all over the globe. The USO did two things for us Air Force guys at CRB. One was to send Bob Hope to visit us and the other was to send us the USO girls. Both moves were bad.

When Bob Hope arrived, there was the usual fanfare. The day of his performance, we were given instructions to avoid flying anywhere near the show, which was located on a sandy area of the base near the movie theater. Actually, there was nowhere on the base that was not sandy.

That morning, I was scheduled for a combat mission to the North. When I arrived back from the mission, I was late for his show, but went with my back-seater anyway. During the show, a Phantom flew fairly close to the Hope stage as it returned from a combat mission. Hope complained loudly and asked over the microphone for the "authorities" to insure no more Phantoms interrupted his performance.

Now wait a minute, I thought. "Is he here for us, or are we here for him?" Hope seemed to think that we should stop the war, while he filmed his show for later viewing back in the States. Whoever was driving the Phantom might have had battle damage, or he might have needed to fly that particular flight path. It did not matter. Hope was way out of line.

The USO girls were not much better. The USO has done a lot of great things for our servicemen in many wars and also during peacetime. They are a dedicated organization and meant only the best for us. For that, they deserve a vote of thanks from all of us who have served.

With the best of intentions from the USO, the USO girls were bad for the war. The idea was for the servicemen (us) to have a "touch of home" as represented by the girls. Any red-blooded man appreciates a good-looking woman—right?

The first time I saw one of the USO girls, I was floored. She was wearing a mini-skirt. It was the first time that I and most of us had seen one. They were the current rage back home. The result of the minis was predictable. It was like waving the proverbial red cape in front of a bull.

We called the USO girls the "Donut Dollies." They apparently thought that serving us donuts would improve our morale. The Donut Dollies changed the social equation of the war. The guys who had recently arrived swarmed around them. The USO said that they were there for our morale, which was just not the case. The Donut Dollies seemed more interested in all the attention that they were getting and were obviously not interested in doing anything for the group. Their attitude seemed to be that they should be the center of attention. I noticed that most of the older guys, older as far as combat, held back. Not once in the entire time that they were over there, did any Donut Dolly approach me. In fact, I cannot recall one time when even one word was exchanged with one of them, either by me or anyone around me. They expected us to approach them, which I refused to do. It was very similar to the Bob Hope situation. Were they in Vietnam for us or were we there to further inflate their sense of self-importance?

I say the above with knowledge that to many, Bob Hope is sacred when it comes to support of our troops in all wars. There can be no doubt that Hope has benefited our country and provided diversion and hope for our military during wartime.

The change in the social equation I referred to was that the focus of many of the guys changed. War is an incredibly serious business. To do a good job in war and to stay alive, a pilot has to be totally focused on his job. And his job was not to chase a mini skirt. Flying combat takes a lot of thought, concentration and emotional energy. The nurses understood. The Donut Dollies did not.

When there are a lot of men and a definite shortage of women, men tend to compete for the few. This situation can be explosive. There is really no place for men to compete for the attention of women in a wartime environment. It is really a man's world during war and that is not about to change. We needed a pilot group that was unified without individual disputes or competitions.

To lose his focus, a combat pilot invites quick death. In the cockpit, he must think entirely of his mission and not about what he might do or say with a woman back at the base. To have "issues" with fellow pilots in a combat flight can be deadly. The presence of the USO girls was absolutely the worst thing that our government could have done for us. One thing they could have done was send us more bombs. We were short of bombs, not blondes.

A much better way of improving pilot morale, or any combatant's morale, was to send them on R&R. On R&R we can choose our own donuts.

The attitude of the new guys, who competed so heavily for the female attention, was to change. Their outlook became very different after viewing life from the viewpoint of the constant threat of impending death. It ages a man and changes his perspective.

TRANSPORTATION:

We were given no ground transport for the pilots. Some of the other officers got Jeeps, but there was no real need for us to have our own. Walking was good for us and we were always "borrowing" someone's Jeep or truck.

It was considered dangerous to leave one's keys in one's Jeep. One morning when I was just getting off my Command Post night shift, I returned to the Squadron Quonset just as the phone rang. As the nearest pilot, I picked up the phone. The guy on the other end of the line could not speak very good English. But I did get the message. With a very thick accent, the Korean stated "we have one of your pilots here who crashed into our roadblock. What would you like us to do with him?" I told the Korean we would be right down. Before he hung up, the Korean told me that the pilot was naked and needed clothing.

Just as I hung up, someone came running in to report that the Chaplain's Jeep was gone. Mild-mannered and quiet Gary Bennett had decided to have his own party. This was the same Gary Bennett who had violated the only rule of the "O" Club and worn his sidearm into the Club. He was responsible for the occasional monsoon leak that dripped from the bullet hole in the roof. On that particular morning, Gary's heavenly inspiration was to choose God's Jeep.

Gary was a good pilot and a good guy who was well liked and respected by the pilots. This was just another example of how the pressures of war can affect combatants who need to be able to "let off steam." For the rest of us, his actions were a welcome interlude from the seriousness of war.

COMMUNICATION LOOPS:

While in SEA, it became evident that communications traveled in certain contained channels. I am referring to the verbal communications between pilots and I came to refer to them as communication loops.

Pilots who flew a particular type of aircraft had their own loop. It consisted of all the bases that housed the same-type planes and the pilots who flew those planes. The usual pattern of travel and visitations were between those same pilots. The Phantom pilots had theirs. The F-100 pilots had theirs. The Navy pilots that flew off the carriers had theirs.

My good fortune was that I was able to connect the dots on many occasions. The "O" Club was one place that connected the loops. We were visited by many officers from all over SEA. Navy pilots also visited when landing from carriers. We had many visitors that flew off the Carrier Oriskany (CVA-34). Ours was a good and safe environment. The R&R Center was another connection point. The Special Action FACS connected the loops from all over South Vietnam, "Tiger Hound" and "Talley Ho."

The Thud pilots never visited Cam Ranh. They were pretty insular and awfully busy. They just had no time to visit other bases outside of Thailand. Other than chatting over drinks, like the French 75s or MIG 15s at their Officer's Club at Kadena in Okinawa, my only connection to them was to visit their Thai bases.

The Command Post was another point of connection. Talking to 7th Air Force daily connected me to their input. The visit of the Big Eye crews plus other inputs from other Elint crews expanded the net of connectors. The Command Post was a perfect place to listen and learn.

Our Intelligence reports were located in a vault at Flight Ops that allowed us easy access. Since I had spent my time in Okinawa as an Intelligence Officer, I had been awarded an Intelligence AFSC (proficiency code). I spent considerable time analyzing the SEA Intelligence reports. They were much more interesting than reading the Stars and Stripes.

The visits of President Johnson and Defense Secretary McNamara provided additional information about bomb shortages from their confidential meetings, of which I had been informed by the Cam Ranh Media Officer who attended.

My many trips throughout Thailand, including visits to the Thud Bases and the CIA, were equally informative. All of these things were open channels for a curious mind. By virtue of joining many of these loops of communication, I was able to do what most could not do. And that was finding out what the hell was really going on.

When I started to write this book, I had many sources for information: The declassified Rules of Engagement documents formed the initial basis. My combat diary and memory of personal experiences provided another. The many declassified agency reports and books written provided further information. But it was the conversations that I had with so many throughout SEA that helped me pull much of it all together and form the basis for this book.

> *"Every gun that is made, every warship launched, every rocket fired, signifies in the final sense a theft from those who hunger and are not fed, for those who are cold and not clothed."*
>
> General of the Army Dwight David Eisenhower

CHAPTER EIGHTEEN
"Spook" Heaven
CIA in Laos

> *"Experts often possess more data than judgement."*
>
> General Colin Powell

The Thud pilot was troubled by my question.

My trip had taken me from Korat to Takhli to continue my discussions with the F-105 guys who, along with Korat, formed the nucleus of our air campaign against Hanoi- Haiphong. My question had to do with the anti-aircraft artillery that they had to deal with since arriving in Thailand.

These pilots faced more defensive guns in the vicinity of Hanoi-Haiphong than WWII bomber pilots ever faced over the Ruhr Industrial Region in Germany or their capitol, Berlin. While Air Force Intelligence in 1966 was reporting 10,000 AAA guns in the Red River Valley, post-war research has placed the number at closer to 7,000- 8,000 as compared to the German defensive guns that numbered slightly in excess of 2,100 for all of Germany.

After landing, the C-130 pilot had informed us that, "we will be gassing up here in Takhli and the two of us will be having lunch. If you are going on with us, our destination is Udorn. We will overnight there." He asked us who would be continuing on and a few responded. They gave us a time to depart for the on-base cafeteria and then return to the aircraft in plenty of time before departure. Since I was planning to stay for the evening, his announcement meant little to me at the time. Before reporting to the F-105 Wing Operations and considering lunch, I elected to walk around the base to get a feel for it.

During my walk, I met several pilots and struck up a conversation with those willing to stop and talk. My impressions were the same as I felt at Korat. The fighter pilots already seemed to consider themselves dead. Their eyes told a story that was very difficult for another pilot to witness.

To each of them I had requested their thoughts on how best to suppress the AAA in an attack. Maybe, just maybe, I could have my questions answered without having to trouble the Thud Wing to schedule tactics meetings.

The look on the troubled pilot's face betrayed his gut feelings. Their rates of loss at both Thud bases were horrendous. He continued, "It doesn't seem to matter where we place them in the flight, their guns still fire." He hesitated for a long time. "Yesterday my flight lost two to the guns at Yen Bai." I was embarrassed. They didn't need me here. After thanking him, I turned around and retraced my steps back to the Flightline.

My trip had taken me on a C-123 from Cam Ranh, first to Tan Son Nhut outside of Saigon and then on to Don Muang, outside of Bangkok. There I grabbed a C-130 scheduled to depart within the hour and flew

293

on to Korat, where I spent the evening after having tactics meetings with several squadrons. This C-130 had picked me up the next day on a direct flight to Takhli.

Looking along the tarmac, I could see the lineup of Thuds much farther down. Their huge airframes seemed menacing, even at a distance.

The 105s were given the Thud moniker because so many of them bailed out over the mountains to the west of Hanoi and wreckage of their aircraft was strewn all over the mountain that was nicknamed "Thud Ridge." Someone thought the name "Thud" was what an aircraft might sound like slamming into a mountain. At least that was the story told to the rest of us. If true, it was in bad taste, but the name stuck.

The name "Thud" was actually an affectionate tribute to the Thunderchief, the largest single-seat aircraft ever to be flown by the Air Force. Of the 833 airframes manufactured, SEA claimed almost half of them.

Wing DO Colonel Allen had not been specific in his orders, which gave me a lot of latitude to be creative. My mission to determine how the F-105s were employing the Cluster Bomb Units in combat was complete. I had satisfied the 12th TFWs need. Now it was my turn to satisfy my need.

Much later, Colonel James Allen, deputy commander of the 12th, later became a General Officer. After he was given his third star, he became Superintendent of the Air Academy. After he was given his fourth star, he became Commander of Military Airlift Command (MAC), the same command that owned the C-130 on which I was riding.

When I had returned, the 130 was still parked and the refueling hoses were still connected to the fuel intake port on the top of a wing. The engines were still shut down and it gave me time to climb the stairs and enter the cockpit. After informing the crew that I would be continuing on with them to Udorn, they welcomed me back and invited me to ride with them in their cockpit jump seat. In a short time, we were airborne again and headed north.

UDORN ROYAL THAI AIR FORCE BASE:

We landed at Udorn Royal Thai Air Force Base shortly after noon. As I climbed down the stairs from the aircraft, a Lieutenant Colonel met me by name. I was stunned. I had no idea how or why they found out that I was coming? He introduced himself and indicated he was commander of the attached recce squadron. They flew the F-101, which was built by McDonnell Douglas in Saint Louis, just like the F-4.

Actually, it was only a half squadron on TDY and their status was as a detachment. Their job was to run the recce tracks across the more important North Vietnamese targets after they had been hit by the fighter-bomber attacks. Those were not easy missions. The RF-101 and RF-4Cs sustained severe loss rates throughout their stays in SEA.

The speedy 101s would fly over the F-105 targets after they had been hit and report Bomb Damage Assessment. The Thud targets had too many defenses and the slower FAC aircraft were never employed for BDA. The F-101 cameras were the scorecards of Thud success.

The condition of Udorn was far more primitive than at Ubon. We were close to the northern border of Thailand, which was the southern border of Laos. This part of the country was remote and unpopulated and it was jungle terrain similar to that down south at Ubon.

The Colonel picked up my bag in spite of my objections. To have a Colonel carrying a Lieutenant's duffle bag just did not seem right. As we walked to his waiting Jeep, he asked if I had eaten lunch. When I told him that I hadn't, he announced that, "I would like to show you something."

THE CIA IN THAILAND:

My attentive and gracious pilot-host then took me on a tour. The Flightline of the 101s, where we were standing, was nothing to write home about. However, the other side of the base was another story. It housed the CIA pilots and aircraft. Here was clandestine warfare at its finest.

The CIA side of the Flightline did look remote and even had a touch of stealth. Tall trees ringed the sides as if protecting and gave a covert impression. The CIA Flightline had aircraft of every description. The aircraft were all props and rotors without a jet to be seen. Big Jolly Greens (helicopters) crowded one side of the separate runway. Some were painted dark green while at least one was the dark of night. On the other side of the runway were parked the prop-driven fighters positioned with the green wall of the jungle as a backdrop. Some of the props were T-28s fighters and showed more than one country-insignia on their sides. Several were painted black.

In response to my question, I was told that the slotted receivers on the sides of each fixed-wing aircraft allowed easy mounting and removal of country insignia. The CIA pilots would just mount the insignia of choice during their pre-flight checks and off they would go to fight for whatever country they wanted to be that day.

My host introduced me to several CIA pilots. One had just arrived at the Flightline and had a flight to prepare for. He wore a Hawaiian shirt, shorts and rubber sandals. "Yes" he said in response to my question, "this is the uniform I fly in." Since the average life expectancy of the CIA pilots was only six months, I figured that they should have their choice of flying garb.

In the following month, I was offered money to fly those same black choppers for the CIA. They came to visit Cam Ranh and requested an interview. They offered $800 per month, which was certainly in excess of what I was then making. But, I didn't sign up to get rich. There were other "rewards." My allegiance was and would remain with the Air Force.

Out of curiosity, I asked the CIA guy some questions: "If I get shot down, will you send anyone to rescue me?" His answer was "no." I continued, "If I get shot down will you admit that I am an American. His answer was again "no." I then told him that I didn't want his job.

After satisfying my curiosity, my Udorn recce Commanding Officer then announced, as he jumped back into his jeep, "We're going to lunch." With barely enough time to join him, we were off. We went bouncing our way along the rutted road, where we soon reentered the jungle. I wondered what he was doing and where we were going, but I decided that I was on an adventure and "what the heck."

As we bounced along under the jungle canopy, my mind had visions of the Philippines and eating lunch out of bamboo bowls. Deeper into the thick jungle we drove. Suddenly, as if from nowhere, two burly Americans holding serious weapons and wearing green and brown camouflage fatigues stopped us. After a brief discussion, the guards quickly opened their gate and let us through. Recce pilots must be frustrated fighter pilots as this Pilot-Colonel negotiated the road very quickly. It felt like I was "jinking" to avoid AAA as we roughly maneuvered along, surrounded by the trees, the shadows and flora of a dense jungle.

The transformation was remarkable. One minute we were doing our formula one routine and the next we were out in the open and staring at a Holiday Inn. At least it looked like a Holiday Inn. Holiday Inn-Udorn turned out to be a CIA hotel, complete with swimming pool, dining room, snack bar and serious bar. This turned out to be home to my host and it was apparent that he was not sleeping under thatch and chicken wire.

In my entire life I have never seen anything to compare. Here we were in a remote jungle. Here we were at a major clandestine airfield housing some of the CIA assets for fighting their "secret" war in Central Laos. And here we were munching cheeseburgers and drinking cokes. To me it was a metaphor for the entire war.

AIR COMMANDOS:

Declassified USAF Rules of Engagement documents mention Air Commando activities in Laos that go back to at least 1961. The USAF Air Commandos, headquartered and trained at Hurlburt Field in Florida, flew extensive combat missions using the prop-powered A-1H and the venerable, prop-powered T-28 aircraft. Most of their initial activity was in South Vietnam.

My flights in the A-1H at Hurlburt and, as an 18-year-old, the T-28 at Moore Field outside of McAllen, Texas, proved to me that both are formidable and high-powered weapon systems. Propeller-driven aircraft have a much more immediate response to throttle advancement than most jet-powered aircraft. It took our Continental Airlines jet transports eight seconds to reach full power from idle. While the Phantom had a rapid power increase with a throttle advance, there is still a quicker response in propeller-driven fighters such as the T-28. The T-28 Trojan and the surprisingly large A1Hs were workhorse aircraft for the CIA, Commandos, Air America and Continental Air Services in clandestine operations throughout the old French Indochina.

THE TANGLED WEB — CIA AIRLINES IN LAOS:

BIRD AND SONS: Bird and Sons was a California-based construction company that performed projects in Laos as early as 1960. In 1960, William H. Bird created the Bird and Sons Air Division and they initially flew five C-46s on Laotian cargo runs. That operation slowly grew until they had 350 employees and 22 aircraft of varying description. Bird and Son's Air Division worked on contract to various outfits including the United States Agency for International Development. USAID operations were headquartered in Bangkok. Bird and Sons was also on contract to the Central Intelligence Agency.

The complement of aircraft flown by Bird and Sons included Bell helicopters, Beech, Cessna, Dornier, Douglas and a Lockheed Ventura. This motley batch of 22 planes was sold in April of 1965, along with the rest of BirdAir, to Continental Air Services (CAS) or (CASI).

CONTINENTAL AIR SERVICES: In the 1960s, Continental Airlines won what was later called the MAC contract, only the initial signed contract was with the USAF Military Air Transport Service or MATS. It was only later that MATS became MAC, short for Military Airlift Command. Continental aircraft and crews operated throughout the Pacific in the 1960s, ferrying military personnel to and from the war.

Continental's President Bob Six decided that there was money to be made in the burgeoning conflict in SEA. In April 1965, he created what he called the Southeast Asia Division of Continental Airlines, Inc., also known as Continental Air Services or CAS (sometimes referred to as CASI).

Initially, CAS had no aircraft or crew members. Later that year, it purchased the entire Air Division of Bird & Sons Construction Company. Prior to the Continental purchase, BirdAir had flown war-related flights with Asian crewmembers out of Savannakhet, Laos. Six established his administrative headquarters in Vientiane, Laos. Later, headquarters for flight operations was established at Udorn RTAFB, Thailand. CAS started hiring Caucasian pilots as opposed to the all-Asian crews flown by Bird and Sons.

Bird and Sons mainly operated transport aircraft, which included C-130s from the USAF. The 130s and other Bird Air transports were used in the evacuation of ex-guerrilla troops in Laos in addition to a set schedule transporting mostly cargo. The scheduled flights for CAS included a cargo "milk run" from Bangkok through Udorn to Vientiane, Laos.

CAS established flight contracts with: United States Agency for International Development (USAID), United States Embassy in Vientiane (USOM), Raymond Morrison and Knutson (RMK) Construction Company and its affiliate Brown Root and Jones (BRJ), and the "Customer." "Customer" was generally known as the Central Intelligence Agency (CIA).

According to the recently declassified report, "The War in Northern Laos," by the US Air Force History Office, CAS "also developed contracts to provide both aircraft and pilots to fly Air Commando FAC (missions) in Laos." The report goes on to say, "one unusual and highly successful mission for CAS pilots known as Project "Brush Cargo" involved flying specially equipped Dornier 28 aircraft over Laos to intercept enemy radio signals." The Dornier 28 "Skyservant" is currently in the military inventory of 21 countries.

When I was flying with Continental Airlines, I had a discussion with the only CAS pilot to transfer to the Airline. He conferred to me that CAS had 42 T-28s and A1Hs retrofitted for combat and were flying attack and FAC missions in Laos and Cambodia. Subsequent research has failed to confirm that story although the discussion of the Raven FACs in Chapter Nineteen does shed light on their combat role.

What is known is that CAS pilot Emmett Kay was taken prisoner by the Pathet Lao and released as part of a "prisoner" exchange on September 18, 1974. Reportedly, several more CAS pilots were classified as MIA and 14 pilots and crew members were reported as killed.

The participation of CAS in the "Secret War" has itself largely remained a secret. It is evident that CAS deserves some of the same recognition given to Air America by our government as its contribution to the conduct of the war was almost as significant.

CIVIL AIR TRANSPORT (CAT): This Chinese airline performed a variety of operations in behalf of the CIA during the Korean War and the "Secret War" in Laos. CAT even issued CIA citations and medals for operations. In 1957, CAT signed an agreement with the CIA for operations in Laos. If this report is correct, then it takes the CIA in Laos back to within three years of Dien Bien Phu. However, the usage of CAT would probably have been limited to cargo transport.

VEKA AKHAT AIRLINES (VAA): Veka Akhat Airlines was formed by the CIA in 1960. It started with three aircraft with an unspecified mission. After several years, VAA was absorbed into the CIA.

XIENG KHOUANG AIR TRANSPORT (XKAT): XKAT started with four aircraft using Thai pilots. The four aircraft were supplied by: (2) C-47s from the CIA; (1) from Air America and (1) from Continental Air Services.

SOUTHERN AIR TRANSPORT: Created by Air America for unspecified duties in Southeast Asia.

AIR ASIA: Created by Pacific Corporation for unspecified duties in SEA. Pacific Corporation appears to be currently non-existent, but it was affiliated with Air America.

When the author returned to the United States, he contacted the CIA to see if there were any pilot jobs available at the CIA. The duty officer replied that the CIA did not have pilots. However, he stated that Air Asia was hiring.

AIR VIETNAM: Air Vietnam shared flight hangars with CAS throughout SEA, but in particular at Tan Son Nhut. Maintenance for Air Vietnam was performed by CAS, Air Asia and China Airline. Air Vietnam participated in joint ventures with CAS, which included leasing aircraft to Foreign Air Travel Development, Inc. The nature of the joint ventures is unknown.

BOUN OUM AIRWAYS (BOA): This Laotian airline was started in 1964 by the CIA, using Laotian Prince Boun Oum as the ostensible owner. BOA used resources, including aircraft, from Air America. They started with an inventory of nine aircraft.

BOA initially used Asian pilots, but later contracted for Continental Air Services pilots. The CAS pilots, flying BOA Dornier 28 aircraft, flew night missions over the Ho Chi Minh Trail in what was called "trail recon." Initially, BOA/CAS flew in support of CIA Project "Hardnose," which later became Project "Hark." Both these projects were related to HCMT intelligence.

In 1967, BOA was shut down due to its high loss rate, and was integrated into CAS.

AIR AMERICA: That Air America operated in Laos as an arm of the CIA was one of the worst kept secrets in SEA. They started their Laotian operations in June of 1960 flying four USAF H-19A helicopters. Later, it expanded to include other choppers, transports and T-28s.

Udorn was one of the bases that supported Air America. Nakhon Phanom (NKP), which was located along the Mekong to the east of Udorn, also supported clandestine air operations. The T-28s were widely used by Air America and other clandestine air services as prop-driven fighter aircraft. American prop-driven aircraft had been shot down as early as 1961.

The attempted rescue on June 6, 1964 of Naval Lieutenant Chuck Klussman, the first American jet to be downed by enemy fire in SEA, has been reported in another chapter. In a declassified CIA report by William M. Leary, he mentions the Air America side of the rescue. Two Air America choppers were sent in to rescue Klussman but the rescue was unsuccessful. Leary reported that this was the first use of Air America helo assets to attempt a rescue and that the two chopper pilots involved were untrained in rescue operations. Later, intense training did ensue and the Air America choppers became very adept at rescue.

In an earlier chapter, I mentioned that John Robertson and I flew a replacement F-4C down to Ubon to replace one that had been shot down. At the time I went to Bangkok, rescue attempts were being made for the two downed F-4 pilots. When John sent word that we would not be authorized to fly combat, he requested that I leave quickly and get back to Ubon.

My C-130 flight back to Ubon was diverted up to Udorn as a Medivac. At Udorn we picked up an unconscious Laotian Colonel and flew him back to a hospital in Bangkok. After we offloaded the Laotian, we reversed our direction and went to Ubon. Until recently, I had no idea that the Medivac had anything to do with the rescue of the MacDill based pilots who were TDY at Ubon. Recently declassified CIA documents state that the Colonel, who later died, was part of a two-helicopter operation by Air America to rescue the two pilot acquaintances of mine that were downed two days after we arrived at Ubon. The rescue was partially successful and one of the two F-4C pilots was returned to Ubon, but the two Air America choppers were badly shot up in the rescue and the Laotian Colonel was in one. The other F-4 pilot was captured and spent the remainder of the war in captivity.

At Udorn, I was also told of Air America operations that flew into North Vietnam in advance of a planned major attack, such as those against the Paul Doumer Bridge in Hanoi or the POL storage facilities located there. The Air America guys worked in conjunction with Laotians in capturing hilltops in North Vietnam along the proposed flight tracks for the incoming and outgoing Thai-based fighter bombers. They brought in 55-gallon drums filled with gas, parked their choppers and waited for downed airmen.

The French-built Paul Doumer Bridge was one of those targets which required repeated rescue attempts for pilots downed in the many attacks by the F-105s out of Korat and Takhli. The Thuds reportedly lost 59 aircraft in the vain attempt to knock out the bridge. That loss figure has not been confirmed. F-4s out of Ubon eventually knocked it down with smart bombs.

While Air America is widely known, its affiliated airlines are largely unknown. As mentioned above, Air America's affiliates included: BOA, Air Asia, XKAT, and Southern Air Transport.

The largest interrelationship between the clandestine airlines in Laos was between Air America and Continental Air Services. Air America and CAS shared and interchanged aircraft and even aircrews.

The large inventory of transport aircraft owned by Air America attests to its primary mission, which was transport of people and cargo in support of the Secret War effort. The Meo and Hmong tribesmen in Laos were allied with the CIA and the CIA regularly dropped provisions to the Meo, Lao and Hmong villages as well as their troops.

After 1964, Air America was relied on more and more by our government in the Search and Rescue mission, particularly to rescue pilots downed in Laos and North Vietnam.

A lesser-known mission was direct air combat. According to the Air Force History Office declassified report on the war in Laos, "a cadre of Air America pilots (who were) trained to fly Laotian combat aircraft, was kept at the US Embassy (in Vientiane), and was called upon when necessary."

Information on the MIA and KIA figures for the clandestine air forces is extremely hard to find. Prior to 1972, the figures are unknown. That includes aircraft shot down and aircrew members killed. But between April 1972 and June 1974, Air America lost 23 aircrew members killed in Laotian flight operations.

NAKHON PHANOM ROYAL THAI AIR FORCE BASE (NKP):

A major part of clandestine flying operations in SEA was carried out from Nakhon Phanom Royal Thai Air Force Base (NKP), which is located 365 miles NE of Bangkok on the Mekong River. The Mekong serves as the border between Thailand and Laos.

The use of NKP goes back to the beginning of the air war in Laos. In the 1950s, after Dien Bien Phu fell, the Viet Minh sent combat units into the Kingdom of Laos to support the Communist army known as the Pathet Lao. Later, NKP was used to fight the Pathet Lao.

In 1962, the US Navy Sea Bees sent a construction battalion to NKP to enhance our American air presence in Thailand and Laos. Air America sent units to NKP at an unspecified time after completion of this construction of support facilities for air operations.

In June of 1964, the USAF Pacific Air Rescue Center was shifted from Tan Son Nhut in SVN to operate out of NKP. On February 2, 1966, the Thai government approved the stationing of combat units of the Air Commandos, under the control of PACAF, at NKP.

NKP was known to many pilots who operated in Laos as Tacan Channel 89. It eventually housed units that were assigned missions for recce, S&R, cargo, fighter and FAC. The USN also maintained a presence there.

Aircraft assigned to NKP included: T-28 Trojan, A-1E Skyraider, A-26 Invader, O-1 Bird Dog, O-2 Skymaster and the OV-10 Bronco. This is just a partial list of the many different aircraft types eventually staging out of NKP. In addition to other American air combat units, the USAF had the 602nd Tactical Fighter Squadron stationed there. The fighter and FAC units operated in the Barrel Roll area of Central Laos.

STUDIES AND OBSERVATIONS GROUP (SOG):

The CIA involved itself in other clandestine operations. As an example, in January, 1964, MACV created a Studies and Observations Group (MACV-SOG) for the conduct of strategic reconnaissance missions in all of what had been Indochina. Its purpose was: the capture of enemy prisoners; the rescue of downed pilots; the conduct of operations to retrieve prisoners of war throughout SEA; conducting clandestine agent team activities and psychological operations.

According to the SOG, it was disbanded in 1972 after participation in most of the significant SEA campaigns including: "The Gulf of Tonkin Incident, "Steel Tiger," "Tiger Hound," "Commando Hunt," "Lam Son 719," the TET Offensive, the Cambodian Campaign, and the Easter Offensive."

It is interesting to note the reference from the SOGs own documents that they were involved in the Gulf of Tonkin Incidents. That the SOG was involved in the OPLAN-34-Alpha missions has been noted in another chapter. While MACV and the CIA jointly provided the crews, equipment and plans, the missions were controlled by the SOG.

However, the Gulf Incidents were exclusive of OPLAN-34 operations. The fact that the intelligence-gathering Task Force Desoto entered the Gulf on the same day that the OPLAN-34 boats entered was only coincidental.

That the SOG states it was involved in the Tonkin Incidents makes one wonder in what capacity? As reported by the NSA and CIA, the Gulf Incidents were purportedly only between United States Navy ships and the North Vietnamese Navy. How would the Studies and Observations Group be involved? Was the story conveyed to me by the "Dress Rehearsal" pilot in Chapter Three the truth? If so, was there a connection between what he participated in and the SOG?

It was the MACV-SOG that conducted the OPLAN 34-Alpha missions that are described in Chapter Three concerning the Gulf of Tonkin Incident. The OPLAN 34 fast boats were crewed by personnel recruited by the CIA and were under joint control by MACV and the CIA. The SOG was the MACV operating arm for clandestine operations.

In 1965, the SOG also conducted reconnaissance missions on the ground in Southern Laos to observe the NVN use of the HCMT System. The operation using American troops was known as "Shining Brass" and its equivalent using all-Vietnamese recon units was known as "Leaping Lena."

A similar cross-border recon operation was initiated in 1967 by SOG into Cambodia called "Daniel Boone." This operation was augmented by the support of Huey gunships and USAF Special Operation Squadrons called "Green Hornets."

In 1969, "Commando Hunt" was an SOG anti-infiltration effort in Southern Laos controlled from Danang and a similar effort in Cambodia controlled from Ban Me Thuot.

The SOG was a large operation. While authorized 394 Americans, the units and elements included: 1,041 US Army troops, 476 US Air Force personnel, 17 Marine troops, 7 CIA paramilitaries with support from

3,068 Special Commando troops and 5,402 South Vietnamese and "third-country" civilian employees. The number of military personnel and civilians, either assigned or working for MACV-SOG, totaled 10,210.

"HEAVY CHAIN":

Another of the MACV-SOG operations involved use of four modified USAF C-130Es and two A-26s also modified for special operations. The aircraft were assigned to the 1198th Operational, Evaluation and Training Squadron based at Norton AFB in Southern California.

In December, 1964, the C-130Es were transferred to the CIA and were sanitized by being stripped of all identifying markers and plates to ensure deniability if the aircraft were lost on discrete operations. According to a participating pilot, USAF Brigadier General (ret.) Dan Pemberton (USAFA 62), the aircraft were loaded with special equipment including: terrain following radar for night or inclement weather missions; Inertial Navigation Systems (INS) which were completely internal and had the ability to navigate to specific sites by coordinates with no need to rely on external navigation aids; electronic eavesdropping and jamming equipment plus two that were modified for 250KIAS airdrops. Several had the Fulton Recovery System equipment installed. The C-130s were primarily used for night missions in Laos.

In June, 1967, the A-26s started low-level dropping of supplies at night to CIA-related forces in Laos. Also in 1967, the modified C-130Es began operations utilizing USAF aircrews wearing civilian clothing without carrying any identifying documentation. This operation, called "Heavy Chain," was created for "unconventional warfare" and flew a variety of missions.

One of those bizarre missions involved overflying Burma (Myanmar) for night landings in India out of their base at Tahkli, Thailand. The ground crews supporting these very clandestine missions were reported by participating CIA operatives as Tibetans. The participating Air Force pilots were as confused at this as the author.

CIA IN PARAMILITARY AIR OPERATIONS — FROM THE "SECRET WAR" TO THE "HORSE SOLDIERS":

The success of the CIAs use of airpower in paramilitary operations is mixed. Much more recently than Laos, the "Agency" was involved in the hugely successful initial military actions in Afghanistan, as detailed in the excellent book on the clandestine battle called "The Horse Soldiers." Military specialists from multiple services and agencies were part of a force of about fifty. The specialists included Navy Seals, Army Delta Force, CIA Paramilitary and others. This tiny handful of troops initially won the Afghan War. They accomplished it by essentially acting as ground-based Forward Air Controllers moving with the tribal forces and directing American airpower against the forces of the Taliban.

In Laos, although there were mistakes made by both the CIA and the military, the loss of the SEA War was the fault of our civilian leadership and not the fault of the CIA involvement any more than it was the fault of our military. The clandestine war in Laos was only a part of the overall operation and its success or failure was dependent on the outcome of the larger war in South Vietnam. The use of the CIA created divided command and control, which was detrimental to the overall effort, but that was the fault of the civilian control and not the CIA. They did their best and were under many of the same constraints as our military.

Airpower alone cannot win a war. To win, we need to have sufficient and capable forces on the ground to occupy. In the case of Laos, we needed substantial ground forces to block the HCM Trail System and stop the flow of supplies to the Viet Cong and the North Vietnamese Army troops operating in South Vietnam and Central Laos. We needed friendly forces at the points of acceptance of supplies in North Vietnam. The very fact that the United States made Laos the most bombed country in the history of aerial warfare attests to the need to have forces on the ground. We accomplished nothing positive with our massive bombing campaign.

When Kennedy made the initial decision not to use American ground troops in Laos, the eventual failure of the Laotian portion of the mission was guaranteed. The massive bombing was not supporting a large enough and capable enough force on the ground to sufficiently influence the course of events.

What was the purpose of our subterfuge in the aftermath of our signing of the 1962 Geneva Accords on Laos? The North Viets had violated the Accords literally before the ink was even dry. In effect, they nullified the Accords. We had aerial photos of their Laotian troop concentrations and should have made the North Viet violations public. Why didn't we?

Why create secret ground and air units? Just who were we trying to misinform and why? We were justified in the utilization of much larger ground forces that could have blocked the HCMT flow of supplies rather than trying to rely on a sophisticated air campaign that, in the end, resulted in failure.

Control of the air is needed to insure victory, but only if there are sufficient forces on the ground. Control of the air allows us to interdict their supply lines, supply warehousing, transportation, communications, radar, command and control and war-making capacity. It allows us to support our ground forces from the air and deny the same interdiction and close-air-support to the enemy. Our best chance for victory in any war relies on the coordinated and sufficient efforts of all our forces: land, sea, air and, if necessary, space.

THE PSYCHOLOGY OF THE LAOTIAN & NORTHERN AIR CAMPAIGNS:

Regarding Laos, there is a significant lesson to be learned by our huge use of bombing in a failed war. Other than angering the Laotians, what did the bombing accomplish? There is sufficient evidence that heavy bombing does not necessarily weaken the resolve of a people. Instead, it often strengthens it.

During World War II, the heavy German bombing of London famously strengthened the resolve of the British. Did the heavy American bombing of the Germans weaken their resolve? If it did, there is scant evidence to prove it. There were no known demonstrations of their populace against the war and their war production actually increased during the heaviest stages of the combined Anglo-American bombing campaign.

The use of airpower did cause Japan to surrender, but only because of the use of the Atom Bomb. The resolve of the Japanese themselves was still strong.

If the anger shown by the Laotians against downed American pilots is any indication, the most bombed nation in the history of aerial warfare still showed strong resolve.

In the 1990s, former Defense Secretary Robert McNamara ventured to Hanoi to discuss the war with his former enemies. He asked General Giap, leader of the enemy forces, whether the bombing campaign against the North had significantly weakened the resolve of the North Viet people. He was greatly surprised when Giap replied that the bombing had the opposite effect and actually strengthened the resolve of his countrymen. The results of the war seemed to validate his statement.

McNamara, as stated in the USAF Rules of Engagement documents, indicated that he felt a prime reason for "Rolling Thunder" was the positive effect that the bombing campaign would have on the population of the South. Again, he was mistaken. How could a major objective of our bombing campaign against the North possibly be a morale booster, as stated by McNamara, to those Vietnamese in the South who were also victims of the same bombing?

From what I saw of the South Vietnamese, they were a collection of diverse groups and not a unified people. Most were just poor, uneducated peasants that wanted to be left alone. The reaction of the Southerners to our bombing was predictable. The South Vietnamese had no love for a country that continually bombed and tore up their country. To so many of them, we were another Western country trying to impose our will on a poor Asian nation.

> *"It had all the earmarks of a CIA operation; the bomb killed everybody in the room except the intended target."*
>
> William F. Buckley Jr.

CHAPTER NINETEEN

"Eyes in the Sky"

Forward Air Control and Clandestine Conflict

"Those who cannot remember the past are condemned to repeat it."

George Santayana

Forward air control is provided for ground troops in close-air-support to ensure that strikes hit the intended targets and that the strikes do not injure or kill friendly troops or civilians. The task is carried out by a forward air controller, who can either be on the ground or in a fixed or rotary-winged aircraft circling within visual distance.

The use of forward air controllers (FACs) in SEA was essential due to the dense jungle terrain that made target identification very difficult. High performance fighter-bombers often fly too fast to properly pick up jungle targets and distinguish between friendly and enemy troops and potential civilians. The close-air-support of friendly troops in SEA made the use of FACs mandatory in Laos and South Vietnam. For a time, FAC control was used in Tally Ho, but that was changed when the Triple A became more intense in the North Vietnamese Panhandle.

FACs in SEA were either flying in light planes with good visibility or on the ground with the troops, usually at battalion level. There was not one FAC-controlled mission that I flew in SEA that did not have an airborne controller. Ground controllers were assigned to Army divisions, but they must have handled propeller strikes because I never talked to one over the radio.

With the exception of Laotian missions, the Air Force FACs in SEA usually flew alone, which was different than the Army observer aircraft. The US Army also flew O-1s as did the Air Force, but they usually had a pilot and an officer observer, called an Air Liaison Officer or ALO. At the time I was flying and fighting in SEA, the O-1 Bird Dog was the aircraft of choice and the FACs did a splendid job of identifying potential targets and controlling airstrikes.

There were no obvious criteria for selection of airborne-controller pilots, but ground controllers were usually chosen from among the fighter pilot fraternity. MacDill pilots were occasionally chosen by Air Force personnel for assignment to Army battalions and MacDill was a favorite location to select FACs for the Army First Air Cavalry Division, known as the 1st Air Cav. This was the Army's first full-helicopter division and they were stationed near the coast at An Khe in the Central Highlands.

After my graduation from the US Army's parachute training, I was designated as a "Jump FAC." On one occasion, I participated in a training operation in Florida where I was assigned to an Army Battalion and acted as a ground FAC. The fact that I had become "one of them" by becoming a paratrooper did help.

Operationally, the practicality of parachuting in to a forward ground operation was questionable. In this particular operation, I controlled F-4C drops in a heavily wooded area. As I watched the F-4s approach, I imagined myself in their cockpits with the visual of the forest below. My commands to them might be, "turn right 10 degrees" or similar directives. Since the pilots might not have a visual of the target, I would line-them-up and might transmit, "Drop on my command...Ready...drop." Visualizing the trajectories of the dropped munitions was essential. It helped to have a fighter pilot controlling those strikes.

Sometimes the presence of Air Force pilots within Army battalions created unintended situations. The 1st Air Cav got into some rough fighting. Twice, to my knowledge, Air Force pilots selected as ground FACs from MacDill got into firefights where all the rest of the Army officers in a battalion were either killed or wounded. This left an untrained pilot leading a battalion-sized force against the VC or NVN regular army units. One of our guys ended up in hand-to-hand combat with a VC.

What the airborne FACs did was officially called "visual reconnaissance." They were assigned sectors and as they flew constantly over their sector they became familiar with the terrain, and learned to detect any changes that might indicate enemy forces or positions hidden under the jungle canopy.

The Bird Dogs (FAC aircraft) were slow and unarmored. It was very dangerous work, but the enemy usually did not fire at them to avoid discovery. However, there were 223 airborne FACs killed in the War. Often, the FACs would visit Cam Ranh Officer's Club and we would get a chance to socialize with the voices we heard on our missions. It was good to match a face with a voice, which provided a bond if and when we connected on another strike.

Initially, the FAC aircraft were equipped with three different radios. One was an FM radio for constant contact with the ground forces. Another was a UHF radio for the fighters and a third was a VHF for contact with the Air Force Tactical Control operation. All three radios were in constant use to ensure coordination of air support requests and approvals and to properly brief the fighter pilots when they came in on a target.

When a FAC spotted a potential target, he radioed the area control and stated the nature of the target and, if necessary, stated the type of munitions that were acceptable or preferable. The area control then found a flight with a load of munitions and enough gas to make the target and get back to base plus an alternate airfield, if necessary.

FACs were concerned with destruction of the targets they had selected, sometimes days before accepting a flight of fighter-bombers. This often might compete with a flight's concern for fuel remaining.

FIGURING FUEL:

When planning a flight, commercial pilots as well as combat pilots figure the fuel required for the mission or trip and allow enough excess fuel to fly to an alternate airfield in case the landing runway or airfield is unusable. There are many reasons that a runway might be unusable in addition to bad weather. In a combat environment, runways often might become unusable. Aircraft crash on runways. Aircraft may lose munitions on runways. Many events require time to clear the runways before landings are resumed.

In SEA, the often very heavy monsoonal rains could close an airfield. We had it happen at Cam Ranh several times in 1966. The monsoons could create visibility problems down to almost zero-zero conditions. In those situations, Cam Ranh would close and alert inbound flights to seek alternates. Thus, during any combat mission, the flight leaders needed to monitor the fuel condition of each aircraft in a flight. A lead would continually recalculate fuel necessary to: complete a mission, fly back to a base, and then, if necessary, fly to a secondary base.

That did not always work. As evidenced by my combat diary, flights may be tasked for different targets several times during a single mission. Diverts were common. The flight lead always had to refigure his flight's fuel anytime a divergence from the planned flight occurred. Overuse of afterburner when returning from long missions was a major culprit of lost, but sometimes needed fuel.

When I was diverted to try to find a VNAF pilot who had been shot down in the Delta, I searched and searched until my planned fuel to get to an alternate was exhausted. The desire of all of us to rescue a fellow pilot also caused my flight to exhaust the fuel needed to get back to Cam Ranh. We then calculated how much time we had left to search if we landed at the nearest airfield, in this case Bien Hoa. The situation always dictated and sometimes pre-planning had to be scrapped, if warranted. It is always a pilot's decision.

The in-flight loss of alternate fuel sometimes resulted in dangerous situations. When flying in England, I participated in a flight where our alternate fuel was exhausted. When I returned to RAF Woodbridge, Suffolk County was experiencing a very heavy snowstorm and no snow-removal equipment was operating. The runways could not be seen. Everything was covered in a thick blanket of snow.

Flying a precision approach, in this case a Ground Controlled Approach (GCA), I landed on a wide expanse of white without ever seeing the runway. Many of us had to do the same whenever the situation dictated.

In Vietnam, the plan was for FAC requests to be made to control, control then contacted a flight lead to give target information. Often, the way it worked was just the opposite. The flight lead would be the first to contact. Sometimes a FAC would contact control and no flights would be available. Then, the FAC would wait until a flight was located. Often, locating a flight consisted of waiting for flights to check in with loads that were not expended over their intended targets. This often happened. Depending on the nature of the target, sometimes alert flights were launched in response to a request from a FAC. The usual alert load was napalm and the gun, which was perfect for close-air-support in the event ground troops got involved in a firefight.

Normally, if a combat flight was unable to expend its load of munitions, it was caused by a variety of reasons. Twice I was targeted against a bridge in the North only to find the bridge underwater. Sometimes a target area would be socked-in by weather. Sometimes a sector FAC could not become airborne and the particular target would have to be aborted.

When a Northern flight was unable to accomplish its primary mission, it often would turn south and cross the borders back into South Vietnam with a full load of bombs or other munitions. When that happened, the flight lead would call an area Control Center and tell him his situation. That information would include the flight location, munitions load and how much fuel he had remaining (stated as allowable time-on-target). The Control Center would then try to find a FAC with a target. Often the FAC would have called the Center to make a request long before the fighters offered their services. Frequently, when flights reported in to a Control Center that they had ordnance to expend, there were no waiting FAC requests. In that case, FACs tried to "scare up" targets. This was when it could get a bit dicey. In that situation, FACs occasionally would find very questionable targets. One that comes to mind was when we were targeted against a lone farmer tilling his field. On that particular flight, I was lead. I intentionally threw my bombs in the jungle a safe distance away from the farmer. Without anything being said over the radio, the other three pilots followed suit. It was a disgusting and unmilitary target.

After a successful attack that was FAC-controlled, the FAC would then fly back to the target to assess the damage and would relay his bomb-damage-assessment (BDA) to the flight lead as the flight departed. In high-threat areas, the FACs occasionally did not get close enough to the target to make an accurate visual assessment. In that case, we often would get estimates.

Due to the usual heavy jungle foliage, it was often necessary for a FAC to mark the target with some type of white smoke. This could also be due to poor visibility or an obscuration of the target. Occasionally, we would arrive at a target after another flight had hit and the area would be obscured by bomb smoke and tree foliage. Often the first aircraft in a flight would create so much smoke that it would obscure the target for the rest of the flight. Smoke and foliage were the usual common culprits for visual target acquisition.

Initial marking of the target by the FAC would either be a smoke grenade or what we called a "Willy Pete," which was a white phosphorous rocket. This created white smoke that really stood out against the dark-green tree canopy. The FAC would call out direction and meters of the target from the smoke. This worked out very well, even though we could not see a target and would be dropping on what we saw as the foliage of the green jungle canopy. We relied heavily on the FACs.

During 1966, there were 250 FACs operating in South Vietnam and Thailand. The following year, that number had more than doubled and the pilots were flying more than 10,000 sorties a month.

Organizationally, the FACs flew as part of Tactical Air Support Squadrons (TASS). The TASSs were based at the following locations during my combat year of 1966: 19th TASS based at Bien Hoa; 20th TASS based at Danang; 21st based at Nha Trang and the 22nd at Binh Thuy. The 504th Tactical Air Support Group operated in Thailand. The 20th TASS was later moved to Chu Lai to support the American and 1st Air Cav Divisions.

HISTORY:

The first FAC to be killed, along with his Vietnamese counterpart, was in South Vietnam flying out of Bien Hoa Air Base on October 15, 1962. By the end of the war, there were many more. The locations where they were shot down and killed may be of interest: Laos- 55; North Vietnam- 6 with one taken as POW; Thailand- 5; Cambodia- 8 and the rest, 149, in SVN. This only covers official Air Force FACs and not Raven or other clandestine units.

In 1961, the Air Force sent five FACs to Bien Hoa AB to train the South Vietnamese Air Force in directing strikes while flying the O-1 Bird Dogs. Each of the FACs was a fighter pilot with experience in air-to-ground delivery. The American pilots flew with South Vietnamese FACs but only the South Viets could control strikes, which had to be approved by the SVN government.

In December 1961, the Tactical Air Control System was established as part of Air Force Operation "Farm Gate" to handle air operations, which included airborne forward air control.

In February 1962, an Air Operations Center (AOC) was set up at Tan Son Nhut Air Base, located near Saigon. The AOC was the center of the command and control network for the FACs. On April 15, 1962, a Marine Observation Squadron entered Vietnam and began to fly with the Air Force. They served as de facto FACs.

The initial performance of the South Vietnamese FACs was poor. However, American FACs were also experiencing problems with rough terrain, limited sight lines and problems with communication. The Air Force determined the need to expand those participating in the FAC network to make it more reliable. To that end, they initially set up Tactical Air Control Parties, which were the predecessor of the later-developed Tactical Air Control Centers.

In early 1963, the war escalated and the VNAF needed more FACs. Additionally, the VC began to attack truck convoys and FACs were tasked to protect them. The FAC response was very successful as no escorted convoy was ambushed during the early part of the year.

To Americans in 1963, there was no knowledge of our involvement in any war in Southeast Asia. No announcements were forthcoming from our government. It was not until the August, 1964 Gulf of Tonkin Incidents that any announcements were made. The entire effort in Laos and the rest of SEA, starting in 1957, was unknown. Presidents Eisenhower, Kennedy and Johnson were all very quiet.

To facilitate the expansion of FAC activity, the USAF activated the 19th Tactical Air Support Squadron at Bien Hoa in July. The 19th trained SVN pilots in forward air control, visual reconnaissance, combat support and how to properly observe. After a year, the 19th turned its equipment over to the VNAF (South Vietnamese Air Force).

THE TRUONG SON STRATEGIC SUPPLY ROUTE:

In 1961, a decision was made in North Vietnam to significantly upgrade a system of transport routes into South Vietnam. The route system had actually been in operation since 1954 and was a primary reason for the presence of North Vietnamese or Viet Minh troops in Laos. After the Geneva Accords split Vietnam into two countries, the Viet Minh never missed a beat. After Dien Bien Phu, they continued the sustained effort to unify their country and that took the form of supplying an armed insurrection against what they considered a Western puppet regime in South Vietnam.

The major construction effort in Laos took them until 1964, which resulted in 3,000 miles of roads and trails that entered southern Laos from three passes through the Annamite Mountains in North Vietnam: Keo Neua Pass; Mu Gia Pass and Ban Karai Pass. After 1964, the construction continued at a reduced rate so that by wars-end, the trail and road system had expanded to over 12,000 miles.

All of the routes through the Annamite converged at Tchepone, Laos. The North Viets supported the vast army of builders by shipping supplies by air to the Tchepone Airport, which also was a visible morale booster for the laborers in the difficult clearing and construction.

The North Viets named the system the Truong Son Strategic Supply Route, although it was a system of routes instead of one route. It became known to the rest of the world as the Ho Chi Minh Trail.

Part of the road and trail system went into and through Cambodia, where the Communists stockpiled large amounts of military supplies. The North Viets were ingenious in their creation of different methods of transport. As mentioned in other chapters, they employed pack mules, bicycles and even elephants. The bicycles were retrofitted to carry up to 400 pounds of supplies per bike. It might even be said that they invented the Mountain Bike with its wide tires.

Worth repeating is the ignorant strategic decision by McNamara that concentrated our huge effort against their dispersal system instead of their supply concentrations in the north.

The FACs controlled much of the effort to destroy supplies on the HCMT, but there were other efforts and operations carried out by every military branch of our armed services, plus the DOD, CIA and others. It was a huge effort, largely controlled electronically by Task Force Alpha at Nakhon Phenom, described in another chapter.

Our combat efforts against the trail were both day and night operations. The 606th Special Operations Squadron flew black C-123Ks out of NKP against the Trail at night. Sometimes they had the support of FACs such as "Nail" to drop flares and offer other assistance. Their job was "killing trucks at night on the HCMT."

The Cambodian access to SVN from the HCMT was normally along the northern border separating Cambodia from South Vietnam. This access included a major road crossing that led directly to Pleiku in the SVN Central Highlands. West of a line connecting Pleiku with Ban Me Thuot, another major SVN town, lie four rivers that cross the border. Rivers offer an exceptional ability to transport heavy loads with the ease and speed of boats. The Viets floated barrels of supplies at night down the rivers from Laos for pickup downstream in South Vietnam. Rivers also provided relatively safe crossings at night.

The United States Army established a string of Special Forces Camps along the border in an attempt to stop this cross-border traffic. Many small, dirt airstrips accompanied this effort and provided access for Army spotter planes, Air Commando prop fighters, VNAF props and Forward Air Controllers.

In 1965, I attended AGOS (Air-Ground Operations School). This was a joint Army- Air Force school based at jungle-shrouded Eglin Air Force Base just outside of Fort Walton Beach, Florida. Eglin is a huge base with lots of auxiliary fields. Hurlburt Field is designated Eglin Auxiliary Field Number 10 and was the headquarters of the Air Commandos. While at AGOS, I visited Hurlburt and talked two Commando pilots into allowing me to fly with them on range missions.

It was slow flying as co-pilot on the lumbering A-1Hs. Pattern speed was 160 knots and while in a bombing dive, the speed stayed at 160. The large engine nacelle and propeller acted as a giant speed brake. One of the two pilots that I flew with at Hurlburt was later killed flying strikes for the Commandos in SEA.

THE NORTHERN LAOTIAN ROAD SYSTEM:

The northern part of the Laotian road system did not go through the Annamite Mountains, but instead directed supplies into northern and central Laos. This was not the Truong Son or HCMT road system but, for lack of a better name, it could be called the Northern Laotian Road System.

Instead of providing supplies and troops to South Vietnam and what was known to most as the Vietnamese War, the northern roads provided supplies to the Pathet Lao and North Vietnamese Army that controlled certain areas of Laos and protected that road system in the Laotian War.

Air Force Operation "Barrel Roll" was tasked against this part of Laos that was centered on the Plain of Jars. This part of the Laotian "Secret War" was essentially a civil war involving several armies and pseudo armies, including the North Vietnamese Army, in force.

The northern road system originates in Hanoi, with two roads connecting Hanoi with Dien Bien Phu and Sam Neua. Dien Bien Phu was the site of the titanic battle that ended the First Indochina War. Dien Bien Phu, where the French Foreign Legion surrendered, is located just across the border from Laos and the North Vietnamese road through Dien Bien Phu connects with a Chinese road on the Laotian side. That roadway connects China with northern Laos, Burma and Thailand in the mountainous north of Laos. China must have felt that this area was its to control, because Chinese MIGs patrolled the skies above this portion of Laos without contest from American or Laotian fighters. Chinese troops were also reported to be protecting their roads in Laos from the ground. With all that attention, China must have considered it a major strategic asset.

For the North Viets, the more important roadway was the one going through Sam Neua in northeastern Laos. This route connected Hanoi directly with the contested Plain of Jars, where the Communist Pathet Lao fought the Royal Lao and Neutralist Armies. This was the area of northern Laos that saw most of the military action. This was also the area that saw the greatest use of the Raven FACs, the NKP Air Commandos and the CAS and CIA combat aircraft.

Sam Neua was the capital of the Pathet Lao. The road through Sam Neua, with its airfield, runs directly to Ban Ban. Similar to Tchepone in the south, Ban Ban was the major crossroads for the NVN supply network in the north. It lays just to the east of the Tranninh Plateau on which sits the Plain of Jars. Roads running west out of Ban Ban connect it to the modern capital at Vientiane as well as the ancient capital at Luang Prabang.

A further supply connection was provided by Hanoi through the northern part of the Annamites. It is the roadway through Barthelemy Pass that connects Muong Sen in NVN with Nong Het in Laos. The road continues from Nong Het directly to Ban Ban.

THE SIHANOUK ROAD:

There was another branch of the North Vietnamese supply system called the Sihanouk Road or Sihanouk Trail, which brought supplies up from the Port of Kompong Son on the Gulf of Thailand or as sometimes called, the Gulf of Siam. Siam is the ancient name for Thailand.

Depending on who is doing the talking, the name of the series of access routes has been called both the Sihanouk Trail and the Sihanouk Road. Whatever the name, the system was effective and allowed the enemy a different entry that was more or less "off the radar" for most of our counter-supply operations.

Kompong Son Bay lies a relatively short distance from the swampy southern edge of the South Vietnamese Mekong Delta. The Road may have gotten its name from the village of Sihanoukville, which lies on the extreme southern edge of the Bay. Sihanouk was also the name of one of Cambodia's former rulers. The Bay offered shelter for offloading of supply ships that came from North Vietnam and from the many other Communistic nations participating in the SEA War.

The Road takes two routes from Kampong Son Bay, one to the capital at Phnom Penh and the other along the Gulf of Siam directly to Kampot and then to the coastal border village of Ha Tien. This offers the most likely routing of seaborne supplies to the VC.

The Delta region of SVN also offered the border crossing of three major rivers, two of which were branches of the mighty Mekong. River access to SVN promised easier transport for much larger cargo loads.

The central part of the Cambodian-South Vietnam border offers five road crossings. This routing was probably shared by transport from the Ho Chi Minh Trail system to the north and the Sihanouk Road system to the south.

As long as the United States was forced to interdict the movement of supplies "in transit" instead of at the source, the use of Forward Air Controllers to counter this vast network of supply access to South Vietnam was essential.

FACS IN LAOS & CAMBODIA:

Everyone who flew in Laos, including the 606th guys, was aware of the very dangerous situation they faced if they were downed for any reason in Laos. As mentioned in another chapter, the "Sandy" rescue guys told us at Cam Ranh that the Laotians would often attack downed airmen with machetes and the Sandy crews would not find much left. That certainly accounts for the absence of many pilots known to be prisoners of the Pathet Lao.

Colonel John Halliday, a member of the 606th at NKP, stated: "They don't take prisoners in northern Laos. Those people have never heard of the Geneva Convention. They kill you outright in terrible, violent ways."

For the FACs flying in Laos, this posed a critical problem. The extent of the American bombing of Laos and the FACs that controlled that bombing has been kept as secret as the war itself. According to Wikipedia, "Laos became the most bombed nation in history. The BBC agrees that approximately the same tonnage of bombs was dropped on Laos as was dropped in the entirety of World War II. As a result, 20% of the Laotian population became refugees, largely relocating because of the bombing." Every Laotian bomb was controlled by a FAC. As a result, the clandestine American "Raven" pilots flying in Laos had the highest FAC casualty rate of the entire SEA War at 50%.

Casualty figures are usually reported as including both killed, injured and wounded. Sometimes those figures may include missing-in-action. Some consider casualties as only meaning those killed-in-action. The initial records regarding casualty losses in the Korean War incorrectly included killed and injured from the entire Pacific Region. Casualty figures from the various battles in our Civil War are not consistent and have often led to confusion and misunderstandings of the comparative intensity of engagements.

In 1964, the U.S. obtained permission for aerial interdiction strikes along the just completed Ho Chi Minh Trail. Since the U.S., due to the Geneva Accords, could not legally send military personnel to Laos, the USAF initially enlisted what were called Combat Controllers dressed as civilians to direct the air strikes. Their call sign was "Butterfly" and they flew in unmarked U.S. Army aircraft piloted by Air America crews that were contracted to the CIA.

The supposed Gulf of Tonkin Incident in 1964, galvanized American military action in SEA. The number of FACs increased dramatically and, as of January 1965, there were 144 USAF airborne FACs in addition to 68 VNAF FACs operating in the combat theater. The number, if any, of Laotian Air Force FACs flying at that time is unknown.

Our Rules of Engagement mandated a FAC to direct all air-delivered ordnance expended in South Vietnam as well as Laos. By April, 1965, five Tactical Air Support Squadrons, which included the FACs, composed the Air Force combat units of the 504th Tactical Air Support Group. The Group's main purpose was logistics, maintenance and administrative functions. But they also contained 250 Bird Dog FACs for all of South Vietnam.

The Bird Dogs were supposed to be assigned, two each, to the Army maneuver battalions, but instead were assigned to brigades. The FACs lived and worked with the brigades and battalions that needed them for operations.

In 1965, Operation "Steel Tiger" was initiated for the southern portion of the Trail and Operation "Barrel Roll" was started for the Northern Laotian Road System. The northern operation supported the Laotian forces fighting the Communists as well as the interdiction on the northern Trail. All of these strikes were FAC directed.

By September 1965, the first Airborne Command and Control Center was launched. The ABCCC became the inflight nerve center for the Vietnamese & Laotian Air Wars. It kept track of all aircraft and served to ensure the proper execution of the fragged missions. It also acted as a central control agency in the diversion of the strike force to secondary and sometimes more lucrative targets. As it expanded, the ABCCC became a 24-hour-per-day program directing all air activity in the war.

In April, 1966 the "Hillsboro" ABCCC directed my rescue from the hills of southern Laos near Route 9 of the HCMT. In 1966, the Air Force increased FAC areas to include the Covey region, in Route Pack One, of North Vietnam. FACs in Covey directed air strikes, but occasionally adjusted gunfire from Navy ships if a Marine artillery spotter was flying with them. As part of the Covey effort, the Marines pioneered the Fast FACs in Vietnam using two-seat F9F Panther jets. Once the Covey area was developed by the Fast FACs, the Marines flew them deep into the HCMT System.

By 1966, the USAF FACs began controlling strikes against the HCMT from both east and west. Most of the strikes from the east came from Cam Ranh Bay and Danang. Those from the west came out of Thailand, unless they were Royal Laotian Air Force prop fighters, which very rarely operated in Southern Laos.

During 1966, another FAC unit was created for Laos as a successor to the "Butterfly" program. This program was known as the "Raven" FACs. The Ravens, which are described later in this chapter, were temporarily assigned to the 56th Special Ops Wing at Udorn, Thailand and operated throughout Laos. They carried no identification and wore civilian clothing. They flew unmarked O-1s, U-17s and T-28s, with Laotian Commanders in their back seats.

The difference between the Raven FACs and the Covey and Nail FACs was that the Ravens could attack any target throughout Laos, while the others had to operate in their assigned areas.

The Air Force effort to increase the insufficient number of FACs continued until full-manning was finally achieved in December 1969. The Air Force effort got help from other sources. The Marine FAC contingent came ashore in its entirety in May, 1966. In June, the Australian FACs began their integration into the American FAC program, which would continue until December 1971. New Zealand sent several FACs to join the Aussies, who were with the Americans.

The US Army had at least seven aviation companies of O-1 Bird Dogs operating in Vietnam. They directed strikes occasionally as well as performing their primary job of artillery direction and visual recce. The control of airstrikes by these Army troops was not authorized, but was done anyway due to the scarcity of Air Force FACs.

The Marine FACs were called Tactical Air Coordinators- Airborne or TACAs, and operated in support of Marine F-4B air units stationed primarily at Danang and Chu Lai. Much of the Marine close-air-support work occurred in and south of the DMZ. They, along with the Air Force, were really stretched to provide the necessary control for the increasing number of airstrikes. Marine F-4Bs provided the majority of close-air-support for their ground units but our Air Force F-4Cs also gave supplemental help, especially off of Alert when Marine ground units were engaged in serious firefights.

The U.S. Army 220th Recon Airplane Company "Catkillers" operated under the control of the 3rd Marine Division in the I Corp area and their airborne controllers were the only authorized Army units to direct airstrikes. They were given the Marine designation of TACA.

Sustained Cambodian air operations started on April 30, 1970, when American and Vietnamese ground forces attacked Cambodian territory in order to destroy VC destined supplies and areas of VC troop sanctuary. The initial air strikes occurred in January, 1969 when over 100 B-52s on a single strike dropped a prodigious number of bombs on Cambodia.

In 1970, The ground forces eventually withdrew, but the FAC-supported bombing strikes continued. A detachment of the 19th TASS, out of Bien Hoa, patrolled Cambodia in support of friendly Cambodian troops using the call sign "Rustic." For communication with the French-speaking Cambodes, the Rustic FACs flew with French speaking interpreters. Rustic FACs continued to support the non-communist Cambodian forces until termination of the air strikes on August 15, 1973.

"COVEY" FACS:

When our fighter flights were connected by radio to FACs and heard the call sign "Covey," we knew that we would be given targets in the southern portion of Route Pack One, which was part of the Southern Panhandle of North Vietnam. Very occasionally, the Coveys directed strikes in Tiger Hound.

The US Marines also flew with Covey, usually in the Demilitarized Zone (DMZ) or in the coastal areas near Vinh Linh. The Finger Lakes region of Route Pack One was a Covey-controlled area which was repeatedly hit by the 12th TFW. The Finger Lakes were deadly to the 12th. Twice I was targeted against the Lakes at the end of a bombing "pause" and I approached the targets with dread. The Finger Lakes claimed half of my "C" Flight pilots on one attack and Cam Ranh lost several other planes nearby.

Most of the time when we hit the Lakes, it was disarmingly quiet. They had a lot of guns, but seldom used them because of holdups in their ammo distribution network. After bombing halts or pauses, they were always ready and their AAA guns were loaded. On those occasions, all hell broke loose and flak was heavy and often intense.

It was on one of those deadly Covey missions that our FAC had part of his wing shot off at the same time that my lead picked up a shell through his wing. I was continually showered with pieces of flak bouncing off my canopy as the Covey FAC barely made it back to Dong Ha, just south of the DMZ.

During the war, the Coveys lost 30 pilots killed while flying out of Danang and Pleiku. Their losses were more than any other FAC call sign, including Raven. While the Ravens had a 50% casualty rate, there were many more Coveys and thus they had more opportunities for losses.

DOG FACS:

The 12th Wing worked with the "Hound Dog" FACs on many of our missions against Tiger Hound. "Hound Dogs" and their neighbors, the "Bird Dogs," operated in both Tiger Hound and across the border in South Vietnam, often in the Khe Sanh area next to the border.

The Hound Dogs controlled our Laotian strikes centered in the Ban Houie Sane area, which included all three Laotian Tiger Hound airfields at Saravane, Attopeu and Tchepone that were under enemy control. Attopeu was heavily defended with AAA, but Tchepone was the heaviest defended area that I struck in Laos.

All the HCMT routes converged on Tchepone. The North Vietnamese Army fiercely protected those crossroads and Tchepone had a heavier defensive reaction than many of the targets we hit in North Vietnam.

In fact, hitting Tchepone felt like hitting the far North. It was surrounded by AA Artillery guns and they never suffered for a lack of artillery shells. Mobile SAM sites were reported to be located in the area. It was never completely known if a SAM site was manned or not, unless of course they were firing at you. The SAM sites were surrounded by heavy, automatically integrated small-to-medium caliber AAA guns, so the danger in getting close to a SAM site was twofold.

Due to the heavy defensive fire, the Hound Dogs understandably only controlled our Tchepone strikes from a distance and usually could not provide Bomb Damage Assessment (BDA). Sky Spot radar control sometimes sent my flights to Tchepone to drop from altitude.

Since our aircraft were not equipped with the electronic sensors that warned other base aircraft of radar paints and radar lock-on's by enemy ground and airborne radars, we had no way of knowing if MIGs, SAMs or AAA were locked on and prepared to fire. When dropping bombs from straight and level with surface-to-air missile sites just below us, we were very "alert." The 85 and 100 mm anti-aircraft guns could reach far above our maximum operating altitudes. Our Intelligence in Vietnam reported that the 100s could reach 100,000 feet, but that has been disputed by other sources.

The Hound Dogs and Bird Dogs were very active during my tour, but were replaced in 1967 after losing a total of 4 Hound Dogs and 7 Bird Dogs.

"NAIL" FACS:

The "Nails" operated out of Nakhon Phenom with the 23rd Tactical Support Squadron. NKP was large enough that it was able to support many different and varied missions for Thailand and Laos. Supporting the clandestine wars were units of the USAF Air Commandos flying prop fighter-bombers. Five Air Commando Squadrons operated out of NKP, often with the Nails against the HCMT. Air Commando Squadrons at NKP included the 1st, 22nd, 602nd, 606th, and 609th.

Of interest, there was a special operation located in the jungle about 300 yards off the base at NKP. It was called "Task Force Alpha" or TFA. TFA was a "geek" outfit that had a facility that rivaled what I saw with the CIA in the jungles outside Udorn. TFA monitored the HCMT. It was a "big screen" control with electronic and visual monitoring stations. Reportedly, TFA included deluxe facilities for recreation as well as operation. Cafeterias, bowling alleys and swimming pools were included as part of what the Air Force was providing for its high-tech operators. As I referred to the CIA facility at Udorn as Holiday Inn-Udorn, this USAF facility could be considered The Marriot-Nakhon Phanom.

The "Nails" covered air operations in Steel Tiger, Barrel Roll and into North Vietnam. Research information is very spotty on the Nail FACs. Occasionally on my flights in the North and Laos, we would hear reference to "Nail" Forward Air Controllers. They stayed at NKP for a long time during the war, flying the O-1s, O-2s and the OV-10s.

"Nail" was part of the clandestine war being fought out of Nakhon Phanom. Their missions were east and southeast of the Ravens and they were within easy reach of the northern half of Route Pack One.

"Nail" was initially known as "Gombey." During the Nail transition from O-2s to the OV-10s, it temporarily changed its call sign to "Snort." The Nails shared FAC operations at NKP with the "Candlesticks" of the 606th flying the UC-123Ks. There's was a unique FAC night mission acting out of NKP that acted as a "Flareship" for other fighter-bombers. Some of the transport sized FAC planes, like the UC-123s, actually carried offensive munitions including napalm and participated in the night strikes.

The "Nails" lost almost as many pilots as the Ravens, with 22 killed during their stay at NKP.

RAVEN FACS — THE REAL WILD WEST:

Many Americans can remember Steve Canyon, a mythical character of old who was depicted as a heroic pilot. When FACs were introduced to and schooled about FAC operations in SEA, they were told about a project called "Steve Canyon" and then told nothing else about it. The FAC teachers and trainers were very secretive and none of the questions about what it entailed were ever answered. As intended, it was a mystery fueled by the FAC program. To qualify for the unknown program, a FAC pilot had to have flown a "Bird Dog" O-1 in SEA for a minimum of six months.

After six months in combat, if curiosity got the best of the FACs, they could again ask about the program. Again, they were told next to nothing other than to be asked, "Are you willing to take a chance?" The program might have been Air Force, but its control and implementation was strictly CIA. They wanted cowboy fighter pilots to man their Bird Dogs. Later, they relaxed the fighter pilot requirement, but still wanted the fighter-pilot-types. Fighter- pilot-types who were willing to take chances and fly rough missions, but fly them in a wild west style with no sheriff to tell them how to do it. The CIA screening system tended to select experienced and aggressive FACs who were not very amenable to being restricted by regulations.

Those who said "yes" to the question "are you willing to take a chance," were flown to Udorn RTAFB in the extreme north of Thailand and just 40 miles south of the capital of Laos, Vientiane. Vientiane was due west of the large, clandestine Thai airbase of Nakhon Phanom, or as the Americans liked to call it, NKP.

Background:

On July 23, 1962, the United States and the Democratic Republic of Vietnam (North Vietnam) signed the Geneva Accords guaranteeing the neutrality of the Kingdom of Laos. The Accords called for the withdrawal of all foreign troops from Laos. This was the second set of Geneva Accords regarding the formerly French Indochina. The first was in 1954 and that one established the split of Vietnam into North and South.

Since the defeat of the French at Dien Bien Phu in 1954, North Vietnam had stationed troops in Laos. The United States also had a small number of advisors, which it quickly withdrew from Laos after signing the Accords. However, the North Vietnamese ignored the Accords they had just signed and left over 4,000 of their troops in Laos. They were intent on the maintenance and building of their supply corridor to the South, with eventually became the HCMT. They also were intent on securing a victory for their Communist brothers, the Pathet Lao. The North Vietnamese representatives repeatedly stated that they had "no military presence in Laos" even though the 4,000 troops were still stationed there.

The Laotian government was concerned. The Laotians were a poor and backward people who were no match for the powerful Viet Minh, who had a victorious, large, well-trained and well-equipped army poised on the eastern flank of Laos.

Laotian Prince Souvanna Phouma, the Prime Minister of Laos, was concerned about this violation of the Accords before they even had a chance of implementation. He turned to America and asked for military assistance.

To avoid the appearance of violating the Accords, President John Kennedy directed the USAF to perform covert operations in Laos to counter the North Vietnamese threat.

The problem for Laos and our Air Force was that the North Vietnamese had helped create a Communist insurgency inside Laos in the form of a growing guerrilla army called the Pathet Lao. Together, the troops of the Pathet Lao and the Viet Minh created a very serious threat.

The United State Air Force began to conduct air strikes against Communist military positions, particularly in the Plain of Jars in the North Central part of Laos. These strikes were initially all performed by prop-driven aircraft. It soon became apparent that, for the safety of civilians, some means of control of the air strikes was necessary.

The bombing strikes, which began later in 1962, were assisted by a variety of efforts at control. Ground markers, including bamboo arrows, were sometimes used as were smoke grenades dropped from a hodge-podge of aircraft types. Each was meant to show the pilots flying the strikes where the controllers wanted the bombs. The controllers were coordinating with the rudimentary ground forces and the strikes were in support of ground operations.

The air strikes were sometimes independent operations against known supply depots or encampments. But most of the strikes were in support of Laotian ground troops. This posed a problem as there were a variety of small "armies" operating in the areas of the air strikes.

Hmong, Meo and Lao tribesmen were allied with the Central Intelligence Agency, which had been operating in Laos at least since 1960 and had affiliated airline contractors operating there at least since 1957. The CIA establishment of Air America was partially to provide the transport of food and supplies to the tribesmen. The developed loyalty of both the Meo and Hmong was really directed to the CIA more than it was to the Kingdom of Laos. Another "army" operating in Laos was the Neutralists, who were not allied with either the Royal Lao Army or the Pathet Lao. To further complicate the issue, the Laotians had employed Thai nationals as mercenaries. In 1968, a unit of the Thai Border Police participated in the defense of Lima Site 85, a radar location that supported the air strikes into North Vietnam. The major battle initiated by the North Viets was far from the Thai border and resulted in the largest loss-of-life for USAF ground troops in the entire SEA War.

Those who got involved in the makeshift airstrike control efforts included the Thai nationals and Hmong tribesmen as well as Americans. Most had little or no specialized training in close-air-support of fighter strikes. Both Continental Air Services (CASI) and Air America pilots would sometimes serve as ad hoc Forward Air Controllers and control the Air Force fighter-bomber attacks. While these Americans had no formal training as FACs, they were veterans of air-to-ground operations and proved effective.

The US Army had been lightly involved in Laos for a time prior to the 1962 Accords. Army Airborne Liaison Observers (ALOs), the "Butterflies," flew the slow-flying O-1 Bird Dogs to act as "spotters" for the ground troops. The pilots the ALOs flew with were supposed to be from the Royal Laotian Air Force, but often were CIA-contracted pilots from either Air America or Continental Air Services. In war, pragmatism often rules. The objective was victory and various "non-standard" methods and approaches were used. If the book doesn't work, throw out the book.

With the step-up in military activity created by Kennedy's orders, the Air Force decided to significantly increase its prop-driven air forces. In April 1964, it deployed Detachment 6, 1st Air Commando Wing to Udorn Air Base in Thailand. That decision was followed in 1965 with the establishment of the Headquarters 2nd Air Division/13th Air Force at Udorn.

Soon it was apparent that the Butterflies were not enough. In November 1964, the Air Force sent its first rated officer to augment the Butterflies. He was stationed at LS 36, a dirt strip near Ka Khang in Laos. He directed strikes by Royal Lao Air Force prop fighters, either while riding in an Air America helicopter or from observation posts on mountaintops.

By April 1965, the first night mission was flown over the HCMT by high-performance fighters. The combined Air Force and Navy sortie rate into Laos soon increased to 1,000 per month. That year also saw, "Prairie Fire" teams of Special Forces troops being air dropped into the HCMT. In the escalating conflict, the B-52s struck Mu Gia Pass on December 11, 1965. This attack proved much more effective than the abortive attack against the pass earlier in the year. In April, 1966, the command of 7th/13th Air Force changed to 7th Air Force at Udorn.

The Hatching of the Ravens:

The Raven FAC program was officially "hatched" on May 5, 1966. It began with two pilots on 90-day temporary duty (TDY), working out of borrowed Air America aircraft. The two pilots had been FACs directing airstrikes on both sides of the DMZ. When they returned to their home base at NKP, they were told that the twin sins of unauthorized aerobatics and the destruction of furniture at a party would be forgiven if they volunteered for a secret program. They were later joined by a third pilot and thus began the Raven-flying support of the Royal Lao Army.

As recommended by the CIA, the Raven FACs would be flying and not observing as did the Butterflies. Instead of the Butterflies in the backseats of the fore and aft seated Bird Dog cockpit, Meo interpreters, called Robins, would occupy and act as observers.

The Raven fighter pilots flew in unarmed and unarmored Bird Dogs. They were responsible for: observation and airborne recce; the marking of enemy targets using smoke rockets; the directing of Air Force air strikes onto the marks, and the reporting of bomb damage assessment to the fighters and to ground troops after the strikes.

As any casual reader of this book knows, the military loves to name projects and operations. The Ravens were code-named "Palace Dog," which certainly was in the same kennel as Tiger Hound and the Hound and Bird Dogs.

It was in 1967 that the Palace Dogs really began to bark. The three active Ravens were augmented with three more stationed at NKP that commuted. At the same time, the Air Force supplied Bird Dog aircraft without any markings of national insignia. They were considered "clean" but with slotted receivers capable of mounting any insignia.

By November, the Raven head count had increased to eight. The number would continue to increase to keep up with the swelling tide of Laotian airstrikes, but would never number more than 22 assigned at any one time.

The chronic shortage of Ravens meant that they flew an incredible number of missions and hours, as much as 14 hours in a day. Air Force fighter bases in Thailand and South Vietnam as well as Navy aircraft carriers would send flights to Laos and, due to the lack of available Raven's, had as many as six fighters stacked at various altitudes, waiting for their turn to bomb.

Some Ravens flew until their supply of marking rockets was exhausted and their canopies were filled with grease pencil notes on air strikes. Some returned desperately low in fuel. One pilot ran out of gas and "dead sticked" three times on return from his long missions. Another pilot directed more than 1,000 sorties of tactical air, flying more than 280 hours in a single month. That is an incredible number of hours anytime and when one considers it was combat, the number bordered on the unbelievable.[62]

Whenever President Johnson called another of his innumerable and counter-productive short bombing halts, bombing pauses, cease fires or any other name he chose to call them, the results would often overwhelm Laos. The halts or pauses never involved Laos. While Cam Ranh would sometimes park its aircraft during a halt, other bases continued bombing, but just shifted it from North Vietnam to Laos. Additionally, the permanent halts to missions against North Vietnam did not mean combat air attacks would stop. The flights were merely shifted from the semi-public war in North Vietnam to the secret war in Laos. When Johnson declared his November 1, 1968, total moratorium of attacks against the North, the four Ravens working northeastern Laos were buried.

After the November cessation of the Air War against the North, a meeting was held in Saigon with the 7th and 13th Air Forces. It was decided that 60% of all tactical air strikes in all of Southeast Asia were to be flown against Laos.

To facilitate the increased number of strikes, the position of Head Raven was created to act as a liaison officer. The number of Ravens in Laos more than doubled to handle the increased work load. On the Plain of Jars, General Vang Pao's Meo Army, reinforced with Hmong fighters, used this increased tactical air as a form of airborne artillery and his Army became dependent on it.

Recruits:

In addition to the six months FAC flying requirement, the fledgling Ravens had to pledge at least six more months remaining on their combat tour. They had to have at least 100 hours of flying time as a fighter pilot, and at least 750 total hours flying time. Those who did volunteer did so without knowledge of their destination.

They were assigned to the 56th Special Operations Wing at Nakhon Phanom Royal Thai AFB and, since they would not be operating out of NKP, they were called Detachment 1. The 56th wrote temporary duty orders that sent them by air to Udorn, Royal Thai AFB due west of NKP.

When they arrived at Udorn, they were sent to their "headquarters," which turned out to be a small, non-descript, shack-like building located in a remote part of the airbase. This was also headquarters for the CIA-front airline called Air America. Air America had administrative control over the Ravens. It was at the shack that the Ravens drew their pay and received their mail. But, as the Air America administrators would inform them, "we will not be controlling you," which begged the question of who would be their bosses?

It was not until they were briefed at the US Embassy in Vientiane that they were given their official chain of command. They only tangentially belonged to the US Air Force. Officially, they would report to the Air Force Air Attaché at the Embassy.

Normally, Air Attaches are attached to embassies as are the intelligence gathering agencies, such as the CIA. Normally, Air Attaches are in the Air Force chain-of-command and report to the Pentagon. Like so many other things in our Laotian involvement, the Raven chain-of-command was different in Laos. The Air Attaché reported directly to the Ambassador. This meant that *officially* the Raven FACs would be working

---

Author's Notes: 62. *Dead sticking means that a pilot lands after running out of gas. It is a tricky maneuver not recommended to any but the most experienced. It used to be taught to Air Force pilots in training. However, the Air Force now recommends against it.*

for the Ambassador.

This, however, did not answer the question, "Who were their "real" bosses? For those Ravens who were assigned to Long Tieng, on the Plain of Jars, the answer would come soon enough.

At the Embassy, the pilots were stripped of all military identification and gear. They were supplied with US Agency for International Development identification and they changed into civilian clothing to be worn for their entire tour of duty. They also were told that they should consider themselves Forest Rangers working for the United States Agency for International Development or USAID. There was even one unconfirmed report that pilots were offered small CIA-created pills composed of lethal shellfish toxin.[63]

The program was of concern to the primitive forces of the enemy. When entering or departing the Embassy, photos were reportedly taken by Pathet Lao operatives so that the identity of the Ravens could be established by the enemy.

The files and records kept on Air Force pilots participating in such unorthodox combat created significant problems that could affect a pilot's career. With the CIA involved, records fabrication climbed to new heights. Since the Raven missions were so secret, and their records so convoluted, they were referred to as "Sheep-dipped" pilots. Associated problems of insurance became so complicated that the CIA created its own insurance company to insure the Ravens, Air America pilots, Continental Air Services pilots and its own CIA pilots.

In 1966, Udorn, located just down the road from Vientiane, was a center for the clandestine air wars being fought in Thailand, Laos and North Vietnam. It, along with NKP, provided extensive air resources for rescue, intelligence-gathering and an increasing air-to-ground strike capability using propeller-driven aircraft.

Udorn was headquarters for the CIAs own air force, as was witnessed by the author on his 1966 visit to the F-101 Recce detachment and to the CIA Flightline. They had their own pilots in addition to those on contract. That visit is detailed in another chapter. Sometime after the author's visit, Udorn was upgraded to support F-4C recce and fighter-bomber aircraft. It also worked in conjunction with the Phantom's "Night Owl" missions being flown out of Ubon Air Base, located almost due south of Udorn.

For the Ravens, Udorn also meant evening recreation at the Club. When they were first escorted to the "Club," the recruits expected the usual Air Force Officer's Club. After all, Udorn was a leased United States Air Force base, even though it was owned by the Thais. When escorted to the "Club" at Udorn, they wound up at the Air America Club. Even though the Udorn Officer's Club was casual, the small Air America Club was even moreso and a lot rowdier. In addition to the Ravens and Air America pilots, those carousing at the Air America Club included CIA and Continental Air Services pilots.

From either the capital or from Udorn, the fledgling Ravens were flown to their operating bases. A few stayed at Vientiane, but others were sent to Luang Prabang, Pakse, Savannakhet, Na Khang (Site 36) and, the assignment of choice, Long Tieng on the Plain of Jars.

Long Tieng:

The accommodations at any of the Raven bases were not what might be considered deluxe. There was no heating or air conditioning; there were open latrines, and they took showers under cold, 55-gallon water drums. There were no cafeterias in the Wild West. The Ravens were required to purchase and cook their own

Author's Notes: 63. The extremes that the CIA-controlled operations used to mask their identity verged on the ridiculous. Just who were they trying to kid?

food, and clean up after their meals.

The "air chariots" for these throw-back air warriors were not much better. Their O-1 Bird Dogs were fore and aft two-seaters without armor. They were high-wing monoplanes with excellent visibility but with a top speed of only 115 mph, which came as a shock to fighter pilots. The 530-mile range did allow for extended loiter times in combat areas.

The actual operational control and decision making was also pretty "rustic." The primary base for command and control was Long Tieng. It was there, on the Plain of Jars, that the Meo General Vang Pao held court.

Long Tieng was also called Site 20 Alternate or just "Alternate." The use of the term "alternate" was to confuse curious people into thinking an alternate must be a minor installation. Long Tieng was anything but minor. It was home to many Royal Lao Air Force pilots and there were so many CIA operatives and pilots that they called it "Spook Heaven" as the CIA-types were referred to by many as "Spooks."

Long Tieng, the "Secret City," became the second largest city in all of Laos. To keep the secret subterfuge, CIA pilots and operatives were not to be referred to as CIA, but instead were to be called CAS. CAS was supposed to stand for Controlled American Source, but that also stood for those other CIA-controlled pilots from Continental Air Services. For this reason, it is probable that Continental pilots were referred to as CASI, instead of simply CAS.

Into this alphabet soup were dropped the Ravens. As finally explained to the Ravens, "in the field" or operational control of them would be in the hands of the CIA and "native" Generals. "Native" meant General Vang Pao, head of the Meo Army and de-facto head of the Meo Tribe.

Decisions on flying and fighting for the Ravens were made every night over dinner at the home of General Pao. Included in his "court" were Meo Officers, Lao Officers, Hmung soldiers, Intelligence types, CIA operatives and the Raven pilots.

Because there were so few of them, the Ravens were often forced to fly seven to eight missions per day. Until the Air Force started to get serious about their mission, they had to rely on substandard maintenance and fuel that was sometimes contaminated with dirt and water. Battle damage in the form of bullet holes were patched by the Ravens themselves with what was called 100-mile-per-hour "Typhoon" Tape.

Added to the considerable woes of the Ravens caused by unreliable fuel and unreliable aircraft, were the unreliable Lao combat pilots that they were controlling. Often the Ravens, out of frustration, would jump out of their Bird Dogs and jump into combat-loaded Laotian T-28s to fly the bombing missions that the Lao pilots refused to fly. The Ravens might have been "cowboy" pilots, but they were as professional as any flying for America. Their courage was unquestioned and their accomplishments were many. They were fighter pilots who wanted to fight for what they considered was right.

Aircraft Maintenance:

In the beginning, both the O-1s and the later-supplied U-17s had severe maintenance problems. Maintenance repair was spotty and performed by poorly trained Lao mechanics, Air America technicians and even the pilots themselves.

The piston engines were tuned for optimum performance at Udorn's low altitude and they would run lean in the highlands of Central Laos. Of critical concern was engine life. Normal wear and tear allowed for an average engine life of 1800 hours. For the overworked O-1s in Laos, that dropped to 400 hours. The combat loads required for takeoff overloaded the Bird Dogs. The required short-field takeoffs necessitated very high engine power settings. Engine failures became epidemic. During the increased work load at the end of 1968, eighteen engine failures occurred to the Ravens in the last quarter of that year. December 1968 was a very bad month, but it got worse. One of the Ravens reported that 26 engine failures occurred in just the month of February, 1969.

Something drastic had to be done. The O-1s were cycled through Udorn to have their fuel tanks cleaned. Some of them had the accumulation of 18 years of crud and mud contaminating the tanks.

In May 1969, Air Force piston-engine mechanics were sent to Laos at the ratio of one mechanic per two FAC aircraft. Engine problems then drastically dropped.

The Air Force also sent crews to repair the severe battle damage being inflicted on the Ravens. Anti-aircraft artillery was being moved in ever-increasing numbers into Northern and Central Laos and their fire could be intense and accurate. The Raven's aircraft were known to take up to 50 battle-damage bullet hits in a single sortie. This sort of intensity was not only bad for aircraft, but could be harmful to a pilot's health.

RULES OF ENGAGEMENT (ROE):

The ROE extended their ubiquitous presence to Laos and its unorthodox war. The rules were extensive and complex. They included that American pilots could not hit SAM sites under construction. We had to wait until they were operational. In the North, we could not hit MIGs at an air base. We had to wait until they had flown to altitude, were properly identified and "showing hostile intentions" before we could attack.

The same was true for the slower-flying fighters. They could not hit hospitals or within a certain distance from pagodas. When the enemy found out these restrictions, they used the hospitals and pagodas for ammo storage, troop shelters and as sites for emplacement of their anti-aircraft artillery guns, the AAA or as sometimes called "triple A."

An entire chapter in this book is devoted to the disastrous consequences to the war-effort due to the imposition of the "rules." To those of us tasked to abide by the "rules," they were an amalgamation of stupidity. Was this an effort by our political leaders to assuage their collective guilt at leading such an ill-conceived and wrong war? Was this another example of their lacking the courage to cease our participation as well as lacking the courage to fight to win? To those of us forced to fight with our hands tied, it was very apparent that no fighter pilot or FAC had been involved in the creation of the Rules of Engagement.

To make matters worse for the FACs, the different Corp areas of South Vietnam had different "rules" from each other and from Laos. For instance, different Corps had different distances from pagodas that must be protected from airstrikes. These variances were huge causes for confusion. South Vietnam was split into four different operating Corps and Laos was split into operating regions. It got so comical that an Air Force General, John D. Lavelle, remarked that "We finally found out why there are two crew members in the F-4. One is to fly and the other is to carry the Rules of Engagement."

To be effective at all, the FACs were forced to repeatedly break the rules. This was confided to me several times by close and long-term friends who served in SEA as both Slow and Fast FACs. As an example, on one of my bombing strikes the controlling FAC stated that he was "temporarily moving the border" between South Vietnam and Cambodia.

The value of Laos for the FACs was that they usually did not have to put up with non-combat US Army or US Air Force types, who didn't have anything better to do than oversee and criticize the combatants. Just as the Air Force had an overabundance of desk pilots who wanted their resume to include combat as well as combat pay, the Army in SEA had less than 20% of its number in the infantry. Too many of the non-combatants were there to ensure the pilots followed the "rules." Since the Air Force FACs supported Army operations, they were sometimes subject to the same harassment as their Army ALO counterparts.

There was never a great number of Ravens flying at any one time. Prior to the Ravens, the Butterflies only had four operating in all of Laos. In 1967 there were only six Ravens. During the ten years that the Ravens flew, there were a total of 161 pilots. Since their Raven tours lasted on average of about six months, that meant the average number of Ravens operating in Laos at any one time was eight.

At the end of his tour, one Raven calculated that 90% of the Raven aircraft had been hit by ground fire and that 60% of those had been downed by enemy fire at some point. Out of the 161 Ravens that eventually served, 23 were killed and over 60 wounded. Not counted in those killed was US Army Embassy Attaché Joseph Bush, who was killed directing a strike in support of the overworked FACs. The losses were the second highest loss rate of all the FAC call signs.

For a more in-depth, exciting, and informative look at the life of the Ravens and the CIA in Laos, I suggest reading Christopher Robbins' excellent books "The Ravens" and "Air America."

DELTA FACS:

While FACs in South Vietnam were each assigned a sector, there was one FAC outfit allowed to go anywhere. In that, they were similar to the Raven FACs in Laos. Both the Ravens and the Delta FACs were unique.

Delta originated as part of Project "Leaping Lena" on May 15, 1964. Its purpose was for the US Special Forces to train ARVN Special Forces for missions in the HCMT area of Laos. Their initial action had five teams of 8 men each that were parachuted into Laos. The North Vietnamese Army was waiting for them and probably had information from its vast spy network within South Vietnam. Only five of the 40 men survived. The US only trained and did not participate.

In October, 1964, "Leaping Lena" was re-designated Project "Delta" with American Special Forces in control serving alongside their South Vietnamese counterparts. The Delta unit moved its main base to Nha Trang Air Base and half of the team was sent to Dong Ba Thin to train the 91st South Vietnamese Ranger Battalion.

The Delta mission at Nha Trang consisted of handling six hunter-killer teams, each composed of four US Special Forces troops and six to eight South Vietnamese Army Special Forces troops. The South Viet troops were part of the 91st Rangers. The unit at Nha Trang was designated Detachment B-52, 5th Special Forces Group.

As Academy classmate, John F. Flanagan of Detachment B-52, explained to me, "We are the Special Action FACs." The Deltas mission included operational and strategic recce into long-held Viet Cong areas and to direct air strikes on them. They also were to conduct bomb-damage assessment (BDA), conduct small-scale-recce and hunter-killer operations, capture and interrogate VC/NVA, tap communications, bug compounds and offices, rescue downed aircrews and prisoners of war, emplace point minefields and other booby traps, conduct psychological operations, and perform counter-intelligence. They were to focus on base areas and infiltration routes in the border areas along Laos. Other than that, they didn't have much to do.

At the time of his departure from Detachment B-52, Captain, later Brigadier General, John Flanagan was the longest serving Delta FAC pilot.

ANZAC FACS:

Australian and New Zealand pilots also participated in the FAC mission in South Vietnam. Initially, the Aussie's were assigned to the 19th TASS at Bien Hoa and later were included in the 20th at Danang. All told, 36 Aussies and 2 New Zealanders flew. They were integrated into the USAF chain-of-command and were part of the American units in everything except uniforms and source of combat pay. To qualify, a pilot had to have flown either the F-86 or French Mirage fighter aircraft, plus other flight time criteria. Some of the FACs came from the F-86 squadron that Australia had based at Ubon, Thailand. Those Ubon Sabre crews flew combat and suffered losses as well as their Phantom neighbors across the runway.

The mix of US Army Air Liaison Officers (ALOs) and US Air Force FACs often became blurred. They served the same purpose. Some Aussies flew as pilot observer and others simply as backseat observers. They were often referred to as FAC/ALOs. All the 38 Anzac FACs attended the USAF FAC School at Binh Thuy Air Base in South Vietnam. Some Aussies flew as back-seat observers in F-4Cs, which were later used as Fast FAC aircraft.

The duties of the Anzac FACs and often the ALOs included: artillery and naval gunfire adjustment; visual and photo recon.; convoy escort; resupply; psychological warfare; radio relay; combat support liaison plus the usual air control of fighter strikes. The FACs and ALOs were literally jacks of all trades in that they performed whatever functions were needed by the Army, Air Force and, on occasion, Navy.

FAST FACS:

As the efforts of the FACs became more effective, the North Viets reacted by gradually improving their antiaircraft defenses and tactics. In addition, they deployed SAMs southward. Their troops started to use the shoulder-fired SA-7 Grail surface-to-air missile. This posed a very serious threat to the fighter forces and we had to change tactics. It also posed a threat to the FACs. The Grail was a heat-seeking missile and propeller planes also emitted a heat pattern, although little compared to that of a jet aircraft like the two-engine Phantom.

As the war dragged on, more and more of the North Viets and their Communist brothers operating AAA guns, started targeting the FACs themselves without consideration of the hornet's nest they might create.

By 1967, the Air Force decided that the slower, prop-driven aircraft used in Route Pack One were too vulnerable. The Air Force response was to create the Fast FACs. The Marine's had pioneered the effort and the Air Force improved it with faster aircraft.

F-100 Super Sabre Fast FACs, call sign "Misty," were armed with 20mm cannon and two rocket launchers for marking targets. The Super Sabres were fast enough to survive in a high-threat area. In 1968, the 8th TFW at Ubon started using F-4s as Fast FACs under the call sign "Wolf." Later, other Phantom Fast FAC units were deployed, including at Udorn and at NKP. The Phantom Fast FACs at Udorn were designated "Laredo."

The Fast FACs developed a potent combination mission using an additional photo recon plane in conjunction with Misty. The photo recon guys performed visual recon as well as pre and post-strike photo assessment of targets for BDA. This led to an increase of strike control and the tripling of accurate bomb damage assessment. Depending on the target area, they also involved the slow FACs to get immediate BDA, even before the smoke from the strike had settled. It thus reduced photo recon losses by not allowing the enemy defenses to concentrate on an already struck target. With the recce planes employed immediately after a strike, the enemy was often unprepared and the defensive reactions were much less than they would have been with the recce birds flying a day or two later.

FAC losses still ran high, in spite of tactics changes. In the three years following their introduction in July 1967, 42 Fast FACs were shot down. In spite of the heavy losses, they continued the daytime program, since it was so successful.

Night Owl Fast FACs began flying missions on October 18, 1969 to supplement the already successful daytime "Wolf" operations. They used laser designators to guide 500#, 1,000# and 2,000# bombs to target. Because of the heavy weight of the 2,000-pounders, the Phantoms did not mount them underwing, instead mounting them centerline. The program lasted barely three months before being cancelled in January 1970, due to excessively high aircraft loss rates.

SLOW FACS:

The slower O-1 and O-2 aircraft used by the FACs were originally developed for other uses. No amount of retrofitting could make up for the deficiencies of the aircraft for FAC use. The Air Force needed and wanted an aircraft specifically designed and developed for FAC missions.

The O-1 Bird Dog had done wonderful work, but it had its shortcomings. The Bird Dog was too slow to timely arrive over targets. It was vulnerable to enemy small arms fire and its small size limited its payload. The radio system allowed use of only one radio channel at a time. It lacked night instrumentation.

The O-2 Skymaster offered many improvements. It had twin engines for greater safety, reliability and it had greater speed. It could carry more equipment and ordnance. It had night instruments, but the O-2 also had limitations.

In 1968, the Air Force delivered the first purpose-built FAC aircraft, the OV-10 Bronco. The Bronco was armored, was nearly twice as fast as the Bird Dog, and carried its own onboard ordnance for attacking "targets of opportunity." The Bronco also had excellent visibility. The pilot was able to lean outboard in the bubble canopy and see directly below the plane. This capability also allowed greater pilot security. It had self-sealing fuel tanks, which certainly helped pilots of shot-up planes from losing precious fuel. In case of malfunctions, backups were available for every system, which drastically improved maintenance reliability. The provision of ejection seats was a pilot favorite.

One of the more important innovations was the installation of eight radios. Each had a scrambler system to disguise messages and all could be used simultaneously. To summarize, it appears that the designers had input from the pilot users.

However, the Air Force has a fault that it repeatedly makes. Once an aircraft design has been adopted, avionics have been selected, the weights of allowable munitions are included and engines are picked, the Air Force often then continually loads additional permanent items on board that become part of the aircraft and add to its overall weight. Most of the time, the same engines are left on the aircraft and they are tasked with lifting the increased weight. This makes for "underpowered" aircraft. These "add on" items should wait until a follow-on model is designed with more powerful engine thrust. Bronco pilots complained that their beautiful plane became underpowered with all the "junk" attached to it after it was built. While the additional items may be considered as very important, from a pilot's standpoint the most important consideration is that the craft has sufficient power to do the job and get the pilot out of emergencies or critical situations. To most pilots, there is no such thing as an "overpowered" aircraft.

By 1968, there were 668 FACs "in country" scattered at 70 FAC locations throughout South Vietnam. The VC daylight activity, in areas largely surveilled by FACs, ceased. This led to another shift, this time to night Slow FAC operations using the O-2.

The Fast & Slow FACs found advantages in cooperating with one another. If a Slow FAC started picking up AAA, he would call in the Fast guy. If the Fast guy could not make out enough detail in target observation, he could call in a Slow guy to loiter and observe.

The Navy, not to be outdone by its Marine and Air Force brethren, created its own FAC squadron on January 3, 1969. The Naval Light Attack Squadron 4, using Marine OV-10s, was stationed at Binh Thuy and Vung Tau. They mixed the missions and used the Broncos for both FAC work and light combat strike. This unit flew 21,000 combat sorties before its disbandment on April 10, 1972.

The FACs pioneered many of the weapons and tactics used today. The O-2s, using flares and Starlight night vision scopes, directed air power against a night-crawling enemy. The Laotian experimentation with laser guided bombs was controlled by FACs. Their efforts helped lead the way toward more sophisticated development, which was featured nightly on television showing the precision bombing in Iraq.

The development of the Fast FACs led to more modern versions used very effectively in the heavily defended skies over the Balkans, Iraq and Afghanistan.

Even with their need and success, the United States closed down the Forward Air Control function at the end of the SEA War, only to be briefly opened later for special operations.

During the SEA War, FACs participated in every major action against the enemy including the Covey portion of Rolling Thunder. In all the SEA war theaters, American fighter-bombers dropped over four times the weight of bombs dropped in all of World War II, 9.5 million tons. Most of that tonnage was under FAC control. In summary, the airborne Forward Air Controllers in Southeast Asia were a huge success.

In August, 2015, Presidential Candidate Jeb Bush called for the re-establishment of the airborne Forward Air Controllers to better facilitate target identification, location and strike control in the American air action against the forces of ISIS in Syria.

The loss of the Air Wars had nothing to do with how the FACs controlled the targets. It had everything to do with the targets not allowed to be hit, the lack of centralized control and the fact that there was no ground force capable of protecting and consolidating the bombing successes.

The reincorporation of airborne FACs into the identification and control of any future air attacks against ground targets should be strongly considered by the Pentagon and whatever administration is running our country. While the visuals provided by airborne cameras have been a significant addition to our intelligence gathering and target control, there is really no substitute for human "eyes in the sky" that can visualize an entire landscape and make quick, human judgments on what is witnessed. Success in our air attacks against ground targets will be realized when decision making is returned to the battlefield and the time between situation identification and countermeasures is severely reduced or eliminated.

Some might wonder why a book with anti-war overtones would be advising how to win wars. There is no conflict. I am against war and that thought is repeated in quotes by military leaders throughout this book. While we must do whatever is within our power to eliminate wars, there are still necessary wars that will need to be fought in our national future. My position is that, if we are forced to fight a war, we should fight it in a manner that insures victory in the shortest possible time and with the minimum amount of destruction and death to all participants.

Just as Aristotle decreed that a society has a warrior class that embodies its spirit and courage, America needs a strong military presence and it needs to remain vigilant to external threats.

An apt analogy on national protection is the owner who makes his home so protected against a break-in that a thief is persuaded to rob another home. That was the motivation behind Sweden and Switzerland establishing such strong militaries that Hitler decided against any invasion and instead sought to engage in trade.

My fervent wish is that those future wars will be minimized in number; minimized in duration and minimized in the caused destruction and loss of life. If we are forced to fight a war, we should do it with sufficient force, sufficient resolve, sufficient efficiency and sufficient ingenuity to win quickly, consolidate quickly and quickly leave the battlefield.

"Television brought the brutality of war into the comfort of the living room. Vietnam was lost in the living rooms of America— not on the battlefields of Vietnam."

Marshall McLuhan

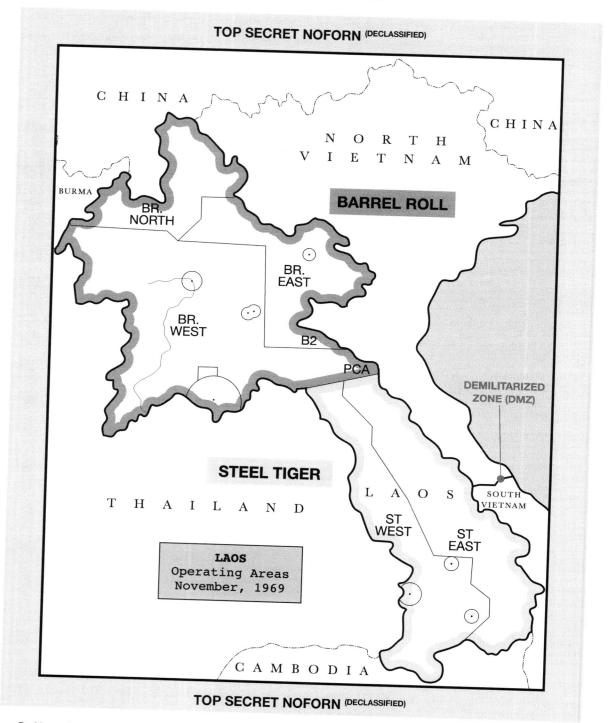

By November, 1969, the Laotian operating area of Barrel Roll expanded to all of northern Laos and was split into east, west and north, all depicted in orange (dark outline). Steel Tiger was expanded to all of southern Laos and split into east and west, depicted in yellow.

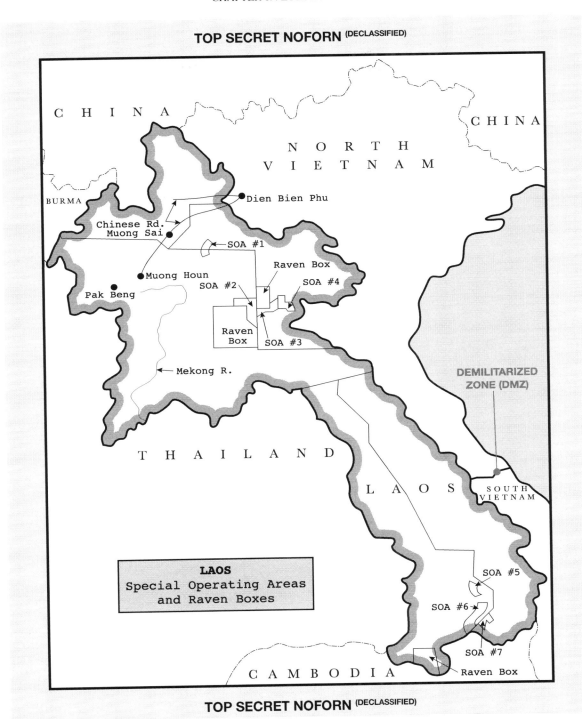

Laotian Special Operating Areas (SOAs) and Raven Boxes — *The boxes were specific for the Raven FACs.*

BOOK 4: ASPECTS OF WAR

BOOK FIVE
Marching Home

BOOK 5: MARCHING HOME

CHAPTER TWENTY

Welcome Home

An Airport Incident

> *"It is fatal to enter any war without the will to win it."*
>
> General of the Army Douglas MacArthur

My war was really split into two separate and distinct wars. The first war lasted three months, from April through June. Looking back, I am surprised that my total war lasted only nine months. From a time standpoint, that equated with the air battles of the famed American Flying Tigers, who flew in behalf of Nationalist China on WWII missions against Imperial Japan in China and Burma. The entire time that the Tigers were flying combat was only six months. In combat, it seems you have flown and fought for an eternity.

My first combat mission was against Laos and continued flights during those first three months were against Laos and South Vietnam. During those three months, I flew 45 combat missions, 16 of which were against the infiltration and supply routes from North Vietnam through Laos into South Vietnam, known to us as "Tiger Hound." The rest were air-to-ground against the South with one that was a prelude of missions to come: a MIG Screen over the Gulf of Tonkin.

My second war started in July and ended on my last combat flight late in December. From July 1 through a mission on August 28 the targets and combat missions got more and more intense as we started to focus on the North. From August 30 through the end of the year, we were really in what can be called "the hell of war."

Part of the tragedy was that the Air War just kept going on and on for year after year. During my war, we hadn't accomplished much toward a resolution of the conflict. We tried our best but, due to reasons I discuss in this book, it was not to be.

From that first Phantom loss of the 45th TFS on June 9, 1965 to the last Phantom combat loss on June 16, 1973, the Air Force lost a total of 443 F-4Cs, Ds and Es. The final combat Phantom loss of the war was an F-4E. The actual final non-combat Phantom loss was an F-4D on June 29, 1973 during landing at Udorn, Thailand. The pilot was flying a ferry mission and lost an engine on final approach. Hostilities ceased in SEA for the United States on August 15, 1973.

The USAF Recce version, the RF-4, lost another 83. The U.S. Navy, flying the B and J models, lost 128 and the U.S. Marines, also flying the B & J models, lost 98 Phantoms. For all the services, F-4 losses to MIGs totaled 90 and 205 to the more lethal Surface to Air Missiles (SAMs). Other than operational losses, the vast majority of the 752 total F-4 losses were due to Automatic Weapons (AW) and the Anti-Aircraft Artillery (AAA). The term automatic weapons or AW often is used interchangeably with the lower caliber AAA (14.5mm up to 23mm) that were radar-controlled and shot down so many at altitudes up to 5,000 feet

AGL. The equally lethal higher caliber AAA could reach us at any of our operating altitudes.

From the initial Phantom loss on June 9, 1965, for which John and I flew its replacement to Ubon, until I flew my first combat mission, the Air Force lost a total of 19 Phantoms. During my war, we lost an additional 49 for a total of 68. After I left, the USAF lost 375 Phantoms during an additional 78 months of combat. The last year of sustained attacks against the North, 1967, saw the greatest loss of Air Force Phantoms of any year with 92 being shot down. That became a sort of benchmark. Comparing the following years with 1967, the percentage loss rates were: 1968, 68%; 1969, 71%; 1970, 36%; 1971, 32%; 1972, 92% and 1973, 7%.

The most losses were sustained in that final full year of Northern air combat and the year of the Linebackers in 1972. If only the United States had shown the same resolve as it did in December, 1972, we would not have suffered nearly the losses. When we did show resolve, North Vietnam came to the bargaining table and worked out an agreement to stop the war, all within a month of the cessation of Linebacker II. Without the will or a plan to win, those losses can only be considered tragic.

Five of my December missions were flown by Pearl Harbor Day on December 7th. By then, I had accumulated 139 missions and my goal was 150. It was then that the Wing and the 559th got serious and tried to talk me out of any more missions. I had to beg and argue for more. They relented.

Colonel Allen felt that I had had enough. He awarded me a medal for my Command Post service and replaced me on December 14. The monsoons came that month and it poured. The Wing was still flying tough missions to the North and I was left to fly the pansy missions to the South. I was pissed.

After I flew my 148th mission, my squadron commander suggested that I might want to take a vacation during Christmas. It seemed he considered me the last relic of the prior regime. However, I jumped at the opportunity to spend Christmas elsewhere, and he set up orders for me to legitimize my trip. It was to the Bullpup Simulator at Clark. The Bullpup is an air-to-ground missile that we had never fired at Cam Ranh. I found out after my return that the simulator had been broken for a year. My commander also cut me orders for Hong Kong.

On December 30, after spending a delightful time in Hong Kong, I grabbed another MAC cargo flight back to SEA. None of the flights that particular day went directly to Cam Ranh, so I chose a flight that took me to Nha Trang and told the pilot that it was "close enough." Nha Trang, as described before, is a beautiful former French resort town. After landing, I met an Army guy who had a jeep and was heading to Cam Ranh. He gave me a lift.

The trip down to CRB was not via the coast, but a bit inland. It was only 15 miles, but my grunt driver cautioned that we would be driving through Viet Cong-controlled territory. There would be only two of us in the jeep and I had no weapon with me. We launched anyway.

The driver's main concern was a high hill about half way down. Apparently, he had experienced trouble transiting that area before and had received sniper fire from the hill.

The combat team, of an unarmed Air Force guy riding shotgun for an armed Army grunt, bumped down the gravel road heading south. By the time we got in the vicinity of the hill, he had already speeded up. When we reached the base of the hill we were screaming. The jeep careened as we "jinked" from side to side at a high rate of speed. The mad dash was uneventful as we received no fire. After the hill, we just coasted the rest of the way. I wondered what posed the greatest danger, the hill or the Jeep?

As we drove on that last leg, the Army sergeant asked me about drugs on base. He had heard rumors about another Army camp and wondered if we had similar problems at our Air Force base. I told him that I heard nothing and that it seemed highly unlikely. Everybody was busy and I had not seen any evidence among the enlisted guys or the pilots. In those days, it was just not something that was done.

The sergeant was heading toward Cam Ranh Army to the south of the air base and was able to drop me off within a mile of my destination. Hauling my duffle, I walked casually along the Flightline, finally arrived at our Squadron Ops. It was evening, but there was still some light outside. The afternoon missions had already been flown and the night missions were no longer being flown. Flight Operations was deserted.

When I walked in, it hit me instantly. My name, which had been prominently displayed on the Plexiglas wall boards, was no longer there. I was shocked. I had been deleted and was not listed anywhere. The mission's board, the organizational boards of Plexiglas, nothing contained my name. It was as if I never existed.

That night I slept a restless sleep. What was going on? Most all of the guys in my squadron were "new faces." I was the old head. All of the original pilots from the base were long gone. I suspected that they had used my absence to cleanse the squadron of my presence and history. What about my two remaining missions?

As one of our backseaters had told me, I was the last of the "replacement pilots" for the Phantom. Until he told me, I had not realized that was how I was categorized. With my arrival at Cam Ranh, I became the first of the replacement pilots. The backseater had actually been on base for a longer time than I had and had apparently followed my flying. So many of these guys were rooting for me to do well because they were backseaters and I was the first one of them to be upgraded.

He had asked, "Are you looking over your shoulder?"

He had been keeping track and there had been a total of 14 Phantom replacement pilots sent to all the bases in Southeast Asia by the time they terminated the program. I was not sure of his overall numbers, but he was correct regarding Cam Ranh. I had been the first. All of the other thirteen pilots had been shot down and either killed or taken prisoner. I had been the first, but I was also the last.

When the Club opened for breakfast, I was there. I remember being surprised that it opened so early. It seems that it was six o'clock for the early missions. Mine was an early mission. I had gotten used to my hours at the Command Post and I was always on duty at six in the morning.

After breakfast, I wandered down to the Flightline. The feeling seemed different. As I strolled along, it was almost like seeing the base for the first time. The Quonsets, trailers and all the other types of structures were clean from a recent downpour. At the Flightline, the F-4s seemed menacing as they sat waiting for their first pilots of the day. Brown-green birds of prey, waiting to pounce. Their camouflage coloring seemed to blend into the color of the hills in the distance. The Flightline was deserted and in that peaceful time between sun-up and the launches to the North. I strode into Operations.

My squadron CO was there. We were the only ones in the large central ops room. He seemed to have known that I had arrived back and that I might be coming down to ops early. It was almost like he had been waiting for me. I looked around and then back at him. "What gives Major?" The actual words of his reply have been etched into my memory to the time of this writing, "Russ, the war is over for you. You have done enough and it is time for you to go home."

I was stunned.

No amount of arguing would convince him that I deserved two more missions. He said, "the Wing has requested that you be relieved of duty." The orders had to have come directly from Colonel Allen. He added, "the Wing has also authorized me to cut you R&R orders for wherever you want to go and to stay for as long as you wish."

It was the last day of the year. Before I had left for Hong Kong, I would have not known the day or the date. I was already starting to readjust.

I picked Bangkok.

Adda took time off from her work at the Agency for International Development and met me at Don Muang. That night we went to the Imperial and had steaks. The buildings of downtown Bangkok seemed different. They seemed larger and stood out with more clarity and they reflected deeper colors.

I had not realized the mental and emotional state in which I had lived. It was as though a heavy weight had been lifted. It was not like I had consciously been under a great deal of tension. I was not, and had enjoyed some aspects of combat, which might seem difficult for others to understand. Most fighter pilots like challenges and the greatest challenge I had ever known was to lead a flight against a heavily defended target, destroy that target and get my guys back safely. But that night my feelings there in Bangkok were hard to explain. As I admitted to Adda, "This feels weird."

On January 7, 1967, I caught a flight out of Don Muang and headed back to Saigon. I had tried to get a hop taking me to Clark or anywhere else, but I had no choice. The MAC (Military Airlift Command) charters back to the States were exclusively flown out of Saigon. I had to process out of SEA in Saigon and it was there that I had to catch my flight back to civilization.

I am not even sure which airline had been chartered. My perceptions were vaguely aware that it was not a MAC cargo plane, but that it was an airliner. As I look back, I think if was Continental, but I can't be sure. This meant I would be sitting on actual seats and not hammocks slung along the side of the plane. I was grateful for that.

My comrades on the flight back were almost all enlisted men from the U.S. Army. The war for these guys had been out in the jungles where they had been suffering in the heat and humidity, fighting mosquitos as well as the Viet Cong with absolutely horrible combat conditions. My war had been spent sleeping between clean sheets in air-conditioned comfort; sipping Courvoisier cognac; listening to classical music and resting peacefully in the knowledge that our base was secure from attack.

The flight attendants were all smiles. During the flight, one of them told me that the flights out were always happy flights. Years later I was again told that same thing by another Continental stew. For her, everyone was going home and she was feeling in a happy mood as well. As she explained, it was the flights into Vietnam that bothered her. She was completely aware that many of those soldiers and sailors on the flights would not ever be going home except in a coffin.

Twelve years later, I flew the inaugural for what would be over four years in the South Pacific for Continental and got to fly with some of the "old head" flight attendants who had flown MAC. I often wondered if I had flown with any of them on that final flight. There were few of those flight attendants who got married and fewer still left flying out of the group. The MAC women were the most senior flying for Continental and they were all flying South Pacific. My guess was that I had flown with some of those same women on my departure that day.

When the wheels lifted off the Vietnamese runway, the guys all cheered. I didn't. My feeling was one of quiet relief. I was thankful to be alive and in a contemplative mood. Memories surfaced in bits and pieces. As we climbed away from Saigon and the Southeast Asian War, I thought of a similar liftoff in a transport plane from a small dirt strip somewhere in South Vietnam. I don't even remember where it was. I just remember it had an awfully short runway and I was on some boondoggle to get away from Cam Ranh. It was not an R&R. It was just an overview trip to experience some of the rest of the war.

On that boondoggle, the aircraft on which I was a passenger was a C-124 cargo plane of ancient vintage. As we lumbered down the short runway and jerked into the air, we began to encounter ground fire. At the time, I was up in the cockpit as an observer. It was in the evening and the waning light allowed the crew and me to easily see the bullets careening through the sky. Not sure if those were tracers, but they were plainly visible as they sliced toward us.

The crew members seemed unconcerned as if it was an everyday event. We took several hits that could be heard puncturing our aircraft skin. They reminded me of the sickening sound that I heard when the rescue chopper that had just landed in Laos had been hit right in front of me. This time, the irony did not escape me. I wondered if I was destined to be shot down as a passenger in a prop-driven transport after having escaped being killed in a fighter on a combat mission. It was a wild ride and gave me a new appreciation for the courage and skill of the cargo drivers. Very seldom did we see the shells being fired at us in the F-4. Of course, we didn't fly that many night flights.

On this particular ride, it was very serene. There were no bullets to say goodbye to us and remind us of what we were leaving. There was not even much turbulence. The cheering soon subsided and the soldiers were left to their own thoughts. Mine wandered from the excitement of the C-124 flight to my coming journey.

My parents were to meet me at Travis Air Force Base just outside of Fairfield in Northern California. Travis serves the same purpose for the Pacific as McGuire serves for the Atlantic. In the parlance of modern airlines, the two massive transport bases were our "hubs."

Emotions are strange things. Stranger for men than I have observed they are for women. Mine had been pushed very deep by the war. They were under the surface, not consciously acknowledged by me. I suppose it was a defense mechanism, but I had become blasé about the death of my friends. I had buried my emotions and they would take some conscious searching to resurrect. With each combat death from the Phantom bases throughout SEA, I had become more immune, more emotionally empty. I had wondered about my own total lack of emotional reactions when buddy after buddy was killed or captured. How much had I changed? Would I ever get those emotional feelings back? I had no answers and those questions would remain unanswered. For now, I was content. As I gazed out the window at the towering cumulonimbus clouds, I could take a deep breath and relax. I was going home to California and an extended stay before venturing on to further flying in England.

As our aircraft approached the mainland, I was filled with trepidation. How would I react on meeting my parents after all that time apart? How would I feel? Judy had decided to wait and fly out from Virginia to meet me at my parent's home in Fillmore. What would I say to her?

On descending the boarding steps, I was surprised to see my brother Dave and his wife Joan. We had been somewhat estranged for quite some time. It was hurtful that he only wrote me once in all the time I was in Vietnam and that letter had been accusatory. I knew that the only reason he had come to welcome me home would have been if he had been pressured by my parents. Our greetings were somewhat awkward.

We were an Anglo-Saxon family and we did not hug. Shaking hands was the limit of our outward display of family emotions. I felt out of place. Part of me felt like I wanted to return to what was familiar. Momentarily, I felt a strong urge to leave. To return to Vietnam and the war that had been my life.

The lights of the terminal and parking lot seemed very bright. Even though it was night, the glare from the lights was similar to that felt when facing a sunny day after having had eye drops from the optometrist. The glare was so bright it hurt. Back in SEA, night lighting had always been subdued. It accentuated the feeling that at Travis I was on foreign soil.

Many might think that a reunion like that would be filled with joy. I could see it in the eyes of my parents and my mother's eyes were brimming with tears. For me, it was not joy. It was a strange feeling and more of a realization of the need for adjustment. The strongest feeling was of relief and a final realization that I had lived through it all.

My next duty station was RAF Bentwaters in Suffolk County, England, United Kingdom. I would continue to fly the F-4, only this time I would be flying for NATO as part of the European War Plan. It was a prime assignment and I felt excited.

My next leg on my journey from Asia to Europe took me from Travis by car to Southern California, where I spent time with my family. My buddy, Jim Annis, flew out and we spent a week skiing in the Tahoe area before my return to Fillmore. From Los Angeles, I was ticketed to Tampa, Florida to renew my MacDill acquaintances.

After my arrival in Tampa, a party was arranged at the Bennett Apartments. While there, an old girlfriend of Spike Nasmyth's got a little drunk and spoke out loud, wishing that I had been the POW instead and that her boyfriend Spike was with her at the Bennett that night. How does one respond to such a comment? Even though it was the alcohol talking, I understood her longing for Spike. But her wishing for me to change places and be a POW made it more than an awkward scene. I left shortly thereafter.

The next morning, I boarded another commercial flight and flew to Washington D.C., where I met Judy and spent a delightful week with her and her family in Culpeper, Virginia. Judy, driving a new VW bug, took me north and deposited me at McGuire Air Force Base in New Jersey for the last leg of my journey.

My memories of the exact details of the event are a little fuzzy. I was walking down the concourse at Tampa toward my waiting plane. The woman was somewhere in her 20s and was reasonably attractive with long, straight, dirty-blonde hair that dropped below her shoulders. Her floral dress fell several inches below her knees and was either a dark blue or green.

I was dressed in my uniform jacket with tie. The uniform ribbons located on the left side of my jacket below my pilot and jump wings had not been updated with the medals I had earned in SEA. That would come later with several squadron presentations in England. As I strode down the concourse toward my waiting gate and the plane that would take me north, the woman darted out of a group and came directly toward me.

She screamed something unintelligible and then spat on my uniform. I was stunned. There was no time for any comment or action, for she hastily retreated back to the sanctuary of her group. It had happened so quickly that others may not have noticed or if they did notice, they did not care. No one came up to me and it was probably fortunate that none did. I am not even sure how I managed to wipe off her spit?

The Pacific Stars and Stripes as well as pilots who later joined our Wing had partially prepared us for the hostile reception that might await us once back on American soil. But I was not prepared for such a greeting. Nobody would be prepared. My inner being seethed in anger and disgust. While part of my mission had been to defend our citizens' rights, including a defense of the American right to protest, this was different. It was a betrayal.

My awareness included a strong anger at my government for placing us in such a situation. The anger included the Military and its insane "Sortie War" that endangered our pilot's lives. But this was different. Couldn't these people see that we had to follow orders? The public had elected Johnson as President. If they felt so inclined, spit on him.

This was not a case of us committing inhumane actions similar to the Germans in WWII. We were fighting a war at the behest of the American people as represented by their elected Executive and Legislative Branches of our government. We were fighting it on the basis of the Geneva Conventions. Was this our "reward" for coming close to death too many times to count? How stupid and ignorant could they be? The intensity of my anger made me feel like striking back.

A later chapter will detail the intense frustration we all felt. We had an obligation to obey the lawful orders of our civilian leaders. Willful disregard and disobeying direct orders would constitute treason and a collective disobedience by the military would mean the end of America as we knew it. Could not these people understand? Did they even try?

This was my welcome home from combat.

Other than my family and friends, nobody from the public ever approached me with a thank you. Mostly, there was confusion on the part of people who wondered why we were not winning. Since I was a professional military man, I could not share my intimate thoughts with strangers or acquaintances. I could not speak against our government or military, even though I had a strong urge to let loose with my frustrations. Mine was a dilemma shared with countless military men who were coming home.

Soldiering on, I quickly regained my composure and completed my Tampa Airport concourse walk. As I moved toward my waiting gate, I pondered my ultimate return and how I would relate to the public. By the time I reached the gate area, I vowed never to wear my uniform in public again.

I never did.

Two years later, that and all the rest of my uniforms went into the trash, which was a fitting metaphor for an airman's return from combat without honor to a divided and hostile nation.

"I must study politics and war that my sons may have liberty to study mathematics and philosophy."

President John Adams

CHAPTER TWENTY-ONE

Without Honor

Return to California

> *"I've learned that something constructive comes from every defeat."*
> Former NFL Coach Tom Landry

Over the next two years, I flew out of RAF (Royal Air Force) Woodbridge located in Suffolk County in East Anglia, England. My assignment was to RAF Bentwaters, which was just a half-hour drive from Woodbridge. RAF Woodbridge was an auxiliary field assigned to Bentwaters.

Our primary mission was nuclear and we would spend a third of our lives sitting behind barbed wire at the end of the runway on alert status. Our home was the "Alert Shack" located next to the Alert Hangars housing our nuclear-loaded Phantoms. My NATO (North Atlantic Treaty Organization) assigned nuclear target was in Poland on what was essentially a one-way mission, since we did not have enough fuel to make it back to England.

In the latter half of my European stay, we were working seven-day weeks. Vietnam had been declared an "exceptional national emergency" and that meant air, naval and ground units were being moved from Europe to the Far East. On our supposed weekly "day off," we planned the "buffer zone" penetration flights that took us at 200 feet over Germany heading for the buffer zone, which was just short of the Iron Curtain.

Our job on the penetration missions was to scare up the air defense radars of the anti-aircraft artillery (AAA) and surface to air missiles (SAM) sites so that our listening stations could note frequencies and triangulate for their locations. The main difference between these Warsaw Pact defensive sites and those in SEA was that those east of the Iron Curtain were largely stationary.

My return from NATO flying to the United States was subdued. My final mission was on November 1, 1968, leading a flight of four to the bombing range associated with Soesterberg Royal Netherlands Air Force Base in Holland. Part of me was glad to be gone from flying due to the situation in SEA. Part of me would sadly miss flying such a wonderful aircraft and the social life and shared mission that we all had in common. Flying fighters was the most exciting thing that I have ever done and fighting in a war was the fulfillment of what I was trained to do. I would miss it all.

More importantly, the only true statement a military man can make in opposition to a political situation like we had in SEA was to hit them in the pocket book. As long as I was in uniform, my loyalty obligated me to do nothing or say nothing publicly against my country or the Air Force. The only way for me to properly and publicly condemn the situation was for me to sever my commitment to the Air Force.

I knew that the Air Force had no choice but to tailor its actions to the dictates of our governmental leaders, but they were still my only available target and by getting out, it was costing them. Being only a junior officer provided me with little power to effectuate any meaningful change.

Politically, I had already exhausted what little power I had by visiting Washington, prior to my arrival in England, to alert two members of the House Armed Serviced Committee to the fact that we were fighting China.

Militarily, my thinking at the time was that those of us dissatisfied with the way the war was being run could perhaps make a change, but we would have to do it collectively by leaving the service. There was no mechanism available for military men to state their grievances against a political decision on how to wage war, nor should there have been. We were obligated by our oath of allegiance to carry out our military role in defense of those decisions.

The year prior to my final flight, the Chief of Staff of the Air Force, General Joseph P. McConnell, had sent me a letter stating that I had "certain skills (that) are essential to the most effective accomplishment of the Air Force mission." He went on to say that my "particular qualifications were carefully weighed, due to the unusual requirements resulting from our national effort in Southeast Asia." The point of the letter was that he had obligated me and, I assumed others with the same skill sets, to stay another year past our severance dates. A copy of that letter is included in the Support Section of this book. SEA was again reaching out to ensnare me.

The Pentagon made a last-ditched attempt to keep me in the Air Force just before that final November flight. They sent a full Colonel from Washington all the way to RAF Woodbridge to try to talk me out of quitting. He told me that I was the sole reason for his trip. The Air Force gesture honored me. The Colonel told me that my file at Air Force personnel had been "flagged for rapid advancement." However, I felt that this "gesture" might have been fabricated in order to get me to change my mind. My mind was already made up.

My reply, "Colonel, you are way too late" was not met by surprise. He had been on similar missions and they had all ended the same. My suggestion to him was to spend his planned time with me on his own "boondoggle" to London. He liked the idea and met it with a smile. As he mentioned, he figured it had been a useless mission, and probably one of many tasked by the Pentagon to try to quell the massive departures from the forces then taking place. Those losses were also part of the tragedy that was SEA. The Force had been massively depleted of qualified pilots through resignations as well as the huge losses in aircrews and aircraft due to enemy defenses.

Part of my consideration on separating from the Air Force had to do with my possible return to Southeast Asia on another combat tour. I was willing to risk my life a second time, if the war could have been considered just or if it was being fought in the right manner. On both counts, SEA did not qualify. Others, who felt the same as I, thought that it was inconceivable that the Air Force would re-train the aging bomber pilot force from SAC and attempt to put them into our high-performance fighters. It did not make sense and seemed to guarantee a degradation of effectiveness. Since it did not make sense, we thought our return to combat was assured. Since it did not make sense, that is exactly what happened.

At the time, the additional year tacked on to my commitment was the most that they could do, since I had already put in my separation papers. If I had not done so, I felt that my return to combat would have been just a matter of time.

Departing England, I flew on an Air Force cargo plane from Mildenhall to McGuire AFB in New Jersey and set up shop at the McGuire VOQ (Visiting Officer's Quarters). There, I would wait for my car to arrive from England.

My separation from the Air Force occurred on November 15th, 1968.

When I was finally reunited with my MG, I started traveling westward on the Pennsylvania Turnpike, I relished the rolling hills that were so green and lush. It was a strong reminder that this was the America that I had grown to love. With my MG leading the way, the trip across America offered many reminders of just what a wonderful country we do have. It is worth honoring and protecting.

On arrival, there was no welcome from anyone other than my immediate family and friends. To those of us returning, it was a lonely march. There were no parades or speeches. But while we might have marched home alone, we did return.

My eternal gratitude to my country for providing me with an excellent advanced education and allowing me to fly the fastest operational fighter in the world. That experience has given me a deeper sense of satisfaction and accomplishment than I could have ever gotten had I chosen another life path. Thank you America.

My return to Southern California was on New Year's Eve, 1968, two years to the day after I had returned to Cam Ranh and found out from my squadron commander that my war was over.

Throughout this book, I have referred to military men with reference to the Southeast Asia War. This is not meant as any slight to military women, who are increasingly taking on significant tasks in the defense of our country. But this book deals with a past war. Of the over 58,000 Americans killed in that conflict, only eight were women.

STRENGTH AND HONOR:

I have mentioned the part that "psychic pay" has to do in the defense of our country. For evaluators like Robert McNamara, the partial-payment of our military men and women in psychic pay would have been considered very "cost-effective." McNamara was representative of many civilians in our government, past and present, who do not understand the inner values that motivate our military people.

None of us joined the military to get rich. Money had little to do with why we signed up. Part of the reason was and is a sense that the able-bodied and able-minded members of our society have an obligation to defend our soil, our organization and our system of values. Perhaps it was naiveté, but we fighter pilots considered it honorable to be willing to defend our country with, if necessary, our lives.

My return home to the United States was not unlike most of the rest of our military men who returned. While our purpose in becoming military men and fighting for our country involved honor, we symbolically marched home without honor.

Historically, prior to the 20th Century, the last great armies that marched in defense of a democratic republic were the Legions of Rome. Any modern military man or woman would understand the motivations of the Roman Legionnaires as repeated in salutation during the Hollywood film Gladiator: "Strength and Honor."

While there are still forces bent on our destruction, we may be forced to engage in the evil of war. While it is fitting to honor those whose participation in combat risks everything for the benefit of the many, it makes no sense to honor the evil itself. And while the necessity of war might rear its evil head at any time, an equal evil exists in showing weakness and not having prepared for the possibility of war.

"Weakness and ambivalence lead to war."
President George H. W. Bush

CHAPTER TWENTY-TWO

Agony of the Scorned
Civilian Primacy

> *"Generals are not in the business of commenting on the correctness or incorrectness of the President's decisions."*
>
> General Norman Schwarzkopf

The founding fathers of these United States managed to create some amazing compromises. It is unsure if even they realized how their decisions would manifest themselves as the population of the republic increased a hundredfold.

Regarding the military, there were two collective decisions that have had a profound and lasting impact on how we now work as a nation. The most important was to have all military men take an oath of allegiance to the Constitution of the United States and not to the President. Thus, the military pledges its very life to uphold a system and not an individual. It guarantees support of the legislative and judicial branches as well as the executive and how they interrelate as defined by the Constitution.

Any action by the executive to alter the constitutionally protected rights of the legislative or judicial could be met by force as the military has a primary pledge to uphold our structure and not its leader.

The second decision of the creators of our system insures that the military itself is subservient to the democratically-elected leadership by making the President the Commander in Chief of the entire military establishment. Thus, the commanding General Officers and Fleet Admirals of all of our military forces are below the President in the Chain of Command. The General Staff, led by the Joint Chiefs of Staff, is also beholden to the President. It is a huge insurance against a military coup d'état.

While the President is the Commander in Chief of our military, he or she should never consider that means the unqualified support of our military for the President. The President should never forget that he or she is obliged, just as our military is obligated, to defend our Constitution.

When the military pledges "Duty, Honor and Country," their duty is clearly defined. It is to serve at the wishes of the elected representative of the people as long as those wishes do not conflict with our Constitution.

The military oath of allegiance, sworn by every military man and woman, pledges them to protect our Constitution. While they are under the President in the Chain-of-Command, their oath of allegiance is not to the President. If there is a conflict between the two, the military's primary allegiance is to the Constitution. Thus, we have created a system where there has never been any attempt or even the rumors of an attempt by any branch of the military of the United States or any group within the branches to usurp authority. To present-day Americans this may not seem much of an issue, but it is almost unique in the histories of governments all over the globe.

The importance of that allegiance by the most powerful military that the world has ever known cannot be overemphasized. The importance of the American President being the Commander in Chief of that military also cannot be overemphasized. Both requirements are responsible for the stable relationship that has existed between the executive branch and the military since the creation of the United States.

Civilian primacy, or the control of the military by our civilian government, is an almost religious conviction of the Officer Corps of all our military services. The military zealously protects those rights and it is an extremely important foundation cornerstone of the stability that protects our way of life. The conviction of our military officers to protect the right of a President to exert final control over the military structure is one of our national, largely unknown, treasures.

The Officer Corps does not want a General Officer to control the enormous power of our military. The final determination of whether we stay at peace or go to war must be made by the civilian authority and not the military authority. The Officer Corps does not want the military to make political decisions as it does not want the politicians to make military decisions. In SEA, President Johnson showed the folly of an unschooled politician trying to make military decisions. After the separate missions have been defined, both the political and the military should remain separate.

The decision of going to war is a political and not a military one. The civilian authority in the form of the executive branch has to make that decision. The Constitution also guarantees that the Legislative Branch must approve any decision to go to war, although that authority has been blurred recently. Once that political decision has been made and approved, then it is up to the military to carry out the civilian dictates.

The participation of the Legislative Branch has been muddied since Vietnam, and that relationship with the Executive Branch has to be clarified as it relates to the authorization to war. The military has no place or authority in that discussion, nor would it want it.

Regarding the correct relationship between the military and the Executive, I vividly recall reading a letter placed in the John Sherman Room at the Mansfield, Ohio Public Library. Both Union Generals Grant and Sherman were from Ohio. The John Sherman Room was named after General William T. Sherman's brother. The letter was from President Abraham Lincoln to Union Commanding General Ulysses S. Grant during the American Civil War. Lincoln's admonishment to Grant was simply, "win the war." It was Lincoln's decision to militarily confront the rebelling Confederate States, but he was leaving it up to the military on how to conduct that confrontation.

Prior to our Civil War, Confederate General Robert E. Lee was asked by the American military to lead the Northern Union forces, but he instead chose to honor his home State of Virginia and pledged to Confederate President Jefferson Davis to follow his orders. Lee's sense of allegiance thus passed from Virginia to the Confederacy.

After his surrender to Grant, Lee considered that the Confederacy was no more and that Virginia would be rejoining the Union. His duty was then to serve the Union. Lee was responsible for insuring, in April 1865, that the remaining Confederate forces surrendered peacefully and that the defeated Southern Armies did not direct their soldiers to continue fighting in the hills in a protracted guerrilla war.

Most have considered that Lee was surrendering the bulk of the Confederate Army when he met Grant at Appomattox. That was not the case. Confederate General Joseph E. Johnston had an army in North

Carolina that was three times the final size of the Army of Northern Virginia under Lee. Contrary to popular perception, Lee did not control the Confederate Armies. He only controlled the Army of Northern Virginia. Lee did not have the authority to surrender Johnston's Army yet he had the respect of and influence over General Johnston and those other leaders of Confederate armies farther west.

Lee was not only influential in the surrender of Johnston, but he convinced General Nathan Bedford Forrest to surrender rather than heading with his forces into the hills. Both Generals Lee and Grant were fellow graduates of West Point. Grant accepted the surrender of Lee with full military honors and considered that Lee was still a professional American military officer.

That sense of duty imbued in both Grant and Lee toward each other and to the civilian leaders who ordered their actions are two of many examples throughout our history of the proper relationship that must exist between the military and the civilian authorities. Never can the military be allowed to cross the line and disobey the direction given them by our President. The dedication of the Officer Corps is the glue that assures that compliance.

President Harry Truman's firing of General Douglas MacArthur in 1951 was another example of securing the proper relationship. MacArthur crossed the line and disobeyed the direction of the President. He tried to make policy regarding the use of nuclear weapons against China during the Korean War. Thus, he directly contradicted the Constitutional guarantee for those decisions to be made by our civilian, elected authority.

THE ANGER:

During the 1960s and 70s, there was a deep anger within many Americans against their government for our involvement in the Vietnam War. There was a considerable lack of understanding in the minds of a large number of our citizens on exactly why we were there in the first place. What was the purpose of a war in a remote and largely unknown part of our world? What was the threat to the United States? The fact that we still had national conscription (draft) helped to stoke the anger, but there was more to it than that.

That deep anger at the carnage shown nightly on their televisions manifested itself in reaction against the government. President Johnson decided not to seek reelection in 1968 primarily due to the resentment against the Vietnam War. Many Americans, who considered themselves patriotic and willing to send their sons to battle in behalf of their beloved country, were confused. Kennedy and Johnson were both at fault for not preparing the populace by educating them on our reasons. Perhaps if they themselves had properly educated themselves on the purported reasons, they might have decided differently on our participation?

When I was at the Academy, I read a book from their library titled "Blueprint for World Conquest." The author of the book whose name was placed prominently on the cover, was the then-leader of China, Mao Tse-Tung. I have been unable to locate that book since. In the book, Mao wrote that the first thrust for his plan of world conquest would be through Southeast Asia. Was the book written by Mao? Was it a fabrication? If it was true that Mao planned world conquest to start with a thrust through SEA, then this alone would justify a counter action against a Communist takeover of SEA.

A book titled "Blueprint for World Conquest" was published, but it was a compilation of documents from the first meeting of the Communist International held in Moscow in 1920. While the book did recommend military force for the expansion of Communism and the conquest of the world, it did not specify geographic areas.

Since this is strictly a military discussion, whether our government had adequate justification for entering a war in that part of the world or not is somewhat irrelevant. The fact that our government seemed oblivious to the enmity that had existed for over a thousand years between the Vietnamese and the Chinese, was also irrelevant. A decision had been made. Rightly or wrongly, our government made a choice and then directed the military to initiate actions against the Communists.

THE AGONY:

Even though we now have a totally professional military consisting entirely of volunteers without any form of draft, the military is still a reflection of our society. The current positive attitude of our people toward our military and the men and women who participate is essential. We cannot afford to alienate the very people we depend upon to defend us, no matter what the cause.

All the draftees and the vast majority of our military personnel served only in Vietnam and not in the rest of Southeast Asia. Those who participated in actions outside of Vietnam were professional volunteers.

Whether our military soldiers, sailors or airmen are draftees, professionals, reservists or National Guard, our military people need to feel they are serving in a just cause and that they are supported by the very people they are tasked to defend. While it may seem a stretch to some that a fight halfway around the world is actual defense of our country, it is to those who have to risk their lives in conducting the fight.

Many Americans were hostile to the war and that hostility spilled over to those involved in the fighting. After our military people returned from SEA combat, their reception was anything but cordial and often hostile. After my return, that hostility was seemingly everywhere.

From a combatant's perspective, I saw that the military was forced to fight a "holding action" without doing the things necessary to guarantee victory. That was an agony in itself, but we had no choice. The military was only following the orders of our civilian government.

At the Pentagon decision-making level, I saw us fly bombing missions without bombs to satisfy an insane competition between the US Navy and the US Air Force. On a National decision-making level, I saw us not even considering an invasion of North Vietnam or Laos while the NVN armies operated with impunity in Laos, Cambodia and South Vietnam. I participated in and witnessed a secret war that certainly was no secret to the enemy. At the base decision-making level, I saw our military leaders refuse to admit we had a bomb shortage yet still schedule bombing missions against heavily defended targets with minimal or no bomb loads.

The correct description of our fighter-pilot feelings was overwhelming frustration. There was anger too, but most of all was the overwhelming sense of frustration and agony at being placed in such a position, when we were facing death on a daily basis.

I saw enough to cause me to turn away from my support of the war before even a month was up on my combat tour. Yet, I could not waiver from the necessity of my following orders. Many of our citizens were angry at us for not refusing to fight a war we did not support. We got that anger both individually and collectively. Yet we had no choice.

It was agony to feel so alone, yet it was necessary.

CAN IT HAPPEN HERE?

I have repeatedly heard that a situation like the ascendency of the Nazi's could never happen here as it did in Germany. I disagree. We are not so just that we would deny authoritarianism, if the situation were desperate enough.

Look at our treatment of Japanese Americans during WWII. We now condemn it, but then we supported it. Look at the current attitude of many Americans toward Muslims, when it was just a few that, in the name of Allah, killed 3,000 in New York and Washington. While some Muslims act brutally, it is unfair to blame all Muslims. If a small minority of Muslims continues to behave in a brutal manner toward the West, it remains to be seen if American can retain its support of the innocent. Americans historically will go to extremes to protect what they believe is right, whether that belief is right or not.

We gave the Federal government significantly heightened powers during the Depression. The level of authority given to Roosevelt would have been unthinkable in earlier times for our then-young government.

It can happen here.

CROSSING THE RUBICON:

What would have happened if our military men had succumbed to the entreaties of our fellow citizens and refused to fight in SEA?

The Roman experience is an example of what could happen. Rome started out as a democratic republic. Citizen-soldiers manned their army, considered at the time the strongest ever fielded. Instead of being technologically advanced beyond that of their enemies or potential enemies, as we are in the American military, the Roman's used engineering, superior organization and equipment to create a military advantage. While engineering can be considered technology, it is the electronically-driven technology of which I speak. The Romans transferred their military dominance to dominance in trade and their citizens used that commercial power to create a style of luxurious living that was the envy of the entire world. Does that sound familiar? Their society was very close to ours, even with a time-distance of 2,000 years. That Republic lived for more than 200 years, just as has the American Republic.

For those 200 years, the Roman Army did the bidding of the Roman Senate. They conquered much of what is now Europe and North Africa. However, they did not have a principle of military subservience to the civilian government of Rome.

When General Julius Caesar marched from encampment in Celtic Gaul (now France) his army was going to Rome. He was using the power of his victorious army to "influence" Rome on the value of his political leadership as well as military. His marching armies were ordered by the Roman Senate to travel no further than the Rubicon River. It was a specific order from the Republic of Rome for the Roman Army to stop. Caesar defied the Senate and his troops went along with his decision.

When Caesar reached Rome itself, he was declared Emperor and Rome ceased to be a democratic republic and instead became a totalitarian empire. The power of a disobeying military had toppled democratic Rome.

NO TURNING BACK:

Once the military decides, within itself, to disobey the lawful orders of our civilian government, a line will have been crossed. Once a precedent is set, there is no reason that commanding generals have to settle with commanding just a single action to satisfy an angry populace. Once that line is crossed and the military disobeys, there really is no turning back. The table is set for total disobedience. Once the Generals feel that they have a better idea of how our country can and should be run than the civilians and they feel that they have the country behind them, then our democracy and way of life are imperiled.

World history is replete with stories of militaries overthrowing elected governments. It has even happened in England under Cromwell.

Americans need to define the difference between those who create policy and those who are ordered to carry it out. The anger against the military in Vietnam should have been aimed at the civilian leaders and not the military. For those of us in the military who were so condemned, it was an agonizing period.

> *"If we don't end war, war will end us."*
>
> H. G. Wells

CHAPTER TWENTY-THREE
The "Forgotten Ones"
Residue of Defeat

"Only strength can cooperate; weakness can only beg."
General of the Army Dwight D. Eisenhower

When I sat beside the burned-out Laotian log in an attempt to hide from the North Vietnamese soldiers, I wondered why the voices in the woods had not captured me. They knew where I was. There seemed to be enough of them that surrounding me would not have been a problem. If they knew where I was, why didn't they come and get me?

The 10 passes made by the Army Rescap aircraft had made it very clear to the North Viet soldiers exactly where I was located, if there had been any doubt. As I sat on the hillside, it became clear. The soldiers were not interested in me. They were more interested in the rotor-bladed aircraft that would be sent to rescue me. As long as they controlled the rescue aircraft, they controlled me. If they captured or killed me and I would have had no further radio contact with the rescue overhead, then the chance to shoot down a rescue helicopter was lost. Keep me alive and on the run and they had a good chance of also capturing the chopper and crew.

That idea was reinforced when I was attempting to climb the Laotian hill on top of which stood my salvation in the form of a Marine chopper. The Viet gunners hidden in the clump of trees could have shot me at any time. I was in the open and very close to their position. Yet they waited for the chopper to land, and when they did start to fire, it was not at me or the chopper door gunner who ran down to haul me the rest of the way. Their bullets were reserved for the chopper, just as they had been for the first rescue helicopter to land. If they had shot me, then the more lucrative target of the chopper would have flown away.

To me, the answer had everything to do with value. The value was in the chopper. Disable the chopper and they have me, the machine and the chopper crew.

When I consider what might have happened if the Marines had not stationed a second helicopter on strip alert at Khe Sanh, my thoughts turn to prisoners of war (POWs). My mind had already been made up, even at that early stage of my war. If necessary and possible, I would bail out over North Vietnamese controlled territory rather than that of the Pathet Lao. My choice was to eject over one of the MIG bases.

Laos was a very primitive country and North Vietnam seemed the far more civilized of the two. If I was to become a POW, I would have preferred to be a POW of the Viets and not the Laotians.

What would have happened to me and the Marine chopper crew if the helicopter had been disabled and we had all been captured? What happened to the USAF, US Navy, US Marine and US Army pilots and crewmembers who were actually captured in Laos during the period from 1961 through 1973? What happened to the civilian pilots and crews contracted with the CIA? What happened to the CIA pilots themselves?

THE CIA, AIR AMERICA AND CONTINENTAL AIR SERVICES (CAS):

When the CIA came down to Cam Ranh to ask me if I would fly black choppers for them in Laos, I refused for several reasons. The main reason was, of course, that I was an Air Force pilot and owed my allegiance to the Air Force. The secondary reasons were based on the "no" answers that I got from the CIA to my questions. I had asked, "If I am shot down will you rescue me?" Additionally, "If I am shot down, will you admit that I am an American?"

The leaders of our clandestine war against the Communists would turn their backs on us if we were shot down. If I was CIA and was shot down, the lack of rescue almost guaranteed that I would end up a prisoner. If they were unable to admit that I was an American, then my value to the prison wardens would be considerably lessened because my country would not want me, would not attempt to rescue me or even seek my release. To the CIA, I would already have been forgotten.

The CIA had its own Air Force. It did not have to rely on contract-airlines like Air America or CAS to do the clandestine fighting. Initially, the major work of the contract airlines was to transport goods and people. Later, a significant rescue mission was added. Their contribution to the actual fighting was not the same. However, if reports that I have heard from the contract pilots were correct, those contractors did participate in some of the fighting with combat-equipped T-28s and A-1Hs. The reports of CAS pilots on standby at the U.S. Embassy in Vientiane for combat duty also confirms.

What happened to the pilots of the CIA and its contracted airlines after being shot down or having mechanicals to their aircraft and being forced down and captured? Significant research has not shed any light on CIA air losses or any CIA or affiliated pilots being repatriated at the end of the SEA War, with the exception of an exchange for the release of one Air America pilot. Air America did report that it had 14 aircraft crewmembers killed in Laos, but that was just for a limited portion of their time in Laos.

THE "SECRET" WAR:

Some Americans are conversant with the fact that we had American aircraft flying combat against the North. That we were being downed with missiles fired by Russians or that we were being shot down by artillery manned by Chinese and Koreans was unknown. That we were fighting Chinese, Korean and even Russian MIGs was also unknown. The entire "Secret War" in Laos, both in the air and on the ground, was shrouded in mystery.

The US Air Force, Navy and Marines lost the astounding total of 1,557 fixed-wing aircraft in North Vietnam and Laos during the course of the SEA War. This figure does not include rotary-wing (helicopter) losses nor does it include US Army losses.

Also astounding is the knowledge that 500 of those 1,557, or 32.1% of the total, were downed in Laos. Five hundred planes in a remote "Secret War" that was largely unknown. Five hundred planes and more than 600 crewmembers downed and often lost. Those figures don't even include those of our clandestine air forces and the CIA. They also don't include the losses of those early US Army spotter planes that are also shrouded in mystery. The ten passes made over my hidden position on the ground in Laos were all flown by US Army spotter planes.

THE U.S. ARMY SECURITY AGENCY (ASA):

The US Army Security Agency flew a significant number of intelligence aircraft during the war. Those included modified fixed-wing Special Electronic Mission Aircraft (SEMA) such as the Beaver, Otter, Caribou, Seminole, Neptune and Mohawk planes as well as helicopters.

My trip to Nha Trang to visit the Army intelligence guys shed light on the 144th Aviation Company based at Nha Trang. They flew the highly-capable OV-1 Mohawk, which was the only fixed-wing aircraft built specifically for the Army's intelligence mission. It had both a day and night visual photo and infrared surveillance capability plus a side-looking (SLAR) radar.

While it is very difficult to ascertain the number of US Army aircraft shot down in Laos and North Vietnam, their losses were significant. I was certainly aware of the Army presence when so many of their O-1 Bird Dog spotter planes suddenly appeared in the skies over me while I was running in Laos. Several of the photos included in this book were taken by Army observers flying in the O-1s.

According to Wikipedia, the United States Army lost 65 Mohawks while the Army claims 67 of their fixed-wing Mohawks were shot down during the SEA War. The Army claims to have lost 72 dead airmen in those losses. Most of those were reportedly lost in Laos or North Vietnam, but some were in Cambodia. During one seven-month period while I was flying in 1966, the Army lost 28 Mohawks in Laos and NVN. We also lost 297 Army Bird Dog O-1s, many of these in Laos. What happened to those pilots?

Hobson, the author of the authoritative book on fixed-wing losses in SEA "Vietnam Air Losses," does not list a single OV-1 loss during the entire war up to the end of 1966. His book only lists USAF, USN and Marine fixed-wing losses. How many of the 364 US Army fixed-wing losses were in Laos? What happened to those pilots?

The US Army lost 5,086 helicopters during the SEA War. It is unknown how many of these were due to combat in Laos and the fate of their pilots is also unknown.

POW RELEASE NEGOTIATIONS & MISSING IN ACTION:

In January, 1973, Henry Kissinger, Secretary of State in the Nixon Administration, opened negotiations with North Vietnam on a settlement of the Vietnamese War. Part of that settlement had to do with the repatriation of our POWs who had languished in prison in Hanoi and surrounding villages. American aviator Everett Alvarez spent more than eight years in the North Viet prisons. Those who were shot down and captured during my part of the War spent six years. It was far longer than any such military captivity in the history of our Republic.

During the heat of an air battle, the method and results of a "shoot down" may not be witnessed by other pilots. The other pilots in an attack are usually very busy dodging defensive weapons and delivering their bomb loads on their targets. They are usually unable to visually record some of the events of an attack, such as how other pilots faired if shot down. I can attest to that, having seen how intense an attack against the North could be with heavily defended targets. It all happens very fast. Usually, an attack by tactical fighter-bombers lasts no more than several minutes and against targets such as in the North, often just a matter of seconds.

While Laos was not quite as intense as the North, there were certain Laotian targets that had significant AAA protection and there were SAM sites throughout much of Laos. Some of those sites were unoccupied but others housed the deadly missiles. Whatever the cause, when pilots were shot down they often would end up classified as Missing in Action.

As time progressed, the names and numbers of the pilots shot down and captured in North Vietnam became better known. However, the names and numbers of those shot down and missing in Laos remained a mystery.

Kissinger himself admitted the problem in his book "Years of Upheaval," published in 1982, that "Equally frustrating were our discussions of the American prisoners of war or missing in action. We knew of at least 80 instances in which an American serviceman had been captured alive (in Laos) and had subsequently disappeared. The evidence consisted of either voice communications from the ground in advance of capture or photographs and names published by the Communists."

THE AGREEMENT:

Less than a month after the December, 1972 B-52 raids on North Vietnam, on January 27, 1973, an agreement to end the war and restore peace in Vietnam was signed in Paris. Thus, when America finally showed resolve and convinced the North Viets we were serious about the execution of the war, North Vietnam came to the bargaining table. Conflict resolution came as the result of a show of strength and not weakness as had been shown for years under both Johnson and Nixon.

Signatories to the agreement were the United States, North Vietnam, South Vietnam and the South Vietnamese Provisional Revolutionary Government (PRG). The PRG was the political arm of the Viet Cong. The agreement provided for the release of many of the pilots held in North Vietnamese prisons.

"Operation Homecoming" was the name given to the last repatriation of US POWs by the North Vietnamese. It began on February 12, 1973 and ended March 29, 1973. Few Americans alive and aware at that time can forget the jubilation when our pilots were freed at Gia Lam airfield in the North and flown by three USAF C-141s to Clark AFB in the Philippines. It was a joyous affair. In addition to the 141s, a C-9 was sent to Saigon to pick up those POWs released in the South.

President Nixon proclaimed, **"All of our POWs** are coming home!" Of course, this is the same Nixon who announced to the American public that "I am not a crook."

The actual agreement of the four parties consisted of a preamble, and nine chapters covering 23 articles and four protocols. Chapter VII, Articles 21 and 22 outlined the future relationship between the US and the Republic of North Vietnam (DRV). One of the principles stated: "Preliminary US studies indicate that the appropriate programs for the US contribution to postwar reconstruction will fall in the range of $3.25 billion of grant aid over five years. Other forms of aid will be agreed upon between the two parties. This estimate is subject to revision and to detailed discussions between the Government of the United States and the Government of the Democratic Republic of Vietnam (DRV)."

Thus, the exchange of POWs was actually based on a reconstruction agreement between the DRV and the US that had the US supplying $3.25 billion in grant aid, plus other help, making the total aid package valued in excess of $4 billion.

Anyone who has had anything to do with negotiations knows that you don't give everything away before you receive payment. Ho was still alive at that point and was too cagey an operator to have made that mistake. The prisoner release for "Operation Homecoming" was actually supposed to be just the first release of prisoners instead of being the last.

In April, 1993, Harvard scholar Stephen Morris discovered a document in a Soviet archive indicating that Vietnam may have misled the Americans about the numbers of POWs it held at the war's end. The document, a translation of writings allegedly prepared by NVN General Tran Van Quang, stated that NVN held 1,205 American POWs as of September 1972, just a few months before the release of the 591 POWs in Operation Homecoming. Several independent analysts, including Kissinger and former National Security Advisor Zbigniew Brzezinski, said the document appeared authentic.

That the North Viets failed to release the rest of the prisoners is no mystery as the United States Congress failed to authorize the promised aid and all of Southeast Asia received no reconstruction or other monies promised in the agreement for the prisoner release.

MISSING REPRESENTATION:

The list of those governments attending the negotiations shows one glaring discrepancy. Even though the Laos Patriotic Front (LPF) sent a representative, he was just an observer. The LPF was the political arm of the Pathet Lao. The Pathet Lao, which held an unknown but significant number of American prisoners, did not participate in the debate of their fate.

Even though 32.1% of American "out of country" warplanes were shot down in Laos, not one prisoner of the Pathet Lao was ever released in Operation Homecoming. There were 10 prisoners from Laos who were released, but one was a Canadian citizen and the other nine were pilots who bailed out in that portion of Laos under the control of the North Vietnamese Army. The nine American pilots were not handed over to the Pathet Lao and, instead, they were sent directly to NVN POW camps.

The areas of Laos controlled by North Vietnamese Army troops varied from year to year and it makes sense that any American pilot captured in NVN Army controlled areas would be sent directly to NVN prisons. What is hard to conceive is this: if 67.9% of air combat losses amounted to more than 400 pilot-prisoners of the North Viets, why did 32.1% of the losses yield only nine pilot-prisoners in Laos? Were the rest all killed or what? The fact remains that the only American pilots to ever make it back to America from Laotian prisons were Chuck Klussmann in 1964 and Dieter Dengler in February, 1966, and those two had escaped.

At the time of the POW release, the United States claimed that there were 1350 POWs or MIAs in North Vietnam and Laos. Only 591 of the claimed 1350 were released, leaving 759 unaccounted for. In the declassified CIA report "Enemy Prisons in Laos," it is stated that more than 60 POWs were being held by the Pathet Lao. In 1969, the USAF estimated 61 POWs were in Laos. Numerous reports claim sightings of "Caucasian" prisoners in the Pathet Lao cave prisons. Other estimates have the number of American prisoners in Laos as much higher.

Kissinger and Le Duc Tho, representing the DRV, negotiated for weeks about the Laotian prisoners. Kissinger held fast to the American position that the prisoner exchange should be controlled exclusively through the DRV. Le Duc Tho argued that Laos was a sovereign nation and that they could handle their own negotiations. Their impasse on Laos seemed to reflect on the Vietnamese prisoners. After two weeks of intense, but fruitless, negotiations with the North Viets, our government suddenly claimed that the other 759 reported prisoners, mostly pilots, were dead.

That claim seemed to be refuted by comments made just prior to the subsequent failure of Congress to authorize any reconstruction money, effort or supplies. Secretary of State William P. Rogers three times called for restraint by members of Congress in making adverse comments on the aid issue. He further stated "At least until American troops are out of Vietnam and (until) all American prisoners are released. His comment was made much later than the actual prisoner release, which certainly indicates that the American government realized it was leaving many POWs behind.

The New York Times later added that Secretary Rogers asked the Senate Foreign Relations Committee that the controversy over aid be kept to a minimum for at least another month or so, which would "allow the release of American prisoners to be completed." These comments and negotiations were also made much later than the actual release of the 591 prisoners in Operation Homecoming. Scroll up to Nixon's comment made to the American public on the earlier repatriation of American POWs. Nixon promised that "ALL of our POWs are coming home."

A STATEMENT OF VALUE:

During the negotiations held in Paris, back in Laos the Pathet Lao emphatically stated that any release of Pathet Lao prisoners of war would be done on Lao soil. It seemed apparent that the Laotian Communists wanted in on the action. While the agreement hammered out between Kissinger and Le Duc Tho included a lot of money for the DRV, no money or assistance was promised for Laos. The Pathet Lao was cast aside.

Laos is an extremely poor and backward country. My feelings, when I was over there, were that it was almost a Stone Age country. When the Pathet Lao learned that it had been left out in the cold regarding reparations, it had to have considered what, if anything, it had of value from the long war that was so brutal to their country.

To the Pathet Lao, if the United States was not interested in freeing its POWs, it seems reasonable that they would consider selling the POWs to the highest bidder.

A defector from the Czechoslovakian Republic, before the collapse of the Warsaw Pact, claims that more than 100 American POWs from the SEA War were processed through his country enroute to the Soviet Union.

If this claim is correct, it seems that the Pathet Lao was able to find a "highest" bidder for its prisoners. Whatever the Soviets planned to do with the pilots is cause for conjecture, but they did the same to American officer-prisoners at the end of the Korean War.

BETRAYAL:

When I sat on that Laotian hillside contemplating my next move, I had total assurance that our military would come in to attempt to rescue Paul and me. There was no question in my mind. It is part of what makes our military strong. Our soldiers, sailors and airmen know that our military has our back and will do their utmost to fight for our lives.

However, when it comes to the political arm of our country, many of us have no such assurance that we would be "rescued." Henry Kissinger and Richard Nixon did what was politically expedient for their careers and left our airmen, who were captured in Laos and North Vietnam, to a future not much better than death.

Since exposure to the truth would give a very negative impression to the world, somewhere in Russia must exist a very secret location housing the remnants of our pilot forces from the Korean War and the sizable pilot forces from Southeast Asia. Either that or the pilots were killed after the Soviets were done with them.

THE GENEVA CONVENTION AND WATER BOARDING:

The United States is a signatory to the Geneva Conventions on the conduct of war and the treatment of prisoners of war (POWs). The Conventions specifically prohibit torturing of prisoners.

We are under a very different situation regarding the nature of our current enemies. They may not belong to identifiable military units while on the "battlefield" and don't wear uniforms, but they still operate violently in a military fashion. They are enemy combatants. Consideration must be given to treatment of those captured combatants regarding torture. By any logical definition, water boarding is torture. Water boarding is in violation of the Geneva Conventions.

When politicians make statements advocating water boarding, they do so in violation of those Geneva Conventions. While most of our enemies and potential enemies, past and present, don't conform to the Conventions, we should still operate on a higher plane than they and stand for certain higher standards of behavior.

Should the United States advocate the use of water boarding for those prisoners we hold, it condemns our military men to the same sort of treatment, and worse, whenever our soldiers, sailors and airmen are captured.

MARCHING HOME:

While I and the rest of us that endured the war in SEA can lay claim to dishonor and repudiation when we came "marching home" from war, we were the fortunate ones.

The level of our governmental betrayal of those entrusted to fight its wars is almost incomprehensible. This is just another reason that clandestine wars should never happen. The "Secret Wars" in Laos were so secret that our public did not know of their existence and the result was that our fighting men who participated were thrown to the wolves with a fate hard to imagine. With secret wars, there is no accountability.

After SEA, the level of necessary trust between the military men and our government was broken. Our military has to believe that it is fighting a just war and that, if necessary, our government will fight long and hard to gain the release of anyone captured. Nixon, like Johnson before him, seemed to be making decisions based on pragmatism and popularity rather than on humanity or loyalty.

If, at the time of the POW release and their own "marching home," the American public would have known about the POWs that we were leaving behind in both Laos and North Vietnam, the outcry might have encouraged a changed approach by the Nixon Administration. The lack of accountability by those entrusted with making decisions regarding the Clandestine Wars condemned those airborne warriors, who fought in behalf of our country, to an unimaginable life and death.

They were and are "the forgotten ones."

> *"Prison is designed to break one's spirit and destroy one's resolve…*
> *with the idea of stamping out that spark that makes each of us human."*
>
> Nelson Mandela

BOOK 5: MARCHING HOME

BOOK SIX

Lessons

CHAPTER TWENTY-FOUR

Rules of Engagement
The McNamara Legacy

> *"If men make war in slavish obedience to rules, they will fail."*
> Commanding General of the Union Armies Ulysses S. Grant

When I graduated from the United States Air Force Academy, my intention was to make the Air Force a career. The intent and motivation were strong. But, my service as a fighter pilot in the Southeast Asian War (Vietnam) changed my plans. The lack of resolve displayed by the United States caused me and many of my fellow pilots to leave the Air Force.

As mentioned previously, what has been called the Vietnam War was really the Southeast Asian War. It involved the active participation of the Southeast Asian countries of China, Vietnam, Laos, Cambodia, The Philippines and Thailand. In addition, Cuba, Russia and other Warsaw Pact countries sent personnel and equipment. The Cubans were in charge of the infamous Hanoi Hilton and the Russians manned the SAM sites. North Koreans manned AAA guns and flew MIGs against us. A half-million Chinese soldiers worked to repair bomb damage. Chinese manned many of the MIGs with which we fought and manned much of the AAA that shot us down. South Korean, Australian and New Zealand troops and equipment fought along our side. It was truly an international war.

The United States displayed a fear of further active involvement by the Chinese and the Soviet Union and this fear impacted how we fought the war. That fear was embodied in the severe restrictions imposed on United States Naval and Air Force fighter-bomber aircraft. Twenty years after the United States withdrew from Saigon, the Air Force and Navy declassified certain documents that detailed the severe restrictions placed on our pilots as they fought against North Vietnam and their allies in the operation called "Rolling Thunder."

The U.S. Navy participated from aircraft carriers stationed in the Gulf of Tonkin. The U.S. Air Force participated from bases such as Danang and Cam Ranh Bay in South Vietnam and Ubon, Korat, Udorn and Takhli in Thailand. Special operations from other bases and from clandestine air forces also supported the effort. The tools were there for our victory, but the tools were not utilized in an effective manner. The restrictions on our air war were detailed in the Rules of Engagement and the information from the declassified reports on the "Rules" clearly shows that much of that blame may be attributed to the Secretary of Defense under President Johnson, Robert S. McNamara.

The following narrative includes personal experiences and many references to declassified intelligence reports on the Rules of Engagement that ruled our USAF and USN conduct of the War. Excerpts from those declassified reports will show that our Department of Defense, under the leadership of Secretary Robert McNamara and President Lyndon Johnson, restricted our military actions to the extent that we were unable to mount a sustained offensive and were unable to attack the targets necessary for victory in the war.

BOMBING HALTS:

While operating against the North, I had to "stand down" many times from missions due to a series of American bombing halts. Those self-imposed bombing halts only succeeded in allowing the North to resupply their AAA and AW guns, especially those at a distance from their sources of supply. The halts also allowed the North to repair the damage caused by the significant efforts of the military to close off sources of supply.

To our pilot's eyes, bombing halts were closely related to the destructive Rules of Engagement in that they were both self-imposed rules that denied us the ability to win.

My combat diary only lists two bombing halts. The reality was that there were many more. I do recall that I managed to leave Cam Ranh for Okinawa or Thailand during some of these halts. My memory recalls 12 bombing halts from the start of the war until I left in January of 1967. However, I cannot verify my memories. What I have verified is that all the bombing halts were not listed or admitted.

The first halt was on May 13, 1965, and it was for four days. The second was on December 24th, 1965 and lasted 37 days. According to Dean Rusk, stated in a recorded interview at the LBJ Library, "I must confess that President Johnson's disappointment in the 37-day bombing pause made a lasting impression on him, because he was very skeptical from that time onward that anything could be done on any sort of bombing halt."

This statement by Rusk flies counter to Johnson's actions. According to the report The USAF in SEA, 1961 to 1973, "President Johnson also approved briefer bombing shutdowns to permit celebrations of TET, Buddha's birthday, Christmas, New Year's Day, Easter," any cause for celebration.

The ostensible purpose of the bombing halts was to bring NVN to the bargaining table. Unfortunately, none of the halts achieved that American objective. The concept of halts came from the meetings between Rusk, McNamara and Johnson, without the judgment of any military man included.

Rusk, who served on General Marshall's War Planning Staff during World War II, should have known better. He stated in the above interview that, "I suggested that, as an alternative to adding substantially to our forces, that we consider a very serious bombing halt, at least in those areas of NVN that were most directly involved in the battlefield in the South."

The lesson that should have been learned was that stopping the bombing did not achieve anything toward getting the North Viets to the bargaining table. That lesson should have been learned time and again. Timidity does not win wars. It was the massive Linebacker II bombing campaign in 1972 that drove the North Viets to the bargaining table so quickly that an agreement was signed within a month. If you want to bargain, do it from strength and not from weakness.

Associated Press reported that "there were nine pauses of varying duration, mostly during holiday periods, before Johnson ordered all bombing north of the 19th parallel halted on March 31, 1968." All bombing throughout North Vietnam was halted on November 1, 1968. In my opinion, there were far more than nine.

The fact that some of the bombing halts never got in our history books may have been that they were unknown outside the military. Another was the varying descriptions used. Bombing halts, bombing pauses, cease fires, stand downs, bombing cessations and other names all amounted to the same thing.

We pilots cringed each time we flew a mission against those guns after a bombing halt. Usually that meant intense flak on the next mission against any protected target. What did the halts accomplish toward winning the war? They certainly helped our enemy recover from the damage we had taken so long to sustain. An air interdiction campaign has to be sustained or it is for naught. That this repeated action by President Johnson was in gross violation of the time-tested Principles of War, does not seemed to have mattered to our politicians.

There were other situations and times where I was privileged to hear, read about, witness or participate in actions or events that gave me great concern about the conduct of the war and about the apparent lack of resolve of our national leaders to lead us on a course designed to win the war.

What I was told, read, witnessed or participated in caused me to wonder what was the real policy behind our actions? Of primary concern were the many restrictions against the use of our planes in the conduct of our missions against our enemy. The American government seemed to be doing everything in its power to keep us from winning the war.

The first of two USAF intelligence reports called "Project CHECO, Southeast Asia Report- the Evolution of the Rules of Engagement for Southeast Asia from 1960 to 1965, was declassified on July 3, 1991. The second, with the same name, defined our restrictions from January 1, 1966 to November 1, 1969." It was declassified on April 28, 1994. Both reports were originally classified Top Secret NOFORN, which means it was off-limits to all foreign nationals.

As has been mentioned in another chapter, the 559th TFS reached Okinawa by flying two tanker-assisted non-stops called Trans Pacs. The first was from MacDill AFB in Tampa, Florida to Hickam AFB in Hawaii. The second hop took us from Hawaii to Naha AB in Okinawa.

While in Hawaii, our squadron was given a briefing on the intelligence situation in SEA. The importance of the briefing was underscored by the fact that the briefer was the Commander of PACAF (Pacific Air Force) Intelligence himself. He stated that we might be among the first USAF Phantom squadrons committed to the war and he wanted to brief us himself. The 45th TFS preceded us by several months, only their destination was Thailand where they became the first Air Force Phantom squadron to actually engage in combat. The 45th lost an aircraft in combat the same day as our briefing.

In the briefing, we were shown intelligence photos of eight Surface-to-Air Missile sites armed with the SAM II missiles. We were told that the DOD had placed the sites off limits to targeting. That denial of our ability to bomb the SAM sites continued until the Russians had constructed more than 100 of them. Only then were the restrictions lifted and we added them to our target lists. From a targeting standpoint, this hesitation made no sense.

From a pilot's perspective, the experience of one Navy fighter-bomber pilot is illuminative. He reported spotting and counting 111 SA-2s being loaded on a railroad car in the Hanoi marshaling yards. He was "denied permission to bomb them." As he stated, "We have to fight all 111 of them, one at a time." This is a stark example of what the Rules of Engagement meant to the SEA Air War.

The narrative that follows includes excerpts from those de-classified reports. The direct quotes from the reports are included with *italics*.

THE "RULES OF ENGAGEMENT"- NORTH VIETNAM:

The policy of gradualism which characterized the Rolling Thunder bombing campaign over North Vietnam since its inception in 1965 continued until late in 1968. This gradualism was forced on the military by our civilian leaders. It *illustrated the continuing validity of the maxim that "war is an extension of national policy."* Our national policy of "gradualism" was possibly the major mistake of the war. President Johnson and Secretaries Rusk and McNamara were the authors of "gradualism." Its level of its success can be attributed to its results. We lost the war.

The Rules of Engagement are national policy translated to the battlefield. Each change, or threat of change, to the US political relationship with other nations, whether Allies, enemies, or potential enemies, was reflected in a corresponding alteration of the Rules of Engagement for the Vietnam conflict.

There were a number of cases during these years in which to attempt to improve the image of the war on the home front dictated change (to the Rules). In other words, it was not military considerations but instead political considerations that often dictated how the war was being fought.

The Rules document covering the period from 1960 to 1965 has many of the same concerns relating to political pressure being exerted on our military to limit the size and scope of our war. In a March, 1965 statement from the Pacific Commander (CINCPAC), *the US military actions were circumscribed by political necessity on many occasions. There were certain political constraints which would remain in effect until the U.S. "signals" were properly read in Hanoi, Peking (Beijing) and Moscow… Restrictions should be lifted gradually in order to preserve the sensitive agreements which had been reached by painstaking political negotiation.* In other words, the Johnson Administration felt politics was primary and military considerations were secondary in a War. The report again uses the term "gradual" when it referred to the implementation of airpower. The fallacy of gradualism is that by slow escalation you announce your intentions to the enemy in advance and allow him to make adjustments and import defensive equipment in a timely fashion.

The report goes on to say: *The rules established for conduct of air operations to-date have taken a number of forms. These have included geographic and political restraints; limitations on the size, frequency and altitude of flights; and restrictions on weapon types employed. In combination, they have posed a challenging, sometimes frustrating succession of problems for the commanders and staff officers charged with the planning and conduct of an effective campaign… Several of the constraints that still exist, limit the capability of our forces to conduct a campaign that will achieve the desired objective.* The repeated discussions and exchanges, which have been generated at all levels by these constraints, have centered mainly on the specific proscriptions rather than on the fundamental policy considerations which underlie them. This was the conclusion of the 1965 report and it laid the problem at the feet of the civilian authorities.

Just what were the political constraints imposed on the military and what was their cause? Referring to the 1969 report: *In a 1967 interview in "US News and World Report," a French journalist and editor, Rene Dabernat, said that Communist China had informed the United States in the spring of 1966 it would not become involved in the Vietnam War, if the U.S. refrained from invading North Vietnam, as well as (refraining) from bombing North Vietnam's (Red River) dikes. Dabernat said that statements by President Lyndon B. Johnson and other U.S. officials demonstrated that they had "agreed to these conditions."* This is in line with the restrictions imposed on us by the Air Force. That same month a *newspaper article written by Edgar Ansel Mowrer stated the United States had a promise from Red China not to intervene in*

Vietnam as long as the <u>US refrained from blockading Haiphong as well as not attacking North Vietnam</u>.

This was unprecedented. Never in my knowledge has a non-combatant nation dictated the terms of how a war is to be fought by a combatant nation. This type of agreement would obviously be subject to the strictest of classifications. However, the passage of time usually allows the content of important secret agreements to emerge. Nothing has ever emerged showing such an agreement in other wars fought by the United States.

Furthermore, *it was the Secretary's (McNamara) view that an intensive air campaign designed to interdict completely war-supporting materials might result in a direct confrontation with the Soviet Union. <u>Bombing of the port facilities, he said, or mining of the harbors would seriously threaten Soviet shipping</u>.* Therefore, McNamara determined that the military-recommended bombing of the dikes, blockading of Haiphong, or mining all the harbors were to be restricted and made "off limits." The fact that the "Soviet shipping" was carrying war supplies to be used against us seemed not to have registered on or mattered to McNamara.

McNamara used his own counsel and repeatedly disregarded the collective opinions of the military. Before we became embroiled so heavily in SEA, the US Navy and US Air Force both evaluated the F-111 design pushed by McNamara. He wanted to develop another aircraft similar to the F-4 that could be used by all the services. If we could again develop a common aircraft that would suit our different requirements, it would be very cost effective. He referred to the "commonality" of parts as a significant cost savings.

The F-111 was designed with an elongated fuselage. This design was good for high speeds in excess of Mach at lower altitudes, which allowed for low-level, under-the-radar penetration for nuclear strikes. The F-105 is a similar, but shorter, design. The Air Force spent 125,000 man hours in evaluating the design of the F-111 and finally turned it down. One of the reasons that it turned the F-111 down was that the Air Force needed a smaller fighter able to turn much tighter in combat. An elongated fuselage does not turn very tightly and is very vulnerable to enemy air defenses. The US Navy also turned it down. I have no idea how many man hours the Navy employed in its analysis?

McNamara thought about it over a weekend and decided to disregard the opinions of both the Navy and Air Force. Apparently, he considered himself smarter than the collective wisdom of the military. After it was built, it was found that the F-111 would not fit on the elevators of half the aircraft carriers in the Navy fleet. Of course the Navy had realized that, but McNamara failed to consider that important "detail." Thus, the aircraft was useless as a Navy weapons system. That colossal arrogance carried over to his management (some say mismanagement) of the SEA War.

The Air Force could not use the F-111 design because it did not fit their fighter need. Thus they had to re-designate the F-111 as a bomber, as evidenced by the "B" portion of the B-111. McNamara's futile attempt to save the Department of Defense money resulted in a huge waste of money through the purchase of a deficiently-designed bomber that the Air Force and Navy did not need. Such was the wisdom of our wartime Secretary of Defense.

McNamara's disregard for military judgment manifested itself in many ways. It was also manifest in his selection of subordinates and advisors. My participation in the MacDill briefing of Robert W. Comer, who was Secretary McNamara's Department of Defense "expert" on fighter aircraft, has already been mentioned in this book. The briefing was disturbing. It was my first example of how McNamara and his team thought that they had all the answers and did not need input from those entrusted to operate the equipment or make military decisions. It was a flaw that would eventually prove fatal.

What was even more troubling was that Comer might have had the correct performance figures that were stated by MacDonald-Douglas, but the figures were totally wrong when it came to operational performance. Aircraft that are production models don't behave like the test aircraft that manufacturers use when formulating performance data. Aircraft that have many hours of use in sometimes severe conditions simply don't behave like the book says they should. It is the same with cars. After 200,000 miles, a car does not perform the same as when it was driven from the dealership.

The purpose of Comer's visit to MacDill should have been to learn actual performance. Comer left the briefing without learning a thing. What was most troubling about my briefing of Comer is that he was later named as the personal representative of President Johnson to the SEA War.

Comer was doing the same thing that his boss McNamara was doing. He was making decisions and passing judgment on incorrect data. In McNamara's case, he based many of his decisions about the progress of the air war on bomb damage assessment (BDA) figures. He was using the same criteria he used as President of Ford Motor Company. Only data from the production floors of automotive plants are not the same as data resulting from the "field" in a war. He wanted wartime data and he was given wartime data. Only those entrusted with BDA were often unable to properly assess BDA due to smoke and foliage. Yet he still got his data, even though it was often grossly inflated and "manufactured" by ground or air controllers.

His emphasis on "body count" as a measure of performance gave him wildly inflated figures. Often, I was on missions when the Forward Air Controllers would be unable to see anything after we hit with our bombs, bullets and napalm. Many of our targets were under the dense canopies of the rainforest. After a napalm attack, the burning would create dense smoke that makes assessment impossible. Fragmentation bombs create a great deal of dust and smoke. The smoke often totally obliterated any viewing of the entire target area. Yet the FACs were required to have a BDA and they would often say, "Well that should have killed maybe 10 of them," and that would be what was reported.

Since the Rules of Engagement in place from 1960 through the end of 1965 did not have the effect desired by McNamara, *a Commander's Conference was held in Honolulu, from January 17 to 31st in 1966. At the conference, a stronger approach was suggested. Three tasks were proposed to accomplish the objectives of the forthcoming 1966 Rolling Thunder campaign:*

(1) Reduce, disrupt and harass the external assistance being provided to North Vietnam.

(2) Destroy in depth those resources already in NVN which contribute most of the support of aggression. Destroy or deny use of all known permanent military facilities. Harass and disrupt dispersed military operations.

(3) Harass, disrupt and impede movement of men and materials through the southern NVN into Laos and SVN.

The conferees made it clear that, although they recognized the interrelationship of all three tasks, they believed that successful accomplishment of the first two would have the greatest impact on the enemy. **Disruption of external assistance would require attacks on and the mining of harbors and the ports of Haiphong, Hon Gay, and Cam Pha, as well as interdiction of the two main rail lines leading to the Chinese border from Hanoi. The task of destroying resources already in NVN must concentrate on POL systems, power plants, and military facilities.** *The interdiction effort in the southern part of NVN was less* *destructive of the war-making resources, but was, nevertheless, a vital part of the overall package of tasks.*

While the military commanders in Hawaii were arriving at these conclusions, Defense Secretary Robert S. McNamara viewed things differently. The Defense Department (Chief) was satisfied that the limited 1965 Rolling Thunder offensive had achieved its objectives...To DOD (McNamara's) eyes, the primary objectives of bombing NVN were to strengthen the morale of the South Vietnamese by showing US determination and continued support; to reduce the flow of men and equipment from the North to the South, or to increase the cost of that flow to the North Vietnamese by bombing infiltration routes and the military sources of supply; and to put political pressure on NVN to halt their subversion campaign in the South. The Defense Secretary recognized (his) *key to achieving these objectives was in the interdiction of the lines of communications (LOCs) in southern NVN rather than in attacks on entry ports and military storage supplies farther north.*

Just as in the case of the F-111s, McNamara disregarded the collective opinion of the entire uniformed military and substituted his own flawed judgment. History has shown us how competent that non-military judgment turned out to be. Again, McNamara denied us the ability to attack concentrations and instead dictated attacking dispersals.

When I was in SEA, I overflew Haiphong many times. Ships were continually seen offloading supplies to barges and lighters who then took the supplies up the Red River to Hanoi. Much of these supplies were assumed to be military. Those were the bullets that eventually made it to the South. Those were the bullets that killed American servicemen. Which begs the question, why were we fighting a war if we are not allowed to use the weapons necessary to win the war? If our leaders are so cautious (cowardly) that they succumb to the threats of the Chinese and Soviets, then we had no business involving ourselves in the war in the first place.

At the start of the conflict, the ostensible reason for fighting in Vietnam was to counter a possible thrust by Red China through Southeast Asia. That would have been the only justifiable reason to involve ourselves in a civil war. But if we were there to counter China, why were we allowing China to dictate our actions? Was Johnson too cowardly to admit his cowardice to the American people?

The application of military power should never be used except as a last resort and then only if all diplomatic efforts have been exhausted. The application of political limits on a military operation is justifiable. But a military has to be able to maneuver within the political constraints. We were fighting against North Vietnam as well as the Viet Cong. The presence of division-sized units of the North Vietnamese Army in South Vietnam and in Laos made both the North and Laos legitimate targets for invasion. We had every right to invade North Vietnam to move the war from defensive to offensive and accomplish our objective, assuming our objective was to defeat the enemy. What better way to rid the South of North Vietnamese troops than to invade the North and force them to recall their troops from the South to defend the North. President Johnson should have imposed HIS terms on the Chinese and not vice versa. Sometimes the very threat of an action is enough to convince an enemy as long as the enemy is convinced of the sincerity of the threat.

One of the abiding tenants of the military is loyalty up and loyalty down. This means that commanders are responsible to support and show loyalty to their subordinates as well as their superiors. We were showing loyalty to the Constitution and Johnson by obeying Johnson's orders to go to war. He was under obligation to the military to show the same loyalty by supporting us and giving us the necessary tools (equipment and policy) to complete our mission. Here we go back to the objective of the war. What was the objective? If we have no overall objective, we can't develop a successful plan to complete our mission. If we have no political objective, we have no mission.

MCNAMARA'S BODY COUNT:

When Secretary of War McNamara declared that "body count" was an important "objective" of our missions, I lost whatever positive thought I had left on the conduct of the War. After McNamara singled out bodies as an objective, the FACs did their best to insure we had body counts, whether the counts were assured or not.

As a professional military man, my job was to help solve, through military action, the objectives that diplomacy was unable to solve. The objectives had to do with national interest. If our national interest was to kill people, then I was in the wrong business.

Wars kill people, of course, but the killing and destruction must have an objective. They must only be a means to an end coinciding with our national objective. Killing must never be an end in itself. When the means becomes the end, it is time to reconsider.

To this day I have a strong distaste for Jane Fonda, often referred to as "Hanoi" Jane, and that distaste is almost universal among military men. However, when she called the fighter pilots "trained killers" she was right with regard to SEA. McNamara's focus on "body count" insured that she was right, which was very troubling to fighter pilots tasked to deny and not necessarily to kill.

General Momyer, commander of 7th Air at the time of my fighting, said that there was no target in SEA worth the loss of one of our front-line fighter-bombers. Most of us fighting would have agreed. The F-4 was better at being an air superiority or interdiction weapon and should have remained such in a primitive war like SEA. An aircraft specifically designed for close-air-support should have been used. An aircraft equipped with multiple, internally-mounted cannon and with a fuel capacity to stay "on target" much longer than the Phantom or other high-performance fighter-bombers should have been employed. The F-4 was a good choice for some of our interdiction missions and those missions requiring us to protect against MIGs. But, the close-air-support missions and those against the HCMT should have been employing an A-10-type aircraft.

The killing of the greatest number of the enemy is never the proper objective of our military. Killing has to have purpose and the purpose of war is not to kill, but to deny.

OBJECTIVES:

When our civilian leaders decide to go to war, they should define the political objective. The political objective that Lincoln gave to Grant was simply, "win the war." It should be left to the military to define the military objectives needed to accomplish the political objectives.

The Israelis showed in their Six-Day War how air wars should be fought. Strike hard and fast and destroy as much as necessary in the shortest possible time. Abide by the Principles of War. They won the war in six days. The casualty figures on both sides were low. They accomplished their political objective with a low body-count.

Another lesson that can be learned from the successful Six-Day War involved the size of the force and their comprehension of the threat severity. Sometimes a larger sized military force can be detrimental for the overall mission. A larger size often results in greater inefficiencies. Conversely, too small a size can negate our mission as happened in Iran on the rescue mission under President Carter.

When America attacked the Iraqi forces in Kuwait, we abided by the Principles of War and we won our limited objective in 100 hours. We had a limited objective which we accomplished by killing a limited number of the enemy because we did it in a limited time. A professional military should try to kill as FEW of the enemy as possible, while still accomplishing its objectives. If the killing of many of the enemy is necessary to accomplish our objectives, then we need to do it. But killing should never become an objective in and of itself.

By forcing a stalemate, McNamara made the objective to be killing the greatest number of the enemy instead of breaking the NVN's will and ability to fight. With killing as the objective imposed by our civilian leaders, we pilots became nothing more than killers instead of professional airmen entrusted to carry out an air campaign in support of reasonable political objectives.

Even if we did not invade, denial of the enemy's source of supplies was essential. Since his source for supplies came on the NE or NW rail routes or by sea, it was necessary for us to impede that supply as much as possible and to do so at its source where it was concentrated. Johnson and McNamara denied us that ability to properly impede their sources of supply.

BOMBING POPULATION CENTERS:

When we attacked the North, we were not allowed to attack population centers. The enemy used this restriction to secure his supply routes. The North Viets would run their railroad trains at night or day, speeding between each town. Their early warning radar system would alert them if American planes were coming their way. If we were, they would park their trains within towns until the threat of our planes was gone. Additionally, they placed their AAA guns within civilian neighborhoods.

In WWII, if the enemy used civilian areas for military purposes, the civilian areas became legitimate military targets. In North Vietnam, it was different. We could not bomb the towns under threat of courts martial, even if they had the lucrative and ammo-laden trains parked inside their city limits. Make no mistake, I am not advocating the bombing of civilian populations as we did on a wholesale basis during WWII. On the contrary, I am advocating against it. However, I am advocating that we bomb them if any enemy uses the centers to house military targets.

Our precision bombing capability means that in future wars we can identify military targets within population centers and use that precision to eradicate. However, it is war and we will never be able to create foolproof bombing methods or equipment. Mistakes will be made and those mistakes will be both human and material. Our expectations should never be that targets will be miraculously destroyed without any collateral damage to civilians. In those instances, pilots may be encountering severe defensive reactions or their bombs might malfunction. The onus should never be on our aircrews. It should be on an enemy for being so callous as to endanger its own civilian population centers by placing military targets in close proximity.

An F-104 pilot was actually courts martialed for a bombing mistake in combat in Vietnam. To a pilot force risking its life under trying conditions, this was a huge mistake on the part of the military, but a mistake forced on the military by Johnson and his incompetent lieutenants.

If you want maximum productivity from pilots as well as other combatants, you applaud their efforts and do not punish them. Those responsible for making mistaken decisions, like a courts martial, should have been required to fly in our back seats to see for themselves what we were up against.

There were occasions when flights were bombing targets near North Viet towns. As sometimes happens in dropping heavy bombs, the release mechanisms might hang up and the bomb might not properly separate from the MER (Multiple Ejection Rack) or TER (Triple Ejection Rack) that held it. In our operations, several bombs that hung up in this manner finally released when the pilot was climbing out and pulling "Gs." When that happens, the bombs often are thrown for miles. Sometimes those thrown bombs impacted inside North Vietnamese towns. On one of my combat missions, we were attacking along the Mekong River. As I dropped a can of napalm, it did not release until I started pulling off the target and in the climb. The bomb released while I was in the climb and it thus had the trajectory of the F-4. It continued to climb and sailed end-over-end for miles, finally landing in Cambodia.

In the North, invariably the thrown bombs that inadvertently landed in villages would ignite secondary explosions. This meant that the town either was hiding trains with munitions or it had warehouses that held munitions. Either way, the towns that did that should have become legitimate military targets. They never were.

This created a dilemma. I often was targeted to destroy villages in the South. Those villages didn't necessarily pose a military threat. They almost never held munitions. Yet we were ordered not to hit villages in the North that did pose a military threat and held munitions. Added to that, the villages in the South were supposedly our allies and we were sent to SEA to protect the South Vietnamese. The villages in the North were supposedly our enemy. In other words, we could attack our civilian allies, but could not attack our civilian enemies.

This is just another example of unintended consequences caused by a not-thought-out policy. The sad result of much of the policy dilemma was that some of our pilots held back and didn't do the damage that might have been needed against an entrenched foe.

With the substantial support of other Communist countries in supplies, money and manpower, North Vietnam created a huge and sophisticated AAA (Anti-Aircraft Artillery) system, which was the cause of many of our air losses. A simple solution was available to eliminate this huge threat to our aircrews: bomb the dikes on the Red River. This would not only flood out most of the AAA batteries, but it would severely hamper agriculture production. However, we could not do this. The Chinese had a good evaluation of what bombing the dikes would do and they did not allow it. It is hard to imagine an American government showing such a lack of will or resolve in allowing a foreign government, and a hostile one at that, to dictate what we would and would not do in war.

In January of 1967, *retired General Curtis Lemay, in an interview in Washington, said that he would start the progressive destruction of North Vietnamese support and supply bases by closing the Port of Haiphong and other ports.* Lemay was the commanding General of the 8th Air Force in England that bombed Nazi Germany. He later led the B-29 attacks against Imperial Japan. Under Eisenhower as President, Lemay created the Strategic Air Command (SAC). Lemay knew how to fight a war. His recommendations were ignored.

The United States Navy and United States Air Force collaborated on a joint study focused on winning the war. *The joint CINCPACFLT/CINCPACAF (Commander-in-Chief Pacific Fleet and CINC Pacific Air Force) concept of operations, published in April of 1967 for RP VI (Route Pack Six) wrote that:*

"The primary objective in denying external assistance to NVN is the closure of Haiphong Port and, in conjunction with this, the objective of preventing the enemy from diverting his resupply effort to the NE and NW rail lines and/or the Hon Gai and Cam Pha Ports. Until authority is received which will allow the closing of the ports, no meaningful military campaign can be launched which will achieve the objective of denying external assistance." Until Linebacker II, that authority never was granted.

By making our objective the interdiction of supplies in the southern portion of NVN, we allowed importation of far more of those supplies than we would have if we would have interdicted them at the source as well as enroute. The supplies enroute were often carried by bicycle through areas off-limits to friendly ground forces. Those supplies helped make the SEA War the third most costly in terms of American military deaths than all the wars ever fought by the United States. The deaths in Vietnam were exceeded only by WWII and our Civil War. The total count of servicemen killed was over 58,000. The total number of fixed-wing aircraft losses was over 3,000 with another 1,000 lost when South Vietnam surrendered to the North. With the addition of over 5,000 helicopters lost, the actual aircraft lost to the United States in SEA numbered almost 10,000. In its entirety, the War was a colossal loss to the United States of personnel, equipment, treasure and prestige.

The full text of restrictions against air operations makes one wonder what we could hit as legitimate targets. A careful reading of the list of restricted targets will help explain why the War was impossible to win. The government needed to relax its terribly restrictive Rules of Engagement or we were doomed to failure. The government never did relax them until the Linebacker B-52 raids against Hanoi and even then they were not totally relaxed. By then, the war was lost on the home front for all practical purposes.

Following were the core restrictions written in the Rules of Engagement:

Air operations (against Route Pack VI) are severely circumscribed. This area contains *the three major water entry ports into NVN and one of the two major RR lines from China. Armed reconnaissance by US aircraft was (only) authorized against naval craft which were within a 3 NM limit of the NVN coast or offshore islands.* **Aircraft were to avoid a 30 NM circle around Hanoi and a 10 NM circle around Haiphong. Attacks were forbidden in a 30 NM wide zone along the entire length of NVN and the Chinese border, from Laos to the Gulf of Tonkin. Attacks on populated areas and on certain types of targets, such as hydropower plants, locks and dams, fishing boats, sampans, and military barracks were prohibited. The suppression of SAMs and gun-laying radar systems (AAA) was prohibited in this area as were attacks on NVN air bases from which attacking aircraft might be operating.**

In military eyes, these restrictions had the effect of creating a haven in the northeast quadrant of NVN into which the enemy could, with impunity, import vital war materials, construct sanctuaries for his aircraft, and prop his AAA defenses around the cities of Hanoi and Haiphong.

As mentioned, the mining of harbors and bombing of port facilities was also denied. As pilots, we would have to watch MIGs landing and taking off from Gia Lam, Phuc Yen or any other of their airfields. We could not hit them on the ground. We could not hit them in their traffic patterns. We had to wait until they got to altitude with us so that they then would be in a position to attack us.

The NVN defenses against our air attacks were radar controlled. The MIGs were directed, the AAA was aimed and the SAMs were locked on by ground radar. Yet we could not hit that ground radar defensive system because the enemy located the individual radars in protected areas such as the immune airfields.

In closing, I would like to include the final USAF Summary of the Rules of Engagement for Rolling Thunder:

The Rules of Engagement for Rolling Thunder from beginning to end faithfully mirrored the political aims and limited military objectives of this air campaign. **In the strict military sphere, the ROE established sanctuaries/ restricted areas within which air strikes could not be conducted. Havens were provided within enemy territory, which were used to cache, import, replenish, launch attacks, and to use for political propaganda whenever the sanctuary was inadvertently violated. Interrelated target systems were never authorized. The overriding consideration for avoidance of population centers precluded attacks on military targets in important cities such as Nam Dinh and Thanh Hoa. The agricultural sector of the NVN economy was protected. Anti-dike and anti-crop campaigns were not undertaken. Third country shipping was protected to the extent that prohibited attacks or mining activities against NVN's three major ports.** *Taken collectively these restrictions, while reducing the potential effectiveness of airpower, contributed to the national policy as determined by the Commander-in-Chief.*

Our national policy apparently was to wage a limited war without resorting to victory, which is about as limited as you can get. It is a far cry from the conduct of our forces during World War II and a world away from General MacArthur's admonition that "there is no substitute for victory." Such is the legacy of the Commander-in-Chief, Lyndon Baines Johnson and his Secretary of Defense, Robert S. McNamara.

> *"You are remembered for the rules you break."*
> General of the Army Douglas MacArthur

CHAPTER TWENTY-FIVE
Principles of War
Violations

> *"To introduce into the philosophy of war itself a principle
> of moderation, would be an absurdity."*
>
> Carl von Clausewitz

Successful military commanders are very familiar with what are called the Principles of War. They are taught to all of us at the U.S. Air Force, Naval and Military Academies as they are taught in most military academies throughout the world. War is a science and there are specific rules that must be followed to insure military success. Every major country that fields armies teaches similar basic principles. The principles may be traced to the successes of the Great Captains of history such as Genghis Khan, Hannibal Barca, Alexander and Napoleon Bonaparte.

These universal principles were outlined by the great Chinese military theoretician Sun Tzu back in 610 B.C., were enhanced by the renowned German theoretician Clausewitz and have been followed in varying degrees by militaries ever since.

As standard doctrine, the Armed Forces of the United States have adopted a set of principles similar to Sun Tzu's. The standard doctrines of the militaries of Russia, China and Britain are also very similar. The American Principles apply to all branches of our military including the United States Air Force. Our Principles may be found in U.S. Army Field Manual 22-100 titled "Military Leadership." Simplified, they are: mass, offensive, surprise, security, simplicity, unity of command, maneuver, economy of force and objective.

To compare, Tzu's principles are: provide detailed assessment and planning; recognize different battlegrounds; employ required tactics and strategic attack; provide proper troop disposition; realize weaknesses and strengths of your enemy; employ proper use of military power and successful maneuvering; utilize variations of action; be adaptable; properly utilize terrain; consider attacking with fire; utilize effective intelligence and espionage.

Tzu's principles may be found in his book titled "Art of War," the Chinese translation of which is "Master Sun's Military Rules." Other military theoreticians, including the German Clausewitz, have also formulated principles or rules for military operations. Clausewitz includes many other principles including cutting off the enemy from his line of retreat and relentless pursuit. The German military followed the concepts of Clausewitz and the brilliant tactical maneuvers of Carthaginian General Hannibal Barca to build a formidable military machine that was hugely successful in the initial stages of World War II . Tzu, Clausewitz and others have contributed to modern theory on the conduct of military operations. However, war is changing along with modern guerrilla tactics and an updating of the principles is in order.

War is a deadly business and the running of that business should never be left to amateurs. Successful business leaders may use varying methods, but their successes may also be attributed to adherence to certain basic principles. Business study is based on the elements of past success and the business principles associated with those successes. Military study is no different, however the governing principles are not the same.

The conduct of the SEA War was based on severely restrictive rules placed on the military by Johnson and McNamara. Unfortunately, Johnson took McNamara's lead on many militarily related matters of the War and, also unfortunately, McNamara relied on business principles instead of military rules that had stood the test of time. While some aspects of the rules of modern business success may apply to warfare, McNamara's seeming lack of understanding of military science led to the debacle that SEA became. The military Principles of War that we have today are the same as we had during the SEA War.

The quote by Clausewitz at the start of this chapter does not necessarily mean that moderation should never be part of the military equation. What is clear is that moderation should not be part of the equation if it compromises victory or the accomplishment of the political objective.

TOTAL VERSUS LIMITED WAR:

The modern evolution of war really started with the invention of gunpowder. That led to the machines of war overtaking the logic of war and the result was the carnage witnessed in our own Civil War. That brutal destruction of army against army reached its heights in World War I with the death of millions of soldiers on European battlefields.

World War II saw even more carnage as that war took the brutality of war to new extremes, only this time with the wastage of entire cities. The Germans returned to the total war of Genghis Khan by initiating the destruction of civilian population concentrations. Those occurred during September, 1939 when the Luftwaffe bombed Polish population centers and in May of 1940 when they destroyed Rotterdam by aerial bombing. Japan also initiated the bombing of population centers in China during the 1930s.

The American history of civilian bombings was largely in retaliation against Germany and Japan during WWII. What started out as daylight precision bombing of industrial targets morphed into nighttime carpet bombing of civilian areas using incendiaries. World War II should not be held as the standard of how America should fight its wars. It was a unique set of circumstances created by our location as protected by two oceans and the brilliant strategy and planning of President Roosevelt.

Actual American attacks against cities occurred in our Civil War as Sherman's Union Army laid waste to Atlanta, but without harming civilians. City attacks were partially revisited in Southeast Asia when we initiated the bombings of Hanoi and Haiphong in December, 1972. Due to the situation existing at the time, that bombing was a necessary evil and resulted in the termination of American involvement and thus the saving of countless lives. The addition of cities to the acceptable target lists of air forces has greatly accentuated the danger to modern societies with the advent of atomic and then thermonuclear weapons.

While our current conflict with Muslim extremists poses significant problems for the United States, it pales in comparison to the potential threat of China. Our policy of encouraging the engagement with and the integration of their economy with that of the world economy may nullify that threat. They may become too economically dependent on the West to risk war. However, the independence of the Chinese military from their civilian authority poses significant risks. To the Chinese military, America is their enemy and the flashpoint of that confrontation may be just off the Vietnamese Coast in the South China Sea.

Which way will China go? Will they take the total war concept of Genghis Khan or the more nuanced approach of Sun Tzu? Sun Tzu was very influential in the thinking of Mao Zedong. Younger military officers in the Chinese Army now consider the concepts of Sun Tzu to be outmoded. Will his influence return as the Chinese military gains more sophistication and capability?

Sun Tzu was against total war as we know it. Actually, he felt that "to subdue the enemy without fighting is the acme of skill." Additionally, he felt that "he whose generals are able and not interfered with by the sovereign will be victorious." Apparently, the Chinese of 2,500 hundred years ago were beset with the same problem of civilian interference with military affairs.

Sun Tzu also advocated measured response. He and Clausewitz, the two most influential military philosophers in history, both recognized that war has its basis in the political. Clausewitz, who was initially captivated by the concept of total war as evidenced by his statement that "war is an act of violence pushed to its utmost" later wrote that "the political object, as the original motive of war, should be the standard for determining both the aim of the military force and also the amount of effort to be made." Thus, he was an early advocate of limited war without even realizing it.

Sun Tzu felt that the "worst (military) policy is to attack cities." In this, he exhibited a keen awareness of constraints and limitations involved in the "purpose" of a war. He was aware that the civilian populace is critical to long-term success of any action and intimately involved in any purpose or objective of a war.

As mentioned in another chapter, America has to become used to the concept of limited wars. While our objective should always be to achieve victory, victory comes with many faces. Victory is achievement of an objective, which does not necessarily equate with destruction of another's military or its will to resist. It could be considered "limited victory."

China, under Mao, flirted with the concept that nuclear wars were winnable. With the current industrialization of China and the subsequent massive urbanization, that concept may have undergone a revision?

BE PREPARED:

One of the siren calls America often hears, especially at the end of conflicts, is to disarm and use the money, previously used for military spending, for other purposes. That is an extremely dangerous course. During World War II, the United States irreversibly crossed a line and became a Superpower. The Free World depends on America's strength. We cannot afford, for many reasons, to give up that responsibility and disarm. To do so would disrupt the world as we know it. To do so would imperil our values and way-of-life. Perhaps the greatest of the Principles of War is to be prepared. We no longer have the luxury of time to train soldiers, airmen and sailors with the protection of two vast oceans for our continent. We no longer have the time to design and build sophisticated weapons of war when wars are won and lost in much shorter time. Those luxuries are virtues of the past.

The example of three countries accentuates the maxim that the best way to avoid war is to be adequately prepared for war. Those counties are Switzerland, Sweden and Thailand. Each has continually maintained significant military capabilities and that strength has allowed each to avoid war since before the Napoleonic Wars.

THE DESTRUCTION OF CARTHAGE:

Perhaps the most graphic example in history of the dangers inherent in disarmament involved Ancient Rome and the Cartheginian Empire. At the time of the Punic Wars, the city-state of Carthage (located in the modern state of Tunisia) was the strongest military and commercial force in the world. The rising power of Rome conflicted with the established power of the Phoenician (Punic) colony. That conflict escalated into military action that became the Punic Wars, starting in 246 B.C.

The Cartheginian General Hannibal Barca famously crossed the Alps in 218 B.C. and ravaged Italy for sixteen years, virtually destroyed every Roman Army sent against him in the second of the three Punic Wars. At Cannae, Hannibal killed more Roman soldiers in eight hours than Americans were killed in eight years of Vietnam. He was invincible. Yet he showed mercy for Rome itself and declined to attack that city. After Cannae, Rome stood exposed with only a rudimentary home guard of 5,000 to protect it.

The Cartheginian political leaders felt that by showing mercy to Rome, that Rome would no longer be as interested in war as a means of expansion and, instead, would rely on trade and commerce as did Carthage. With the military threat seemingly receded, Carthage felt that their money could be better spent than on the military. They valued commerce rather than war. Instead of staying militarily strong and protecting its populace, Carthage unilaterally disarmed. They disbanded Hannibal's army and retired him to the Eastern Mediterranean. They mistakenly felt that Rome had the same desire for peace as Carthage. The Romans, however, considered that act as one of weakness and had presented Rome with an unmatched opportunity.

In 149 B.C., the Romans initiated the third of the Punic Wars and attacked the city itself. Carthage, a city of over a million people, was eventually conquered and utterly destroyed in 146 B.C. Its "crime" had been to rival Rome in naval power, commercial power and influence with other region states. Three years of siege had reduced the population to 50,000 by the time of eventual capitulation. The initial population of over a million had either been starved to death, had been killed with the relentless Roman siege weapons, or had managed to escape the city to live a life of nomadic existence. Those remaining were sold into slavery.

The Romans dismantled every building and wall in the city and for seventeen days, burned it to the ground. The democratically elected Roman Senate voted to destroy the city. The land on which the city had rested was sown with salt so extensively that the earth was as dead as its former inhabitants. Carthage was turned into a desert wasteland.

If the reader considers that we might now be more civilized, consider modern examples of genocide. Consider the very recent Russian and Chinese military adventures into Ukraine and the islands of the South China Sea. The world is still in a primitive state and dictates eternal vigilance. Don't let Carthage happen to America.

SOUTHEAST ASIA WAR VIOLATIONS OF CURRENT PRINCIPLES:

Following is a simplified assessment of the violations of those Principles of War in SEA that led to our first military defeat.

MASS: Concentrate combat power at the decisive place and time.

SEA Violations: We violated Mass by our decision to employ gradualism in the buildup of our forces. Our enemy was able to plan and react with counter force.

Reason for violation: Political constraint.

OFFENSIVE: Seize, direct and exploit the initiative.

SEA Violations: When we allowed the Chinese to deny us the ability to attack North Vietnam with ground forces; denied us the ability to bomb the Red River dikes from the air; denied us the ability to mine the harbors, as well as other military denials, we lost the initiative and we condemned ourselves to fighting a defensive war against an enemy who had guaranteed sanctuaries that denied access to our military forces. Our political decisions seemed designed "not to lose" which guaranteed a defensive instead of an offensive war.

The moment we allowed the Chinese to set their own principles for the conduct of our war, was the moment we guaranteed that the best we could hope to accomplish would be stalemate. Stalemate meant that we were merely killing and destroying for no stated or productive reason.

Weakness and cowardice elicits boldness and audacity.

Reason for violation: Political weakness.

OBJECTIVE: Direct every military operation towards a clearly defined, decisive and attainable objective.

SEA Violation: Our political leaders did not state clearly defined political objectives of the war. Without those political objectives, it was almost impossible to define decisive and attainable military objectives. Due to the extremely severe and limiting Rules of Engagement, any successful air operation in SEA was forced to have an objective that was very limited in scope.

Since we were involved in two civil wars, a defined political objective would have been to inspire the populace toward a defined end. There was no such inspiration.

Reason for violation: Political indecisiveness.

SURPRISE: Strike the enemy at a time, at a place, or in a manner for which he is unprepared.

SEA Violations:

The South: The rules in place in South Vietnam during the war dictated that the American military had to get the consent of the ARVN (Army of the Republic of Vietnam) leaders before we initiated any military operation. We made the political and military mistake of not insisting that certain operations and target types be excluded from that requirement. The ARVN leadership was totally infiltrated with Viet Cong sympathizers and our notification of the ARVN was effective notification to the VC as to time, place and intensity of any operation.

The North: In the air portion of the war, by severely restricting the targets that could be hit in the North, the Rules of Engagement effectively eliminated much of the element of surprise. Additionally, the astounding revelation by Secretary of State Dean Rusk that we were notifying the North Vietnamese, "in advance" through the Swiss, of the location of the following-day's targets is difficult to fathom. One does not have to know the Principles of War to understand the stupidity of such action. Our civilian leaders thus totally eliminated any semblance of surprise for our Air Force and Naval airmen and directly contributed to the death of many. This Johnson Administration action is further explained in Chapter Twenty-Six, "Why We Lost."

Reason for violation: Political ignorance, cowardice and an inability to manage.

SECURITY: Never permit the enemy to acquire an unexpected advantage.

This is an area that really was strictly military and I thought we did a good job of providing security to the best of our abilities.

SIMPLICITY: Prepare clear, uncomplicated plans and clear, concise orders to ensure thorough understanding.

SEA Violations: Our military orders were clear enough, but those that came from our politicians made the job of proper military planning and force application an extremely complicated and limiting process. A proper answer to how our country dropped the ball on this one may be found in the declassified Rules of Engagement documents that are partially included in this book.

Reason for violation: The clear reason for the establishment of this principle was the need for clarification of orders leading to an accomplishment of a war's objectives leading to victory. In SEA, it was inconceivable that the clarity of orders would be meant to deny the accomplishment of those objectives.

UNITY OF COMMAND: For every objective, ensure unity of effort under one responsible commander.

SEA Violations: Unity of command allows decisions to be made quickly as situations dictate. The chains of command forced on the military by the awkward and cumbersome communications and control rules required by our politicians, allowed for many missed military opportunities and needless pilot deaths. One needs to look no further than the situation regarding operations in Laos and the political intervention that was part of those operations.

This principle should have been structured by the Pentagon and then left up to its selected overall field commander to implement. The air war had essentially three components of command. The US Navy and US Air Force both had independent air targeting without a defined, single commander for theater air operations. The clandestine air forces also operated independently of any centralized theater command. The paramilitary forces under the control of the CIA should have been under the direct operational control of a central military authority.

Reason for violation: President Johnson's apparent content with divided command and control.

MANEUVER: Place the enemy in a position of disadvantage through the flexible application of combat power.

SEA Violations: I thought that the military did the best it could with consideration of the constraints under which it operated. However, the insistence by Johnson that he and his unofficial and incapable War Council have the final approval on targeting, air attack routing, offensive actions, attack limitations, munitions and attack methods helped insure that our operations were extremely inflexible and entirely predictable for the enemy regarding our Air War. We had the capability to employ our massive combat power in an effective manner and we were prevented from doing so.

Our American pilots became, in effect, "sitting ducks" since the enemy was informed by the American Government, in advance, as to locations of targets to be hit and at what time the planes would arrive. This information, though shared with the enemy, was never disclosed to military pilots flying missions over North Vietnam.

The creation by North Vietnam and China of mobile SAM batteries and mobile AAA regiments, were thus poised to move from target to target as advised daily by our State Department. The death and imprisonment of many American pilots can be laid at the feet of Rusk, McNamara and Johnson.

Reason for violation: The political intervention in strictly military matters is self-evident. Our political leaders may limit the scope of military actions, but within that scope the leaders must provide our military the means of winning a victory by accomplishing the goals presented. The Rules of Engagement dictated by McNamara insured an inflexibility of application of air power.

ECONOMY OF FORCE: Allocate maximum essential combat power to primary efforts. Allocate minimum essential combat power to secondary efforts.

SEA Violations: We used high performance aircraft against marginal targets, which begged for a more appropriate application of available equipment. We did manage to use a preponderance of force, where allowed, but we did it in a manner that was not "cost effective."

The primary use of air power in its interdiction efforts in North Vietnam should have been used against incoming transport of supplies and at the points of concentration of those supplies. McNamara's satisfaction with attacking the supplies after they got into the distribution network was a clear violation of economy of force.

Primary air efforts dealt with targeting. The industrial, agricultural and population bases were made off-limits by the Rules of Engagement and they thus denied our military the ability to employ "primary" efforts.

In a 1980s study, it was determined that fully "82% of the Vietnamese War veterans who saw heavy combat strongly believed the war was lost because of lack of political will."

Reason for violation: Lack of political courage to order air strikes where necessary to accomplish military success.

Modern war demands the use of similar principles as those used over 2,600 years ago. It also requires force integration for more effective applications of those forces. The Pentagon is moving in the right direction by revising the command structure of the military by combining elements of the various services to deal with the different types of threats to our country. Equally important is that modern, limited war requires integration of the political as well as the military in the initial determination of objectives.

To that end, I have taken the liberty of putting together a suggested list of modern Principles of War. These are provided as "food for thought." Other, more capable, military minds can add to, subtract from and further define. While content may vary, the main suggestion here is to bring the Principles in line with modern conditions, thought and requirements.

The following suggested Principles of War, while considered essential for successful military operations, should also govern decisions and actions of the political arm of our decision-making apparatus. The political portion of decision-making should be familiar with and take into account the Principles when making decisions on objectives and limitations for war.

Adherence, by both political and military leaders, to the below-proposed Principles will give the United States the best chance of continuing our almost unblemished record of military success and will, more-importantly, provide, by showing strength, unity and prudence, the best chance for peace in an ever-changing world. Strength, in this context, includes strength of will as well as strength of force.

PROPOSED PRINCIPLES OF WAR FOR POLITICAL AND MILITARY LEADERS:

Evaluation: Evaluate all possible non-military, alternative solutions to political and diplomatic problems. Evaluate the application of all possible military options. Consideration of military solutions should only be done as a last resort after all other options have been exhausted.

Preparation: Train, plan and equip for all possible contingencies prior to conflict. Simulate wartime conditions during peacetime operations. Insure sufficient quantities of trained personnel and equipment are available to fight foreseeable conflicts. Identify potential enemies and evaluate their strengths and weaknesses. Develop equipment to maximize utility for all potential military actions. To insure support, properly prepare and inform the citizens. Establish effective intelligence to determine intent and capabilities of real and potential enemies.

Technical: Maintain emphasis on research to develop both offensive and defensive electronic weapons and engineering advancements in both weaponry and equipment.

Coalition: Unite worldwide political and military entities and organizations in a common cause.

Objectives and Focus: Clearly define political and military objectives and limitations. Primary focus should be on those objectives.

Responsibilities: Clearly delineate the responsibilities and authorities for the political and military as well as for the different organizations involved.

Communications: Orders and communications at all levels should be simple, clear and concise.

Unity of Command: Command and control authority should be under one theater commander for all military operations, including paramilitary.

Battlefield Assessment: Completely assess all battlefield conditions, including terrain, defenses, enemy capabilities, difficulties, human and environmental, before initiating military operations.

Force Application: Apply manpower, equipment and weapons with consideration of utility, size, economy, positioning, intensity, duration and objective. Quickly, continually and relentlessly apply a preponderance of force with consideration of the proper mix of land, sea, and air power. Provide sufficient reserves.

Tactics: Tactical decisions should be in compliance with overall strategic objectives and should be made to maximize speed, maneuverability and efficiency.

Offensive: A war cannot be won without concentration on offensive operations.

Surprise: Never allow your enemy to know your plans or operations. Strike unpredictably with regard to time, intensity and place.

Security: Secure your positions from enemy knowledge or action.

Troop Protection: Civilian and military leaders need to provide maximum protection and support for our military personnel consistent with operations. If necessary, rescue should always have highest priority as well as efforts to return prisoners-of-war from captivity.

Population Centers: Carrying war to the population centers should be avoided, unless the enemy locates military or military-related equipment, personnel or operations within the centers.

Target Selection: The selection of targets to be attacked should be consistent with the overall focus of the campaign and done to maximize the damage done to the ability and/or desire of the enemy to wage war. Target selection should be done to minimize damage to civilians or their dwellings.

Adaptability and Flexibility: Adapt to changing tactical conditions. Be flexible and unpredictable in tactical operations.

Persistence and Determination: Be persistent and relentless in following a course of action to its satisfactory conclusion. Follow up an advantage and act with determination to pursue and, without pause, destroy the enemy's ability and/ or desire to wage war.

Consistency, Patience and Time: Be consistent with the strategic plan of action to accomplish the overall objectives. Use patience in the accomplishment of those defined objectives. Wisely use time to determine the most advantageous moment to commence or alter operations.

Post-War Occupation & Securing Lasting Peace: In advance, have a comprehensive occupation plan in place to secure peace and maintain law-and-order. To win the populace, provide means to insure the safety, security, health and welfare of the population and provide sufficient food, medicine, equipment and supplies needed for adequate living. To insure lasting peace, while still installing strict occupational controls over an enemy population, its citizens should be treated with respect and dignity.

> *"The two most powerful warriors are patience and time."*
> Leo Tolstoy

CHAPTER TWENTY-SIX
Why We Lost
An Evaluation

> *"Let us conduct ourselves so that all men wish to be our friends and all fear to be our enemies."*
>
> Alexander the Great of Macedonia

The list of those who contributed to our loss in Southeast Asia is long. President Lyndon Baines Johnson and his Secretary of Defense, Robert S. McNamara, made about as many mistakes as could be made in SEA. Secretary of State Dean Rusk, a timid man, was also partially responsible. But they were not the only ones who made mistakes. There were many contributors and causes deserving of mention. Johnson's primary mistake was expanding Kennedy's war. Vietnam and the rest of SEA was a war that was fought in the wrong place, for the wrong reasons and fought in the wrong manner. As has been shown, those making mistakes go back to Truman and include all the Presidents from him to Nixon. Actually, President Roosevelt is also due some criticism.

AMERICAN EFFECT ON ASIAN HISTORY:

After the end of World War I, President Woodrow Wilson was shut out of post-war determinations of how the world would be structured by the winning countries that had suffered so many casualties. The war started in 1914 and the US was a late comer in 1917 and therefore had much fewer casualties than France and Great Britain. Those two countries made the determinations about the political disposition of postwar Europe and their draconian conditions sowed the seeds for World War II.

After World War II, Roosevelt was determined that he would not be left out. He became part of the handful of countries that made the post-war determinations after World War II. The primary actors were Great Britain under its Prime Minister Winston Churchill, the Soviet Union under its dictator Joseph Stalin and Roosevelt.

During the final months of WWII, the second of three conferences between the victorious allies occurred at Yalta in the Russian Crimea. The meeting lasted from February 4th through the 11th 1945, just two months before Roosevelt died. At Yalta, Roosevelt was ailing and Churchill's military was exhausted.

Stalin's Red Army menaced Eastern Europe and Stalin was able to dictate to the weaker Anglo Saxon Nations. Roosevelt made the same mistake made after WWI, by playing God with the disposition of other countries in the postwar world. His biggest mistake was that he even attended the Yalta Conference, since he was too ill to handle those discussions.

While most of the discussions involved postwar Europe, a promise was made by Stalin to enter the war against Imperial Japan. By February 1945, America had a very good idea of approximately when we would have the Atomic Bomb. Yet we still naively asked the Soviet Union to enter the conflict. At Yalta, Stalin promised that he would declare war against Japan three months after the surrender of Germany.

The American concern about Japan, after the defeat of Germany, had to do with the anticipated invasion of the Japanese home islands. The American military estimated a million American casualties with an invasion of Japan proper.

Stalin also gained the agreement of Churchill and Roosevelt that the Soviet Union could gain control over Southern Sakhalin Island. Sakhalin, one fifth the size of all of Japan, is located just to the north of Japan's Hokkaido Island. Stalin also was given postwar control over the Kuril Islands, east of Sakhalin. The Kuril Islands are comprised of 56 small islands that stretch 730 miles from Hokkaido to the Kamchatka Peninsula in Russia.

The invitation to the Soviets to attack Japan was curious in that the Soviets had no experience in storming beaches or island invasions, nor did they possess the equipment to do so. The Japanese troops, reportedly to have been 4 million men strong, were located on their home islands. America feared it would lose more men in the invasion and defeat of Japan than it had lost in all its other wars combined. While we wanted the Soviet manpower, how would it be utilized without a seaborne invasion capability? While significant numbers of Japanese troops still occupied Manchuria, the American concern was not with those troops. The American Army had the European experience of its D-Day invasion. They also had the Pacific experience of island landings under General MacArthur. The Navy and Marines had significant island hopping experience under Admiral Chester Nimitz, but the Soviets had no such training, experience, or equipment.

The storming of beaches was a talent that the American military possessed in abundance that was missing from every other army in the world, including the Red Army.

At the time of the German surrender, the Red Army was almost entirely in Europe, occupying the ground wrested from the Wehrmacht. It is assumed that they used the three-month hiatus, between the German surrender and the Soviet attack against Japan, to move troops to positions opposite Manchuria and within easy reach of the Korean Peninsula.

As it was, Stalin invaded exactly as promised, three months after the German surrender on May 8, 1945. The declaration of war against Japan by the Soviets occurred on August 8, 1945. However, that was two days after the United States dropped the Atomic Bomb on Hiroshima and only a week before the surrender of Japan. The United States fought an intense war against Japan for almost four years without territorial acquisitions, yet the Soviets fought for a week and got the Kurils and Southern Sakhalin for its "efforts."

My point here is that we seemed to do a horrible job of figuring out the postwar world and managed to negate much of what we did in our own fighting against the Axis Powers and equipping the Soviets.

The other Asian promise made at Yalta involved Korea. Stalin promised to insure a continuance of a unified Korean Peninsula. After the Soviet's declaration of war against Japan, they quickly moved troops down and into the northern part of Korea. By action, the Soviets nullified the Yalta provision promising a continuance of the unification of Korea. They ended up splitting the country. Stalin proved immediately that he was not to be trusted, yet we continued to do so.

The Soviet efforts in Asia at the end of WWII created the problems that exist even to this day. Their material, money and manpower support of revolutionary efforts created two split nations in Asia: Korea and Vietnam. The positioning of their troops also provided a boost to Mao's fight against the Nationalist Chinese under Chiang Kai-shek.

American territorial acquisitions were temporary. Islands such as Iwo Jima and Okinawa were eventually returned to Japan. Island chain protectorates, such as the Marshalls and Caroline Islands, were eventually given their own political independence. America has continued to provide infrastructure repair using our Naval Construction Battalions. Sakhalin and the Kurils still remain under Soviet ownership and control.

Other than our continued military presence on Okinawa, the architecture of post-world-war Asia shifted decidedly in favor of the Communists. Our commitment of troops to Korea ended in stalemate. Our commitment of troops to SEA also ended in a temporary stalemate when we decided to remove our troops from the area. At the time of our military involvement in SEA, the Communist dominance of the Asian mainland contributed significantly to the eventual success of North Vietnam in the SEA War.

The entire situation in Asia after the end of WWII is partially the fault of the aging and infirmed Franklin Roosevelt. His guilt should be added to the other five Presidents who were involved in the Southeast Asia quagmire.

Truman was the President who made the post war decisions, but Roosevelt laid the ground work at Yalta. Roosevelt was particularly remiss by leaving Truman in the dark on so much of what was going on during WWII. The mistakes that Truman made regarding the political architecture of Asia are Roosevelt's mistakes. Truman was so much in the dark that Roosevelt never informed him of the Manhattan Project. Thus, Truman heard about the existence of the Atomic Bomb after the death of Roosevelt in April, 1945.

As mentioned, Truman's mistake was made in 1946 when he failed to stand up for the historical American principle of anti-colonialism and instead supported the reinstatement of French Colonial rule over all of Indochina.

Eisenhower compounded the mistake in 1954 by militarily supporting the French Foreign Legion in its final battle against the Viet Minh, Dien Bien Phu. Both Truman and Eisenhower failed to consider the legitimate aspirations of a native people who had been under the colonial yoke of France since the 1700s. Eisenhower also oversaw the initial movements of ground units into SEA in 1960 and possibly as early as 1957.

Kennedy continued the covert introduction of further ground forces as well as the initial engagement of Commando air as well as CIA- controlled air units in 1961. The mistakes of both Presidents included an inability to realize that Communism was not monolithic and that the Vietnamese hated the Chinese. It was a failure of Intelligence.

Vietnam was basically a civil war pitting a puppet Southern regime that was placed to serve the interest of a foreign power against a brutal, but nationalistic, Northern regime that wanted a united Vietnam free of interference from any foreign power, including the Chinese. Ho Chi Minh was willing to use whatever political and military ideology that was necessary to fulfill his dream of an independent and prosperous Vietnam. It was no place for American involvement.

Johnson compounded past mistakes by fabricating the Gulf of Tonkin Incidents and lying to the American people about the level and timing of our involvement. He capitulated to China by allowing it to determine how the entire SEA effort was to be fought. China, when they realized that Johnson was cowardly and would yield to their demands, denied us the one action that would have placed the Air Force and Navy on a path toward winning the air portion of the war and that was the denial of bombing of the Red River dikes.

Additionally, our government created safe havens in the North for our enemy to use in the conduct of its war against our air units.

The Chinese also denied us the action needed to place our enemy on the defense, and that was a ground invasion of the North and Laos. The very fact that Johnson turned cowardly and allowed our course to be so dictated is difficult to comprehend. It made murderers out of those of us charged to carry on the stalemate.

PRESIDENT JOHNSON AND THE JOINT CHIEFS OF STAFF:

Johnson's daily telephone calls from the White House to 7th Air Headquarters in Saigon clearly shows a civilian trying to play at war. Did he somehow think that he was more capable of making military decisions than those trained and entrusted to do it?

Johnson's relationship with the leaders of the military services that were members of our Joint Chiefs of Staff is telling. In 1965, at the effective start of the larger SEA War, the leaders of the Joint Chiefs of Staff were all combat veterans. In November of that year, the Joint Chiefs were composed of: US Army General Earl Weaver, who was Chairman; General Harold Johnson, Chief of Staff of the Army; General Wallace Greene, Commanding General of the Marines, Chief of Naval Operations Admiral David L. McDonald and General John McConnell, Chief of Staff of the Air Force. Each of the five military leaders was into his third war and very capable of proper military leadership in Southeast Asia.

It is imperative that any President and his representatives work well with the Joint Chiefs in planning and executing any war. There needs to be respect shown by both the political and military leaders with each other. War is indeed a people business.

Marine Corp Lieutenant General Charles Cooper (ret.), then a junior officer, participated as a single-support officer during a pivotal meeting of the Joint Chiefs with President Lyndon Johnson in November of 1965. His job was to hold up the easel. This meeting was a defining one from the standpoint of where the war was going and how it would be fought.

To show how Johnson respected and treated the military leaders of our country, reference is made to a book written by General Cooper, "Cheers, Tears: A Marine's Story of Peace and War," which included his eyewitness account of that pivotal meeting between President Johnson and the Joint Chiefs.

The Joint Chiefs proposed to Johnson that their military judgment was to take decisive measures to avoid a protracted conflict and insure a shortened war. General Douglas MacArthur often stated that America should never get involved in a war on the Asian mainland. Yet here we had a burgeoning war on that same massive landmass.

The Joint Chiefs proposed mining Haiphong Harbor to minimize seaborne transport of supplies. They also proposed a complete blockade of the North Vietnamese coast. Finally, they stated that we should mount a massive bombing campaign with Air Force B-52s pounding the Hanoi- Haiphong industrial complex.

According to General Cooper, after the presentation by the Joint Chiefs, President Johnson turned away from them in the Oval Office and seemed to contemplate their proposals. Then he whirled around and "screamed obscenities, he cursed them personally, he ridiculed them for coming into his office with their "military advice." Noting that it was he who was carrying the weight of the free world on his shoulders, he called them filthy names: shitheads, dumb shits, pompous assholes, and used the F-word as an adjective more freely than a Marine in boot camp would use it. He then accused them of trying to pass the buck for World

War III to him. It was unnerving, degrading."

Such was the extreme lack of respect shown by Johnson, not only for the unanimous recommendations of the Joint Chiefs, but for the military leaders themselves. The comment about WWIII is telling. His concern with the possible intervention of the Chinese seemed an obsession that verged on fear. The Chiefs themselves evaluated that the possibility of Chinese intervention, in the event of massive American military actions, was small.

THE EFFECT OF TET:

In November of 1965, our ground forces learned a valuable lesson in the Ia Drang Valley of South Vietnam. The Viet Cong massed its forces and was decimated by the American forces. In February 1968, the VC and NVN military forces again massed during the TET Offensive and were hugely decimated by American and South Vietnamese forces with ample support of ground artillery and airborne bombing and gunnery. However, it seems that the intention of the North Vietnamese General Giap in creating the TET Offensive was not military, but political.

The *Wall Street Journal* published an interview with a Mr. Bui Tin who served on the General Staff (equivalent of our Joint Chiefs of Staff) of the North Vietnamese Army. He received the unconditional surrender of South Vietnam on April 30, 1975. During the interview, Mr. Tin was asked if the American antiwar movement was important to Hanoi's victory. Mr. Tin responded that "it was essential to our strategy." He further stated that the North Vietnamese leadership listened to the American evening news broadcasts, "to follow the growth of the American antiwar movement." Visits to Hanoi made by persons such as Jane Fonda, former Attorney General Ramsey Clark and others "gave us confidence that we should hold on in the face of battlefield reverses."

He went on to say, "America lost because of its democracy; through dissent and protests it lost the ability to mobilize to win." As a member of the General Staff, Tin was advised by General Vo Nguyen Giap, commander of the NVN and VC forces, that the 1968 TET Offensive "had been a defeat (for us)."

After TET, the VC main force and irregular troops were judged not to be viable as military forces for the remainder of the war and the organized ground operations of the enemy were then carried out by the NVN regular units. The overall casualty figures from TET show the extent of our victory. Of the 80,000 Viet Cong soldiers that started the offensive, in less than two weeks over 45,000 were killed at a loss of a little more than 1,500 American deaths. A large part of the huge enemy losses was due to the use of our artillery and airpower. However, the calculated risk by the legendary North Vietnamese General Vo Nguyen Giap worked and the decisive American military victory turned into a decisive American political defeat.

The major reason was the reaction of the unprepared American public to the heavy loss of American life after three known years of warfare. The public had not been properly informed or conditioned by Johnson. He had allowed unfettered media access to the war resulting in a public turned strongly against the Administration.

When Air Force Operation "Rolling Thunder," our air attack against North Vietnam, began in 1965, only 15% of Americans considered themselves "doves" or against the war. That left 85% either with no opinion or as "hawks" who favored military action. By January 1968, that "dove" figure had increased to 28%.

TET started on January 31, 1968, when the Viet Cong regular and irregular forces attacked American and ARVN positions throughout Vietnam. The battles were intense, but by February 10th the forces of the Viet

Cong were largely crushed.

After TET, the political dominos started to fall. First General Westmoreland asked for 200,000 additional troops and was refused by Johnson. Then on March 31st Johnson announced that he would not seek or accept the nomination for another term as President. The very next day, April 1st, Johnson ordered a halt to all bombing north of the 19-degree latitude, which excluded most of North Vietnam. That same month, another poll showed that 42% of Americans now considered themselves "doves" and they outnumbered "hawks" 42%-41%. On November 1, 1968, Johnson increased his moratorium on bombing to include all of North Vietnam and the Demilitarized Zone. The message was clear to the military and political leaders of North Vietnam. Militarily we had them on the run, but politically they had us on the run.

The cessation of bombing in the North also spelled doom for the military air campaign. The total stoppage of the bombing campaign was ordered less than three months before he left office. This was another clear sign to our military and to their military that the President of the United States was possessed with a defeatist attitude. Yet we continued to fight year after year.

After TET, had we struck militarily by invading the North with ground troops and drastically altering the Rules of Engagement for our Air War, we could have been on a path to victory in a war that should not have been. The past mistakes and half-hearted attempts to win had precluded Johnson from being able to implement those needed changes.

Unfortunately, our significant TET victory came too late, as our political and public will crumbled and our eventual military defeat was assured due to the public's perception of the war and our lack of political will to do what was necessary to win.

Stalemate should never be an accepted objective of war. Yet this seemed to be the political objective that evolved under Johnson. "Creeping Objective" is an appropriate description of how our national focus changed as it "evolved" under Johnson. How was our public to correctly identify our objective if that objective seemed in a constant state of flux?

THE NEED FOR AGGRESSIVE ACTION:

From a military standpoint, after TET the only effective enemy force left in the South were the North Vietnamese Army regulars. What better way to eliminate the NVN soldiers in the South than invade the North? With an invasion, the Northern leaders would have been forced to do for us what we could not do for ourselves, and that was to recall all their soldiers in the South to return to their home soil to fight for the North. With one stroke, we would have eliminated the threat to the South.

It would have forced them on the defensive and provided us with the initiative in providing for a peace that would satisfy our national interest, while still preserving part of the economy and culture in the North. Instead of negotiating from weakness, as Kissinger was forced to do, we would then have been able to negotiate from a position of strength.

McNamara also shares in the blame. The Rules of Engagement promulgated by McNamara guaranteed at best a stalemate in the Air War. They were so restrictive as to deny an American ability to win.

The failure to understand and comply with the Principles of War that pertained to all aspects of how any war should be fought also placed us squarely on a path to eventual defeat.

Johnson was ignorant about war and yet he played at being General. It was a deadly game played with the lives of those he entrusted to fight the war, without the necessary policy weapons needed to win. He completely failed in his use of politics as a necessary part of the military process of waging a victorious war.

In SEA, our military was at fault by allowing munitions shortages to occur and then lying to our government about the existence of the shortages. To the airmen entrusted to fight (both Navy and Air Force), the Pentagon seemed more interested in the contest between Naval Air and Air Force Air than the defeat of our common enemy. It sent planes on bombing missions with either reduced bomb loads or with no bomb loads at all. Perhaps it was the lack of a goal stated by the political arm that encouraged the Pentagon to create its own side objective.

At the Thai Thud bases, the Air Force sometimes loaded no bombs for Northern bombing missions. Instead they loaded ball ammo in the guns of the jets and called the missions armed recce to seek out "targets of opportunity." Ball ammo is practice ammo and does not explode. Thus, it is only marginally effective. This was the Air Force answer to our recurring shortage of bombs. They stayed with the same number of missions whether they had bombs or not. To the fighter pilots, the Pentagon's mantra was "a sortie is a sortie, whether it is effective or not."

MILITARY OBJECTIVES OF AIR TARGETING:

While the military objectives of air targeting are usually closely guarded secrets, one can identify some of them from other wars such as World War II: Denial of the industrial capacity of the Germans to sustain major armies in the field is certainly one. The systematic pounding of population centers to affect public morale is another. Sinking of Japanese supply ships to starve their outlying islands of food and munitions is a third. To be effective, there has to be an overall objective to air operations. There has to be a purpose.

Hitler's classic mistake in targeting during the "Battle of Britain" was allowing his emotions to change a crucial military objective instead of following a consistently sound course of action. His overall military objective for Britain was to successfully invade their island nation. He called it Operation Sea Lion.

The main obstacles to accomplishment of his objective of invasion were the fighter pilots of the Royal Air Force (RAF), who mounted a spirited defense of their islands. To counter the RAF, the Luftwaffe determined that they needed to deny the British fighter pilots their weapons of war. They decided to hit the British factories responsible for production of fighter planes. The Luftwaffe determined that the most vulnerable component for the British fighters were needed ball bearings for their fighter aircraft engines.

At the time of the Battle of Britain, Sweden provided 58% of the total supply of military ball bearings to the Germans and 31% of the overall supply to Britain. Militarily, the bearings were used in submarine and aircraft engines, tanks and guns. Fifteen percent of the overall British supply came directly from Sweden, while the rest of the Swedish 31% came from other nations using Swedish manufacturing equipment. Almost all the remaining 69% of needed ball bearing production came directly from British manufacturing plants.

During the Battle of Britain, 1,700 British war planes were sitting idle in wait of their needed engine ball bearings. The entire Battle and the safety of Britain hung in the balance. The Luftwaffe concentrated its bombing raids against the manufacturing plants supplying this needed component. According to the RAF, Britain was one week away from losing the Battle due to the depleted supply of aircraft. Those aircraft were not in the air due to lack of ball bearings caused by the relentless German bombing campaign.

During the latter stages of the Battle of Britain, British bomber aircraft were re-targeted against German cities. Reportedly, this tactic enraged Hitler and he vowed revenge against British cities. Whatever the reason, the Luftwaffe changed its targeting focus to that of British cities one week short of a "ball bearing" victory against the RAFs fighter forces in the Battle of Britain. That change of focus allowed for the eventual victory by our British allies.

The point in this narrative is that there has to be a meaningful purpose in an air bombing campaign and the campaign needs to stick to that purpose through its needed conclusion.

To a fighter pilot in the "trenches" of the Southeast Asian War, there seemed little purpose in our efforts. We, of course, were not privy to the reasons that certain air campaigns were initiated, but we could certainly speculate.

The close-air-support of our ground forces was certainly a clear and beneficial objective. It made us pilots feel good to be so supportive of our troops. Our MIG Screen mission over the Gulf was another clear objective. It was helping our Navy fighter pilot brothers by protecting their aircraft carriers as well as our own intelligence gathering aircraft. MIG Cover for the strike aircraft and those engaged in clandestine electronic warfare was a third.

But it was what we were not targeted against that caused us the greatest concern. Evaluation of McNamara's Rules of Engagement from the "user" end was frustrating. We could not hit the MIGs at their home bases. We could not hit them in their traffic patterns. We had to wait for them to reach an altitude from which they could attack us. We joked that our government was trying to be sporting. If so, it was deadly sport.

We were not allowed to hit the North Vietnamese port facilities. The Navy was not allowed to mine their harbors. Yet, their harbors were their main sources of supply. It made no sense to allow the enemy freedom to unload their supplies of war and not hit them where those supplies were concentrated. Instead we allowed them to disperse their supplies. Cam Ranh was targeted against single trucks and similar small targets after the North Viets were allowed to disperse their concentrations of supplies. Our targeting of their supply network was similar to our targeting of the MIGs. As shown in a previous chapter, our Secretary of Defense did not allow us to hit the enemy where they were most vulnerable. Instead, he directed us to hit them where we were most vulnerable. For the fighter pilots, it was not an academic matter. Those were real bullets being fired at us.

One of the more glaring examples of a lack of sustained purpose involved the Northeast and Northwest railways that linked Hanoi with its suppliers from China, Russia and the Warsaw Pact countries of Europe. Interdiction is that part of an air war where bombers are targeted against locations deep within an enemy's area of control. Those targets may involve vital industries, communication, agricultural, transportation, air defenses, etc. Any target that weakened an enemy and lessened his ability to fight effectively should be fair game. In the case of the NE and NW railroad lines, we targeted them heavily. However, just like the ball bearings in Britain, that targeting has to be sustained. In the case of the railroads, we pulled back. It did no good to bomb their railway tracks if they could repair those tracks and continue to move needed war supplies.

The insane bombing halts insisted by Johnson were purportedly an attempt to get the enemy to the bargaining table. Trouble with that approach is that we needed something with which to bargain. To the pilot in the trenches, the bombing halts allowed the enemy to repair damage and resume use of the railroad lines. Another obvious affect was that they were also able to supply their anti-aircraft weapons that were at a distance from their sources of supply. While the interrupted focus on the railroads was bad enough, the later change of target emphasis almost entirely away from the railroads was a further compounding mistake.

The importance of the railroad lines to the enemy cannot be overemphasized. As mentioned, China had over a half million men tasked with repairing the damage in North Vietnam that our air interdiction campaign caused to the railroad tracks. North Vietnam had its own work crews diligently working and even threw in the 300 French prisoners from their First Indochinese War.

It was greatly discouraging to our pilots to see so many pilots and aircraft lost in an air campaign, just to see the focus of that campaign shifted. It made no military sense and was just a waste of human and material resources. It also brought into question just how these crucial military decisions were made?

THE CRUCIBLE OF DECISIONS:

During the SEA War, military decisions by our national administration were made each Tuesday at lunch meetings chaired by President Johnson. From the start of the "Rolling Thunder" bombing campaign in March, 1965, President Johnson and his lunch companions decided such things as targets, number of sorties allowed, tactics, what munitions to use against which targets, even approach corridors flown by our fighter-bombers.

The rest of this "targeting committee" consisted of Secretary of State Dean Rusk, Secretary of Defense Robert McNamara, Walt Rostow and Bill Moyers. What qualified these leaders to be making such important military decisions?

Walt Rostow was an economist who served as Special Assistant for National Security Affairs to President Johnson from 1966 to 1969. Bill Moyers was a journalist who served as Press Secretary to President Johnson from 1965 to 1967. President Johnson was a teacher before he became a politician. He taught government, public-speaking and the humanities. Dean Rusk had university degrees in political science and law with a stint at Oxford. McNamara had degrees in economics. Not one participant had educational or work experience in physics or engineering. I mention physics and engineering because of the many decisions this group made concerning munitions that would be employed against specific targets. Many of those decisions defied logic.

Rusk did have a stint as a war planner in WWII, but that would not prepare a man to make valid decisions on how to attack a target from the air and with what munitions should be used to destroy a target. It would make any attack pilot sick to know that his life was in the hands of decision-makers ignorant of what they were supposed to be deciding.

Not one of this original group had any actual combat experience. Not one representative of the armed services or Joint Chief of Staff was present. This sorry state of affairs lasted until late fall of 1967, when a military General Officer was finally invited to attend. By then the irrevocable damage had been done. Within seven months of this belated addition of a professional, by the spring of 1968, Rolling Thunder would be severely restricted and then totally terminated.

Everything about the Tuesday lunches was wrong, not only the lack of expertise of the participants, but the organizational aspects. Targeting should have been decided at the Pentagon level by experts and consistent with an overall plan that was in concert with the objectives of the war. The methodology of the attacks and the weapons employed to accomplish the missions should have been decided by military men with combat-pilot experience. If there are those who disagree with me, I only have to point to the fact that America lost the war to prove that we did many things wrong.

With the termination of Rolling Thunder, our attack aircraft would not revisit the North until 1972, when

Nixon employed the Linebacker attacks. Thus, the entirely civilian lunch participants would make military decisions on more than 80% of all the Rolling Thunder targets without the assistance of any military men, let alone a combat fighter-bomber pilot. It is no wonder that their "military decisions" resulted in abject failure. A military man is left to wonder if any of the participants was even aware of the existence of the "Principles of War"?

As previously mentioned, the matching of the munitions loads on our aircraft with the targets to be destroyed, bore no semblance to reality during these meetings. You cannot destroy a well-constructed bridge with rockets, but you can with larger fragmentation bombs. The "targeting committee" chose rockets, not missiles, rockets.

Roads were chosen for targets because of the mistaken belief that a large number of bombs, precisely placed, can knock out a road. The Communists could call upon huge numbers of personnel to fill in bomb craters so that any closure of a road was for only a short time, usually less than a day before repairs were completed and the road was back in use.

One has to use explosive, fragmentation bombs to create bomb craters. Napalm is not explosive and not fragmentation. Napalm is an incendiary bomb. Yet the "targeting committee" chose napalm to "bomb" the roads. What did they think we were doing, burning dirt?

Throughout this book there are references to the Johnson Administration's commendable concern for avoidance of civilian casualties. Johnson also repeatedly stated he did not want to harm North Vietnam's agricultural economy and had offered, on several occasions, to fund the rebuilding of North Vietnam's industrial base after cessation of hostilities. What he seemed unable to grasp was that we first had to defeat North Vietnam.

While advanced post-war planning is essential, an assumption of victory can be, as shown in SEA, extremely counter-productive. In planning the tactics of a war, it is also counter-productive to base target-selection judgment on post-war considerations. Target what is necessary to win a war, and do not allow post-war planning or considerations to interfere with target-selection or our method of fighting.

For those of us flying and fighting, a common refrain was often heard: "how can they be so stupid?" When awareness finally dawned, the reality of our situation was evident. We pilots were just pawns in a gristly game being played by our politicians. The researched discoveries of wartime action and policy just reinforced that notion.

ANALYSIS OF DEFEAT:

Much later, McNamara and Rusk seemingly began to realize what they had done and questioned their own policies and decisions. But the rest of them, Johnson, Nixon and Kissinger, were coldly-calculating politicians who seemed more concerned with avoiding policies that might hurt them politically rather than for the well-being of our military men and for the honor and benefit of the United States.

Consider their disregard of the POWs who they left behind. This is just another terrible example of the callous disregard that these amoral politicians had for the military. These military men had committed their lives to serve their country and these politicians rewarded that patriotism by insuring their deaths at the hands of a barbaric enemy. Treason may be too strong a word to describe some of their actions, but it comes close.

A war such as SEA, that lasted so long and ended in disaster, created a great many post-mortems. Even

Dean Rusk, one of those responsible for many of the failed policies, seemed to have second thoughts of the wisdom shown. As he stated, "Coming back to (a discussion of) the point of gradualism, looking back on it, the question arises as to whether we might have prevented further North Vietnam efforts against South Vietnam had we put in more troops sooner, but the gradual response left it open to North Vietnam to speculate that if they just did a little bit more, they'd be able to overcome what the Americans were willing to do." This is political speak for "our policy of gradualism may have prolonged the war?"

Our government contracted several "think tanks" to do post-war analysis. BDM Corporation was one selected to make a post-war analysis of why we lost. Their conclusion: "the Communist Vietnamese leadership outlasted America's 8-year effort in SEA and finally reunited Vietnam by force of arms. A major factor contributing to their success was the remarkable logistical support they created with an integrated network of bases, sanctuaries and lines of communication. The sanctuaries (created by the Rules of Engagement) gave them the trump card that enabled them to fight a protracted war and outlast the U.S. commitment to the Republic of Vietnam."

BDM was a think-tank provider of analysis to the U.S. Army Air Defense forces. They started out in the 1950s as Braddock, Dunn and McDonald and eventually they were purchased by and became part of TRW.

The British Broadcasting Company (BBC) was another entity that provided analysis, but did it on its own. It stated that "more bombs fell on Laos than in all of World War II and 30% (of those bombs) failed to detonate." This was not my experience. Bombs dropped from aircraft in my flights behaved, on average, quite well. If the BBC was referring to the CBUs, we had no way of knowing if all the bomblets exploded. Our 12th Wing participated in a significant way in the Laotian War, but our rate of ordnance malfunction was surprisingly small. Malfunctions did happen, but our bombs, even those that were left over from WWII, performed well.

Part of the problem in SEA is being repeated in Syria in our battle against ISIS. Reportedly, more than half of our flights in Syria are returning with unexpended ordnance loads. If these reports are true, there has to be a corrective response.

Late in my war year in 1966, the CIA calculated that "it cost the United States $8.70 to inflict a dollar's worth of damage to the North Vietnam war effort." There are many explanations, some of which are mentioned in this book, as to why our productivity was so poor. Unexpended ordnance loads are one of them.

In a desert war like the Middle-East, returned munitions loads usually mean that target approvals have not been given. This is one example of why our recent wars have been so wasteful and not cost-effective. We should go on the propaganda offense and alert the world of the practice by our desert-enemy of using civilian areas for military purposes. Place the onus of civilian deaths on them instead of waiting for them to show the world visual proof of civilian deaths caused by our military actions.

Our military expends a great deal of effort and money to place a bomb on an attack aircraft over a target. The total number of maintenance hours to allow each fighter-bomber to fly one hour of combat airtime is significant. It takes a huge team to make it happen. Each time we fail to make each bomb count, we fail the efforts of that entire team. Returning to base with unexpended bombs is just as bad as my stupid failure to arm the bombs over the target. It is imperative to make the entire process of placing a bomb effectively on a target to be as smooth and seamless as possible. It takes constant fine-tuning, constant training and consistent policies.

The last month of my war, December 1966, the prestigious Rand Corporation, another think-tank, wrote a report on the effectiveness of Rolling Thunder: "The main <u>constraints</u> on air operations (were): (1) Keeping civilian casualties to a minimum, (2) Limiting attacks to (purely) military objectives, and (3) Avoiding actions which might provoke China or the USSR."

"The U.S. failure to-date to undertake a max effort to deny access to imports by sea or over land— attributable evidently mainly to the fear of provoking and activating the USSR and China—thus emerges as the outstanding gap in the logic of the United States' coercive strategy against North Vietnam." Victory in SEA was a concept that, like honor, seemed to have been out-of-fashion in Washington. "Even if an escalation in tempo, with the current restrictions (ROE) in place, there is no indicator that Rolling Thunder would bring about the desired outcome 'within an acceptable time period.'"

In August, 1967, the Senate Armed Services Committee reported: "The fact that the air campaign has not achieved its objectives to a greater extent cannot be attributed to the inability or impotence of air power. It attests rather to the fragmentation of our air might by overly-restrictive controls, limitations, and the doctrine of "gradualism" placed on our aviation forces. (This) prevented them (our forces) from waging the air campaign in a manner and according to the timetable, which was best calculated to achieve maximum results."

Timing in war is everything. In an air campaign, the best results will be obtained by hitting the enemy hard and fast, before he has a chance to recover or repair damage. Once that advantage has been gained, uninterrupted and relentless attacks must be continued. The objective is to destroy the enemy's current war-making, communication and transportation capacity and follow it up with ground occupation to solidify the air action.

One salient point that is often overlooked when evaluating Vietnam is that those sent had only one year to spend in SEA. In WWII, combatants from the U.S. were in for the duration. One result of the rapid turnover, at least of the fighter forces, was a lack of continuity. Lessons learned were often lost.

ULTIMATE BETRAYAL:

While the above acts and omissions of Johnson together portray a compelling set of causes for our defeat, one act stands out above all others: Dean Rusk served as Secretary of State from January 21, 1961, through to January 20, 1969, first under President John Kennedy and later under President Lyndon Johnson. Nearly twenty years after our defeat in SEA, former Secretary Rusk acquiesced to an interview with Peter Arnett on a CBS documentary called the "Ten Thousand Day War."

The results of that interview have been extracted from a book by Air Force General Pete Piotrowski called: "The Secret War and Other Conflicts." In the book, Arnett, formerly of CNN, asked, "it has been rumored that the United States provided the North Vietnamese government the names of the targets that would be bombed the following day. Is there any truth to that allegation?"

To everyone's astonishment, Rusk responded, "Yes, we didn't want to harm the North Vietnamese people so we passed the (information on our) targets to the Swiss Embassy in Washington with instructions to pass them to the NVN government through their embassy in Hanoi." He went on to say, "all we wanted to do was demonstrate to the North Vietnamese leadership that we could strike targets at will, but we didn't want to kill innocent people. By giving the North Vietnamese advanced warning of the targets to be attacked, we thought they would tell the workers to stay home."

Mr. Arnett opined that this "would be a treasonous act by anyone else." I cannot agree with Arnett on treason, for Rusk and McNamara clearly had good intentions. At least they seemed good based on their limited views. However, it is almost incomprehensible to me and anyone associated with the Air Force or Navy to absorb the enormity of this admission. With this revelation coming at such a long time after the war, it is sad to consider that the triad of Johnson, McNamara and Rusk seemed to consider the lives of the unknown North Viet civilians as more important than those of us entrusted to carry out the missions under their orders. In retrospect, this was an act of blatant treachery. Had this information been known at the time, we would have been justified to refuse to fly any missions until the notifications had ceased.

The North Vietnamese were well equipped with mobile AAA guns and mobile Surface to Air Missiles. With a day's advance notice, they could use the same mobile guns and missiles to move to and position around each target as identified. To give an enemy advanced notice of intended targets is an astounding piece of information.

The entire focus of our bombing efforts over North Vietnam was to destroy the selected targets with minimal loss of personnel and equipment. By telegraphing our intent in advance, we insured that our bombing effectiveness was reduced in addition to the huge increase in danger to the aircrews. We were fighting a war and it is the responsibility of the civilian authority to give American soldiers, sailors and airmen the best equipment and protection possible. By this act of advance notice, a great many more airmen were killed and aircraft destroyed. Even more pilots had to spend a significant portion of their lives in Vietnamese captivity.

The enormity of this admission is so profound as to question the sanity and intelligence of those responsible. More probable is the consideration that the evidence of cowardice at the very top of our national leadership led to the many decisions that prolonged the war and greatly escalated the number of deaths.

To a fighter-bomber pilot who had many friends shot down over heavily defended targets in North Vietnam, the issues are far more visceral. This is another example of rank amateurs leading our disastrous effort. What were the motivations that caused Rusk, McNamara and Johnson to make such an unfathomable decision? Did they even consider the aircrews?

> *"Civilized society is perpetually menaced with disintegration through the primary hostility of men towards one another."*
>
> Sigmund Freud

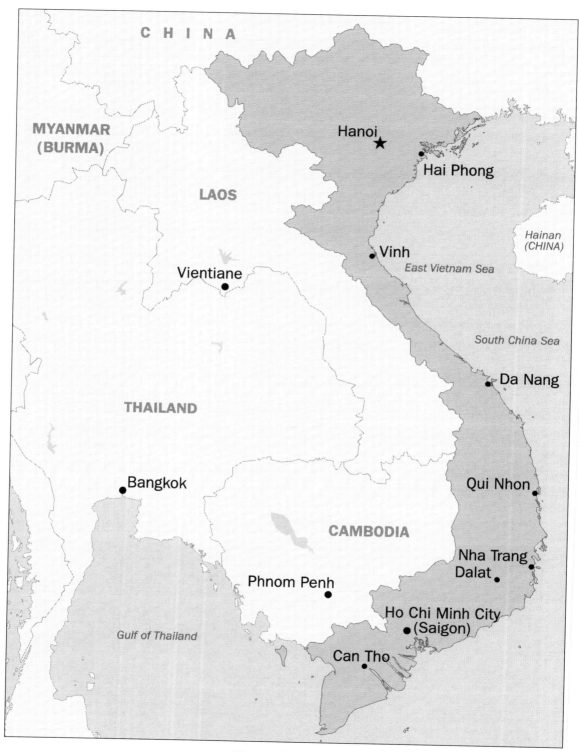

Vietnam Post-1975

CHAPTER TWENTY-SEVEN
Without Purpose
America's Longest War

> *"There has never been a protracted war from which a country has benefited."*
>
> Sun Tzu

Determination of the exact dates of the starts and stops of American wars is an inexact science. Even the names of some of our wars have been marked by controversy. As of the writing of this book, America has been involved in 13 wars. Some might contest and maintain either 11 or 12. My criteria for selecting what might qualify as wars were the individual purposes for initiating each war. For example, our two wars with Iraq each had a different purpose, as did our current war in Afghanistan.

It has been stated that the War of 1812 was, in reality, an extension of our Revolutionary War. While there is some justification for that view, the War of 1812 was due mainly to the forced impressment of over 10,000 American sailors on British warships to assist in the British war against Napoleon. Britain may have continued to treat us as a colony, but our objectives were different from those in the Revolutionary War. While it was an affront to our sovereignty, the impressment of sailors was also detrimental to our commerce with other nations.

The wars against Iraq and Afghanistan have also been categorized in different ways. The 1st Iraqi War was to drive the Iraqis out of Kuwait and to eliminate the threat to the Saudi Arabian oil fields. The Afghan War was to attack the Taliban who supported al Qaeda, the terrorist group responsible for the attacks on the World Trade Center and the Pentagon.

The 2nd Iraqi War was stated by our government as an effort to rid the Middle East of a brutal dictator who used Chemical Weapons of Mass Destruction (WMDs) on his own people as well as in its war with Iran. Iraq also had a rudimentary nuclear weapons program that was thought to still be in operation.

With appreciation of the validity of other views and with the exception of our Southeast Asia War, I have made the following, generally-accepted determinations of the durations of our chronologically-listed wars. The dates listed are not the overall dates of the duration of the wars. They just pertain to the time of American involvement:

Indian Wars	291 Years	(1607 to 1898)
Revolutionary War	3,059 Days	(4/19/1775 to 9/3/1783)
War of 1812	1,071 Days	(6/18/1812 to 12/24/1814)
Mexican- American War	648 Days	(4/25/1846 to 2/2/1848)

Civil War	1,458 Days	(4/12/1861 to 4/9/1865)
Spanish-American War	229 Days	(4/25/1898 to 12/10/1898)
World War I	584 Days	(4/6/1917 to 11/11/1918)
World War II	1,346 Days	(12/7/1941 to 8/14/1945)
Korean War	1,128 Days	(6/25/1950 to 7/27/1953)
Southeast Asian War (Vietnam)	8,606 Days	(6/8/1956 to 12/31/1979)
1st Iraqi War	42 Days	(1/17/1991 to 2/28/1991)
Afghan War	5,000+ Days and counting (10/7/2001 to…)	
2nd Iraqi War	3,193 Days	(3/19/2003 to 12/15/2011)

The start date of our SEA War is very ambiguous. Some claim it began with the American Naval Air attacks against North Vietnam on August 5, 1964, after the purported Gulf of Tonkin Incidents. This book has served to show that American troops, ships and aircraft had actually participated much earlier, and that American air combat action in South Vietnam occurred prior to 1962. Ground units were fighting prior to 1961.

American clandestine ground and air units fought in Laos, possibly as early as the 1950s, although the actual participation dates of civilian clandestine air units and the timing of our military participation remains a deep mystery.

Often participation can only be determined through lists of combat casualties. In Laos, that source was largely denied due to the clandestine air forces: Bird and Sons, Continental Air Services, and Air America among others, that did not publish their lists of wounded, dead or missing.

The Department of Defense, in an attempt to clarify, stated that November 1, 1955 was the official start date of the Vietnam War as that was when the DOD created its SEA War casualty list. While casualty figures often include the wounded, the first-known American military death of the war was Air Force Tech Sergeant Richard B. Fitzgibbon Jr., who died on June 8, 1956, and is the first chronologically-listed death on the Vietnam War Memorial Wall in Washington D.C.

Various pundits have also selected 1956 as the start date due to the establishment in that year of the Military Assistance Advisory Group (MAAG) in Saigon by the U.S. Military. The MAAG replaced a similar group from France that left Vietnam after their defeat at Dien Bien Phu.

Others select 1959, which was the year that Ho Chi Minh declared the start of the "People's War." Also in 1959, two U.S. soldiers were killed in a guerrilla attack on Bien Hoa Airfield outside Saigon. In 1960, the North Vietnamese formerly formed the National Liberation Front, later commonly referred to as the Viet Cong. Actually, some cadres of the Viet Minh were located in the South and those formed the basis for the establishment of the Viet Cong. Helicopter gunships arrived on the U.S. Helicopter Carrier Cole on December 11, 1961, along with 400 American military personnel to assist the South Vietnamese Army (ARVN). All of these have been used as starting dates and there are good arguments in support of each.

With the still-secret dates of the initiation of operations by our surrogates and our own early forces in Laos, the selection of an earlier date makes sense. The author has joined others who have chosen the date of the first death on June 8, 1956 as the starting point of our SEA War. Since much of our early American participation in the "secret wars" in both South Vietnam and Laos was by air units, it is highly appropriate

398

that the first death of an airman should mark the official starting date.

As for the date of termination, every source that I consulted has listed the ending as the date that the American military evacuated our Embassy and other personnel as Saigon fell to North Vietnamese Army troops on April 30, 1975. The facts do not support that listing, especially in any comparison to the Afghanistan War.

Several independent sources have stated that combat-related deaths for the U.S. military in SEA continued after the North Vietnamese troop's victorious conquest of the South in 1975. In the four years from 1976 through the end of 1979, the United States lost, on average, 192 military men killed per year in "combat related" operations, with the worst year being 1978 with 447 deaths. What operations were they performing?

The official Department of Defense figures for fatal casualties in the Afghan War list the total number of American military deaths from combat and other causes in Afghanistan, Pakistan and Uzbekistan from the start of that war on October 7, 2001 until October 1, 2015 as 2254 deaths. This averages out to be 161 fatalities per year due to all causes.

Thus, the average number of our military killed in SEA, after the supposed end to hostilities, is higher than the average number killed in Afghanistan during the years of a supposed "hot" war. For these reasons, I have listed the end-date for our Southeast Asian War as the end of 1979, a year when we lost 148 killed.

This book categorizes several times that the Chinese and Vietnamese, even with the Chinese support given North Vietnam during the SEA War, were enemies. This has again been shown by Vietnamese actions and support for the defunct Trans Pacific Trade Pact negotiated by the United States and widely viewed as a counter to China.

Of interest, for three weeks and six days in February, 1979, the Chinese People's Liberation Army (PLA) fought a very hot border war against the Vietnamese Army, then-composed of the remnants of the ARVN, Viet Cong and the North Vietnamese Army, plus recruits.

By Vietnamese estimates, they lost 26,000 soldiers killed while the Chinese estimate that 57,000 PLA troops and another 70,000 Chinese militia troops were killed. Perhaps the disparity between the casualty figures resulted from the Vietnamese being so battle-tested after so many years of warfare.

The root cause for that short but deadly war was Chinese distrust of the intentions of the Soviets and Vietnamese, due to the Vietnamese invasion of Cambodia and their war against the Cambodian surrogates of China. This war that killed so many, occurred just 10 years after Chinese troops, AAA units and fighter aircraft left North Vietnam.

Basing a determination of the start date for any war on listed deaths has its own risks. Prior to 1960, the United States military experienced only three known deaths in Southeast Asia. In 1960, we had five as the escalation began. What complicates the issue is that in the 23 years subsequent to our final-day evacuation of Saigon, our military experienced 834 deaths in SEA. The final combat death listed for SEA was in 1998. One is left to wonder what was the manner of their deaths?

Military record-keeping is also an inexact science. After 1953, it was commonly listed that American deaths in the Korean War numbered around 50,000. That was the official DOD figure for many years. Later, it was discovered that that figure included military deaths from various causes throughout the Pacific Region. The figure that had been quoted for decades was then revised down to 33,000.

If one agrees with my above-stated, starting-date criteria, it is apparent that the SEA War is the longest in our history. For the current Afghan War to qualify, hostilities would have to continue in that conflict until April 30, 2025, exactly 40 years to the day of the American evacuation of Saigon (Ho Chi Minh City) by helicopter.

No description of our war in Southeast Asia can avoid the adjective of tragic. To most Americans, it seems impossible to comprehend that our elected government would send American military people to a far-off war without any intention to win, but that is what happened.

We fostered death and destruction without a goal; without a purpose. It was a graphic display of why we must consider very carefully before we ever again decide to commit our military and only then if we have clearly defined and obtainable objectives.

On the political front, how many times did President Johnson need to convince himself that our bombing halts were futile gestures? What kind of hubris would guide a leader who would or could not recognize that, if the rules you are using do not work, you change the rules?

President Dwight Eisenhower, himself a highly successful five-star General of the Army, stated on October 21, 1966, that President Johnson showed "hesitation, indecision, and even timidity in Vietnam." Johnson's actions or lack of actions kept the war alive. In the face of such determined resistance, every policy and every decision of consequence seemed destined to prolong the war and create an endless stalemate. Other current and former military leaders spoke even more forcefully, in terms often unprintable, that Johnson was destroying the fabric of our military and forcing our people to question American "exceptionalism" by his inept leadership. Unfortunately, Johnson had created a situation that could not be easily rectified, even with his departure from the Oval Office.

History has shown that avoidance of war is accomplished by showing strength, not weakness. Potential aggressors usually have a calculus that avoids strengths and, instead, concentrates on apparent enemy weaknesses. Southeast Asia has graphically shown us that during peacetime, our military should be as strong as we can possibly make it, other governmental requirements considered.

TRAGIC BYPRODUCT OF WAR, THE POWS:

Before our River Rat pilots' "first real reunion" with the returned POWs, I had wondered how they could have mentally and emotionally maintained with their long incarceration in a war that they were intimately aware was not being fought to win. What must have been their thoughts? Did they have any trust left for our politically leaders? Our war-without-end placed our POWs in an untenable situation. They survived with their honor intact and with a surprisingly strong demonstration of mental and emotional stability after their return. How did they do it?

The "rock" on which they seemingly based their survival was not our country, but in themselves. That is not to say that some did not rely on their faith in God or that many did not still support the government that did not support them. They showed a resilience that transcended those considerations. During most of their confinement, they were kept separated.

Through ingenious methods they communicated. They built a reliance on their chain-of-command that provided hope. They trusted their group. My profound respect goes to all of these men who were able to create methods and organization to better withstand an untenable and inhumane situation. I also credit strong leadership from within their group. It is extraordinary what they managed to accomplish. While the POWs stood firmly behind their pledge to uphold the Geneva Conventions for prisoner conduct, they used common sense against a very brutal enemy who tortured them and behaved in an inhumane manner in violation of every convention on how to properly treat prisoners.

PREPARING FOR WAR:

The current method of practice by the Air Force in preparation for war is unknown to this writer, but I would imagine that several of the lessons that should have been learned in SEA have not become part of our "institutional memory." Two of those practices led to many unnecessary deaths and loss of valuable aircraft. Those practices can be corrected with proper training.

Stateside practice for war in overseas locations should contain the realism of the actual conditions of war. One of our mistakes in SEA has been repeatedly mentioned in this book. That was the use of multiple bombing, rocketry or gunnery passes against our targets. This was suicide and a suicide learned in practice.

When we practiced at controlled bombing and gunnery ranges, we would use the standard racetrack pattern of bomb release on the target, which was usually a spot on the ground surrounded by concentric circles to show miss distances. The use of single bomb drops in a standard pattern was necessary for safety and for learning how to drop and getting closer to the target. However, training should take the practice one step further. The final proficiency check-out of a pilot should contain the realism of warfare. It should insist on a single pass and a varied pattern of attack for all the aircraft in an attack formation. The standard racetrack pattern needs to be discarded for a varied attack using different attack vectors and dive angles. The bomb release should include all carried bombs and the aiming point should be short of the target with the objective of "walking" the bombs through the target. "One pass and haul ass" should be the graduation motto for our airmen in training.

A second lesson was never learned while I was in SEA. From all the accounts I was able to review after leaving; it was not learned later in the war. That unlearned lesson was the stateside practice of parking aircraft in neat and tidy rows on the tarmac. Back in the United States, Maintenance personnel learned to make the Flightlines orderly by parking aircraft so that the noses were in a straight line.

This was great for peacetime and made our Air Force bases neat and orderly. Yet those same practices were carried into war. For the Viet Cong attacking our Air Force bases in Vietnam, this greatly simplified their ranging problems when attacking. Their mortar operators needed to find the proper distance from their mortars to our aircraft. If they located their mortars perpendicularly to the neat lines of our aircraft, once they found the range they could "walk" the mortars down our neat lines.

Repeated attacks against our South Vietnamese airfields left the same carnage of neat lines of burning hulks that had once been state-of-the-art aircraft. We never learned. To avoid this unnecessary wastage of valuable inventory, we need to practice random parking and revetment screening during peacetime.

Our stateside practices need to show the realism of warfare, for it is in practice where we instill those methods that need to be second nature when pilots are confronted with the reality of a heavily defended target. It is in practice where ground personnel learn the lessons necessary for immediate action when confronted with a penetration of our base defenses. Those practices also need to be periodically reviewed to ensure that the changing nature of air warfare is reflected in a corresponding change in the way we prepare for that warfare.

Another aspect of the SEA war might also have been overlooked. That is the issue of pride in accomplishing a challenging task. Much of the airborne effort in SEA was sustained by the pride of the ground and air crews. However, there are different degrees of pride. It is better if a war is personalized for the warrior and for the support personnel. For example, in SEA the Air Force no longer inscribed the names of the pilots and crew chiefs on the sides of the fighter aircraft like they did during WW II and Korea. The result was a depersonalization of the war for individual participants. That depersonalization was counter-productive. Pride can be very "cost-effective."

TRANSFORMATIVE WARS:

Our Revolutionary War was a war of creation. While it had a significant, positive result, the number of battle deaths attributed to the war years was few. General Washington won by avoiding conflict, due to a comparative disadvantage in forces, and only occasionally did he engage. The results were transformative in that we became a unique country consisting of many individual parts (our States). With relatively few battle deaths, we created a nation.

While the reasoning of Great Britain may have been to maintain control by keeping us divided into thirteen individual colonies, the result of our decision to federalize and the considerations that went with that decision has created a blueprint for which other areas of the world, most notably Europe, can unite.

While the Revolutionary War did transform us from a controlled to a controlling nation, the two really transformative wars in our national history are the Civil War and World War II. Both wars created massive mobilizations of combat troops and the creation of a huge number of machines of war. These two wars resulted in the deaths of huge numbers of troops and sailors, far exceeding any of our other American wars. The reasons that those two wars were so transformative was that they severely altered how we were viewed by the rest of the world, altered how we viewed the rest of the world and changed us from a non-militaristic nation into a militaristic one. The aftermath of both transformative wars was that we changed from being reactive to active to the events of the world around us.

Many of those who helped create the United States came to our shores looking for a new start and participated in our remarkable westward expansion. That expansion was galvanized and pushed by the significant numbers of troops remaining from our Civil War battles. In two short decades those troops quickly won the remaining Indian Wars and transformed the United States into one of three massive and far-reaching nation-states of the 19th, 20th, and 21st Centuries. We also rejected confederation and, instead, remained a federated system.

Many of those who settled in what became the United States did so to avoid the incessant wars on the European Continent. Yet it was our participation in a war on that same continent that transformed the United States from a peaceful, middle-tiered nation with a small and weak military into the strongest military and industrial nation that the world had ever known.

It remains to be seen if the Southeast Asian War will itself become somewhat transformative. Will our national experience with and newfound knowledge of the brutality of war caused by our Indochinese quagmire lead us to a more balanced military approach to international relations and a more prudent use of our vast military resources?

Avoidance of war should be a prime motivator for the United States. But we also must have the will and strength to fight a war to win if it is absolutely necessary for the most critical of our national interests. We would be well-served to heed Teddy Roosevelt's oft-mentioned admonition to "speak softly, but carry a big stick," which obviously means to be cautious and prudent in any military commitment, but insure that when we do commit, it is with an overwhelming force of arms and will.

Former Secretary of State Madeline Albright famously asked, "What is the purpose of having such a superb military if you don't use it?" She missed the point. Contrary to what she and other politicians might think, the purpose of our military is to preserve the peace through strength, not wage war.

In future wars, a guiding rule should always be followed to insure success: leave military decisions up to the professionals. Simply stated: Define the objectives; give them the tools; celebrate their victories.

> *"Victorious warriors win first and then go to war, while defeated warriors go to war first and then seek to win."*
>
> Sun Tzu

EPILOGUE

Southern California

> *"To be prepared for war is one of the most effective means of preserving peace."*
>
> Continental Army General George Washington

My return to California was with a mixed-bag of feelings. Friends, acquaintances and even family members avoided any discussion of the war or my participation in it. At the time, my impression was that my family wanted to avoid burdening me with recollections of unpleasant times. My impression of friends and acquaintances was of indifference. Not once did anyone ever ask me to describe or explain my experiences in Southeast Asia. Discussions with my only sibling, my brother, ended in arguments and were subsequently avoided.

In retrospect, the attitude of the American public was understandable. Americans hate to lose. It is like rooting for your favorite team only to find that it not only lost, but did not play the game to win. Americans were confused and angered. Many did not want to single out military participants, but they felt let down, disillusioned and even betrayed.

One of my first actions on getting home was to pull out my standard issue canvas duffle bag. From it, I pulled out all my flight suits, fatigues, khakis, formal wear and threw them in the trash. All the paraphernalia of war, the photos, my combat diary, the mission cards, the confidential mission results, my notes, letters, etc., all went into a box which quickly found its way to the attic and became a forgotten part of my past.

As time has passed, I have resurrected some of the memories of that time in my life. I remembered enough so that I could speak intelligently with the occasional high school history class that had an interest in and a curiosity about a forgotten war.

It is often said that time heals and it has. We have witnessed a renewed respect by the public for those fighting overseas. Cars sport yellow-ribbon decals that admonish others to "Support our Troops." Patriotic celebrations excite a new generation. It is all to the good.

But for those of us who did fight and came home to an indifferent and hostile reception, there is a deeply buried part of us all that will remain embittered. For us, the time for recognition has passed. It is best to move on and only look back to learn what not to do. The human part of it is better left forgotten.

Southeast Asia should be remembered as a lesson on how not to do things. It seems that it may become the last truly intense and sustained air war in our history. The direction is toward unmanned vehicles. Removing the avionics and human systems in fighting aircraft will allow designers to create airborne weapon systems capable of sustaining "G" forces far in excess of those that can be endured by a man. It is a good direction.

The lessons that first need to be decided and then learned and maintained by our nation have to do with the current and future relationship between our military and with our elected, civilian leaders. Until world societies become truly civilized, we will be forced to fight future wars. America should be prepared structurally, emotionally as well as physically for those wars.

Commanding General of the Continental Army during our Revolutionary War, George Washington, learned first-hand of the devastation created by war, first as an officer in the British Army and later as leader of the American Continental Army. The father of our country served us first in war and later in peace as our first President. He fervently desired to preserve and protect our country and to that end repeatedly stated a desire to maintain a strong military presence to preserve the peace, but also maintained a "first wish" as stated below:

> *"My first wish is to see this plague of mankind, war,*
> *banished from the earth."*
>
> Commanding General & First President George Washington

Support Information

SUPPORT INFORMATION

The Author's Acknowledgments & Thanks

My thanks to those who gave their energy and time to proof and read this book for content, organization, style and text, while offering many other valuable suggestions.

In Southern California:
Julie & Dr. Robert Davey, PhD*;* United States Air Force Academy (USAFA) Class of 1962: Julie is a published author of four books, including "Cry Wolf" for which she has sold the movie rights and "Writing for Wellness." A graduate of Colorado Women's College, she is a former journalist in Texas and Professor of Journalism at Fullerton (California) College. Julie has worked for the benefit of others all her life, most notably with the City of Hope and with Native Americans in Alaska. Julie is due significant thanks for her major support, suggestions and proofing skills.

Julie's husband Bob was an Instructor Pilot in the Air Force. He earned his MBA from Pepperdine University, his MS and his PhD in Aeronautics from Cal Tech. He served as Professor of Aerospace Engineering at Cal Poly University and also served as Mayor of Duarte, California. With three other Officers, Bob was tasked by the Pentagon to do a mathematical study and evaluation of the conduct of the War in Southeast Asia.

Bob is also the published author of "The Moon War." (Laguna Niguel)

USAF Brigadier General (ret.) Daniel Pemberton*, USAFA Class of 1962:* Dan is a Vietnam War combat-veteran transport pilot. In Guam, Dan flew as Captain for Air Micronesia, a subsidiary of Continental Airlines as well as flying Captain for American Airlines. He was commander of the Air National Guard unit at Naval Station Ventura County, California.

A Command Pilot in the Air Force, he was awarded the Meritorious Service Medal, (2) Air Medals and an Air Force Commendation Medal. Dan was part of the clandestine transport forces flying missions for the CIA from Thailand during the Vietnam War. (Thousand Oaks).

Gary Wartik*, J.D.:* Gary is a business counselor who worked twelve years for the City of Thousand Oaks, California as Director of Business Development. He received his MPA at USC and his law degree from SFV College of Law . He served as Director of the Camarillo Chamber of Commerce and for many years in Sacramento as Legislative Analyst, writing many of the documents that became California law. A specialist in writing private and municipal business development plans, Gary is currently owner of Vision Economics-805-987-7322. (Camarillo)

In Alabama:
USAF Colonel (ret.) James R. Annis*, USAFA Class of 1962:* Jim is a Vietnam combat-veteran Electronic Warfare Officer (EWO). He participated in the massive B-52 raids against North Vietnam and Laos. His flying rating is as a Master Navigator who earned the Legion of Merit and (2) Air Medals. He received his MBA from Inter American University and his MS from the University of Tennessee.

Jim was officer-in-charge of the huge declassification effort for all SEA-related documents of the US Air Force and US Navy. For this book, he supplied the Project CHECO Rules of Engagement documents as well as several important reports and documents from USAF educational facilities in Alabama. For ten years, Jim served as Professor at the University of Tennessee (Montgomery).

In Arizona:

USAF Major General (ret.) Don Shepperd, *USAFA Class of 1962:* Don is a Vietnam combat-veteran fighter pilot and "Misty" Fast FAC, while flying the F-100. He was Commander of the United States Air National Guard as well as CNN Military Analyst from 1994 through 1998. He has written or edited several published books including: "Misty," "Fly Girl," "The Friday Pilots," "Bury us Upside Down," and "Those Red Tag Bastards" about the exploits of the exceptional Air Academy Class of 1962. Don was a Command Pilot in the Air Force and was decorated with the following medals: Silver Star, Legion of Merit, Distinguished Flying Crosses (3), Meritorious Service Medals (2), Air Medals (16) and an Air Force Commendation Medal. He received his MS from Troy State (Tucson).

Carolyn Goodenough:

My heartfelt thanks to my wife, Carolyn, who has read, corrected and suggested. She graduated from Cal State Northridge and retired from management at State Farm Insurance. Carolyn was the Grant Writer for United Way of Ventura County, California. She also is Grant Writer for the Assistance League of Conejo Valley (California). She possesses writing and proofing skills in abundance. Without her support and understanding, this book would not have happened. She has been a part of this from the beginning. (Pine, Arizona & Thousand Oaks, CA).

559th Tactical Fighter Squadron GIBs (Guys in Back):

My thanks and respect go to all the GIBs who flew the back seats of the Air Force Phantoms in SEA. Piloting is all about control, and to fly any aircraft without that control is difficult. Flying GIB was a much harder job than flying as Aircraft Commander.

With apologies for not remembering his name, my thanks also go to the GIB at Cam Ranh Bay who gave me the photo that was enlarged for the cover of this book. From his back seat vantage point, he shot the photo of an Operation "Big Eye" 559th Fighter Squadron Phantom prowling the skies over the Gulf of Tonkin. He suggested I "might be able to use it someday." Thank you, (Cam Ranh Bay, Vietnam).

Additional thanks go to: Ann McCrea Borden for help on organization; Barbara Carillion for help on proofing; Laura Seiler for help on indexing; Vince Williams our graphic artist who helped on book set up and text transfer, photos, maps and the dust cover; Alex Harwick, Harry Paddon, Steve Mettler, and posthumously, Freeman Marcy for combat content; Albert E. Gilligan (Association of Graduates) on awards for the Class of 1962 at the United States Air Force Academy, Colorado.

Bibliography

REPORTS, LISTS, DESCRIPTIONS, INTERVIEWS AND ARTICLES:

France:
"The USAF in France 1950-1967"...Jerry McAuliffe
"French Indochina"... Wikipedia.org
"The French in Vietnam" .... www.askasia.org
"Letter from Ho Chi Minh to President Harry S. Truman- 2-28-1946"
    National Archives .... www.archives.com
"Ho Chi Minh and Truman" The Fletcher School of International Politics,
    Tufts University, GMAP P230 ....Professor Lee
"French Actions in Recent Gold Crisis"
    Secret NoForn-Declassified...CIA Report in 1968
"France and the Atlantic Alliance" - Secret-Declassified ....CIA Report in 1967
"What Price Freedom?" .... www.renocitizen.com/french

World War II & Korea:
"World War II History"... www.wwiifoundation.org
....www.taphilo.com/ history
....www.armyairforces.com
"Pearl Harbor: Fifty Years of Controversy" - Institute of Historical Review ....Charles Lutton
"Lyndon Baines Johnson-His Time in Townsville and the Bombing Raid on LAE"
    "TOW 9," June 9, 1942 ....www.ozatwar.com
"Did Swedish Ball Bearings Keep the Second World War Going?"
    Economic History Society of Britain, Eric B. Golson
        http://www.ehs.org.uk/press/how-ball-bearings-could-have-changed-
        the-course-of-the-second-world-war
"Defense of the Reich".. Wikipedia
"Anti-Aircraft Artillery"... www.globalsecurity.org
"Korean War Battle Deaths" - Dept. of Veteran's Affairs ....www.va.gov
"GDP Per Capita"...http://useconomy.about.com

Southeast Asian War and the Aftermath:
"Gulf of Tonkin Incident: Reappraisal 40 Years Later"
    DOD Historian Edward Drea ....www.historynet.com
"Gulf of Tonkin Incident"... Wikipedia
"List of Vietnam War Flying Aces" .... Wikipedia
"Vietnam War Casualties" .... Wikipedia
"Vietnam War Statistics" .... www.Izsally.com/archives

"USAF in Thailand".. Wikipedia

"Air Aces"   ....www.aces.safarikovi.org

....W10.ru/Korea/Vietnam

"Air Interdiction - a definition" .... Wikipedia

"Air Force Deaths in SEA" - National Archives ....www.archives.gov

"Chinese Air Force Fighter Divisions"

Air Power Australia.. www.ausairpower.net

"Oral History Interview with Secretary of State Dean Rusk- 9/26/69"

Interviewer: Paige E. Mulhollan - Accession #74-245, LBJ Library

"SEA Air Belligerents"...www.khmerairforce.com

.... www.airwarvietnam.com

"TET Offensive of 1968- A Simpler Version" - John D. Dennison.........www.1stcavmedic.com

"The TET Offensive" .... www.USHistory.org

"The Vietnam Veteran's Memorial"..........................www.thewall.usa.com/summary

.... www.eaa.org

"C-130 Operations in Vietnam"..www.TheAviationZone.com

"45th Tactical Fighter Squadron"....................................... World e-book Library

"Vietnam, the First "Tanker War" - Ellery D. Wallwork, Air Mobility Command History Office

"Forward Air Controllers in the Vietnam War" .... Wikipedia

"FAC Call Signs"... www.fac-assoc.org

"FAC Losses in SEA".. www.24hourcampfire.com

.... www.amc.af.mil

"Royal Australian Air Force FACs in Vietnam" .... https://home.earthlink.

....net/aircommando

"Forward Air Controller Deaths in SEA" - American Legion....................www.legion.org

"List of Aircraft Carriers in Service" .... Wikipedia

"William Westmoreland: Biography" - Spartacus Educational ....www.spartacus.school.co.uk

"U.S. Intelligence in Vietnam" - General Bruce Palmer Jr.

Secret-Declassified ....CIA Report in 1984

"Communist Insurgency in Thailand"

Secret-Declassified ....CIA Report in 1966

"The Effects of Soviet and Chinese Involvement in the War on Vietnamese Communists"

Top Secret- Declassified .... CIA Report

"The Vietnam War, 1964-1969: A Chinese Perspective" - Xiaoming Zhang

Associate Professor, the U.S. Air War College .... www.jstor.org

"The Chinese Threat in the Vietnam War" - John W. Garver

"The Rules of Defeat: The Impact of Aerial Rules of Engagement on USAF Operations in North

Vietnam, 1965-1968" - Major Ricky J. Drake, School of Advanced Airpower Studies,

USAF Air University

"A Viet Cong Memoir".. Truaong Nhu Tang

BIBLIOGRAPHY

"Battle Casualty Lists" . . . . www.iCasualties.org

"Sino- Vietnamese War of 1979" . . . . Wikipedia

"Vietnamese War Fixed-Wing Aircraft Losses". . . . . Wikipedia

"More Aerial Intelligence Systems used during the Vietnam War"

    U.S. Army Command History Office

"National Vigilance Park" - NSA/CSS

"Vietnamese Defense against Aerial Attack". . . . . www.vietnam.ttu.edu

    Barton Meyers - Brooklyn College, New York University

"North Korean Pilots in Skies over Vietnam"

    Merle Pribbenow - CIA S. Vietnamese language specialist - Saigon

    Wilson Center - North Korean International Documentary Project

"Washington Management of the Rolling Thunder Campaign" - Dr. Mark Jacobsen

    Navy History and Heritage Command

"Tactical Command & Control of Carrier Operations" - Admiral James L. Holloway III

    . . . . www.history.navy.mil

"The USAF in SEA: 1961- 1973" . . . . www.dtic.mil

"The USAF in SEA- 1968" - Jacob Van Staaveren, Office of Air Force History

    Declassified Top Secret

"Operation Rolling Thunder". . . . . Wikipedia

"Rolling Thunder- Anatomy of a Failure" - Col. Dennis M. Drew . . . . www.au.af.mil

"Rolling Thunder" - Air Force Magazine, John T. Correll

"The Air Force in the Vietnam War" - Air Force Association, John T. Correll . . . .

"To Hanoi and Back, USAF and NVN 1966- 1973" - Wayne Thompson

    USAF History and Museums Program

"Rolling Thunder to Linebacker: U.S. Fixed-Wing Survivability over North Vietnam"

    LCDR Douglas M. White, U.S. Command and General Staff College for the Rand Corporation

"Route Pack Six" - Air Force Magazine . . . . www.airforcemag.com

"Vietnam Bomb Halt- Gain or Loss?" - Associated Press

    Eugene (Oregon) Register Guard - November 21, 1968

"Viet Cong and Vietnam People's Army Logistics and Equipment" . . . . Wikipedia

"Weapons of War: The Five Deadliest Air Defense Missiles" - The National Intent

    . . . . www.thenationalintent.org

"Surface to Air Missiles" . . . . Wikipedia

"AGM- 12B "Bullpup". . . . . Wikipedia

"AGM- 45 "Shrike" . . . . Wikipedia

"AGM- 78D "Standard ARM". . . . . Wikipedia

"Soviet Fire-Control Radars". . . . . www.users.sch.gr

"SA-2, High Altitude SAM" - The Military Factory . . . . www.militaryfactory.com

"Rolling Thunder and the Law of War" - W. Hays Parks, Air University Review
 The author has chosen not to quote from this excellent report. He recommends the reader read
 it in its entirety: www.airpower.maxwell.af.mil/airchronicles/aureview/1982/jan-feb/parks.html
"The Missile Men of North Vietnam"
 Vietnam Ministry of Foreign Affairs - Foreign Press Center . . . . www.presscenter.org.vn
"Soviet SAM Site Configuration" - Air Power Australia . . . . www.ausairpower.net
"AAA & SAMs: A Short Operational History of Ground-Based Air Defense"
 Kenneth P. Werrell
"Electronic Countermeasures in the Air War against North Vietnam 1965- 1967"
 Bernard C. Nalty and techniques - An authoritative, book-sized (103 pages)
 discussion that the author recommends. www.allworldwars.com/tactics
"Radar Bombing during Rolling Thunder- Ryan's Raiders and Combat Sky Spot"
 . . . . www.thefreelibrary.com
"Patterns & Predictability: The Soviet Evaluation of Operation Linebacker II"
 Dana Drenkowski & Lester W. Grau . . . . .www.fmso.leavenworth.army.mil

SEA - "Secret War" in Laos:
"CIA Air Operations in Laos, 1955-1974 - NSA Historian William M. Leary
 Supporting the "Secret War" . . . . www.cia.gov
 "Continental Air Services" . . . . www.america.net/casihistory
"CIA Activities in Laos" . . . . Wikipedia
"Raven Forward Air Controllers" . . . . Wikipedia
"Military Assistance Command-Vietnam – Studies and Observations Group" . . . . Wikipedia
"1198th Operational Evaluation and Training Squadron" . . . . Wikipedia
"Project Delta" . . . . Wikipedia
"Site Lima 85, Laos" . . . . Wikipedia
"Southern Laos-Ho Chi Minh Trail - 1967" . . . . www.wikiwand.com
"Laos: Most Heavily Bombed Place" - Simon Ingram, BBC News . . . . www.news.bbc.co.uk

SEA - Communications:
"On Watch - Profiles from the NSAs past 40 Years"
 Top Secret Umbra & Secret Spoke - declassified
"A Special Historical Study of SIGINT Support to Air Operations in SEA- 1965 to 1971"
 Thomas N. Thompson, Historian
 Top Secret Umbra - declassified, U.S.A.F. Security Service . . . . .www.nsa.gov

Western Pacific:
"U.S. Relations with the Federated States of Micronesia"
 U.S. Department of State - Bureau of East Asian and Pacific Affairs

HEADQUARTERS PACAF (USAF) DE-CLASSIFIED REPORTS:

"Evolution of the Rules of Engagement for Southeast Asia- 1960-1965"

Project CHECO Report - Top Secret NOFORN - September 1966

Albert F. Simpson Historical Research Center - Maxwell AFB, Alabama

"Rules of Engagement - Jan 1, 1966-November 1, 1969

Project CHECO Southeast Asia Report - Top Secret NOFORN*- 1976

Albert F. Simpson Historical Research Center - Maxwell AFB - Alabama

Author's Note: These two reports describe in detail the Rules of Engagement that tied the hands of the US Air Force to the extent that America could have never hoped to win the Vietnamese War. The "Rules" largely affected our targeting in SEA and led to our defeat.

NOFORN means that no foreign nationals are allowed to read it.

CHECO means Contemporary Historical Evaluation of Combat Operations.

PUBLICATIONS:

"MIG Sweep"- Publication of the Red River Valley Fighter Pilots Association

"Vietnam"- Weider History . . . . www.Historynet.com

BOOKS- PUBLISHED & UNPUBLISHED:

Civil War:

"April 1865- The Month that Saved America" - Jay Winik - Harper Collins

World War II & Korea:

"Infamy: Pearl Harbor and Its Aftermath" - John Toland - Doubleday

"Admiral Kimmel's Story"- The Truth about Pearl Harbor - H. Regnery Company
Admiral Husband E. Kimmel

"Okinawa- The Last Battle" - Historical Division- US Army, Charles E. Tuttle Company

"Marine" - General Chesty Puller, USMC

Southeast Asian War:

"Vietnam Air Losses–USAF, USN & Marine Corps Fixed-Wing Aircraft Losses in Southeast Asia 1961- 1973" - Chris Hobson.
This is the most authoritative book you will find on the subject. The organizational and equipment loss rates included are from this book.

"Vietnam Above the Treetops" - Brig. Gen. John F. Flanagan / Praeger (USAFA- 62)

"Misty"- Fast FACs in SEA, Edited by: Major General Don Shepperd, USAF (ret.) (USAFA- 62)

"Feet Wet- Reflections of a Carrier Pilot" - Rear Admiral Paul T. Gillchrist, Presidio USN (ret.)

"Cherries - A Vietnam War Novel" - Casualty Lists of the Vietnam War (WordPress)
. . . . www.cherrieswriter.wordpress.com

"Encyclopedia of the Vietnam War - Volume I"
Spencer C. Tucker, Editor
Michael R. Nichols

"A Bright and Shining Lie: John Paul Vann and America in Vietnam" - Neil Sheehan
    This is the best book that the author has ever read on the subject of the Ugly America that made
    such a mess of SEA and treated its own citizens with such contempt.
"Phantom Reflections" - Mike McCarthy, Stackpole Military History Series
"Secrets of the Vietnam War" - Albert A. Nofi . . . . www.books.google.com

SEA - "Secret War" in Laos:
"Sundowner Days- Recollections of a (Naval) Fighter Pilot" - Unpublished; Freeman Marcy
"Flying through Midnight- A Pilots Story of his Secret Missions into Laos"
    John T. Halliday - Scribner
"The Blood Road - The Ho Chi Minh Trail" - John Prados, John Wiley and Sons
"The Secret War and Other Conflicts" - General Pete Piotrowski
    ISBN (International Standard Book Number) 978-1-4931-6187-4
"Air America"- Clandestine CIA Air War" - Christopher Robbins
"The Ravens- FACs from Nakhon Phanom" - Christopher Robbins
"Honor Denied" - Allen Cates
"Here there are Tigers: The Secret Air War in Laos" - Reginald Hathorn
"The War in Northern Laos" (declassified)
    Victor B. Anthony & US Air Force History Office; Richard R. Sexton
"War in Laos" - Kenneth Conroy Squadron, Signal Publications

SEA- Political:
"The Years of Lyndon Johnson- Means of Ascent" - Robert A. Caro, Random House
"Rendezvous with Destiny" - Michael Fullilove, Penguin Press
"Dereliction of Duty" - H.R. McMaster, Harper Collins
"The Making of a Quagmire: America and Vietnam during the Kennedy Era" - David Halberstam
"The Fog of War: Lessons from the Life of Robert S. McNamara" - James G. Blight
"In Retrospect: The Tragedy & Lessons of Vietnam" - Robert S. McNamara
"Argument without End - In Search of Answers to the Vietnam Tragedy"
    Public Affairs, Perseus Books Group
"Into the Quagmire- Lyndon Johnson and the Escalation of the Vietnam War"
    Robert S. McNamara, Brian Van DeMark, Oxford University Press
"Secrets- a Memoir of Vietnam and the Pentagon Papers" - Daniel Ellsberg, Viking
"Cheers, Tears: A Marine's Story of Peace & War" - General Charles Cooper, USMC
"Blueprint for World Conquest" - Communist International Kessinger Legacy Group
"Blueprint for World Conquest" - Mao Tse Tung (Mao Zedung)
    The author read this book at the Air Academy Library in 1962. The book detailed how China
    would conquer the world militarily with an initial thrust through Southeast Asia. Research has
    been unable to relocate it.

SEA- Prisoners of War (POWs):

"The Men We Left Behind" - Mark Sauter & Jim Sanders, National Press Books

"Kiss the Boys Goodbye" - Monika Jensen-Stevenson & William Stevenson

"Hanoi Release John Nasmyth" - Virginia Nasmyth, V. Parr Publishing

"2355 Days- A POW's Story" - John "Spike" Nasmyth, Orion Book (F-4C Pilot, 12th TFW)

"The Vietnam War" www.gx2527leftinvietnam.com

Iraq and Afghan Wars:

"Horse Soldiers- US Soldiers who rode to Victory in Afghanistan" - Doug Stanton, Simon & Schuster

"It Doesn't Take a Hero" - Gen. H. Norman Schwarzkopf, Bantam Books

AGENCY SOURCES- INTERNET ADDRESSES:

U.S. Central Intelligence Agency (CIA) . . . . www.cia.gov
  Research- Publications - Freedom of Information Act, FOIA search

U.S. National Security Agency (NSA). . . . . .www.nsa.gov
  Library- Publications- FOIA
  Electronic Reading Room - FOIA search - The Gulf of Tonkin

U.S. Department of State (DOS) . . . . www.state.gov milestones-Charters

U.S. Department of Defense (DOD) . . . . .www.defense.gov/search

U.S. Navy (USN) . . . . www.usnavy.com

. . . . .www.navy.mil

U.S. Air Force (USAF). . . . . .www.airforce.com

U.S. Army (USA) . . . . www.usarmy.com

. . . . .www.army.mil

U.S. National Archives. . . . . .www.archives.gov/ research

. . . . www.nsarchive.gwu.edu/

United Nations (UN) - Atlantic & UN Charters. . . . . .www.un.org

Glossary & Reference
Abbreviations, Codes, Names, Operations, Projects, Terms

AAA . . . . Anti-Aircraft Artillery

AB . . . . Air Base

AB . . . . Afterburner

ABCCC . . . . Airborne command and control center

ABS . . . . Air Base Squadron

ABW . . . . Air Base Wing

AC . . . . Aircraft Commander

A/C . . . . Aircraft

ACCS . . . . Airborne command and control squadron

ACG . . . . Air Commando Group

ACS . . . . Air Commando Squadron

ACT . . . . Air Combat Tactics (Dog fighting)

ACW . . . . Air Commando Wing

AD . . . . Air Division

ADC . . . . Air Defense Command- former USAF, prior to 1968

ADC . . . . Aerospace Defense Command

ADF . . . . Automatic Direction Finder

ADVON . . . . Advanced Echelon

AEW . . . . Airborne Early Warning

AEW&C . . . . Airborne Early Warning & Control

AF . . . . Air Force

AFB . . . . Air Force Base

AFC . . . . Air Force Cross (decoration)

AFM . . . . Air Force Manual

AFP . . . . Air Force Pamphlet

AFROTC . . . . Air Force Reserve Officer Training Corp

AFSC . . . . Air Force career-field designation code

AFSC . . . . Air Force Systems Command

AFSSO . . . . Air Force Security Service Office

AGL . . . . Actual ground level; refers to altitude

AGM . . . . Air-to-Ground Missile

AGM-45 . . . . Shrike air-to-ground missile

AGM-78 . . . . Standard ARM air-to-ground missile above ground level as opposed to altitude above sea level

AGOS . . . . Air-Ground Operations School

AID . . . . Agency for International Development

AIG . . . . Address Indicator Group

418

AIRA . . . . Air Attaché
ALQ-51 . . . . Self-protection jammer pod
ALQ-71 . . . . Re-designation of ORC-160 jammer
ALQ-94 . . . . Deception jammer- F-111
ALQ-101 . . . . Self-protection jammer pod
ALQ-119 . . . . Self-protection jammer pod
ALR-18 . . . . Jamming transmitter for B-52
ALT-6 . . . . Jamming transmitter for B-52
ALT-22 . . . . Jamming transmitter for B-52
ALT-28 . . . . Jamming transmitter for B-52
AMEMB . . . . American Embassy
ANG. . . . . Air National Guard
AOC. . . . . Air Operations Center
AOC. . . . . Air Officer Commanding
AP . . . . Air Police
APGC . . . . Air Proving Ground Center
APP . . . . Appendix
APS-95 . . . . Search radar- EC-121D
APX-40 . . . . IFF recognition set
APC-37 . . . . UHF radio
ARC-109 . . . . EC-121D radio
ARCP . . . . Air Refueling Contact Point
ARCT . . . . Air Refueling Contact Time
ARM . . . . Anti-Radiation Missile
ARRG . . . . Air Rescue & Recovery Group
ARRS . . . . Air Rescue & Recovery Squadron
ARRW. . . . . Air Rescue & Recovery Wing
ARS . . . . Air Refueling Squadron
ARS . . . . Air Rescue Squadron
ARVN . . . . Army of the Republic of Vietnam
AS . . . . Attack Squadron (Navy)
ASOC . . . . Air Support Operations Center
ASW. . . . . Anti-Submarine Warfare
ATC . . . . USAF Air Training Command
AW . . . . Attack Wing (Navy)
AW . . . . Automatic Weapons
AWADS . . . . Adverse Weather Aerial Delivery System
AWC . . . . Air War College
"Able Mable" . . . . RF-101 photo reconnaissance over Laos
Able Sugar . . . . Out-of-control; ape shit

Abort . . . . Terminating a flight, mission or strike

Acquisition Radar . . . . Detects targets @ 100 miles + & tracks them to within range of five fire-control radars

Ailerons . . . . Control surfaces on wings of an aircraft that control turn and bank

Air America . . . . CIA-front force fighting in Laos. Headquartered at Udorn AF, Thailand

Air Asia . . . . CIA-front air force

Air Attache' . . . . US Air Force officer assigned to each American Embassy

Air Commandos . . . . Guerrilla air units flying prop combat planes, mainly A1Hs and T-28s. Headquartered and trained @ Hurlburt Field in Florida

Air Division . . . . Organizational unit of USAF- usually two Wings

Airevac . . . . Evacuation by air

Air Force Academy . . . . . Established in 1955, it is the military academy for the USAF. Located in Colorado. Similar to Annapolis and West Point.

"Airpatch" . . . . Call sign for Cam Ranh Bay Command Post

Air-to-Air . . . . Protective cover for strikes or Elint aircraft against MIGs

Air-to-Ground . . . . Dive bomb, napalm, gunnery and rocket attacks

Albrook AFB . . . . Former base in the former Panama Canal Zone which housed Jungle Survival School

Alert-Air Defense . . . . . . Air defense intercept launch from mobile units located at end of runway

Alert-Close Air Support . . . . Close-air-support strike launch from mobile units located at end of runway

Alert-Nuclear . . . . Nuclear launch in the event of total war

"Alpha" Squadron . . . . . . Primary USAF Tactical squadron designated for worldwide alert; 559th TFS served as Alpha for Tibet

Annam . . . . Previous name of Vietnam

Annamite Mountains . . . . Between southern NVN and southern Laos

Annapolis . . . . City in Maryland, home to the US Naval Academy

Anchors . . . . USAF refueling tracks (racetrack) designated by colors. Tracks were located over northern Laos for refueling attack strikes against NVN or MIG Screen missions over RP5 and RP6A and RP6B (Route Packs). Brown and Tan Anchor tracks were located over South China Sea for pre and post-strike missions against NVN, especially for flights out of Cam Ranh Bay (CRB) or Danang

Anchor Tracks . . . . Racetrack patterns flown by tankers over the Gulf and Laos

Anzac . . . . Australia & New Zealand Army Corp

Apollo Program . . . . Picked fighter pilots to guide the Apollo spaceships on orbital missions that eventually landed men on the moon.

"Arc Light" . . . . SAC tactical B-52 operations in SEA prior to Linebacker attacks

Area Target . . . . Non-specific target defined as a general attack area

A Shau . . . . Along with Ia Drang, site in S. Vietnam where the US scored a significant victory over the VC due to their massing of troops.

Atlantic Charter . . . . Signed on August 14, 1941 by the US and UK and later by all Allied countries. Stated the goals of WWII that included self-govt. for all peoples. Violated by the US after WWII when it supported the re-imposition of French control over Indochina.

A1Es and Hs . . . . Propeller-driven aircraft used by: USAF, USN, VNAF, RLAF and Air America in SEA

A-4 . . . . USN & USMC attack aircraft

A-6 . . . . USN & USMC all-weather attack aircraft

A-7 . . . . USAF & USN attack aircraft

A-10 . . . . "Warthog" close-air-support aircraft developed after SEA

BARCAP . . . . Barrier Combat Air Control

BDA . . . . Bomb Damage Assessment

BLC . . . . Boundary Layer Control- hot air shot over the F-4 wings to lower stall and landing speeds

BLU . . . . Napalm

BOQ . . . . Bachelor Officer's Quarters

BR . . . . Barrel Roll mission

BS . . . . Bombardment Squadron

BS (P) . . . . Bombardment Squadron Provisional

BW . . . . Bombardment Wing

BW (P) . . . . Bombardment Wing Provisional

BX . . . . Base Exchange

BZ . . . . Buffer Zone

Backseater . . . . Co-Pilot in Phantom II

Ball Ammo . . . . TP (Target Practice) gun rounds- Non-explosive

"Bango" . . . . F-4s out of Thailand

Ban Houei Sane . . . . Military Intelligence center just inside the Laotian panhandle from SVN; site of a major battle of the TET Offensive

Banjo . . . . Call sign for DMZ (Demilitarized Zone)

Barrage Fire . . . . Multiple launches in quick order by SAM batteries

Barrage jamming . . . . . . Distribution of power over wide frequency Band

Barlock . . . . GCI Radar

"Barrel Roll" . . . . Air interdiction campaign in Laos in support of Royal Lao forces against Pathet Lao and North Vietnamese forces.

Barrel Roll . . . . Aircraft roll revolving around a fixed axis

Barrier . . . . Cable at each end of runway to stop out-of-control aircraft

Base Operations . . . . Headquarters for non-combat operations

"Bat Cat" . . . . Elint (electronic intelligence) program using EC-121

Beagle . . . . Red Chinese medium bomber at time of SEA War

Bear . . . . Russian heavy bomber powered by four variable-pitch, counter-rotating turboprops

Beeper . . . . Sound emitted over radio (Guard Channel) indicating ejection

"Beer" City . . . . Huge outdoor area on Cam Ranh Peninsula reserved for beer storage

"Bell Tone" . . . . Early (1961) air defense detachment at Don Muang

Benjo ditch . . . . Open ditch carrying sewage

Bien Hoa . . . . Multi-purpose VNAF base near Saigon

"Big Eye" . . . . USAF MIG Screen missions off Haiphong in support of Yankee Station carriers. USAF EC-121 airborne warning and control aircraft. Later called "College Eye." Supported by CRB F-4C aircraft

"Big Look" . . . . USN MIG Screen missions in support of Yankee Station carriers; flew F-4Bs & Js

Bingo . . . . Low fuel callout- "No shit bingo" means emergency condition

Bird . . . . Pertains to aircraft- (also) British slang for women

Bird and Sons . . . . CIA-fronted propeller driven air force- Operated in Laos. Primarily transport aircraft- Sold inventory to CAS

Bird Dog . . . . Small, propeller-driven spotter planes

Black Choppers . . . . Usually identified Air America or other clandestine helicopters operating in Laos. Based at Udorn and NKP

Black 130s . . . . C-130s operating in clandestine mode over North Vietnam

"Black Spot" . . . . HCM Trail night strike operation using C-123K with sensors

"Blind Bat" . . . . USAF C-130 Flareship Operations

Blockhouse . . . . Radar intercept center on Okinawa

"Blue Tree" . . . . Photo recce over NVN

Boondoggle . . . . A wasteful or impractical project or activity. Also refers to a whimsical trip or mission

Boxer . . . . 12th TFW call sign

"Brown Cradle" . . . . Elint upgrade for EB-66; USAF C-130 flareship operations

Buff . . . . Nickname giver to B-52; Big, Ugly, Fat, Fucker

Bullpup . . . . Air-to-ground missile controlled from cockpit

Burner . . . . Afterburner- Raw fuel shot into tailpipe for significant increase in power and acceleration.

Burn through . . . . Juncture at which radiated power of radar transmitter overcomes a jamming signal. Generally at arrange of 8-10 miles.

"Buying the Farm" . . . . . . Getting killed in an aircraft accident or shootdown

B-52 . . . . Boeing developed heavy bomber owned by SAC–carried 108, 750# bombs

B-57 . . . . Canberra bomber operated in Laos- highest bomb accuracy rate of any jet in SEA

B-66 (RB-66, EB-66) . . . . . Elint (Electronic Intelligence) aircraft

B-111 (F-111) . . . . Formerly F-111- McNamara's Mistake (one of many)-used terrain following radar for all-weather attacks in SEA. Many aircraft lost on missions in SEA and never found.

CAG. . . . . Commander Air Group (Navy)
CAP . . . . Combat Air Patrol - flying cover
CAS . . . . Close air support - Air attacks in support of ground troops
CAS . . . . Continental Air Services - Wholly owned subsidiary of Continental Airlines that was CIA-front for fighting in Cambodia and Laos; also known as CASI
CAS . . . . Controlled American Source - Name given in Laos for CIA operatives
CBU. . . . . Cluster bomb units
CBs . . . . Naval Construction Battalions; "Sea Bees"
CCK. . . . . Ching Chuan Kang AB., Taiwan
CCTW. . . . . Combat Crew Training Wing
CCTS . . . . Combat Crew Training Squadron
CCK. . . . . Ching Chuan Kang Air Base, Taiwan. Formerly Kung Kuan Air Base
CDS . . . . Container Delivery System
CEA . . . . Circular error actual - Average miss distance from target
CG. . . . . Commanding General
CHECO . . . . Contemporary Historical Evaluation of Combat Operations
CHMAAG. . . . . Chief, Military Advisory and Assistance Group
CIA . . . . Central Intelligence Agency
CILH . . . . Central Identification Lab - Hawaii
CINCPAC. . . . . Commander in Chief, Pacific Area
CINCPACAF . . . . Commander in Chief - Pacific Air Forces
CINCPACFLT. . . . . Commander in Chief - Pacific Fleet
CMSgt. . . . . Chief Master Sergeant
Col. . . . . Colonel
CO. . . . . Commanding Officer
COD. . . . . Carrier On-Board Delivery
COIN . . . . Counterinsurgency
COMUSMACTHAI . . . . . Military Advisory Chief - Thailand
COMUSMACV. . . . . Military Advisory Chief - South Vietnam.
CONUS . . . . Continental United States
CRA. . . . . Cam Ranh Army
CRB . . . . Cam Ranh Bay
CRC . . . . Control and reporting center
CRN. . . . . Cam Ranh Navy
CRP . . . . Control and reporting post

CSG . . . . Combat Support Group

CSAF . . . . Chief of Staff- Air Force

CTG . . . . Carrier Task Group (Navy)

CVSG . . . . Anti-Sub Carrier Air Group

CVW . . . . Carrier Air Wing

CW . . . . Cricket West

Cambodes . . . . Cambodian soldiers used as mercenaries by the Viet Cong and by the United States

Cambodia . . . . Country in SEA that was once part of French Indochina

"Candlestick" . . . . Flareship operations using C-123 & C-130s

"Carolina Moon" . . . . . . Special ops against Thanh Hoa Bridge using C-130s

Cart Start . . . . Explosive cartridge start of an aircraft jet engine without external compressed air support. Used for alert launches

Carriers (Aircraft) . . . . . . Used in SEA in 1965-1966: Oriskany, Kitty Hawk, Ranger, Hancock, Ticonderoga

Cat Shot . . . . Carrier launches using a steam catapult

C. Turner Joy (USS) . . . . . Naval Destroyer involved in bogus Gulf of Tonkin Incident on August 4, 1964

Central Command. . . . . . . All-service command based at MacDill AFB in Florida; controls Middle Eastern wars and operations; succeeded Strike Command

Chaff . . . . Radar reflectors (usually aluminum strips); Dispensed from aircraft to confuse enemy radar

Chaff Bomb . . . . Leaflet dispenser modified to scatter chaff. Contains explosive charge

Chiang Kei-shek . . . . Leader of the Nationalist Chinese

Chicoms . . . . Chinese Communists

Chopper . . . . Helicopter

Chu Lai . . . . Marine Air Base on Central Coast of SVN

Clark AFB . . . . Closed due to the eruption of Pinatubo; largest USAF base in world during SEA War; main staging and command base

Class 26 . . . . Destroy an aircraft

Clean . . . . Without bombs

Clicks . . . . Kilometers

Close-Air-Support. . . . . . Aircraft strikes against troops in support of Army or Marines

"College Eye" . . . . Formerly Big Eye; Task force of EC-121Es providing early warning of air attacks from the North

"Combat Lancer" . . . . . . Initial deployment of F-111 to Thailand

"Combat Skyspot" . . . . . (aka Skyspot); Misque (MSQ) Radar for controlled bombing. Used for anti-SAM missions from Cam Ranh Bay (CRB)

"Combat Talon" . . . . . . Special operations using C-130s

Combat Tree. . . . . IFF (Identification Friend or Foe) detection system

Comfy Boy . . . . Reports on ECM activity in SEA

Comfy Coat . . . . Reports on ECM activity in SEA

Commando Club . . . . TACAN (Tactical Air Navigation) & TPQ-81 radar site in Northern Laos (Lima 85)

"Commando Hunt" . . . . . . Interdiction campaigns against HCMT in northern Laos

"Commando Sabre". . . . . . USAF F-100 fast, high-threat FAC operations (Misty Operations)

"Connie" . . . . Air Force Elint aircraft operating in Gulf of Tonkin- Controlled Big Eye Phantoms on MIG Screen-Monitored Enemy Strike Frequency (EC-121)

"Constant Guard" . . . . . . Tactical Aircraft deployment to SEA in 1972

Continental Air Services . . . CIA-fronted air force in Laos and Cambodia. Purchased transport inventory (28) of Bird and Sons. Author interviewed former CAS pilot who said that CAS had 42 fighter planes in SEA- (T-28s and A-1Hs)

Contrails. . . . . Telltale vapor condensation trails in atmosphere following the wake of an . . . aircraft

Coreolis Force. . . . . The force created by the motion of the earth through space that gives cyclonic direction to the rotation of clouds and water. Effects rotational direction of storms. The direction of cyclonic storms in Southern Hemisphere is opposite than that in the Northern Hemisphere

Corps . . . . Division of South Vietnam into four operating or Corps areas

Counter . . . . In SEA, refers to a mission over North Vietnam. Did not refer to Gulf missions

Covey . . . . FAC call sign for operations in southern Laos & NVN.

Crown . . . . Airborne rescue command post. Crown and Sandy's visited CRB to discuss threats to pilots downed in Laos (later renamed King)

C-119 . . . . "Connie" operating Elint over Gulf of Tonkin-controlled Big Eye Phantoms

C-124 . . . . Short runway transport used in SEA

C-130 . . . . Workhorse cargo plane used extensively in SEA - longest running production in aviation history-still being built. More C-130s produced than any other aircraft in history.

C-130 Gunship . . . . C-130 equipped with Vulcan Cannon 20 MM Gattling gun w/100 rounds per second firing-rate

DER . . . . Double Ejection (bomb) Rack

DEROS . . . . Date Eligible for Return from Overseas

DFC . . . . Distinguished Flying Cross (decoration)

DIA . . . . Defense Intelligence Agency

DME. . . . . Distance Measuring Equipment

DMZ. . . . . Demilitarized Zone separating North and South Vietnam

DO. . . . . Director of Operations

DOD. . . . . Department of Defense

DR. . . . . Dead Reckoning- Navigational direction figured without the aid of ground stations or INS (Inertial Navigation System)

DPMO. . . . . Defense POW Missing Personnel Office

DRV . . . . Democratic Republic of Vietnam (North)

Danang . . . . Vietnamese City on the north coast of what was South Vietnam. Site of MCAS in Vietnam War; ancient name Tourane

Dead Sticking . . . . Landing without power

Delta. . . . . The southern, South Vietnamese area south of Saigon; Mekong Delta

Delta Dagger F-102

Dengler, Dieter . . . . Navy pilot downed flying A1E; one of only two men to escape from a Pathet Lao prison.

Dien Bien Phu. . . . . Site of last battle of the Indochina War

"Dinging in". . . . . Crashing

Divert . . . . Flying a divert mission. Diverted from primary target

Dixie Station . . . . Along with Yankee Station was position for USN carriers operating in SEA. Dixie, in South China Sea was for SVN. Yankee was for NVN

"Dog Fight". . . . . Refers to fighting between fighter aircraft. Maneuvering to get into other aircrafts rear position to shoot a gun or fire an IR missile

Don Muang . . . . American AB in Thailand, outside of Bangkok

Donut Dollies . . . . USO girls assigned to Vietnam for morale

Drag chute. . . . . Aircraft chute used to slow an aircraft on landing

Drone . . . . Remotely-controlled pilotless aircraft

Duty Officer. . . . . Officer temporarily in-charge due to absence of more senior officers

ECM. . . . . Electronic Counter Measures (Electronic Warfare)

ECS . . . . Deputy Chief of Staff- Air Force

Ens . . . . Ensign

ETA . . . . Estimated Time of Arrival

ETE . . . . Estimated Time Enroute

EW . . . . Electronic Warfare

Ewar. . . . . Electronic Warfare

EWO . . . . Electronic Warfare Officer

"Eagle Pull". . . . . Evacuation of personnel from Cambodia in April, 1975

East China Sea . . . . Ocean surrounding Okinawa

Element . . . . Flight of two fighter aircraft

Elevators . . . . Control surfaces on aircraft's tail that controls climb or descent

Elevons . . . . Large control surfaces on F-4 wings that operated like a combined elevator and aileron

Elint . . . . Electronic Intelligence
European War Plan . . . . . . NATO Nuclear attack against the Warsaw Pact countries
EA-1 . . . . Ewar (electronic warfare) A-1
EA-3 . . . . Ewar Douglas Skywarrior
EA-6 . . . . Ewar A-6
EB-47E . . . . Ewar B-47 medium strategic bomber
EB-66 . . . . Ewar RB-66

FAC . . . . Forward Air Controller - Usually airborne but also includes ground FACs
FAR . . . . Laotian ground forces
FCS . . . . Fighter Commando Squadron (Navy)
FG . . . . Fighter Group (Navy)
FIS . . . . Fighter Interceptor Squadron (Navy)
FIW . . . . Fighter Interceptor Wing (Navy)
FLIR . . . . Forward Looking Infra-Red (IR)
FNG . . . . Fucking New Guy
FOD . . . . Foreign Object Damage - Damage to jet engines
FS . . . . Fighter Squadron (Navy)
FTW . . . . Flying Training Wing (Navy)
FW . . . . Fighter Wing (Navy)
FWMAF . . . . Free World Military Assistance Forces
Faceplate . . . . NATO designation for MIG-21
Fan Song . . . . Fire control radar for the SA-2 SAM system. Was target for Shrike Missile
and "Wild Weasel" crews.
Farmer . . . . NATO designation for MIG-19
"Farm Gate" . . . . Detachment of 4400 CCTS (Air Commandos) in SVN; flew strike missions
in SEA by December 1961
Feet Dry . . . . Over land, primarily naval air term
Feet Wet . . . . Over water, primarily naval air term
Ferret . . . . E-recon aircraft or mission
Finger Lakes Region . . . . . Area near Vinh Linh in the NVN panhandle where the 12 TFW and 559th
TFS lost a lot of aircraft
Fire can . . . . Soviet radar used by NVN for AAA up to 100mm
Firepower Demonstration . . . Use of live bombs and rockets to simulate wartime conditions
Flak . . . . Shrapnel expended from airborne explosions of AAA shells
Flag Poling . . . . Pilots having affairs with wives of other pilots in same unit
"Flaming Dart" . . . . US air attacks against NVN in February, 1965
Flight Operations (Ops) . . . . Flightline site for squadron operations
Flight . . . . Airborne flight refers to group of aircraft flying together. Organizationally

refers to one-fourth of the aircraft and personnel in an Air Force squadron

Flight Control . . . . Ground-based for regional control of strike aircraft

Flightline . . . . Squadron Operations, Maintenance, Aircraft

Formosa . . . . Former name for Taiwan

Fort Benning . . . . US Army fort in Georgia; site of jump school

Fragged . . . . Subject to frag orders

Frag Orders . . . . A partial or fragmented part of a general order. Used from headquarters to detail and control daily flight operations in SEA. Aircraft targeting orders are frag orders

"Freedom Train" . . . . Air campaign against NVN in spring, 1972, Targets between DMZ & 20th Parallel

"Frequent Wind" . . . . . . Evacuation of US personnel from Saigon, April 1975

Fresco . . . . NATO designation for MIG-17

Futima MCAS. . . . . Marine air facility on Okinawa

F-4. . . . . McDonald Douglas Phantom II fighter-bomber; highest loss rate of any fighter in SEA

F-5. . . . . Fighter version of T-38; flew in SEA as part of Skoshi Tiger

F-84 . . . . Flown by 12th TFW @ MacDill

F-86 . . . . Flown by Australian Air Force at Ubon

F-100 . . . . Widely used in SEA

F-102 . . . . Used in air defense of Okinawa

F-105 . . . . "Thunderchief", Workhorse for USAF war against NVN out of Thailand

GCA. . . . . Ground Control Approach- Radar assisted approach to a runway

GCI . . . . Ground Control Intercept. Enroute radar tracking of aircraft

GIB . . . . Guy in Back- A backseater in an F-4

GPA-122 . . . . Auto recognition equipment for IFF

GRADS . . . . Ground Radar Aerial Delivery System

GVN. . . . . Government of South Vietnam (SVN)

"G"s . . . . Pulling Gs refers to "gravity" forces exerted on the human body. One G equals weight of one person

"G" Suit . . . . Worn by pilots and plugged into pneumatic system of aircraft. Exerts air pressure on lower extremities by action of bladders to force blood . back into the brain of the pilot during high stress maneuvers

Geneva Accords. . . . . . . Split Vietnam into two countries after French defeat at Dien Bien Phu

General Ma . . . . Commander of Royal Laotian Air Force

Gia Lam. . . . . Major MIG base near Hanoi

"Giant Dragon" . . . . U-2 recce ops in SEA (see Lucky Dragon)

"Giant Scale" . . . . SR-71 recce ops in SEA (see Habu)

Giap . . . . Vo Nguyen Giap - North Vietnamese General who masterminded defeats of French and Americans

Gimp . . . . Evasive maneuver of drones against fighters

"Glowing Heat". . . . . SR-71 deployment to and from Kadena AB, Okinawa

"Green Python" . . . . RF-101 photo recce from Udorn

Green Berets . . . . Army Special Forces

Guard Channel . . . . Emergency Channel monitored by all aircraft using UHF radios

Guidance beacon . . . . Signaling device that tells weapons controllers SAM trajectories

Guided bombs. . . . . Ordnance directed by crew using TV or laser beams

Guideline Missile . . . . . . NATO designation for missile in SA-2 system

Gulf . . . . Gulf of Tonkin, located off North Vietnam and China

Gun . . . . The F-4 externally mounted 20MM Vulcan Cannon with 100 rounds per second firing rate

Gunships . . . . Choppers armed with door guns for fighting; also refers to the AC-130s armed with Gattling Cannons

HC. . . . . Navy Helicopter Combat Support Group

HC-130P . . . . Tanker version of C-130

HCMT. . . . . Ho Chi Minh Trail (see below)

HD. . . . . High-Drag bombs - Usually the "snake eye"

HEAT . . . . High Explosive Anti-Tank (rocket)

HEAP . . . . High Explosive Anti-Personnel (rocket)

HEI . . . . High Explosive Incendiary-explosive ammunition for the gun - causes fires

H&MS. . . . . Marine HQ and MX (Maintenance) Squadron

HQ. . . . . Headquarters

HU. . . . . Navy Helicopter Utility Squadron

"Habu" . . . . SR-71 flights over SEA

Hainan. . . . . Hainan Island off the south coast of China and part of China

Haiphong . . . . Second largest city and major port for North Vietnam

"Hammer". . . . . Call sign for 391st TFS at Cam Ranh Bay and part of the 12th TFW

Hanoi . . . . Capitol of North Vietnam & now Vietnam

Hanoi Jane . . . . Jane Fonda, anti-war activist

Harness . . . . Worn by pilots on entering aircraft cockpit. Harness strapped into ejection seat.

Hat Rack . . . . Drone recognition device for MIGs/SAMs

Hawk Missiles . . . . Conventional tipped air defense missile used in Vietnam

"Hawkeye" . . . . Experimental RC-47 RDF operations

Heat . . . . Refers to the Sidewinder Missile- In heat means Sidewinders are selected to fire on weapons selection panel

Heat Seeking Missiles . . . . American Sidewinder and Soviet Atoll

Hercules Missiles . . . . . . Nuclear-tipped air defense missiles controlled by the U.S. Army

High Drag . . . . Accurate retarded bombs with fins; HD

Hillsboro . . . . (also Hillsboro Control) USAF C-130 airborne command post operating over Steel Tiger area - Hillsboro directed rescue of author from Laos

"Hilo Hattie" . . . . Experimental USAF RDF photo and infra-red recce ops using HC-54s

"Hit the Silk" . . . . Bail out; parachute

Hmung . . . . Native soldiers used as American mercenaries; native of Vietnamese Central Highlands and Laos; of Chinese extraction

Ho Chi Minh . . . . Political leader of North Vietnam and Viet Minh against French and Americans

Ho Chi Minh Trail . . . . . (also HCMT) Network of roads, trails, and tracks running from NVN (often using My Gia Pass) through Laos and Cambodia into SVN for infiltration of supplies and troops

"(Operation) Homecoming" . . Repatriation of POWs from Hanoi and SVN in February and March of 1973. Did not repatriate pilots from Laos

Hooch . . . . Structure used in SEA - Usually of thatch and bamboo. Common use - Home

Hound Dog . . . . FACs in Tiger Hound

Howitzer. . . . . Artillery piece

Hungry's . . . . F-100 Super Sabre fighter-bombers that operated in South with special operations in North

Hunter-Killer . . . . Teams & tactics that employ detection aircraft and munitions-carrying aircraft

Hurlburt Field . . . . Eglin Auxiliary # 10; home of the Air Commandos

ICC . . . . International Control Commission

ICBM . . . . Intercontinental Ballistic Missile

ID . . . . Identification

IFF. . . . . Identification Friend or Foe- electronic equipment on board aircraft that can encode ground radar image for identification and communication (can identify an emergency and type of aircraft)

IFR . . . . Instrument Flight Rules

ILS . . . . Instrument Landing System- Airport operated system that projects a tracking beam. Aircraft instrumentation with ILS will automatically provide movement guidance to maintain the beam.

INS . . . . Inertial Navigation System- Litton designed navigation system used by the F-4 in SEA - entirely internal to the aircraft and allowed accurate navigation to targets in enemy controlled territory

IO . . . . Intelligence Officer

IP . . . . Instructor Pilot

IP . . . . Initial Point

IR . . . . Infra-red

IRBM . . . . Intermediate Ballistic Missile

"Igloo White" . . . . Elint system to detect HCMT movement in Laos

Immelman . . . . Maneuver where an aircraft reverses direction

Incendogell (jell) . . . . . . Jellified gas used in napalm

"In Country" . . . . South Vietnam

Indochina . . . . French Indochina colony comprising Laos, Cambodia and Vietnam

Infrared (IR) . . . . Going IR means going with Sidewinder shot

Intel . . . . Intelligence

Interdiction . . . . Long-range fighter-bomber missions to hit supply, airfields, communication, transportation and command and control

"Iron Hand" . . . . Aircraft suppression of AAA (anti-aircraft artillery) and SAMs (surface-to-air missiles)

Iwakuni Air Base . . . . . . Marine facility on Honshu, Japan

JATO . . . . Jet Assisted Take Off

JCS . . . . Joint Chiefs of Staff

JGS . . . . Joint General Staff (South Vietnam)

JOC . . . . Joint Operations Center

JPRC . . . . Joint Personnel Recovery Center

JTF . . . . Joint Task Force (Navy)

JTF- FA . . . . Joint Task Force- Full Accounting

J-79 . . . . Jet engine; 17,000 pounds of thrust; F-4 equipped with two J-79s

JP-4 . . . . Low-grade fuel used by Air Force Phantoms

JP-5 . . . . Low-grade fuel used by Marine Phantoms

Jolly Green Giants . . . . . Large choppers used in SVN and Laos

"Jinking" . . . . Maneuvering of fighter aircraft from side-to-side and up and down to evade radar tracking by the AAA batteries

Jolly Green Giant . . . . . . Call signs and affectionate name for USAF HH-3 and HH-53 SAR helicopters

Jump Training . . . . Army parachute training

Joker . . . . Emergency fuel

"Jungle Jim" . . . . Code name for Air Commandos out of Hurlburt Field, Eglin, Florida; operation that flew air combat strikes in SEA early in the war

KBA . . . . Killed by Air

KIA . . . . Killed in Action

KM . . . . Kilometer

KWF. . . . . Killed While Flying

Kadena AFB. . . . . On Okinawa and home to 18th TFW of F-105s

Kep . . . . Major MIG airfield in North Vietnam

Khe Sanh . . . . Important Special forces camp in South Vietnam established in August of 1962. Later transferred to the US Marine Corps. Used for monitoring of HCMT. Protected by 105 MM Howitzers similar to French defenses of Dien Bien Phu. Was base for helicopters sent to rescue author in April, 1966 aircraft downing.

Kill Ratio . . . . Percentage amount of expected kills in a designated area

King. . . . . USAF HC-130 airborne rescue command post (formerly Crown)

Klussman, Chuck . . . . . . First American jet pilot downed in SEA on June 6, 1964; flying Navy recce plane; one of only two to escape Pathet Lao

Korat RTAFB . . . . F-105 base in Thailand

KC-135 . . . . Boeing Tanker aircraft used extensively in SEA - -Pilots often used heroic measures to save "fuel-starved" fighter-bombers

LAPES . . . . Low- altitude Parachute Extraction System

LARA . . . . Light, Armed Recce Aircraft

LAU . . . . Mighty Mouse 2.75" rockets

LAX . . . . FAA designation for Los Angeles International Airport

LGB . . . . Laser Guided Bomb (smart bomb)

LLTV . . . . Low-light Television

LNRS . . . . Limited Night Recovery System

LOC . . . . Line of Communication

LOR . . . . Letter of Reprimand

LORAN . . . . Long-Range Aid to Navigation

LPF . . . . Laos Patriotic Front (political arm of the Communistic Pathet Lao)

LS . . . . Landing site

LSO . . . . Landing Signal Officer (Navy)

Lt. . . . . Lieutenant

Lt. (jg) . . . . Lieutenant Junior Grade (Navy)

Lt. Cdr. . . . . Lieutenant Commander (Navy)

Lt. Col. . . . . Lieutenant Colonel (Marines, Air Force, Army)

LZ . . . . Landing zone

Lao Tribesmen . . . . CIA aligned tribe in Central Laos

Laser Weapons . . . . Light beam directed weapons that were evaluated on later Laotian missions

Lead . . . . Flight leader

Lighters . . . . Transport boats that offloaded ships off Haiphong Harbor for transport up the Red River to Hanoi

Lima Site . . . . Temporary landing site in Laos, used by SAR forces, Ravens, Air America, Bird and Sons, CAS, or Special Forces. CIA created and used similar sites in NVN

"Linebacker I" . . . . Air campaign against NVN, April to October, 1972; Primarily used Phantoms.

"Linebacker II" . . . . Air campaign using B-52s against NVN in 1972-Linebacker II were the devastating Hanoi raids of 18- 30 December

Line-Up Card . . . . Used by pilots on missions for the line-up of crew and mission info

Long Tieng . . . . Laotian base that was headquarters for the clandestine air forces operating in Laos; Became second largest city in Laos.

Luang Prabang . . . . . . City in the central part of northern Laos that is also the name for ancient Laos

"Lucky Dragon". . . . . . . U-2 recce ops in SEA (see "Giant Dragon")

Luzon . . . . Largest and northernmost island in the Philippines

MAAG . . . . Military Air Advisory Group- based in foreign countries to train nationals to fly

MAC . . . . Military Airlift Command

Mach . . . . Speed of sound

MACV . . . . Military Advisory Chief- South Vietnam

MACVSOG . . . . Military Assistance Command, Vietnam, Studies and Observation Group

MACTHAI . . . . Military Advisory Chief - Thailand

MAG . . . . Military Advisory Group- American detachments sent to foreign countries to advise

MAG . . . . Marine Aircraft Group

MATS . . . . Military Air Transport Service - Preceded MAC

MAW . . . . Marine Aircraft Wing

MCAS . . . . Marine Corps Air Station

MDA . . . . Minimum Descent Altitude - Area minimum to insure clearance of mountainous terrain

MER . . . . Multiple Ejection Rack - used to carry bombs on F-4s- Usually mounted centerline

MIA . . . . Missing in Action

MIG . . . . Soviet aircraft type- Manufactured by Mikoyan Guerevich

MIG- 17 . . . . Single engine/ single seat interceptor

MIG- 19 . . . . Supersonic single engine/ single seat interceptor

MIG-21 . . . . Short-range, supersonic, single engine and seat
MIGCAP . . . . MIG defense combat patrol
MIGs . . . . Enemy aircraft operated by the Chinese, Russian, and Vietnamese in SEA;
    MIG 17s, 19s and 21s operated in SEA
MIL . . . . Millimeter settings on cockpit-mounted bomb aiming device
MM . . . . Millimeter
MNDs . . . . Maintenance Non-Deliveries- method of evaluating maintenance efficiency
MP . . . . Military Police
MSgt. . . . . Master Sergeant
MTU . . . . Marine Task Unit
MX . . . . Maintenance
MacDill AFB . . . . Home of Central Command; home of 12th and 15th TFWs during SEA War
Mach . . . . Speed of sound which varies with altitude (i.e. density of air)
Maddox (USS) . . . . American destroyer that took part in the questionable Gulf of Tonkin Incident
    on August 2, 1964.
Magnetron . . . . Vacuum tube to generate jamming power
MaGuire AFB . . . . Major MAC hub for Atlantic; located in New Jersey
Mandrake . . . . Russian U-2- Type reconnaissance plane
Mao Zedong (Mao Tse-tung) . Chinese Communist who led the victorious forces that defeated the
    Nationalists under Chiang Kai Shek and controlled all of China, with the . . .
    exception of Taiwan, by 1949
Mariana Islands . . . . American protectorates that lie in same chain as Guam; main islands are
    Saipan, Tinian and Pagan
Mark 82 . . . . "Snake Eye" high drag, retard bombs with fins
Matchsticks . . . . As in "made matchsticks"- refers to a wasted mission against trees
Markettime . . . . SAR call sign
"Market Time" . . . . USN air and surface patrols along SVN coast to interdict VC supplies
Martin Baker Company . . . . Maker of the ejection seats on the Phantom
"Mayday" . . . . Radio distress call usually meaning a plane was "going in"- Crashing
McDonnell Aircraft . . . . . Manufacturer of Phantom; located in Saint Louis; later merged with Douglas
to form . . . . McDonnell- Douglas
Medevac . . . . Evacuation (usually by air) for medical reasons; Airevac
Mekong . . . . Mekong River which originates in China and marks the political boundary
between . . . . Thailand and Laos and between Vietnam and Cambodia- Mekong Delta is
    important rice . . . . growing area
Meos . . . . Hill people of Laos who were allied with the CIA
MIG Cover . . . . Flying in air-to-air protection of Elint or Strike aircraft over NVN.
MIG Screen . . . . Flying as barrier aircraft against MIGs flying over the Gulf - Usually
    protecting the aircraft carriers
Mighty Mouse . . . . Unguided 2.75" rockets- also LAU; Fired from pods carrying 19 each.

Mike-Mike . . . . MM- Millimeter; 20 mike-mike refers to use of the 20 millimeter cannon shells

Misque . . . . Radar stationed at Dong Ha that controlled the Sky Spot missions

"Misty" . . . . Clandestine FAC (forward air controller) missions. Radio Call sign of Commando Sabre F-100 fast FAC aircraft; Name of book edited by Major General Don Shepperd, USAF (Ret.)

Mobile Control . . . . In SEA, was pilot sitting in a jeep at end of runway to check condition of landing aircraft- Had radio contact with tower and aircraft

Monkeys . . . . As in "killed monkeys" - refers to a wasted mission against the jungle

Monsoons . . . . Torrential tropical rains that affected SEA air operations

Montagnards . . . . Hill people of the Central Highlands of South Vietnam, who were allied with the U.S.

Mu Gia Pass . . . . The "funnel" through the Annamite Mountains that fed supplies, equipment and troops into the Ho Chi Minh Trail

"Mule Train" . . . . USAF C-123s in SVN in January, 1962

NAS . . . . Naval Air Station

NASA . . . . National Aeronautics and Space Administration

NATO . . . . North Atlantic Treaty Organization

NCO . . . . Non-Commissioned Officer

NE . . . . Northeast

NFO . . . . Naval Flight Officer (navigator)

NKP . . . . Nakhon Phanom Royal Thai Air Base- Thai base along the Mekong used by the CIA, Thai and USAF units

NLF . . . . National Liberation Front- Political arm of Viet Cong (VC)

NM . . . . Nautical mile

NOFORN . . . . American document classification code that does not allow foreign nationals access

NORAD . . . . North American Air Defense Command - Joint command of the United States and Canada- HQ in Colorado Springs

NSA . . . . National Security Agency

NVA . . . . North Vietnamese Army

NVN . . . . North Vietnam

NW . . . . Northwest

Naha . . . . Capitol of Okinawa; Name of Air Base on Okinawa

"Nail" . . . . Radio call sign of FACs operating over SVN and Laos; Part of 23rd TASS

Nakhon Phanom (NKP) . . . . Rescue, transport, recce, clandestine airfield located in Thailand on the Mekong River

Nama Nui . . . . Red light district in Naha that houses the "Teahouse of the August Moon"

Napalm . . . . Jellied gas dropped in aluminum canisters during SEA War
Nape. . . . . Napalm
National Liberation Front (NLF). Viet Cong
Navaid. . . . . Navigational aid
Negritos . . . . Negro Pygmies that preceded the Philippinos to the Philippine Islands; used
      to train USAF pilots in jungle warfare
Neutralists. . . . . Non-aligned third Laotian army during SEA War
Nguyen Sinh Cung . . . . . Birth name of Ho Chi Minh
Niagra . . . . USAF strike operations in defense of Khe Sanh in 1968
"Night Owl". . . . . Radio call sign and ops by 8th TFW for night FAC and interdiction ops over
      HCMT- Lost 40 F-4Cs
Noise . . . . Jamming signal on radar scope/ clutter
North . . . . North Vietnam
Northbrook . . . . SAR call sign
"No Shit" Bingo. . . . . . . Super Emergency fuel state

OER. . . . . Officer Effectiveness Report
OG. . . . . Operations Group (Navy)
OJT . . . . On the job training
OL. . . . . Operating Location
OPREP . . . . Operations report
OPS . . . . Operations- Usually refers to Squadron
OPW. . . . . Operations or Wing Operations
OSS . . . . Office of Strategic Services- US Intelligence Agency formed during WWII
      that preceded CIA
OWC . . . . Officer's Wives Club
"O" Club . . . . Officer's Club - Exclusive dining, drinking, discussing and carousing facility
Ocean Station November . . . Stationary ship west of Hawaii used for navigation
Okinawa. . . . . Main island in the Ryukyu Island chain located between Japan and Taiwan
"Old Heads". . . . . Older members of a group in term of time and not age
"Out-Country" . . . . Laos or North Vietnam

PACAF . . . . Pacific Air Force- command headquarters in Hawaii
PACOM . . . . Pacific Command
PARC . . . . Pacific Air Rescue Center
PAVN . . . . People's Army of North Vietnam (NVN)
PCS . . . . Permanent Change of Station (as opposed to TDY (temporary duty)
PDJ . . . . Plaine des Jarres (Plain of Jars, Laos)

PI . . . . Philippine Islands

PIO . . . . Public Information Officer - Usually one assigned per Air Force Wing

PI Troops . . . . Philippine mercenaries

PJ . . . . Parachute Jumper

PK . . . . Pleiku in Central Highlands of SVN; Peacock Control

PL . . . . Pathet Lao

PMDL . . . . Provisional Military Demarcation Line

POL . . . . Petroleum, Oil, Lubricants

POL Storage. . . . . Refers to oil storage depot

POWs . . . . Prisoners of War

PRG . . . . South Vietnamese Provisional Revolutionary Government (political arm of the Communistic Viet Cong)

PSO . . . . Pilot Systems Operator - USAF rear seat pilot in F-4

PSP . . . . Metal plating used for parking aircraft in SEA - Pierced Steel Planking

PW. . . . . Prisoner of War; also POW

"Pad" . . . . The Alert Pad - trailer located at the end of .the runway housing pilots for an immediate launch

Panama . . . . GCI call sign located at Danang on Central Coast

Panhandle . . . . Southern portion of Laos or North Vietnam

Panoramic scan receiver . . . Determines bearing of enemy radar

"Parrot" . . . . Another name for an IFF that "squawks"

Passive tracking. . . . . . . Radar operators tracking source of jamming without using tracking beam

Pathet Lao . . . . Communist Laotian Army- allied with Viet Minh

Pathfinders . . . . Marine special ops units - clandestine infiltration ops in Laos and NVN for observation of HCMT traffic

"Patricia Lynn" . . . . RB-57 recce ops using advanced infra-red sensors and cameras. Used extensively in Laos

"Pave Aegis" . . . . C-130s mounted with 105 MM howitzers

"Pave Arrow" . . . . Development program for laser weapons

"Pave Eagle" . . . . Elint recce for data used by Igloo White sensors

"Pave Knife" . . . . Development program for laser weapons

"Pave Nail" . . . . Night observation system used by OV-10s

"Pave Pronto". . . . . AC-130A Gunship II program

"Pave Spectre" . . . . AC-130E Gunship II program

"Pave Way" . . . . Laser, electro-optical or IR guidance system for bombs. Developed in Laotian ops and later used effectively in Desert Storm

"Peacock". . . . . GCI call sign located at Pleiku in Central Highlands

Pedal Shaker . . . . Physical indication of impending stall in F-4

Pedro . . . . Call sign and name for HH-43 rescue choppers

"Penlight". . . . . GCI call sign controlling missions in Laos

Phan Rang. . . . . Fighter base in SVN located south of CRB

Phantom. . . . . F-4C or other models of the F-4; F-4B flown by Marines and Navy

Phantom. . . . . Call sign for the 559th TFS

"Phyllis Ann" . . . . USAF RC-47 and EC-47 RDF operations

Pickle . . . . Dropping a bomb

Pickle Button . . . . Mounted on control stick for dropping bombs

"Piece of cake" . . . . Easy

"Pierce Arrow" . . . . USN strikes following purported Gulf of Tonkin incident

"Pipe Stem" . . . . RF-101 photo recce detachment at Tan Son Nhut AF, Saigon in 1961

Pipper . . . . Red, laser-type dot on cockpit windscreen marking aiming point for bombs and gun

Pistol . . . . Another name for the Gattling gun

Plaines des Jarres . . . . . . Central Laotian plain

"Pocket Money". . . . . . . Aerial mining ops against NVN harbors in May, 1972

Post-target turn . . . . Change in direction after bomb release

"Prairie Fire" . . . . Clandestine cross-border ground recce in Laos and NVN by US Special Forces for strike control and BDA purposed (later renamed Shining Brass)

Port Call . . . . Date of flight or ship departure

Powerglide . . . . SAR call sign

Primary . . . . Refers to primary target

Principles of War . . . . . . Time-honored rules of warfare

Probe and drogue . . . . . . Aerial refueling method using intake pipe inserted into flexible tanker hose

Propane Bomb . . . . Developed but not used in Gulf War; aerosol bomb of significant size

"Proud Deep" . . . . Reactive strikes against NVN in 1971 in response to SAMs near DMZ

Pulse repetition . . . . Number of radar pulses per second

Punch Out. . . . . Eject from an aircraft- Bail out

Pyramid . . . . GCI call sign in South Vietnam

QRC-128 . . . . Installed in fighters to jam communication between the ground controllers and interceptors

QRC-160A-1 . . . . Self-protection aircraft jamming pod

QRC-248 . . . . Device to interrogate NVN IFF transponders

QRC-335 . . . . "Wild Weasel" noise and deception jammer

Quonset Hut . . . . A lightweight, prefabricated, corrugated, galvanized steel hut of semi-circular design. Based on the British Nissen Hut from WWI and named after Quonset Point, Rhode Island.

RA . . . . Reconnaissance/ Attack

RAF . . . . Royal Air Force (British)

RAT . . . . Ram Air Turbine on Phantom to drive gun

RB . . . . Reconnaissance/ Bomber

RCZ . . . . Radar Control Zone

RCR . . . . Runway Condition Rating - rates level of "slippery' conditions- Was important at CRB due to coral dust on runways and ablation of surface on aluminum runways

RDF . . . . Radio Direction Finder - Means of locating other aircraft by use of voice transmissions

RESCAP . . . . Flying cover or CAP for rescue missions

RF . . . . Reconnaissance/ Fighter

RHAW. . . . . Radar Homing and Warning

RIO . . . . Radar Intercept Officer - Non-pilot flying in back seat of Marine and Navy F-4s

RKG. . . . . Royal Cambodian Government

RLAF . . . . Royal Laotian Air Force

RLG . . . . Royal Laotian Government

RMK . . . . Raymond, Morrison and Knutson - Construction company that did much of the work on Cam Ranh peninsula; Used stronger Korean workers.

R&R . . . . Rest and Recuperation; also Rest & Relaxation - boondoggles where pilots got away and rested from combat

ROE. . . . . Rules of Engagement

ROK . . . . Republic of Korea (South)

ROTC . . . . Reserve Officer Training Corp

RP . . . . Route Pack

RPM. . . . . Revolutions per Minute for turbine blades in a jet engine

RR. . . . . Railroad

RS . . . . Reconnaissance (recce) Squadron

RSI . . . . Research Studies Institute

RT . . . . Rolling Thunder

RTAB . . . . Royal Thai Air Base (also RTAFB)

RTAFB . . . . Royal Thai Air Force Base

RTF . . . . Reconnaissance task force

RVAH . . . . Navy Heavy Reconnaissance (Recon) Attack Squadron

RVN. . . . . Republic of Vietnam (South)

RVNAF . . . . Republic of Vietnam Air Force or Armed Forces

RW . . . . Recon Wing (Navy)

RWT. . . . . Road Watch Team

Radar . . . . "In radar" was pilot reference to having selected Sparrow missile on his weapons selection panel

Radar Homing and Warning . Device that warns of radar tracking & location

Radome . . . . Radar cover located on front end of Phantom

"Ram" Patch . . . . Symbol of the 559th TFS

"Ranch Hand". . . . . USAF C-123 defoliation and herbicide unit

Rapid Roger. . . . . Unsuccessful plan to use one squadron of F-4s at Ubon for two squadrons of pilots operating day and night.

Ravens. . . . . USAF FAC pilots operating clandestinely in Laos

Recce . . . . Reconnaissance; either armed or photo Recon Reconnaissance (recce)

Red Crown . . . . USN early warning and air control ship stationed in northern Gulf of Tonkin to support air ops over NVN

Red River Valley . . . . . . Refer to the valley where Hanoi and Haiphong are located. Red River originates in China; Principal river in NVN; Had over 7,000 AAA guns during war.

"Replacement Pilots" . . . . . Individual pilots arriving on a SEA base after units have deployed; name given to initial Phantom replacements at Cam Ranh

Retards . . . . High drag bombs with fins

Ripple . . . . Bomb release where all bombs stored on MERs and TERs release simultaneously so that they "walk" through the target

River Rats . . . . Red River Valley Fighter Pilots Association. Membership criteria is having flown against Route Packs 5 & 6 in North Vietnam

Rivet Bounder. . . . . Deception jammer activated by Fan Song

Rivet Top . . . . EC-121K used as a NVN airborne command post

"Rolling Thunder" . . . . . USAF air campaign against North Vietnam from March, 1965 to October, 1968

Rote . . . . Temporary squadron rotation

Route Packs . . . . (aka Route Packages) Numbered geographical areas of NVN designed by CINCPAC to organize Rolling Thunder ops. Seven areas numbered from south to north with Route Packs Five and Six being the toughest (Red River Valley). RP6 divided into RP6A and RP6B

Royal Laotian Army
& Air Force . . . . Rightist units fighting the Communistic Pathet Lao

Rudders . . . . Control surfaces on tail of aircraft; controls yaw. Large rudder of F-4 used to fly plane at times

Rules of Engagement . . . . . Specific rules established by DOD that limited action of USAF and USN pilots in carrying out their missions; threat of courts martial for pilots . . who violated

"Rustic" . . . . FAC call signs when operating over Cambodia

Ryan's Raiders . . . . F-105s that conducted night raids against NVN

Ryukyu Group. . . . . Island group located between Japan and Taiwan; Okinawa is the principal island

RB-66 (EB-66) . . . . Elint aircraft that flew tracks over NVN

SA . . . . Small arms

SA . . . . Special Action

SA FACS . . . . Special Action FACs

SAC . . . . Strategic Air Command

SALOA . . . . Special Arc Light Operating Area

SAMs . . . . Surface to Air Missiles in SEA; SAM refers to the SAM 2 & shoulder-mounted SA-7, both manufactured in Russia

SAM "Break" . . . . Called over strike frequency to alert pilots that a SAM had launched. All aircraft usually broke or dove toward the ground whenever it was called

SAR . . . . Search and Rescue

SATS . . . . Short Airfield- Tactical Support

SEA . . . . Southeast Asia

SEAL . . . . Sea/ Air/ Land/ Commando (Navy)

SEATO . . . . Southeast Asia Treaty Organization

SF . . . . Special Forces

Sgt. . . . . Sergeant

SIGINT . . . . Signals Intelligence

SL . . . . Steel Tiger mission

SMSgt. . . . . Senior Master Sergeant

SOA . . . . Special Operating Area

SOP . . . . Standard Operating Procedures

SOS . . . . Special Operations Squadron (AF)

SOS . . . . Save Our Ship (oceanic distress call)

SOW. . . . . Special Operations Wing (AF)

SRS . . . . Strategic Recce Squadron (Navy)

SRW. . . . . Strategic Recce Wing (Navy)

SS . . . . Strategic Squadron (Navy)

SSgt.. . . . . Staff Sergeant

SSZ . . . . Special Strike Zone

STOL . . . . Short Take Off & Landing

SVN . . . . South Vietnam

SW. . . . . Strategic Wing (Navy)

Sabre . . . . F-86 Fighter used extensively in Korean War

Safe Areas . . . . Safe ejection areas with "friendlies" on the ground

Sampan . . . . Fishing boats used by the Vietnamese and Chinese

Sandy . . . . Radio call-sign of A-1 rescue escort ops. Pilots referred to the Crown guys as "Sandys." The USAF lost 201 Sandy's in SEA and the USN lost 65

Scrambler . . . . Coding system that distorts a telephone transmission and clarifies on receipt

Secondary . . . . Additional explosions from target area after strike; usually meant ignited ammunition storage depot

Self-protection pod . . . . . Aerodynamic, externally carried, fighter radar jamming pod

"Senior Crown" . . . . USAF SR-71 high-altitude, high speed recce program (also see Habu and Giant Scale)

Seventeenth (17th) Parallel . . Rough dividing line between North and South Vietnam

Shadow . . . . Radio call sign and name for AC-119 gunship (the Shadow knows)

Sharkbait . . . . 557th TFS call sign

Sharpe . . . . Admiral in charge of Pacific Fleet in 1966

"Shining Brass" . . . . Clandestine cross-border ground recce into Laos and NVN by Special Forces for strike control and BDA (formerly Prairie Fire)

"Shiny Brass" . . . . Infiltration operation into "Tiger Hound" using Philippinos, Thai and Laotian troops

Shrike Missile . . . . Operated by Iron Hand flights- radar homing anti-SAM

Shufly . . . . USMC helicopter detachment in SVN

Sidewinder Missile . . . . . Infrared heat-seeking missile- Usual F-4 load of four

Sihounoak Road (Trail) . . . . This Cambodian routing originated in the Gulf of Siam with two land routes into SVN and three river routes. It also sent supplies up to connect with the Ho Chi Minh Trail System into SVN

Singles. . . . . Dropping one bomb at a time

"Silver Dawn". . . . . USAF Elint aircraft over Gulf of Tonkin

"Skoshi Tiger" . . . . USAF operational test and evaluation program out of Bien Hoa in SVN; Evaluated the F-5s for combat.

Skunk Works . . . . Lockheed hangar at Burbank Airport where the SR-71, U-2, X-15 and F-104 were developed

Sky Spot. . . . . Ground radar-controlled bomb drop against SAM and other sites. Normally used during overcast weather conditions. Dong Ha "Misque" radar controlled flights. CRB used HDs

Smart Bombs . . . . Bombs with internal electronics for target acquisition and aiming

Snake Eye . . . . Mark 82, high drag bomb sometimes called a retard - Used tail fins

Sortie . . . . One flight flown by one aircraft

Sortie War . . . . The competition between the USAF and Navy brass which caused additional, unnecessary strikes against the North. Aircraft sent to targets with no bombs; Aircraft sent on strafing runs with ball (target) ammo

"South" . . . . Refers to South Vietnam

South China Sea. . . . . . . Off the coast of Vietnam, which also includes the Gulf of Tonkin

Spad . . . . Call sign and name for A-1 aircraft (see Pave Spectre)

Spare . . . . Aircraft used as potential replacement in event of an aircraft malfunction on the ground or in the air

Sparrow Missile . . . . Radar guided missile used by F-4; Usual load was four Sparrows and four Sidewinders

Special Forces . . . . Army units in SEA commonly called Green Berets

Special Jamming . . . . . . Disruption of the guidance down link on an SA-2 missile

Spectre . . . . Call sign and name for C-130 gunship

Spooky . . . . Call sign and name for AC-47 gunship equipped with Gattling cannons

Spoon Rest . . . . NVN acquisition radar used in SA-2 system

Spot Jamming . . . . Concentration of all power on a narrow frequency range

Squadron . . . . Primary operating USAF combat unit comprised of four Flights. Phantom . . squadrons (full strength) had 48 pilots and 18 to 24 planes

"Squares" . . . . As in filling squares; refers to the squares on Plexiglas wall charts; means fulfillment of specific requirement

Squawk . . . . When the IFF "Parrot" is transmitting

Stan Eval . . . . Standardization and Evaluation- Officers assigned to establish and insure upkeep of minimum standards in Air Force units

Standard Arm (AGM-78) . . . Replacement missile to the Shrike; used to attack the SA-2 Fan Song emissions

Stand-off jamming . . . . . Long-range jamming out of SAM reach

Stargazer Frequency . . . . Common UHF over the South China Sea

Stars and Stripes . . . . . . Military newspaper in the Pacific

Stead AFB . . . . Home of the so-called "torture school" for USAF survival training; has been closed.

"Steel Tiger" . . . . Operational name for strike area in Southern Laos

Stick . . . . Air Force - Control column where fighter pilot controls turn and bank. Bomb release button, trim and trigger also on stick. Trigger is for missiles or gun

Stick . . . . Army- String of helicopters

Stinger . . . . Call sign and name for AC-119 gunship

Stinger Missile . . . . American, shoulder-mounted SAM

Stopcock . . . . An engine; means to cut-off engine power

Strafe . . . . Firing cannon or "gun" at ground targets

Strategic . . . . Worldwide or macro outlook and tasking

Strike . . . . A ground attack mission against a specific target

Strike Command . . . . . . Predecessor of Central Command; all-service command in charge of DOD wars and operations in the Middle East; located at MacDill AFB in Tampa, Florida

Strike Frequency . . . . Common radio frequency used by American Air Force units in an attack. Also common frequency used by Chinese and Vietnamese MIGs over North Vietnam

Subic Bay . . . . Major USN ship docking and repair facility in the Philippines during the SEA War

Summary Court . . . . Legal name for Officer assigned by USAF to Conduct the legal affairs of a pilot shot down and killed, taken prisoner or MIA

"Sunshine Pilots" . . . . . . Name given to pilot Lieutenants that were not allowed to fly night missions at CRB

Super Sabre F-100

Sweep jamming . . . . Concentrated power beam swept over wide frequency band

Sweep modulator . . . . . . Random energy bursts into jamming barrage by self-protection pods flown by fighters

TAC . . . . Tactical Air Command: Fighter- bomber command controlling all units in CONUS. Similar to USAFE and PACAF

TAC(A) . . . . Tactical Air Controller (Airborne)

TACG . . . . Tactical Air Control Group (Navy)

TACAN . . . . Tactical Air Navigation- navigational aid used extensively in SEA

TACC . . . . Tactical Air Command Center- Forward located center that controls tactical fighter strikes.

TACG . . . . Tactical Air Control Group

TAOR . . . . Tactical area of responsibility

TARCAP . . . . Target CAP (Combat Air Patrol)

TAS . . . . Tactical Airlift Squadron (Navy)

TASG . . . . Tactical Air Support Group

TASS . . . . Tactical Air Support Squadron (FACs)

TAW . . . . Tactical Airlift Wing

TBG . . . . Tactical Bombardment Group

TBS . . . . Tactical Bombardment Squadron

TCG . . . . Troop Carrier Group

TCG . . . . Tactical Control Group

TCS . . . . Troop Carrier Squadron

TCW . . . . Troop Carrier Wing

TCW . . . . Tactical Control Wing

TDY . . . . Temporary Duty

TER . . . . Triple Ejection Rack

TET . . . . Vietnamese Holiday; usually refers to the TET Offensive by the NVN Army in February 1968

TEWS . . . . Tactical Electronic Warfare Squadron

TF . . . . Task Force (Navy)

TF-77 . . . . US Carrier Task Force off Viet coast

TFG . . . . Tactical Fighter Group (Navy)

TFG . . . . Task Force Group (Naval carrier)

TFR . . . . Terrain Following Radar- F-111 (B-111) flown out of Thailand equipped with TFR lost many planes lost due to unexplained reasons. Pilots blamed the TFR

TFS . . . . USAF Tactical Fighter Squadron

TFW . . . . USAF Tactical Fighter Wing

TG . . . . Tactical Group

TOT . . . . Time over Target

TP . . . . Target Practice ammo for the gun; also called ball ammo. Used extensively in SEA for targets

TRIM . . . . Trails, Roads, Interdiction, Multi-sensor

TRS . . . . Tactical Reconnaissance Squadron

TRW . . . . Tactical Reconnaissance Wing

TS . . . . Top Secret

TSgt. . . . . Technical Sergeant

TSN . . . . Tan Son Nhut Air Base, Saigon, South Vietnam

TUC . . . . Time of Useful Consciousness

Tactical . . . . Regional or micro outlook and tasking of units

Tactical Air Control Center . . North Sector Control agency established in 1966 for the Air War over NVN

"Tailgate" . . . . Personnel or cargo exiting the dropped tailgate of a transport in-flight

Takhli RTAFB. . . . . F-105 operating base in Thailand

Tally Ho . . . . Code or target area name for southern Panhandle of NVN. Part of Route Pack I (RP1); FAC controlled region including areas Peter, Paul, Mary, Ford and Banjo)

Tan Son Nhut . . . . Military airfield near Saigon

Target fixation . . . . Pilot fixating on a target at the expense of surroundings; often resulted in crash and pilot's death

Targets of Opportunity . . . . Targets that are selected by the pilot of a fighter-bomber that are his to choose, subject to the Rules of Engagement.

Tarmac . . . . Incorrect but common usage to describe an airfield's aprons and ramps where aircraft taxi and are parked.

Taxi Pilot . . . . A duty position "pulled" by pilots for needed ground movement of aircraft. Usual movement was from maintenance bays to the Flightline

Teaball. . . . . Weapons Control Center @ NKP

Terrain masking . . . . Radar protection afforded by ridges and hills

Test Pilot . . . . At squadron level was responsible for checking aircraft out in flight after maintenance repair

Thai Bases	Takhli, Korat, Nakhon Phanom, Udorn, Ubon, Don Muang
Thunderchief	Official nickname for the F-105
"Thud"	Unofficial nickname for the F-105
Thud Ridge	Ridgeline used by F-105s for terrain masking as they approached Hanoi from the NW
"Tiger Hound"	Air interdiction operating area in southeastern Laos. Steel Tiger was reduced in size and renamed Tiger Hound. The 12th TFW flew over 9,000 sorties against Tiger Hound in early 1966
Top Gun	Highest rated pilot
"Torture" School	Stead AFB in northern Nevada, since closed; known for its "POW training" which was part of its Survival Training School
Tourane	Ancient name for the City of Danang and surrounding area
Track-while-scan	Fan Song radar detection of additional aircraft other than tracked target
Trans Pac	Movement of aircraft across the Pacific
Travis AFB	Primary MAC base in CONUS for Pacific; near Fairfield, California
Trigger	Mechanism on control stick of fighters that could fire gun or missiles, depending on setting on the weapons control (or selection) panel
Trim	Method of "fine-tuning" aircraft controls by adjustment of the ailerons
"Triple Nickel"	Nickname for 555th TFS
Trojan	Nickname for T-28
"Trojan Horse"	SAC U-2 recce ops in SEA (also see Giant Dragon and Lucky Dragon)
Trolling	Missions when Ewar aircraft or fighters attempt to trigger enemy radar in order to locate transmitters
"Tropic Moon III"	B-57 fitted with LLTV (Low-light TV) and other sensors for night missions against HCMT
Typhoon	Pacific hurricane
T-28	Trojan; workhorse propeller-driven fighter aircraft used extensively by: USAF Air Commandoes; SVN Air Force; Air America; Continental Air Services; Royal Laotian Air Force; Royal Thai Air Force
T-33	Discontinued Air Force basic trainer that was version of the F-80 Shooting Star
T-37	Twin-engine Cessna built primary trainer
T-38	Basic Air Force trainer that replaced the T-33; trainer version of the F-5 fighter
UHF	Ultra High Frequency
USAAC	United States Army Air Corps
USAAF	United States Army Air Force
USAF	United States Air Force

USAFE . . . . United States Air Force in Europe - tactical forces

USAFSS. . . . . USAF Security Service

USAID . . . . United States Agency for International Development

USMC. . . . . United States Marine Corps

USN . . . . United States Navy

USO . . . . United Services Organization

USS . . . . United States Ship

USSR . . . . Union of Soviet Socialist Republics

Ubon. . . . . Name of Thai city in east; location of primary F-4 base for USAF in Thailand

"Up Country" . . . . Area of the northern part of South Vietnam - Usually refers to the
mountainous areas

"Up to speed" . . . . Ready to go; proficient

U-2 . . . . Single turbojet, single seat, high altitude reconnaissance aircraft

VA . . . . Attack Squadron (Navy)

VAL . . . . Attack Squadron- Light (Navy)

VC. . . . . Viet Cong- Guerrilla army fighting the U.S. in South Vietnam

VE Day . . . . Victory in Europe- WWII

VF. . . . . Fighter Squadron (Navy)

VFP . . . . Light Photo Squadron (Navy)

VFR . . . . Visual Flight Rules

VHF . . . . Very High Frequency

Viets . . . . Vietnamese

VJ Day . . . . Victory in Japan- WWII

VMA . . . . Marine Attack Squadron

VMA (AW) . . . . Marine All-Weather Attack Squadron

VMCJ . . . . Marine Composite Recce Squadron

VMF (AW) . . . . Marine All- Weather Fighter Squadron

VMFA . . . . Marine Fighter Attack Squadron

VMGR . . . . Marine Aerial Refueller Transport Squadron

VMO . . . . Marine Observation Squadron

VNAF . . . . Vietnamese Air Force (South)

VOR . . . . VHF Omni Directional Range

VORTAC . . . . VOR/ TACAN

VOQ . . . . Visiting Officer's Quarters

VP . . . . Patrol Squadron (Navy)

VPAF . . . . Vietnamese People's Air Force (NVN)

VQ . . . . Fleet Air Recce Squadron (Navy)

VR . . . . Fleet Logistics Support Squadron

VRC . . . . Tactical Support Squadron (Navy)

VSF . . . . Anti-Submarine Fighter Squadron (Navy)

VW . . . . Fleet Early Warning Squadron (Navy)

VW . . . . Fighter Wing (Navy)

VW . . . . Attack Wing (Navy)

Vector . . . . Heading

Vector homing and warning . . EW equipment that warns of enemy radar tracking and furnishes a bearing to
hostile . . . . transmitter

Vichy . . . . French government during WWII that was controlled by Nazi Germany

Viet Cong . . . . Regular and guerrilla (irregular) units operating in South Vietnam;
Distinctive from Regular NVA (North Vietnamese Army) units.

Viet Minh . . . . Guerrilla units fighting the French in the Second Indochina War. Later
became the North Vietnamese Army in the North and the Viet Cong in the
South.

Vo Nguyen Giap . . . . Military genius who led the Viet Minh to victory over the French; also led the
VC and NVN . . . . Army victory over the United States

Vulcan Cannon . . . . External stores mounted centerline on the Phantom; 20 MM Gattling Cannon.
On the F-4E and subsequent models, the cannon was internally mounted.

WSO . . . . Weapons Systems Officer (navy)

WW II . . . . World War Two

WWS . . . . Wild Weasel Squadron- USAF Anti-SAM

WX . . . . Weather

Warsaw Pact . . . . Six nation European alliance of Communistic nations at the time of the
existence of the Soviet Union: East Germany, Poland, Bulgaria, Rumania,
Hungary, Czechoslovakia

Warthog . . . . Name for A-10, USAF close-air-support attack aircraft

"Water Glass" . . . . F-102 air defense in SVN in 1962 and 1963. The air defense detachments in
SVN and Thailand in the very early stages of the SEA War show the concern
of policymakers with possible Chinese air intervention

"Water Pump" . . . . Program located at Udorn, Thailand that was started in 1964 to train Laotian
pilots

West Point . . . . Name of the US Army Military Academy @ West Point, New York

Wheelus Air Base . . . . USAF base in Libya, seven miles to east of Tripoli; used to train all USAFE
fighter-bomber pilots in bombing, rocketry and gunnery; discontinued by
Kaddafi and later used by Soviets

Whiplash . . . . Code name for F-105s operating against Steel Tiger

"Wild Weasel". . . . . USAF F-100Fs, F-105Fs and Gs and F-4Cs fitted with radar homing and warning gear for neutralization and destruction of radar controlled weapons. Did not start until SAM network included over 100 sites. Wild Weasel was one of the most dangerous operations of the War

Whiskey . . . . Call sign for the 558th TFS

Willy Pete . . . . White Phosphorous flare - Tool of FACs for marking targets.

Wing. . . . . Organizational unit of USAF- comprised usually of .four squadrons, but can have less

Yankee Station . . . . Position in Gulf of Tonkin for US aircraft carriers for ops over NVN and Laos

"Yankee Team" . . . . Early US air recce ops in northern Laos comprised of USN and USAF units

Yoke . . . . Control column on military and civilian transport aircraft

Yontan . . . . Abandoned Japanese Zero base in Okinawa; used by DOD as multi-service, multi-use facility

Z . . . . Greenwich Mean Time

Zero . . . . Japanese primary fighter plane in World War II

Zuni Rockets . . . . Very accurate, unguided, non-controllable 5" rocket often mounted on Marine or Navy A-4 aircraft. Zuni rockets are fired from individual tubes as opposed to the Mighty Mouse rockets fired from pods.

Letter from the Chief of Staff

DEPARTMENT OF THE AIR FORCE
OFFICE OF THE CHIEF OF STAFF
UNITED STATES AIR FORCE
WASHINGTON, D.C.

15 NOV 1967

Captain Russell E. Goodenough, FR63856
78th Tactical Fighter Squadron
APO New York 09405

Dear Captain Goodenough

Due to the unusual requirements resulting from our national
effort in Southeast Asia, the Secretary of the Air Force
and I have determined that it is essential to retain
selected Regular officers for one year beyond the date of
requested separation. Consequently, your application for
separation has been approved to be effective 22 March 1969.
We are required to take this action because the continued
efforts and leadership of officers possessing certain skills
are essential to the most effective accomplishment of the
Air Force mission. I want you to know that your particular
qualifications were carefully weighed against the needs of
the Air Force and it was decided that there is an overriding military need for your services.

It is our desire that you remain on active duty for the additional year. If continued service will cause an extraordinary hardship, you may submit a new application on that
basis through appropriate channels to USAFMPC.

I express to you my appreciation for what I know will be
your response to the challenge of our increased operational
requirements.

Sincerely

J. P. McCONNELL, General, USAF
Chief of Staff

Index

An index has not been created for this self-published, short-print edition. Whenever a publisher prints its own edition, a complete index will be prepared and incorporated into the book to allow use for research or reference.

Russ Goodenough
RussFromCal@gmail.com

National Geographic Map - North Vietnam

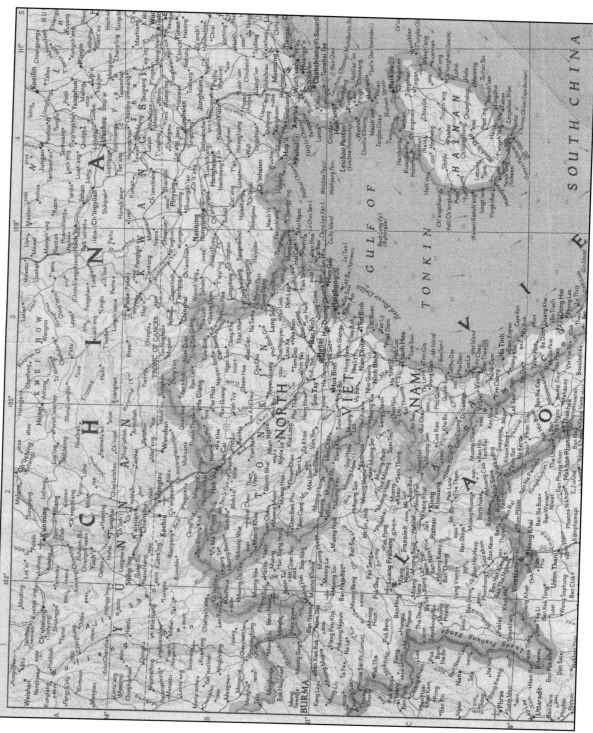

National Geographic Map - South Vietnam

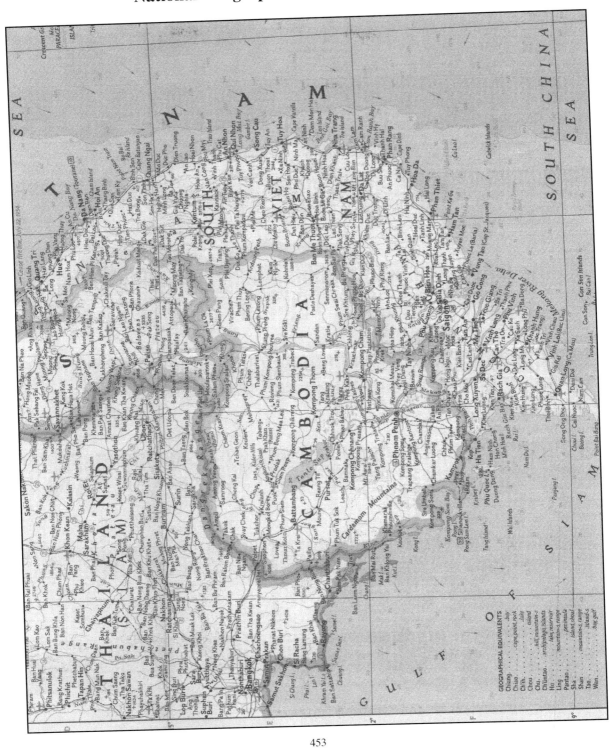

50309978R00265

Made in the USA
San Bernardino, CA
19 June 2017